Revolutionizing Supply Chains Through Digital Transformation

Manal Benatiya Andaloussi
Chouaib Doukkali University, Morocco

IGI Global
Publishing Tomorrow's Research Today

Published in the United States of America by
IGI Global Scientific Publishing
701 East Chocolate Avenue
Hershey, PA, 17033, USA
Tel: 717-533-8845
Fax: 717-533-8661
Website: https://www.igi-global.com E-mail: cust@igi-global.com

Library of Congress Cataloging-in-Publication Data

Names: Benatiya Andaloussi, Manal, 1986- editor.
Title: Revolutionizing supply chains through digital transformation / edited by: Manal Benatiya Andaloussi.
Description: Hershey PA : IGI Global Scientific Publishing, [2025] | Includes bibliographical references. | Summary: "This book offers a comprehensive examination of how digital innovations are not only transforming supply chains but are also fundamentally redefining the value creation process across industries"-- Provided by publisher.
Identifiers: LCCN 2024053095 (print) | LCCN 2024053096 (ebook) | ISBN 9798369344279 (hardcover) | ISBN 9798369344286 (paperback) | ISBN 9798369344293 (ebook)
Subjects: LCSH: Supply chain management--Technological innovations. | Artificial intelligence--Industrial applications.
Classification: LCC HD38.6 .R48 2025 (print) | LCC HD38.6 (ebook) | DDC 658.70285--dc23/eng/20250131
LC record available at https://lccn.loc.gov/2024053095
LC ebook record available at https://lccn.loc.gov/2024053096

British Cataloguing in Publication Data
A Cataloguing in Publication record for this book is available from the British Library.

Table of Contents

Detailed Table of Contents

transformation of supply chain operations. Finally, the chapter provides a business case highlighting the purpose of ontologies, an algorithmic concept similarity assessment, and the usefulness of ontology in developing operational service design.

Despite the extensive discussion on the benefits of BDA in supply chains, there remains a lack of systematic understanding of how BDA can be effectively linked to Supply Chain Optimization (SCO). This document explores the cumulative published literature from 2014 and 2024, so as to ascertain the impact of big data analytics on supply chain optimization. 64 articles were selected from diverse academic journals, and from these articles, information was gathered, analyzed, and organized. The results shows that Big data is often used for making predictions in SCO; big data analytics has a lot of difficulties dealing with large amounts of data related to managing the supply chain, which include too much data, problems with data quality, keeping data safe and private, difficulty in analyzing data, ability to grow as needed, and complicated supply chains. The study recommends that big data projects should begin with specific goals instead of just hoping people will use them. Starting with small test projects can help show the benefits of big data analytics.

In the food industry, consumer preferences constantly keep on changing and as a business; it is inevitable to have robust supply chain to meet the changing market demands. This dynamic consumer behaviour drives different market trends and demand for expected personalised experiences while using products and services. This chapter will discuss these two important pointers, ever changing landscape of consumer behaviour and role of supply chain agility in dealing with it. Case studies will be used to demonstrate the transformative effect of supply chain agility practices. These practices majorly consist of flexible manufacturing process, real time data analytics and collaborative partnership. Furthermore, need of risk management and resilience is to be considered to put proactive measures in place for seamless supply chain operations. The future trends and challenges will also be covered in this chapter, primarily due to emerging technologies and the changes in regulations shaping the direction of agile supply chains within the food sector

This chapter explores the integration of smart manufacturing principles and Industry 4.0 technologies to optimize production management within supply chains. As manufacturing processes increasingly embrace digitization and connectivity, production management plays a pivotal role in ensuring efficiency, flexibility, and responsiveness throughout the supply chain. The chapter delves into advancements such as cyber-physical systems, the Internet of Things (IoT), artificial intelligence (AI), and advanced robotics, and their impact on reshaping traditional production management practices. These technologies enable real-time monitoring, predictive maintenance, and demand-driven production. Through practical examples and case studies, the chapter demonstrates how the seamless integration of Industry 4.0 technologies enhances production planning, scheduling, and execution, leading to improved productivity, reduced lead times, and greater customer satisfaction. Furthermore, it addresses the challenges and considerations of implementing smart manufacturing initiatives.

Throughout history, manufacturing systems paradigms have evolved significantly to meet the changing needs of society, from dedicated transfer lines to evolvabe production systems (EPS). Evolvable Production Systems are designed for swift response to market changes, pose a complex integration challenge due to component heterogeneity. Ontology-based semantic tools facilitate this integration by providing a common language for components. This chapter reviews the evolution of manufacturing systems paradigms by the emergence of Industry 4.0 technologies. It also explores the ontology-based semantic tools for EPS integration and reviews the existing ontologies for manufacturing systems. It highlights representative ontology development methodologies and concludes with future trends in ontology-based evolvable manufacturing systems development.

Blockchain technology has been recognised for its potential to improve transparency, traceability, and security in the financial industry, prompting the RBI to push banks to implement it into their operations. Blockchain has applications outside banking and finance, including in agro-food supply chains, land record administration, intellectual property rights, voting systems, cybersecurity and healthcare management. Despite its great potential, blockchain technology is still in the early stages of adoption in India's agro-food supply chain. This study conducts a rigorous literature review and expert questionnaire survey to identify the key barriers and opportunities for blockchain implementation in agricultural supply chain management. The findings aim to improve digital strategies connected to blockchain, assisting decision-makers in overcoming considerable challenges and deciding the best course of action. By solving these issues, blockchain can empower farmers, minimize food waste and promote a more efficient, secure, and sustainable agro-food supply chain in India.

The COVID-19 pandemic, started in late 2019, rapidly expanded into a global crisis, showing the critical importance of an effective vaccine supply chain. This unique situation prompted governments, pharmaceutical companies, and research institutions to came together for a historic effort, leading to the development and approval of vaccines within a year. The pandemic highlighted the issues of traditional vaccine supply chains, particularly in ensuring efficient and equitable distribution across developed and developing countries. It also highlighted areas of vulnerability in supply chain structures globally including storage, transport and production structures. As a result, the crisis boosted the use of modern digital technologies such as AI and Blockchain, which were instrumental in predicting the demand for vaccines and maintaining the security of records. Ahead, innovations such as the metaverse, augmented reality, and digital twins provide the prospect for redefining even further the distribution of vaccines, collaboration, learning, and even supply chain management.

This chapter explores the impact of technological advances on purchasing practices and their influence on the performance of Moroccan companies, focusing on crucial aspects such as the impact of information technology, machine learning techniques, and the resolution of logistical challenges. The study underlines the importance of digitization for Moroccan businesses and policymakers, highlighting the critical role of technology adoption in promoting the procurement sector. It identifies the main drivers of digitization adoption, including organizational, technological, environmental, and human aspects, while addressing ethical considerations, such as data privacy and the impact on employment. This chapter demonstrates how digitization and AI can improve business performance and competitiveness in the purchasing function. It provides guidelines for Moroccan companies and policymakers to navigate this digital transformation effectively.

The fifth-generation (5G) technology is a next-generation communication technology that enables significantly faster data transmission, lower latency, and greater connectivity compared to its predecessors. Integrating 5G technology in supply chain management offers a competitive advantage by optimizing operations, enhancing real-time monitoring, improving logistics, and enabling advanced automation through the Internet of Things (IoT). This chapter explores how 5G technology can revolutionize supply chain management by providing a detailed overview of its value propositions, such as facilitating real-time data exchange, enhancing logistics optimization through better route planning, and supporting IoT-driven automation for more efficient inventory management. Additionally, it discusses the role of 5G in enabling seamless connectivity across supply chain networks, thus improving visibility and decision-making processes. By evaluating emerging trends and potential developments, this study aims to provide valuable insights for researchers, practitioners, and industry stakeholders on the impact of 5G technology on supply chain activities, highlighting both opportunities and challenges in its implementation.

The focus of our chapter is to determine the extent to which lean manufacturing and lean digital 4.0 are complementary when it comes to reducing waste in the production chain. Indeed, Industry 4.0 is increasingly presented as a must for improving productivity and ensuring economic growth in manufacturing companies. On the other hand, many companies have already partially or fully implemented Lean principles and tools. A number of aspects remain to be clarified regarding the existing links between Industry 4.0 and the Lean approach: is there a hierarchy, improvement or complementarity between the two approaches? What are the links between the two approaches? This chapter seeks to highlight the links that exist between the two approaches in terms of continuous improvement and operational performance. To this end, we have highlighted the principles and technologies proposed by lean manufacturing and Industry 4.0 respectively. We have also discussed the theory of constraints, which has been applied in lean manufacturing circles.

Foreword

In an era where digital transformation is no longer a choice but a necessity, the comprehensive study of its impact on supply chains is both timely and critical. The book "Revolutionizing Supply Chains Through Digital Transformation" offers an insightful and thorough exploration of how emerging technologies are reshaping the landscape of supply chain management. It is a remarkable contribution to the field, bringing together a collection of case studies and theoretical analyses that not only illuminate current trends but also pave the way for future developments.

As a scholar and practitioner in the areas of supply chain management, logistics, information systems, and digital transformation, I have witnessed firsthand the profound shifts that these technological advancements have triggered across industries. This book is particularly valuable as it provides a well-rounded view of these changes, from the theoretical underpinnings of digital transformation to practical applications in various sectors. The editor has curated a selection of chapters that address both the opportunities and the challenges that come with this rapid technological evolution.

What sets this book apart is its strategic structure, which guides the reader through the complexities of digital transformation in a logical and coherent manner. The initial chapters lay a solid foundation by exploring the new forms of value creation enabled by digital technologies. Subsequent chapters delve into specific technologies—such as the Internet of Things (IoT), Big Data Analytics, blockchains and Artificial Intelligence—and their direct impact on supply chain management. This approach not only provides a deep understanding of each technology's role but also demonstrates their interconnectedness and collective impact on optimizing supply chains.

The inclusion of case studies across different industries further enhances the book's practical relevance. These case studies not only illustrate the theoretical concepts discussed but also provide real-world examples of how companies are successfully navigating the challenges such as supply chain disruptions in times of crisis, and leveraging the opportunities presented by digital transformation. This practical orientation makes the book a valuable resource for both academics and practitioners, offering insights that are directly applicable to the strategic management of supply chains.

Moreover, the book does not shy away from addressing the broader implications of digital transformation, such as sustainability, waste management, and the role of emerging technologies like 5G. These topics are crucial as we move towards more resilient and sustainable supply chains, and their inclusion underscores the editors' commitment to providing a comprehensive overview of the field.

In conclusion, "Revolutionizing Supply Chains Through Digital Transformation" is an essential read for anyone involved in supply chain management, logistics, or digital transformation. It provides a well-rounded, in-depth analysis of how digital technologies are transforming the supply chain landscape, offering both theoretical insights and practical guidance. I am confident that this book will serve as a valuable reference for researchers, practitioners, and students alike, contributing significantly to the ongoing discourse in this rapidly evolving field.

Youssef DHIBA
Faculty of Legal, Economic and Social Sciences, Hassan II University, Mohammedia, Morocco

Preface

In the modern business landscape, the confluence of digital technologies with supply chain management has ushered in an era of unprecedented change and opportunity. The concept of supply chain management (SCM), once rooted in traditional logistics and operational efficiency, has evolved into a sophisticated, technology-driven discipline.

"Revolutionizing Supply Chains Through Digital Transformation" offers a comprehensive examination of how digital innovations are not only transforming supply chains but are also fundamentally redefining the value creation process across industries. This comprehensive guide delves into the integration of technologies such as Internet of Things (IoT), artificial intelligence, blockchain, and big data analytics, reshaping the way businesses manage their supply chains. From enhanced visibility and transparency to predictive analytics and autonomous decision-making, this book provides insights into how companies can leverage these advancements to optimize operations, reduce costs, and gain a competitive edge in the global marketplace. This book bridges the gap between theory and practice, offering a blend of academic rigor and real-world application. By synthesizing the latest research findings, case studies, and industry best practices, it serves as a valuable resource for scholars, researchers, and practitioners in the fields of supply chain management, operations management, logistics, and information technology. This book brings together insights from leading experts and researchers, presenting a multifaceted exploration of the challenges, opportunities, and future directions of digital SCM. Through its in-depth analysis and actionable insights, it not only contributes to advancing scholarly discourse but also equips professionals with the knowledge and tools needed to navigate the complexities of the digital supply chain landscape.

At its core, this book is about the intersection of digital transformation and supply chain management. Digital transformation refers to the integration of digital technologies into all areas of a business, fundamentally changing how companies operate and deliver value to customers. In the context of SCM, digital transformation is driving new levels of efficiency, agility, and resilience. Technologies such as Artificial Intelligence (AI), the Internet of Things (IoT), blockchain, big data analytics, and 5G are enabling companies to streamline operations, improve decision-making, enhance transparency, and respond more rapidly to market changes.

This book provides a deep dive into how these technologies are being applied within supply chains to create new forms of value. Each chapter addresses a specific aspect of digital SCM, offering both theoretical insights and practical applications.

The relevance of digital transformation in supply chains cannot be overstated. In today's globalized and highly competitive market, supply chains must be more agile, resilient, and efficient than ever before. The COVID-19 pandemic has further highlighted the vulnerabilities in traditional supply chains, pushing companies to accelerate their digital transformation efforts. Digital technologies have become essential tools for managing disruptions, optimizing operations, and staying competitive in a rapidly changing environment.

Moreover, the growing importance of sustainability and the need to address environmental challenges have made digital transformation even more critical. Digital tools are not only helping companies improve their operational efficiency but are also enabling them to reduce their environmental footprint, enhance transparency, and meet regulatory requirements. This book addresses these pressing issues, offering insights into how companies can leverage digital technologies to build more sustainable and resilient supply chains.

The primary audience for this book includes academics, researchers, and students in the fields of supply chain management, operations management, and digital transformation. It is also an invaluable resource for practitioners, including supply chain managers, operations executives, and business leaders who are responsible for driving digital transformation initiatives within their organizations. Additionally, policymakers and regulators will find the book useful for understanding the implications of digital transformation in supply chains and for shaping policies that support innovation and sustainability.

The book is designed to cater to both those who are new to the topic and those who have a deep understanding of SCM and digital technologies. For newcomers, the book provides a solid foundation in the key concepts and technologies driving digital transformation in supply chains. For experts, it offers advanced insights and practical case studies that can inform and inspire their own digital transformation efforts.

The chapters in this book are organized in a sequence that reflects a logical progression from foundational concepts to advanced applications, creating a cohesive narrative that guides the reader through the complexities of supply chain digital transformation. We begin with a literature review that lays the groundwork by exploring the new forms of value creation enabled by digital transformation. This establishes a theoretical basis that informs the subsequent chapters, which delve into specific technologies and their impact on supply chain management. The book then transitions to examining the role of key technologies such as the Internet of Things, Big Data Analytics, Blockchain and Artificial Intelligence, highlighting their transformative effects on supply chain optimization, agility, and decision-making.

The chapters on smart manufacturing, Industry 4.0, and ontology-based semantic tools build on this foundation, showing how these technologies are being integrated into production management to optimize supply chain operations. The discussion then shifts to the practical applications and challenges of implementing these technologies, illustrated by case studies in different contexts, such as the pandemic crisis, and different industries, such as food and agriculture.

Finally, the book addresses the broader implications of digital transformation in supply chains, including waste management, decarbonization, and the potential of emerging technologies like 5G to further revolutionize supply chains. Each chapter is strategically placed to build upon the previous one, ensuring a smooth transition and creating a synergistic flow that enhances the reader's understanding of the subject matter. This structure not only highlights the interconnectedness of the various elements of digital transformation but also emphasizes their collective impact on the future of supply chain management.

Chapter 1: Digital Transformation towards New Forms of Value Creation: Literature Review

This foundational chapter offers a comprehensive literature review on the evolving nature of value creation in the digital age. It examines how digital transformation is reshaping traditional business models, leading to the emergence of new value creation paradigms. The chapter highlights key theories and concepts that explain the relationship between digital technologies and value creation, providing strategic recommendations for companies looking to optimize their digital value chains. It also discusses the challenges and opportunities associated with this transformation, making it an essential read for understanding the broader context of digital SCM.

Chapter 2: The Impact of Digital Transformation on Supply Chain Management: Opportunities, Challenges, and Future Directions

This chapter delves into the specific impact of digital transformation on SCM. It explores the opportunities that digital technologies offer for improving supply chain efficiency, visibility, and sustainability. The chapter also addresses the challenges that organizations face in adopting these technologies, such as technological integration, data security, and change management. By examining the future directions of digital SCM, the chapter provides practical advice for companies navigating their digital journeys. This chapter is crucial for understanding the strategic implications of digital transformation in supply chains.

Chapter 3: The Seminal Role of Internet of Things in the Digital Transformation of Supply Chain Management

The Internet of Things (IoT) plays a pivotal role in the digital transformation of supply chains, as this chapter thoroughly explores. By examining IoT's impact on various sectors, including agriculture, healthcare, and logistics, the chapter illustrates how IoT technologies are enhancing supply chain transparency, inventory management, and risk mitigation. The chapter also discusses the challenges associated with IoT adoption, such as data privacy and security concerns, and advocates for strategies to overcome these barriers. This chapter is essential for understanding how IoT is driving innovation in SCM.

Chapter 4: Convergence of Service Oriented Architecture with Internet of Things for Business Information Systems

This chapter discusses the integration of Service-Oriented Architecture (SOA) with the Internet of Things (IoT) to enhance business information systems. It explores how these technologies can be combined to create decision support systems in supply chain management, utilizing data communication networks and protocols for effective data collection and processing. The chapter also emphasizes the importance of semantic interoperability, facilitated by ontologies and similarity assessment methods, and highlights practical business cases to demonstrate the application of the proposed system architecture.

Chapter 5: Big Data Analytics for Supply Chain Optimization: Harnessing Data for Strategic Supply Chain Decisions

Big data analytics is a powerful tool for optimizing supply chains, as explored in this chapter. The chapter investigates the challenges and opportunities associated with big data analytics in SCM, including issues related to data quality, privacy, and scalability. It also provides practical recommendations for companies looking to leverage big data for strategic decision-making. By examining case studies and real-world examples, the chapter demonstrates how big data analytics can drive significant improvements in supply chain performance, making it an invaluable resource for practitioners.

Chapter 6: Supply Chain Agility: Adapting to Consumer Preferences in the Food Industry

In the rapidly changing food industry, supply chain agility is crucial for meeting evolving consumer preferences. This chapter discusses the importance of flexibility, real-time data analytics, and collaborative partnerships in achieving supply chain agility. It also explores the role of risk management and resilience in maintaining seamless supply chain operations. Through case studies, the chapter illustrates how agile supply chain practices can transform business operations and drive competitiveness in the food industry. This chapter is essential for understanding how supply chains can adapt to changing market demands.

Chapter 7: Integrating Smart Manufacturing and Industry 4.0 Technologies for Production Management Optimization in Supply Chains

This chapter explores the integration of smart manufacturing principles and Industry 4.0 technologies in optimizing production management within supply chains. It highlights how technologies such as cyber-physical systems, AI, and advanced robotics are reshaping traditional production management practices. By providing real-world examples and case studies, the chapter demonstrates how these technologies can enhance production planning, scheduling, and execution, leading to improved productivity and customer satisfaction. The chapter also addresses the challenges of implementing smart manufacturing initiatives, making it a valuable resource for those interested in the future of production management in SCM.

Chapter 8: Ontology Based Semantic Tools for Evolvable Manufacturing Systems Integration

Manufacturing systems have evolved significantly over time, and this chapter examines how ontology-based semantic tools facilitate the integration of evolvable production systems. The chapter reviews existing ontologies for manufacturing systems and explores future trends in ontology-based evolvable manufacturing systems development. It also highlights the importance of semantic interoperability in integrating heterogeneous components within manufacturing systems. This chapter is particularly relevant for those interested in the evolution of manufacturing systems and the role of semantic tools in SCM.

Chapter 9: Leveraging Blockchain Technology in Indian Agri-Food Supply Chains: Examining the Challenges and Opportunities

Blockchain technology has the potential to revolutionize agri-food supply chains, and this chapter examines its application in the Indian context. By conducting a rigorous literature review and expert survey, the chapter identifies the key barriers and opportunities for blockchain adoption in agricultural supply chain management. It also discusses how blockchain can enhance transparency, traceability, and sustainability in the agri-food sector. The chapter provides valuable insights for decision-makers looking to implement blockchain technology in their supply chains, making it an essential read for those interested in the intersection of blockchain and SCM.

Chapter 10: Post COVID-19 Vaccine Supply Chain: Challenges, Disruptions, and Digital Transformation

This chapter examines the challenges and disruptions in the COVID-19 vaccine supply chain, highlighting the critical role of digital transformation in addressing these issues. The rapid development and distribution of vaccines exposed vulnerabilities in traditional supply chains, particularly in storage, transport, and equitable distribution. The adoption of AI, Blockchain, and emerging technologies like the metaverse and digital twins has been pivotal in overcoming these challenges, offering new prospects for future supply chain management and resilience in the healthcare sector.

Chapter 11: Study of the Impact of Artificial Intelligence and the Digitalization of Purchasing Practices on Economic Performance

This chapter explores the impact of AI and digitalization on purchasing practices and their influence on the economic performance of Moroccan companies. It discusses the drivers of digitization adoption, including organizational, technological, environmental, and human factors. The chapter also addresses ethical considerations related to data privacy and employment. By providing guidelines for navigating digital transformation in the procurement sector, the chapter offers practical advice for companies and policymakers. This chapter is crucial for understanding how AI and digitalization are transforming the purchasing function in SCM.

Chapter 12: Transforming Supply Chains: Exploring the Role of 5G Technology

5G technology has the potential to revolutionize supply chain management by enabling faster data transmission and more reliable communication. This chapter explores the impact of 5G on SCM, highlighting its value propositions and ability to support supply chain operations. The chapter also discusses emerging trends and developments related to 5G technology and offers insights into its potential impact on supply chain activities. This chapter is essential for understanding how 5G technology can enhance supply chain performance and competitiveness.

Chapter 13: Managing Waste within Supply Chain: from Lean Manufacturing to Lean Digital 4.0

Lean manufacturing and Industry 4.0 technologies have the potential to significantly reduce waste within supply chains. This chapter explores the intersection of these two approaches, examining their complementarity and impact on operational performance. The chapter also discusses the role of digital tools in enhancing the efficiency and effectiveness of waste management processes. By providing practical examples and case studies, the chapter demonstrates how companies can achieve continuous improvement through Lean Digital 4.0 practices. This chapter is crucial for those interested in waste management and sustainable supply chain practices.

Chapter 14: Towards Decarbonized Transportation: A Comprehensive Review of Global Challenges and Digital Transformation

Transportation is a major contributor to global carbon emissions, and this chapter examines the role of digital transformation in addressing these challenges. It provides a comprehensive review of the progress and future prospects of decarbonization in the transport sector, focusing on digital technologies that optimize operations and reduce emissions. The chapter also discusses the role of government policies and industry initiatives in supporting decarbonization efforts. This chapter is essential for understanding the intersection of digital transformation and sustainability in the transportation sector.

As we move into an increasingly digital world, the importance of digital transformation in supply chains cannot be overstated. The technologies and strategies discussed in this book are not just theoretical concepts; they are practical tools that companies can use to build more efficient, resilient, and sustainable supply chains. By embracing digital transformation, companies can not only navigate the complexities of the modern business environment but also seize new opportunities for growth and innovation.

"Revolutionizing Supply Chains Through Digital Transformation" is a comprehensive exploration of how digital technologies are reshaping supply chain management. By covering a wide range of topics, from theoretical foundations to practical applications, the book provides valuable insights for companies, researchers, and policymakers. The book emphasizes the importance of embracing digital transformation to build resilient, efficient, and sustainable supply chains capable of thriving in the face of disruption. Whether you are a business leader, a researcher, or a student, this book offers the knowledge and strategies needed to navigate the complexities of digital SCM in the modern world.

Benatiya Andaloussi Manal
Chouaib Doukkali University, Morocco

Acknowledgment

Deep gratitude is extended to the editorial team for their unwavering support and exceptional guidance throughout the development of this book. The dedication, professionalism, and insightful feedback provided were crucial in shaping the final manuscript. The expertise in managing the complexities of this project has significantly contributed to its success. The commitment to excellence and assistance in realizing the vision of this work are greatly appreciated.

Sincere appreciation is expressed to the reviewers for their invaluable contributions to this book. The detailed reviews, constructive criticism, and expert advice offered have greatly enhanced the quality and rigor of the content. The time and effort dedicated to providing thorough evaluations were essential in refining and perfecting the manuscript. The dedication to academic excellence and pivotal role in bringing this book to completion are deeply acknowledged.

Chapter 1
Digital Transformation Towards New Forms of Value Creation: Literature Review

Ahmed El Hammoumi
Faculté Polydisciplinaire de Taza, Morocco

Mohammed El Hammoumi
Faculté des Sciences Juridiques, Économiques, et Sociales de Fès, Morocco

ABSTRACT

Purpose The research aimed to assess how digital transformation has altered traditional value creation paradigms in companies, identifying new forms of value generated by this transformation. The ultimate goal was to provide strategic recommendations for companies looking to leverage digital transformation for enhanced value creation, emphasizing best practices and innovative approaches to optimize the digital value chain. Research methodology The study focused on analyzing and interpreting various theories and concepts, shedding light on the relationships between digital transformation and new forms of value creation, while highlighting changes in value creation processes. Results The study highlights the crucial role of digital transformation in redefining new forms of value creation and opportunities for innovation and competitiveness. It provides insights into the opportunities and challenges that companies face in this evolving business environment.

DOI: 10.4018/979-8-3693-4427-9.ch001

PURPOSE

The research aimed to assess how digital transformation has altered traditional value creation paradigms in companies, identifying new forms of value generated by this transformation. The ultimate goal was to provide strategic recommendations for companies looking to leverage digital transformation for enhanced value creation, emphasizing best practices and innovative approaches to optimize the digital value chain. This assessment was based on previous studies and case analyses in this field.

RESEARCH METHODOLOGY

The study focused on the analysis and interpretation of various theories and concepts, as well as previous studies and case analyses, to illuminate the relationships between digital transformation and new forms of value creation. It aimed to highlight changes in value creation processes by examining how digital transformation impacts these processes.

RESULTS

The study highlights the crucial role of digital transformation in redefining new forms of value creation and opportunities for innovation and competitiveness. It provides insights into the opportunities and challenges that companies face in this evolving business environment. Indeed, to maximize value creation, companies must understand the value creation models and choose the one that best aligns with their strategic objectives and organizational context.

Research limitations

The theoretical approach of this research could benefit from empirical analysis. Additionally, testing the results on a representative sample opens up prospects for future research. A temporal and contextual extension could further enhance the relevance of the findings.

Originality/value

This theoretical study makes a substantial contribution to understanding digital transformation's impact on value creation in the business context. It stands out for its innovative contribution, shedding new light on how digital transformation influences new forms of value creation, offering valuable perspectives for research and innovation.

Contributions and Conclusion

Digital transformation has redefined the boundaries of value creation, facilitating the emergence of new business models based on digital platforms. This enables dynamic and scalable value capture through intelligent exploitation of networks and technologies.

In conclusion, digital transformation is more than just a technological evolution; it is a key driver of value creation for companies, offering unprecedented opportunities for innovation and competitiveness, reshaping how companies interact with customers in an increasingly digital marketplace.

INTRODUCTION:

The development of the digital world has led to the emergence of innovative technologies, which have accelerated the digitization of the economy and significantly changed organizational management methods. This change, characterized by the use of Big Data, artificial intelligence, and the Internet of Things, entails significant changes in the functions of businesses. Companies of all sizes and nationalities attach great importance to the adoption and use of these new tools, while questioning their utility. To succeed in their digitization, they must undergo an internal modification that concerns organizational models, corporate culture, and work techniques.

Traditional organizational models are being questioned by digitization, which requires an experimental approach to foster adaptability. In a constantly evolving scientific and technological world, this represents a major challenge for businesses. Although its name is recent, digital transformation is a process that has evolved over time, moving from a reflection on the "What" and "Why" to a reflection on the "How" and ultimately the creation of value.

Digitization enhances various aspects of the business, including quality, cost reduction, and convenience (Cavelius F. et al., 2018). However, to fully leverage its benefits, digital transformation must be implemented correctly.

Despite the growing interest of researchers and professionals in the relationship between digital transformation and value creation, this topic remains complex and sparks numerous debates and scientific research.

In this context, this chapter aims to contribute to understanding the impact of digital transformation on forms of value creation by exploring business digitization today, the concept of value creation, and examining how digitization influences economic models and business ecosystems.

1. LITERATURE REVIEW AND SITUATIONAL STATEMENT:

1.1. from Digital Transformation to the Evolution of Value Creation in the Digital Era: Fundamental Concepts and Dynamics

Companies seeking to thrive in the digital era must understand digital transformation and its impact on value creation in a world where technology constantly redefines paradigms. To emphasize value creation in the digital era, this chapter first examines the conceptual foundations of digital transformation.

- **Conceptual Foundations of Digital Transformation**

Digital transformation, which involves the integration of digital technologies into all aspects of the business, is an ongoing process that profoundly alters internal processes and creates a new business ecosystem. The transition to Industry 4.0 is facilitated by the adoption of smart technologies, thereby increasing productivity and competitiveness (Winasis et al., 2021). To successfully transition to Industry 4.0, characterized by the connectivity and interconnection of products and processes, leaders must provide strong support (Frank et al., 2019; Florek-Paszkowska et al., 2021).

According to Vial (2019), digital transformation goes beyond a mere IT strategy; it combines IT and business strategy, requiring alignment between digital strategy and organizational transformation. The SMACS approach provides a framework for the effective use of digital technologies, based on key technological drivers such as social, mobile, analytics, cloud, and security.

Finally, digital transformation is not only focused on technological advancements; it also represents a fundamental change in how companies perceive their IT, considering it as a key strategic element for value creation and capture (Van Alstyne, Parker, & Choudary, 2016). To succeed in this transition to a new business environment, top management must actively commit. This involves questioning the organization and the company's strategy.

External Digital Trend Keys

- ubiquitous connectivity
- abundance of information
- global supply chains
- improvement in IT cost/performance
- growth of cloud computing
- emergence of Big Data

-scope of the digital business strategy
- scale of the digital business strategy
- speed of decision-making
- source of value creation and capture

PERFORMANCE

Main Organizational Changes

-limitations of traditional economic models
- cross-functional role
-new mandate for information technologies and information system management
-increased familiarity with information technologies

Figure 1. The Various Keys to the Digitalization Strategy

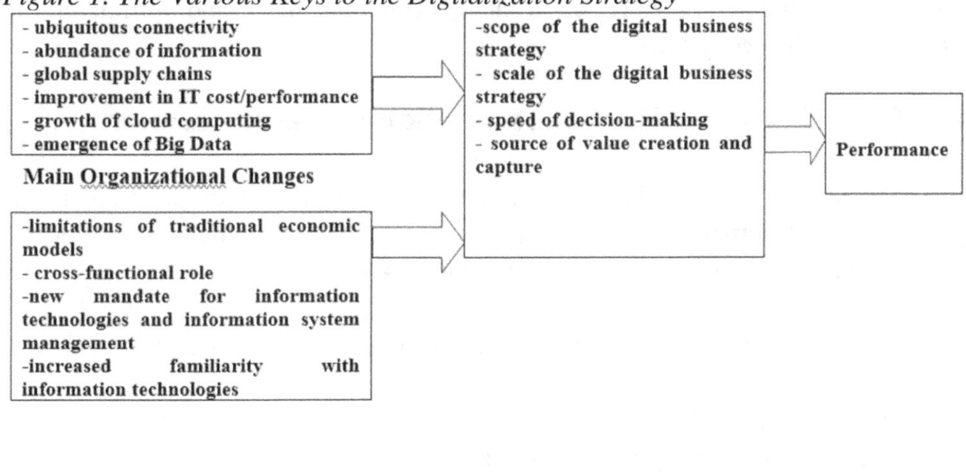

- **Evolution of the value creation concept in the digital age:**

In the context of businesses, value creation is a complex concept influenced by the expectations of both internal and external customers. It can manifest in various ways, including increasing dividends for shareholders, boosting margins for executives and employees, and enhancing comfort and efficiency at work for employees. It also encompasses social, ethical, and environmental factors. Individual preferences determine value (Smith, 2020).

One of the nine fundamental elements of the economic model is value creation, which describes how an organization creates, delivers, and captures value to differentiate itself from its competitors (Osterwalder & Pigneur, 2010).

Globalization and the diffusion of new technologies, particularly digital ones, have profoundly altered the ways in which businesses create value. These changes have led to a shift towards companies seeking to organize the economy around them, exerting increasing influence (Rifkin, 2014).

Traditional methods of value creation have been transformed by the digital revolution, favoring the increasing outsourcing of tasks and directing businesses towards their core activities (Coase, 1937). New economic models have emerged, emphasizing the role of users and networks in value creation (Shapiro & Varian, 1999).

By introducing integrated access service ecosystems for users, platforms such as Google, Facebook, Amazon, and the Apple Store have redefined value creation. These platforms employ a variety of business models, including data collection, marketplace creation, and mobile application hosting (Van Alstyne, Parker & Choudary, 2016).

According to Van Alstyne and colleagues, beyond merely maximizing individual products and services, platforms introduce a paradigm shift by emphasizing user communities, interactions between producers and consumers, and optimizing the total value of the ecosystem.

1.2. The effect of digital transformation on value creation:

At the dawn of the digital revolution, the shift from value creation based on tangible assets to the emphasis on user experience reveals how digitization is radically transforming traditional mechanisms of value creation.

- **New paradigms of value creation: from tangible value to user experience.**

Digitization has shifted the paradigms of value creation by emphasizing user experience over tangible goods. This underscores the increasing importance of satisfying and engaging customers beyond the mere utility of products or services. Digitization is the driving force behind this transformation, which has a significant impact on how businesses interact with their customers. Value creation now pivots towards providing memorable and personalized experiences, acknowledging that customers' perception of value is influenced by intangible factors such as emotion and customization. Traditionally, value creation has focused on the intrinsic qualities of offerings (Pine and Gilmore, 1998; Normann and Ramirez, 1993).

Apple and other innovative companies have demonstrated the importance of differentiation through functional, aesthetic, and intuitive products (Normann and Ramirez, 1993), while services like Uber and Airbnb have revolutionized their sectors by offering seamless and customizable user experiences. Digitization is crucial to this transition towards an experience economy, enabling rich and personalized interactions across digital platforms and paving the way for even more immersive user experiences through emerging technologies such as virtual and augmented reality (Choudhury and Harrigan, 2014; Kumar and Reinartz, 2018).

The crucial shift from tangible values to user experience in value creation strategies in the digital age is illustrated by this pivot towards user experience as the core of value creation, a crucial strategy for businesses seeking to retain their customer base and stand out in a competitive landscape.

- **Impact of digitization on value creation processes.**

By significantly altering traditional methods of production, customization, and distribution of goods and services, digitization profoundly redefines the foundations of value creation in the business world. Companies are embracing the digital age by utilizing advanced technologies such as artificial intelligence, robotics, and the Internet of Things (IoT) to transform their internal processes, enhance efficiency, and pave the way for continuous innovation (Brynjolfsson and McAfee, 2014). This digital transformation is evident not only in the optimization and automation of operations but also in the ability to offer highly personalized and engaging customer experiences.

Digitization liberates businesses from many operational constraints, reducing costs and improving quality. Smart factories, for example, are an excellent example of this evolution, where predictive analytics and connected sensors optimize production and maintenance (Brynjolfsson and McAfee, 2014). Furthermore, the exploitation of big data and predictive analytics fosters unprecedented customization of offerings, specifically addressing the expectations and preferences of consumers. Spotify, with its personalized music recommendations, is an excellent example, demonstrating how algorithms can enhance the user experience by utilizing analysis of individual listening habits (Verhoef et al., 2015).

Moreover, digitization enables the emergence of innovative economic models that redefine methods of value creation. The rise of subscription-based services or platforms facilitating micro-scale transactions demonstrates how businesses can capture new sources of revenue and expand their market. For example, Instagram has created a new channel for advertising revenue by integrating non-intrusive ads into its audience (Parker and Van Alstyne, 2019).

In summary, digitization allows businesses to radically rethink their value creation processes as a catalyst and driver of transformation. By leveraging digital technologies, companies not only streamline their operations but also reinvent their relationship with customers, offering personalized experiences and developing resilient and innovative economic models that foster sustainable growth in the digital economy.

1.3. The dimensions of value creation in the digital era

Revolve around multiple facets, including the strategic use of data, dynamic collaboration through digital platforms, and customization to meet the unique needs of each individual, thus redefining the very foundations of innovation and business success.

- **Personalization and adaptation to individual needs**

Digitization has revolutionized businesses' ability to personalize their products and services to meet the individual needs of their customers, going far beyond simple minor adjustments to offer unique and tailored experiences to each client. In an increasingly competitive and customer-centric business environment, personalization has become imperative for companies. Digitization has played a crucial role in enabling businesses to collect, analyze, and effectively leverage data to understand the specific needs of each customer and provide them with tailored solutions (Verhoef et al., 2017).

A key strategy for personalization involves using predictive analytics to anticipate customers' needs and offer relevant products or services before they explicitly request them. For instance, e-commerce companies utilize machine learning algorithms to recommend products based on customers' purchase histories and browsing behaviors, thereby providing a personalized and intuitive shopping experience (Chen et al., 2018).

Furthermore, digitization enables businesses to personalize the customer experience across various touchpoints such as websites, mobile applications, social media, or messaging services. Through seamless integration of customer data across these channels, companies can provide a consistent and smooth experience, thereby enhancing customer loyalty and engagement (Rust et al., 2018).

Personalization extends beyond products and services but also encompasses sales and customer service processes. For instance, AI-powered chatbots can offer personalized and real-time assistance, proactively addressing customer queries and providing recommendations based on their specific needs (Verhoef et al., 2017).

In conclusion, digitization has significantly enhanced businesses' ability to personalize their offerings and adapt to the individual needs of their customers. By harnessing data and digital technologies, companies can create unique customer experiences, thereby strengthening their competitiveness and long-term customer loyalty.

- **Utilization of data to optimize processes and decisions**

The use of data to optimize processes and decisions has become a crucial element of business strategy in the era of digitization. Companies leverage the vast amounts of available data to make more informed decisions, improve operational efficiency, and drive innovation.

This use of data has become imperative for companies seeking to remain competitive in an ever-evolving business environment. Digitization has enabled the collection and analysis of vast amounts of data from various sources, thereby providing companies with valuable insights into their internal operations, customer behaviors, and market trends (LaValle et al., 2011).

Process optimization relies on using data to identify inefficiencies, bottlenecks, and improvement opportunities in business operations. For example, companies can employ process analysis techniques to map and model their workflows, thereby identifying unnecessary or redundant steps and proposing solutions to streamline them (Davenport and Harris, 2007). Similarly, predictive analytics can be utilized to anticipate equipment failures and plan maintenance proactively, thereby reducing unexpected downtime and associated costs.

When it comes to decision-making, data plays a crucial role by providing factual information to inform strategic choices. Companies can utilize data analysis techniques such as data mining, machine learning, and predictive analytics to identify trends, detect patterns, and assess past performance (Provost and Fawcett, 2013).

Utilizing data to optimize processes and decisions also presents challenges, particularly regarding the quality and confidentiality of the data. Companies must ensure that the data used for decision-making is accurate, reliable, and relevant, while also complying with regulations regarding data protection and user privacy (Wamba et al., 2015).

In conclusion, leveraging data to optimize processes and decisions is a critical element of business strategy in the digitalization era. By harnessing available information, companies can enhance their operational efficiency, make more informed decisions, and remain competitive in the market.

- **Collaboration and Co-creation through digital platforms**

Collaboration and co-creation through digital platforms represent a significant evolution in how companies interact with their customers, partners, and other stakeholders. Digital platforms facilitate connection and collaboration between geographically distant individuals and organizations, thereby fostering innovation and joint value creation.

Digital platforms have radically transformed how businesses collaborate and co-create value with their stakeholders. Through these platforms, companies can create online spaces where users can connect, share ideas, collaborate on projects, and contribute to innovation in a seamless and effective manner (Chesbrough et al., 2018).

Collaboration through digital platforms enables companies to leverage collective intelligence by gathering ideas, skills, and resources from diverse backgrounds. For instance, crowd sourcing platforms allow businesses to submit challenges or problems to an online community, soliciting creative and innovative solutions from people worldwide (Howe, 2008). Similarly, internal collaboration platforms enable employees from different teams, departments, or regions to work together on common projects, fostering cross-functional collaboration and organizational synergy.

Co-creation through digital platforms involves the active participation of customers and other stakeholders in the design, development, and improvement process of products and services (Prahalad and Ramaswamy, 2004). For example, software industry companies use open-source development models, allowing external developers to contribute to the source code and thus enrich the features and quality of the final product (von Hippel et al., 2016). Similarly, consumer goods companies can invite their customers to participate in design competitions or product testing programs, thus gathering valuable feedback to enhance their offerings.

Digital platforms also play a crucial role in facilitating partnerships and strategic alliances between businesses. Online marketplace platforms, for example, enable companies to sell their products and services to a wide audience through a shared digital infrastructure (Parker and Van Alstyne, 2019). Similarly, resource-sharing platforms, such as carpooling platforms or housing rental platforms, allow individuals and businesses to collaborate to optimize the use of assets and resources.

In conclusion, collaboration and co-creation through digital platforms represent a fundamental shift in how businesses innovate and create value with their stakeholders. By leveraging these platforms, companies can expand their reach, access new ideas and skills, and foster innovation in a collaborative and open manner.

1.4. Emerging Value Creation Models:

- **Demand Economy: Providing Tailored Solutions through Data Analysis**

The demand economy, facilitated by data analysis, represents a major shift in how businesses interact with their customers. By using data to understand customers' needs and preferences deeply, companies can provide tailored solutions that precisely meet the expectations of each individual.

Demand economy, powered by data analysis, offers businesses the opportunity to provide tailored solutions that precisely meet the individual needs of their customers. Rather than offering standardized products or services, companies leverage vast amounts of available data to deeply understand customer behaviors, preferences, and needs, enabling them to offer personalized and highly relevant offerings (Kannan et al., 2016).

Data analysis enables businesses to segment their market based on specific customer characteristics such as age, gender, geographic location, purchasing habits, and product preferences. These segments can then be used to personalize offerings and communications, thus providing a more relevant and engaging customer experience (Verhoef et al., 2017).

Another key application of data analysis in the demand economy is product recommendation. Machine learning algorithms analyze customer purchase and browsing data to identify patterns and correlations, enabling businesses to recommend products and services that align with the individual interests and needs of each customer (Chen et al., 2018). These personalized recommendations help increase sales and improve customer satisfaction by streamlining the purchasing process and providing relevant suggestions.

Furthermore, data analysis enables businesses to anticipate the future needs of customers and offer proactive solutions. By identifying purchasing trends and behaviors, companies can anticipate customer needs and provide relevant products or services before they are explicitly requested, thereby enhancing customer loyalty and satisfaction (Kumar and Reinartz, 2018).

In conclusion, the demand economy, fueled by data analysis, represents a major evolution in how businesses interact with their customers. By deeply understanding customer needs and preferences, companies can provide tailored solutions that offer significant added value, thereby strengthening loyalty, satisfaction, and profitability.

- **Monetization of Platforms and Social Networks**

Monetization of platforms and social networks has become a central economic model in the digital economy. Companies leverage their online audiences to generate revenue through various strategies, such as advertising, premium subscriptions, sales of products or services, and many others.

Monetizing platforms and social networks has become a crucial element of business strategy in the digital economy. Companies leverage the vast audiences and user engagement on these platforms to generate revenue in various ways.

Advertising represents one of the primary revenue sources for many platforms and social networks. Companies pay to display targeted ads to users based on their demographic characteristics, interests, and online behavior. Platforms utilize sophisticated algorithms to precisely target ads and maximize their effectiveness, thus generating significant revenue through clicks, impressions, or user actions on the ads (Evans, 2016).

Furthermore, some platforms and social networks offer premium subscription models, allowing users to pay a fixed amount to access additional features or exclusive content. For example, music streaming platforms offer paid subscriptions to access ad-free music, better audio quality, and advanced customization features (Chen et al., 2019). Similarly, professional social networks like LinkedIn offer premium subscriptions to access advanced job search and professional networking features.

Selling products or services is another monetization strategy for certain platforms and social networks. For example, e-commerce platforms integrated into social networks allow businesses to sell their products directly to their followers, providing a seamless and transparent shopping experience (Feng et al., 2017). Similarly, social media influencers can monetize their audience by promoting products or services from partner brands, often for a fee or commission for each generated sale.

Finally, some platforms and social networks utilize mixed revenue models, combining multiple sources of income to maximize profitability. For instance, a video streaming platform might offer a premium ad-free subscription while displaying ads for free users, while also providing e-commerce features to purchase products or services related to the viewed content (De Vries et al., 2017).

In conclusion, monetizing platforms and social networks represents a crucial economic model in the digital economy. By leveraging their vast audiences and user engagement, businesses can generate significant revenue through advertising, subscriptions, selling products or services, and other monetization strategies.

- **Integration of Artificial Intelligence and Automation to Create Value**

The integration of artificial intelligence (AI) and automation has become a key strategy for creating value in many sectors. By harnessing AI's capabilities to analyze data, make decisions, and execute tasks autonomously, businesses can enhance operational efficiency, drive innovation, and deliver more personalized customer experiences.

The integration of artificial intelligence (AI) and automation offers considerable potential to create value across a wide range of industries and business domains. By combining AI's capabilities to process and analyze massive datasets with automation to execute tasks autonomously, businesses can achieve significant efficiency gains, reduce operational costs, and innovate in delivering products and services (Bughin et al., 2017).

In the realm of data management, AI is employed to analyze complex datasets and identify patterns, trends, and insights that are challenging to detect using traditional methods. For instance, machine learning algorithms can be utilized to predict customer behaviors, detect fraud, optimize logistics operations, or recommend personalized products or services (Davenport and Ronanki, 2018).

Automation, on the other hand, enables businesses to carry out repetitive or routine tasks autonomously, thereby freeing up human resources to focus on higher-value tasks. For instance, robots and automated systems can be employed in manufacturing to assemble products, in logistics to manage warehouses and shipments, or in call centers to respond to customer inquiries automatically (Manyika et al., 2017).

By combining AI and automation, businesses can create autonomous systems capable of making decisions and acting in real-time without human intervention. For example, autonomous vehicles use AI algorithms to detect obstacles, interpret traffic signals, and make driving decisions, thus providing increased safety and convenience for drivers (Thrun et al., 2006). Similarly, automated trading systems leverage AI-based predictive models to make real-time investment decisions, thus capitalizing on opportunities in financial markets (Gan et al., 2018).

In conclusion, the integration of artificial intelligence (AI) and automation holds substantial potential for creating value across various business sectors. By harnessing the capabilities of AI to analyze data and make decisions, and using automation to perform tasks autonomously, companies can enhance operational efficiency, boost innovation, and offer more personalized customer experiences, thereby strengthening their competitiveness in the market.

1.5. Situational statement:

In order to offer a thorough examination of prior research on digital transformation and value creation, we will look at a few scholarly publications and case studies that have addressed this subject. With an emphasis on the several models and theories of digital transformation, this section will highlight the key discoveries and contributions of previous research.

- In 2014, Gawer carried out a study titled "The Business Model of Platforms: A Research Overview." This study looks at how digital platforms foster relationships amongst various user groups to create value. Gawer places a strong emphasis on the value of network effects and the ways in which platforms can result in open innovation and economies of scale. The findings demonstrate how platforms provide value by facilitating productive user interactions and offering supplementary services that improve the ecosystem.

Uber, an American multinational company built around a mobile application that links users, was the subject of a case study. Uber connects drivers and passengers through a platform model. This case study investigates how Uber has used real-time data and mobile technologies to revolutionize the transportation industry. The findings demonstrate how Uber's innovative platform has facilitated resource optimization, enhanced customer satisfaction, and quick international growth.

- In 2012, McAfee & Brynjolfsson carried out a second study titled "Big Data: The Management Revolution." The impact of big data on value generation and decision-making is covered in this article. The writers demonstrate how businesses can use data to streamline processes, enhance goods and services, and create more winning marketing campaigns. The findings show how big data used strategically can result in major competitive advantages, especially when combined with predictive and prescriptive analytics. For instance, Google's search engine and advertising services are powered by enormous amounts of data. This case study examines how Google uses data to provide advertisers with insightful information. Moreover, Google has become one of the most profitable businesses in the world because to the monetization of data through targeted advertising.
- In 2021, Verhoef et al. carried out research on "The Influence of Digital Transformation on Customer Experience." The impact of digital transformation on the customer experience is investigated in this study. Verhoef and his associates pinpoint crucial digital levers, such personalization, interactivity, and service continuity, that can improve consumer contact. The findings suggest that digital technologies provide enhanced personalization and improved consumer happiness, hence resulting in elevated loyalty and sustained value. Apple, for example, has a user-centric strategy to offer a distinctive consumer experience through its goods and services. In order to build a seamless and interesting ecosystem, Apple blends hardware, software, and services, as this

case study examines. Additionally, Apple's flawless user interface increases client loyalty and keeps profit margins high.

- In 2016, Don and Alex Tapscott carried out a study titled "Blockchain Technology and Digital Transformation: A Comparative Study." The study looks at how blockchain technology helps with digital transformation by offering corporate transaction security, transparency, and efficiency solutions. The findings demonstrate how blockchain technology can revolutionize company models by fostering new kinds of trust and cooperation in online transactions.
- In 2014, Andrew McAfee, Didier Bonnet, and George Westerman conducted a research titled "Digital Transformation and the Creation of New Business Models." This study demonstrates how innovative technology and business strategies are adopted by top digital transformation organizations in order to generate value and set themselves apart from rivals. The findings show that for digital transformation to be successful there needs to be a clear vision and a well-thought-out plan.
- In 2017, Peter Weill and Jeanne W. Ross carried out a follow-up study titled "How Digital Transformation Creates New Business Value." According to the report, businesses may generate value through digital transformation by enhancing operational effectiveness, creating new goods and services, and reimagining client interactions. The significance of embracing new technology and making investments in digital capabilities is emphasized.
- Klaus Schwab performed a research in 2018 titled "The Impact of Digital Transformation on Business Models: Evidence from a Global Survey." Schwab examines the impact of digital transformation on conventional business paradigms in this study. The findings demonstrate that businesses are better positioned to generate value and satisfy evolving customer expectations when they successfully incorporate digital technologies into their operations and product/service strategy.
- In 2016, Viktor Mayer-Schönberger and Kenneth Cukier carried out a second study titled "The Role of Big Data in Digital Transformation: A Quantitative Study." The influence of big data on digital transformation is quantified in this study. The findings show that businesses may generate significant additional value by using big data to enhance decision-making, optimize operations, and create new products.

Depending on the methodology employed, prior research indicates that digital transformation can provide benefit in a number of ways.

- ✓ Platform Model: Generates value by utilizing network effects and promoting interactions.
- ✓ Data Model: Produces insightful data for operational optimization and decision-making.
- ✓ Customer Experience Model: By providing individualized and interesting encounters, this model increases customer happiness and loyalty.

2. PROPOSAL FOR A RESEARCH MODEL ON THE VALUE CREATION PROCESS IN THE DIGITAL AGE:

This research model illustrates how digital transformation leads to a series of interconnected processes that contribute to value creation within the enterprise. Each step, from data collection to customer engagement through innovation and process optimization, plays a crucial role in generating overall value for the company.

Digital transformation is a process revolutionizing how businesses operate and interact with their environment. At the core of this transformation lies the extensive collection of data from various sources such as connected devices, online interactions, business transactions, and many others. These vast and varied datasets then fuel advanced analytics, enabling businesses to extract meaningful insights about their customers, operations, and the market as a whole.

One of the primary outcomes of this in-depth data analysis is the ability to personalize products, services, and customer experiences. By understanding individual customer needs, businesses can tailor their offerings precisely, thereby providing significant added value and enhancing customer loyalty.

Simultaneously, digital transformation also fosters continuous innovation. By leveraging digital technologies such as artificial intelligence, the Internet of Things (IoT), and block chain, businesses develop new business models, products, and services. These innovations create new opportunities for growth and differentiation in the market.

En conclusion, la transformation digitale crée de la valeur globale pour les entreprises en améliorant l'efficacité opérationnelle, en stimulant l'innovation, en renforçant l'engagement client et en offrant des expériences personnalisées. Cela se traduit par une croissance des revenus, une meilleure rentabilité et une position concurrentielle renforcée sur le marché.

Digital transformation

Extensive Data collection

Advanced Data analysis

Personalization and customization

Innovation and creation of new

Services
Optimization of internal processes
Customer engagement and loyalty
Creation of overall value

Figure 2. Process of Value Creation in the Era of Digitalization

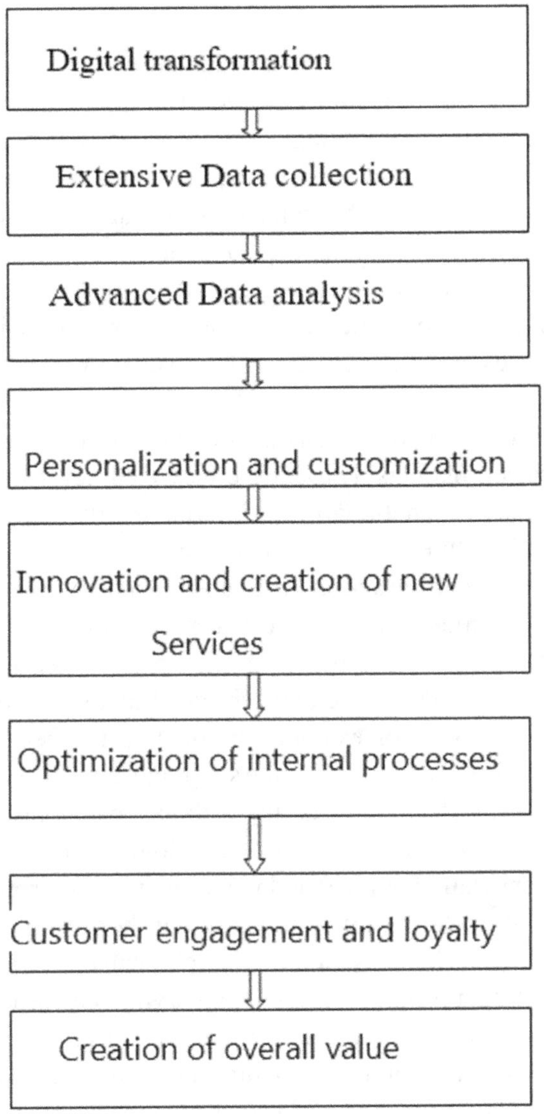

This figure represents the key components of digital transformation, visually illustrating the interconnected processes that lead to digital transformation, showing how different strategies and initiatives contribute to creating overall value for an organization.

3. DISCUSSION OF RESULTS:

Digital transformation represents both a challenge and a major opportunity for businesses in terms of value creation. Indeed, it offers considerable potential for rethinking business models, improving operational efficiency, and better meeting customer needs. However, it also presents significant challenges to overcome.

One of the key advantages of digital transformation is the improvement of operational efficiency. By integrating digital technologies into internal processes, companies can automate certain tasks, reduce errors, and increase productivity. For example, the use of integrated management software optimizes inventory management, human resources, and finances, resulting in cost savings and better resource allocation.

Furthermore, digital transformation offers companies the opportunity to expand their reach and reach new markets. Through increased online presence, companies can reach a wider audience, both nationally and internationally. E-commerce platforms, social networks, and mobile applications enable effective promotion of products and services and facilitate transactions with customers.

Personalization of products and services also constitutes a major advantage of digital transformation. By collecting and analyzing customer data, companies can better understand their needs and preferences, enabling them to offer more targeted and personalized offerings. For example, product recommendations based on a customer's purchase history can enhance the shopping experience and foster loyalty.

However, digital transformation is not without challenges. One of the main obstacles lies in the need to invest in new technologies and infrastructures. Initial costs can be high, especially for small and medium-sized enterprises, and it is often difficult to measure the return on investment in the short term. Additionally, managing data and cybersecurity presents a major challenge, particularly concerning the protection of customer privacy and compliance with data protection regulations.

Finally, digital transformation also involves significant organizational and cultural changes. Companies must adapt their structures and processes to fully leverage new technologies, which can lead to resistance to change from employees. Additionally, training and skills development are essential to ensure that employees are able to effectively use new technologies and adapt to new ways of working.

In conclusion, digital transformation offers considerable opportunities for value creation, but it requires strategic management and continuous adaptation to overcome associated challenges. Companies that succeed in addressing these challenges and fully leveraging the benefits of digital transformation will be better positioned to thrive in an ever-evolving business environment.

CONCLUSION:

The creation of value, through a profitable business model, has been largely modified by the globalization of value chains, as Western companies have refocused on the most profitable activities: upstream and downstream of production, and more particularly on services and customer relations. The digital revolution has ushered in new modes of value creation. Thanks to the multiplier effects of networks, the power of algorithms and a capacity for rapid growth, the business models of digital platforms are capturing a growing share of value.

The polarization of the economic fabric around a few major digital players is becoming a credible prospect. This study examines three types of reaction to this scenario. Firstly, those of governments, whose tax bases, social models and regulatory powers are being challenged by these platforms. Those of other companies are threatened by the risk of subordination to a handful of players, and for customers, whose trust has built the platforms' prosperity. At a time when business models are being invented to extract value from data, it is the customer who will decide how value is allocated, at a time when business models are being reinvented around data. History is far from being written, but value will be created by those who are able to grasp the essence of the economic world that is being redesigned before our very eyes.

REFERENCES:

Choudhury, M. M., & Harrigan, P. (2014). CRM to social CRM: The integration of new technologies into customer relationship management. *Journal of Strategic Marketing*, 22(2), 149–176. DOI: 10.1080/0965254X.2013.876069

-Coase, R. H. (1972). Industrial organization: a proposal for research. In *Economic research: Retrospect and prospect, Volume 3, policy issues and research opportunities in industrial organization* (pp. 59-73). NBER.

Davenport, T. H., & Harris, J. (2007). *Competing on analytics: The new science of winning*. Harvard Business Press.

Howe, J. (2008). *Crowdsourcing: Why the power of the crowd is driving the future of business*. Crown Business.

Gawer, A. (2014). The Business Model of Platforms: A Research Overview. *Journal of Management Studies*.

Evans, D. S. (2016). *Matchmakers: The new economics of multisided platforms*. Harvard Business Review Press.

De Vries, L., Gensler, S., & Leeflang, P. S. (2017). Popularity of brand posts on brand fan pages: An investigation of the effects of social media marketing. *Journal of Interactive Marketing*, 31, 89–100.

Feng, T., Huang, X., & Liu, G. (2017). Social commerce research: Definition, research themes and improvement measures. *Information Systems Frontiers*, 19(3), 447–458.

Davenport, T. H., & Ronanki, R. (2018). Artificial intelligence for the real world. *Harvard Business Review*, 96(1), 108–116.

Gan, G., Jiang, H., & Li, T. (2018). Trading bots and institutional traders on cryptocurrency exchanges. *Journal of Management Information Systems*, 35(1), 333–355.

Frank, M. J., Allen, J. J., Cavanagh, J. F., & Bismark, A. W. (2019). Multiple dissociations between comorbid depression and anxiety on reward and punishment processing: Evidence from computationally informed EEG. *Computational Psychiatry (Cambridge, Mass.)*, 3, 1. PMID: 31149639

Florek-Paszkowska, A., Ujwary-Gil, A., & Godlewska-Dzioboń, B. (2021). Business innovation and critical success factors in the era of digital transformation and turbulent times.

Kannan, P. K., & Li, H. A. (2017). Digital marketing: A framework, review and research agenda. *International Journal of Research in Marketing*, 34(1), 22–45. DOI: 10.1016/j.ijresmar.2016.11.006

Normann, R., & Ramirez, R. (1993). From value chain to value constellation: Designing interactive strategy. *Harvard Business Review*, 71(4), 65–77. PMID: 10127040

Pine, B. J., & Gilmore, J. H. (1998). Welcome to the experience economy. *Harvard Business Review*, 76(4), 97–105. PMID: 10181589

Osterwalder, A., & Pigneur, Y. (2010). *Business model generation: a handbook for visionaries, game changers, and challengers* (Vol. 1). John Wiley & Sons.

LaValle, S., Lesser, E., Shockley, R., Hopkins, M. S., & Kruschwitz, N. (2011). Big data, analytics and the path from insights to value. *MIT Sloan Management Review*, 52(2), 21–32.

McAfee, A., & Brynjolfsson, E. (2012). Big Data: The Management Revolution. *Harvard Business Review*. PMID: 23074865

Mayer-Schönberger, V., & Cukier, K. (2013). *Big data: A revolution that will transform how we live, work, and think*. Houghton Mifflin Harcourt.

Manyika, J., Chui, M., Bughin, J., Dobbs, R., Bisson, P., & Marrs, A. (2017). *A future that works: Automation, employment, and productivity*. McKinsey Global Institute.

Kumar, V., & Reinartz, W. (2018). Creating enduring customer value. *Journal of Marketing*, 80(6), 36–68.

Parker, G. G., & Van Alstyne, M. W. (2019). Innovation, ecosystems, and platforms: A multilevel theory of digital technology. *Journal of Management Information Systems*, 36(2), 354–389.

Prahalad, C. K., & Ramaswamy, V. (2004). Co-creation experiences: The next practice in value creation. *Journal of Interactive Marketing*, 18(3), 5–14. DOI: 10.1002/dir.20015

Provost, F., & Fawcett, T. (2013). *Data science for business: What you need to know about data mining and data-analytic thinking*. O'Reilly Media, Inc.

Rifkin, S. B. (2014). Examining the links between community participation and health outcomes: A review of the literature. *Health Policy and Planning*, 29(suppl_2), ii98–ii106. DOI: 10.1093/heapol/czu076 PMID: 25274645

Rust, R. T., Kannan, P. K., & Peng, X. (2018). *The customer economy: Why customer lifetime value is the key to unlocking great business performance*. Routledge.

-Schwab, K. (2018). The Impact of Digital Transformation on Business Models: Evidence from a Global Survey.

Shapiro, C., & Varian, H. R. (1999). The art of standards wars. *California Management Review*, 41(2), 8–32. DOI: 10.2307/41165984

-Tapscott, D., & Tapscott, A. (2016). *Blockchain Technology and Digital Transformation: A Comparative Study.

Smith, B. J., & Lim, M. H. (2020). How the COVID-19 pandemic is focusing attention on loneliness and social isolation. *Public Health Research & Practice*, 30(2), 3022008. PMID: 32601651

Brynjolfsson, E., & McAfee, A. (2014). *The second machine age: Work, progress, and prosperity in a time of brilliant technologies*. WW Norton & Company.

-Bughin, J., Hazan, E., Ramaswamy, S., Chui, M., Allas, T., Dahlström, P., ... & Henke, N. (2017). Artificial intelligence: The next digital frontier?. McKinsey Global Institute, 1-118.

Chen, J., Chiu, M. L., & Petrescu, M. (2018). Customized product recommendation in e-commerce. *Information & Management*, 55(7), 833–851.

-Cavelius, F., Endenich, C., & Zicari, A. (2018, May). L'impact de la digitalisation sur le role du controleur de gestion. In *Transitions numériques et informations comptables* (pp. cd-rom)

Chesbrough, H., Vanhaverbeke, W., & West, J. (Eds.). (2018). *New frontiers in open innovation*. Oxford University Press.

Chen, Y., Chen, N., & Wen, Y. (2019). The Spotify business model: Redefining the music streaming industry. *Information Systems Management*, 36(2), 116–132.

Thrun, S., Montemerlo, M., Dahlkamp, H., Stavens, D., Aron, A., Diebel, J., Fong, P., Gale, J., Halpenny, M., Hoffmann, G., Lau, K., Oakley, C., Palatucci, M., Pratt, V., Stang, P., Strohband, S., Dupont, C., Jendrossek, L.-E., Koelen, C., & Mahoney, P. (2006). Stanley: The robot that won the DARPA Grand Challenge. *Journal of Field Robotics*, 23(9), 661–692. DOI: 10.1002/rob.20147

Van Alstyne, M. W., Parker, G. G., & Choudary, S. P. (2016). Pipelines, platforms, and the new rules of strategy. *Harvard Business Review*, 94(4), 54–62.

Verhoef, P. C., Broekhuizen, T., Bart, Y., Bhattacharya, A., Dong, J. Q., Fabian, N., & Venkatesan, R. (2017). Digital transformation: A multidisciplinary reflection and research agenda. *Journal of Business Research*, 81, 236–246.

Verhoef, P. C., Broekhuizen, T., Bart, Y., Bhattacharya, A., & Dong, Qi, J., Fabian, N., & Haenlein, M. (2021). The Influence of Digital Transformation on Customer Experience. *Journal of Service Research.*

Verhoef, P. C., Kannan, P. K., & Inman, J. J. (2015). From multi-channel retailing to omni-channel retailing: Introduction to the special issue on multi-channel retailing. *Journal of Retailing*, 91(2), 174–181. DOI: 10.1016/j.jretai.2015.02.005

-Westerman, G., Bonnet, D., & McAfee, A. (2014). Digital Transformation and the Creation of New Business Models

Wamba, S. F., Gunasekaran, A., Akter, S., Ren, S. J. F., Dubey, R., & Childe, S. J. (2015). Big data analytics and firm performance: Effects of dynamic capabilities. *Journal of Business Research*, 70, 356–365.

Von Hippel, E., & von Krogh, G. (2016). Free revealing and the private-collective model for innovation incentives. *R & D Management*, 46(3), 438–451.

-Weill, P., & Ross, J. W. (2017). How Digital Transformation Creates New Business Value

-Vial, G. (2021). Understanding digital transformation: A review and a research agenda. *Managing digital transformation*, 13-66.

Winasis, S., Djumarno, D., Riyanto, S., & Ariyanto, E. (2021). The effect of transformational leadership climate on employee engagement during digital transformation in Indonesian banking industry. *International Journal of Data and Network Science*, 5(2), 91–96.

Chapter 2
The Impact of Digital Transformation on Supply Chain Management:
Opportunities, Challenges, and Future Directions

Mohamed Oualid El Baki
Faculté des Sciences Juridiques, Économiques, et Sociales de Agdal, Morocco

Manal Benatiya Andaloussi
Chouaib Doukkali University, Morocco

ABSTRACT

Digital transformation is reshaping SCM by integrating advanced technologies. This chapter explores the impact of digitalization on SCM, focusing on the opportunities it presents, the challenges organizations face, and the future directions of digital supply chains. Key areas covered include the role of Artificial Intelligence (AI) and Machine Learning in optimizing processes, the use of Internet of Things (IoT) for real-time monitoring, and the implementation of blockchain for improved traceability. The chapter also examines the benefits of digital transformation, such as increased productivity, better visibility, and enhanced sustainability. it discusses the challenges associated with digital adoption, including technological integration, data security, and change management. The findings are the potential of digital technologies and offer practical advice for companies looking to navigate their digital journey and achieve competitive advantages in a rapidly changing environment.

DOI: 10.4018/979-8-3693-4427-9.ch002

1. INTRODUCTION

Supply Chain Management (SCM) plays a pivotal role in the functioning of today's globalized economy. As businesses strive to meet increasing consumer demands, optimize operations, and remain competitive, efficient supply chain management becomes critical. Traditionally, supply chains operated with manual processes, limited data visibility, and siloed systems, often leading to inefficiencies, delays, and increased costs. However, with the advent of digital technologies, the landscape of supply chain management has been undergoing a transformative shift. Digital transformation in SCM refers to the integration of digital technologies across supply chain processes, enabling real-time data sharing, automation, and enhanced decision-making capabilities. This evolution has redefined how organizations manage their supply chains, driving improvements in efficiency, transparency, and agility.

This chapter aims to explore the impact of digital transformation on supply chain management by examining the various opportunities and challenges it presents. Through an in-depth analysis, the chapter seeks to provide insights into how digitalization is reshaping the supply chain landscape, enhancing efficiency, and creating competitive advantages. Additionally, the chapter will look into the future directions of digital SCM, considering emerging trends and technologies that are poised to further revolutionize supply chain operations. The goal is to offer a comprehensive understanding of the significance of digital transformation in SCM and to guide practitioners and researchers in navigating this complex yet promising field.

To achieve the chapter's objectives, the following key research questions will be addressed:

1. **How is digital transformation reshaping supply chain management?**

This question focuses on understanding the fundamental changes brought about by digital technologies in the structure and functioning of supply chains.

2. **What are the key benefits and challenges associated with digital SCM?**

This question explores the advantages that digitalization brings to supply chain management, as well as the obstacles that organizations face in implementing these technologies.

3. **What are the future trends in digital supply chains?**

This question aims to identify and analyze the emerging trends and technologies that are likely to shape the future of digital supply chain management.

2. LITERATURE REVIEW

Historical Perspective

Evolution of Supply Chain Management

Supply Chain Management (SCM) has undergone significant changes over the past several decades. Initially, supply chains were characterized by fragmented and siloed processes, with limited visibility and coordination across different stages of production and distribution. The focus was primarily on cost reduction and efficiency within isolated functions, such as procurement, production, and logistics. However, the rise of globalization and the increasing complexity of markets demanded more integrated and responsive supply chain networks. This shift led to the development of more sophisticated SCM practices that emphasized cross-functional collaboration, strategic partnerships, and the integration of information technologies to enhance visibility and coordination (Christopher, 2016; Chopra & Meindl, 2020).

The Transition from Manual Processes to Digital Solutions

The transition from manual processes to digital solutions marked a pivotal moment in the evolution of SCM. Initially, supply chains relied heavily on manual data entry, paper-based documentation, and labor-intensive processes, which often resulted in inefficiencies, errors, and delays. The introduction of Enterprise Resource Planning (ERP) systems in the 1990s laid the foundation for more automated and integrated supply chain operations. These systems enabled companies to centralize and standardize their data, facilitating better decision-making and coordination across the supply chain. As digital technologies continued to evolve, supply chains began to adopt more advanced tools such as Electronic Data Interchange (EDI), barcode scanning, and radio-frequency identification (RFID) systems, further enhancing the accuracy and efficiency of supply chain processes (Rushton, Croucher, & Baker, 2017).

Theoretical Frameworks

Overview of Relevant Theories in SCM and Digital Transformation

Several theoretical frameworks underpin the study of SCM and digital transformation. One of the foundational theories in SCM is the Resource-Based View (RBV), which emphasizes the importance of strategic resources and capabilities in achieving competitive advantage (Barney, 1991). In the context of digital transformation, RBV suggests that the integration of digital technologies into SCM can be seen as a strategic resource that enhances a firm's ability to compete by improving efficiency, agility, and innovation.

Another relevant theory is the Dynamic Capabilities Framework, which focuses on a firm's ability to adapt, integrate, and reconfigure internal and external resources to respond to rapidly changing environments (Teece, Pisano, & Shuen, 1997). Digital transformation in SCM can be viewed through this lens, as it requires firms to continuously adapt their processes and technologies to remain competitive in a dynamic market.

Furthermore, Transaction Cost Economics (TCE) provides insights into how digital technologies can reduce the costs associated with coordinating and managing supply chain transactions. TCE suggests that digital tools, such as blockchain and cloud computing, can lower transaction costs by increasing transparency, reducing information asymmetry, and automating contractual processes (Williamson, 1985).

Current Trends

Review of Existing Literature on Digital Transformation in Supply Chains

Recent literature highlights the profound impact of digital transformation on SCM. The adoption of digital technologies such as Artificial Intelligence (AI), the Internet of Things (IoT), Blockchain, and Big Data Analytics has led to significant improvements in supply chain efficiency, visibility, and responsiveness. These technologies enable real-time data collection, advanced analytics, and automated decision-making, which collectively enhance the agility and resilience of supply chains (Ivanov, Dolgui, & Sokolov, 2019; Wang, Gunasekaran, Ngai, & Papadopoulos, 2020).

Analysis of the Key Technologies Driving Digital SCM

Digital transformation in SCM is driven by several key technologies. AI and Machine Learning are being used for demand forecasting, inventory optimization, and logistics planning, enabling companies to make more accurate and data-driven decisions. The IoT facilitates real-time tracking and monitoring of goods, improving supply chain visibility and reducing the risk of disruptions. Blockchain technology enhances transparency and traceability by providing a secure and immutable ledger of transactions, which is particularly valuable in industries with complex supply chains, such as pharmaceuticals and food (Kouhizadeh, Sarkis, & Zhu, 2020).

Big Data Analytics allows companies to analyze vast amounts of data from various sources to identify patterns, trends, and correlations that can inform strategic decisions. Robotics and automation are transforming warehousing and distribution processes, leading to increased efficiency and reduced labor costs. Finally, cloud computing is enabling better collaboration and data sharing across the supply chain, making it easier for companies to coordinate with suppliers, partners, and customers (Christopher, 2016).

A notable contribution to this field is the comprehensive bibliometric literature review conducted by Manal Benatiya Andaloussi, titled "A Bibliometric Literature Review of Digital Supply Chain: Trends, Insights, and Future Directions." Andaloussi's work provides an in-depth analysis of the digital supply chain (DSC) by employing bibliometric methods to map out key research themes, influential authors, and prolific journals within the domain. Her study highlights the significant impact of digital technologies on supply chain management, emphasizing trends such as intelligent supply chain management, technologies that drive supply chain performance, and the rise of circular and sustainable supply chains. This review not only synthesizes existing research but also offers valuable insights into the future directions of digital transformation in SCM, making it a critical reference for understanding the evolving landscape of the field.

3. KEY TECHNOLOGIES IN DIGITAL SUPPLY CHAIN

Artificial Intelligence (AI) and Machine Learning

AI and Machine Learning (ML) are transforming supply chain management by providing advanced tools for demand forecasting, inventory management, and logistics optimization. AI algorithms analyze historical sales data, market trends, and external factors (such as weather or economic indicators) to predict future demand more accurately. This allows companies to optimize inventory levels, reducing the risk of stockouts or overstocking (Choi, Chan, & Yue, 2021). In logistics, AI-driven systems optimize routing, load planning, and delivery schedules, resulting in cost savings and improved delivery times. ML models continuously learn from new data, enhancing their predictive capabilities and allowing for real-time adjustments to supply chain strategies (Min, Zacharia, & Smith, 2019).

Internet of Things (IoT)

The Internet of Things (IoT) plays a crucial role in real-time tracking, monitoring, and data collection within the supply chain. IoT devices, such as sensors and RFID tags, are embedded in products, vehicles, and infrastructure, providing continuous data on the location, condition, and status of goods as they move through the supply chain. This real-time visibility allows companies to monitor shipments, manage inventory, and respond quickly to disruptions or delays (Ben-Daya, Hassini, & Bahroun, 2019). For instance, IoT-enabled temperature sensors in the pharmaceutical industry ensure that sensitive products are stored and transported under optimal conditions, reducing the risk of spoilage and ensuring compliance with regulations (Zhong, Xu, & Wang, 2017).

Blockchain

Blockchain technology enhances transparency, traceability, and security in the supply chain by providing a decentralized and immutable ledger of transactions. Each transaction or event in the supply chain is recorded on the blockchain, creating a transparent and tamper-proof record that can be accessed by all authorized parties. This is particularly valuable in industries where trust and traceability are critical, such as food and pharmaceuticals. Blockchain can help verify the authenticity of products, track their origin, and ensure compliance with industry standards and regulations (Kouhizadeh, Sarkis, & Zhu, 2020). Additionally, smart contracts—self-executing contracts with terms directly written into code—automate and streamline processes such as payments and order fulfillment, reducing the need for intermediaries and minimizing the risk of disputes (Saberi, Kouhizadeh, Sarkis, & Shen, 2019).

Big Data Analytics

Big Data Analytics enables the use of vast amounts of data generated across the supply chain to inform decision-making and predictive analytics. By analyzing data from various sources, including IoT devices, social media, and market reports, companies can identify patterns, trends, and correlations that may not be immediately apparent. This data-driven approach allows for more accurate demand forecasting, risk management, and inventory optimization (Wang, Gunasekaran, Ngai, & Papadopoulos, 2020). Predictive analytics, a key component of Big Data Analytics, helps companies anticipate potential disruptions, such as supply shortages or demand spikes, and take proactive measures to mitigate their impact (Ivanov & Dolgui, 2020).

Robotics and Automation

Robotics and automation are revolutionizing warehousing, production, and distribution processes in the supply chain. Automated systems, such as robotic picking and packing, conveyor belts, and autonomous vehicles, enhance the efficiency and accuracy of operations, reducing labor costs and minimizing human error (Wang, Tiwari, & Wee, 2021). In warehouses, robots can perform repetitive tasks such as sorting, lifting, and transporting goods, allowing human workers to focus on more complex activities. In production, automation improves consistency and quality by reducing variations in manufacturing processes. The use of robotics also extends to last-mile delivery, where autonomous drones and vehicles are being tested for efficient and contactless delivery solutions (Greasley & Assanova, 2022).

Cloud Computing

Cloud computing plays a pivotal role in improving collaboration, data storage, and accessibility across the supply chain. By leveraging cloud-based platforms, companies can store and share vast amounts of data securely and efficiently. Cloud computing facilitates real-time collaboration between supply chain partners, allowing them to access and update shared data from anywhere in the world. This improves coordination, reduces the risk of data silos, and enhances decision-making across the supply chain (Wu, Yue, Jin, & Yen, 2016). Additionally, cloud computing supports the scalability of supply chain operations, enabling companies to quickly adapt to changes in demand or market conditions by scaling their IT infrastructure up or down as needed (Cheng, Chen, & Luo, 2015).

4. OPPORTUNITIES OF DIGITAL TRANSFORMATION IN SUPPLY CHAIN

Enhanced Efficiency and Productivity

Digital transformation significantly enhances efficiency and productivity in supply chain management by automating routine processes and enabling real-time data access. Technologies like AI, IoT, and robotics contribute to reducing operational costs and time, allowing companies to streamline their supply chain operations. By optimizing resource allocation and minimizing human error, these digital tools lead to improved overall productivity.

Improved Visibility and Transparency

Digital tools such as IoT and blockchain enhance visibility and transparency across the supply chain by enabling real-time tracking and monitoring of goods and services. This increased transparency helps in ensuring the authenticity of products, reducing the risk of counterfeiting, and enhancing trust among stakeholders. For example, blockchain technology provides a tamper-proof record of transactions, which is particularly valuable in complex global supply chains.

Increased Agility and Responsiveness

The digital transformation of supply chains allows companies to respond more quickly to market changes and disruptions. By leveraging predictive analytics and real-time data, businesses can anticipate demand shifts, manage inventory more effectively, and quickly adapt to new market conditions. This agility is crucial in today's fast-paced business environment, where consumer demands and external factors such as natural disasters or pandemics can cause significant disruptions.

Customization and Personalization

Digital transformation enables greater customization and personalization of products and services. Advanced data analytics allow companies to understand individual customer preferences and tailor their offerings accordingly. This not only improves customer satisfaction but also gives companies a competitive edge by offering products that meet specific consumer needs.

Sustainability

Sustainability is increasingly becoming a priority in supply chain management, and digital transformation plays a key role in achieving eco-friendly practices. Technologies like IoT and big data analytics help companies monitor and manage their resource use more efficiently, reducing waste and lowering their carbon footprint. Additionally, digital platforms can facilitate the adoption of circular economy practices, such as recycling and remanufacturing, further contributing to sustainability goals.

5. CASE STUDIES

Successful Digital Transformation

Several companies have successfully implemented digital transformation strategies in their supply chain management (SCM), demonstrating the potential benefits of adopting new technologies.

Amazon, Walmart, and Maersk are prime examples of how digital transformation can significantly enhance supply chain management. Amazon has set a high standard by utilizing cutting-edge technologies such as robotics, artificial intelligence (AI), and machine learning to revolutionize its warehouse operations. These innovations have optimized inventory management, streamlined logistics, and drastically reduced both delivery times and operational costs. By leveraging advanced analytics and automation, Amazon has established itself as a leader in e-commerce efficiency and supply chain management. Walmart, on the other hand, has effectively harnessed digital technologies to refine its supply chain operations. The company employs blockchain technology to improve the traceability and transparency of its food supply chain, while big data analytics are used to optimize inventory levels and reduce waste. Walmart's implementation of real-time data tracking and predictive analytics has significantly enhanced its supply chain resilience and operational efficiency. Maersk, a global giant in shipping and logistics, has embraced digital tools to enhance its supply chain management. By integrating Internet of Things (IoT) sensors and blockchain technology, Maersk has improved the visibility and traceability of cargo, leading to better management of shipping routes and reduced delays. These digital initiatives have not only increased operational efficiency but also improved customer satisfaction, demonstrating the transformative impact of digital technologies in the logistics sector.

Lessons Learned

From both successful and failed digital transformations, several key lessons have emerged; successful digital transformations often hinge on the seamless integration of new technologies with existing systems. Companies that neglect this integration may face significant operational disruptions and inefficiencies. For instance, firms that embarked on digital transformation without aligning their IT infrastructure with new technologies often encountered substantial challenges. Additionally, effective change management is vital for the success of digital transformation initiatives. Organizations must address employee resistance, provide comprehensive training, and cultivate a culture that embraces technological change. Companies that overlooked these critical aspects frequently struggled with low adoption rates and suboptimal utilization of new technologies. Furthermore, high-quality data and robust security measures are fundamental to leveraging digital tools effectively. Businesses that invested in digital technologies but failed to ensure data accuracy and security often faced issues such as incorrect forecasts and increased vulnerability to cyber threats. Addressing these factors comprehensively is crucial for realizing the full potential of digital transformation and maintaining operational integrity.

Comparative Analysis

A comparative analysis of digital transformation across various industries reveals distinct impacts and applications tailored to specific sector needs. In the retail sector, digital transformation primarily focuses on enhancing customer experience through personalization and real-time inventory management. Retailers utilize technologies to provide tailored shopping experiences and manage stock levels dynamically. Conversely, the manufacturing industry emphasizes the implementation of automation and predictive maintenance technologies to boost production efficiency and minimize downtime. These tools are applied to streamline operations and address industry-specific challenges. In the healthcare sector, digital transformation aims to improve patient care and operational efficiency through the adoption of electronic health records and telemedicine solutions. These technologies facilitate better patient management and remote consultations. On the other hand, the logistics industry leverages digital tools to optimize route planning, inventory management, and supply chain visibility. This focus on enhancing logistics operations reflects the industry's priorities for efficiency and real-time data access. Each industry applies digital technologies in ways that align with its unique operational needs and challenges, showcasing the diverse applications and benefits of digital transformation.

6. FUTURE TRENDS AND DIRECTIONS

The Role of Artificial Intelligence and Automation

Artificial intelligence (AI) and automation are poised to drive significant advancements in supply chain management (SCM), revolutionizing various aspects of the industry. One of the key developments will be the evolution of advanced predictive analytics. AI algorithms are expected to become increasingly sophisticated, enhancing capabilities in forecasting demand, optimizing inventory levels, and predicting potential disruptions. This advancement will enable more proactive and informed decision-making, reducing uncertainty in supply chain operations. Additionally, the integration of AI-driven robots and autonomous vehicles in warehouses and logistics is anticipated to greatly enhance operational efficiency. These autonomous systems will help reduce labor costs, minimize human error, and streamline processes. Moreover, intelligent automation will play a crucial role in transforming routine tasks. AI will facilitate more intelligent automation of functions such as order processing and quality control, allowing human resources to focus on higher-value, strategic activities. Collectively, these advancements will contribute to a more efficient, responsive, and resilient supply chain landscape.

Sustainability in Digital Supply Chains

Sustainability is set to become a central focus in digital supply chains, driven by increasing environmental concerns and regulatory pressures. One significant development will be the adoption of green technologies, including energy-efficient systems and sustainable packaging solutions, which aim to reduce the environmental impact of supply chain operations. Additionally, digital tools will play a crucial role in facilitating the implementation of circular economy practices, such as recycling and reusing materials, thereby minimizing waste and resource consumption. Enhanced data analytics will also enable more precise tracking and reduction of carbon footprints throughout the supply chain, aligning with broader sustainability goals. These advancements collectively highlight the shift towards more environmentally responsible and resource-efficient supply chain practices, underscoring the growing importance of sustainability in the digital era.

Hyper-Personalization

Hyper-personalization is set to become increasingly critical in addressing individual customer needs, driven by advancements in digital technology. One key development will be the ability to offer customized products, thanks to advances in digital manufacturing and 3D printing technologies. These innovations will enable companies to create highly tailored products that meet specific customer preferences. Additionally, AI-driven platforms will facilitate real-time personalization of offers and services, adjusting dynamically based on customer behavior and preferences to enhance the overall customer experience. Furthermore, the use of big data analytics will provide deeper insights into customer preferences, allowing for more accurate and targeted marketing strategies. Collectively, these advancements will empower businesses to deliver a more personalized and engaging experience, reflecting the growing demand for individualized customer interactions in the digital age.

Global Supply Chain Resilience

Enhancing global supply chain resilience will be crucial in mitigating risks and managing disruptions:

- **Risk Management Strategies**: Companies will invest in advanced risk management strategies, including scenario planning and simulation models, to prepare for various disruption scenarios.
- **Diversification**: Diversifying supply sources and manufacturing locations will reduce dependency on single suppliers and regions, improving resilience to global disruptions.
- **Collaborative Networks**: Strengthening collaborative networks and partnerships will enable more agile and responsive supply chains, enhancing overall resilience.

Integration of Emerging Technologies

Emerging technologies will continue to shape the future of supply chain management:

- **Blockchain 2.0**: The evolution of blockchain technology will offer enhanced features, such as improved scalability and interoperability, further boosting supply chain transparency and security.
- **Quantum Computing**: Quantum computing has the potential to solve complex optimization problems in supply chains, enabling unprecedented levels of efficiency and innovation.
- **5G Connectivity**: The deployment of 5G technology will facilitate faster and more reliable data transmission, supporting real-time decision-making and enhanced connectivity in supply chain operations.

Figure 1. Timeline of Digital Transformation in Supply Chains

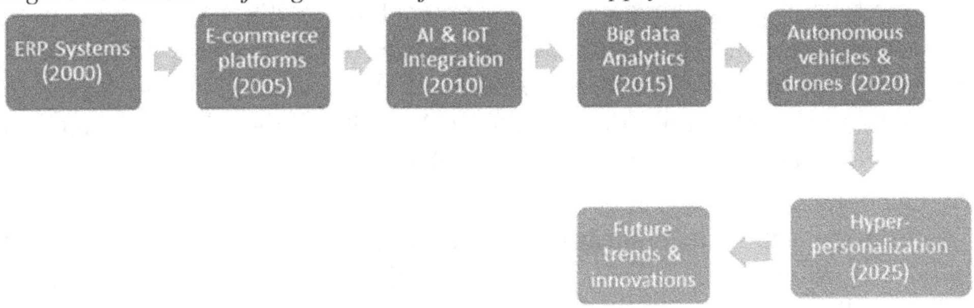

7. CONCLUSION

Summary of Key Points

This chapter explores the profound impact of digital transformation on supply chain management (SCM), revealing several key insights. Digital technologies, including artificial intelligence (AI) and automation, have markedly enhanced operational efficiency, reduced costs, and streamlined processes within supply chains. Innovations such as the Internet of Things (IoT) and blockchain have significantly improved visibility and transparency, providing real-time tracking and fostering greater trust among stakeholders. The adoption of digital tools has also increased agility and responsiveness, enabling supply chains to adapt more swiftly to market changes and disruptions, thus enhancing overall resilience. Technologies like big data analytics and 3D printing are driving hyper-personalization, allowing businesses to meet specific customer needs and preferences with greater precision. Additionally, digital transformation supports sustainability efforts through improved resource management, contributing to more eco-friendly and sustainable supply chain operations. Collectively, these advancements illustrate how digital transformation is reshaping SCM to be more efficient, transparent, responsive, and sustainable.

Implications for Practitioners

For companies aiming to implement digital supply chain management (SCM), several practical recommendations are essential for success. First, prioritize investments in technologies that align with your supply chain objectives, such as artificial intelligence (AI) for predictive analytics and blockchain for enhanced transparency.

Secondly, focus on data security by implementing robust cybersecurity measures to protect sensitive information and ensure compliance with privacy regulations. Embracing change management is also crucial; fostering a culture that supports digital transformation through adequate training and addressing resistance to change will facilitate smoother transitions. Additionally, adopting a holistic approach is recommended, considering the integration of multiple technologies to leverage their combined benefits and achieve comprehensive improvements in supply chain performance. Finally, continuously monitor and evaluate the performance of digital solutions, remaining adaptable to evolving technologies and shifting market conditions. By following these recommendations, companies can effectively navigate the complexities of digital SCM and enhance their operational capabilities.

Suggestions for Future Research

Future research in digital supply chain management (SCM) could explore several promising areas to deepen understanding and improve practices. One key area is the impact of emerging technologies, such as quantum computing, on SCM and how these innovations might integrate with existing systems. Another important focus could be evaluating the effectiveness of digital solutions in achieving long-term sustainability goals and their role in supporting circular economy practices. Additionally, research could examine global resilience strategies through case studies, investigating how various industries manage supply chain disruptions and the effectiveness of different resilience approaches. Lastly, understanding the impact of hyper-personalization on customer satisfaction and loyalty presents a valuable avenue for research, particularly how digital tools can be optimized to enhance these outcomes. Exploring these areas will contribute to advancing knowledge and practices in digital SCM, addressing current challenges and leveraging future opportunities.

REFERENCES

Andaloussi, M. B. (2024). A bibliometric literature review of digital supply chain: Trends, insights, and future directions. *SAGE Open*, 14(2), 1–20. DOI: 10.1177/21582440241240340

Barney, J. (1991). Firm resources and sustained competitive advantage. *Journal of Management*, 17(1), 99–120. DOI: 10.1177/014920639101700108

Baryannis, G., Dani, S., & Antoniou, G. (2019). Supply chain risk management and artificial intelligence: State of the art and future directions. *Computers & Industrial Engineering*, 137, 106024.

Brynjolfsson, E., & McElheran, K. (2016). *The second machine age: Work, progress, and prosperity in a time of brilliant technologies*. W. W. Norton & Company.

Cheng, J., Chen, W., & Luo, C. (2015). Cloud computing in manufacturing: A review of the state-of-the-art. *Enterprise Information Systems*, 9(5–6), 606–625.

Choi, T. M., Chan, H. K., & Yue, X. (2021). Recent development in big data analytics for business operations and risk management. *IEEE Transactions on Cybernetics*, 51(5), 2518–2534. PMID: 31329572

Chopra, S., & Meindl, P. (2020). *Supply chain management: Strategy, planning, and operation* (7th ed.). Pearson Education.

Christopher, M. (2016). *Logistics & supply chain management* (5th ed.). Pearson Education.

Dubey, R., Gunasekaran, A., Childe, S. J., Blome, C., Papadopoulos, T., & Luo, Z. (2017). Big data and predictive analytics and manufacturing performance: Integrating institutional theory, resource-based view, and big data culture. *British Journal of Management*, 30(2), 341–361. DOI: 10.1111/1467-8551.12355

Greasley, A., & Assanova, M. (2022). Robotics and automation in supply chain management. *The Journal of Supply Chain Management*, 58(3), 234–247.

Hazen, B. T., Boone, C. A., Ezell, J. D., & Jones-Farmer, L. A. (2014). Data quality for data science, predictive analytics, and big data in supply chain management: An introduction to the problem and suggestions for research and applications. *International Journal of Production Economics*, 154, 72–80. DOI: 10.1016/j.ijpe.2014.04.018

Ivanov, D., & Dolgui, A. (2020). A digital supply chain twin for managing the disruption risks and resilience in the era of Industry 4.0. *Production Planning and Control*, 31(10), 775–788.

Ivanov, D., & Dolgui, A. (2021). Simulation-based approaches for supply chain resilience and risk management: Recent advances and future perspectives. *European Journal of Operational Research*, 291(2), 482–495.

Ivanov, D., Dolgui, A., & Sokolov, B. (2019). The impact of digital technology and Industry 4.0 on the ripple effect and supply chain risk analytics. *International Journal of Production Research*, 57(3), 829–846. DOI: 10.1080/00207543.2018.1488086

Kache, F., & Seuring, S. (2017). Challenges and opportunities of digital information at the intersection of Big Data Analytics and supply chain management. *International Journal of Operations & Production Management*, 37(1), 10–36. DOI: 10.1108/IJOPM-02-2015-0078

KKol, A., & Pinkse, J. (2020). The role of digitalization in sustainable supply chain management: Insights from the global fashion industry. *Business Strategy and the Environment*, 29(5), 1832–1844.

Kouhizadeh, M., Sarkis, J., & Zhu, Q. (2020). Blockchain technology and the sustainable supply chain: Theoretically exploring adoption barriers. *International Journal of Production Economics*, 231, 107831. DOI: 10.1016/j.ijpe.2020.107831

Kumar, S., & Nair, A. (2021). Sustainability in supply chains: An overview of recent trends and future directions. *Journal of Cleaner Production*, 290, 125260.

Min, H., Zacharia, Z. G., & Smith, C. D. (2019). Artificial intelligence and its impact on supply chain management. *Journal of Business Logistics*, 40(1), 29–37.

Nguyen, T. H., & Vu, H. L. (2020). Hyper-personalization in the digital age: Trends and challenges. *Journal of Retailing and Consumer Services*, 55, 102077.

Rushton, A., Croucher, P., & Baker, P. (2017). *The handbook of logistics and distribution management* (6th ed.). Kogan Page Publishers.

Saberi, S., Kouhizadeh, M., Sarkis, J., & Shen, L. (2019). Blockchain technology and its relationships to sustainable supply chain management. *International Journal of Production Research*, 57(7), 2117–2135. DOI: 10.1080/00207543.2018.1533261

Srinivasan, R., & Swink, M. (2018). An investigation of visibility and flexibility as complements to supply chain analytics: An organizational information processing theory perspective. *Production and Operations Management*, 27(10), 1842–1862. DOI: 10.1111/poms.12746

Tapscott, D., & Tapscott, A. (2020). *Blockchain revolution: How the technology behind bitcoin is changing money, business, and the world.* Penguin Books.

Tjahjono, B., Esplugues, C., Ares, E., & Pelaez, G. (2017). What does Industry 4.0 mean to supply chain? *Procedia Manufacturing*, 13, 1175–1182. DOI: 10.1016/j.promfg.2017.09.191

Wang, Y., Gunasekaran, A., Ngai, E. W. T., & Papadopoulos, T. (2020). Big data analytics in logistics and supply chain management: Certain investigations for research and applications. *International Journal of Production Economics*, 229, 107852.

Wang, Y., Tiwari, M. K., & Wee, H. M. (2021). Impact of robotics and automation on productivity and labor: A quantitative study. *Journal of Manufacturing Systems*, 60, 225–239.

Williamson, O. E. (1985). *The economic institutions of capitalism*. Free Press.

Wu, G. C., Yue, W. T., Jin, Y., & Yen, H. (2016). Cloud computing in logistics service: Framework, simulation, and performance evaluation. *Journal of Computer Information Systems*, 56(4), 331–338.

Zhong, R. Y., Xu, X., & Wang, L. (2017). IoT-enabled smart factory visibility and traceability using laser-scanners. *Advanced Engineering Informatics*, 32, 243–252.

KEY TERMS AND DEFINITIONS

Artificial Intelligence (AI): *A branch of computer science that deals with creating systems capable of performing tasks that normally require human intelligence, such as decision-making and problem-solving.*

Blockchain: *A decentralized digital ledger technology that records transactions across many computers in a way that ensures the security and transparency of the data.*

Big Data Analytics: *The process of examining large and complex data sets to uncover hidden patterns, correlations, and insights that can inform decision-making and strategic planning.*

Internet of Things (IoT): *A network of interconnected devices that collect and exchange data through the internet, enabling real-time monitoring and management of supply chain operations.*

Hyper-Personalization: *The use of advanced data analytics and digital technologies to create highly customized products and services tailored to individual customer preferences.*

Robotics: *The use of robots and automated systems to perform tasks in manufacturing, warehousing, and logistics, enhancing efficiency and reducing human labor.*

Cloud Computing: *The delivery of computing services such as storage, processing, and software over the internet, allowing for scalable and flexible access to resources.*

Supply Chain Resilience: *The ability of a supply chain to adapt to and recover from disruptions, ensuring continuity and stability in operations.*

Chapter 3
The Seminal Role of Internet of Things in the Digital Transformation of Supply Chain Management

A. S. Anurag
https://orcid.org/0009-0005-5790-9084
Central University of Kerala, India

M. Johnpaul
https://orcid.org/0000-0002-1133-0588
Central University of Kerala, India

ABSTRACT

The chapter thoroughly examines the transformative influence of the Internet of Things (IoT) on Supply Chain Management (SCM) by assessing its pivotal role across various sectors and its integration with key technologies. It outlines IoT's communication protocols and categorizes its applications into four types based on the application domain. It showcases IoT's contributions to smart agriculture, disaster management, autonomous vehicles, healthcare, smart homes, industrial automation, and logistics. The chapter emphasizes IoT's advancements in SCM, including transparency, inventory management, risk mitigation, and demand forecasting, facilitated by technologies such as RFID, cloud computing, and blockchain. It also addresses data privacy, security, and adoption barriers, advocating for training, cost-effectiveness, and awareness initiatives. Overall, it underscores the necessity of embracing IoT for SCM optimization while addressing its challenges to ensure

DOI: 10.4018/979-8-3693-4427-9.ch003

a prosperous future.

INTRODUCTION

In the mid-18th century, Great Britain witnessed the dawn of a revolution capable of reshaping the world: the first industrial revolution. This revolution marked the invention of several new innovative technologies and production processes. The production landscape underwent a seismic shift, with machines replacing animal and human labor (Mohajan, 2019). This technological advancement opened doors to mass production, heralding a new era. However, the focus shifted beyond mere production. The distribution of goods emerged as a paramount concern. Unlike the pre-industrial age, post-industrialization facilitated global-scale production, prompting industrialists to strategize efficient and systematic processes for reaching consumers. This notion has evolved and emerged as a cornerstone of modern business practices. Once a mere afterthought, supply chains (SCs) have become indispensable in today's interconnected world.

Supply chain management (SCM) has only recently been recognized as an organizational process. There is no standard definition we can use to describe SCM. However, it is relatively easy to deduct the meaning of the SCM from its name itself. In essence, SCM is the process involved in supplying goods or services to customers promptly and efficiently as per their requirements. Even if the name suggests that these processes are a chain. The actual process of SCM is too complex to conclude that it is a simple chain of processes.

Modern SCM processes are an interconnection of multiple chains that are more like a network than a chain. Martin Christopher acknowledged this in his book (Christopher, 1992); he also defined SCM as a network of interconnected organizations engaged in various production and service delivery stages, ultimately aimed at providing value to end consumers. These organizations are linked upstream (towards suppliers) and downstream (towards customers) and collaborate in different processes to create and deliver products and services efficiently (Christopher, 2011). Christopher also argues that by definition, the term should be changed from 'Supply Chain Management' to 'Demand Network Management.' The modern SCM is more well described with the latter than the former. Hence, the process of SCM starts with the customer demand and ends with the fulfillment of this demand. It is not a linear chain process but a combination of multiple functions or joined chains. According to (Ittmann, 1999), the term became popular through a book by Robert B. Handfield and Ernest L. Nichols in 1999 (Handfield & Nichols, 1999). Since then, various organizations and researchers sought to expand their knowledge in this field. A group of researchers from the University of Tennessee developed a unified definition that states that SCM is the systemic and strategic coordination of traditional business functions within a particular company and across businesses within the SC. This coordinated approach aims to improve the long-term performance of the individual companies and the entire SC (Min et al., 2019). Figure 1 illustrates the process flow in a typical SC. It is to be noted that the figure shows only the four main phases. Each of these phases has multiple chains of processes.

Figure 1. Basic Diagram Illustrating the Flow of Supply Chain Processes (Authors)

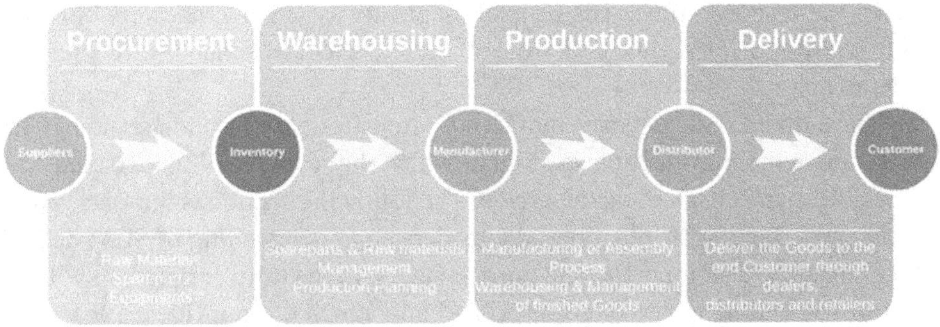

Since the dawn of the first industrial revolution, we have seen several new revolutions with the invention of newer technologies. Electricity acted as a catalyst in the second industrial revolution from 1840, and later, in the late 20th century, we saw the third industrial revolution with the advent of digital technologies (Duarte et al., 2018). In 2011, in Germany, we witnessed the formalization of the next industrial revolution (Rojko, 2017). This new revolution is termed as 'Industry 4.0'. With the industry's evolution, all the industrial processes also evolved, and the most critical change we saw was in the field of SCM, which is now referred to as SCM 4.0. Artificial Intelligence (AI) is the innovative technology that fuelled the emergence of the fourth industrial revolution or Industry 4.0. AI has revolutionized the manufacturing and supply processes. AI technologies such as Machine Learning (ML) (Carbonneau et al., 2008), the Internet of Things (IoT), Big Data Analytics (BDA), Cyber-Physical Systems (CPS), cloud computing (Qi & Tao, 2019), blockchain (Azzi et al., 2019), robotics, metaverse (Yang et al., 2022), additive manufacturing, and edge computing (Nain et al., 2022) have helped SC processes to evolve from a simple assembly line procedure to the SCM 4.0. These technologies, alone or collectively, play an essential role in today's SCM processes. In this chapter, we are going to discuss IoT in detail. Just like SCM, IoT also lacks a single formal definition. According to Rose et al. (2015), British Technology pioneer Kevin Ashton was the first to use the term

'Internet of Things'. He used this term to describe a system that connects physical devices to the internet with sensors or actuators (Rose et al., 2015).

This chapter will discuss IoT and its technologies in detail, such as Wireless Sensor Networks (WSN), RFID, Middleware, Computing Platforms, and Environment monitoring devices. We also discuss the importance of IoT in SCM, highlighting how the IoT can be effectively utilized in managing the inventory, transportation, and production processes to make the SCM process more streamlined. IoT helps organizations track and monitor the movements of their goods and raw materials in real-time. This helps mitigate real-time disruptions in the SC by considerably reducing the response time. The chapter elucidates how IoT empowers organizations to monitor the real-time data from all these devices to enhance efficiency and competitiveness.

We have divided this chapter into five sections for ease of understanding. The first section is the Introduction section, in which the readers will understand what to expect from the chapter and the theme. The following section is the Background and Literature Review, which gives the readers an understanding of SCM and IoT and their history, development, and current status. In the third section, we will discuss how IoT and SCM are interrelated and how much of an influence IoT has in revolutionizing the SCM process. The fourth section will discuss current trends and future developments in the subject before ending with the conclusion. This structure will offer a comprehensive overview of IoT and its impact on SCM.

BACKGROUND AND LITERATURE REVIEW

The IoT is a complex topic to wrap our heads around. The term was first introduced by Kevin Ashton in 1999 (Dave, 2011). Since then, there have been contradicting opinions among researchers regarding the use of IoT. According to the Internet Society (ISOC), some view the IoT as a revolutionary advancement, promising a fully interconnected "smart" world that brings progress, efficiency, and vast economic value to various industries. However, others caution against its potential darker implications, highlighting concerns about surveillance, privacy violations, and security breaches (Rose et al., 2015). This ongoing debate between the promise and peril of IoT contributes to the topic's complexity.

Kevin Ashton initially conceived the idea of IoT while presenting a paper on integrating RFID into Procter & Gamble's SC (Ashton, 2009). Following Kevin Ashton's initial explanation, the concept of IoT evolved from being solely related to RFID to encompassing any devices equipped with sensors or similar technology capable of network connectivity. Subsequently, researchers provided definitions emphasizing that IoT involves a collection of devices connected to the Internet.

IoT is defined as the interconnectedness of everyday objects embedded with intelligence, offering vast potential for innovative applications to enhance the quality of life (Xia et al., 2012). IoT is also defined as a flexible global network infrastructure with self-configuring abilities, adhering to standardized communication protocols, where physical and virtual entities possess unique identities and attributes, enabling intelligent interactions and integration within an information network (Kiritsis, 2011; Li et al., 2012). These definitions can be misleading to some since the term "Internet of Things" is arguably a misnomer, at least in its current context, because it does not exclusively refer to devices communicating over the Internet; rather, it encompasses any network, such as a private LAN, WAN, or local servers, without necessarily requiring Internet access. Therefore, it is reasonable to substitute "Internet" with "network" in IoT. This becomes evident when discussing the four primary communication models commonly employed in IoT.

IoT Communication Models

Device to Device (D2D)

This communication mainly occurs in a wireless environment among smart devices using Bluetooth, Zigbee, and Wifi (Bello & Zeadally, 2016; Swamy et al., 2016). This is the model where smart devices communicate with each other without any intermediate server (Pawar & Trivedi, 2019; Swamy et al., 2016) (Figure 2a). Smart devices, in this context, are devices that are capable of collecting information from their surroundings and communicating it with other devices. These smart devices can be sensors, actuators, or RFID tags, capable of autonomously making decisions with the acquired data. Two D2D models exist: Network-Infrastructure-Dependent D2D Communication and Network-Infrastructure-Independent D2D Communication (Bello & Zeadally, 2016). In the former, the devices communicate over an existing network infrastructure. Bluetooth and WiFi Direct, used in the communication between two phones, are examples of Network-Infrastructure-Dependent D2D Communication. In 'infrastructure independent communication,' devices can communicate directly using protocols and technologies designed for decentralized communication, such as Mobile Ad-hoc Networks or Bluetooth Low Energy (BLE).

Device to Cloud (D2C)

In this communication model, each smart device will connect directly to a cloud server through an application server (Swamy et al., 2016; Zain et al., 2016) (Figure 2b). This connection will facilitate data transfer and control. These types of communication models are used where device-to-device communication is impossible.

In the D2C model, the devices are capable of more intelligent decision-making than the D2D. This is due to the availability of single-point data storage, which facilitates communication between multiple IoT devices. D2C enables extensive data aggregation and analytics, leveraging cloud computing to analyze large data sets in real time, fostering intelligent decision-making while reducing physical data storage and enhancing security through encrypted data transmission from IoT devices to cloud platforms (AutoPi, 2024).

Device to Gateway

In the Device-to-Gateway model, or the Device-to-Application Layer Gateway model, the devices will make use of a gateway to access the cloud, unlike the D2C model, in which the devices are directly connected to the cloud (Figure 2c). This model involves a local gateway serving as an intermediary between smart devices and applications, with the gateway hosting the necessary application software (Swamy et al., 2016). Usually, health-tracking devices or smart watches rely on a smartphone application to connect to a cloud. These devices cannot connect with the cloud directly; hence, they use these applications. This model is commonly used to make new intelligent gadgets work with old systems that do not naturally fit together. However, it can get complicated and costly because you need to create unique software and systems to make them communicate with each other (Zain et al., 2016).

Back-end Data-sharing Model

The data from these IoT devices and sensors can be analyzed and interpreted. So, for analysis, a third party might need to access the data collected by the IoT devices. It is a limitation in all the three models described above that it cannot be used in a situation where there is a need for data sharing with a third party. So, to make this possible, the standard D2C model is modified and extended. This extended D2C model is called the Back-end Data-sharing Model (Figure 2d). The back-end data-sharing model allows users to export and analyze data from smart devices in the cloud alongside other sources, supporting users' ability to share sensor data with third parties (Zain et al., 2016). A backend-sharing system facilitates the collection and analysis of data from individual IoT sources, necessitating a federated cloud services approach or cloud APIs for interoperability (Reddy, 2021).

Figure 2. Illustration of Communication Models of IoT (Authors)

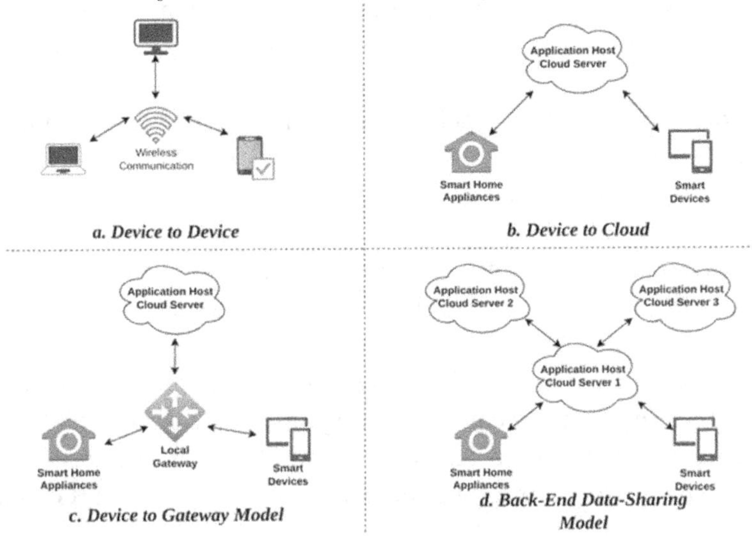

Characteristics of IoT Infrastructure

An efficient IoT infrastructure should possess key characteristics (Figure 3) to yield its full potential. Several authors have already shortlisted the essential characteristics of an IoT infrastructure (Patel & Patel, 2016; Pradeepa & Praveen, 2020)

Connectivity: It is the most critical of all features. The first thing we need in an IoT infrastructure is proper connectivity. As discussed in the previous section, different technologies are used to achieve this. Connectivity provides accessibility and compatibility to the IoT infrastructure (Pradeepa & Praveen, 2020).

Scalability: The second most important thing is the system's scalability. Scalability is the ability of a network system to expand without affecting its performance (Bondi, 2000). An efficient IoT system should be capable of accommodating and identifying numerous devices while it is active.

Intelligence: An IoT infrastructure should be intelligent enough to understand the data it is collecting and should be able to interpret the data to make decisions. The intelligence of an IoT system depends on the intelligence of the devices it is composed of.

Interoperability: This is the ability of two or more devices to share and use information (Patel & Patel, 2016). Hence, it is also an essential characteristic of an IoT infrastructure. It will not be easy to share information and make decisions without interoperability. The IoT devices achieve interoperability by using standard data encryption and algorithms.

Security & Privacy: As with all digital technologies, the issue of data privacy and security comes with increasing usage. A reliable IoT system should be secure. We should make a safe model by securing the endpoints, networks, and data (Pradeepa & Praveen, 2020).

Unique Identity: Identifying each connected device quickly and efficiently is an essential characteristic of a well-designed IoT model. In IoT, each connected device is assigned an ID number based on different criteria, which will help identify and control each device individually.

Remote Monitoring: One of the other unique characteristics of IoT models is their ability to connect remotely. With proper communication models, a user can control and monitor devices remotely.

Data Analytics: The property that made IoT globally famous is data analytics. IoT means collecting data and communicating among the devices and the user. By looking at the shared data, a user can interpret the data and make informed decisions. The data from the IoT devices can be studied to forecast the future (Geeksforgeeks, 2023).

Figure 3. Key Characteristics of an IoT Infrastructure (Authors)

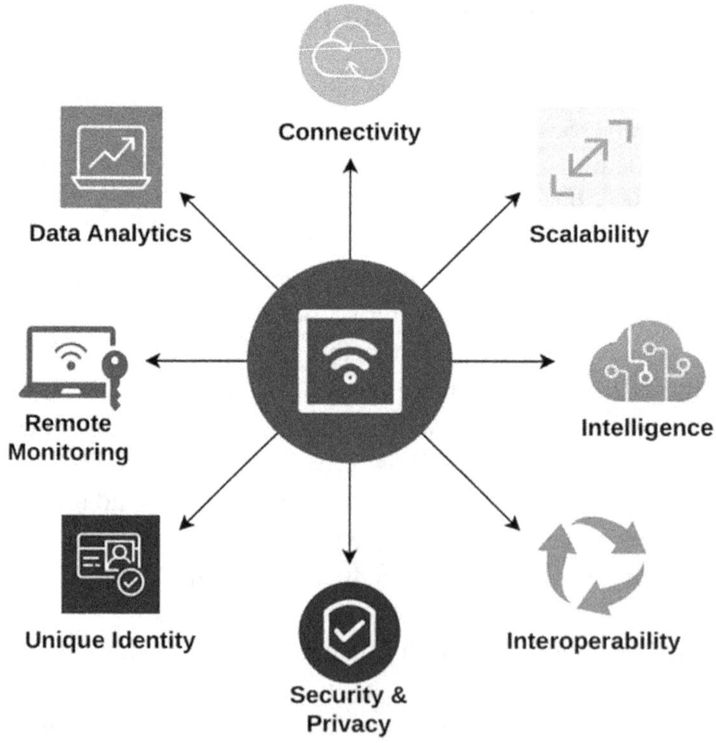

Types of IoT

IoTs are grouped based on the area in which they are being used. Figure 4 illustrates the four major areas and the corresponding versions of IoT. When an IoT model is used for consumer applications, it is a Consumer Internet of Things (CIoT). Common examples of CIoT are smartphones, smart assistants, smartwatches, and smart home appliances. The market for smart home appliances and CIoT are rapidly growing sectors. The latest research shows that the smart home market has an annual growth rate of 13 percent between 2017 and 2023 (Meng et al., 2018). With this increasing market and millions of new smart devices in households worldwide, the CIoT is also bringing new challenges and privacy concerns (Loi et al., 2017). Since the demand for consumer products is high, companies are not giving enough importance to CIoT as other IoT types.

Currently, the most popular type of IoT is the Industrial Internet of Things (IIoT). Since IIoT is one of the pillars of Industry 4.0. With the emergence of smart factories and manufacturing, we see large-scale use of IoT in industrial sectors such as manufacturing, factory automation, and logistics. Even IoT is used in the agriculture and healthcare sectors. The idea behind IIoT is to establish a factory environment that is completely interconnected, transparent, automated, and intelligent, aiming to improve manufacturing processes and efficiency (Dhirani et al., 2021). The IIoT also faces challenges related to its implementation and functioning. IIoT needs to be energy efficient; it needs high intelligence and computing power to achieve efficient real-time performance, coexistence, interoperability, and security (Dhirani et al., 2021).

CIoT focused on smaller areas like homes or private spaces, and IIoT was implemented in large-scale factories and industrial spaces. The Commercial IoT will be implemented in spaces between these two, such as hotels, commercial buildings, and theatre complexes. Even if Commercial IoT is closely related to CIoT, Commercial IoT extends beyond consumer applications to encompass various environments like office buildings, supermarkets, hotels, healthcare facilities, and entertainment venues, offering diverse applications such as environmental monitoring, access control, scheduling, connected lighting, and asset tracking. These applications enhance guest experiences in hotels and restaurants by enabling more efficient monitoring in smart buildings and offices (Hernandez, 2019).

Perhaps the Internet of Military Things(IoMT) is the IoT that seriously focuses on security and privacy. IoMT encompasses a sophisticated network of interconnected entities within the military domain that links various elements to foster continuous communication to coordinate, gather intelligence, and engage with the physical landscape (Cameron, 2018). Unlike the other types of IoT, the IoMT has severe challenges in protecting the physical devices connected to it. A failure of a single device during a war could bring down the entire system, which would be devastating. Since the physical parts of an IoMT should be adequately protected. IoMT was also described as the Internet of Battlefield Things (IoBT) (Castiglione et al., 2017), Military Internet of Things (MIoT) (Yushi et al., 2012), and Internet of Battle Things (Kott et al., 2016).

Figure 4. Types of IoT based on the Field of Use (Authors)

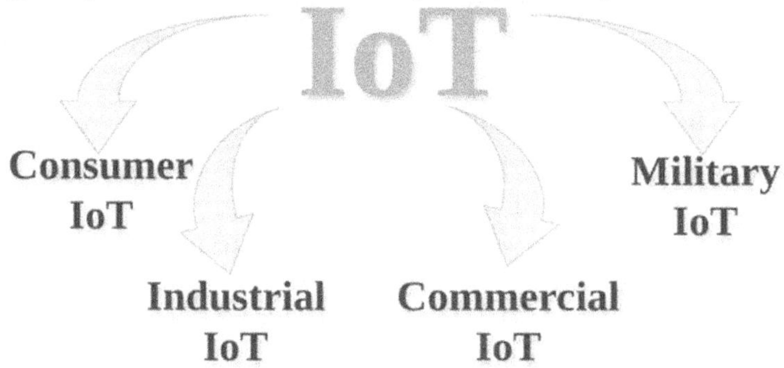

Applications of IoT

IoT has revolutionized many sectors with its dynamic capabilities and relatively simple and user-friendly devices. With its improvements, researchers discover new applications daily, including agriculture, disaster management, navigation systems, healthcare, smart homes, BDA, industries, and logistics (Figure 5).

Agriculture

As the primary sector, agriculture is the first area to benefit from a new innovative technology. The case with IoT is also no different. IoT has influenced the agriculture sector in a highly positive way in the last few decades. Some of the major applications of IoT in agriculture are smart irrigation, which conserves water sources, environment monitoring systems, animal health trackers, plant life monitoring, intelligent machines and tools, product quality, and product traceability (Xu et al., 2022). This is achieved with the help of devices like sensors and actuators. In agricultural fields, sensors continuously monitor diverse environmental factors and farm variables, with commonly employed sensors for temperature, humidity, soil patterns, airflow, location, CO2 levels, pressure, and moisture (Farooq et al., 2020). Even with IoT's success in the agriculture sector, it faces some issues in data management, such as unstable data transmission, hindered data sharing, safety risks during transmission, and inadequate positioning accuracy, diminishing the timeliness of data delivery. Moreover, the extensive software and hardware requirements obstruct the scalability and expansion of the system (Xu et al., 2022). Addressing these issues and concentrating on researchers on less explored issues are crucial to the success of IoT in smart farming.

Disaster Management

Disaster management is a systematic approach involving federal, state, local, and private sector entities collaborating to plan and manage disaster mitigation, rescue, response, and recovery (Shah et al., 2019). According to the international disaster database 'EM-DAT,' the number of mass disasters shows an exponential rise over the years (EM-DAT, 2024). We faced most of these disasters without proper knowledge or technology. However, recently, we have seen the rise of IoT (Ray et al., 2017) as a disaster management system capable of warning and making optimum decisions in the face of a disaster. WSNs are the technology commonly implemented along with IoT for disaster management models (Nandan et al., 2021). WSNs utilize energy-efficient sensor nodes comprising a power source, microcontroller, wireless radio, and various environmental sensors to gather environmental data (Adeel et al., 2019). With the data collected from the environment, the changes can be mapped and analyzed with past data to predict the future possibility of a disaster.

Vehicle Tracking and Navigation Systems

A world of driverless vehicles is not a fictional future. Our world is already filled with autonomous vehicles. There were around 31 million cars worldwide with varying degrees of automation during 2019. This number is expected to hit the 50 million mark this year (Placek, 2023). A reliable navigation system is the backbone of any autonomous vehicle; with the developments in IoT, researchers have achieved this feat rather quickly. Cameras, radars, and LiDARs, among other line-of-sight sensors, are extensively employed in autonomous vehicles and mobile robots to perceive surroundings and make real-time decisions (Zhang & Fisac, 2021). With these devices, the vehicle will collect data from its surroundings, plan its path for navigation, and eventually execute its plan into action. For this purpose to happen in real-time and quickly, a sophisticated system capable of handling numerous devices simultaneously is required. IoT does this in an autonomous vehicle; large volumes of data are collected from millions of simultaneous devices and processed in cloud computing (Khayyam et al., 2020). With further advancements in IoT systems, we will be able to develop something more sophisticated in the future that will change our society as a whole.

Healthcare

One major field that utilizes IoT's power is the healthcare sector. With an increase in the use of smart wearables capable of monitoring primary health conditions, the idea of using complex devices to access all kinds of health data has emerged. Healthcare systems leverage interconnected smart devices to establish an IoT network for healthcare analysis, patient monitoring, and automatic identification of situations requiring physician involvement (Kodali et al., 2015). IoT helps monitor patients' physiological statuses via sensors, gathering and analyzing their information and transmitting analyzed patient data remotely to processing centers for appropriate actions (Babu et al., 2013). Healthcare professionals face specific issues during the implementation of IoT, such as patients might get uncomfortable wearing specific devices, difficulty in removing and repairing some devices, higher cost in implementation, need for high energy for the system, and difficulty in employing encryption techniques (Selvaraj & Sundaravaradhan, 2020). Proper solutions for these challenges are necessary for the responsible use of IoT in healthcare.

Smart Home

Initially, home automation was installing automatic gates and surveillance cameras. Over the years, the trend has changed from simple automated homes to today's contemporary ‘Smart Homes.’ The developments in IoT have also contributed to the development of an efficient smart home. A smart home can monitor the environment, give out alerts on out-of-pattern variations, control installed devices, and bring total intelligence into the home (Malche & Maheshwary, 2017). Even if several protocols are used in IoT-based smart homes across the globe, the most commonly used ones are the BLE, Z-wave, Zigbee, and Thread. Data Security and Latency, mixed-criticality, difficulty in fault identification, and the need to give extra importance to functional safety (AumRaj, 2022) are some of the crucial challenges regarding the IOT implementation in Smart Homes.

Big Data Analytics

IoT plays an essential role in BDA. With the increasing number of Smar Homes, Smart Buildings, and cities, the data generated through IoT devices is also increasing. This large amount of data can be stored and analyzed efficiently by integrating BDA and IoT (Ahmed et al., 2017). The data collected by IoT devices are redundant, heterogeneous, and fluctuating, with considerable noise (Gulia & Chahal, 2020). However, these data are fast growing and can help substantially gain knowledge; hence, with the help of BDA, these Big Data can be stored and handled correctly. Gulia and Chahal (2020) have described four steps in IoT for Big Data processing. The first step is to manage the data sources, including connected devices like sensors and actuators. In the second step, the big IoT data collected by these devices are stored in the Big Data storage system. In this system, the Big IoT Data is converted into big data files, and finally, the report for the data is generated and presented.

Industrial Automation

Like smart homes, we have seen the emergence of smart factories with the development of IoT technologies. With the help of IoT, a conventional factory will transform into a 'smart factory' capable of monitoring and controlling remotely. Industrial automation encompasses various control systems deployed across diverse domains and processes, including motion control, protection systems, and digital control. These processes range from batch production, seen in pharmaceutical and food industries, to continuous processing, such as in electric power and oil and gas sectors, as well as discrete manufacturing, evident in automotive and robotics industries (Breivold & Sandstrom, 2015). Like home automation, similar challenges are faced in industrial automation as well. Managing latency and scalability of data, mixed-criticality, secure Real-time Collaboration, Fault Tolerance, and functional safety is critical in successful industrial automation (Breivold & Sandstrom, 2015).

Logistics and Supply Chain

Logistics and SC are among the most critical IoT functions in an industry. The idea of IoT was born out of the idea of implementing RFID tags in SCs (Ashton, 2009). Hence, it is the first application that IoT has ever had to perform. The latest development in IoT has enabled SCM to access more accurate data, thereby making efficient decisions (Rejeb et al., 2020). Implementing IoT in logistics yields swift and efficient outcomes by enabling real-time tracking of assets, packages, and personnel across the entire value chain. This technology offers automation possibilities to streamline processes, eliminate manual labor, enhance quality and predictability, and cut operating expenses. IoT optimizes collaboration between individuals and network-connected devices while facilitating monitoring and guiding processes toward improved efficiency (Ivankova et al., 2020).

Figure 5. Some of the Application Areas of IoT (Authors)

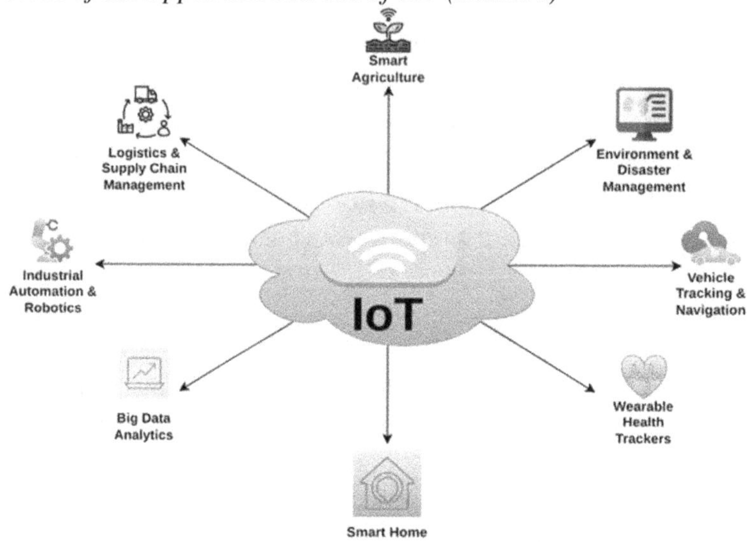

INTEGRATION OF IoT IN SCM

With the rapid digital disruptions happening worldwide, IoT is a unique technology that helps almost every field. The most essential function of today's business is the SCM, and these SCM processes are getting more streamlined with the introduction of IoT. Inventory management, predictive maintenance, SC visibility, environment monitoring, route optimization, risk management, demand forecasting, and warehouse automation are some of the applications of IoT. Several innovative technologies and devices assist IoT in achieving this feat.

RFID and QR Codes

Radio Frequency Identification (RFID) is the cornerstone technology in IoT-enabled SCM. RFID tags transmit encoded data via radio waves, which are then picked up by RFID readers (Weinstein, 2005). This technology revolutionizes the tracking process, enabling seamless monitoring of a product's journey from its origin to its final destination. Moreover, RFID has an extensive application in warehouse management, facilitating efficient sorting and organization of products and raw materials. In addition to RFID, Quick Response (QR) codes are widely utilized for product identification.

NFC

Another significant advancement from RFID technology is Near Field Communication (NFC). Unlike RFID, NFC operates within a concise range, typically within a few centimeters (Ok et al., 2010). NFC is commonly integrated into smartphones and other mobile devices, facilitating contactless payment systems, access control, and seamless data exchange between devices. In SCM, NFC finds applications for authentication, verification, and information exchange during product inspections or inventory checks.

Telematics

Transportation is a crucial aspect of SCM. Telematics systems combine GPS and GPRS technologies and play a crucial role in goods transportation. They enable the planning, monitoring, coordinating, and optimizing motor vehicle operations, focusing on ongoing delivery and distribution processes (Osińska & Zalewski, 2020). These systems utilize advanced vehicular network architectures, on-board computers, the Internet, in-vehicle networks, and mobile telecommunications to improve vehicle operations. Mainly used in the transport sector of the SC, telematics supports various functions essential for efficient transportation management (Bujak et al., 2015). With this system, the entire transportation process of the SCM will be more transparent and reliable.

Cloud Computing

Cloud computing refers to providing computing services over the internet (Montazerolghaem et al., 2020), such as servers, storage, databases, networking, software, and analytics. This approach allows for quicker innovation, adaptable resources, and cost efficiencies. Cloud computing utilizes TCP/IP and advanced computer technologies like fast microprocessors, ample memory, high-speed networks, and robust system architectures based on standard interconnect protocols and mature data center technologies (Gong et al., 2010). SCM Cloud signifies a significant shift in SCM by providing efficient and secure SCM functions while abstracting technical complexities, allowing users to concentrate on functionality and cost. Service providers simplify adoption by selecting requirements and technologies and streamlining user decision-making and implementation processes (Bhoir & Principal, 2014). Cloud computing enables real-time access to SCM data and analytics from anywhere with an internet connection, facilitating quicker decision-making and enhancing overall SC visibility and responsiveness.

Digital Twin

A digital twin is a virtual model of a physical entity or process that gathers data from the real world to accurately represent, validate, and simulate its current and future behavior, serving as a crucial tool for data-driven decision-making and management across various sectors (Botín-Sanabria et al., 2022). Digital twin technology is utilized across diverse sectors, including manufacturing, automotive, healthcare, smart cities, infrastructure, defense, retail, and energy. Within SCM, digital twins replicate and analyze the physical SC, enabling managers to forecast real-world outcomes based on virtual alterations. This capability empowers organizations to experiment with and optimize their SCM processes for increased efficiency.

Blockchain

Blockchain technology is a decentralized database of transaction records, validated and maintained by a global network of computers, where entries are immutable and linked in a chain (Sarmah, 2018). Originally intended to be used in cryptocurrency transactions, within a short span, blockchain technology found its way into almost all fields and applications. Today, blockchain is one of the most critical technologies in SCM. Blockchain technology enables companies to enhance product security, traceability, and transparency across the SC, mitigating counterfeit risks, ensuring regulatory compliance, and fostering trust among partners while also automating and optimizing various SC operations like inventory management, order tracking, and payment settlements (Sardjono et al., 2023).

Apart from these, numerous other technologies are available that are designed to enhance the performance of IoT. IoT can produce remarkable results in SCM when combined with these innovative technologies.

REVOLUTIONIZING SCM

Figure 6. Enhanced Features of IoT-Enabled SCM (Authors)

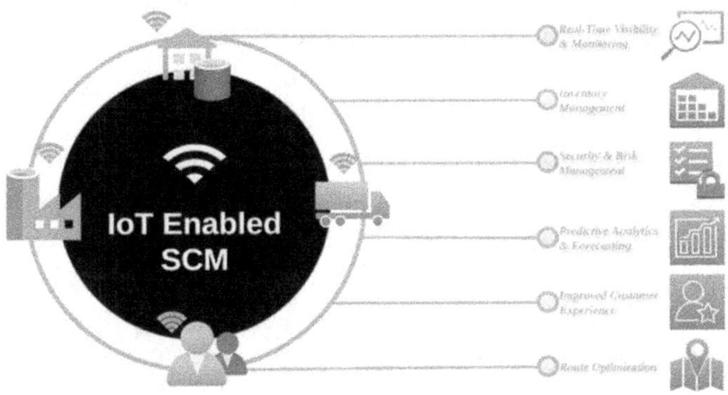

The conventional SC has always struggled to address the issues relating to transparency, inventory management, transportation efficiency, risk mitigation, and demand forecasting. However, the development of Information and Communication Technology (ICT) has introduced a wave of groundbreaking technologies, among which IoT stands out as particularly transformative for SCM processes. Figure 6 illustrates how IoT implementation has revolutionized these critical areas within the SC. By leveraging IoT devices and connectivity, businesses can achieve unprecedented transparency in their processes, optimize inventory management with real-time tracking, streamline transportation logistics, proactively mitigate risks through data-driven insights, and enhance demand forecasting accuracy. This integration of IoT technologies marks a significant shift in traditional SCM paradigms, offering newfound efficiency, resilience, and agility to SC operations.

Real-Time Visibility and Monitoring

Visibility in SCs is crucial for businesses. Visibility is how well an SC stakeholder can understand the transactions and functions in an SC, from a product's origin to its consumption. IoT technology can provide real-time tracking and data accessibility across all stakeholders, enhancing coordination, integration, and performance improvement, fostering internal and external integration among processes, suppliers, and customers (Ahmed et al., 2021). A properly visible SC can improve decision-making, stakeholder collaboration, customer satisfaction, and responsiveness to unexpected events.

Inventory Management

Inventory management involves tracking available stock levels at various stages of production, serving as a vital tool for industries experiencing growth in demand to prevent delays and ensure efficient operations (Jayanth et al., 2017). Inventory management is a critical function of an organization that can drastically affect its functioning. It tracks the level of raw materials, work-in-process components, and finished products to optimize costs and improve customer satisfaction (Mashayekhy et al., 2022). IoT technology leverages technologies like RFID tags, barcodes, GPS trackers, sensors, robots, smart shelves, and intelligent packaging to manage the inventory successfully.

Security and Risk Management

In SC operations, IoT is vital for addressing inherent security risks, including those arising from natural disasters, geopolitical events, pandemics, labor strikes, demand fluctuations, transportation delays, cybersecurity threats, and limited visibility, which can all result in substantial financial losses for companies. By gathering and sharing real-time data across the SC, IoT enables businesses to anticipate potential risks and disruptions, respond swiftly to emerging threats, and make informed decisions (Meng, 2021). By harnessing IoT technologies, businesses can strengthen their risk management strategies, enhance operational efficiency, and establish a more resilient SC ecosystem capable of navigating uncertainties and disasters effectively.

Predictive Analytics and Forecasting

Predictive analytics uses data mining techniques to forecast future outcomes based on historical data (Mishra & Silakari, 2012). Predictive analytics in SCM utilizes advanced techniques to forecast demand, optimize inventory, and improve decision-making, which is crucial for organizations striving to stay competitive in a dynamic business landscape by addressing challenges like demand variability, disruptions, and inventory management effectively (Oyewole et al., 2024). IoT enhances predictive analytics by providing a continuous stream of real-time data from connected devices.

Improved Customer Experience

Making a business profitable depends on maintaining Customer satisfaction (Choi, 2019). IoT technology offers numerous advantages for enhancing customer satisfaction across various business sectors. IoT facilitates better service delivery by enabling real-time operations monitoring and fostering improved communication channels between staff and customers. Additionally, it enhances operational efficiency and optimizes resource utilization, streamlining workflows and automating routine tasks. This automation frees up staff to concentrate on delivering more critical customer services, leading to personalized experiences and efficient problem resolution (Ahmed et al., 2022). Ultimately, these combined benefits result in heightened customer satisfaction and enriched service experiences, making IoT implementation a valuable strategy for businesses seeking to optimize customer relations.

Route Optimization

IoT technology can be leveraged to enhance the efficiency of vehicle transportation routes in several ways. IoT devices enable real-time tracking and monitoring, anticipate maintenance requirements proactively, and dynamically optimize routes using live data (Yu et al., 2021). This interconnected network enhances coordination, minimizes errors, and boosts operational efficiency by facilitating communication between vehicles, drivers, and central dispatch systems (Yu et al., 2021). By leveraging IoT technology in vehicle transportation routes, companies can achieve cost savings, improve customer satisfaction, and streamline logistics operations.

BARRIERS IN IoT IMPLEMENTATION

We have explored how IoT can significantly enhance SCM processes. Numerous organizations have upgraded their traditional SCM systems to incorporate IoT technology, positioning themselves for a competitive advantage in today's fast-paced market. However, like all new technologies, IoT implementation encounters several barriers. To maintain their edge, organizations must promptly identify and address these obstacles.

Data Security and Privacy

Ensuring the security and privacy of data stands as a paramount concern in the integration of IoT systems. With vast amounts of data flowing throughout the IoT network, there exists a significant risk of vulnerability to external cyber-attacks. Data security concerns pose a substantial barrier to the widespread adoption of IoT technology. According to (de Vass et al., 2021), many employees express unease about the data security implications of this emerging technology. Such perception among staff members could hinder the adoption of IoT solutions.

Integration Issues

Developing a scalable IoT system poses challenges as it comprises a network of devices spread across various locations, with some sensors in constant motion, necessitating adaptability to dynamic environments. Consistent internet availability and robust connectivity are critical for the seamless operation of devices far from each other. Besides internet availability, the demand for substantial computational power, preemptive fault detection, considerable energy consumption, and societal acceptance are significant barriers to integrating IoT into the conventional SCM (Mukhopadhyay & Suryadevara, 2014).

Investment and Training Requirements

The success of IoT as a new technology heavily relies on the level of investment stakeholders are willing to commit and the extent of training provided to managers and employees. De Vass et al. (2021) noted that many organizations are focused on their current workflows and existing technologies, which hinders their interest in adopting new technologies. The prolonged investment period required for IoT and uncertain returns has made organizations increasingly hesitant to embrace such innovations. Another significant barrier to the implementation process is higher management's lack of awareness and understanding of the technology (de Vass et al., 2021).

Employee Resistance to Change

Throughout history, employees have shown a degree of resistance to new technologies. This resistance stems from employees' preference for the safety of familiar practices over the uncertainty of change. They are often more inclined to accept new technology only when adequately educated about its benefits. Trust-related concerns primarily drive resistance (Brou & Janssen, 2015). Staff members perceive new technology as a hurdle, alongside resistance from both internal and external stakeholders, as well as resistance to surveillance (de Vass et al., 2021), which collectively serve as a significant barrier to IoT implementation.

REAL-WORLD EXAMPLES OF IoT IMPLEMENTATION

Volvo

Volvo employs Autonomous Guided Vehicles (AGVs) in their production process, providing flexibility but posing battery-related challenges. When the battery voltage drops below 22V, AGVs stop functioning, causing production delays and preventing the manufacture of roughly two engines weekly (Zabeu, 2023).

In an online article, Volvo Group revealed that they have addressed the issue with the help of IoT solutions utilizing Long Range Wide Area Network (LoRaWAN) technology. According to the article, they equipped each AGV with LoRaWAN sensors to monitor battery voltage levels and detect any drops below 23V or battery failures. These sensors transmitted data through a private LoRaWAN network within the factory, directly connected to Volvo Group's secure Ethernet network. This setup enabled the maintenance team to receive timely notifications about AGV battery status and any issues, allowing them to efficiently move affected AGVs to charging stations without disrupting production (Volvo, 2023). By leveraging LoRaWAN IoT technology, Volvo Group established a predictive maintenance system to monitor and manage AGV battery concerns effectively, enhancing manufacturing operations.

Tesla

Tesla is one of the companies that has implemented IoT technologies efficiently. The Tesla car is equipped with advanced driver assistance systems that use IoT technologies like cameras, sensors, and onboard computers to enable the car to steer, accelerate, and brake automatically, enhancing driving safety and convenience. The auto-steer feature assists the driver in keeping the car within a marked lane, providing an additional layer of safety and convenience (Anand, 2023).

According to an online article by Medium, the main benefits of incorporating IoT in Tesla's cars include Cost-efficiency, Convenience and User-friendliness, Efficient Network Updates, Increased overall Efficiency, and Enhanced Safety. The article also showcases an incident where IoT allowed Tesla to fix around 30,000 cars remotely with a software update, showcasing IoT integration's damage control and efficiency benefits (Rastogi, 2022).

FUTURE TRENDS IN IoT

The future of the IoT has tremendous potential for significant advancements, particularly with the integration of edge computing and the continued evolution of AI and ML. According to Adeusi et al. (2024), with the integration of edge computing and the advancements in AI and ML, the IoT will be able to enhance its capabilities and efficiency to new levels (Adeusi et al., 2024).

The enhanced predictive analytical capabilities of IoT have the potential to transform SCM significantly in several key ways. Improved data processing speeds can bolster real-time decision-making within SCM operations. Advanced AI and ML technologies enable more efficient management of IoT devices, facilitating the precise collection and processing of data across the entire SC network. In the future, technologies such as digital twins and blockchain are anticipated to impact IoT positively (Park & Park, 2024). The expected implementation of 6G communication technology will further contribute to these advancements. As these technologies develop, they will unlock new potential for integrating IoT with blockchain and digital twins, leading to more sophisticated applications within SCM processes. Park and Park (2024) suggest that utilizing technologies such as edge AI, blockchain, cloud computing, fog computing, and edge computing-based data intelligence can enhance the overall performance and security of IoT networks while mentioning that Implementing measures that enhance user privacy and build trust in IoT systems is essential for their widespread adoption.

Sial et al. (2024) discuss several key points regarding the future of IoT technology, particularly in relation to supercapacitors and their applications. The future development of supercapacitors is focused on improving their energy density, power density, and cycling stability, which are critical for the efficient operation of IoT devices. By utilizing ML models, researchers can make accurate predictions about capacitance and lifespan, which will aid in material selection and design strategies for supercapacitors. With highly advanced capacitors, the design of more durable and efficient IoT devices will become more facile. Furthermore, the authors highlight that cloud-based solutions will be essential for scaling IoT applications. These solutions provide the necessary flexibility to adjust resources based on demand, which is crucial for the widespread adoption of IoT technologies (Sial et al., 2024).

Building sustainable IoT systems will be crucial for the future success of the technology. As the cybersecurity risks associated with sustainable IoT become more evident, there will be an increasing demand for enhanced security frameworks and standards to safeguard systems, sensors, and data from digital threats. This includes the development of trust and reliability frameworks to ensure safe and secure operations across diverse environments (Salam, 2020). Energy harvesting represents a major strategy for enhancing the sustainability of IoT systems. According to Katz et al. (2024), energy harvesting enables IoT devices to operate autonomously without frequent battery replacements or external power sources. By capturing energy from renewable sources such as solar power and radio waves, IoT devices can significantly reduce their carbon footprint. This approach aligns with green technology principles and supports sustainable development by promoting the use of clean energy (Katz et al., 2024). As such, energy harvesting will be a pivotal component in the advancement of sustainable IoT systems in the future.

CONCLUSION

In this chapter, we have delved into various applications of IoT, particularly its pivotal role in enhancing SCM. Despite its accompanying challenges, IoT unquestionably represents the technology of the future. IoT's most prevalent communication protocols are D2D, D2C, Device to Gateway, and the Back-end Data-sharing Model. D2D facilitates direct wireless communication, while D2C enables devices to link directly to cloud servers. Device to Gateway involves a local gateway acting as an intermediary, and the Back-end Data-sharing Model enables seamless data sharing. A flexible IoT infrastructure is paramount, ensuring accessibility and compatibility across diverse technologies. The system needs to be able to handle numerous devices without compromising performance.

IoT is categorized into four main types based on their usage areas. CIoT focuses on applications like smart home appliances, smartphones, and wearables. IIoT has become vital with the emergence of Industry 4.0, enhancing manufacturing processes and efficiency across various sectors, including manufacturing, factory automation, logistics, agriculture, and healthcare. Commercial IoT finds applications in hotels, commercial buildings, and entertainment venues, extending beyond consumer products. IoMT prioritizes security and privacy, enabling continuous communication in military domains.

IoT enables smart irrigation, environment monitoring, and intelligent machines in agriculture, aids disaster management through predictive analysis and monitoring, supports navigation and perception in autonomous vehicles, facilitates patient monitoring and remote data transmission in healthcare, enables environmental monitoring and device control in smart homes, transforms traditional factories into smart ones through remote monitoring and control in industrial automation, and allows real-time tracking of assets, packages, and personnel in logistics and SCM, thereby enhancing collaboration and streamlining processes for increased efficiency.

The integration of IoT into SCM has led to significant advancements in transparency, inventory management, transportation efficiency, risk mitigation, and demand forecasting. Technologies such as RFID, QR codes, NFC, telematics, cloud computing, digital twins, and blockchain have played crucial roles in enhancing SCM processes through IoT. Real-time visibility and monitoring provided by IoT have improved coordination, integration, and performance among stakeholders. Efficient inventory management is facilitated by IoT by utilizing technologies like RFID tags, sensors, and intelligent packaging, resulting in cost optimization and enhanced customer satisfaction. IoT supports security and risk management in SCM by anticipating potential risks, responding promptly to emerging threats, and making informed decisions based on real-time data. Predictive analytics and forecasting leverage IoT in SCM to forecast demand, optimize inventory, and improve decision-making, which is crucial for competitiveness in dynamic business environments. Enhanced customer experience is achieved through IoT by enabling real-time monitoring of operations, enhancing communication channels, and streamlining workflows for personalized experiences. Route optimization benefits from IoT by enabling real-time tracking, proactive maintenance, and dynamic route optimization using live data, leading to cost savings and improved customer satisfaction.

Despite the numerous practical applications of IoT, it is essential to address the challenges it faces to succeed. One primary concern is data privacy and security, as many worry about the vulnerability of the large data flows within the system. Additionally, digital illiteracy and lack of knowledge about modern technology pose barriers to IoT adoption by businesses. Staff resistance due to unfamiliarity with the technology is also a significant obstacle. Overcoming these challenges requires providing training for users, ensuring the cost-effectiveness of systems, and raising awareness of the potential benefits of IoT. Furthermore, increased research on the topic, facilitated through academic and organizational collaboration, is crucial for better understanding and advancing the technology.

REFERENCES

Adeel, A., Gogate, M., Farooq, S., Ieracitano, C., Dashtipour, K., Larijani, H., & Hussain, A. (2019). *A Survey on the Role of Wireless Sensor Networks and IoT in Disaster Management*. DOI: 10.1007/978-981-13-0992-2_5

Adeusi, K. B., Adegbola, A. E., Amajuoyi, P., Adegbola, M. D., & Benjamin, L. B. (2024). The potential of IoT to transform supply chain management through enhanced connectivity and real-time data. *World Journal of Advanced Engineering Technology and Sciences*, 12(1), 145–151. DOI: 10.30574/wjaets.2024.12.1.0202

Ahmed, E., Yaqoob, I., Hashem, I. A. T., Khan, I., Ahmed, A. I. A., Imran, M., & Vasilakos, A. V. (2017). The role of big data analytics in Internet of Things. *Computer Networks*, 129, 459–471. DOI: 10.1016/j.comnet.2017.06.013

Ahmed, M., Abdou, M. Y. K., & Elnagar, A. M. (2022). The Impact of Implementing the Internet of Things (IoT) on Customer Satisfaction: Evidence from Egypt. [JA-AUTH]. *Journal of Association of Arab Universities For Tourism and Hospitality*, 22(2), 365–380. DOI: 10.21608/jaauth.2022.123022.1304

Ahmed, S., Kalsoom, T., Ramzan, N., Pervez, Z., Azmat, M., Zeb, B., & Ur Rehman, M. (2021). Towards Supply Chain Visibility Using Internet of Things: A Dyadic Analysis Review. *Sensors (Basel)*, 21(12), 4158. DOI: 10.3390/s21124158 PMID: 34204434

Anand, D. (2023, January 10). *IOT in Tesla (Automotive industry)*. Medium. https://medium.com/aictespices-iot-club-blog-contest-2023/iot-in-tesla-automotive-industry-b1d0871e3363

Ashton, K. (2009). That "internet of things" thing. *RFID Journal*, 22(7), 97–114.

AumRaj. (2022). *Challenges of IoT in Smart Home Automation*. AumRaj. https://aumraj.com/challenges-of-iot-in-smart-home-automation/#:~:text=The%20home%20appliances%20are%20connected,issues%20in%20smart%20home%20automation

AutoPi. (2024). *Device to Cloud Communication*. Autopi.Io. https://www.autopi.io/glossary/device-to-cloud-communication/

Azzi, R., Chamoun, R. K., & Sokhn, M. (2019). The power of a blockchain-based supply chain. *Computers & Industrial Engineering*, 135, 582–592. DOI: 10.1016/j.cie.2019.06.042

Babu, B. S., Srikanth, K., Ramanjaneyulu, T., & Narayana, I. L. (2013). IoT for Healthcare. [IJSR]. *International Journal of Scientific Research*, 5(2), 322–326.

Bello, O., & Zeadally, S. (2016). Intelligent Device-to-Device Communication in the Internet of Things. *IEEE Systems Journal*, 10(3), 1172–1182. DOI: 10.1109/JSYST.2014.2298837

Bhoir, H., & Principal, R. P. (2014). Cloud Computing For Supply Chain Management. *INTERNATIONAL JOURNAL OF INNOVATIONS IN ENGINEERING RESEARCH AND TECHNOLOGY [IJIERT], 1*(2).

Bondi, A. B. (2000). Characteristics of scalability and their impact on performance. *2nd International Workshop on Software and Performance*, 195–203. DOI: 10.1145/350391.350432

Botín-Sanabria, D. M., Mihaita, A.-S., Peimbert-García, R. E., Ramírez-Moreno, M. A., Ramírez-Mendoza, R. A., & Lozoya-Santos, J. de J. (2022). Digital Twin Technology Challenges and Applications: A Comprehensive Review. *Remote Sensing (Basel)*, 14(6), 1335. DOI: 10.3390/rs14061335

Breivold, H. P., & Sandstrom, K. (2015). Internet of Things for Industrial Automation — Challenges and Technical Solutions. *2015 IEEE International Conference on Data Science and Data Intensive Systems*, 532–539. DOI: 10.1109/DSDIS.2015.11

Brou, P., & Janssen, M. (2015). Effects Of The Internet Of Things (IoT): A Systematic Review Of The Benefits And Risks. *The Fifteenth International Conference on Electronic Business*, 217–222.

Bujak, A., Topolski, M., & Miler, R. K. (2015). Telematics as a tool of efficient supply chain management. *Archives of Transport System Telematics*, 8(2), 8–12.

Cameron, L. (2018). Internet of Things Meets the Military and Battlefield: Connecting Gear and Biometric Wearables for an IoMT and IoBT. *IEEE Computer Society*. https://www.computer.org/publications/tech-news/research/internet-of-military-battlefield-things-iomt-iobt

Carbonneau, R., Laframboise, K., & Vahidov, R. (2008). Application of machine learning techniques for supply chain demand forecasting. *European Journal of Operational Research*, 184(3), 1140–1154. DOI: 10.1016/j.ejor.2006.12.004

Castiglione, A., Choo, K.-K. R., Nappi, M., & Ricciardi, S. (2017). Context Aware Ubiquitous Biometrics in Edge of Military Things. *IEEE Cloud Computing*, 4(6), 16–20. DOI: 10.1109/MCC.2018.1081072

Choi, D.-H. (2019). Impact of Internet of Things (IoT)'s Service Quality on the Hotel Customer Satisfaction. *International Journal of Recent Technology and Engineering, 8*(2S6), 362–366. DOI: 10.35940/ijrte.B1069.0782S619

Christopher, M. (1992). *Logistics and Supply Chain Management: Strategies for Reducing Costs and Improving Services*. Financial Times.

Christopher, M. (2011). *Logistics & Supply Chain Management* (4th ed.). Pearson Education Limited.

Dave, E. (2011). How the next evolution of the internet is changing everything. *Internet of Things : Engineering Cyber Physical Human Systems*.

de Vass, T., Shee, H., & Miah, S. (2021). IoT in Supply Chain Management: Opportunities and Challenges for Businesses in Early Industry 4.0 Context. *Operations and Supply Chain Management: An International Journal*, 148–161. DOI: 10.31387/oscm0450293

Dhirani, L. L., Armstrong, E., & Newe, T. (2021). Industrial IoT, Cyber Threats, and Standards Landscape: Evaluation and Roadmap. *Sensors (Basel)*, 21(11), 3901. DOI: 10.3390/s21113901 PMID: 34198727

Duarte, A. Y. S., Sanches, R. A., & Dedini, F. G. (2018). Assessment and technological forecasting in the textile industry: From first industrial revolution to the Industry 4.0. *Strategic Design Research Journal*, 11(3). Advance online publication. DOI: 10.4013/sdrj.2018.113.03

EM-DAT. (2024). *Inventorying hazards & disasters worldwide since 1988*. https://www.emdat.be/

Farooq, M. S., Riaz, S., Abid, A., Umer, T., & Zikria, Y. (2020). Role of IoT Technology in Agriculture: A Systematic Literature Review. *Electronics (Basel)*, 9(2), 319. DOI: 10.3390/electronics9020319

Geeksforgeeks. (2023). *Characteristics of Internet of Things*. Geeksforgeeks.Org. https://www.geeksforgeeks.org/characteristics-of-internet-of-things/

Gong, C., Liu, J., Zhang, Q., Chen, H., & Gong, Z. (2010). The Characteristics of Cloud Computing. *2010 39th International Conference on Parallel Processing Workshops*.

Gulia, P., & Chahal, A. (2020). Big Data Analytics for IoT. [IJARET]. *International Journal of Advanced Research in Engineering and Technology*, 11(6), 593–603. DOI: 10.34218/IJARET.11.6.2020.054

Handfield, R. B., & Nichols, E. L. (1999). *Introduction to Supply Chain Management*. Prentice Hall.

Hernandez, M. (2019). *IoT: Consumer & Commercial vs. Industrial - Main overview*. Ubidots.

Ittmann, H. W. (1999). Introduction to Supply Chain Management by Robert B. Handfield and Ernest L. Nichols. *Informs*, 111–114.

Ivankova, G. V., Mochalina, E. P., & Goncharova, N. L. (2020). Internet of Things (IoT) in logistics. *IOP Conference Series. Materials Science and Engineering*, 940(1), 012033. DOI: 10.1088/1757-899X/940/1/012033

Jayanth, S., Poorvi, M. B., & Sunil, M. P. (2017). *Inventory Management System Using IOT.*, DOI: 10.1007/978-981-10-2471-9_20

Katz, M., Paso, T., Mikhaylov, K., Pessoa, L., Fontes, H., Hakola, L., Leppäniemi, J., Carlos, E., Dolmans, G., Rufo, J., Drzewiecki, M., Sallouha, H., Napier, B., Branquinho, A., & Eder, K. (2024). Towards truly sustainable IoT systems: The SUPERIOT project. *JPhys Photonics*, 6(1), 011001. DOI: 10.1088/2515-7647/ad1c6a

Khayyam, H., Javadi, B., Jalili, M., & Jazar, R. N. (2020). Artificial Intelligence and Internet of Things for Autonomous Vehicles. In *Nonlinear Approaches in Engineering Applications* (pp. 39–68). Springer International Publishing., DOI: 10.1007/978-3-030-18963-1_2

Kiritsis, D. (2011). Closed-loop PLM for intelligent products in the era of the Internet of things. *Computer Aided Design*, 43(5), 479–501. DOI: 10.1016/j.cad.2010.03.002

Kodali, R. K., Swamy, G., & Lakshmi, B. (2015). An implementation of IoT for healthcare. *2015 IEEE Recent Advances in Intelligent Computational Systems (RAICS)*, 411–416. DOI: 10.1109/RAICS.2015.7488451

Kott, A., Swami, A., & West, B. J. (2016). The Internet of Battle Things. *Computer*, 49(12), 70–75. DOI: 10.1109/MC.2016.355

Li, Y., Hou, M., Liu, H., & Liu, Y. (2012). Towards a theoretical framework of strategic decision, supporting capability and information sharing under the context of Internet of Things. *Information Technology and Management*, 13(4), 205–216. DOI: 10.1007/s10799-012-0121-1

Loi, F., Sivanathan, A., Gharakheili, H. H., Radford, A., & Sivaraman, V. (2017). Systematically Evaluating Security and Privacy for Consumer IoT Devices. *Proceedings of the 2017 Workshop on Internet of Things Security and Privacy*, 1–6. DOI: 10.1145/3139937.3139938

Malche, T., & Maheshwary, P. (2017). Internet of Things (IoT) for building smart home system. *2017 International Conference on I-SMAC (IoT in Social, Mobile, Analytics and Cloud) (I-SMAC)*, 65–70. DOI: 10.1109/I-SMAC.2017.8058258

Mashayekhy, Y., Babaei, A., Yuan, X.-M., & Xue, A. (2022). Impact of Internet of Things (IoT) on Inventory Management: A Literature Survey. *Logistics (Basel)*, 6(2), 33. DOI: 10.3390/logistics6020033

Meng, L. (2021). Using IoT in Supply Chain Risk Management, to Enable Collaboration between Business, Community, and Government. *Smart Cities*, 4(3), 995–1003. DOI: 10.3390/smartcities4030052

Meng, Y., Zhang, W., Zhu, H., & Shen, X. S. (2018). Securing Consumer IoT in the Smart Home: Architecture, Challenges, and Countermeasures. *IEEE Wireless Communications*, 25(6), 53–59. DOI: 10.1109/MWC.2017.1800100

Min, S., Zacharia, Z. G., & Smith, C. D. (2019). Defining Supply Chain Management: In the Past, Present, and Future. *Journal of Business Logistics*, 40(1), 44–55. DOI: 10.1111/jbl.12201

Mishra, N., & Silakari, S. (2012). Predictive Analytics: A Survey, Trends, Applications, Oppurtunities & Challenges. [IJCSIT]. *International Journal of Computer Science and Information Technologies*, 3(3), 4434–4438.

Mohajan, H. K. (2019). The First Industrial Revolution: Creation of a New Global Human Era. *Journal of Social Sciences and Humanities*, 5(4), 377–387.

Montazerolghaem, A., Yaghmaee, M. H., & Leon-Garcia, A. (2020). Green Cloud Multimedia Networking: NFV/SDN Based Energy-Efficient Resource Allocation. *IEEE Transactions on Green Communications and Networking*, 4(3), 873–889. DOI: 10.1109/TGCN.2020.2982821

Mukhopadhyay, S. C., & Suryadevara, N. K. (2014). *Internet of Things: Challenges and Opportunities* (pp. 1–17). DOI: 10.1007/978-3-319-04223-7_1

Nain, G., Pattanaik, K. K., & Sharma, G. K. (2022). Towards edge computing in intelligent manufacturing: Past, present and future. *Journal of Manufacturing Systems*, 62, 588–611. DOI: 10.1016/j.jmsy.2022.01.010

Nandan, A. S., Singh, S., Malik, A., & Kumar, R. (2021). A Green Data Collection & Transmission Method for IoT-Based WSN in Disaster Management. *IEEE Sensors Journal*, 21(22), 25912–25921. DOI: 10.1109/JSEN.2021.3117995

Ok, K., Coskun, V., Aydin, M. N., & Ozdenizci, B. (2010). Current benefits and future directions of NFC services. *2010 International Conference on Education and Management Technology*, 334–338. DOI: 10.1109/ICEMT.2010.5657642

Osińska, M., & Zalewski, W. (2020). Determinants of Using Telematics Systems in Road Transport Companies. *European Research Studies*, 28(2), 474–487. DOI: 10.35808/ersj/1604

Oyewole, A. T., Okoye, C. C., Ofodile, O. C., & Ejairu, E. (2024). Reviewing predictive analytics in supply chain management: Applications and benefits. *World Journal of Advanced Research and Reviews*, 21(3), 568–574. DOI: 10.30574/wjarr.2024.21.3.0673

Park, H., & Park, S. (2024). Emerging Trends and Challenges in IoT Networks. *Electronics (Basel)*, 13(3), 513. DOI: 10.3390/electronics13030513

Patel, K. K., & Patel, S. M. (2016). Internet of Things-IOT: Definition, Characteristics, Architecture, Enabling Technologies, Application & Future Challenges. *International Journal of Engineering Science and Computing*, 6122–6131.

Pawar, P., & Trivedi, A. (2019). Device-to-Device Communication Based IoT System: Benefits and Challenges. *IETE Technical Review*, 36(4), 362–374. DOI: 10.1080/02564602.2018.1476191

Placek, M. (2023). *Autonomous vehicles worldwide - statistics & facts*. Statista.

Pradeepa, K., & Praveen, M. (2020). A Survey on Routing Protocols With Security in Internet of Things. *Solid State Technology*, 63(4).

Qi, Q., & Tao, F. (2019). A Smart Manufacturing Service System Based on Edge Computing, Fog Computing, and Cloud Computing. *IEEE Access : Practical Innovations, Open Solutions*, 7, 86769–86777. DOI: 10.1109/ACCESS.2019.2923610

Rastogi, H. (2022, May 5). *IoT in Tesla: Applications, Benefits and Potential Risks*. Analytic Steps. https://analyticssteps.com/blogs/iot-tesla-applications-benefits-and-potential-risks

Ray, P. P., Mukherjee, M., & Shu, L. (2017). Internet of Things for Disaster Management: State-of-the-Art and Prospects. *IEEE Access : Practical Innovations, Open Solutions*, 5, 18818–18835. DOI: 10.1109/ACCESS.2017.2752174

Reddy, A. M. (2021). A Review on Iot Enabling Technologies and Back-End Data-Sharing Model. *Journal of Electronics. Computer Networking and Applied Mathematics*, 11(11), 41–47. DOI: 10.55529/jecnam11.41.47

Rejeb, A., Simske, S., Rejeb, K., Treiblmaier, H., & Zailani, S. (2020). Internet of Things research in supply chain management and logistics: A bibliometric analysis. *Internet of Things : Engineering Cyber Physical Human Systems*, 12, 100318. DOI: 10.1016/j.iot.2020.100318

Rojko, A. (2017). Industry 4.0 Concept: Background and Overview. [IJIM]. *International Journal of Interactive Mobile Technologies*, 11(5), 77. DOI: 10.3991/ijim.v11i5.7072

Rose, K., Eldridge, S., & Chapin, L. (2015). The internet of things: An overview. [ISOC]. *The Internet Society*, 80(15), 1–53.

Salam, A. (2020). *Internet of Things for Sustainability: Perspectives in Privacy.* Cybersecurity, and Future Trends., DOI: 10.1007/978-3-030-35291-2_10

Sardjono, W., Arum, I. R. M., Rahmasari, A., & Lusia, E. (2023). Impact of Track and Trace (T&T) in Industrial Revolution 4.0 of the Pharmaceutical Industry (Pharma 4.0). *E3S Web of Conferences, 388*, 03014. DOI: 10.1051/e3sconf/202338803014

Sarmah, S. S. (2018). Understanding Blockchain Technology. *Computing in Science & Engineering*, 8(2), 23–29.

Selvaraj, S., & Sundaravaradhan, S. (2020). Challenges and opportunities in IoT healthcare systems: A systematic review. *SN Applied Sciences*, 2(1), 139. DOI: 10.1007/s42452-019-1925-y

Shah, S. A., Seker, D. Z., Hameed, S., & Draheim, D. (2019). The Rising Role of Big Data Analytics and IoT in Disaster Management: Recent Advances, Taxonomy and Prospects. *IEEE Access : Practical Innovations, Open Solutions*, 7, 54595–54614. DOI: 10.1109/ACCESS.2019.2913340

Sial, Q. A., Safder, U., Iqbal, S., & Ali, R. B. (2024). Advancement in Supercapacitors for IoT Applications by Using Machine Learning: Current Trends and Future Technology. *Sustainability (Basel)*, 16(4), 1516. DOI: 10.3390/su16041516

Swamy, N., & Nayak, S., & M N, V. (2016). Analysis on IoT Challenges, Opportunities, Applications and Communication Models. *International Journal of Advanced Engineering* [IJAEMS]. *Management Science*, 2(4), 75–78.

Volvo. (2023). *Volvo Group implements a new Internet of Things (IoT) network to make factories smarter*. https://www.volvogroup.com/en/news-and-media/news/2023/mar/volvo-group-implements-a-new-internet-of-things-iot-network-to-make-factories-smarter.html

Weinstein, R. (2005). RFID: A technical overview and its application to the enterprise. *IT Professional*, 7(3), 27–33. DOI: 10.1109/MITP.2005.69

Xia, F., Yang, L. T., Wang, L., & Vinel, A. (2012). Internet of Things. *International Journal of Communication Systems*, 25(9), 1101–1102. DOI: 10.1002/dac.2417

Xu, J., Gu, B., & Tian, G. (2022). Review of agricultural IoT technology. *Artificial Intelligence in Agriculture*, 6, 10–22. DOI: 10.1016/j.aiia.2022.01.001

Yang, J., Wang, X., & Zhao, Y. (2022). Parallel Manufacturing for Industrial Metaverses: A New Paradigm in Smart Manufacturing. *IEEE/CAA Journal of Automatica Sinica, 9*(12), 2063–2070. DOI: 10.1109/JAS.2022.106097

Yu, Q., Wang, Y., Jiang, X., Zhao, B., Zhang, X., Wang, X., & Liu, Q. (2021). Optimization of Vehicle Transportation Route Based on IoT. *Mathematical Problems in Engineering*, 2021, 1–10. DOI: 10.1155/2021/1312058

Yushi, L., Fei, J., & Hui, Y. (2012). Study on application modes of military Internet of Things (MIOT). *2012 IEEE International Conference on Computer Science and Automation Engineering (CSAE)*, 630–634. DOI: 10.1109/CSAE.2012.6273031

Zabeu, S. (2023, March). *Volvo adopts IoT to monitor autonomous vehicles on the production line*. NetworkKing The IT Monitoring Magazine. https://network-king.net/volvo-adopts-iot-to-monitor-autonomous-vehicles-on-the-production-line/

Zain, I., Rehan, A., & Ashraf, J. (2016). Internet of Things. *International Journal of Engineering Development and Research*, 4(3), 1088–1092.

Zhang, Z., & Fisac, J. F. (2021). *Safe Occlusion-aware Autonomous Driving via Game-Theoretic Active Perception*. DOI: 10.15607/RSS.2021.XVII.066

KEYWORDS AND DEFINITIONS

Big Data Analytics: Process of analyzing and interpreting 'Big Data' to understand the nature and pattern of something to make an informed decision

Blockchain: A database consists of blocks of data interconnected chronologically to form a data chain.

Cloud Computing: Process of delivering computing services like storage, servers, and databases

Internet of Things: A collection of physical devices interconnected through a network for data transfers

Logistics: Moving the goods to a customer with the help of transportation facilities

SCM 4.0: Supply chain Management integrated with intelligent technology like AI, Machine learning, and IoT.

Sensor: A device that can detect the change in a particular environment factor and can convert the change into corresponding electrical signals to be measured by a computer.

Supply Chain Management: Monitoring and managing all the Processes involved in moving goods or services from a producer to a customer.

Wireless Sensor Network: A network of interconnected wireless sensors that are capable of transmitting data wirelessly.

Chapter 4
Leveraging Internet of Things Applications With Service-Oriented Computing for Supply Chain Operations

Kamalendu Pal
https://orcid.org/0000-0001-7158-6481
University of London, UK

ABSTRACT

Globalization and digitalization have shaped supply chain operations management in recent years. There is a growing focus on using the Internet of Things (IoT) to develop decision support systems for supply chain operations. These systems collect and process business operational data to create services for stakeholders. The chapter introduces a knowledge-based approach to designing and implementing these operational service supports based on relevant web services. Emphasizing the critical role of semantic interoperability is accomplished through ontologies and similarity assessment methods. The practical application of these theoretical concepts is not just a possibility but a reality, and this demonstration will engage the business stakeholders, making them feel reassured about the feasibility of the digital transformation of supply chain operations. Finally, the chapter provides a business case highlighting the purpose of ontologies, an algorithmic concept similarity assessment, and the usefulness of ontology in developing operational service design.

DOI: 10.4018/979-8-3693-4427-9.ch004

INTRODUCTION

The rich tapestry of commercial trading, woven between countries and continents, has been a cornerstone of human civilization since ancient times. This historical significance of global trade, which was a vibrant exchange of goods such as rice, wheat, spices, textiles, metals, petroleum products, and other essential commodities, connects us to the roots of our profession. The Silk Road, the Spice Route, and a myriad of interconnected trade networks were the threads that initiated trade patterns, which have since flourished with the advent of industrialization (Bardhan, 2003) and globalization (Stiglitz, 2017).

While the fundamental concept of global trade remains unchanged, the process of moving goods and money from point A in one country to point B in another has evolved into a complex and multifaceted operation. This operational business practice now encompasses financing trade, tracking and tracing goods along supply chains, and verifying the quality of those goods through provenance and product pedigree. As global trade has expanded, these operational business processes have multiplied and become more intricate. The demands of increased trade volume among more participants – business financiers, partners as importers and exporters servicing different market segments, freight forwarders, customs and port authorities, regulatory governing bodies, and insurance providers- have complicated these business practices. This evolution underscores the critical importance of understanding and managing supply chain operations, emphasizing the urgency and significance of digitization of business processes (Pal, 2017a) (Pal, 2017b) (Pal & Karakostas, 2014).

The business world recognizes the significant potential of robust supply chain management (SCM) in connecting regular activities and distribution operations to drive a company's growth and profitability. The SCM system procures raw materials, transforms them into intermediate and finished products, and delivers them to customers with impeccable service provisions, thus playing a crucial role in driving growth. Integrating information and material flows in the demand and supply process enhances logistical resource allocation, management, and control, increasing productivity, reducing operational costs, and effective customer services. SCM also involves managing supply chain facets, ensuring customer product delivery, and providing value-added services (Pal, 2018a) (Pal, 2018b) (Pal & Yasar, 2023) (Pal et al., 2024). These value-added services, such as personalized product recommendations, predictive maintenance, and real-time order tracking, are designed to enhance the customer experience and increase customer loyalty. Reverse logistics, the handling of products returned to the company, is an integral part of this process, as it ensures a comprehensive approach to supply chain management despite the potential for substantial losses.

Figure 1. Supply Chain Management Process

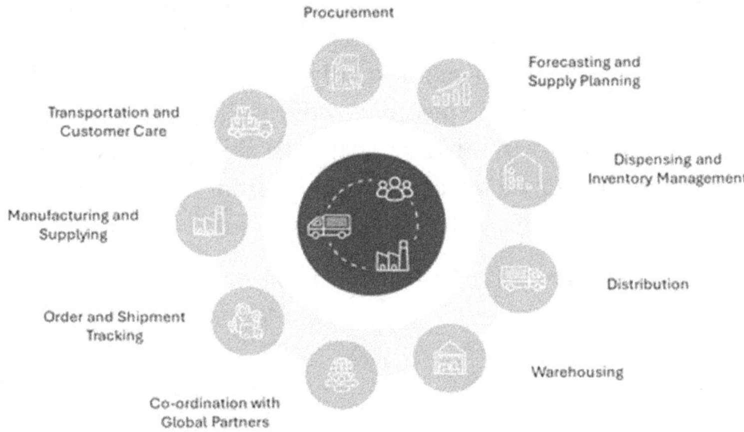

Strategically, SCM can be dissected into various business processes, each with unique activities. These processes are not just a series of tasks, but they form the backbone of the supply chain, each playing a crucial role in the smooth operation of the entire system. They include forecasting and supply chain planning, procurement, transportation and customer clearance, manufacturing and supplying, order and shipment tracking, coordination with global partners, warehousing and receiving, distribution, and dispensing and inventory management. Figure 1 presents a visual representation of these strategic business processes, which are more sequential in practice, as shown in the diagram. It describes a continuum based on a straightforward concept – using a better understanding and knowledge of the world for industrial SCM systems to make better decisions within a business objective function.

Historically, the beginning of the SCM initiative was characterized by relatively static models codified in rules defined by humans to provide the best possible representation of the real physical world. However, the landscape of SCM is rapidly changing. In recent decades, these model-driven business operation practices have not been adequate enough to manage global supply chain operations effectively. The evolution from these static models to dynamic ones is a testament to the progress and innovation in the field of SCM.

Modern SCM is a local or regional concern and a global phenomenon. It is on a trajectory of multi-decade progression towards greater sophistication, addressing the challenges of increasing product varieties, fulfilment options, and customer engagement at the lowest possible cost. A 'nexus of business processes and technology forces ', which refers to the intersection of strategic business activities and technological advancements, is driving unprecedented change in supply chain and retail operations in one sector or region and across all business sectors globally. In this way, SCM depends on business process operation practice and technology architecture to bring innovation and offer value-added services to customers. Instead of a static model, the current generation supply chain management is driven by increasingly dynamic models, made possible by the availability of digital data points from everywhere, the ability to sense this data, the ability to process this data, the ability to react to this data, and the ability to learn from it over time.

Figure 2. A Digital Supply Chain Operations Scenario

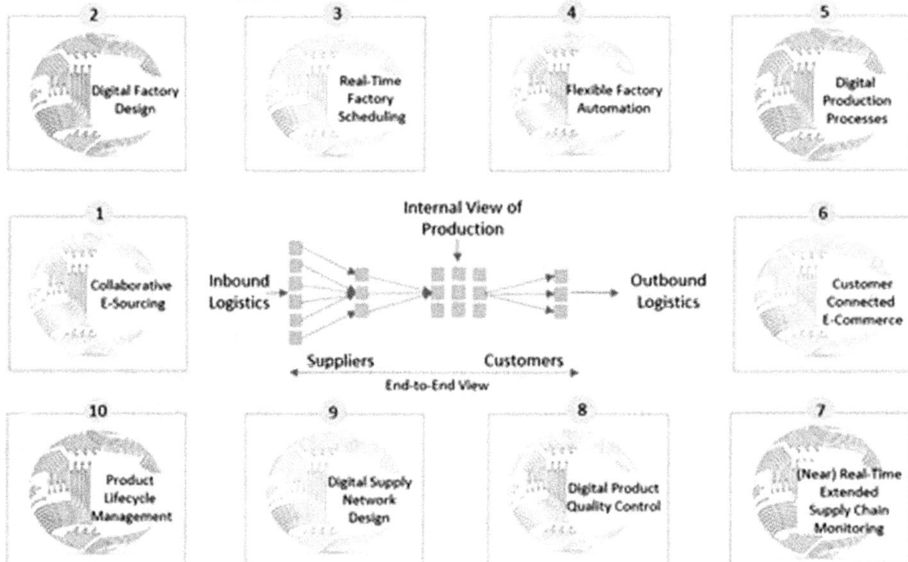

Furthermore, these models will provide much more accurate representations of the natural world at any given time. In other words, computer representation of the supply chain will become time-synchronized with the physical real world; as digital data from the supply chain is processed and intelligent adjustments are made, the digital and the physical become one. Not only will the models be commingled with physical reality through digital data, but the logic that runs software against these models will transition from a rules-driven paradigm to a learning paradigm. In the 'digital phase' of modern supply chain management, which refers to the era of advanced digital technologies, machine learning is driving real facet of digitation of the mainstream of enterprise software.

With numerous opportunities to digitize various aspects of supply chain operations, business organizations often take a structural approach to automate essential services. This chapter describes the strategic decision-making process within the supply chain. It achieves this by presenting a series of digitized business scenarios covering inbound, internal, outbound, and end-to-end operation activities, as shown diagrammatically in Figure 2. The digitization of business processes takes a new dimension with the deployment of information and communication technologies (ICT). This structured approach breaks down the supply chain into a series of digital scenarios, enhancing the efficiency and effectiveness of operations and inspiring a future where the potential of digitization is fully realized, reassuring of the benefits of this transformation.

The chapter presents a strategic framework for robust decision-making based on a clear understanding of the outcomes that an industrial sector wants to achieve. It emphasizes the empowerment of business strategists, like you, to think about which areas they want to focus on, assess their level of achievement to date, and prioritize their efforts. Figure 2 presents a snapshot of the framework that consists of business partners collaborative electronic sourcing, digital factory design, real-time factory scheduling, flexible factory automation, digital production processes, customer-connected electronic commerce, near real-time extended supply chain monitoring, digital product quality control, digital supply network design, and product lifecycle management. However, the detailed discussion regarding this framework is beyond the scope of this chapter.

Real-world industrial sectors like manufacturing, healthcare, transportation industry, retail business, and environmental monitoring are increasingly reliant on obtaining relevant sensor data. Processing this data in real-time from all operational value chain components is crucial for these sectors to maintain efficiency and competitiveness. Implementing an intelligent industry involves integrating connectivity into industrial products and related services using service-oriented computing and the Internet of Things (IoT). This integration aims to capitalize on intelligence and actionable knowledge for machines, allowing for autonomous collaboration among machines and integrating products and additional value-added services. Service-oriented computing has significantly transformed the service consumption and delivery platform, revolutionizing how businesses and users engage with IT resources across various industrial domains. Its impact on the supply chain is particularly noteworthy, as it optimizes processes and enhances the overall customer experience. The emerging IoT further extends the service-oriented concept beyond computing and communication to include the physical field devices and hardware, enabling real-time monitoring and control of the supply chain. By using the data collected from sensors, machines, devices, and people in the industrial production processes as well as the virtual world, data analytics can identify relations and patterns to gain valuable insights for optimized operations and to provide services to customers such as machine failure prevention and real-time production performance improvement. Service-oriented computing and IoT technologies enable organizations to pursue new revenue streams based on the extracted insights regarding performance footprint and autonomous operation, opening up exciting new possibilities for business growth and profitability.

This comprehensive chapter provides an extensive review of the latest trends in IoT-based business applications and the challenges related to interoperability. It explores how semantic web technologies, frameworks, and information models can play a crucial role in supporting the automation of industrial business operations, highlighting their potential in IoT applications. The chapter covers two crucial aspects of industrial IoT ecosystems: (i) the fundamental concept of IoT and its information systems architectural issues, and (ii) interoperability, service-oriented computing, and the significance of business processes ontology design for operational service implementation. In conclusion, the chapter addresses pertinent issues and challenges for future research, ensuring a comprehensive understanding of the field.

The rest of this chapter provides an overview of how service-oriented computing is merging with IoT technologies to create business information systems for industrial applications. It also examines notable research in this area. The chapter ends with concluding remarks and outlines a future research agenda.

RELATED ADVANCES AND RESEARCH WORKS

In recent years, modern industrial application paradigms (e.g., Industry Four, Industry Five) have dominated the business world of information systems design and development. Within these applications, service-oriented computing, and the Internet of Things (IoT) technologies are essential in heterogeneous services integration, fostering a collaborative environment for information sharing and decision-making (Pal & Yasar, 2020) (Pal & Yasar, 2023). This collaborative nature of decision-making, where everyone's input is valued, is a crucial benefit of these technologies. At the same time, the concept of cyber-physical systems (CPS), the Industrial Internet of Things (IIoT), modern data communication technologies, service-oriented computing, and artificial intelligence-based techniques are ushering in a new dawn for industrial applications integration, where everyone is part of a larger community.

Figure 3. Different Characteristics of IioT Based Information Systems

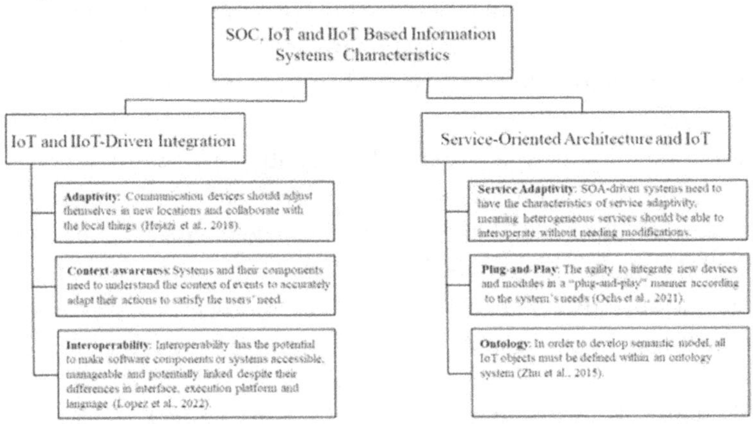

As mentioned before, there is a diversity of protocols in the IoT domain, and various challenges are faced when integrating heterogeneous information. Academics and practitioners have presented different system integration enablers frameworks and their components to achieve various aspects of information system deployment for industrial applications.

Figure 4. Interoperability Between Applications and Enablers

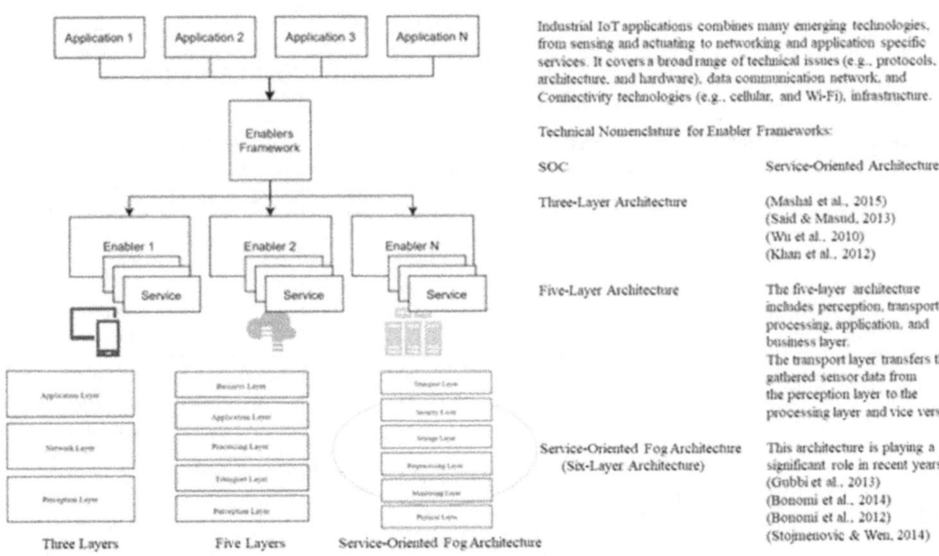

IIoT is revolutionizing the operation of industrial information systems, enabling them to sense and acquire information from the operating environment in new ways. IoT and IoT systems need different characteristics to be considered at the time of design and implementation to improve the benefits of interconnected objects in a network (Razzaque et al., 2016) (Schneider et al., 2018). The diagrammatic representation in Figure 3 highlights some of the essential characteristics.

Convergence of SOC with IoT technology often provides an agile information system with various design challenges. In order to deal with this, researchers often use a unique information system design techniques and with a common theme of Enablers Framework (EF) component that act like interface proxy. A simple interoperability between applications and enablers is shown in Figure 4.

Recent Research Work on Service-Oriented IoT

Several studies have investigated the application of Web paradigms and protocols to service provisioning. Traditional context-aware frameworks have several limitations when it comes to developing context-aware services consists of various research issues: (i) if the context is constantly changing (such as location), a context-aware service must be invoked with the updated context data. Consequently, the service must be invoked multiple times, which increases network traffic and the cost of using the service, (ii) large messages: sending a large message to the context manager. Table 1 represents some of the recent research works.

Table 1. Some of the Recent Research Works on Context-Aware Semantic Service Provisioning

Reference	Domain	Proposed Solution	Web Technology	Context Aware	Context Reasoning	Strength
(Kim et al., 2016)	Smart home	Middleware Architecture	OWL	Yes	Yes	1.Context inferring 2.Sensor abstraction 3.Rule based context aware service selection
(Gochhayat et al., 2016)	General	Architecture	SOA	Yes	No	1.Minimizes overhead of communication and processing
(Sciullo et al., 2020)	General	WoT Store Platform	W3C WoT Micro-service oriented	No	No	1.Resource dynamic discovery 2.Simplified management

continued on following page

Table 1. Continued

Reference	Domain	Proposed Solution	Web Technology	Context Aware	Context Reasoning	Strength
(Ibaseta et al., 2021)	Building	Architecture Real-World Application	W3C WoT Cloud	No	No	1.Interoperable 2.Scalable 3.Energy consumption 4.Real-world Application
(Ortiz et al., 2022)	Hospital	Architecture	Event riven SOA Cloud, Fog, and Edge	Yes	No	1.Integrated edge, fog, and cloud computing 2.Situational-aware 3.Event-Driven SOA

The above research review leads to the presentation of the proposed system architecture in the following section.

OVERVIEW OF THE FRAMEWORK

The proposed framework uses model-theoretic semantics modelled in ontologies for IoT-generated data modelling. It helps to gather detailed information regarding the characteristics of IoT devices based on their technical requirements. The advantages of this encoding are – (i) interconnecting different classification systems to represent capabilities and properties of constituent parts, (ii) translating characteristics or properties among compound constituent parts, and (iii) aggregating basic properties into complex properties based on the constituents of a superordinate system. Those concepts can be used and adapted for the IoT to enhance the use of IoT devices by connecting them as a group, creating coordination between IoT devices, and improving their interoperability.

One of the main objectives of this framework is to define an IoT architecture, which can also be used for other applications. The design principle in Apparel Business Semantic Data Management (ABDDI) is that any physical/real-world object in the global textile and clothing business can have a virtual representation through a Virtual Object (VO). A VO uses a semantic representation of the functionality and conceals the varied identity of the real-world object. Multiple VOs can be combined to form a Composite Virtual Object (CVO) that provides more compact and reliable services. In simple, CVOs are combined to form a service request. Thus, the ABDDI architecture has three layers: VO, CVO, and Service, as shown in Figure 5.

Figure 5. RFID Tagging Level at Different Stages in the Apparel Manufacturing Network

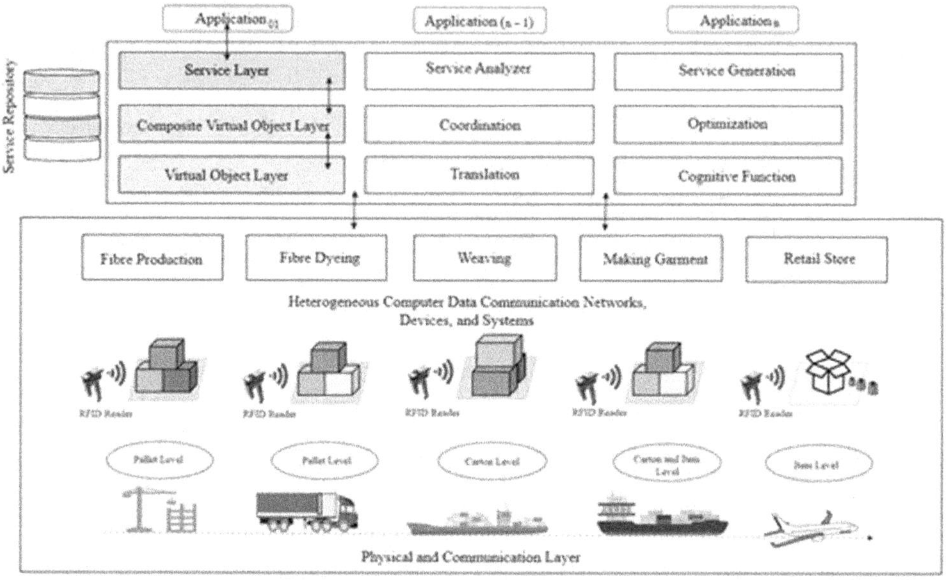

The functionalities of the three layers are presented below:

- **VO layer**: The VOs represent real world objects in the digital format. End-users can search semantically and retrieve information from any existing VO. Also, actuation can be done through the VO.
- **CVO layer**: In this layer, VOs are combined to form a service request. This layer caters to functionality to search and query categories of CVOs semantically for service provision, ensuring reliable and efficient service delivery.
- **Service layer:** This layer is the dynamic heart of the system. It receives requests from users and analyzes them to determine the categories of CVOs needed for service accomplishment. It then performs service composition and orchestration, adapting to the ever-changing cloth and textile business environment with agility and responsiveness. The Service layer is crucial as it ensures that the right services are provided to the users at the right time, enhancing the overall efficiency of the system.

The ABDDI system has other components: a registry and a control unit. Every layer in this framework has a registry referencing the available VOs, CVOs, and services. These registries provide methods to semantically search and query existing VOs, CVOs, and services. The control unit, a key component, regulates access to the VOs, CVOs, and services based on the level of the end-user requirements.

KNOWLEDGE REPRESENTATION AND REASONING APPROACH

Description logics (DLs) (Baader et al., 2002) are a family of knowledge representation languages with a rich historical significance. They have been widely used in ontological modelling, providing a key foundation for the Web Ontology Language (OWL) as standardized by the World Wide Web Consortium (W3C). The use of DLs in knowledge representation predates the advent of ontological modelling in the context of the Semantic Web, with the first DL modelling languages emerging in the mid-1980s.

DLs, as their name suggests, are logics, with most DLs being decidable fragments of first-order logic. This characteristic equips them with *formal semantics*, a precise specification of the meaning of DL ontologies. These formal semantics not only enable the unambiguous exchange of DL ontologies between human and computer systems but also empower logical deduction to *infer additional* information from the facts stated explicitly in an ontology.

The chapter underscores the indispensable role of DLs in knowledge representation for pervasive computing within the global apparel supply chain. DL-based systems, akin to database management systems (DBMS), are crucial for comprehending complex descriptions. In DL, elementary descriptions, comprising of atomic concepts and roles, serve as the foundation for constructing complex descriptions using concept constructors. The use of abstract notation, with A and B for atomic concepts, R for atomic roles, and C and D for concept descriptions, enhances understanding of the system. Table 2 highlights vital DL constructors and their related examples, integral to the DLs explored in this chapter.

Table 2. Description Logics Set of Constructors

Constructor Name	Syntax	Explanation
Top concept	T	Universal concept. All the objects in the domain.
Bottom concept	⊥	The empty set.
Atomic concept	A	All objects belong to set A.
Atomic negation	¬A	All the objects do not belong to set A.
Conjunction	C⊓D	The objects belong to both C and D sets.
Disjunction	C⊔D	The objects that are in the extension of either C or D or both
Value restriction	∀RC	All the objects are participating in the R relation, whose range is all the objects belonging to the C set.
Existential restriction	∃RC	At least one object participating in the relation R.
Concept definition	A ≡ C	Concepts represent sets of elements and can be viewed as unary predicates.

Resource Representation and Reasoning in Description Logics

The most important and well-known service characterizing reasoning in DL checks for specificity hierarchies by determining whether a concept description is more specific than another one or, formally, if there is a *subsumption* relation between them.

Figure 6. Definitions 1 and 2

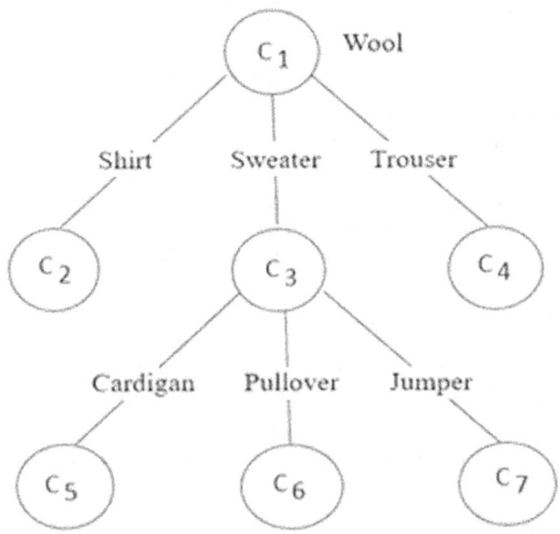

It is worth showing how to model concept collections formalized in ALN (D) according to a compact lossless representation. Such modelling allows for finding commonalities in resource annotations formalized in DL.

Figure 7. Definitions 3-7

Definition 1 (Subsumption): *Give two concept descriptions, C and D, and a TBox τ in a DL L; one can say that D subsumes C τ(C ⊑τ D)concerning if for every model of τ, $C^I \subset D^I$. In a particular case, two concepts are equivalent if they subsume each other.*

For example, consider the following concept descriptions, referring to different garment types in an apparel supply chain network: G_1 = *SweaterBodyGarment* ⊓ ∀ *hasMain.Colour.Red*, and G_2 = *UpperBodyGarment* ⊓ ∀ *hasMain.Colour.Red*. Then using TBox reasoning – the concept inclusion can be achieved, and the output will be *Sweater* $\sqsubseteq_T$ *UpperBodyGarment*. Hence, given the model, knowledge expressed by G_1 is more specific than the one required by G_2 concerning the reasoning mechanism and the definition of G_2 subsumes G_1.

Based on subsumption, new reasoning mechanisms can be defined in DLs. The ABDDI system development uses several non-standard reasoning mechanisms (e.g., Least Common Subsumer – LCS).

Definition 2 (Least Common Subsumer): *Let C_1, ..., C_p be p concept descriptions in a DL L. A Least Common Subsumer (LCS) of C_1, ..., C_p, denoted by LCS (C_1, ..., C_p) is a concept description E in L. state that the following conditions hold: (i) $C_h \sqsubseteq E$ for h = 1, ..., p; (ii) E is the least L–concept description satisfying (iii), i.e., if E′ is an L–concept satisfying $C_i \sqsubseteq E'$ for all i = 1, ..., n, then $E \sqsubseteq E'$.*

Figure 8. Definitions 8-9

Definition 3 (Concept Components): *Let C be a concept described in a DL L, with C formalized as* $C^1 \sqcap \ldots C^m$. *The Concept Components of C are defined as follows: if* C_j, *with* $j = 1, \ldots, m$ *is either a concept name, a negated concept name, or a concrete feature or a number restriction, then* C_j *is a Concept Component of C; if* $C_j = \forall R.E$, *with* $j = 1 \ldots, m$, *then* $\forall R.E^k$ *is a Concept Component of C, for each* E^k *Concept Component of E.*

Definition 4 (Subsumption): *Give two concept descriptions C and D, and a TBox* τ *in a DL L; one can say that D subsumes C* $\tau(C \sqsubseteq_\tau D)$ *concerning if for every model of* τ, $C^I \subset D^I$. *In a particular case, two concepts are equivalent if they subsume each other.*

Definition 5 (Least Common Subsumer): *Let* $C_1, \ldots, C_p$ *be p concept descriptions in a DL L. A Least Common Subsumer (LCS) of* $C_1, \ldots, C_p$, *denoted by LCS* $(C_1, \ldots, C_p)$ *is a concept description E in L. state that the following conditions hold: (i)* $C_h \sqsubseteq E$ *for* $h = 1, \ldots, p$; *(ii) E is the least L–concept description satisfying (iii), i.e., if E' is an L–concept satisfying* $C_i \sqsubseteq E'$ *for all* $i = 1, \ldots, n$, *then* $E \sqsubseteq E'$.

Definition 6 (r-Common Subsumer, Informative r-Common Subsumers): *Let* $C_1, \ldots, C_p$ *be p concept descriptions in a DL L, and let be* $k \leq p$. *An r-Common Subsumer (r-CS) of* $C_1, \ldots, C_p$ *is a concept* $D \neq \top$ *such that D is an LCS of at least* $r = k/p$ *concepts among* $C_1, \ldots, C_p$. *One can define a particular case as Informative r-Common Subsumers (IrCS) that specific r-CSS for which* $r < 1$.

It is worth showing how to model concept collections formalized in ALN (D) according to a compact lossless representation. Such a modelling framework allows for finding commonalities in resource annotations formalized in DL.

Definition 7 (Concept Components): *Let C be a concept described in a DL L, with C formalized as* $C^1 \sqcap \ldots C^m$. *The Concept Components of C are defined as follows: if* C_j, *with* $j = 1, \ldots, m$ *is either a concept name, a negated concept name, or a concrete feature or a number restriction, then* C_j *is a Concept Component of C; if* $C_j = \forall R.E$, *with* $j = 1 \ldots, m$, *then* $\forall R.E^k$ *is a Concept Component of C, for each* E^k *Concept Component of E.*

Semantic Similarity Assessment

Before describing the proposed approach's theoretical framework, the employed reasoning services will be shortly recalled in the following subsection to make the chapter self-contained. Furthermore, the proposed algorithmic concept of similarity measurement is presented in this section.

In ABSDM, the similarity between concepts C_i, C_j can be expressed by a number, and its values can fall between 0 and 1. It may be viewed as a one-directional relation, and its larger values imply a higher similarity between the concepts. The concept similarity is described as follows:

Figure 9. Definition 10

Definition 8 (Aggregate Collection Matrix): *Let $S_1, \ldots, S_n$ be an aggregate collection, with $S_i = C_{1i}, \ldots, C_{pi}$ for $i = 1 \ldots n$. Let $D \in \{D_1, \ldots, D_m\}$ be the Concept Components deriving from all the concepts in the aggregate collection. The Aggregate Subsumers Matrix is defined as $A = (a_{ij})$, with $i = 1 \ldots n$ and $j = 1 \ldots m$, such that for each i, $a_{ij} = v$, with $0 \leq v \leq p_i$, where v is the number of concept descriptions in S_i subsumed by the component D_j.*

Definition 9 (Aggregate Model): *Let $S_1, \ldots, S_n$ be an aggregate of concept collections; for $i = 1 \ldots n$, S_i is a concept collection descriptions s_{ki} with $k = 1 \ldots p_i$. An Aggregate Model for $S_1, \ldots, S_n$ and each of this element consists of the pair of items - <E, G> with the following characteristics: (i) E represents the subsumers matrix deriving from the collection $C_1, \ldots, C_p = \cup(C_{ki})$, with $i = 1 \ldots n$ and $k = 1 \ldots p_i$, whose elements e_{kj} are calculated by using prognostications to subsumption; and (ii) G is the collection subsumers matrix deriving from the input collection $S_1, \ldots, S_n$, whose elements a_{ij} are calculated by using information stored in E. In this computation, each row i in G is related to an aggregate collection S_i, defined as a collection of description C_{ki} whose subsumption relationship with components deriving from $S_1, \ldots,$ Sn is stored in E. To this modelling, values a_{ij}, for each component D_j, are determined as Concept Component Relative Cardinality $RC_{D_j}^{S_i}$.*

EXAMPLE OF A BUSINESS SCENARIO

A simple apparel manufacturing scenario is used to present a part of ABDDI algorithmic computation. Semantic IoT-based product flow in a retail outlet is considered. Each product is described using semantic-enhanced IoT as an ALN (D) concept expression in OWL language. As the retail apparel product arrive or depart the shop, they are scanned by the gate RFID readers; reading events, including semantic annotation extracted from tags, are fed to a semantic Data Service Management Service (DSMS), which computes Concept Components and subsumption test through a reasoning mechanism.

Figure 10. Algorithm for Semantic Similarity Computation

Definition 10 (Concept Similarity): An ontological concept (C) similarity (∂) is considered a *relation*, and it can be defined as $\partial C \times C \rightarrow [0, 1]$. In simple, it is a function from a pair of concepts to a real number between *zero* and *one*, expressing the degree of similarity between two concepts such that:

1. $\forall C_1 \in G, \ \partial(C_1, C_1) = 1$
2. $\forall C_1, C_2 \in G, \ 0 \leq \partial(C_1, C_2) \leq 1$
3. $\forall C_1, C_2, C_3 \in G, \ IF \ Sim_d(C_1, C_2) > Sim_d(C_1, C_3) \ THEN \ \partial(C_1, C_2) < \partial(C_1, C_3)$

The above properties provide the range of semantic similarity functions $\partial(C_i, C_j)$. For exactly similar concepts, the similarity is $\partial(C_1, C_1) = 1$; when two concepts have nothing in common, their similarity is $\partial(C_1, C_2) = 0$. In this way, the output of the similarity function should be in the closed interval [0, 1]. Here Sim_d represents the semantic distance, and (C_1, C_2, C_3) represent three concepts of graph G. In CSIA, the following semantic similarity (∂) function has been used for computation purposes:

$$\partial(C_1, C_2) = \frac{1}{deg \cdot Sim_d(C_1, C_2) + 1}$$

Where C_1 and C_2 represent two concepts, and 'deg' represents the impact of semantic distance on semantic similarity, it should be between $0 < deg \leq 1$. A weight allocation function is used, as shown below, to compute the semantic similarity between concepts:

$$w(C_m, C_n) = \left[\max(depth(C_m)) + \frac{OrderNumber(C_n)}{TNodes(G) + 1} + 1 \right]^{-1}$$

Where C_m *and* C_n represents two nodes directly connected, $\max(depth(C_m))$ represents the maximum depth of the node C_m (the depth of the root node is equal to 0 and 1 for the nodes directly connected to the root node and so on), TNodes(G) and OrderNumber(C_n) represent the total number of nodes in concept graph G and the order number of the node (C_n) between their siblings. The detailed description of these mathematical formalizations is beyond the scope of this chapter.

Let us consider a situation that allows a user to purchase a sweater from an online business. This example considers how a request is matched with the service advertised for wool garments selling service. An algorithm (i.e., ALGORITHM 1) tries to perform semantic matching for a relevant sweater.

The algorithm takes two ontological concepts, the root node (root), and the concepts graph (G), as input and computes a semantic similarity between the concepts as output.

The part of the concept hierarchy used in this example is shown in Figure 5. Each node of this hierarchy represents a concept. The experimental comparison considers semantic similarity among Wool, Shirt, Sweater, Trousers, Cardigan, Pullover, and Jumper. The proposed algorithm (i.e., Algorithm-I) provides semantic similarity between concepts with a higher score than the path similarity algorithm.

Figure 11. The Hierarchical Concept Relationships

```
Algorithm I
input: two concepts (C1, C2), the root node (root), concepts graph (G)
output: semantic similarity value between two concepts
begin
if C1 and C2 are same concept then Simd = 0
else
    if C1 and C2 are directly connected then Simd = w (C1 , C2)
    else
        if idirect path connection exist then
            Spath01 = ShortestPath (G, C1, RootN)
            Spath02 = ShortestPath (G, C2, RootN)
            Simd = w(Spath01) + w(Spath02) – 2*w(CSPath]
        end if
            ∂(C1, C2) = 1 / (deg·Simd+1)
    end if
end if
return ∂
end
```

Table 3. The Results of Various Similarity Measures

	C_1	C_2	C_3	C_4	C_5
C_1	1.00	0.25	0.50	0.20	0.20
C_2	0.25	1.00	0.50	0.33	0.16
C_3	0.50	0.50	1.00	0.25	0.16
C_4	0.20	0.33	0.25	1.00	0.20
C_5	0.20	0.16	0.16	0.20	1.00
	C_1	C_2	C_3	C_4	C_5
C_1	1.00	0.48	0.65	0.51	0.38
C_2	0.48	1.00	0.65	0.51	0.38
C_3	0.65	0.65	1.00	0.71	0.48
C_4	0.51	0.51	0.71	1.00	0.59
C_5	0.38	0.38	0.48	0.59	1.00

(a) Path similarity (b) The proposed method

In Table 3, (a) represents the outcome of path similarity (Jandl et al., 2019), while (b) highlights the results of the algorithm proposed for use in ABDDI. Within ABDDI, the similarity measure offers a high degree of flexibility and customization, enabling the incorporation of user preferences. This concept encompasses two primary facets. Firstly, users have the ability to specify the relative importance of similarity assessment parameters through an advanced search interface. Secondly, in addition to presenting a singular ranking for each potential service, the system can also furnish more comprehensive results, such as varying values for recall and the extent of match, aimed at assisting users in pinpointing the timeliest service.

FUTURE RESEARCH DIRECTIONS

Ontology, as a foundational declarative knowledge representation model for SOC-based services, is a field ripe for future research. The lack of a universally agreed-upon ontology that encompasses all concepts used by the services currently results in partner organizations having varied interpretations of semantics in their services. However, the potential impact of future research on ontology alignment is significant. It could lead to partner organizations harmonizing their ontologies and establishing mutual understanding, enabling autonomous information integration from different sources and facilitating service-based application interoperability. This potential impact should inspire optimism and hope for the future of SOC-based services.

While many academic and industry proposals have aimed to tackle interoperability issues in IoT-based information systems, significant challenges persist. The absence of standards and innovative technologies poses major obstacles in developing IoT-based service applications. This underscores the need for research advancements to create semantically interoperable platforms spanning different IoT domains. It's a call to action for future work in this area, particularly in developing standards and technologies. Potential contributions are crucial in addressing these challenges and in future research ontology alignment related exercise will play an important role.

In summary, a more thorough evaluation of the current research solutions that enable industry digitalization is needed. This evaluation, along with more case studies and field studies, requires a collaborative effort from all stakeholders. Further research should include practical initiatives to address critical industry-specific challenges, such as timeliness and safety. It is important to note that these initiatives will be using various software-based tools, which are crucial in the context of digitalization.

CONCLUSION

The IoT-based industrial applications face various challenges, such as low-memory devices and network limitations, which underscore the urgent need for reliable software architectures. These challenges, including [specific challenges], highlight the pressing need for dependable software architectures. The recent focus on the convergence of service-oriented computing and IoT offers a promising solution to these challenges. This convergence, leveraging the robust infrastructure of the service orientation, can alleviate these issues. As a result, the demand for dependable software architectures has never been more pressing. These architectures are crucial to meet the quality requirements of new emerging technologies and the complex quality challenges they bring. This chapter presents a few industry-specific application reviews on service orientation and IoT technology-based software architectures.

The chapter has meticulously gathered, evaluated, and synthesized the reviewed architecture knowledge, including design technologies, application area, and evaluation related to advantages. This knowledge is invaluable as the current trends are promising, and there is increasing interest in designing scalable service-oriented IoT technologies for use in different application areas. This growing interest opens up possibilities for the future of service-providing technologies and highlights several opportunities for further academic study. In addition, IoT applications rely on real-time context data and allow information to be sent to drive users' behaviours in intelligent supply chain environments. These IoT-based solutions are mostly tailored for vertical applications and systems, utilizing knowledge only from business areas. However, to realize IoT's full potential, these specialized silo applications must be replaced with horizontal collaborative applications, including knowledge acquisition and sharing capabilities.

Overview of the impact of globalization and digitalization on supply chain operations management. It includes the emerging trends of increased Internet of Things (IoT) utilization for decision-support systems in supply chain operations. Gathering and analyzing business operational data to provide services for stakeholders is essential. Designing Decision-Support Systems Using IoT and Data Processing Systems. In addition, a knowledge-based approach to designing and implementing operational service supports is presented in this chapter with the help of a business case.

REFERENCES

Aazam, M., & Huh, E. N. (2014). "Fog computing and smart gateway based communication for cloud of things," in Proceedings of the 2nd IEEE International Conference on Future Internet of Things and Cloud (FiCloud' 14), 464–470, Barcelona, Spain, August 2014. DOI: 10.1109/FiCloud.2014.83

Atzori, L., Iera, A., & Morabito, G. (2011). IoT: Giving a social structure to the internet of things. *IEEE Communications Letters*, 15(11), 1193–1195. DOI: 10.1109/LCOMM.2011.090911.111340

Baader, F., Calvanese, D., McGuinness, D., Nardi, D., & Patel-Schneider, P. (Eds.). (2002). *The Description Logic Handbook*. Cambridge University Press.

Bardhan, P. (2003). *International Trade Growth and Development: Essays*. Wiley-Blackwell. DOI: 10.1002/9780470752777

Barnaghi, P., Presser, M., & Moessner, K. (2010). "Publishing Linked Sensor Data", in *Proceedings of the 3rd International Workshop on Semantic Sensor Networks*.

Berners-Lee, T. (2000). *Weaving the Web: The Original Design and Ultimate Design of the World Wide Web by its inventor*. Harper Business.

Bonomi, F., Milito, R., Natarajan, P., & Zhu, J. (2014). *"Fog computing: a platform for internet of things and analytics," in Big Data and Internet ofThings: A Road Map for Smart Environments*. Springer.

Bonomi, F., Milito, R., Zhu, J., & Addepalli, S. (2012). "Fog computing and its role in the internet of things," in *Proceedings of the 1st ACM MCC Workshop on Mobile Cloud Computing*, 13–16, 2012. DOI: 10.1145/2342509.2342513

Bordel Sánchez, B., Alcarria, R., Sánchez de Rivera, D., & Robles, T. (2018). Process execution in CyberPhysical Systems using cloud and Cyber-Physical Internet services. *The Journal of Supercomputing*, 74(8), 4127–4169. DOI: 10.1007/s11227-018-2416-4

Broy, M., Cengarle, M. V., & Geisberger, E. (2012). Cyber-Physical Systems: Imminent Challenges. In Large-Scale Complex IT Syst. Dev., Operat. and Manag. - 17th Monterey Workshop, volume 7539 of LNCS, 1–28.

Cardoso, J., Sheth, A., Miller, J., Arnold, J., & Kochut, K. (2004). Quality of service for workflows and web service processes. *Journal of Web Semantics*, 1(3), 281–308. DOI: 10.1016/j.websem.2004.03.001

Cheng, H., Xue, L., Wang, P., Zeng, P., & Yu, H. (2017). Ontology-based web service integration for flexible manufacturing systems. In 15th Int. Conf. on Ind. Inf., pages 351–356. IEEE. DOI: 10.1109/INDIN.2017.8104797

Ciortea, A., Mayer, S., & Michahelles, F. (2018). Repurposing Manufacturing Lines on the Fly with Multi-agent Systems for the Web of Things. In Proc. of the 17th Int. Conf. on Autonomous Agents and Multi-Agent Systems, pages 813–822. Int. Found. for Autonomous Agents and Multiagent Systems / ACM.

Colitti, W., Steenhaut, K., Caro, N. De., (2011). "Integrating Wireless Sensor Networks with the Web", Extending the Internet to Low power and Lossy Networks (IP+SN).

Colucci, S., Di Noia, T., Pinto, A., Ruta, M., Ragone, A., & Tinelli, E. (2007). A Nonmonotonic Approach to Semantic Matchmaking and Request Refinement in E-Marketplaces. *International Journal of Electronic Commerce*, 12(2), 127–154. DOI: 10.2753/JEC1086-4415120205

Cory, A., Henson, J., Pschorr, K., Sheth, A. P., & Thirunarayan, K. (2009). "Sem-SOS: Semantic sensor Observation Service", in *Proceedings of the International Symposium on Collaborative Technologies and Systems*.

Courbis, C., & Finkelstein, A. (2005). Weaving Aspects into Web Service Orchestrations, in *Proceeding of International Conference of Web Services (ICWS '05)*, July 2005. DOI: 10.1109/ICWS.2005.129

De Virgilio, R., Di Sciascio, E., Ruta, M., Scioscia, F., & Torlone, R. (2011). Semantic-based rfid data management. In *Unique Radio Innovation for the 21st Century* (pp. 111–141). Springer. DOI: 10.1007/978-3-642-03462-6_6

Jakl, A., Schoffer, L., Husinsky, M., & Wagner, M. (2018), Augmented Reality for Industry 4.0: Architecture and User Experience, In Proceeding of the 11th Forum Media Technology, CER-WS, 38-42.

Jandl, C., Nurgazina, J., Schoffer, L., Reichl, C., Wagner, M., & Moser, T. (2019). SensiTrack – A Privacy by Design Concept for Industrial IoT Applications, In *Proceeding of the 24th IEEE International Conference on Emerging Technologies and Factory Automation*, 10-13 September, Zaragoza, Spain, 1782-1789. DOI: 10.1109/ETFA.2019.8869186

Jeschke, S., Brecher, C., Meisen, T., Ozdemir, D., & Eschert, T. (2017), Industrial Internet of Things and Cyber Manufacturing Systems, In Industrial Internet of Things, Springer, 3-19.

Keskinock, P., & Tayur, S. (2001). Quantitative analysis of Internet-enabled supply chain. *Interfaces*, 31(2), 70–89. DOI: 10.1287/inte.31.2.70.10626

Lasi, H., Fettke, P., Kemper, H.-G., Feld, T., & Hoffmann, M. (2014). Industry 4.0. BISE, 6(4):239–242. Lastra, J. L. M. and Delamer, I. M. (2006). Semantic Web Services in Factory Automation: Fundamental Insights and Research Roadmap. *IEEE Transactions on Industrial Informatics*, 2(1), 1–11.

Lee, H. L., & Billington, C. (1992). Managing supply chain inventories: Pitfalls and opportunities. *Sloan Management Review*, 33(3), 65–77.

Lee, J., Kao, H.-A., & Yang, S. (2014). Service Innovation and Smart Analytics for Industry 4.0 and Big Data Environment. *Procedia CIRP*, 16, 3–8. DOI: 10.1016/j.procir.2014.02.001

Lefort, L., Henson, C., Taylor, K., Barnaghi, P., Compton, M., Corcho, O., Garcia-Castro, R., Graybeal, J., Herzog, A., Janowicz, K., ... (2005). "Semantic Sensor Network XG Final Report", 2011, W3C Incubator Group Report, https://www.w3.org/2005/Incubator/ssn/XGR-ssn/

Li, L., & Horrocks, I. (2004). A software framework for matchmaking based on semantic web technology. *International Journal of Electronic Commerce*, 8(4), 39–60. DOI: 10.1080/10864415.2004.11044307

Lobov, A., Lopez, F. U., Herrera, V. V., Puttonen, J., & Lastra, J. L. M. (2008). Semantic Web Services framework for manufacturing industries. In Int. Conf. on Rob. and Biomim., pages 2104–2108. IEEE.

Maass, W., Filler, A. (2006). Towards an infrastructure for semantically annotated physical products. INFORMATIK 2006–Informatik für Menschen–Band 2, Beiträge der 36. Jahrestagung der Gesellschaft für Informatik eV (GI).

Marrella, A. (2018). Automated Planning for Business Process Management.

Minor, M., Montani, S., & Recio-García, J. A. (2014). Process-oriented Case-based Reasoning. *Information Systems*, 40, 103–105. DOI: 10.1016/j.is.2013.06.004

Monostori, L. (2014). Cyber-physical Production Systems: Roots, Expectations and R&D Challenges. *Procedia CIRP*, 17, 9–13. DOI: 10.1016/j.procir.2014.03.115

Montenegro, G., Kushalnagar, N., Hui, J., & Culler, D. (2007). "Transmission of IPv6 packets over IEEE 802.15.4 networks," Internet proposed standard RFC, vol. 4944.

Müller, G. (2018). Workflow Modeling Assistance by Casebased Reasoning. Springer Fachmedien, Wiesbaden. Ocker, F., Kovalenko, I., Barton, K., Tilbury, D., and VogelHeuser, B. (2019). A Framework for Automatic Initialization of Multi-Agent Production Systems Using Semantic Web Technologies. *IEEE Robotics and Automation Letters*, 4(4), 4330–4337.

Pal, K. (2017a). Supply Chain Coordination Based on Web Services. In Chan, H. K., Subramanian, N., & Abdulrahman, M. D. (Eds.), *Supply Chain Management in the Big Data Era* (pp. 137–171). IGI Global Publication. DOI: 10.4018/978-1-5225-0956-1.ch009

Pal, K. (2017b). "A Semantic Web Service Architecture for Supply Chain Management", In 8th International Conference on Ambient Systems, Networks and Technologies (ANT 2017), 999-1004, Procedia Computer Science 109C. DOI: 10.1016/j.procs.2017.05.442

Pal, K. (2018a). "Ontology-Based Web Service Architecture for Retail Supply Chain Management", In 9th International Conference on Ambient Systems, Networks and Technologies (ANT 2018), 985-990, Procedia Computer Science 130. DOI: 10.1016/j.procs.2018.04.101

Pal, K. (2018b). "*A Big Data Framework for Decision Making in Supply Chain",* In M. V Kumar, G. D. Putnik, J. Javakrishna, V. M. Pillai, L. Varela (Edited); IGI Publication, September 2018, USA, Chapter 1, IGI Global Publication, Hershey PA, USA.

Pal, K. (2020). "Information Sharing for Manufacturing Supply Chain Management Based on Blockchain Technology", in Dr Idongesit Williams (Eds.), Cross-Industry Use of Blockchain Technology and Opportunities for the Future, Chapter 1, May, IGI Global Publication, Hershey PA, USA. DOI: 10.4018/978-1-7998-3632-2.ch001

Pal, K., & Karakostas, B. (2014). A Multi Agent-Based Service Framework for Supply Chain Management, In the proceeding of International Conference on Ambient Systems, Networks and Technology. *Procedia Computer Science*, 32, 53–60. DOI: 10.1016/j.procs.2014.05.397

Pal, K., & Ul-Haque, A. (2000). "*Internet of Things and Blockchain Technology in Apparel Manufacturing Supply Chain Data Management*", In the proceeding of 11th International Conference on Ambient Systems, Networks and Technologies (ANT-2020), Procedia Computer Science, pp. 450- 457, April 6-9, Warsaw, Poland.

Pal, K., & Ul-Haque, A. (2023). "*Internet of Things Impact on Supply Chain Management*", In the proceeding of 14th International Conference on Ambient Systems, Networks and Technologies (ANT-2023), Procedia Computer Science, 478-485. DOI: 10.1016/j.procs.2023.03.061

Pal, K., Ul-Haque, A., & Shakshuki, E. (2024). "*Supply Chain Transport Management, Use of Electric Vehicles, Review of Security and Privacy for Cyber-Physical Transportation Ecosystem and Related solutions*", In the proceeding of 15th International Conference on Ambient Systems, Networks and Technologies (ANT-2020), Procedia Computer Science, 135-142, April 23-25, Hasselt, Belgium. DOI: 10.1016/j.procs.2024.06.008

Puttonen, J., Lobov, A., & Lastra, J. L. M. (2013). Semantics-Based Composition of Factory Automation Processes Encapsulated by Web Services. *IEEE Transactions on Industrial Informatics*, 9(4), 2349–2359. DOI: 10.1109/TII.2012.2220554

Puttonen, J., Lobov, A., Soto, M. A. C., & Lastra, J. L. M. (2010). A Semantic Web Services-based approach for production systems control. *Advanced Engineering Informatics*, 24(3), 285–299. DOI: 10.1016/j.aei.2010.05.012

Russomanno, D. J., Kothari, C. R., & Thomas, O. A. (2005). "Building a Sensor Ontology: A Practical Approach Leveraging ISO and OGC Models", in the 2005 International Conference on Artificial Intelligence, 637-643.

Ruta, M., Colucci, S., Scioscia, F., Di Sciascio, E., & Donini, F. M. (2011). Finding commonalities in RFID semantic streams. *Procedia Computer Science*, 5, 857–864. DOI: 10.1016/j.procs.2011.07.118

Seiger, R., Huber, S., & Schlegel, T. (2018). Toward an execution system for self-healing workflows in cyber-physical systems. *Software & Systems Modeling*, 17(2), 551–572. DOI: 10.1007/s10270-016-0551-z

Stiglitz, J. (2017). Globalization and its Discontents Revisited: Anti-Globalization in the Era of Trump,Penguin.

Swaminathan, J. M. (2000). *Supply chain management.* International Encyclopedia of the Social and Behavioural Sciences, Elsevier Sciences.

Zhu, W., Zhou, G., Yen, I. L., & Bastani, F. (2015). A PT-SOA Model for CPS/IoT Services, In *Proceedings of the 2015 IEEE International Conference on Web Services*, New York, NY, USA, 27 June – 2 July 2015. DOI: 10.1109/ICWS.2015.91

Chapter 5
Big Data Analytics for Supply Chain Optimization:
Harnessing Data for Strategic Supply Chain Decisions

Divyeshkumar Vaghani
https://orcid.org/0009-0005-4983-5257
Gannon University, USA

ABSTRACT

Despite the extensive discussion on the benefits of BDA in supply chains, there remains a lack of systematic understanding of how BDA can be effectively linked to Supply Chain Optimization (SCO). This document explores the cumulative published literature from 2014 and 2024, so as to ascertain the impact of big data analytics on supply chain optimization. 64 articles were selected from diverse academic journals, and from these articles, information was gathered, analyzed, and organized. The results shows that Big data is often used for making predictions in SCO; big data analytics has a lot of difficulties dealing with large amounts of data related to managing the supply chain, which include too much data, problems with data quality, keeping data safe and private, difficulty in analyzing data, ability to grow as needed, and complicated supply chains. The study recommends that big data projects should begin with specific goals instead of just hoping people will use them. Starting with small test projects can help show the benefits of big data analytics.

DOI: 10.4018/979-8-3693-4427-9.ch005

1. INTRODUCTION

In this current age, there has been a rapid surge in data generation (Choi et al., 2017), leading to a growing interest among management professionals in big data analytics (BDA). While the idea of big data has existed for years, organizations have only recently begun to grasp how it can provide valuable insights into their operations, allowing for improved business decisions. Traditional supply chain management has long been crucial for businesses, focusing on the movement of goods and services from origin to consumption. However, the advent of big data has transformed supply chain optimization significantly. Big data analytics has become vital in this area, offering opportunities to enhance decision-making, increase operational efficiency, and gain a competitive edge (Wang & Alexander, 2015). Companies can leverage big data to manage inventories and streamline production processes, thereby reducing internal costs related to production, sales, and inventory (Xu et al., 2019). The rising volume of data in supply chains necessitates the adoption of analytics to maintain a competitive advantage (Yang, 2022).

Leading businesses that have adopted big data as a new strategy are experiencing transformative improvements in operations. Notable examples include Amazon, which uses big data for inventory management and predictive analytics to anticipate customer purchases and pre-ship products (Ritson, 2014). Wal-Mart processes over a million transactions per hour and employs advanced systems like Radio Frequency Identification (RFID) to manage vast amounts of data (Feng et al., 2014). UPS has also utilized telematics to optimize its global logistics network (Davenport and Patil, 2012). Chen and Zhang (2014) argue that big data holds substantial potential to revolutionize various fields, including business, scientific research, and public administration. Gartner, Inc. defines big data as high-volume, high-velocity, and high-variety information assets requiring innovative processing methods for better insights and decision-making. Typically, big data is characterized by the four Vs: Volume, Velocity, Variety, and Veracity. It involves vast amounts of data in diverse formats—structured, semi-structured, and unstructured—originating from various sources such as transactional systems, GPS devices, and social media. The reliability of this data is also a crucial consideration.

Many businesses are now focusing on big data analytics (BDA) development (Kiron et al., 2014). Digitalization, along with the increasing engagement of users on social media is the driving force behind BDA (Hellerston et al., 2008; Lohr, 2012). The volume of big data exceeds the capacity of traditional software tools and storage systems for efficient data capture, storage, and processing (Kubick, 2012). This surge in data is a key resource for companies amidst the growth of information technology and Industry 4.0 (Tukas et al., 2019). The rapid increase in big data affects numerous areas, contributing to global advancements in science and technology (Manyika et al., 2016). Big data analytics involves using advanced techniques to analyze large datasets characterized by high volume, variety, velocity, value, and veracity to derive meaningful insights for decision-making (Fosso Wamba et al., 2015; Tiwari et al., 2018). The rise of BDA has significant implications for how companies collect, analyze, and process data, leading to improved business operations and forecasting (Arunachalam et al., 2018; Wang et al., 2016; Xu et al., 2021).

Big data analytics enable firms to process extensive, fast-moving, and diverse data to gain valuable insights, thus providing a competitive edge (Fosso Wamba et al., 2017). Historically, supply chain managers relied on traditional data warehouses for insights, but advances in data processing now allow for quicker and more effective decision-making (Galbraith, 2014; Hazen et al., 2014). Improved information processing capabilities can reduce uncertainties, especially in complex operational tasks like disaster relief (Papadopoulos et al., 2017). Effective data management and integration are crucial for linking supply chain management with producers, suppliers, and partners. Addressing challenges in supply chain management requires ensuring visibility and fostering trust and collaboration. Supply chain professionals access data from traditional sources such as POS and RFID, as well as from newer sources like digital click streams, surveillance footage, and social media (Sanders & Ganeshan, 2015).

Supply chain optimization (SCO) involves developing plans to manage supply chains by translating requirements into actionable programs while optimizing outcomes under constraints (APICS, 2017; Supply Chain Council, 2012). The exponential growth of data significantly impacts SCO activities, such as demand forecasting and production planning, driven by advancements in digital technologies and analytics (Waller and Fawcett, 2013). Modern supply chains rely heavily on advanced technologies like sensors and smart devices, which provide real-time demand and supply visibility (Wang et al., 2016; Gunasekaran et al., 2017). Schoenherr and Speier-Pero (2015) argue that extensive data is needed for decision-making to reduce costs and improve product availability.

Organizations that implement big data analytics effectively see better returns on investment (Accenture, 2019). A structured big data strategy can enhance ROI in areas like marketing, purchasing, shipping, and storage (Benabdellah et al., 2016). The complexity of supply chains, characterized by collaboration and integration, often makes competition between supply chains more intense than between individual firms (Antai & Olson, 2010). The use of big data in marketing is increasing, but supply chain professionals have yet to fully exploit its potential to enhance operational efficiency (Srinivasan & Swink, 2017). Many firms still struggle with applying analytical techniques to improve supply chain performance.

As companies expand their IT infrastructure to incorporate big data solutions, they face challenges due to globalization, increasing data volumes, and the demand for more customized products and services. This requires integrating new suppliers and adapting supply chain operations for global application, considering regional specifics and competitor offerings. The focus is shifting towards managing risks and bottlenecks, as well as improving transparency across the supply chain (Smart Service Wet Working Group, 2014). Big data solutions must be tailored to each company's unique needs and environment. This often begins with developing a comprehensive data strategy to clarify the value drivers and goals of new IT solutions. Examples of big data strategy targets and potential uses are illustrated through specific use cases (Jeseke et al., 2015).

The Thomson Reuters Web of science tool was utilized to find out how many "big data" articles were published in the past ten years; 64 articles that were related to the study were found, and from these articles, information was gathered, analyzed, and organized.

The manuscript is structured as follows. Section 2 explores the background and literature of big data and supply chain optimization. This is followed by Section 3 where the author presents a detailed overview of the research methods used for the review process. Next, was discussion of findings in Section 4, where the main objectives of the study were addressed. In section 5, the study was concluded, and a way forward was proposed.

1.1 Statement of the Problem

In recent years, the rising interest in Big Data has prompted organizations to integrate Big Data Analytics (BDA) into their supply chains (SC) (Dubey et al., 2018). SC leaders aim to gather valuable insights that enhance their ability to forecast, identify patterns, and boost competitive advantage (Lamba & Singh, 2017). Analytics are reshaping how supply chain management (SCM) processes data, both through internal systems integration and external channels such as mobile devices, social media, and the Internet of Things (IoT) (Chavez et al., 2017).

Despite the extensive discussion on the benefits of BDA in operations and supply chains, there remains a lack of a systematic understanding of how BDA can be effectively linked to Supply Chain Optimization (SCO). This understanding is crucial for evaluating the financial investment and skill development required for BDA adoption and implementation (Brinch et al., 2018; Hofmann & Rutschmann, 2018; Lai et al., 2018). Existing literature on the relationship between BDA and SCO either provides a broad view of BDA's impact on various SCO issues (e.g., Tiwari et al., 2018; Wang et al., 2016) or focuses on developing conceptual and analytical models for specific SCO tasks (e.g., Zhong et al., 2015a). However, these perspectives fall short in guiding decisions on prioritizing BDA investments for particular SCO needs.

The complexity of managing supply chains is critical for industries competing in the global market, where it involves handling material and information flow between different entities, particularly in the context of digital information flow (Awwad et al., 2018). The explosion of data, rising customer expectations, and the need to maintain a competitive edge have driven organizations to focus on analytics for strategic decision-making. Consequently, competition among companies and their supply chains has intensified. In today's competitive landscape, supply chain professionals are tasked with managing vast amounts of data to create integrated, efficient, and adaptable supply chain operations (Dutta, 2021).

SCM organizations are overwhelmed by data, to the extent that McAfee and Brynjolfsson (2012) observed that "businesses collect more data than they know how to handle." This is particularly true for firms recognized for their data management in areas like warehousing, marketing, or transportation. However, the reality is that these successes are not just isolated examples; they represent a significant shift where failure to adapt could lead to obsolescence. A Sloan Management Review survey reported by Hopkins et al. (2010) found that top-performing companies in analytics outperform their industry peers by up to three times. Although many organizations have high expectations for Big Data Analytics (BDA) in their supply chains, actual utilization remains limited, and many struggle to unlock its full business value (Pearson et al., 2014).

The purpose of this study is to ascertain the impact of big data analytics on supply chain optimization. The additional objectives of the study are to:

i. Assess the applications of big data analytics to supply chain optimization;
ii. Find out the importance of big data analytics in supply chain optimization;
iii. Examine the challenges of leveraging big data analytics in supply chain optimization; and
iv. Ascertain the role emerging technologies play in enhancing the effectiveness of BDA in supply chain optimization.

2. BACKGROUND

2.1 Concept of Big Data

When someone says, "I've received a large dataset!" they usually mean that the data contains a vast number of entries or records, making it complex and rich in information. Likewise, when someone says I've just bought a house!" they usually mean that the house is large in terms of area or number of rooms. Similarly, when referring to "big data," it's essential to understand how this term differs from the usual concept of data. Big data represents an evolving field within Information Technology (Vera-Baquero et al., 2015). Although the term itself is relatively new, the practice of collecting and storing large volumes of data for analysis has long existed. Organizations gather data from various sources such as business transactions, social media, and sensor data or machine-to-machine interactions (SAS Institute, 2024). This data arrives at an unprecedented rate and must be processed promptly. Big Data is characterized by datasets too large for standard computers to handle efficiently (Chen et al., 2014).

The term has become associated with advancements in data storage, management, processing, interpretation, analysis, and visualization (Kaisler et al., 2013). Big data encompasses datasets that exceed the capabilities of traditional data analysis tools (Costello & Prohaska, 2013). It refers to data with a high volume, velocity, and variety, necessitating more advanced methods than those used in conventional database systems for decision-making (Laney, 2001a). Big data enables systems to operate using substantial volumes of real-world data (Van der Aalst, 2012). Big data research emerged prominently in the 21st century, with significant applications in fields beyond 2000. Figure 1 below shows the big data cognitive map.

Figure 1. Big Data Cognitive Map (Rahimi, et al., 2021)

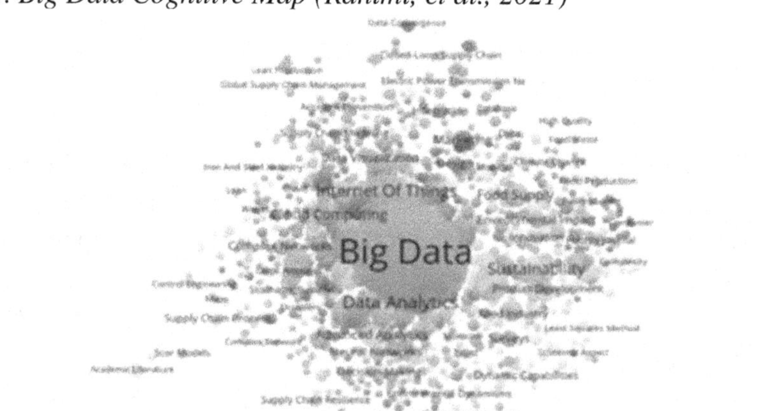

Gartner (2012) defines Big Data as: "High-volume, high-velocity, and/or high-variety information assets that require cost-effective and innovative processing methods to enhance insight, decision-making, and process automation." Laney (2001) introduced the '3Vs' concept to define Big Data:

- **Volume**: This refers to the massive amounts of data stored within IT systems. The challenge here is to manage storage space and ensure data accessibility efficiently. Volume signifies the extensive amount of data collected from various sources over time. For example, in freight data, this includes ERP/WMS order data, tracking information, and freight invoices, generated by sensors, barcodes, and ERP systems. The amount of data is now measured in Zettabytes or Yottabytes, reflecting a scale far beyond traditional database management techniques (Firican, 2017).
- **Velocity**: This describes the speed at which data is generated and needs to be processed. Data is often produced in real-time and must be handled promptly for further use. Velocity concerns the rate of data generation, transfer reliability, storage efficiency, and the speed of extracting useful insights. Technologies like RFID tags, sensors, and smart metering drive the need to manage data streams in near-real-time. With increasing internet accessibility and machine integration, data collection speeds are continuously rising.
- **Variety**: Variety pertains to the different forms of data within the big data environment. It includes both structured data (e.g., numbers in databases) and unstructured data (e.g., emails, videos). Variety involves handling data from diverse sources like IoT devices, mobile platforms, and online social networks. For instance, supply chain data varies widely due to heterogeneous sources and formats, including sensors in manufacturing, highways, retail, and warehouses. The variety of data types is crucial in defining Big Data, which encompasses both structured and unstructured data (Technology, 2018).

In addition to the traditional '3Vs,' Big Data is often described with two more 'Vs' in the '5Vs' concept:

- **Veracity**: This refers to the accuracy and reliability of data. Veracity involves ensuring data is correct and trustworthy, despite potential uncertainty from various sources. It focuses on the quality and accuracy of data, requiring processes to filter and validate information (Benabdellah et al., 2016; Kumar, 2016). Veracity emphasizes that quality is more critical than quantity, highlighting the need for proper metrics around data types and sources.
- **Value**: Value pertains to the insights that data can provide to support decision-making. It is the most crucial yet elusive aspect of the '5Vs.' The value of a dataset is determined by the insights gained through analysis and the return on investment from acquiring and analyzing the data (XSNET, 2017). Figure 2 below shows the evolution of big data framework from 1997 to 2016, while figure 3 shows the 4v's of big data.

Figure 2. Big Data Framework Evolution During the Time (Wang et al., 2016)

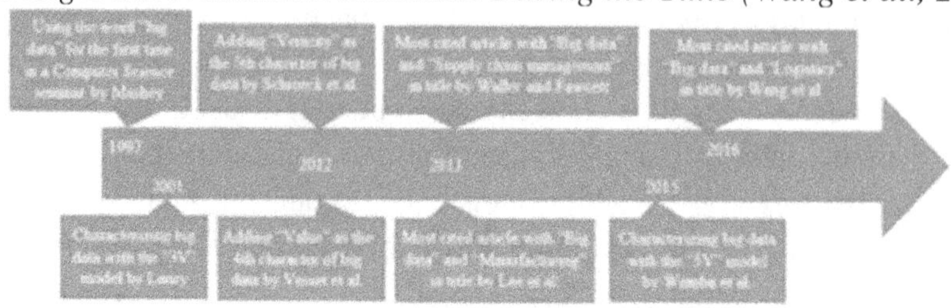

Figure 3. The Four V's of Big Data (Bughin, 2016)

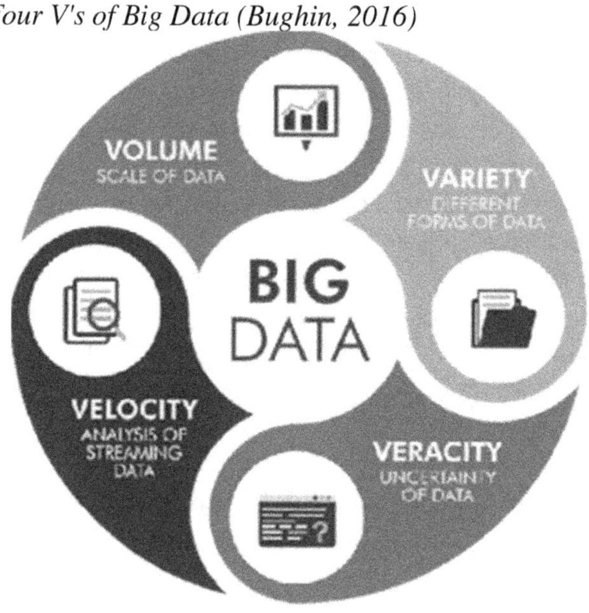

2.2 Concept of Big Data Analytics

Data analytics involves examining raw data to draw conclusions about the information it contains. This process uses algorithmic techniques to uncover previously unknown or hidden patterns and insights from large datasets. While traditionally focused on inference, analytics can also offer prescriptive insights, which significantly impact research and technology by helping businesses achieve a competitive edge. Big data analytics refers to the application of advanced analytical methods to very large and diverse datasets, including structured, semi-structured, and unstructured data from various sources, ranging from terabytes to zettabytes. This approach helps reveal hidden patterns, correlations, market trends, and customer preferences. Advanced analytics enables organizations to identify changes and determine how to respond effectively. It is particularly useful for discovering new customer segments, finding optimal suppliers, associating products, and understanding sales trends. Organizations are increasingly implementing various analytics tools and techniques, such as data mining, statistical analysis, data visualization, artificial intelligence, and machine learning, which are well-suited for large, multi-petabyte datasets.

The value of big data is realized when businesses use it to make data-driven decisions. To achieve this, organizations must employ efficient methods to convert large volumes of rapidly changing and varied data into actionable insights. Analyzing big data allows researchers and businesses to leverage their data to uncover new opportunities, leading to smarter business decisions, more efficient operations, higher profits, and a competitive advantage. Big data analytics can be seen as a component within the broader process of extracting knowledge from big data.

According to Tonidandel et al. (2018), big data analytics (BDA) is emerging as a crucial tool for managing and reporting substantial datasets that traditional tools cannot handle, transforming them into new information (Dubey et al., 2018). BDA involves using advanced methods like predictive analytics, statistics, data mining, and artificial intelligence for large, unstructured datasets (Barbosa et al., 2018). Major companies, such as Amazon, utilize predictive analytics through BDA to forecast shipments from over 200 global distribution centers (Storey & Song, 2017), while Walmart processes order analytics from millions of transactions, including RFID data, totaling approximately 3 petabytes (Heller, 2017). Scholars recognize BDA as a significant driver of value creation and business process improvement (Wang et al., 2016). Since the 2010s, there has been a notable increase in specialized and diverse publications on BDA, including literature reviews, original research, case studies, and surveys.

Despite widespread belief in the benefits of BDA for supply chains, its actual use remains limited, and many organizations struggle to extract meaningful insights. Often, companies and researchers are uncertain about which analytic methods and techniques to apply for specific business activities and purposes (Tonidandel et al., 2018; Hazen et al., 2014). Big Data projects require significant investment in preliminary research to identify the most suitable BDA methods for specific supply chain processes and available data. Additionally, BDA often involves advanced methods beyond traditional statistics, as they address complex and unstructured data (Dubey et al., 2018). Consequently, data scientists and managers invest considerable time and effort in analyzing and selecting appropriate analytic techniques through reviews and specifications.

2.3 Evolution of Data Analytics Tools

As organizations began to adopt data analytics in the late 1990s and early 2000s, they encountered several challenges. At that time, data was less accessible and primarily controlled by IT departments. Analysts spent considerable time gathering and preparing data rather than analyzing it. Their goal was to develop accurate and reliable solutions to business problems while keeping the results simple enough for business users to understand. During this period, tools such as SAS for backend data inference and modeling, Oracle and Teradata for comprehensive solution development, IBM CPLEX for large-scale optimization problems, and Cognos and MicroStrategy for visualization through reports were commonly used.

By the late 2000s, companies like Google and Facebook, along with other internet-based firms, began to explore and analyze new types of data, which later became known as big data. In addition to data generated from internal operations, new sources included public data, social media, and mobile devices. Analysts recognized that this new data was distinct in nature, encompassing unstructured formats such as text, images, audio, and video, and came in much larger volumes than traditional internal data. This shift led to the creation of new tools and technologies, including Hadoop, which offered distributed data storage and processing with low cost, flexibility, and scalability; Python and R, open-source programming languages with extensive libraries for statistical analysis; and Tableau, Looker, and Microsoft Power BI, popular for developing, customizing, and building interactive and visually appealing web dashboards.

2.4 Concept of Supply Chain Optimization

A supply chain consists of four interconnected components: transportation, marketing, warehouse management, and procurement (Awwah et al., 2018). Supply chain optimization (SCO) is concerned with the movement of goods, services, and information from their origins to customers through a network of linked entities and activities (Seyedan & Mafakhen, 2020). SCO is tasked with establishing and maintaining connections between various entities involved in acquiring raw materials and delivering the final product to the end user (Halo, 2018). This network includes various businesses, from producers and central organizations to wholesalers, retailers, customers, and end users. Besides physical flows of goods, the supply chain also involves the flow of information and financial transactions (Darvazeh et al., 2020).

The supply chain for a product encompasses the network of companies and facilities involved in converting raw materials into a finished product and distributing it to customers (Sovza, 2014). Strategic planning incorporates the needs and capabilities of material suppliers, service providers, and customers, as companies view their operations through the lens of supply chain interactions and strategies (Stank et al., 2001). The challenge of synchronizing operations across all aspects of a business is known as Supply Chain Optimization (SCO). Copacino (1997) emphasizes the importance of integration in his SCO definition: "The new vision of Supply Chain Management connects all the players and activities involved in turning raw materials into products and delivering those products to consumers at the right time and place in the most efficient manner".

The Supply Chain Operations Reference (SCOR) model outlines the business activities associated with meeting customer demand. It includes several sections and revolves around five key management processes: Plan, Source, Make, Deliver, and Return. The Plan process aligns aggregate demand with supply to develop strategies that meet sourcing, production, and delivery needs. The Source process involves procuring goods and services to satisfy planned or actual demands. The Make process transforms products into their finished state to meet these demands. The Deliver process is responsible for providing finished goods and services to customers. Lastly, the Return process manages the return of materials from customers to address product defects, ordering issues, or maintenance needs. The latest version of the SCOR model introduces an additional management process: Enable. This process supports the planning and execution of supply chain activities and is fundamental to all other processes.

By defining supply chains through these processes, the SCOR model can describe both simple and complex supply chains using a unified set of definitions. This approach allows various industries to be connected and provides a comprehensive view of supply chain operations. Consequently, modern logistics practice has evolved from a solely internal focus to include collaboration across the entire spectrum of supply chain participants (Stein & Voehl, 1998).

2.5 Sources of Supply Chain Data

Big data can generally be categorized into three types based on its structure: structured, semi-structured, and unstructured (Rozados & Tjahjono, 2014). Structured data typically consists of standardized numbers and text stored in organizational databases, such as transaction records, which are relatively straightforward to analyze with minimal data preparation (Minelli et al., 2013). In contrast, unstructured data encompasses a variety of formats, including text, audio, video, geospatial information, emails, and internet logs. This type of data requires substantial effort in processing before it can be used in analytic models to derive insights (Dubey et al., 2018; Minelli et al., 2013).

Supply chain data sources are diverse and extend beyond traditional structured data sources like core transactional records (Minelli et al., 2013). Modern organizations analyze data from internal systems related to production and operations, as well as more complex external sources such as smart objects, clickstream data, and social media data collected from online platforms (Rozados & Tjahjono, 2014; Xu et al., 2021).

To classify big data sources in the supply chain by their structure and the volume and velocity of data generated from over 50 sources, Seyedan and Mafakhen (2020) reported that data from transactions, RFID, Point of Sale (POS) systems, sensors, and social media were the top contributors. These sources were rated at 87%, 42%, 41%, 43%, and 43% respectively for data generation and analytics. Figure 4 shows the classification and sources of data.

Figure 4. Classification and Sources of Data (Awwad, et al., 2018)

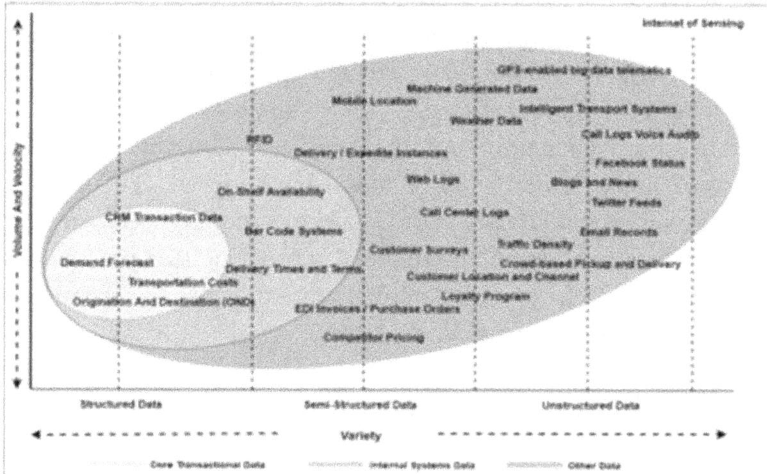

Big data analytics includes several steps: gathering and storing data, cleaning it up, exploring the data, creating models and algorithms, and showing the results clearly. According to Berisha et al., (2022), the big data analysis process usually has these steps: collecting data, storing data, processing data, analyzing data, showing data visually, making decisions, and improving over time. The big data analysis often needs to be repeated. This is because new data is collected and new insights are found, so the process might happen several times. The process can be changed to meet the specific needs of different businesses and organizations. Big data analysis can be divided into four main types (Tamilsevi, et al., 2018): batch processing which is used for analyzing past data to make predictions about the future, usually in the context of time series data; stream processing which is received continuously in real-time and is analyzed quickly to provide estimates; Online Transaction Processing (OLTP) which focuses on handling tasks related to transactions, such as online banking and updating customer information by call center staff; and interactive queries and analysis which allows for very quick searches on large amounts of data from various sources (Ribeiro, et al., 2015). Figure 5 shows the flow in the process of big data.

Figure 5. Flow in the Process of Big Data (Iheukwumere, et al., 2024)

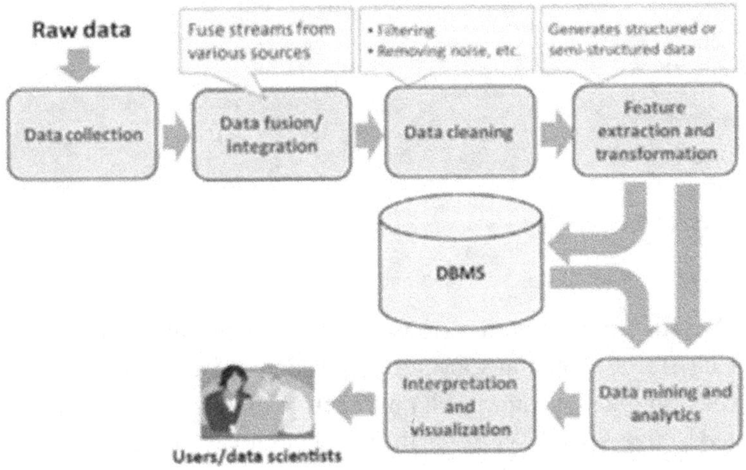

The way data behaves in today's growing and unpredictable global supply chains means that using big data analysis and machine learning has become essential for managing supply chains. Supply chains are collecting a huge amount of data, including different types like videos, pictures, blogs, files, online activity, location data, and information from sensors, devices, and social media. In supply chain, data can be divided into different types: customer information, shipping details, delivery updates, order records, sales figures, store information, and product details (Constante, et al., 2019). Figure 6 below shows that taxonomy of supply chain data.

Figure 6. Taxonomy of Supply Chain Data (Seyedan & Mafakhen, 2020)

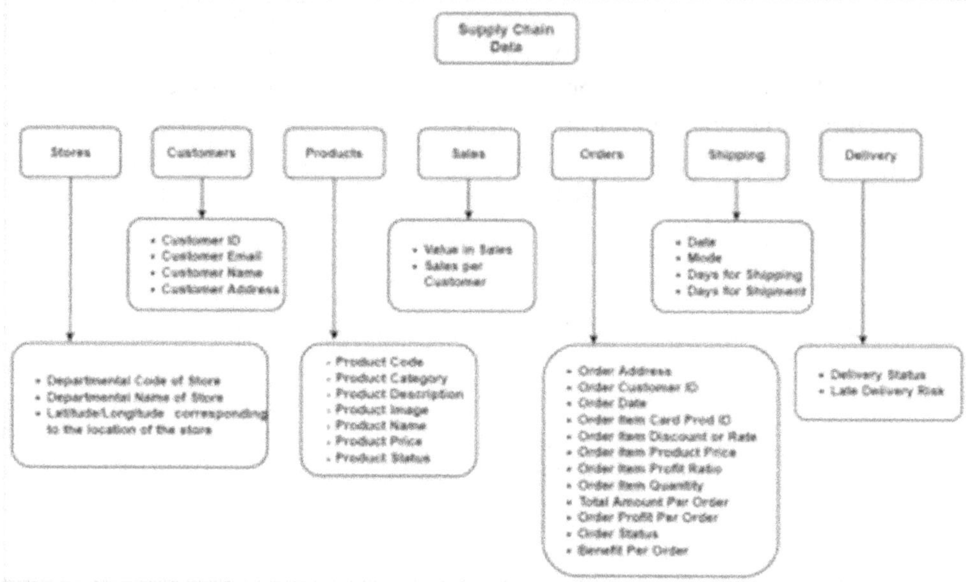

Supply chain data comes from various separate sources, including sales, inventory, manufacturing, storage, and transportation (Seyedan and Mafakhen, 2020). There are many sources of big data in supply chains, each with different advantages and challenges related to size, speed, type, worth, and accuracy (Lee and Mangalaraj, 2022). Using different types of data that vary in time and place highlights the importance of big data analysis in managing supply chains. To make demand predictions more accurate, we should closely look at supply chain data to better understand market trends, customer habits, suppliers, and technologies. Looking at data to find trends and patterns can help make future predictions more accurate, which can lower supply chain costs (Ali, et al., 2017; Bian, et al., 2016).

Analyzing supply chain data has become more complicated for several reasons: (1) there are more supply chain players involved, (2) the setups of supply chains vary widely based on whether products are similar or different, (3) these players are interlinked in various ways, (4) there are unknown factors in how these parts behave, (5) there is often a lack of information about the supply chain players, (6) manufacturing and production teams are working together more to better meet different customer needs, and (7) more companies are using digital tools and technologies like blockchain to monitor their supply chain activities (Buyukozkan & Gocer, 2018).

Big data analytics (BDA) is being used more and more in supply chain optimization (SCO) (Nguyen, et al., 2018) It helps with several tasks like choosing suppliers (Choi, et al., 2018), reducing sourcing costs (Huang and Handfield, 2015), managing risks in sourcing (Miroslav, et al., 2014), researching and developing products (Zhang, et al., 2017), planning and controlling production (Shu, et al., 2016), managing quality (Krumeich, et al., 2016), maintenance and diagnosis (Guo, et al., 2016), warehousing (Chuang, et al., 2014), picking orders (Ballestin, et al., 2013), controlling inventory (Alyahya, et al., 2016), and transportation (like smart transport systems (Cui, et al., 2016) and planning logistics (Shan and Zhu, 2015)). BDA also helps in managing demand, including forecasting (Jun, et al., 2014), sensing demand (He, et al., 2015), and shaping demand (Marine-Koig and Anton, 2015). One important use of big data analytics (BDA) in supply chain optimization (SCO) is to make accurate predictions, especially about how much product will be needed. This helps to lessen the bullwhip effect, which is when small changes in demand cause bigger fluctuations in supply (Munir, 2019; Rostami-Tabar, et al., 2019). Table 1 presents the challenges and uses of big data in an organized manner.

Table 1. Challenges and Uses of Big Data

S/N	Aspect	Details	References
1.	Challenges in Analyzing Supply Chain data	There are more supply chain players involved	Buyukozkan & Gocer, 2018
		The setups of supply chains vary widely based on whether products are similar or different	
		These players are interlinked in various ways	
		There are unknown factors in how these parts behave	
		There is often a lack of information about the supply chain players	
		Manufacturing and production teams are working together more to better meet different customer needs	
		More companies are using digital tools and technologies like blockchain to monitor their supply chain activities	

continued on following page

Table 1. Continued

S/N	Aspect	Details	References
2.	Uses of Big Data Analytics (BDA) in Supply Chain Optimization (SCO)	Choosing suppliers	Choi, et al., 2018
		Reducing sourcing costs	Huang and Handfield, 2015
		Managing risks in sourcing	Miroslav, et al., 2014
		Researching and developing products	Zhang, et al., 2017
		Planning and controlling production	Shu, et al., 2016
		Managing quality	Krumeich, et al., 2016
		Maintenance and diagnosis	Guo, et al., 2016
		Warehousing	Chuang, et al., 2014
		Picking orders	Ballestin, et al., 2013
		Controlling inventory	Alyahya, et al., 2016
		Transportation (like smart transport systems	Cui, et al., 2016
		Planning logistics	Shan and Zhu, 2015
		Managing demand, including forecasting	Jun, et al., 2014
		Sensing demand	He, et al., 2015
		Shaping demand	Marine-Koig and Anton, 2015

Source: Author's computation, 2024.

2.6 Methods of Big Data Analytics

Big data analysis uses different methods because of the large amount of data involved. This data is too big to be handled by regular database systems. It also comes in quickly (velocity) and comes from many different sources, including social media, emails, and messages (variety) (Wisner, Tan & Leong, 2012). Big data analytics is a complete way to handle, process, and look at large amounts of data (in terms of size, types, speed, accuracy, and usefulness) to create useful information. This information helps with quick actions, measuring performance, and gaining a competitive edge. It involves using advanced methods to find important information from big data, which makes decision-making easier. It's a special kind of complex data that cannot be easily stored, managed, or examined by traditional methods. This data comes from unknown sources and has many different aspects, making it difficult to understand because it is complicated and constantly changing (Sun, Chen & Yu, 2016).

Supply chain analytics looks at information and uses different methods to help make better decisions about how goods move in the supply chain. In other words, supply chain analytics looks at data to help make better decisions about meeting demand and providing supplies. After looking at the research, we found three main types of advanced analysis methods: descriptive, prescriptive, and predictive (Hahn, et al., 2015)

Prescriptive Analytics

Prescriptive analytics is an advanced way of analyzing data. It uses specific methods to look at different choices and suggest the best solution for a particular situation. As the name implies, it offers a solution to a specific issue. One way is to use machine learning with neural networks. This method uses models to find the best values (or weights) for the neurons by using sets of training data. Once the neural network model is trained, it can recommend the best actions to help achieve the business goal based on certain business information. Simulation is a tool that helps predict outcomes. When used with the right search or optimization methods, it can also guide decisions effectively. Prescriptive analytics tells us not just "What will happen", but also "What the company should do". It gives suggestions on what actions to take for the best business results. Prescriptive analytics is the best type of advanced analytics because it can recommend the best solutions.

Prescriptive analytical models are complicated. When used well, prescriptive analytics can greatly improve how an organization makes decisions. New technologies like cloud computing have made it much simpler to use these complicated models. Companies that have experts in data analysis and strong computer resources are using special analytics tools to improve their production and inventory choices, enhance customer experiences, and ensure that the right products are delivered at the right time. Airlines use advanced models to decide how to best sell their seats at different prices. They consider factors like travel needs, demand, buying habits, and timing to make the most money. More and more companies understand that big data analytics can help them get ahead of their competitors. Because of this, they are choosing the right analytics tools to lower costs, improve service quality, and increase their profits.

Prescriptive analytics uses methods and formulas to find and evaluate different solutions. Examples of prescriptive analytics include simulations and finding the best solutions. Tiwari shares a list of important data analysis methods for supply chains. These methods include sorting things into groups (classification), predicting outcomes (regression), grouping similar items (clustering), finding relationships (association), showing data in pictures (visualization), understanding meanings (semantic analysis), analyzing graphs (graphical analysis), improving processes (optimization), and testing scenarios (simulation) (Tiwari et al., 2018). Prescriptive Analytics uses data from different processes like Manufacturing, Logistics, Transportation, and Warehousing, as well as new methods like Cyber Physical Systems in the Industry 4.0 trend.

Predictive Analytics

Predictive analytics is the ability to guess what might happen in the future and to understand future results better. It is a more advanced type of analysis that uses statistics and machine learning. It helps find groups, patterns, and unusual cases, and to guess what might happen in the future, making it a useful tool for predicting. The basic idea of predictive analytics is probability. It uses the information the user has and tries to guess the missing information. It helps answer the question, “What might happen?” When models are set up correctly, predictive analytics can help make complicated predictions in marketing and sales. This helps a company to make achievable goals, manage expectations, and plan well. Predictive data analytics involves quickly analyzing current and past data to predict what might happen in the future. This technology uses machine learning and computer methods to learn from available data (Siegel, 2013). Predictive analytics can bring great benefits to businesses and individuals alike. Additionally, predicting things has been recognized as an important area of study for the future (Elragal & Klischewski, 2017).

The tools used for predictive modeling depend on how complex the model is. Some commonly used tools are SAS, MATLAB, R, and Python, among others. These tools work by bringing together past data from different systems like sales, inventory, customer management, and employee records. They look for trends in this data and use methods like random forest and Generalized Linear Model (GLM) to make predictions. They also use K-means clustering to group similar data together. Finally, we can use simulations to help predict what might happen in certain decision-making situations.

One use of predictive analytics is to create credit scores. These scores help financial services figure out how likely a customer is to pay on time. Other business uses include figuring out how sales may finish at the end of the year, predicting how much stock will be needed, guessing what items a customer might buy together, and looking at other buying habits of customers. Even though predictive analytics has many benefits, it's important to remember that forecasting is just an educated guess. How accurate it is depends on how good and reliable the data is.

Descriptive Analytics

Descriptive analytics does what its name implies: it describes or summarizes data and turns it into something useful. This is the simplest kind of analysis, and nearly 90% of companies today use it. Descriptive analytics looks at past data by combining or exploring it. It is the first step in using big data effectively. However, it is very useful because it shows us how people acted in the past, which can help us understand how different things might affect the organization in the future. Descriptive data analytics looks at past business events, trends, patterns, and reasons to help understand what happened. Descriptive analytics can be done in different ways, such as regular reports and dashboards, custom reports, detailed data searches (OLAP), alerts, and data viewing (Siegel, 2013).

Descriptive analytics tries to find problems and chances in the current processes and operations. It collects information from a lot of data and tells us "what has happened." and "what is happening right now." GPS, RFID technology, and sensors gather information in real-time. This information is then summarized and turned into useful details about where goods are and how much is available in a supply chain. This information helps managers make the needed changes.

Most of the numbers we use come from descriptive analytics, which includes simple calculations like averages and standard deviations. Descriptive models use simple math and statistics to find important figures that show patterns in past data. STATA, MS Excel, and SPSS are older tools used for descriptive analytics. Now, R and Python are becoming more popular in the industry because they have many free libraries and are easy to develop and use. Descriptive analytics helps an organization understand what has happened in the past regarding its production, inventory, sales, operations, finances, and customer behavior (Nguyen, Zhou, Spiegler, Ieromonachou, & Lin, 2017). Figure 7 below shows the different methods of data analytics.

Figure 7. Analytics Framework by Tom Davenport (Gurobi Optimization, 2019)

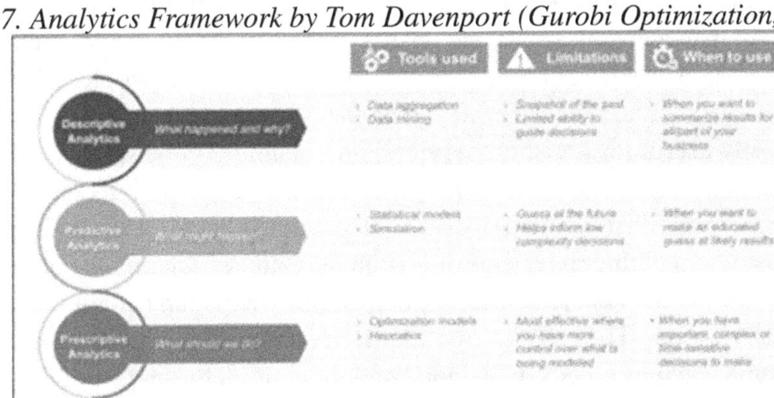

3. RELATED WORKS

BDA in SCO is a mixed topic because it combines ideas from different fields. Business challenges don't usually come in the form of clear data problems. Even when there is a lot of data available, people often struggle to use it effectively in their complicated decision-making processes that can help improve the business. Barratt et al. (2014) argue that they saw the importance of exploring how big data analytics (BDA) can be used in supply chain optimization (SCO).

Oncioiu et al. (2019) study looked at how supply chain management and big data analytics can help Romanian supply chain companies. The study used a method that involves numbers and took a survey, using a questionnaire to gather information. There were 205 managers in the study, and the collected data were examined using SPSS software. This involved looking at frequency tables, contingency tables, and main component analysis. The results show that companies are worried about understanding new methods and tools, like cloud computing and security technology, which need to be carefully looked into.

Vitari and Raguseo (2018) studied how businesses can use their ability to manage digital data to improve their financial success. They also looked at whether other factors affect this relationship. The study looked into these questions to reach its goals: 1) How much do companies that have strong Digital Data skills perform better financially. 2) How do the conditions in a company and its industry affect the link between its Digital Data skills and financial performance. The researchers tested their ideas using special modeling techniques and by collecting data from a financial database and a survey of sales managers from 125 companies. It was found that having strong digital data skills helps companies do better financially. This effect is stronger for newer companies in fast-changing and rich environments.

Brinch et al., (2018) used a combination of different methods. It first involved a Delphi study that looked at how big data is applied in supply chain management using a modified SCOR process framework. They also sent out a questionnaire to supply chain managers to explain the results of the Delphi study and to check how big data is actually used in practice. The study shows that when people talk about big data, they focus more on how to collect data than on how to manage and use it. Big data is mostly useful for logistics, services, and planning rather than for sourcing, manufacturing, and returns. Also, supply chain leaders are adopting big data slowly.

Bhattacharjya, Ellison, and Tripathi (2016) studied how e-retailers use Twitter to help customers with delivery questions quickly and efficiently. Li et al. (2018) looked at how big data analytics (BDA) helps improve demand chain management by using BDA tools. They discovered that BDA allows companies to learn about their customers' habits, needs, behaviors, and thoughts. This understanding is very important for making customers happier. So, BDA is important because it helps supply chain partners share information more easily and efficiently. Brandau and Tolujevs (2013) used a data mining method to gather information from location and sensor devices. They wanted to find out what caused problems in the logistics process to ensure that goods move smoothly. Meanwhile, Pang, Zhao, Yan, et al. (2021) talked about using big data to greatly lower the differences in predicting the environment. Hopkins and Hawking (2018) shared a real example where a truck used technology like GPS, information about locations, and cameras to make driving safer, encourage better driving habits, and cut down on fuel use and carbon dioxide emissions. In the same way, Sugrue and Adriaens (2021) talked about how short sea shipping and inland waterways can help logistics by making things work better or getting the most value for costs.

3.1 Gaps analysis

Even though we know a lot about Big Data Analytics in Supply Chain Processes, we point out three important areas that need more study. First, the studies show that there are varied contributions on different parts of the planning process (like production, logistics, and product development). These studies focus mainly on how big data analytics is used for specific supply chain activities. It doesn't give a clear picture of how the different big data analysis methods and techniques connect to the entire supply chain process, and whether there are benefits from using big data methods alongside the sources of big data (Hofmann and Rutschmann, 2018). There is no clear summary showing how BDA connects to the whole process of SCO. There is a lot of interest in studying how big data analytics (BDA) helps with short-term decisions rather than with more strategic, long-term decisions (Koot et al., 2021) The role of BDA in long-term focus is not often studied (Xu et al., 2021) Since big data analytics (BDA) is still a new and changing technology, it's unclear how supply chain experts can decide what to focus on in their research and work related to it. We think that studying big data analytics (BDA) in supply chains should be practical and focused on the future. The goal is to connect what we learn from research with how things work in the real world.

4. METHODOLOGY

In recent years, there have been a lot of improvements in how we collect and study large amounts of data. The Thomson Reuters Web of Science tool was used to find out how many "big data" articles were published in the past ten years. The search plan was created by first finding the important places to get information. A wide range of databases was chosen to access many different types of publications.

Journal articles, conference papers, dissertations, theses, books, magazine articles, newspaper articles, and trade journals. I looked for information in databases like EBSCO, Emerald, and Scopus. We also looked online to find more materials. White The identified keywords were directly related to BDA (for example, Big Data Analytics includes things like big data, analytics, advanced analytics, predictive analytics, data science, and supply chain analytics. These keywords were then grouped with phrases like "Supply Chain Optimization" or "SCO" to make sure they fit with this study. The search area for the text was changed based on the database (like Title, Abstract, Keywords, etc.)

We experimented with various title and topic searches in the Web of Science. We found that the best choice was to use "big data" in the title search and the other keywords in the topic search. For example, when we searched for articles about "big data" and "supply chain optimization", we found 574 articles. Some of these articles didn't relate to what we were studying. On the other hand, looking for articles from 2014-2024 that have both "big data" and "supply chain optimization" in the title showed us only 143 articles, and many important articles were missing. We looked for articles from the same years that had "big data" in the title and focused on "supply chain optimization". We found 64 articles that were related to our study. We used the same method as in many other review papers (Mishra et al., 2018; Nguyen et al. 2017). We gathered information, analyzed it, created different categories, and assessed the papers. Figure 8 shows the inclusion and exclusion criteria for the search.

Figure 8. PRISMA Flow Chart Showing the Inclusion and Exclusion Criteria

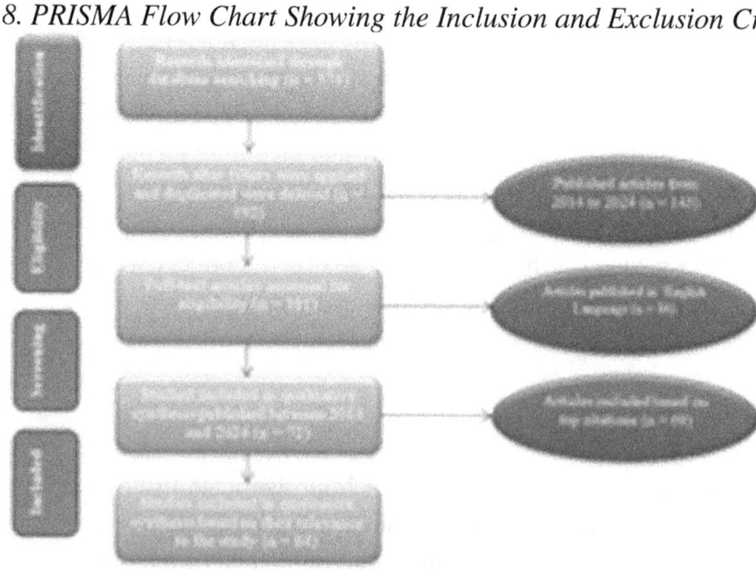

Figure 9 shows how many articles have been published from 2014 to 2024 that have "big data" in their title, along with the topics of "supply chain", "supply chain optimization", and "business". Figure 9 shows that the number of publications in this area has been growing in recent years. It's important to note that not many studies on big data were released before 2014. Figure 10 shows the distribution of reference papers by publication, and Figure 11 shows the distribution of reference papers by type.

Figure 9. Number of Publications with "Big Data" in Title (Thomson Reuters Web of Science).

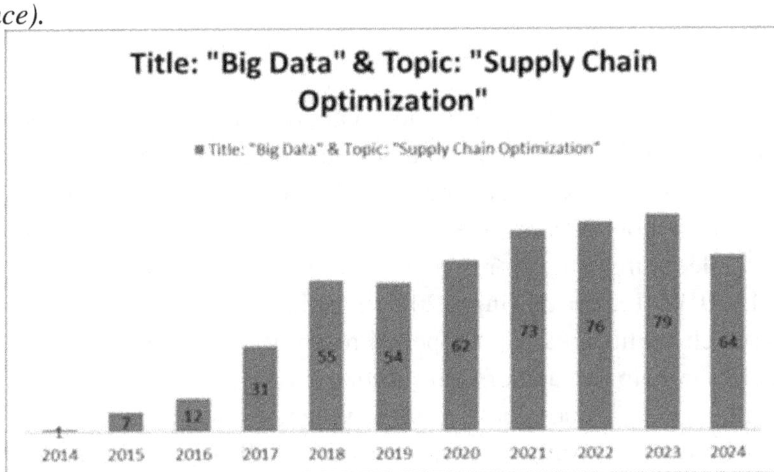

Figure 10. Distribution of Reference Papers by Publication

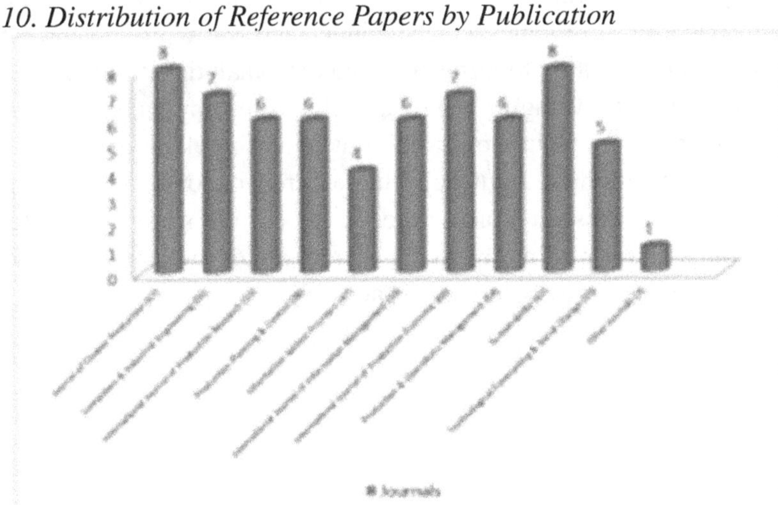

Figure 11. Distribution of Reference Papers by Type

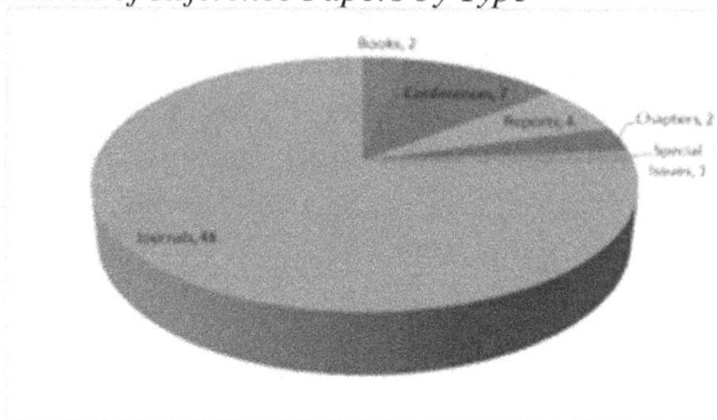

Advancements in technology have led many researchers and professionals to use big data analysis in areas like manufacturing, logistics, and other parts of the supply chain. Also, because the advantages of big data analysis have drawn in many more researchers, more papers have been written that look at previous studies and suggest possible future paths for research (Barbosa et al., 2018; Dubey et al., 2019; Gupta et al., 2019a; Lamba & Singh, 2017; Rialti et al., 2019). Figure 9 shows that a lot of research in this area has happened recently. This means a new review of the literature can help researchers who want to work on big data in supply chain management. Also, our study looks at improving the supply chain.

The qualitative data from 64 journal articles will be analyzed using content analysis. This method will help identify key themes, patterns, and insights within the data, facilitating a detailed exploration and interpretation of the perspectives from these sources. The results of a detailed exploration of how big data analytics enhances supply chain optimization (SCO) were presented and discussed. The result were presented in four sub-themes which included applications of big data analytics to supply chain optimization, importance of big data analytics in supply chain optimization, challenges of leveraging big data analytics in supply chain optimization, and the role of emerging technologies in enhancing the effectiveness of BDA in supply chain optimization. In a nutshell, the researchers conducted a grouped and systematic selection of research procedures in the current study by checking, collecting, grouping, and exploring the major themes under investigation. The review is now based on each of the objectives of the study.

5. RESULTS AND DISCUSSION

5.1 Application of Big Data Analytics in Supply Chain Optimization

Supply chain management includes designing, planning, executing, controlling, and monitoring how goods and information move. When we talk about optimizing supply chains, it specifically looks at how to work together with other members in the supply chain. The goal is to make sure that what is available (supply) matches what is needed (demand) and to improve how goods, services, and information are delivered. Research shows that using BDA (Big Data Analytics) is helpful for planning main supply chain activities like sales, buying materials, making products, and delivering them (Sanders, 2016; Souza, 2014; Talwar et al., 2021; Wang et al., 2016).

Big Data analysis can make supply chain optimization better by helping to predict demand, speeding up new product development, improving how we work with suppliers, lowering risks in the supply chain, and creating reliable and efficient supply chain plans. According to ComputerWorld (2024), using big data and data analysis in a supply chain helps companies improve in key areas like managing risks, predicting customer needs, responding quickly, assessing the supply chain, and making the entire process more efficient.

Big data analytics is increasingly being used in supply management for various tasks like picking orders, storing goods, planning logistics, researching and developing products, managing demand, shipping products, handling purchasing, and managing sourcing risks (Seyedan & Mafakhen, 2020). Big data analytics is used in every part of supply chains, including storage, finance, healthcare, manufacturing, buying, sales management, and transportation. Lodermann et. al (2021) found that supply chain analytics includes these key areas: managing demand, improving inventory, running warehouses, fulfilling orders, analyzing supplier performance, studying costs, handling risks, and measuring performance.

The main goal of using big data in supply chain management is to make better predictions and reduce the bullwhip effect (a situation where small changes in demand cause bigger changes in supply). Supply chain analytics looks at many different areas, all of which help make the supply chain better and more effective (Rostani-Tabar, et al., 2019). Big data analytics can be used in these parts of supply chain management:

Demand Management/Planning

Demand management means looking at past data and market trends to guess what people will want in the future. Demand management helps identify new market trends and understand why problems happen. This allows one to look at things from the customer's perspective and take action based on what customers need. Predicting how much people will want to buy has always been hard for managing supply chains. However, using big data can help figure out things like customer loyalty, demand signals, and the best prices (Saeid et al., 2020; Mejri et al., 2021). To keep good relationships with customers, it's important to provide the correct products to the right people. By using predictive analytics, companies can determine how likely a problem is to happen and what effects it might have. Getting accurate forecasts is very important for planning and meeting demand. Recent discussions agree that using data from social networks created by users and customer reviews can greatly enhance demand forecasting and lower forecasting mistakes. This improvement happens for both the medium-term and short-term forecasts (Brinch et al., 2018). This is clear to professionals and could lead to demand planning in supply chains that is based entirely on data (Roßmann et al., 2018).

As customer needs keep changing, big data analytics (BDA) helps companies forecast what customers want by analyzing more and more data. A study by Kato and Kamoshida (2020) used data on the economy and population to create models that predict the demand for different body types in Japan. They made these predictions for each month, looking up to 36 months into the future. Using all the big data available helps customers understand what they want in fashion products. It can also suggest items that customers might be willing to buy later on (Ren, Chan, and Siqin 2020). Being able to accurately predict how well sales will do is very helpful for future growth. It greatly affects marketing plans and how to manage stock, allowing managers to create effective strategies for the market (Lau, Zhang, and Xu 2017). One more benefit of studying big data for real demand planning is creating a sustainable supply chain that focuses on consumers. This can be done by analyzing data from Twitter to understand how people feel about different topics and their buying habits. This gathered information helps improve competitiveness and keep things up-to-date (Yuan et al., 2018).

Procurement Planning (PRC)

Clearly, lowering costs and making customers happy are two main goals for those in charge. To reduce rising driving costs and help make better decisions, organizations need effective ways to turn large amounts of different data into useful information (Gandomi and Haider 2015). The possibilities of using big data analytics (BDA) are vast, but they depend on the different technologies, tools, and skills that can be accessed for BDA. These technologies, tools, and skills have been successful in many ways. They help measure how complicated it is to size purchase orders, understand the costs involved, and identify processes that often have clear and simple mistakes. This can help decision-makers become more aware of their choices by analyzing well-known methods for measuring complexity (Bock and Isik 2015).

Procurement planning (PRC) means planning what to buy and the materials needed. It involves deciding how much to purchase by looking at the list of materials needed, how long it will take to get them, and the limits on how much can be produced. BDA can help create better sourcing strategies and improve the process of choosing suppliers by using decision-making methods that consider multiple factors. It does this through tools that assess costs or risks to evaluate suppliers. Getting this information helps companies have more influence in negotiations and improves their teamwork with important suppliers.

Production and Manufacturing

Researchers explored the various ways big data analytics (BDA) can be used in manufacturing. They looked at different types of data and found that using this data can help reduce the time it takes for customers to receive their orders and also support sustainability efforts. For example, Kumar et al (2016) developed a new system called Map-Reduce which was created to automatically find patterns in problems related to faults in steel plate manufacturing. This system helped to solve issues with uneven data and aimed to reduce the number of faults that happen during production. The method suggested by Xu, Chen, and Zheng (2016) used a mix of different techniques to handle big data analytics in order to make better decisions.

Production planning (PRD) involves creating a big picture plan, organizing production tasks, and scheduling work. It determines how to use the available production capacity in one or more facilities, especially when demand changes with the seasons. It also helps make short-term decisions about the size of batches and the order of tasks on the machines. Research on using Big Data Analytics (BDA) for production planning is clearly more developed than for other areas. This is because it takes advantage of real-time data from the Internet of Things (IoT) and smart devices. Using various data analysis methods, big data helps improve predictions about how long tasks will take, scheduling production, managing the shop floor, and handling materials. It also aids in planning inventory for in-house production and in deciding how to allocate resources based on the types of products being made. Also, gathering helpful information about customers' personal traits and preferences in a situation where products are customized for each individual has been seen as a way for designers to make choices based on what customers really want. When thinking about how to prioritize maintenance, Bumblauskas, et al (2017) explained that BDA helps set standards to predict when a specific part will fail. This way, it can be replaced on time. It also involves getting a complete service proposal to meet the suggestions made by the analysis.

Inventory Management

An inventory management system helps with ordering items, keeping track of stock, buying products, and checking if the physical stock matches the records. Inventory control is an important part of managing the supply chain. It helps organizations keep track of their stock so they can meet customer needs while also keeping costs low. The goals of inventory management are to predict how much products will be needed, keep the right amount of stock, reduce storage costs, keep customers happy, prevent running out of products, and make order processing faster and more accurate by improving how items are picked and delivered. This also involves making sure data is correct, having clear visibility of stock, and managing risks (Saied, et al., 2020; Cohen, 2015).

Many research studies show that big data analytics (BDA) is useful when everyone can see the inventory clearly. For example, Demey and Wolff (2016) showed a model called Semantic Inventory Management for the International Space Station (SIMISS). Possible places for lost items are figured out using three-dimensional context clues; space, time, and people. Demey and Wolff (2016) showed that using SIMISS can lower the cost of sending supplies for long missions to the International Space Station. It also helps save crew members' time and makes sure the mission is successful (Zheng and Wu 2017).

Logistics and Transport Optimization

Supply chain companies aim to use logistics to make customers happy by choosing the best delivery methods based on what customers prefer when shopping online. They focus on getting the right item to the right person in the right place. Big data analysis helps find better routes for transportation, choose the best types of transport, and decide where to place warehouses by looking at traffic patterns and customer locations, among other factors. People use big data analytics to help with transportation in health care (Brouer et al., 2016) and to fix planning issues in shipping industries (Mehmood & Graham, 2015). Distribution planning is about organizing how materials move within the production system, how goods are transported to customers, and how they are moved between different places in the distribution process. There is a substantial amount of data coming from both internal sources (such as GPS and shipping details) and external sources (such as traffic and weather). This creates a big opportunity for Big Data Analytics (BDA) to help make logistics better and improve route planning. Using big data analytics (BDA) in planning how to deliver goods helps to make the planning process faster, reduces delays, allows for better tracking of items, improves guesses on when trucks will arrive, and leads to better fuel use and vehicle upkeep.

Big Data Analytics (BDA) can greatly improve how we make decisions in logistics in a few main ways: (a) accurately predicting when problems will happen, (b) showing the path of deliveries clearly, (c) keeping track of the vehicles, and (d) guessing what customers will do. Chen and Kezunovic (2016) studied weather data using fuzzy logic to create plans for reducing the effects of weather. This helps utility operators make better predictions about outages and improve their real-time operations, including scheduling maintenance (Zhong et al., 2016). Mishra and Singh (2020) studied data from sensors used in a truck monitoring system. They discovered that using predictive analysis can provide useful information, like telling when parts need to be repaired or replaced before they actually break. It can also give advice on driving habits for different road conditions to both drivers and fleet owners.

Accurate Prediction

Quick and correct predictions are one of the biggest benefits of big data analysis that supply chain businesses can use to improve their operations. As stated by Nguyen, et al (2018), research on logistics and transportation offers little insight into improving routes in real-time using simple data. On the other hand, there is a lot of research about improving manufacturing processes in real-time using models and simulations. By using the right optimization methods, it's very likely that logistics and transportation workers can apply similar big data analytics (BDA) techniques to improve real-time routing problems and make their supply chain operations better. Helping BDA in the supply chain is not just about assessing it. It's really about making changes to improve how things work and to support better decision-making.

Big data analytics has changed the way companies do maintenance by helping them check how their equipment is doing, plan maintenance better, improve safety, save money, and use data to make smarter choices. This leads to more reliable and better-performing equipment. Companies can lose their customers if they don't meet what customers want. Also, a company's reputation can be hurt if they don't complete orders or only do part of them. In today's world, it's important to give the right product to the right person at the right time and place to keep customers happy and loyal. Smart companies will use Big Data to understand their customers better. This helps them predict what customers need, know their likes and dislikes, and create a special experience with their brand.

5.2 Importance of Big Data Analytics to Supply Chain Optimization

In supply chain optimization, using big data has become more common. Top companies like Dell, Apple, and Samsung are using big data to improve their supply chain operations and finding new business opportunities (Yu et al., 2018) Getting supply chain information from different places, like visits to customer websites, feelings shared on social media, and changing contracts, is seen as an important part of using big data to improve supply chain skills (Bansal et al., 2020) Also, getting data in real-time is very important, especially in situations like the ongoing operations of fusion devices, where data needs to be looked at and saved immediately (Zilker et al., 2010) Getting real-time data is important for good communication and managing the large and complicated data found in businesses, consumers, and banks.

After gathering the data, the next step is very important. It's very important to have ways to work with big sets of data, and making sure the data is clean and reliable is crucial. This is especially important for using big data to help with operations and decision-making in different parts of a business during the whole process of making products in a smart factory (Li et al., 2019) Also, strategic sourcing, which includes smart buying and coordinating within the company, has been recognized as a key factor in making supply chains more flexible. This highlights how important data processing methods are for improving supply chains (Chiang et al., 2012).

With new technology in the Supply Chain, the amount of data being created is growing quickly. Before Information Technology was used in Supply Chain, the information was recorded using physical papers. Most of the information about how materials move is now being recorded as organized digital data. Since Supply Chains now operate all over the world, they gather a lot of data from many processes, and this data is created very quickly. This can be called Big Data. Also, marketing and sales teams are now using both unstructured and structured data to understand customer needs better and to make supply chain processes more cost-effective. Using Big Data can greatly help in areas like creating new products, predicting what customers want, making supply decisions, improving delivery processes, and gathering customer opinions. Table 2 shows how Big Data helps in different areas of business (Iheukwumere, et al., 2024).

Table 2. Percentage of Big Data Contribution in Supply Chain Optimization

Name Of The Business Operations	Contribution To The Businesses (%)
Marketing	45
Operations	43
Sales	38
Risk Management	35
IT Analytics	33
Finance	32
Product Development	32
Customer Service	30
Logistics	22
HR	12
Other	12
Brand Management	8

Source: Iheukwumere, et al., 2024.

Looking at data is very important because it helps us understand things better, which can greatly affect choices in managing the supply chain. Using big data analysis helps improve how we plan, make decisions, and prepare supply chains. This makes supply networks more alert and flexible (Vincent et al., 2021; Sakib, 2021). Using big data in supply chain and business management helps companies see their operations more clearly, understand how their performance is doing, and gain insights into customer behavior. It also provides up-to-date information that makes it easier to make decisions (Liu & Yi, 2016).

5.3 Challenges of Integrating Big Data Analytics into Supply Chain Optimization

Industries that depend on data have several challenges with big data analytics. These challenges include cleaning and putting together data, storing large amounts of data, handling complicated data, keeping data private and secure, preparing the necessary infrastructure, and managing big data effectively (Wang, et al., 2020; Ikegwu, et al., 2022). According to Wang et al. (2016), the main problems with big data analysis are: complicated data formats, extremely high dimensions, limited ability to handle large amounts of data, and constant uncertainty. Big data analytics has many problems, like how to gather, combine, and save large amounts of data without needing lots of technology and software. The huge amount of data and the continuous flow of data are the two biggest challenges for big data analysis.

The problems with using Big Data Analytics in Supply Chain can be divided into two types: Organizational Challenges and Technical Challenges (Arunachalam, Kumar, & Kawalek, 2017). The problems and difficulties related to organizational challenges are as follows:

- **Time-Consuming**: Things like having a lot of Big Data, the complicated nature of the supply chain, the goals for understanding the data, and outside issues like not having access to the data make the analysis process slow. Handling the huge amount of data created by the supply chain can put a lot of pressure on systems and tools used for analysis (Stefanovic & Milosevic, 2017).
- **Insufficient resources**: To get better results, it's important to have real-time data. The supply chain creates complicated data for connected parts of a business, so gathering and storing this data should be made easier. Using big data in supply chain optimization (SCO) needs advanced technology, which can be difficult for smaller companies that don't have many resources (Rehman et al. 2016). Advanced technologies and systems need strong and flexible computer networks. They also require the use of RFID systems to track and trace things for easy data sharing. However, the limited number of tags in RFID systems creates new security and privacy problems that organizations need to deal with (Chen et al., 2015). Additionally, the problems with different blockchain systems working together in supply chain management show that we need widespread steps to help overcome technology challenges (Hassan et al., 2024; Kayikci & Subramanian, 2022).
- **Privacy and security issues**: Dealing with important supply chain information can be risky. This includes the chance of data leaks, people getting access without permission, and the wrong use of data (Shahzad et al., 2020). These risks get worse because there is more and different types of data being created in supply chains. This makes it very important for organizations to have strong data security measures in place. Ways to keep data safe include using advanced technologies like AI, machine learning, and proactive blockchain to solve problems with collecting, analyzing, and processing data (Shahzad et al., 2020). Also, using blockchain to protect privacy and organize data can help solve privacy and security problems when sharing lots of data in supply chains (Tang et al., 2023).
- **Behavioral problems**: Supply chain risks and inventory costs can increase if decision-makers react strongly to small changes in the physical world, making the "bullwhip effect" worse. Because there is a lot of Big Data, decision

makers may mistakenly find connections that seem important but do not really mean anything. Using big data in supply chain management requires important changes in how the organization works and its culture. It's important to think about how to manage changes to help move to a decision-making process that relies on data (Liu et al., 2023).

- **Data Quality**: The quality of the data that is stored and used can impact how well the analytics techniques work. Data is not physical and has many different aspects depending on where it comes from and how it is used. To get dependable results for making decisions, the data needs to be of good quality and consistent. The different kinds of data and sources used in the supply chain can impact how good the collected data is. Making sure that data from different sources is clear, consistent, and combined well is a big challenge in supply chain analysis. This is because the data can come from many places and in different formats.
- **Lack of Skills**: When a company can't use the data well, it weakens the quality of the insights gained from analyzing the data. The methods we use to study, calculate, predict, and display data need to be changed or improved based on how complicated or large the data is (Arunachalam et al., 2017) Looking at the complicated supply chain data can be tough because it needs advanced tools and methods to understand it well. This is important to help make decisions and turn insights into useful plans.

5.4 Role of Emerging Technologies in Enhancing the Effectiveness of BDA in Supply Chain Optimization

To understand how Big Data will change supply chain optimization in the future, we need to look at new technologies and the rules that are being set. Using artificial intelligence (AI) and machine learning (ML) is becoming an important way to improve supply chains (Alvarez-Rodriguez et al., 2018) This integration helps create better tools for analyzing data in supply chains, which improves decision-making and makes operations more efficient (Orieno et al., 2024; Oncioiu et al., 2019) In addition, using big data analysis in logistics and supply chain management is thought to offer ideas for future research and development in this area (Babatunde et al., 2021; Govindan et al., 2018) Around the world, changing rules about how data can be used in supply chain optimization is very important to think about. Changing rules and regulations are affecting how businesses use Big Data in managing their supply chains. Companies need to pay attention to following these rules (Ezeigweneme et al., 2024; Al-Shorman et al., 2023) Also, using big data analytics to predict demand in supply chains needs more study, especially in closed-loop supply chains.

Emerging technology in supply chains include using machine learning to help prevent financial risks in supply chains (Lei et al., 2023; Lukong et al., 2022) This means looking closely at whether it's important and urgent to use AI technology to find money problems in supply chains. Also, creating an AI tool to assess financial risks in the supply chain is an important progress in this area (Luo et al., 2022) The use of AI and machine learning in different areas, like supply chain optimization, is likely to become more important in the next few years (Naved, 2022). Also, researchers have looked at how using big data predictions in supply chain optimization affects decision-making; they found that using these predictions helps make better decisions in supply chain operations (Patrick et al., 2022)

In a nutshell, emerging technologies to improve supply chains will focus on combining AI and machine learning, better data analysis tools, and new rules about how data can be used in managing supply chains. Research shows that using big data, machine learning, and predictive analytics helps improve supply chains. This highlights how technology and rules are changing around the world.

6. CONCLUSION

In recent years, big data analytics has developed as a field that brings together statistics, machine learning, data mining, and analysis. It helps us understand how we can create insights and predictions from both organized and unorganized big data. Big data has been used in supply chain optimization in many areas to help different industries. It has been helpful in taking care of machines before they break, managing storage and shipping, improving relationships with suppliers, ensuring good quality, managing what customers want, and handling risks. Big data analytics has a lot of difficulties dealing with large amounts of data related to managing the supply chain. The study found several challenges, including too much data, problems with data quality and combining different data, keeping data safe and private, difficulty in analyzing data, ability to grow as needed, and complicated supply chains.

Big data analysis can help companies understand what they need for their business. Many companies make plans for growing their business based on a rise in demand, which can happen when businesses are doing well overall. However, they need to think about the fact that if the market slows down, they might end up with many empty warehouses and unused factories. Big data helps these companies guess which way the market will go and make plans for growth using this information.

Both the research and the experiences of companies using big data analytics in manufacturing show that there are more real-life examples than academic studies. Researchers will probably create new ways to use big data in manufacturing, like finding methods to get better results while spending less time and money. Big data is often used for making predictions in research, but there aren't many studies that look at how accurate those predictions are. In addition to the quality of the data itself, how accurate big data analysis is depends a lot on how good the model used for the analysis is. We still need to find ways to check how accurate big data analysis methods are.

6.1 The Way Forward

As companies focus on using big data analysis, they should first identify a clear reason for doing so, like solving a problem or taking advantage of an opportunity. According to Watson, big data projects should begin with specific goals instead of just hoping people will use them. Starting with small test projects can help show the benefits of big data analysis. It's normal to start a big data project by looking at goals that focus on the customer. The different examples talked about earlier show many areas that have gained from big data analysis. No matter the situation, it's important that the pilot project solves a problem related to a specific business goal. The pilot project should help solve a business issue and show how useful big data analytics can be for the company and its partners. To make big data projects successful, it's important to have strong support from leaders and a good match between business goals and analytics plans. At the beginning, the sponsor might be the Chief Information Officer (CIO), but later it could change to other executives in charge of specific functions as new business chances come up.

To make good use of big data, companies need to create a culture where decisions are based on data, not just on gut feelings from managers. To create a culture where decisions are based on data, we can encourage sharing data, offer more training in data analysis, and explain how using data can help make better choices. Workplace training should focus on teaching tech skills and digital know-how, but it also needs to include training in important soft skills for the future. The workplace is changing quickly because of new technology like AI, automation, and data analysis tools. Workers should be willing to try new ways of doing their jobs and be ready to adjust quickly. They also need to work well with others to handle the changes happening around them. In the long run, big data should be an essential part of how the organization works. The organization needs to have someone in charge of big data, like a chief analytics officer. Data science should also be recognized as an important skill in the organization.

REFERENCES

Al-Shorman, H., Eldahamsheh, M., Attiany, M., Al-Azzam, M., & Al-Quran, A. (2023). Potential effects of smart innovative solutions for supply chain performance. *Uncertain Supply Chain Management*, 11(1), 103–110. DOI: 10.5267/j.uscm.2022.11.005

Alvarez-Rodriguez, U., Sanz, M., Lamata, L., & Solano, E. (2018). Quantum artificial life in an ibm quantum computer. *Scientific Reports*, 8(1), 14793. Advance online publication. DOI: 10.1038/s41598-018-33125-3 PMID: 30287854

Antai, I., & Olson, H. (2013). Interaction: A new focus for supply chain vs supply chain competition. *International Journal of Physical Distribution & Logistics Management*, 43(7), 511–528. DOI: 10.1108/IJPDLM-06-2012-0195

APICS (2017). Supply Chain Operations Reference Model, v12.0, Supply Chain Operations Management.

Arunachalam, D., Kumar, N., & Kawalek, J. P. (2017). Understanding big data analytics capabilities in supply chain management: Unravelling the issues, challenges and implications for practice. *Transportation Research Part E, Logistics and Transportation Review*. Advance online publication. DOI: 10.1016/j.tre.2017.04.001

Awwad, M., & Pazour, J. (2018). Search Plan for a Single Item in an Inverted T k-Deep Storage System. *Military Operations Research*, 23(1), 5–22.

Babatunde, F. O., Omotayo, A. B., Oluwole, O. I., & Ukoba, K. (2021, April). A Review on Waste-wood Reinforced Polymer Matrix Composites for Sustainable Development. [). IOP Publishing.]. *IOP Conference Series. Materials Science and Engineering*, 1107(1), 012057. DOI: 10.1088/1757-899X/1107/1/012057

Bansal, P., Gualandris, J., & Kim, N. (2020). Theorizing supply chains with qualitative big data and topic modeling. *The Journal of Supply Chain Management*, 56(2), 7–18. DOI: 10.1111/jscm.12224

Barbosa, M. W., Vicente, A. C., Ladeira, M. B., & Oliveira, M. P. V. (2018). Managing supply chain resources with big data analytics: A systematic review. *International Journal of Logistics*, 21(3), 177–200. DOI: 10.1080/13675567.2017.1369501

Barratt, M., & Oke, A. (2007). Antecedents of supply chain visibility in retail supply chains: A resource-based theory perspective. *Journal of Operations Management*, 25(6), 1217–1233. DOI: 10.1016/j.jom.2007.01.003

Benabdellah, A. C., Benghabrit, A., Bouhaddou, I., & Zemmouri, E. M. (2016, Nov. 29 2016-Dec. 2 2016). *Big data for supply chain management: Opportunities and challenges.* Paper presented at the 2016 IEEE/ACS 13th International Conference of Computer Systems and Applications (AICCSA).

Berisha, B., Meziu, E., & Shabani, I. (2022). Big data analytics in cloud computing: An Overview. *Journal of Cloud Computing (Heidelberg, Germany)*, 11(24), 24. DOI: 10.1186/s13677-022-00301-w PMID: 35966392

Bhattacharjya, J., Ellison, A., & Tripathi, S. (2016). An Exploration of Logistics-Related Customer Service Provision on Twitter: The Case of e-Retailers. *International Journal of Physical Distribution & Logistics Management*, 45(9/10), 979–1006.

Bian, W., Shang, J., & Zhang, J. (2016). Two-way information sharing under supply chain competition. *International Journal of Production Economics*, 178, 82–94. DOI: 10.1016/j.ijpe.2016.04.025

Brandau, A., & Tolujevs, J. (2013). Modelling and Analysis of Logistical State Data. *Transport and Telecommunication Journal*, 14(2), 102–115. DOI: 10.2478/ttj-2013-0009

Brinch, M. (2018). Understanding the value of big data in supply chain management and its business processes. *International Journal of Operations & Production Management*, 38(7), 1589–1614. DOI: 10.1108/IJOPM-05-2017-0268

Brinch, M., Stentoft, J., Jensen, J. K., & Rajkumar, C. (2018). Practitioners understanding of big data and its applications in supply chain management. *International Journal of Logistics Management*, 29(2), 555–574. DOI: 10.1108/IJLM-05-2017-0115

Brinch, M., Stentoft, J., Jensen, J. K., & Rajkumar, C. (2018). Practitioners understanding of big data and its applications in supply chain management. *International Journal of Logistics Management*, 29(2), 555–574. DOI: 10.1108/IJLM-05-2017-0115

Bughin, J. (2016) "Big data, Big bang?," Journal of Big Data, pp. 3(1), 2.

Bumblauskas, D., Gemmill, D., Igou, A., & Anzengruber, J. (2017). Smart Maintenance Decision Support Systems (SMDSS) Based on Corporate Big Data Analytics. *Expert Systems with Applications*, 90, 303–317. DOI: 10.1016/j.eswa.2017.08.025

certain investigations for research and applications. International Journal of Production Economics, 176, 98-110. .DOI: 10.1016/j.ijpe.2016.03.014

Chavez, R., Yu, W., Jacobs, M. A., & Feng, M. (2017). Data-Driven Supply Chains, Manufacturing Capability and Customer Satisfaction. *Production Planning and Control*, 28(11–12), 906–918. DOI: 10.1080/09537287.2017.1336788

Chen, M., Mao, S., Zhang, Y., & Leung, V. C. (2014). *Big data: related technologies, challenges and future prospects*. Springer International Publishing. DOI: 10.1007/978-3-319-06245-7

Chen, P. C., & Kezunovic, M. (2016). Fuzzy Logic Approach to Predictive Risk Analysis in Distribution Outage Management. *IEEE Transactions on Smart Grid*, 7(6), 2827–2836. DOI: 10.1109/TSG.2016.2576282

Choi, T. M., Wallace, S. W., & Wang, Y. (2017). Big data analytics in operations management. *Production and Operations Management*. Advance online publication. DOI: 10.1111/poms.12838 PMID: 26766385

Choi, Y., Lee, H., & Irani, Z. (2018). Big data-driven fuzzy cognitive map for prioritising IT service procurement in the public sector. *Annals of Operations Research*, 270(1–2), 75–104. DOI: 10.1007/s10479-016-2281-6

Cohen, M. A. (2015). Inventory management in the age of big data. *Harvard Business Review*.

ComputerWorld. (2018). *Overcoming 5 Major Supply Chain Challenges with Big Data Analytics*.

Constante, F., Silva, F., & Pereira, A. (2019) DataCo smart supply chain for big data analysis. Mendeley Data. vg2k6. 5.DOI: <ALIGNMENT.qj></ALIGNMENT>10.17632 /8gx2f

Copacino, W. C. (1997). *Supply Chain Management: The Basics and Beyond. APICS Series onResource Management*. St. Lucie Press.

Costello, T., & Prohaska, B. (2013). Trends and strategies. *IT Professional*, 15(1), 64. DOI: 10.1109/MITP.2013.5

Cui, J., Liu, F., Hu, J., Janssens, D., Wets, G., & Cools, M. (2016). Identifying mismatch between urban travel demand and transport network services using GPS data: A case study in the fast growing Chinese city of Harbin. *Neurocomputing*, 181, 4–18. DOI: 10.1016/j.neucom.2015.08.100

Darvazeh, S. S., Vanani, I. R., and Musolu, F. M. (2020) Big data analytics and its application in supply chain management. New Trends in the use of Artificial Intelligence for the Industry 4.0.

Davenport, T. H. (2014). How Strategists Use "Big Data" to Support Internal Business Decisions, Discovery and Production. *Strategy and Leadership*, 42(4), 45–50. DOI: 10.1108/SL-05-2014-0034

Demey, Y. T., & Wolff, M. (2016). SIMISS: A Model Based Searching Strategy for Inventory Management Systems. *IEEE Internet of Things Journal*, 4(1), 1–1. DOI: 10.1109/JIOT.2016.2638023

Divyeshkumar, V. (2024). An Analysis of the Impact of Human-Computer Interaction on Artificial Intelligence in Healthcare. *NeuroQuantology : An Interdisciplinary Journal of Neuroscience and Quantum Physics*, 22(3), 95.

Divyeshkumar, V. (2024). Balancing Safety and Decision-Making Algorithms in AI-Driven Autonomous Vehicles. *NeuroQuantology : An Interdisciplinary Journal of Neuroscience and Quantum Physics*, 22(3), 112.

Divyeshkumar, V. (2024). Block-chain based data provenance and integrity verification. *International Journal of Science and Research Archive*, 12(1), 2516–2533.

Divyeshkumar, V. (2024). Leveraging Electronic Health Records (EHR) for Enhanced Patient Care. *International Journal of Current Science Research and Review*, 7(5), 2963–2971.

Dubey, R., Gunasekaran, A., Childe, S. J., Luo, Z., Fosso Wamba, S., Roubaud, D., & Foropon, C. (2018). Examining the role of big data and predictive analytics on collaborative performance in context to sustainable consumption and production behaviour. *Journal of Cleaner Production*, 196, 1508–1521. DOI: 10.1016/j.jclepro.2018.06.097

Dutta, B. (2021) Big data in supply chain management: Impacts and applications. https://www.analyticssteps.com/ blogs/big-data-supply-chain-management-impacts-and-applications

Elragal, A., & Klischewski, R. (2017). Theory-driven or process-driven prediction? Epistemological challenges of big data analytics. *Journal of Big Data*, 4(19), 19. DOI: 10.1186/s40537-017-0079-2

Ezeigweneme, C. A., Umoh, A. A., Ilojianya, V. I., & Adegbite, A. O.Chinedu Alex EzeigwenemeAniekan Akpan UmohValentine Ikenna IlojianyaAbimbola Oluwatoyin Adegbite. (2024). Review Of Telecommunication Regulation And Policy: Comparative Analysis USA AND AFRICA. *Computer Science & IT Research Journal*, 5(1), 81–99. DOI: 10.51594/csitrj.v5i1.703

Feng, Q., & Shanthikumar, J. G. (2018). How research in production and operations management may evolve in the era of big data. *Production and Operations Management*, 27(9), 1670–1684. DOI: 10.1111/poms.12836

Firican, G. (2017). *The 10 Vs of Big Data.*

Fosso Wamba, S., Akter, S., Edwards, A., Chopin, G., & Gnanzou, D. (2015). How 'big data' can make big impact: Findings from a systematic review and a longitudinal case study. *International Journal of Production Economics*, 165, 234–246. DOI: 10.1016/j.ijpe.2014.12.031

Fosso Wamba, S., Gunasekaran, A., Akter, S., Ren, S. J. F., Dubey, R., & Childe, S. J. (2017). Big data analytics and firm performance: Effects of dynamic capabilities. *Journal of Business Research*, 70, 356–365. DOI: 10.1016/j.jbusres.2016.08.009

Galbraith, J. R. (2014). Organization design challenges resulting from big data. *Journal of Organizational Design*, 3(1), 2–13. DOI: 10.7146/jod.8856

Gandomi, A., & Haider, M. (2015). Beyond the Hype: Big Data Concepts, Methods, and Analytics. *International Journal of Information Management*, 35(2), 137–144. DOI: 10.1016/j.ijinfomgt.2014.10.007

Gartner. (2012). What Is Big Data? Ghosh, D. (2015, 14-15 Sept. 2015). *Big Data in Logistics and Supply Chain management - a rethinking step.* Paper presented at the 2015 International Symposium on Advanced Computing and Communication (ISACC).

Govindan, K., Cheng, T., Mishra, N., & Shukla, N. (2018). Big data analytics and application for logistics and supply chain management. *Transportation Research Part E, Logistics and Transportation Review*, 114, 343–349. DOI: 10.1016/j.tre.2018.03.011

Gunasekaran, A., Papadopoulos, T., Dubey, R., Wamba, S. F., Childe, S. J., Hazen, B., & Akter, S. (2017). Big data and predictive analytics for supply chain and organizational performance. Journal of Business Research, 70, 308-317. http://dx.doi .org/. jbusres.2016.08.004.DOI: 10.1016/j

Guo, S. Y., Ding, L. Y., Luo, H. B., & Jiang, X. Y. (2016). A Big-Data-based platform of workers' behavior: Observations from the field. *Accident; Analysis and Prevention*, 93, 299–309. DOI: 10.1016/j.aap.2015.09.024 PMID: 26614050

Hahn, G. J., & Packowski, J. (2015). A perspective on applications of in-memory analytics in supply chainmanagement. *Decision Support Systems*, 76, 45–52. DOI: 10.1016/j.dss.2015.01.003

Hassan, A. O., Ewuga, S. K., Abdul, A. A., Abrahams, T. O., Oladeinde, M., & Dawodu, S. O. (2024). Cybersecurity In Banking: A Global Perspective With A Focus On Nigerian Practices. *Computer Science & IT Research Journal*, 5(1), 41–59. DOI: 10.51594/csitrj.v5i1.701

Hazen, B. T., Boone, C. A., Ezell, J. D., & Jones-Farmer, L. A. (2014). Data quality for data science, predictive analytics, and big data in supply chain management: An introduction to the problem and suggestions for research and applications. *International Journal of Production Economics*, 154, 72–80. DOI: 10.1016/j.ijpe.2014.04.018

He, W., Wu, H., Yan, G., Akula, V., & Shen, J. (2015). A novel social media competitive analytics framework with sentiment benchmarks. *Information & Management*, 52(7), 801–812. DOI: 10.1016/j.im.2015.04.006

Heller, F. (2017) "Technological innovation applied to walmart and tesco's supply chain," Doctoral dissertation, Lisboa, Portugal.

Hofmann, E., & Rutschmann, E. (2018). Big data analytics and demand forecasting in supply chains: A conceptual analysis. *International Journal of Logistics Management*, 29(2), 739–766. DOI: 10.1108/IJLM-04-2017-0088

Hopkins, J., & Hawking, P. (2018). Big data analytics and IoT in logistics: A case study. *International Journal of Logistics Management*, 29(2), 575–591. DOI: 10.1108/IJLM-05-2017-0109

Huang, Y. Y., & Handfield, R. B. (2015). Measuring the benefits of erp on supply management maturity model: A "big data" method. *International Journal of Operations & Production Management*, 35(1), 2–25. DOI: 10.1108/IJOPM-07-2013-0341

Iheukwumere, O. C., Eze, U. F., Otuonye, A. I., & Ikerionwu, C. O. (2024). Big Data Analytics in Supply Chain Management: Applications and Challenges. *International Journal of Novel Research in Computer Science and Software Engineering*, 11(1), 3–6.

Ikegwu, A. C., Nweke, H. F., Arukwe, C. V., Alo, U. R., & Okonkwo, O. R. (2022). Big data for data-driven industry: A review of data sources, tools, challenges, solutions, and research directions. *Cluster Computing*, 25(5), 3343–3387. DOI: 10.1007/s10586-022-03568-5

M. Jeseke, M. Grüner, F. Wieß (2013) "BIG DATA IN LOGISTICS: A DHL perspective on how to move beyond the hype", DHL Customer Solutions & Innovation, 12.

Jun S-P, Park D-H, Yeom J. (2014) The possibility of using search traffic information to explore consumer product attitudes and forecast consumer preference. Technol Forecast Soc Chang. 86:237–53. ORE.2013.10.021.DOI: <ALIGNMENT.qj></ALIGNMENT>10.1016/J.TECHF

Kaisler, S., ... (2013) Big data: issues and challenges moving forward. In: 2013 46th Hawaii International Conference on System Sciences (HICSS), Wailea, Maui, HI, 7–10 January, pp. 995–1004. IEEE. DOI: 10.1109/HICSS.2013.645

Kato, T., & Kamoshida, R. (2020). Multi-Agent Simulation Environment for Logistics Warehouse Design Based on Self-Contained Agents. *Applied Sciences (Basel, Switzerland)*, 10(21), 7552. DOI: 10.3390/app10217552

Kayikci, Y. and Subramanian, N. (2022). Blockchain interoperability issues in supply chain: exploration of mass adoption procedures., 309-328. DOI: 10.1007/978-3-030-87304-2_13

Kiron, D., Prentice, P. K., & Ferguson, R. B. (2014). The analytics mandate. *MIT Sloan Management Review*, 55(4), 1–25.

Koot, M., Mes, M. R. K., & Iacob, M. E. (2021). A systematic literature review of supply chain decision making supported by the Internet of Things and Big Data Analytics. *Computers & Industrial Engineering*, 154, 107076. DOI: 10.1016/j.cie.2020.107076

Krumeich, J., Werth, D., & Loos, P. (2016). Prescriptive Control of Business Processes. *Business & Information Systems Engineering*, 58(4), 261–280. DOI: 10.1007/s12599-015-0412-2

Kumar, M. (2016). *Applied big data analytics in operations management*. Appl Big Data Anal Oper Manage., DOI: 10.4018/978-1-5225-0886-1

Lai, Y., Sun, H., & Ren, J. (2018). Understanding the determinants of big data analytics (BDA) adoption in logistics and supply chain management: An empirical investigation. *International Journal of Logistics Management*, 29(2), 676–703. DOI: 10.1108/IJLM-06-2017-0153

Lamba, K., & Singh, S. P. (2017). Big data in operations and supply chain management: Current trends and future perspectives. *Production Planning and Control*, 28(11-12), 877–890. DOI: 10.1080/09537287.2017.1336787

Laney, D. (2001). *3 D Data Management: Controlling Data Volume*. Velocity and Variety.

Lau, R. Y. K., Zhang, W., & Xu, W. (2017). Parallel Aspect-Oriented Sentiment Analysis for Sales Forecasting with Big Data. *Production and Operations Management*, 27(10), 1–20.

Lee, I., & Mangalaraj, G. (2022). Big data analytics in supply chain management: A systematic Literature Review and Research directions. Big Data Cognitive. *Computing*, 6(17).

Lei, Y., Qiaoming, H., & Zhao, T. (2023). Research on supply chain financial risk prevention based on machine learning. *Computational Intelligence and Neuroscience*, 2023(1), 1–15. DOI: 10.1155/2023/6531154 PMID: 36923907

Liu, P., & Yi, S. (2016). Investment decision-making and coordination of supply chain: A new research in the big data era. *Discrete Dynamics in Nature and Society*, 2016, 1–10. DOI: 10.1155/2016/2026715

Liu, Z., Wang, Y., Cai, L., Cheng, Q., & Zhang, H. (2016). Design and Manufacturing Model of Customized Hydrostatic Bearing System Based on Cloud and Big Data Technology. *International Journal of Advanced Manufacturing Technology*, 84(1–4), 261–273. DOI: 10.1007/s00170-015-8066-2

Lukong, V. T., Ukoba, K., Yoro, K. O., & Jen, T. C. (2022). Annealing temperature variation and its influence on the self-cleaning properties of TiO2 thin films. *Heliyon*, 8(5), e09460. DOI: 10.1016/j.heliyon.2022.e09460 PMID: 35647349

Luo, S., Min, X., & Zhao, J. (2022). Construction of artificial intelligence application model for supply chain financial risk assessment. *Scientific Programming*, 2022, 1–8. DOI: 10.1155/2022/4194576

Manyika, J., Chui, M., Brown, B., Bughin, J., Dobbs, R., Roxburgh, C., & Byers, A. H. (2011). "Big Data: The Next Frontier for Innovation, Competition, and Productivity." Accessed on January 2, 2019. Available at https://www.mckinsey.com/insights/business_technology/ big_data_the_next_frontier_for_innovation.

Marine-Roig, E., & Anton Clavé, S. (2015). Tourism analytics with massive user-generated content: A case study of Barcelona. *Journal of Destination Marketing & Management*, 4(3), 162–172. DOI: 10.1016/j.jdmm.2015.06.004

McAfee, A. (2011, November). What Every CEO Needs to Know About the Cloud. *Harvard Business Review*, 124–132.

Mehmood, R., & Graham, G. (2015). Big data logistics: A health-care transport capacity sharing model. *Procedia Computer Science*, 64, 1107–1114. DOI: 10.1016/j.procs.2015.08.566

Mejri, I., Bouzid, A., Bacha, S., & Layed, S. B. (2021) Forecasting demand using ARIMA model and LSTM neural network: a case of detergent manufacturing industry. International Conference on Innovation and Intelligence for Informatics, Computing, and Technologies (3ICT), 346-353. DOI: 10.1109/3ICT53449.2021.9581762

Minelli, M., Chambers, M., & Dhiraj, A. (2013). *Big Data*. Big Analytics, Big Data, Big Analytics.

Miroslav M, Miloš M, Velimir Š, Božo D, Đorđe L. (2014) Semantic technologies on the mission: preventing corruption in public procurement. Comput Ind. 65(5):878–90. ND.2014.02.003.DOI: <ALIGNMENT.qj></ALIGNMENT>10.1016/J.COMPI

Munir, K. (2019). *Cloud computing and big data: technologies, applications and security* (Vol. 49). Springer.

Naved, M. (2022). A review of the use of machine learning and artificial intelligence in various sectors. *Multimedia Research*, 5(4), 26–31. DOI: 10.46253/j.mr.v5i4.a3

Nguyen, T., Zhou, L., Spiegler, V., Ieromonachou, P., & Lin, Y. (2017). Big data analytics in supply chain management: A state-of-the-art literature review. *Computers & Operations Research*. Advance online publication. DOI: 10.1016/j.cor.2017.07.004

Oncioiu, I., Bunget, O., Turkes, M., Capusneanu, S., Topor, D., Tama , A., Rako , I.-S., & Hint, M. (2019). The impact of big data analytics on company performance in supply chain management. *Sustainability (Basel)*, 11(18), 4864. DOI: 10.3390/su11184864

Optimization, G. "The Power of Analytics," accessed September 8, 2019. http://www.gurobi.com/resources/prescriptive-analytics

Orieno, O. H., Ndubuisi, N. L., Ilojianya, V. I., Biu, P. W., & Odonkor, B. (2024). The Future Of Autonomous Vehicles In The US Urban Landscape: A Review: Analyzing Implications For Traffic, Urban Planning, And The Environment. *Engineering Science & Technology Journal*, 5(1), 43–64. DOI: 10.51594/estj.v5i1.721

Pang, J., Zhang, N., Xiao, Q., Qi, F., & Xue, X. (2021). A New Intelligent and Data-Driven Product Quality Control System of Industrial Valve Manufacturing Process in CPS. *Computer Communications*, 175, 25–34. DOI: 10.1016/j.comcom.2021.04.022

Papadopoulos, T. Gunasekaran, A. Dubey, R. Altay, N. Childe, S. J. and Fosso-Wamba, S. (2017) "The role of Big Data in explaining disaster resilience in supply chains for sustainability," Journal of Cleaner Production, pp. 142, 11081118.

Patrick, W., Anselemo, P., Ronoh, R., & Mbugua, P. (2022). Impact of predictive analytics of big data in supply chain management on decision-making. International Journal of Scientific Research in Computer Science Engineering and Information Technology, 225-238. DOI: 10.32628/CSEIT228423

Pearson, M. (2011b). Predictive Analytics: Looking forward to better supply chain decisions. *Logistics Management*, 50(9), 22.

Rahimi, I., Gandomi, A. H., Fong, S. J., & Ulku, M. A. (2021) *Big Data Analytics in Supply Chain Management: Theory and Applications*. CRS Press: Taylor and Francis Group, London, New York. First edition.

Ren, S., Zhang, Y., Liu, Y., Sakao, T., Huisingh, D., & Almeida, C. M. (2019). A comprehensive review of big data analytics throughout product lifecycle to support sustainable smart manufacturing: A framework, challenges and future research directions. *Journal of Cleaner Production*, 210, 1343–1365. DOI: 10.1016/j.jclepro.2018.11.025

Rialti, R., Marzi, G., Ciappei, C., & Busso, D. (2019). Big data and dynamic capabilities: A bibliometric analysis and systematic literature review. *Management Decision*, 57(8), 2052–2068. DOI: 10.1108/MD-07-2018-0821

Ribeiro, A., Silva, A., & Rodrigues, A. (2015). Data modeling and data analytics : A Survey from a big data perspective. *Journal of Software Engineering and Applications*, 8(December), 617–634. DOI: 10.4236/jsea.2015.812058

Roßmann, B., Canzaniello, A., von der Gracht, H., & Hartmann, E. (2018). The future and social impact of big data analytics in supply chain management: Results from a Delphi study. *Technological Forecasting and Social Change*, 130, 135–149. DOI: 10.1016/j.techfore.2017.10.005

Rostami-Tabar, B., Babai, M. Z., Ali, M., & Boylan, J. E. (2019). The impact of temporal aggregation on supply chains with ARMA(1,1) demand processes. *European Journal of Operational Research*, 273(3), 920–932. DOI: 10.1016/j.ejor.2018.09.010

Rozados, I. V., & Tjahjono, B. (2014). Big data analytics in supply chain management: trends and related research. In: *6th International Conference on Operations and Supply Chain Management*, pp. 2013–2014.

Rußmann, M., Lorenz, M., Gerbert, P., Waldner, M., Justus, J., Engel, P., & Harnisch, M. (2015). *Industry 4.0: The Future of Productivity and Growth in Manufacturing Industries*. Boston Consulting Group.

Saeid, S. D., Iman, R. V. and Farzaneh, M. M. (2020) Big Data Analytics and its Applications in Supply Chain Management. New Trends in the use of Artificial Intelligence for the Industry 4.0.

Sakib, S. (2021). Usage of data analytics in improving sourcing of supply chain inputs. DOI: 10.20944/preprints202110.0103.v1

Sanders, N. R. (2016). How to use big data to drive your supply chain. *California Management Review*, 58(3), 26–48. DOI: 10.1525/cmr.2016.58.3.26

SAS Institute. What is big data. http://www.sas.com/en_us/insights/big-data/what-is-big-data. html

Schoenherr, T., & Speier-Pero, C. (2015). Data science, predictive analytics, and big data in supply chain management: Current state and future potential. *Journal of Business Logistics*, 36(1), 120–132. DOI: 10.1111/jbl.12082

Seyedan, S., & Mafakheri, F. (2020). Predictive big data analytics for supply chain demand forecasting: Methods, applications, and research opportunities. *Journal of Big Data*, 7(1), 53. Advance online publication. DOI: 10.1186/s40537-020-00329-2

Shahzad, A., Zhang, K., & Gherbi, A. (2020). Intuitive development to examine collaborative iot supply chain system underlying privacy and security levels and perspective powering through proactive blockchain. *Sensors (Basel)*, 20(13), 3760. DOI: 10.3390/s20133760 PMID: 32635589

Shan Z, Zhu Q. (2015) Camera location for real-time traffic state estimation in urban road network using big GPS data. Neurocomputing. 169:134–43. https://doi .org/ M.2014.11.093.DOI: 10.1016/J.NEUCO

Siegel, E. (2013). Predictive Analytics: The Power to Predict Who Will Click, Buy, Lie, or Die, Wiley Publishing Smart Service Welt Working Group (2014) "Smart Service Welt: Recommendations for the Strategic Initiative Web-based Services for Businesses", acatech, Berlin.

Souza, G. C. (2014). Supply chain analytics. *Business Horizons*, 57(5), 595–605. DOI: 10.1016/j.bushor.2014.06.004

Srinivasan, R., & Swink, M. (2017). An investigation of visibility and flexibility as complements to supply chain analytics: Organizational information processing theory perspective. *Production and Operations Management*. Advance online publication. DOI: 10.1111/poms.12746

Stank, T. P., Keller, S. B., & Daugherty, P. J. (2001). Supply chain collaboration and logistical service performance. *Journal of Business Logistics*, 22(1), 29–48. DOI: 10.1002/j.2158-1592.2001.tb00158.x

Stefanovic, N., & Milosevic, D. (2017) Model for big data analytics and management. *7th International Conference of Information Society and Technology (ICIST)*, 163-168.

Stein, M., & Voehl, F. (1998). *Macrologistics Management*. St. Lucie Press.

Storey, V. C. and Song, I. Y. (2017) "Big data technologies and management: What conceptual modeling can do," Data & Knowledge Engineering, pp. 108, 50-67.

Sugrue, D., and P. Adriaens. (2021). "A Data Fusion Approach to Predict Shipping Efficiency for Bulk Carriers." Transportation Research Part E: Logistics and Transportation Review 149: 102326. doi:. 2021.102326.DOI: 10.1016/j.tre

Sun, E. W., Chen, Y. T., & Yu, M. T. (2015). Generalized optimal wavelet decomposing algorithm for big financial data. *International Journal of Production Economics*, 2015(165), 194–214. DOI: 10.1016/j.ijpe.2014.12.033

Supply Chain Council (2012). Supply Chain Operations Reference Model. Revision 11.0,. Supply Chain Operations Management.

Talwar, S., Kaur, P., Fosso Wamba, S., & Dhir, A. (2021). Big data in operations and supply chain management: A systematic literature review and future research agenda. *International Journal of Production Research*, 59(11), 3509–3534. DOI: 10.1080/00207543.2020.1868599

Tamilsevi, K., Sumithra, V., & Dhanapriadharsini, K. (2018). Big data analytics using hadoop technology. *IACSIT International Journal of Engineering and Technology*, 5(1), 1507–1511.

Tang, F., Lin, J., Xing, L., Yang, X., He, H., Ma, S., … & Huang, D. (2023). Privacy protection and data coordination mechanism of supply chain based on blockchain.. DOI: 10.1117/12.2685950

Technology, N. J. I. o. (2018). *Why Data is the Next Frontier of Innovation.*

Tiwari, S., Wee, H. M., & Daryanto, Y. (2018). Big data analytics in supply chain management between 2010 and 2016: Insights to industries. *Computers & Industrial Engineering*, 115, 319–330. DOI: 10.1016/j.cie.2017.11.017

Tonidandel, S. King, E. B. and Cortina, J. M. (2018) "Big data methods: Leveraging modern data analytic techniques to build organizational science," Organizational Research Methods, pp. 21(3), 525-547.

Van der Aalst, W. M. (2012). A decade of business process management conferences: personal reflections on a developing discipline. In *Proceedings of the International Conference on Business Process Management* (pp. 1-16). Berlin: Springer. DOI: 10.1007/978-3-642-32885-5_1

Vera-Baquero, A., Colomo Palacios, R., Stantchev, V., & Molloy, O. (2015). Leveraging big-data for business process analytics. *The Learning Organization*, 22(4), 215–228. DOI: 10.1108/TLO-05-2014-0023

Vincent, A. A., Segun, I. B., Loretta, N. N., & Abiola, A. (2021). Entrepreneurship, agricultural value-chain and exports in Nigeria. *United International Journal for Research and Technology*, 2(08), 1–8.

Waller, M. A., & Fawcett, S. E. (2013). Data science, predictive analytics, and big data: A revolution that will transform supply chain design and management. *Journal of Business Logistics*, 34(2), 77–84. DOI: 10.1111/jbl.12010

Wang, G., Gunasekaran, A., Ngai, E. W., & Papadopoulos, T. (2016). Big data analytics in logistics and supply chain management: Wang, G., Gunasekaran, A., Ngai, E.W.T., Papadopoulos, T. (2016). Big data analytics in logistics and supply chain management: certain investigations for research and applications. *International Journal of Production Economics*, 176, 98–110. DOI: 10.1016/j.ijpe.2016.03.014

Wang, L., & Alexander, C. (2015). Big data driven supply chain management and business administration. *American Journal of Economics and Business Administration*, 7(2), 60–67. DOI: 10.3844/ajebasp.2015.60.67

XSNET. (2017). *Updated for 2017: The V's of Big Data: Velocity*. Volume, Value, Variety, and Veracity.

Xu, J., Pero, M. E. P., Ciccullo, F., & Sianesi, A. (2021). On relating big data analytics to supply chain planning: Towards a research agenda. *International Journal of Physical Distribution & Logistics Management*, 51(6), 656–682. DOI: 10.1108/IJPDLM-04-2020-0129

Xu, L., Gao, R., Xie, Y., & Du, P. (2019). To be or not to be? Big data business investment decision making in the supply chain. *Sustainability (Basel)*, 11(8), 2298. DOI: 10.3390/su11082298

Yang, S. (2022). Analysis for supply chain management: Evidence from toyota. *BCP Business & Management*, 34, 1204–1209. DOI: 10.54691/bcpbm.v34i.3160

Yuan, H., Xu, W., Li, Q., & Lau, R. (2018). Topic Sentiment Mining for Sales Performance Prediction in e-Commerce. *Annals of Operations Research*, 270(1–2), 553–576. DOI: 10.1007/s10479-017-2421-7

Zheng, M., & Wu, K. (2017). Smart Spare Parts Management Systems in Semiconductor Manufacturing. *Industrial Management & Data Systems*, 116(2), 322–348. DOI: 10.1108/IMDS-06-2016-0242

Zhong, R. Y., Huang, G. Q., Lan, S., Dai, Q. Y., Chen, X., & Zhang, T. (2015a). A big data approach for logistics trajectory discovery from RFID-enabled production data. *International Journal of Production Economics*, 165, 260–272. DOI: 10.1016/j.ijpe.2015.02.014

Zilker, M., Behler, K., Bluhm, T., Heimann, P., Hennig, C., Kroiss, H., Kühner, G., Laqua, H., Lewerentz, M., Maier, J., Neu, G., Raupp, G., Reich, M., Riemann, H., Schacht, J., Spring, A., Treutterer, W., Werner, A., & Zehetbauer, T. (2010). Development and implementation of real-time data acquisition systems for fusion devices with open source software. *Fusion Engineering and Design*, 85(3-4), 378–382. DOI: 10.1016/j.fusengdes.2010.02.014

KEY TERMS AND DEFINITIONS

Big Data: Big data means a data which is very large for a traditional system to process.

Big Data Analytics: Big data analytics has to do with all the methods, processes, and techniques employed to derive insights from big data.

Data Analytics: Data analytics has to do with the steps, and methods used to get useful information from raw data.

Supply Chain: Supply chain has to do with the procedures involved from the production of goods to when it is delivered to the final consumer.

Supply Chain Optimization: Supply chain optimization has to do with the act of making the activities of the supply chain better, easier and faster.

Logistics: Logistics has to do with the movements of customers' goods from the place of manufacture to the place of consumption.

Manufacturing: This is the process of creating new products.

Chapter 6
Supply Chain Agility: Adapting to Consumer Preferences in the Food Industry

Mayuri Vaibhav Kulkarni
https://orcid.org/0009-0005-9557-3809
Independent Researcher, India

Nitesh Behare
https://orcid.org/0000-0002-9338-8563
Balaji Institute of International Business, Sri Balaji University, Pune, India

Puja Bhardwaj
https://orcid.org/0000-0003-1129-5556
Balaji Institute of International Business, Sri Balaji University, Pune, India

Shrikant Waghulkar
https://orcid.org/0000-0002-3767-3765
Ramachandran International Institute of Management, India

Vivek V. Nemane
https://orcid.org/0000-0002-5123-6676
Symbiosis Law School, Symbiosis International University (Deemed), Pune, India

Devkumar P. Mahisekar
https://orcid.org/0000-0002-2143-5455
Pratibha Institute of Business Management, India

Shubhada Nitesh Behare
Independent Researcher, India

Vinod N. Sayankar
Neville Wadia Institute of Management and Research Center, Pune, India

ABSTRACT

In the food industry, consumer preferences constantly keep on changing and as a business; it is inevitable to have robust supply chain to meet the changing market demands. This dynamic consumer behaviour drives different market trends and

DOI: 10.4018/979-8-3693-4427-9.ch006

demand for expected personalised experiences while using products and services. This chapter will discuss these two important pointers, ever changing landscape of consumer behaviour and role of supply chain agility in dealing with it. Case studies will be used to demonstrate the transformative effect of supply chain agility practices. These practices majorly consist of flexible manufacturing process, real time data analytics and collaborative partnership. Furthermore, need of risk management and resilience is to be considered to put proactive measures in place for seamless supply chain operations. The future trends and challenges will also be covered in this chapter, primarily due to emerging technologies and the changes in regulations shaping the direction of agile supply chains within the food sector

1. INTRODUCTION TO SUPPLY CHAIN AGILITY

Agility in the supply chain is the capability to respond quickly and effectively to the probable changes and disruptions in the supply chain environment. Now a day, with changing businesses dynamics as a result of varying consumer demands, global market shifts, natural disasters and political volatility, agility provides critical competitive advantage. An agile supply chain is flexible, adaptable and responsive. It encompasses simplifying the workflow by elimination or minimization of non-value adding activities, stakeholder collaborations, and the application of technology to increase visibility and decision making. Agility can help mitigate risks, reduce lead times, optimize inventory and improve customer satisfaction.

A robust and agile supply chain should be characterized by effective forecasting and demand planning, a multi-sourcing strategy, efficient transportation and logistics network, as well as embracing a digital revolution using artificial intelligence and blockchain. Through perpetual assessment and modification in the supply chain strategies, firm can survive well any risk and benefits from the opportunities accomplishing long term sustainable growth in the evolving market conditions.

1.1. Definition and Importance

1.1.1. Definition of Supply Chain Agility

According to (Sourabhi, 2023), "*Supply chain agility is a supply chain organization's ability to respond efficiently and avoid making knee-jerk reactions to fluctuations in consumer demand as well as the effects of market vulnerabilities such as geopolitical crises, shortages of labour or raw materials, and acts of nature*".

According (GEP, 2021), "*Supply chain agility refers to a company's ability to quickly adjust its strategy, particularly in procurement, inventory management and delivery to meet rapidly changing supply chain requirements. Companies with a high degree of supply chain agility can navigate change with ease, adapt to changing market conditions and take advantage of new business opportunities*".

(Lopienski, 2023) have defined Supply chain agility as *"how quickly and efficiently an ecommerce supply chain can react to changes in the market and customer demand. It also relates to the ability to anticipate, resist, and bounce back from unexpected, disruptive events*".

(Kilpatrick, Delesalle, & Mussomeli, 2022) have defined supply chain agility as *"the capabilities, key performance metrics, and performance expectations related to agility are not as standardized or well defined as they are for supply chain efficiency. And the focus on agility will vary based on a company's overall strategy and the design of the supply chain to support that strategy"*.

1.1.2. Significance of Supply Chain Agility

Changes in the consumer preferences are being observed in the modern food industry. It is evolving continuously due to factors could be like lifestyles, nutritional trends, or diverse cultures. The supply-chain agility facilitates food companies to respond quickly to the diversity in consumer opinions effectively. Firstly, being agile means food manufacturers and retailers to respond quickly to changes in consumer demand (Haq & Boddu, 2015). Businesses can review their production programs, product catalogues and inventory plans in real time, following agile supply chain practices and taking into account the current market situation (Dallasega, Rojas, Rauch, & Matt, 2017). Thus, they can deal with trends and dynamic consumer behaviour avoiding situations of stock-outs or an excess supply. Secondly, supply chain agility promotes rapid product development as well as customized needs of the consumer. Food companies with agile operating processes can introduce a new product swiftly in the market or remodel an existing one to follow the trendy consumer regimen such as plant-based alternatives, dietary restrictions or popular flavours (Thomas, Maître, & Symoneaux, 2021).

On the other hand, seasonal and regional fluctuations in consumer demands can be easily adapted maintaining the agile supply chain. Food companies can adapt to demand variations at different time and region modifying strategies for sourcing, production and shipping methods (Mardenli, Sackmann, & Rhein, 2023). It ensures the consistent supply for sales to enhance the revenue with proper inventory management and least wastage. Additionally, agile supply chain practices build up partnership and communication among the stakeholders including suppliers, manufacturers, distributors and retailers. Through strong ties and differential insights based on real time information, companies can predict changes in consumer demand more precisely and effectively coordinate the activities (Mishra, Pande Sharma, & Chaudhary, 2024). This cooperative strategy leads to faster decision making and issues resolution to quickly match the changing consumer preferences.

1.2. Factors contributing to agility

Significance of agile supply chain is its responsiveness to overcome business disruptions as well as flexible to the changing business environments. The realization of supply chain agility is based on different critical elements. First, Planning is the central part of the activity and involves strategic forecasting, risk anticipation, and contingency planning.

Network orientation brings suppliers, manufacturers and distributors into the decision-making process and collaboration to make quick decisions during a disruption. Flexible supply chain can quickly adjust to changes in demand without much compromise on efficiency. The seamless integration of processes associates different supply chain functions with each other, reducing the completion time for each function and hence increasing agility. Information integration provides real-time visibility and insights to empower decision-making (Anupam, 2015). The factors of supply chain agility in the food industry are relational competencies, sustainability, and service-oriented attributes. The dynamic consumer preferences can only be handled by proper planning and network orientation (Mandal, 2015). Critical factors taxonomies are useful for prioritizing strategies to enhance agility. The other industry sectors like pharmaceuticals employs taxonomies related to flexibility and responsiveness The agri-food sector examines the concepts of the Triple-A Supply Chain (Kontopanou & Tsoulfas, 2022) and the New AAA Supply Chain, taking into account the nature of the product and its sustainability (M., G.T., & N.P., 2021). Overall, a comprehensive approach of combination of planning and network collaboration, flexibility, process integration, and information sharing ensures supply chain agility that supports the competitiveness and sustainability of business growth in the dynamic market.

2. UNDERSTANDING CONSUMER PREFERENCES

Consumer preferences are the driving force behind product development, marketing decisions, as well as supply chain operations in the food industry. Many factors ranging from health consciousness, sustainability objective, convenience needs and cultural distinction determines the consistently changing preferences. Supply chain agility must be priorities to respond to the diverse and complex consumer preferences by the food companies. Popularity for healthy foods like organic, natural and minimally processed options. Moreover, sustainability is also becoming a top priority as consumers prefer food in environmental friendly packaging with sourcing the ingredients in an ethical ways and targeting to minimize the food waste.

Convenience is another major factor that defines consumer choices resulted in the popularity of on-the-go snacks, pre-cooked meals, and meal kits. Cultural diversity also contributes to the diversified choices of taste and ingredient and food companies need to have agility in their supply chains to fulfil the demand of varying preferences. Companies in the food sector that adopt agile supply chain, outperform consumer trends, develop innovative products and stay competitive in the food business (León-Bravo, Moretto, Cagliano, & Caniato, 2019).

2.1. Market Research and Analysis Techniques

Techniques of market research and analysis are imperative in understanding the consumer needs and optimization of the product offerings in the food industry. This research study identified that food values like safety, taste, health, price and environmental concerns differs across demographic groups in three Asian countries. This is where food businesses can offer modified products to cater to the specific desires of various consumer groups. Moreover, consumers are considering the things like local production, environmental sustainability, and product quality. Consumer decisions while choosing products are affected by this trend. It means that food industry players can bring sustainable alternatives in the market that are in line with these values. Market research techniques can be used to devise strategies based on prevailing trends to be more competitive to address the consumer demands in a better way. Marketing research gives thorough understanding of consumer behaviour as well as provides inputs on strategic decision-making so that businesses will remain flexible to the changes in the market (Untari & Satria, 2021).

2.2. Trends Shaping Consumer Choices in Food

Businesses of the food industry need more agility in the supply chain to acutely handle the changing market dynamics and variable consumer expectations. The process of selecting suppliers and evaluating factors that enable the development of supply chain agility can be performed more actively using methodologies like the fuzzy multi-criteria decision-making process and interpretive structural modelling. These methods enable businesses to discover effective and optimal ways for selecting suppliers and make the supply chain process more flexible and responsive. The Analytic Hierarchy Process (AHP) further emerges as an instrumental tool for evaluating stakeholder willingness to support initiatives such as local procurement and shortening the supply chain (Menéndez Molist, Kallas, & Guadarrama Fuentes, 2024). Giving the proper priority to stakeholder preferences and the potential benefit of such strategies will enable a business to make informed decisions toward becoming more agile and better in line with consumer requirements.

The methodologies are evolving in analysis, thus efficiency in the tuning of the supply chain strategy in the food industry. Integration of such methodologies into operations empower businesses to be able to deal with challenge proactively, benefit from opportunities and therefore retain the leading place in a very dynamic market environment. It will thus agility in the supply chain supported by analysis techniques will be very important in meeting the consumer expectations and in turn, the sustainable growth of the food sector.

3. THE IMPACT OF CONSUMER PREFERENCES ON SUPPLY CHAINS

3.1. Case Studies Highlighting Changes in Demand

The consumer preference is factor that has impact on supply chain because it is deciding factor about demanding products and selecting sourcing and distribution strategies. The following case studies demonstrate the relation between consumer preference and supply chain dynamics transformation.

3.1.1. Case Study 1: Beyond Meat

Beyond Meat, the company that offering alternatives of plant-based meat saw an impressive increase in sales catalysed mainly due to popularity of veganism and awareness about the sustainability of food production. Eventually, shift in consumer demand towards healthy and sustainable food resulted into the market for Beyond

Meat food started growing rapidly and consumers started buying the plant-based burgers, sausages and ground meat alternatives offered by the Beyond Meat company (Barpagga, 2023).

However, sudden increase in demand for Beyond Meat food is putting tremendous pressure on food supply chain to secure sourcing of the sufficient amount of plant-based ingredients like pea protein on priority. Furthermore, implemented strategies also need to be reworked to manage production capacities and distribution cycle in stores and restaurants ensuring consistent availability of products.

To overcome these challenges, Beyond Meat companies grow their supplier network to streamline the supply of key ingredients. They formulate their recipes for mass production without altering the taste and quality of the food that consumer demands through investing in research and development. Additionally, they optimize their distribution channels collaborating with distributors and retailers facilitating efficient and timely delivery to meet the consumer requirements. Overall, this case of Beyond Meat demonstrates how shift in the consumer preference towards plan-based food require supply chain to be agile enough for continuous growth and cater to increasing demand for environment friendly protein substitute (Retailer, 2023).

3.1.2. Case Study: Coca-Cola

Coca-Cola, a dominant player in global market of beverage industry, selling sugar rich carbonated drink experienced the downswing in demand for their drink due to increase in awareness about the related health concerns among consumers and preference to the healthier alternatives (Batra, 2023). To retain the market with changing trend, Coco-Cola quickly update their product portfolio adding variety of healthier beverages such as sparkling water, flavour water and low-calorie drinks.

This strategic move to diversify product portfolio, the supply chain of Coca-cola had to undergo through considerable reshaping for sourcing new ingredients for healthier version of beverages, rearrange the product lines for verities of products manufacturing and develop distribution network for consistent supply to the market.

Coca-Cola handled these challenges by improving the agility and efficiency of its supply chain operations. To achieve the objectives Coca-Cola invested in technology and innovations. Use of data analysis and predictive modelling helped to get better control of inventory management and distribution to ensure availability of right products at right places and at right time (HBC, 2023), (Pereira & Shafique, 2023).

Coca-Cola optimized its supply chain adjusting to the changing consumer preferences and successfully managed to minimise the impact of declining demand for sugary beverages by wide -ranging product portfolio. Thus, remain competitive in the growing and dynamic beverage market condition (Pereira & Shafique, 2023).

3.1.3. Case Study: Amazon

Amazon, an e-commerce giant that has set a trend of online shopping for groceries experienced sudden spike in the number of consumers who prefer shopping for food virtually particularly during the Covid-19 pandemic as consumers sought convenience, safety and accessibility. Amazon's grocery supply chain encountered numerous challenges of meeting unmatched demand (Jollivet, 2020).

To overcome these challenges, Amazon speedily setup expanding network of fulfilment centres, find out the more effective delivery routes and improved inventory management systems to ensure timely delivery of groceries to the consumers without straining operations. Furthermore, Amazon made considerable investment to improve efficiency and agility of its grocery supply chain using innovative technologies and automation (Knight, 2015).

As a result of revamping of supply chain by means of technology and innovation, Amazon, managed to respond to changing needs and preferences of consumers and emerged as a leader in online grocery market. This case of Amazon highlighted the importance of supply chain agility to meet varying consumer preferences and ensure long term growth path in the competitive e-commerce segment (Vempati, Crapanzano, Woodyard, & Trunkhill, 2017).

3.2. Challenges Faced by Traditional Supply Chains

Traditional supply chains in food industry have its own limitations which prohibit modification to supply chain agility while responding to changing consumer preferences. First, stakeholders that are in real pressure of food globalization and intensified demand by consumers for foods recognized to be safe and of high quality are agri-food supply chain stakeholders (Webb, 2015). The need to meet the multifaceted expectations of consumers complying with the highly complex international trade regulations put on the layers of complexities. In addition, the perishable nature of food products amplifies supply chain vulnerability and complexity (Mann, Kumar, Kumar, & Mann, 2016). The food supply chain is inherently much more vulnerable than many others industries to disruptions such as transportation delay, temperature fluctuation, risk of contamination etc. Hence, very detailed planning and coordination are required to mitigate these risks.

The COVID-19 pandemic stress the necessity of agility in the supply chain agility raising more new challenges. The fast-changing market conditions and disruptions caused to fresh produce export supply chains have brought to light the need for resilient and flexible operations in a supply chain (Yawson & Yamoah, 2022). The pandemic has also revealed the need for proactive efforts to freeze the critical flaws in the US food supply chain by increasing its resilience and adaptability. The traditional food supply chains must have to address these challenges to make supply chain agile and to continue to stay in line with customer preferences in a rapidly changing market environment (Sodhi, Tang, & Willenson, 2023).

4. STRATEGIES FOR AGILE SUPPLY CHAINS

In the food industry, agile supply chain strategies are crucial to switch in time to conform to customer preference and market demand. These strategies ensure high quality products and services, focusing on flexibility, responsiveness and efficiency. In this chapter, we explore critical agile supply chain strategies.

4.1. Flexible Manufacturing and Production Processes:

Flexible manufacturing and production processes allow food companies to respond promptly to changes in demand patterns by quickly altering production volumes, product variations, and manufacturing schedules (Vachter & Bányai, 2022). The companies can make use of automation and robotics to achieve production line flexibility, hence making it easier to switch from one line to the other with minimal time spent in changeover. The agile manufacturing processes ensures that the food company can produce the right products in the right quantities as per the consumer preference levels with minimal waste and best use of resources (C. & V.S., 2016), (Venugopal & Saleeshya, 2019).

4.2. Just-in-Time Inventory Management:

Just-in-Time (JIT) inventory management is a system of maintaining only the minimum inventory levels to reduce the maintaining costs and achieve more responsiveness towards the consumer demands. JIT in the food industry reduces the amount of food wastage for the producer. It assures the consumer to get the freshest perishable product available on the same day as it is produced. Effective demand forecasting combined with data analytics can be a real boost for food companies to optimize their inventory levels, facilitate more agile procurement processes and enhance visibility across the supply chain to ensure that in such a dynamic environment of continually shifting demand, they can respond effectively (Nassibi, Fasihuddin, & Hsairi, 2022). Implementing JIT inventory management food companies can have a flexible supply chain through real-time visibility of the stock level versus consumer market demand and preference.

4.3. Responsive Distribution Networks:

Responsive distribution networks are instrumental for food companies to ensure fast and efficient delivery of their products across all geographical locations and distribution channels. With the help of technologies such as real-time tracking and route optimization software, food companies can adjust transportation routes for faster products delivery time and minimize the transportation cost (Devadharshini, Praniis, Nishanth, & Jayapal, 2023). Additionally, using third-party logistics providers and following Omni-channel distribution strategies, food companies get an access to consumers at multiple interfaces, such as online, retail, or foodservice outlets to for timely fulfilment of consumer need. Thus, this kind of prompt responsiveness of the food companies addressing the consumer ensures high level of customer satisfaction.

5. TECHNOLOGY ENABLERS FOR SUPPLY CHAIN AGILITY

Technology plays an important role in supply chain agility, especially in the food industry, where quick response to rapidly changing consumer preferences is predominant. Here, we discuss three main technology enablers of supply chain agility.

5.1. Data Analytics and Predictive Modelling

Data analytics and predictive modelling techniques are important for food companies to facilitating them with insights to act upon in real-time and make conversant decisions based on knowledge obtained. These technologies reveal trends and patterns allowing firms to predict the future change in consumer preferences, demand dynamics, and market conditions through extensive datasets inspections. Moreover, employing historical sales data, market intelligence and external varying factors such as weather cycles, predictive models gives more accurate predictions of future demand which helps in supply chain agility (Borucka, 2023). For example, food companies can leverage data analytics to foresee seasonal changes in consumer preferences and respond by managing production schedules and inventory levels accordingly. Furthermore, predictive models can also help organizations to make their procurement processes more efficient so that probable disruptions in supply chain can be ascertained and addressed proactively.

Data analytics and predictive modelling are significant in supply chain management because it can be used to predict first-tier supply chain disruption from historical data analysis. It reveals practical use of these technologies to assess the effectiveness in predicting supply chain disruptions improving supply chain agility. Through careful feature selection and engineering, data analysis helps to determine key predictors of disruption and allow preventive measures to mitigate risks and execute flawless operations.

5.2. IoT (Internet of Things) Applications

The Internet of Things (IoT)provides real-time insights into assets tracking, processes, and inventory transforming the supply chain operations. Sensors, RFID tags, and GPS trackers on IoT devices collect data on different parameters like temperature, humidity and location providing unprecedented clarity across the supply chain. Implementing IoT, food companies with the help of real-time data can quickly detect problems respond with corrective steps strengthening their supply chain agility (Taranya, Rama Devi, & Kavita, 2023). For example, while transporting perishable food, IoT enabled temperature sensors monitor and alert cold chain ensuring adherence to safety standards. If variations beyond permissible limit are detected, the alarm alerts for timely corrective actions immediately to prevent the decaying and preserve the product quality.

The IOT devices collect the relevant real-time environmental data and improve efficiency of supply chain management to a great extent. This increases visibility, traceability, risk management and collaboration to effectively handle the supply chain complexity. Thus, these systems perform better tracking, communication and inventory control at all levels within throughout the supply chain.

IoT is considered as a strategic technology enabler make the operation of the entire supply chain more efficient by collecting updated information about the environment for quick and fact-based decision making. Underscoring the role of IoT in managing demand volatility, cost fluctuations and driving operational excellence, several researches shows how IoT can drastically change the dynamics of supply chain. By leveraging IoT, food companies can optimize the processes within the supply chain, thereby lowering risks and enabling quick respond to the dynamic market demands (Pal & Kant, 2018).

5.3. AI (Artificial Intelligence) and Machine Learning in Demand Forecasting

Demand forecasting has profoundly redefined by artificial intelligence and machine learning algorithms that analyse historical data, market trends and external elements to accurately forecast future demand. These technologies identify complex patterns and relationships and predict more accurate results than traditional forecasting techniques for demand forecasting. In the food industry, keeping the optimal amount of inventory and minimizing understock and overstock situations is critical, accurate demand forecasting plays an important role. Artificial intelligence models consider seasonality, promotions and consumer behaviour variables, allowing companies to tune production, procurement and distribution strategies more effectively. For example, AI-based algorithms for social media and online feedback track growing trends, allowing companies to launch new products matching with the trends and improve the supply chain agility.

Furthermore, AI has implications on other supply chain parameters such as cost, quality and sustainability. Using AI technology in demand forecasting, makes supply chain more agile and perform efficiently putting more focus on IT-supply chain integration (Taseen, Wangyongli, & Ali, 2023). Furthermore, AI capability of excellent levels of accuracy in demand forecasting surpasses its effects other industries other sectors dealing with energy and water apart from the food industry. AI and IoT together termed as AIoT, perform intelligent tasks without human intervention reforming the supply chain management.

6. COLLABORATION AND PARTNERSHIPS IN AGILE SUPPLY CHAINS

In food industry, supply chain agility has an important role to quickly respond to the consumer demand. Core tenets of the agile supply chains are collaboration and partnership. The following three sections then examine in more detail three of the critical aspects of collaboration and partnerships:

6.1. Supplier Relationship Management

Employing an effective supplier relationship management (SRM) practice is one of the fundamental factors to get success in the food industry. It helps in sourcing good-quality food ingredients and ensuring food safety. To develop strong partnership with suppliers, organizations need to work towards improving their procurement processes, risk management and supply chain agility. Adopting Transparent and mutually beneficial relationships with suppliers, companies can gain more visibility across the supply chain, settle on constructive terms and react with agility to changes in demand or market conditions (Burkhart & Bode, 2022) (Kauppila, Valikangas, & Majava, 2020).

Supplier relationship management is more than just transaction relations; it involves collaboration, communication and trust-building to build long-term relations. This could be invaluable to a food company. Trusted partnerships between food company and suppliers assures quality, secure competitive pricing and get timely information regarding market trends and supply chain disruptions. Moreover, clear communication and information sharing facilitates proactive problem solving and improve relation between suppliers and food companies continuously.

Collaboration in supply chains is a new business management paradigm highlighting relationship-based tactics and strategic trust. Adopting collaborative approach beyond individual company across the entire supply chain enables companies to leverage existing strength and resources. It takes importance of working together as a one unit to get the best out of stakeholders have to offer to overcome challenges collectively and achieve common goals.

The supply chain collaboration improves performance of all stakeholders within the chain: companies work more productively, reducing costs and enabling them to respond optimally to changing market dynamics (Smith, 2016). For example, Collaborative Planning, Forecasting and Replenishment (CPFR), by definition, helps match the production and inventory levels correctly with consumer requirements so that the possibility of stock outs and excess inventory is reduced accordingly. In today's highly competitive global markets where consumer preferences have developed the habit of changing at a notice. Collaboration in the supply chain has become necessity to maintain an edge. Companies that are adopting collaboration are capable to adapt to changes in the market, be more innovative and deliver excellent value to their customers.

Moreover, supply chain collaboration moves from traditional open market relationships to more cooperative and coordinated efforts. Key dimensions of collaboration are shared goals, mutual understanding and common incentives that are steering this move. Companies are becoming aware about how close relationships with stakeholders are important to achieve greater success and supply chain operations efficiency (Novijanti, Siagian, & Tarigan, 2023).

6.2. Collaborative Planning, Forecasting, and Replenishment (CPFR)

The process of Collaboration on Planning, Forecasting and Replenishment (CPFR) is one important technique in supply chain management. It helps in the rationalization of inventory enabling collaboration between trading partners towards achieving higher accuracy in demand forecasting. This becomes more applicable for the food industry where demand is typically volatile and shows seasonal patterns. CPFR makes easier to achieve matching of the production and inventory levels with customer demand. In this process, the retailer exchanges the sales data, marketplace intelligence and promotional plans with supplier to let them act in advance for rescheduling production and replenishing inventory. CPFR allows companies to optimize their supply chain operations, reduce stock outs, cut down excess inventory and hence improve response to market fluctuations.

There are many advantages of Collaborative Planning, Forecasting and Replenishment (CPFR) for a supply chain but it also has several challenges and remedies:

Benefits of CPFR:

Improved Forecasting Accuracy and Efficiency: CPFR harmonizes trading partners' activities and through information exchange and shared decision-making, improves both the accuracy and efficiency of forecasting. This ensures a better connection of production and inventory levels to consumer demand, hence less stock outs and excess stock (Zhang & Yuan, 2014).

Enhanced Supply Chain Efficiency: CPFR results into increase in profitability of an organization improving supply chain efficiency through seamless operations and lowering inventory holding. It ensures competitiveness of the companies involved in the supply chain.

Sustainable Production and Consumption: CPFR encourages sustainable production and consumption within the food industry in consistent with some circular economy principles. A company implementing CPFR supports environmental sustainability and corporate social responsibility since it reduces waste and optimizes resource use.

Challenges of CPFR:

Logistics Drawbacks: Drawbacks of logistics limit the performance of short food supply chains (SFSC) and the possible benefits. Current researches are dominated by descriptive studies which offer limited solutions to overcome these problems.

Potential Remedy: SFSCs with technology tools such as route optimization software or through integrated transportation networks can deal with the logistics challenges. Moreover, the use of logistics partners could facilitate the effective transportation and thus the entire supply chain would perform efficiently.

Consumer preferences and pricing: Consumer preferences and pricing in the food supply chain predominantly influences efforts for green innovation. Companies find it difficult to re-orient themselves with changing consumer preferences and with the efforts in competitiveness through pricing strategies in CPFR (He, Lei, & Fu, 2019).

Possible Remedy: To overcome this challenge companies can make use of market research and consumer insights techniques to predict the evolving trends and align their product offerings with the changing business environment. The pricing strategies should be quick and flexible enough to respond to the changing market demands timely. Regular pricing review ensures competitiveness.

Complexity and Organizational Change: The embracement of CPFR practices involves massive organizational change and collaboration across trading partners. Complexity and organizational resistance to change can significantly deter successful embracement of CPFR practices.

Possible Remedy: Companies can setup favourable environment to accept the changes promoting culture of teamwork and communication in the organization. Conducting trainings and change management program communicating benefits and the transition process of CPFR will make employees comfortable with CPFR practices. On another side, clearly defined roles and responsibility for trading partners to perform and establishing effective communication channels for them boost efforts to achieve the set goals and objectives.

6.3. Co-Creation with Suppliers and Retailers

Collaboration and partnerships are some of the factors that make food supply chain agile enabling to respond to changes required by consumer liking and market trends. Co-creation by suppliers and retailers in innovative cooperation drives product and packaging development and marketing strategies for evolving consumer demand. These joint efforts encourage creativity and agility that can be leveraged to align products quickly (Garrigós & Molina, 2020). For example, sourcing sustainable ingredients from suppliers to develop environment friendly products or portray special packaging solutions to attract environment-oriented customers. Additionally, jointly designing and executing a promotional campaign with retailers or working on unique product line to improve brand visibility and thus drive more sales. By tapping into the expertise and resources of their partners, companies can quickly develop products, successfully differentiate brands and also improve customer satisfaction.

Supplier Relationship Management, CPFR and joint creation enhance the agility, responsiveness and modernity of the food industry supply chain. Joint creation improves the visibility of the supply chain by organizing project planning, forecasting and replenishment rates to help in improving the performance of the supply chain. The transition from open market relationships to cooperative partnerships is a must in agile supply chains. Supplier Relationship Management facilitates agility while CPFR brings about financial performance benefits despite the obstacles in collaborative gain sharing. Supplier and retailer co-creation facilitates innovation and competitiveness by integrating the management of value chains and knowledge development with innovation processes (Bettiga & Ciccullo, 2019).

For instance, setting up innovation hub wherein following co-innovation strategies, retailers co-innovate with customers and suppliers breaking innovation barriers and improve competitiveness. An agile supply chain strategy mediates the strategy to the performance together with strategic partnerships with suppliers and customer relationships, thus enhancing the overall supply chain performance.

7. RISK MANAGEMENT AND RESILIENCE

Supply chain agility supports companies not only in the continued adjustment to changes in the market but also to mitigate risks within the relatively changing food industry landscape. Risk management and resilience are also equally key factors toward supply chain agility to help companies steer any disruptions and market volatility. This section brings out the major strategies of risk management and resilience with reference to supply chain agility in the food industry.

7.1. Mitigating Supply Chain Disruptions

In addition to natural disasters, geopolitical consequences and supplier problems, the COVID-19 pandemic has turned the most robust supply chain shaky. The pandemic has acted as an unveiling of the long-standing shortcomings in global supply chains which had subjected the food sector to exceptional experiences (Aday & Aday, 2020). Disruption of the supply chain resulted from lockdowns, travel restriction and labour shortages adversely affected production, distribution and transportation networks hence market experienced food shortage and prices fluctuations. Food businesses applied various approaches in trying to minimize such disruptions. The need of the hour is diversifying sources of suppliers to reduce the overreliance on a single supplier and minimize the risks of localized disruptions creating the risk of shortages. Building alternative logistics routes and distribution channels has proved advantageous for companies to be prepared for transport disruptions and border closures during the pandemic.

Technology solutions have improved resilience management ability in a supply chain. Real-time monitoring systems with sensors and analytics capabilities provide visibility in operations that raises an early warning on any kind of disruption (Al-Banna, et al., 2022). Predictive analysis algorithms crunch data from sources such as weather predictions, market trends and social media and prepare for proactive decisions at the time of predictable disruptions. Moreover, COVID-19 pandemic has pointed out the need for such agility and adaptability in supply chain management is more paramount. Adoption of agile manufacturing practices like modular production setups and flexible workforce arrangements help companies in responding to changes in demand and production capacity. Also alliances and partnerships with local suppliers and distributors empower companies to withstand global disruptions and ensure the continuance of supplies. Another area that has gained a much attention post-pandemic is contingency planning. To ensure business continuity, companies have developed concrete plans considering variety of disruption levels (Romig, 2021). These plans are regularly reviewed and updated by cross-functional teams with simulated exercises used to test effectiveness and identify areas that need enhancement.

7.2. Building Resilience Against Market Volatility

Food companies face uncontrollable challenges due to high market volatility impacting demand patterns, pricing dynamics and supply chain operations. Embracing agile and responsive strategies build resilience against market uncertainty that react to market dynamics effectively. For example, putting demand-based production models in action adjust the levels of production on real-time demand signals, hence reducing the risk of overproduction or stock outs for companies. Additionally, developing cooperative environment by encouraging strong relationships with customers and suppliers, companies can better respond to market fluctuations.

Resilience frameworks have been put forward to assist in the formation of a strong supply chain. These frameworks purposefully mention the importance of business continuity management and organizational resilience in supply chain resilience (Parast, 2022). A thorough approach in building resilience into supply chains via risk management has also been recommended which is adjustable to various applications within the supply chain. Moreover, the measuring of resilience considers risks and associate resilience with the capacity to predict the risks to recover, to be agile and to be time tolerant. This lays a foundation for checking the strategy of risk mitigation.

The ability of organizations to build market volatility resilience will be appreciated once it fully understands the benefits that are associated with resilience not only after a disaster but also in normal operations. This basically involves identifying and controlling factors contributing for the risks associated with production as well as those impacting a wide variety of market-related risks or even disasters. Supply chain strategy and design literature mention the role of supply chain strategy and design in determining the level of supply chain resilience, particularly in uncertain contexts. In providing values to the company, risk management plays very important role, where elements of supply chain re-engineering, collaboration, agility and risk awareness contribute to building supply chain resilience.

7.3. Contingency Planning for Unexpected Events

Contingency planning is the foreseeing of the possibility of undesirable events such as pandemics, economic downturns or changes in the regulatory requirements and be prepared reduce the harshness of adverse impact. Robust contingency planning will be developed from scenario analysis, risk assessment and stakeholder engagement. Companies can work out effective strategies to source from an alternative source by identification of key dependencies in their supply chain (De Matta & Miller, 2018).

Furthermore, cross-functional interaction and periodic simulation exercises help in the assessment of the ability of the contingency plans set in place, thereby bringing in necessary improvements. Best practice for contingency planning includes making supply chain plans resilient to control the disruptions and risks across business operations. Resilience performance metrics for supply chain functions should be in place, hence emphasizing system factors such as flexibility and reliability. Scenario-based analyses assess impacts of potential disasters on vulnerable functions to devise strategy for pre-emptive risk management.

It becomes quite tedious task to integrate risk management and resilience strategies into supply chains with the increasing complexity and vulnerability of global supply chains. This resulted into keeping supply chains operating with challenges. These include shortages, sometimes being out of stock on some items and elongated lead times on some component which are very detrimental to resilience and recovery processes.

Risk management is an area said to deliver a very high quantum of value to companies through various researchers and supply chain experts. It also says that there are no particular strategies that make a supply chain resilient (Monroe, 2019). Instead, deep insight into the supply chain structure and vulnerabilities is must to select an appropriate strategy. Hence selection of appropriate risk management and resilience approach varies with characteristics and challenges of each supply chain under consideration.

8. IMPLEMENTING AGILE SUPPLY CHAIN PRACTICES

Food companies must adopt agile practices for supply chain as it facilitates adapting to new consumer needs and market dynamics. This shall call for multifaceted change management approaches from strategies, employee training and skill development as well as performance measurements and a culture of continuous improvement.

8.1. Change Management Strategies

Successful adoption of agile practices for supply chain in the food industry is depending on the change management to a great extent. Within organization, it is the orchestration that deals with moving from traditional to agile processes, systems and thought processes of the employees about the new agile ones. Clear and transparent communication involving whole staff right from the highest level to the working teams is essential to make them understand the motive behind it for their commitment to ensure the success. Organization can encourage employees to take ownership in the process of change by engaging them and getting input and feedback toward change; hence, resistance to change is minimized.

Another essential step is setting up a separate change management team or task force. This team consecutively manage the implementation process, is held accountable to the process and supports employees in the organization during transition. Probable barriers and challenges in moving toward agile supply chain practices in an organization can be handled effectively having a change management team in place. Good transformation programs are the key to get maximum benefits of agile supply chain practices and avoid failure consequences (Sabri, Optimization of supply chain management in contemporary organizations, 2015). Strategic partnerships with suppliers and strong customer relations are the major negotiators between agile strategies and performance in the supply chain and should be considered in the program (Sabri & Verma, 2015). Additionally, supply chain processes should be continuously change and transform so that organizations will be able to meet the dynamic market demand and remain competitive in the market.

8.2. Employee Training and Skill Development

Proper training of staff and skill acquisition are paramount to any organization wishing to implement agile supply chain practices (Modgil, Singh, & Agrawal, 2023). Human Resource Development (HRD) professionals can have significant contribution providing developmental interventions for critical set of skills required by managers in the supply chain. HRD professionals use their proficiency in training, organizational development and change management to spread deeper awareness about supply chain management within organization. Training programs are must for organizational transformation and can greatly help in improving the supply chain score for the firm. The objective of training programs is comprehensive skill development including both hard skills and soft skills to bridge competency gaps and enhance supply chain performance. The soft skills training makes employees knowledgeable in effective communication, collaboration and problem-solving while the hard skills training makes them well-versed with the technical knowledge and tools necessary for agile supply chain management (Cocolin, DeVarney, & Aqlan, 2018).

Other important areas of training for the employees include new technologies, tools and methodologies applicable to agile supply chain management. For example, employees may undergo training on data analytics, predictive modelling and demand forecasting techniques in order to enhance capability on better decision-making and responsiveness to change in markets. Further, encouraging a culture of constant learning and development motivate employees to always acquire new skills and knowledge, this further strengthens the agility and resilience of the supply chain. Competent staff to practice agile supply chain effectively can be built as a result of investing in employee development. Frequent employee development programs further polishes individual capabilities and to gear up for dynamic changes in the market and act as change drivers towards bettering supply chain performance through the provision of continuous skill development.

8.3. Performance Metrics and Continuous Improvement

Effective monitoring and enhancement in agile practices in the supply chain require setting up performance metrics and promoting culture of continuous improvement. This comprises of defining Key Performance Indicators (KPIs) in line with the objectives of agility like responsiveness, flexibility and efficiency (Routroy & Shankar, 2015). Examples of KPIs are order execution lead time, inventory turnover and on-time delivery performance. Measuring these metrics constantly and analyse the same for the purpose of knowing areas of improvement, companies can take corrective actions in time. Regular reviews and performance assessment boost employees to share best practices and learnings developing a culture of continuous learning and improvement.

The agile supply chain strategies influence positively competitiveness and sustainable growth and financial performance of manufacturing companies (Gangaraju, et al., 2023). The study further finds out important dimensions of an agile supply chain such as quickness, speed and management of cash flow that would make supply chain management more effective. Research findings on the impact of supply chain strategy on firm performance in Saudi Arabia indicated a strong positive correlation of the agile supply chain with firm performance and supply chain integration that mediates the relationship between both agile and lean supply chains with firm performance. In its importance, performance measurement in supply chain management is absolutely relevant, so simulation techniques can be appropriate for the purpose of supply chain performance measurement in a volatile environment (Routroy & Shankar, 2015).

Continuous performance evaluation is relevant for competitive advantage and sustainability of the businesses in agile supply chain practices. The important performance variables properly selected allow procedures of improvement, identification of problems and measuring of performance against plans or best practice. The lean paradigm of supply chain management focuses on cost and time reduction. Thus, a well-defined measurement system increases the probability of success. The techniques that will drive continuous improvements in this area should include fuzzy analytic hierarchy process (FAHP) with the integration of performance value analysis (PVA) for analysing the performance of the agile supply chain (Routroy & Shankar, 2015). Balanced sets of measures together with appropriate performance measurement practices will result in increased performance outcome in the field of supply chain management.

Time constraints and real-time application difficulties poses that curtail the use of available models for measuring agility in agile supply chains. The available information also does not cover any empirical analysis and case studies carried out in the performance metrics and measurements within the supply chain environment in the scenario of Small and Medium-Sized Enterprises.

9. FUTURE TRENDS AND CHALLENGES

The food industry is developing continuously presenting new trends and challenges. It becomes prerequisite for food industry to predict the trends and challenges that will depict future in order to remain agile and efficacious in meeting consumer preferences.

9.1. Anticipated Changes in Consumer Preferences

Consumer preferences for the food industry are experiencing dramatic change toward health, sustainability and convenience with demand for organics, plant-based and locally sourced products. In this context, consumers become more sensible toward the environment and an emerging inevitability of sustainable packaging and production practice becoming more relevant to business operations. Hence, innovation and adaptability of the product offerings and their supply chain strategies both become necessity.

The changing aspects of consumer behaviours and environmental challenge are greatly influencing supply chains. Companies constantly have pressure on them to strengthen their supply chain resiliency. Agile supply chains are now more important than ever for riding out different kinds of supply chain disruptions due to pandemics or even trade conflicts, urging for assessment of sourcing strategies in COVID-19 like pandemic situation (Shamsuddoha, 2023). For instance, keep operations uninterrupted by expanding supplier base purposefully across different regions to reduce regional dependency. Digital transformation holds a lot of potential to reform changing aspects of supply chains gaining visibility end-to-end and real-time insights in line with changing consumer expectations. Breakthrough digital technologies like artificial intelligence and big data are impacting customer behaviour and necessitating organisations to respond quickly to be competitive in the market.

Major environmental events are driving universal shifts of consumer preferences that primarily impact future trends. The extended effects of the COVID-19 crisis might show long-term changes in consumer confidence and spending patterns particularly with the rising environmental awareness adding sustainability concerns into consumer welfare analysis. The mix of product attributes, social influence and individual personality characteristics determine consumer preference for new product variants, highlighting the complex relationship between consumer behaviour and market dynamics. In the dynamic environment of the food business, businesses must adopt changes by employing technology and agility to excel in changing view of food industry (Kohl, et al., 2022).

9.2. Advancements in Technology and Their Implications

The food industry and its supply chains are on the verge of technological revolution guided by the contributions of artificial intelligence, blockchain, and the Internet of Things. The technologies bound to assure further transparency, traceability and efficiency in the supply chain, improving demand forecasting precision, inventory management. Also, ensure food safety and authenticity through unalterable records and real-time monitoring. Implementing these innovations is inevitable for businesses to make sure that they are on par with these technology innovations to effectively interpret need of tech-oriented consumers and retain market competitive advantage. On its own, technology is a necessary facilitator but not sufficient alone. The changes brought about by the technologies in Industry 4.0 make agile supply chains more responsive to market changes and customer requests, thus indicative of the need for more encompassing technologies (Kohl, et al., 2022).

Supply chain management practices are being reformed with combinations of advanced technologies and bring about changes in business processes and supplier network. The investments in information technologies, cloud solutions and advanced analytics is rapidly building space toward better production scheduling and proactive process improvement, reflecting a broader shift toward digitalization (Buntain, 2021). This reformation of supply chains under such technological revolution will affect not only product and component pricing but also the profitability of suppliers and manufacturers. On the other hand, advanced technologies permit management of supply chain disruptions effectively bringing operational efficiency and resilience improvement throughout the supply chain. Recent advancements in technologies such as blockchain, additive manufacturing and machine learning are very likely key to the future of managing supply chains, thus stress the focus on innovation and investment in the field (Bjerkenes & Haddara, 2019).

9.3. Regulatory and Environmental Factors Shaping the Future of Agile Supply Chains

In coming years, regulatory requirements and environmental concerns in food industry are going to bring noticeable change in agile supply chains (Despoudi, 2020). Stringent regulations for food safety enforce quality assurance and traceability systems while the environmental regulations intended toward reduction of carbon emissions and waste will drive sustainability initiatives such as packaging waste reduction and circular economy. Additionally, concerns about climate change and resource inadequacy will push for local sourcing and striving for the carbon footprint reduction associated with food production and transportation. Complying with these changing regulatory and environmental aspects insists for cooperation within the supply chain as well as investment in sustainable practice and technologies.

The fact that both social and environmental challenges bound to affect the supply chains makes it imperative for companies to evaluate and eliminate the upcoming obstacles. Climate change is likely to be a major impacting factor in future product designs underlining the significance of environmental considerations in the future strategies of the supply chain management. Likewise, an integration of lean and agile principles for reducing environmental impacts are gaining more popularity, hence calling for organized research and development of frameworks that would integrate agile practices with sustainability. With government regulations rapidly supporting environmental standards and an increasing number of consumers demanding green products, businesses must adopt agile and green supply chain strategies to enhance their environmental and financial performances in view of changing consumer expectations.

9.4. Potential Challenges and Opportunities in Adapting Agile Supply Chains to Future Trends

In transformation path to adapting agile supply chains to future trends is bumpy and full of jerks of large number of challenges and opportunities as indicated by the findings extracted from insights from academic abstracts:

Challenges:

- The ongoing turmoil and instability in the current business environment have turned out to be the new normal; these pose a remarkable challenge to supply chains in maintaining resilience and agility in an environment of unpredictability (Lauras, Lamothe, Benaben, Andres, & Pol Er, 2015).

- The complex relationship of lean, green and agile practices introduces a new, relatively vague issue in terms of structural integration and stands as a challenge to optimize the efficiency of the supply chain.
- Though the technologies of Industry 4.0 show great progress, for agile supply chains seeking for responsiveness, it remains a lasting challenge in terms of practical implementation of critical enablers including factors such as connectivity, visibility and transparency.

Opportunities:

New methodologies and technologies are vital to enhance supply chain agility and thereby promote productive ground for the development of collaborative platforms promoting agility and adaptability (Lauras, Lamothe, Benaben, Andres, & Pol Er, 2015).

The promising aspect of using Industry 4.0 Information and Digital Technologies would enhance capabilities of agile supply chains to predict and respond to any change in market dynamics and growing customer requirements.

The identification of leading models and frameworks in agile supply chain implementation will be a stepping stone toward future research efforts and offer guidelines to the industry practitioners to ingrain agility to their supply chain operations.

10. CONCLUSION:

In summary, in food industry, ability of supply chain for quick response by to changes in consumer preferences is the key to success to outperform the increasing market competition. Adoption of agility enables companies not only to match with the ever-changing customer demands effectively but also improve its operational efficiency and resiliency. Therefore, flexible processes, technology integration and the collaborative methods give the organization the pathway to pass through uncertainties and exploit market opportunities. However, staying agile over long term need those adaptations and innovations to remain steps ahead of any new emerging trend and challenge. As we look forward to the future of supply chain management within the food industry, it is evident that agility will continue to be mainstay for business success within an ever more dynamic environment adding value for the customer as well as all other stakeholders.

REFERENCES

Aday, S., & Aday, M. (2020, December 01). Impact of COVID-19 on the food supply chain. *Food Quality and Safety*, 04(04), 167–180. DOI: 10.1093/fqsafe/fyaa024

Ajay Guru Dev, C., & Senthil Kumar, V. S. (2016). Analysis on critical success factors for agile manufacturing evaluation in original equipment manufacturing industry-an AHP approach. *Chinese Journal of Mechanical Engineering*, 29(5), 880–888.

Al-Banna, A., Franzoi, R. E., Menezes, B. C., Al-Enazi, A., Rogers, S., & Kelly, J. D. (2022, January). Roadmap to digital supply chain resilience. *Computer-Aided Chemical Engineering*, 49, 571–576. DOI: 10.1016/B978-0-323-85159-6.50095-6

Anupam, G. (2015). Role of responsiveness and process integration in supply chain coordination. *Advances in Management Accounting, 08*(02), 01-08. Retrieved Apr 15, 2024, from https://www.scopus.com/record/display.uri?eid=2-s2.0-84923867319&origin=scopusAI

Barpagga, M. (2023, Aug 17). *Case Study Analysis: The Rise of Plant-Based Meat Alternatives in the Food Industry*. Retrieved May 08, 2024, from https://www.linkedin.com/pulse/case-study-analysis-rise-plant-based-meat-food-mukul-barpagga/: https://www.linkedin.com/pulse/case-study-analysis-rise-plant-based-meat-food-mukul-barpagga/

Batra, T. (2023, Aug 30). *Evolving Tastes: Coca-Cola's Health-Conscious Approach to Beverage Innovation*. Retrieved May 08, 2024, from https://www.linkedin.com: https://www.linkedin.com/pulse/evolving-tastes-coca-colas-health-conscious-approach-beverage-batra/

Bettiga, D., & CicculIo, F. (2019, March 19). Co-creation with customers and suppliers: An exploratory study. *Business Process Management Journal*, 25(02), 250–270. DOI: 10.1108/BPMJ-12-2016-0246

Bjerkenes, M., & Haddara, M. (2019). Blockchain Technology Solutions for Supply Chains. *4th Future Technologies Conference, FTC 2019. 1069*, pp. 909-918. San Francisco: Springer. DOI: 10.1007/978-3-030-32520-6_65

Borucka, A. (2023, May). Seasonal Methods of Demand Forecasting in the Supply Chain as Support for the Company's Sustainable Growth. *Sustainability (Basel)*, 15(09), 7399. Advance online publication. DOI: 10.3390/su15097399

Buntain, M. (2021, Apr). Process Manufacturers Leverage Cloud Computing for Advanced Analytics. *InTech, 68*(02), 01-09. Retrieved May 15, 2024, from https://www.scopus.com/record/display.uri?eid=2-s2.0-85159211081&origin=scopusAI

Burkhart, D., & Bode, C. (2022). TRANSPARENCY IN BUYER-SUPPLIER RELATIONSHIPS: THE WHAT AND WHEN OF SENSITIVE INFORMATION EXCHANGES. *82nd Annual Meeting of the Academy of Management, AOM 2022.* 2022. Seattle: Academy of Management. DOI: 10.5465/AMBPP.2022.37

Cocolin, N., DeVarney, A., & Aqlan, F. (2018). Analysis of soft skills requirements for manufacturing jobs. *3rd North American IEOM Conference. IEOM 2018. 2018,* pp. 1443-1451. IEOM Society. Retrieved May 15, 2024, from https://www.scopus.com/record/display.uri?eid=2-s2.0-85066977758&origin=scopusAI

Dallasega, P., Rojas, R. A., Rauch, E., & Matt, D. T. (2017). Simulation Based Validation of Supply Chain Effects through ICT enabled Real-time-capability in ETO Production Planning. *Procedia Manufacturing*, 11, 846–853. DOI: 10.1016/j.promfg.2017.07.187

De Matta, R., & Miller, T. (2018). *A Strategic Manufacturing Capacity and Supply Chain Network Design Contingency Planning Approach. 2018 IEEE Technology and Engineering Management Conference, TEMSCON 2018.* Institute of Electrical and Electronics Engineers Inc., DOI: 10.1109/TEMSCON.2018.8488401

Despoudi, S. (2020, Jan 01). Green supply chain. In *The Interaction of Food Industry and Environment* (pp. 35–61). Elsevier., DOI: 10.1016/B978-0-12-816449-5.00002-3

Devadharshini, R., Praniis, R., Nishanth, B., & Jayapal, C. (2023). Enhancing Fleet Operations with a Vehicle Route Management Solution. *2nd International Conference on Advancements in Electrical, Electronics, Communication, Computing and Automation, ICAECA 2023.* Virtual, Online: Institute of Electrical and Electronics Engineers Inc. DOI: 10.1109/ICAECA56562.2023.10199496

Gangaraju, P. K., Raj, R., Kumar, V., Akhil, N., De, T., & Kaswan, M. S. (2023). Financial performance in Industry 4.0 agile supply chains: Evidence from manufacturing companies. *The TQM Journal*. Advance online publication. DOI: 10.1108/TQM-07-2023-0214

Garrigós, J. A., & Molina, M. (2020, May 03). Integrating Customers and Suppliers in Retail Co-innovation: Mercadona, the Spanish grocery retailer, uses a co-innovation approach in which customers and suppliers collaborate to create new products. *Research Technology Management*, 63(03), 33–41. DOI: 10.1080/08956308.2020.1733887

GEP. (2021). *WHAT IS SUPPLY CHAIN AGILITY?* Retrieved May 08, 2024, from www.gep.com: https://www.gep.com/knowledge-bank/glossary/what-is-supply-chain-agility

Haq, A. N., & Boddu, V. (2015, January). Analysis of agile supply chain enablers for Indian food processing industries using analytical hierarchy process. *International Journal of Manufacturing Technology and Management*, 29(1-2), 30–47. DOI: 10.1504/IJMTM.2015.066780

HBC. (2023). *SUPPLY CHAIN OVERVIEW*. Retrieved May 10, 2024, from https://www.coca-colahellenic.com: https://www.coca-colahellenic.com/en/about-us/what-we-do/supply-chain

He, J., Lei, Y., & Fu, X. (2019, December 02). Do consumer's green preference and the reference price effect improve green innovation? A theoretical model using the food supply chain as a case. *International Journal of Environmental Research and Public Health*, 16(24), 5007. Advance online publication. DOI: 10.3390/ijerph16245007 PMID: 31835416

Jollivet, A. (2020, May 07). *Amazon & COVID-19: A paradigm shift in grocery shopping behavior and how grocery brands should adapt*. Retrieved May 01, 2024, from https://www.linkedin.com: https://www.linkedin.com/pulse/amazon-covid-19-paradigm-shift-grocery-shopping-how-brands-jollivet/

Kauppila, O., Valikangas, K., & Majava, J. (2020). Improving supply chain transparency between a manufacturer and suppliers: A triadic case study. *Management and Production Engineering Review, 11*(03), 84-91. doi:DOI: 10.24425/mper.2020.134935

Kilpatrick, J., Delesalle, P., & Mussomeli, A. (2022, Apr 01). *The new supply chain equilibrium*. Retrieved May 04, 2024, from www2.deloitte.com: https://www2.deloitte.com/xe/en/insights/focus/supply-chain/supply-chain-agility-efficiency.html

Knight, W. (2015, September-October). Inside amazon. *Technology Review*, 118(05), 62–69. Retrieved May 01, 2024, from https://www.scopus.com/record/display.uri?eid=2-s2.0-85022335891&origin=scopusAI

Kohl, M., Habl, A., Kallali, K., Puff, J., Fottner, J., Oger, R., Lauras, M., & Li, J. (2022, October). Managing supply chains during the Covid-19 crisis: Synthesis of academic and practitioner visions and recommendations for the future. *International Journal of Logistics Management*, 33(04), 1386–1407. DOI: 10.1108/IJLM-07-2021-0375

Kontopanou, M., & Tsoulfas, G. (2022). ANALYZING NEW WAYS TO ADAPT THE TRIPLE-A SUPPLY CHAIN MODEL AND ITS EXTENSIONS IN AGRI-FOOD SUPPLY CHAINS. *Logforum*, 18(03), 285–295. DOI: 10.17270/J.LOG.2022.735

Kontopanou, M., Tsoulfas, G. T., & Rachaniotis, N. P. (2021, November). The compatibility of the triple-a agri-food supply chain with the United Nations Sustainable Development Goals. [). IOP Publishing.]. *IOP Conference Series. Earth and Environmental Science*, 899(1), 012002.

Lauras, M., Lamothe, J., Benaben, F., Andres, B., & Pol Er, R. (2015). Towards an agile and collaborative platform for managing supply chain uncertainties. *6th International IFIP Working Conference on Enterprise Interoperability, IWEI 2015.* 213, pp. 64-72. Nimes: Springer Verlag. DOI: 10.1007/978-3-662-47157-9_6

León-Bravo, V., Moretto, A., Cagliano, R., & Caniato, F. (2019, September 01). Innovation for sustainable development in the food industry: Retro and forward-looking innovation approaches to improve quality and healthiness. *Corporate Social Responsibility and Environmental Management*, 26(05), 1049–1062. DOI: 10.1002/csr.1785

Lopienski, K. (2023, Aug 14). *Supply Chain Agility: 6 Strategies to Improve Agility.* Retrieved May 08, 2024, from https://www.shipbob.com/blog/supply-chain-agility/ : https://www.shipbob.com/blog/supply-chain-agility/

Mandal, S. (2015). Exploring the influences of relational competencies on supply chain agility. *International Journal of Applied Engineering Research: IJAER*, 10(19), 40566–40577. Retrieved April 15, 2024, from https://www.scopus.com/record/display.uri?eid=2-s2.0-84945953275&origin=scopusAI

Mann, H., Kumar, V., Kumar, U., & Mann, I. J. (2016, June). Perishable product supply chains: A fifteen year profile. *Change Management*, 16(02), 11–32. DOI: 10.18848/2327-798X/CGP/v16i02/11-32

Mardenli, A., Sackmann, D., & Rhein, S. (2023). Current challenges in agricultural supply chains: an empirical assessment based on expert perspectives. *2023 International Scientific Conference on The Science and Development of Transport - Znanost i razvitak prometa, ZIRP 2023. 73*, pp. 66-76. Zagreb: Elsevier B.V. DOI: 10.1016/j.trpro.2023.11.893

Menéndez Molist, A., Kallas, Z., & Guadarrama Fuentes, O. V. (2024, March). Assessing the Downstream and Upstream Preferences of Stakeholders for Sustainability Attributes in the Tomato Value Chain. *Sustainability (Basel)*, 16(06), 2505. Advance online publication. DOI: 10.3390/su16062505

Mishra, N. K., Pande Sharma, P., & Chaudhary, S. K. (2024). xRedefining agile supply chain practices in the disruptive era: a case study identifying vital dimensions and factors. *Journal of Global Operations and Strategic Sourcing*. DOI: 10.1108/JGOSS-04-2023-0031

Modgil, S., Singh, R. K., & Agrawal, S. (2023, March 03). Developing human capabilities for supply chains: An industry 5.0 perspective. *Annals of Operations Research*, 336(03). Advance online publication. DOI: 10.1007/s10479-023-05245-1

Monroe, R. (2019). Developing resilience in supply management. In *Mathematical Modelling of System Resilience* (pp. 01-30). River Publishers. Retrieved May 01, 2024, from https://www.scopus.com/record/display.uri?eid=2-s2.0-85106606876&origin=scopusAI

Nassibi, N., Fasihuddin, H., & Hsairi, L. (2022). A Proposed Demand Forecasting Model by Using Machine Learning for Food Industry. *6th International Conference on Future Networks and Distributed Systems, ICFNDS 2022* (pp. 690-694). Tashkent: Association for Computing Machinery. DOI: 10.1145/3584202.3584307

Novijanti, E., Siagian, H., & Tarigan, Z. J. (2023). The effect of supply chain collaboration on supply chain performance through production technology, new product development and product knowledge. *Uncertain Supply Chain Management*, 11(02), 637–650. DOI: 10.5267/j.uscm.2023.2.001

Pal, A., & Kant, K. (2018, February). IoT-Based Sensing and Communications Infrastructure for the Fresh Food Supply Chain. *Computer*, 51(02), 76–80. DOI: 10.1109/MC.2018.1451665

Parast, M. M. (2022, August). Toward a contingency perspective of organizational and supply chain resilience. *International Journal of Production Economics*, 250, 108667. Advance online publication. DOI: 10.1016/j.ijpe.2022.108667

Pereira, E. T., & Shafique, M. N. (2023). The Implementation of Artificial Intelligence in Supply Chain. *6th International Conference on Innovative Computing and Communication, ICICC 2023*. 703, pp. 497-504. Delhi: Springer Science and Business Media Deutschland GmbH. DOI: 10.1007/978-981-99-3315-0_37

Retailer, I. (2023, Sep 21). *India's Changing Food Palette: Embracing Plant-Based Meat*. Retrieved May 08, 2024, from https://www.indianretailer.com: https://www.indianretailer.com/article/retail-business/retail/indias-changing-food-palette-embracing-plant-based-meat

Romig, T. (2021). A collaborative approach to business continuity and organisational resilience when dealing with a major crisis, such as covid-19. *Journal of Airport Management*, 15(03), 226–234. Retrieved May 07, 2024, from https://www.scopus.com/record/display.uri?eid=2-s2.0-85113147420&origin=scopusAI. DOI: 10.69554/XGNV5295

Routroy, S., & Shankar, A. (2015). Performance analysis of agile supply chain. *International Journal of Manufacturing Technology and Management*, 29(3-4), 180–210. DOI: 10.1504/IJMTM.2015.069255

Sabri, E. (2015). Optimization of supply chain management in contemporary organizations. In *Optimization of Supply Chain Management in Contemporary Organizations* (pp. 01-337). IGI Global. DOI: 10.4018/978-1-4666-8228-3

Sabri, E., & Verma, L. (2015). Mastering change management for successful supply chain transformation. In *Optimization of Supply Chain Management in Contemporary Organizations* (pp. 117–147). IGI Global., DOI: 10.4018/978-1-4666-8228-3.ch005

Shamsuddoha, M., & Nasir, T. (2023). Principal Lessons Learned from COVID-19: Prescriptive and Long-Lasting Strategies for Sustainable Supply Chain Improvement. *Understanding Complex Systems*, F1776, 81–105. DOI: 10.1007/978-3-031-45229-1_5

Smith, A. D. (2016). Exploring strategic partnering in supply chain management: Case study of successful practices. In *Supply Chain Management: Practices, Applications and Challenges* (pp. 01-19). Nova Science Publishers, Inc. Retrieved May 08, 2024, from https://www.scopus.com/record/display.uri?eid=2-s2.0-85060522719&origin=scopusAI

Sodhi, M. S., Tang, C. S., & Willenson, E. T. (2023). Research opportunities in preparing supply chains of essential goods for future pandemics. *International Journal of Production Research*, 16(08), 2416–2431. DOI: 10.1080/00207543.2021.1884310

Sourabhi, S. (2023, Nov 09). *Supply Chain Agility: Benefits and Strategies*. Retrieved May 09, 2024, from www.oracle.com: https://www.oracle.com/in/scm/supply-chain-agility/#:~:text=Supply%20chain%20agility%20is%20a,materials%2C%20and%20acts%20of%20nature

Taranya, R. T., Rama Devi, Y., & Kavita, G. (2023). Logistics, traceability in food supply chain management. *4th International Conference on Design and Manufacturing Aspects for Sustainable Energy, ICMED-ICMPC 2023. 391.* Hyderabad: EDP Sciences. DOI: 10.1051/e3sconf/202339101075

Taseen, M., Wangyongli, & Ali, E. (2023). Integration of Artificial Intelligence for Demand Forecasting and Resource Allocation in Renewable Energy Supply Chains. *25th International Multi Topic Conference, INMIC 2023.* Lahore: Institute of Electrical and Electronics Engineers Inc. DOI: 10.1109/INMIC60434.2023.10465757

Thomas, C., Maître, I., & Symoneaux, R. (2021). Consumer-led eco-development of food products: A case study to propose a framework. *British Food Journal*, 123(07), 2430–2448. DOI: 10.1108/BFJ-11-2020-1050

Untari, D. T., & Satria, B. (2021). Integration of supply chain management to business performance and business competitiveness of food micro industry. *Uncertain Supply Chain Management*, 9(03), 705–710. DOI: 10.5267/j.uscm.2021.4.008

Vachter, D., & Bányai, T. (2022). LEAN AND SIMULATION-BASED POTENTIALS IN THE MANUFACTURING PROCESSES OF FOOD INDUSTRY. *Academic Journal of Manufacturing Engineering, 20*(03), 67-73. Retrieved May 08, 2024, from https://www.scopus.com/record/display.uri?eid=2-s2.0-85145951190 &origin=scopusAI

Vempati, L., Crapanzano, R., Woodyard, C., & Trunkhill, C. (2017). Linear program and simulation model for aerial package delivery: A case study of Amazon prime air in Phoenix, AZ. *17th AIAA Aviation Technology, Integration, and Operations Conference, 2017.* Denver: American Institute of Aeronautics and Astronautics Inc, AIAA. DOI: 10.2514/6.2017-3936

Venugopal, V., & Saleeshya, P. (2019, May 04). Manufacturing system sustainability through lean and agile initiatives. *International Journal of Sustainable Engineering*, 12(03), 159–173. DOI: 10.1080/19397038.2019.1566411

Webb, M. (2015). Overview of food safety standards. In *Food Safety, Market Organization, Trade and Development* (pp. 45-58). Springer International Publishing. DOI: 10.1007/978-3-319-15227-1_3

Yawson, D. E., & Yamoah, F. A. (2022, November). Review of Strategic Agility: A Holistic Framework for Fresh Produce Supply Chain Disruptions. *Sustainability (Basel)*, 14(22), 14977. Advance online publication. DOI: 10.3390/su142214977

Zhang, P., & Yuan, A. Q. (2014). A study on CPFR inventory management technology. *4th International Conference on Frontiers of Manufacturing Science and Measuring Technology, ICFMM 2014. 599-601*, pp. 2079 - 2082. Trans Tech Publications Ltd. DOI: 10.4028/www.scientific.net/AMM.599-601.2079

Chapter 7
Integrating Smart Manufacturing and Industry 4.0:
Technologies for Production Management Optimization in Supply Chains

Bassem Chaker
https://orcid.org/0000-0003-1324-2271
OLID Research Laboratory, Higher Institute of Industrial Management, University of Sfax, Tunisia

Chedli Damak
https://orcid.org/0009-0007-2254-792X
OLID Research Laboratory, Higher Institute of Industrial Management, University of Sfax, Tunisia

ABSTRACT

This chapter explores the integration of smart manufacturing principles and Industry 4.0 technologies to optimize production management within supply chains. As manufacturing processes increasingly embrace digitization and connectivity, production management plays a pivotal role in ensuring efficiency, flexibility, and responsiveness throughout the supply chain. The chapter delves into advancements such as cyber-physical systems, the Internet of Things (IoT), artificial intelligence (AI), and advanced robotics, and their impact on reshaping traditional production management practices. These technologies enable real-time monitoring, predictive maintenance, and demand-driven production. Through practical examples and case studies, the chapter demonstrates how the seamless integration of Industry

DOI: 10.4018/979-8-3693-4427-9.ch007

4.0 technologies enhances production planning, scheduling, and execution, leading to improved productivity, reduced lead times, and greater customer satisfaction. Furthermore, it addresses the challenges and considerations of implementing smart manufacturing initiatives.

INTRODUCTION

Smart manufacturing and Industry 4.0 technologies represent transformative forces in modern production management. Smart manufacturing integrates digital technologies with traditional manufacturing processes, creating interconnected, data-driven, and agile production systems. Industry 4.0, known as the fourth industrial revolution, involves the integration of cyber-physical systems, the Internet of Things (IoT), artificial intelligence (AI), and advanced robotics into manufacturing operations. These innovations are revolutionizing production management practices within supply chains, making them more efficient, flexible, and responsive to market demands (Zheng et al., 2018).

The significance of these technologies lies in their ability to enhance operational efficiency, improve product quality, and enable businesses to respond more effectively to evolving customer demands. For example, cyber-physical systems enable real-time monitoring and control, allowing for immediate adjustments in production processes to maintain optimal performance (Lee et al., 2015). IoT devices provide valuable data on equipment performance and process parameters, facilitating predictive maintenance and reducing downtime (Zhou et al., 2015).

To remain competitive in the global marketplace, organizations must embrace digital transformation. This involves adopting advanced technologies that can provide a competitive edge through improved production management. By integrating digital innovations, businesses can achieve significant improvements in productivity, reduce lead times, and enhance customer satisfaction (Bueno et al., 2020).

Despite the significant advancements, there is a lack of clarity on how these technologies can be effectively implemented to maximize their benefits in various manufacturing contexts. This chapter seeks to address the following research problem:

How can smart manufacturing and Industry 4.0 technologies be effectively implemented to enhance operational efficiency, improve product quality, and respond to evolving customer demands in modern manufacturing environments?

To explore this problem, the study is guided by the following research questions:

- What are the fundamental principles and components of cyber-physical systems (CPS) and digital twins in production management?

- How do CPS and digital twins contribute to real-time monitoring, control, and optimization of production processes?
- What are the key challenges and benefits associated with the implementation of CPS and digital twins in manufacturing?
- How can IoT and sensor technologies be deployed for real-time production monitoring and predictive maintenance?

The theoretical foundation of this study is guided in the principles of cyber-physical systems and digital twins, as well as the broader context of Industry 4.0. Cyber-physical systems integrate physical processes with computational resources, enabling real-time monitoring and control. Digital twins are advanced digital replicas of physical assets, processes, or systems, which allow for real-time simulation and optimization. According to (Lee et al., 2015), CPS enable seamless communication between machines, sensors, and control systems, enhancing the ability to monitor, analyze, and optimize production activities dynamically. Similarly, digital twins, as noted by (Shangguan et al., 2019), provide valuable insights into system behaviors, enabling predictive maintenance, process improvements, and enhanced decision-making.

To address these research questions, a mixed-methods approach was employed, combining qualitative and quantitative research methods to explore the implementation and impact of smart manufacturing technologies. A comprehensive review of existing literature on CPS, digital twins, IoT, and Industry 4.0 was conducted to establish a theoretical framework and identify key themes and concepts. Additionally, two in-depth case studies were conducted to illustrate the practical applications of smart manufacturing technologies in real-world settings. The first case study focuses on the implementation of CPS and digital twins in a lean production environment, while the second examines the adoption of Industry 4.0 solutions for mass customization.

Cyber-Physical Systems and Digital Twins in Production Management

In this section, we will introduce the concept of cyber-physical systems and digital twins in the realm of production management. We will start by elucidating the fundamental principles behind cyber-physical systems, emphasizing their role in bridging the gap between the physical and digital domains within production environments. By exploring their application in manufacturing operations, we aim to showcase how CPS enable real-time monitoring, control, and optimization of production processes, leading to enhanced efficiency and productivity. Additionally, we will examine the concept of digital twins and their significance in virtual simulation and optimization of production systems. Through insightful analysis and practical examples, this section will provide a comprehensive understanding of how cyber-physical systems and digital twins are reshaping production management practices, paving the way for improved performance and competitiveness within supply chains.

Fundamental Principles of Cyber-Physical Systems

Cyber-physical systems are integrated networks of physical and computational components that interact in real-time to manage and control production processes. These systems bridge the gap between the physical and digital domains by enabling seamless communication between machines, sensors, and control systems. This interaction enhances the ability to monitor, analyze, and optimize production activities dynamically (Park et al., 2019). CPS employ advanced algorithms and data analytics to facilitate real-time decision-making, thereby increasing efficiency and reducing downtime (Villalonga et al., 2021).

Real-time Monitoring and Control

Real-time monitoring and control are critical for maintaining optimal production performance. CPS use sensors and IoT devices to continuously collect data on equipment status and production parameters, which are then analyzed to predict maintenance needs and optimize operations (Nguyen et al., 2022).

Integration with IoT and Sensor Technologies

Integration with IoT and sensor technologies allows CPS to gather comprehensive data from various sources. This integration enhances the system's ability to provide accurate and timely insights, facilitating better decision-making and operational efficiency (Graessler & Poehler, 2017).

Applications of Cyber-Physical Systems in Manufacturing

The implementation of CPS in manufacturing has revolutionized how production processes are managed and optimized. This integration not only improves the accuracy and efficiency of production operations but also enables real-time responses to changes and disruptions, thereby maintaining high levels of productivity and quality.

Production Process Optimization

CPS optimize production processes by providing real-time data and insights that enable adjustments and improvements. This leads to more efficient use of resources and higher productivity.

Predictive Maintenance

By continuously monitoring equipment conditions, CPS can predict when maintenance is needed, thus preventing unexpected breakdowns and reducing downtime (Havard et al., 2021).

Quality Control

CPS enhance quality control by monitoring production parameters and ensuring that processes remain within specified tolerances. This leads to higher quality products and reduces waste (Villalonga et al., 2021).

Introduction to Digital Twins

Digital twins are advanced digital replicas of physical assets, processes, or systems. They allow for real-time monitoring, simulation, and optimization by mirroring the real-world performance of their physical counterparts. This technology provides valuable insights into system behaviors, enabling predictive maintenance, process improvements, and enhanced decision-making. By integrating digital twins with cyber-physical systems, manufacturers can achieve unprecedented levels of efficiency and accuracy in production management (Shangguan et al., 2019).

Role in Simulation and Optimization

Digital twins play a crucial role in simulating and optimizing production systems. They enable manufacturers to test scenarios and predict outcomes without disrupting actual production, thus facilitating better planning and decision-making (Ma et al., 2020).

Integration with CPS

The integration of digital twins with CPS enhances their ability to monitor and control production processes. This synergy allows for more accurate simulations and real-time optimizations, further improving operational efficiency (Graessler & Poehler, 2017).

Applications of Digital Twins in Production Management

Digital twins have diverse applications in production management, significantly enhancing efficiency and effectiveness. They enable real-time performance monitoring, predictive maintenance, and optimization of production schedules. By simulating various scenarios, digital twins help identify potential bottlenecks and streamline operations. Additionally, they facilitate quality control by providing detailed insights into production processes, ensuring consistent output and reducing waste. These applications make digital twins indispensable for modern manufacturing environments, driving continuous improvement and operational excellence.

Production Scheduling and Planning

Digital twins assist in production scheduling and planning by providing detailed simulations of production processes. This helps in optimizing schedules and resource allocation, leading to improved efficiency (Shangguan et al., 2019).

Real-time Performance Monitoring

Digital twins enable real-time performance monitoring by continuously updating their models based on live data from the physical production environment. This ensures that production processes are running smoothly and efficiently (Nguyen et al., 2022).

Predictive Maintenance and Failure Analysis

By using digital twins to simulate and analyze equipment conditions, manufacturers can predict potential failures and schedule maintenance proactively. This reduces downtime and extends the lifespan of machinery (Ma et al., 2020).

Benefits and Challenges of Implementing CPS and Digital Twins

Implementing cyber-physical systems (CPS) and digital twins offers significant benefits, including enhanced efficiency, real-time monitoring, predictive maintenance, and improved decision-making capabilities. These technologies enable more accurate simulations and optimizations, leading to reduced downtime and increased productivity. However, challenges such as high initial costs, complexity of integration, data security concerns, and the need for advanced technical expertise can hinder their implementation. Addressing these challenges is crucial for maximizing the potential of CPS and digital twins in modern manufacturing environments.

Efficiency and Productivity Gains

The implementation of CPS and digital twins leads to significant gains in efficiency and productivity by optimizing processes and reducing downtime (Villalonga et al., 2021).

Data and Communication Requirements

Effective implementation requires robust data collection and communication networks to ensure that all components of the CPS and digital twins are accurately synchronized (Graessler & Poehler, 2017).

Interoperability and Integration Challenges

One of the major challenges is ensuring interoperability and seamless integration of various components within the CPS and digital twins. This requires standardization and collaboration across different systems and platforms (Havard et al., 2021).

Future Perspectives and Trends

The future of cyber-physical systems and digital twins is poised for significant advancements driven by ongoing technological innovations. Emerging trends such as artificial intelligence, machine learning, edge computing, and 5G connectivity will further enhance the capabilities of CPS and digital twins, enabling more sophisticated data analysis and real-time decision-making. Additionally, the expansion of these technologies into new sectors beyond manufacturing, such as healthcare and smart cities, will open up new opportunities and applications. As these technologies continue to evolve, they will play an increasingly critical role in driving efficiency, productivity, and innovation across various industries.

Advances in AI and Machine Learning for CPS

Future advancements in AI and machine learning will further enhance the capabilities of CPS, enabling more sophisticated analysis and decision-making processes (Villalonga et al., 2021).

Expansion of Digital Twin Applications

As technology progresses, the applications of digital twins will expand beyond manufacturing to include other sectors such as healthcare, construction, and logistics (Nguyen et al., 2022).

Emerging Technologies and Innovations

Emerging technologies such as edge computing, 5G networks, and advanced robotics will further drive the evolution of CPS and digital twins, making them even more integral to modern production management (Park et al., 2019).

IoT and Sensor Technologies for Real-time Production Monitoring

In this section, we will analyze the pivotal role of Internet of Things and sensor technologies in enabling real-time production monitoring within manufacturing environments. We will begin by examining the deployment of IoT-enabled sensors and devices, highlighting their significance in capturing real-time data related to equipment performance, process parameters, and product quality. By utilizing IoT technologies, manufacturers can gain unprecedented insights into the operational status of production facilities, facilitating proactive maintenance, optimization, and decision-making (Syafrudin et al., 2018). Furthermore, we will explore the diverse applications of IoT in achieving real-time visibility and control over production operations. From monitoring inventory levels and equipment utilization to tracking work-in-progress and detecting anomalies, IoT solutions empower manufacturers to enhance efficiency, minimize downtime, and ensure product quality throughout the production process (Chen, 2020). Through comprehensive analysis and illustrative examples, this section aims to elucidate the transformative potential of IoT and sensor technologies in driving operational excellence and competitiveness within modern manufacturing ecosystems.

Deployment of IoT-enabled Sensors and Devices

IoT-enabled sensors and devices are critical components of modern production monitoring systems. These technologies capture real-time data on various aspects of production, including equipment performance, process parameters, and environmental conditions. The deployment of these sensors throughout the production facility enables continuous data collection and real-time monitoring, providing valuable insights for optimizing operations (Zhang et al., 2016).

Real-time Data Capture and Analysis

IoT sensors collect vast amounts of data, which can be analyzed to improve decision-making and operational efficiency. Advanced data processing platforms and big data technologies are used to manage and analyze this data in real-time, enabling proactive maintenance and rapid response to production issues (Nguyen et al., 2022).

Applications in Production Monitoring

IoT technologies have numerous applications in production monitoring. They enable real-time visibility into production processes, helping manufacturers monitor inventory levels, equipment utilization, and work-in-progress. This real-time insight helps detect anomalies early, ensuring prompt corrective actions to maintain production efficiency and product quality (Shahbazi & Byun, 2021).

Benefits and Challenges

Implementing IoT and sensor technologies in manufacturing provides significant benefits, including enhanced operational efficiency, reduced downtime, and improved product quality. However, challenges such as data security, integration complexity, and the need for robust communication networks must be addressed to fully leverage these technologies (Riad et al., 2019).

Future Trends

Future advancements in IoT and sensor technologies will continue to drive improvements in real-time production monitoring. Emerging trends such as edge computing, AI integration, and enhanced sensor capabilities will further enhance the efficiency and effectiveness of production monitoring systems.

AI and Predictive Analytics for Demand-driven Production

In this section, we will explore the pivotal role of Artificial Intelligence and predictive analytics in enabling demand-driven production within manufacturing environments. We will begin by elucidating the fundamental role of AI and machine learning in predicting demand patterns and optimizing production schedules. By leveraging advanced algorithms and historical data, AI systems can analyze complex demand signals, identify trends, and forecast future demand with remarkable accuracy. This enables manufacturers to align production levels with customer demand, minimize inventory costs, and reduce the risk of stockouts or overstocking (Yang Li et al., 2015).

Furthermore, we will focus on the implementation of predictive analytics for predictive maintenance and quality control. Predictive analytics leverages AI-driven algorithms to analyze real-time sensor data, equipment performance metrics, and historical maintenance records to predict potential equipment failures or quality issues before they occur. By adopting predictive maintenance strategies, manufacturers can schedule maintenance activities proactively, minimize unplanned downtime, and extend the lifespan of critical assets. Similarly, predictive analytics can be utilized to identify patterns and anomalies in production processes, enabling proactive quality control measures to ensure consistent product quality and customer satisfaction (Ma et al., 2014).

Predicting Demand Patterns

AI and machine learning algorithms play a critical role in predicting demand patterns by analyzing large datasets to uncover trends and patterns. These insights allow manufacturers to forecast demand more accurately and adjust their production schedules accordingly, ensuring that they can meet customer demands without overproducing or underproducing (Blackburn et al., 2015).

Optimizing Production Schedules

By utilizing predictive analytics, manufacturers can optimize production schedules to align with predicted demand. This involves adjusting production rates, managing inventory levels, and ensuring that resources are allocated efficiently to meet customer needs while minimizing waste and costs (Ghahramani et al., 2020).

Predictive Maintenance

Predictive maintenance uses AI and machine learning algorithms to monitor equipment performance and predict potential failures. This proactive approach allows manufacturers to schedule maintenance activities before issues occur, reducing downtime and extending the lifespan of equipment (Hrnjica & Softic, 2020).

Quality Control

AI-driven predictive analytics can also enhance quality control by analyzing data from production processes to identify patterns and anomalies. This enables manufacturers to implement corrective actions promptly, ensuring consistent product quality and reducing the risk of defects (Verma, 2018).

Benefits and Challenges

Implementing AI and predictive analytics offers significant benefits, including improved demand forecasting, optimized production schedules, reduced maintenance costs, and enhanced product quality. However, challenges such as data integration, algorithm accuracy, and the need for skilled personnel must be addressed to fully realize these benefits (Lade et al., 2017).

Future Trends

Future advancements in AI and predictive analytics will continue to enhance demand-driven production. Emerging technologies such as deep learning, real-time data processing, and advanced sensor networks will further improve the accuracy and efficiency of these systems, driving innovation and competitiveness in manufacturing (Chien et al., 2020).

Robotics and Automation for Flexible Production

This section focuses on the transformative impact of robotics and automation on enabling flexible production within manufacturing environments. We explore the integration of robotics and automation technologies, highlighting their role in enhancing production flexibility and agility. By automating repetitive tasks and streamlining workflows, robotics and automation systems enable manufacturers to adapt quickly to changing production demands, accommodate varying product specifications, and optimize resource utilization. Furthermore, we examine the concept of collaborative robots (cobots) and human-robot collaboration in production environments. Unlike traditional industrial robots, cobots are designed to work alongside human operators, facilitating seamless collaboration and interaction. This collaborative approach enables manufacturers to combine the strengths of human workers—such as dexterity, problem-solving abilities, and adaptability—with the precision and efficiency of robotic systems. By fostering human-robot collaboration, manufacturers can enhance productivity, improve ergonomics, and create safer and more efficient production environments (Giberti et al., 2022).

Integration of Robotics and Automation Technologies

The integration of robotics and automation technologies plays a critical role in enhancing production flexibility. Modern robotic systems are equipped with advanced sensors, control systems, and artificial intelligence capabilities that enable them to perform complex tasks with high precision. These technologies allow manufacturers to automate repetitive and labor-intensive tasks, leading to increased efficiency and productivity (Garcia et al., 2018).

Enhancing Production Flexibility and Agility

Robotics and automation systems enhance production flexibility and agility by enabling quick adjustments to changing production demands. These systems can be easily reprogrammed to handle different tasks and product specifications, allowing manufacturers to respond swiftly to market changes and customer requirements (Wiese et al., 2022).

Collaborative Robots (Cobots) and Human-Robot Collaboration

Collaborative robots, or cobots, are designed to work alongside human operators, facilitating seamless interaction and collaboration. Cobots are equipped with safety features that allow them to operate in close proximity to humans without posing risks. This human-robot collaboration leverages the strengths of both humans and robots, leading to enhanced productivity and improved ergonomics in the workplace (Hildebrandt et al., 2016).

Applications in Flexible Production

Robotics and automation technologies have numerous applications in flexible production, including assembly, packaging, and material handling. These systems can be reconfigured to perform a wide range of tasks, making them ideal for environments where production requirements frequently change (Pan et al., 2012).

Benefits and Challenges

The benefits of implementing robotics and automation in flexible production include increased efficiency, reduced labor costs, and improved product quality. However, challenges such as high initial investment costs, complexity of integration, and the need for skilled personnel must be addressed to fully leverage these technologies (Dean-Leon et al., 2018).

Future Trends

Future advancements in robotics and automation will continue to drive improvements in flexible production. Emerging technologies such as advanced AI, machine learning, and enhanced sensor capabilities will further enhance the adaptability and efficiency of robotic systems, paving the way for more innovative and competitive manufacturing practices (Löfving et al., 2018).

CASE STUDIES AND APPLICATIONS

This section provides a closer look at real-world applications of smart manufacturing technologies and Industry 4.0 solutions through two compelling case studies. In Case Study 1, we examine the implementation of smart manufacturing technologies within lean production environments. In Case Study 2, we shift our focus to the adoption of Industry 4.0 solutions for mass customization in manufacturing.

Through these case studies, this section aims to showcase the practical applications and benefits of smart manufacturing technologies and Industry 4.0 solutions in addressing real-world challenges and driving innovation within manufacturing industries.

Case Study 1: Implementation of Smart Manufacturing Technologies in Lean Production

Lean production environments emphasize efficiency and waste reduction, making them ideal candidates for integrating smart manufacturing technologies. By leveraging IoT, AI, and data analytics, companies can enhance lean practices through real-time monitoring, predictive maintenance, and improved workflow management. For instance, a study demonstrated how IoT-enabled sensors and AI-driven analytics improved machine uptime and reduced maintenance costs in a lean production setting (Zheng et al., 2018).

Case Study 2: Adoption of Industry 4.0 Solutions for Mass Customization

Mass customization presents unique challenges in balancing the efficiency of mass production with the flexibility needed for customization. Industry 4.0 technologies, such as digital twins, advanced robotics, and AI, facilitate this balance by enabling dynamic production processes and real-time adjustments to meet specific customer requirements. A notable case study illustrated how digital twins and AI were used to optimize production schedules and manage resources effectively, allowing for efficient mass customization without compromising quality (Giberti et al., 2022).

Case Study 3: Siemens – Digital Twins in Manufacturing

Siemens implemented digital twins across their manufacturing facilities to enhance operational efficiency and product quality. By creating virtual replicas of their physical assets and processes, Siemens was able to simulate and optimize production workflows, leading to a 30% reduction in time-to-market for new products. Additionally, real-time data from digital twins allowed for predictive maintenance, reducing downtime by 25%.

Case Study 4: General Electric – CPS for Predictive Maintenance

General Electric (GE) adopted cyber-physical systems to improve predictive maintenance in their manufacturing plants. CPS were used to monitor machine health in real-time, analyzing data on vibrations, temperatures, and other critical parameters. This implementation resulted in a 40% reduction in maintenance costs and a 35% increase in equipment lifespan. The proactive maintenance approach also enhanced overall production efficiency and reduced unexpected downtimes.

Case Study 5: Bosch – Real-time Data Analytics for Production Optimization

Bosch leveraged real-time data analytics from CPS to optimize their production processes. By continuously monitoring and analyzing production data, Bosch was able to identify inefficiencies and implement corrective actions swiftly. This approach led to a 15% increase in productivity and a significant reduction in waste, demonstrating the tangible benefits of integrating advanced digital technologies in manufacturing.

Case Study 6: Tesla – Customization and Quality Control with Digital Twins

Tesla uses digital twins to enhance both customization and quality control in their vehicle production. Digital twins allow Tesla to simulate and test various configurations and production scenarios before implementing them on the factory floor. This capability has enabled Tesla to offer highly customized vehicles while maintaining high quality and safety standards, leading to increased customer satisfaction and loyalty.

Impact on Stakeholders

Impact on Employees:

- **Skill Enhancement and Job Enrichment**: The integration of CPS and digital twins requires employees to develop new skills, such as data analysis and digital tool usage, leading to job enrichment and career development opportunities. For example, a study at Siemens revealed that workers who engaged with digital twins experienced improved job satisfaction due to enhanced problem-solving capabilities.
- **Workplace Safety**: IoT sensors and CPS can monitor working conditions in real-time, thereby enhancing workplace safety. For instance, General Electric implemented CPS to monitor machine vibrations and temperatures, significantly reducing workplace accidents.

Impact on Managers:

- **Improved Decision-Making**: Managers benefit from real-time data and analytics provided by CPS and digital twins, leading to better-informed decision-making. A case study from Bosch demonstrated that real-time data analytics enabled managers to optimize production schedules and resource allocation, resulting in a 15% increase in productivity.
- **Operational Efficiency**: The ability to monitor and control production processes in real-time allows managers to swiftly address any inefficiencies or issues, enhancing overall operational efficiency. For example, the integration of digital twins at Procter & Gamble helped managers identify bottlenecks and streamline production, reducing downtime by 20%.

Impact on Customers:

- **Product Quality and Customization**: Customers benefit from higher quality products and increased customization options due to the precise monitoring and control capabilities of CPS and digital twins. For instance, Tesla's use of digital twins has enabled the company to offer highly customized vehicles while maintaining stringent quality standards.
- **Faster Response to Market Demands**: The agility provided by these technologies allows companies to respond more quickly to changing market demands, improving customer satisfaction. Nike's adoption of smart manufacturing technologies has allowed for quicker turnaround times on custom orders, significantly boosting customer satisfaction.

Through these case studies, it becomes evident that the integration of smart manufacturing technologies and Industry 4.0 solutions not only addresses real-world production challenges but also drives significant improvements in efficiency, customization, and overall operational excellence. These examples underscore the transformative potential of these technologies in modern manufacturing.

Challenges and Considerations

In this section, we will analyze the challenges and considerations inherent in the adoption of advanced digital technologies within manufacturing environments. We tackle the critical issue of cybersecurity risks and data privacy concerns associated with interconnected production systems. As manufacturing processes become increasingly digitized and interconnected, the threat landscape expands, with potential vulnerabilities exposing systems to cyber attacks, data breaches, and intellectual property theft. Addressing these risks requires robust cybersecurity measures, including encryption protocols, access controls, threat detection systems, and employee training programs. Furthermore, compliance with data privacy regulations such as GDPR and CCPA is paramount to safeguarding sensitive information and maintaining trust with customers and stakeholders (Leesakul et al., 2022).

Cybersecurity Risks and Data Privacy Concerns

The interconnected nature of modern manufacturing environments exposes them to a wide array of cybersecurity threats. These include potential cyber-attacks aimed at disrupting operations, stealing sensitive data, or compromising intellectual property. To mitigate these risks, manufacturers must implement comprehensive cybersecurity strategies encompassing encryption, access control, and real-time threat detection (Bag et al., 2021).

Technical Integration Challenges

Integrating new digital technologies into existing manufacturing systems can be complex and costly. It requires not only technological upgrades but also significant changes to workflows and processes. This integration challenge is particularly pronounced for small and medium-sized enterprises (SMEs), which may lack the resources for large-scale technological overhauls (Ghobakhloo & Ching, 2019).

Workforce Adaptation and Training

The adoption of advanced digital technologies often necessitates significant changes in workforce skills and roles. Employees need to be trained to work with new systems and technologies, which can be a time-consuming and resource-intensive process. Resistance to change among employees can also pose a barrier to successful implementation (Leesakul et al., 2022).

Regulatory and Compliance Issues

Manufacturers must navigate a complex landscape of regulations related to data privacy and security, such as the General Data Protection Regulation (GDPR) and the California Consumer Privacy Act (CCPA). Ensuring compliance with these regulations is critical to protecting customer data and maintaining trust (Bag et al., 2021).

Cost and Financial Constraints

The financial investment required for implementing advanced digital technologies can be substantial. This includes costs associated with new equipment, software, training, and ongoing maintenance. For many manufacturers, particularly SMEs, these costs can be a significant barrier to adoption (Demartini et al., 2019).

Ensuring Sustainable Implementation

While digital technologies offer numerous benefits, their implementation must be sustainable to ensure long-term success. This involves considering the environmental impact, resource efficiency, and the social implications of technological changes. Adopting sustainable practices can help mitigate the negative effects of digital transformation and support broader sustainability goals (Chatterjee et al., 2021).

Best Practices and Recommendations

In this section, we outline best practices and recommendations for maximizing the success of digital transformation initiatives within manufacturing organizations. Firstly, we emphasize the importance of establishing cross-functional collaboration between production, engineering, and supply chain teams. By ensuring interdisciplinary collaboration, organizations can leverage diverse expertise and perspectives to drive innovation, problem-solving, and decision-making. Cross-functional teams facilitate the integration of digital technologies across different functional areas, ensuring alignment with strategic objectives and operational requirements. Through regular communication, collaboration platforms, and joint initiatives, organizations can streamline processes, minimize conflicts, and accelerate the pace of digital transformation (Abdallah et al., 2021).

Secondly, we underscore the significance of investing in employee training and skills development for digital transformation. As technology continues to evolve rapidly, the demand for digital skills and competencies grows exponentially. Training programs, workshops, and certifications enable employees to acquire the knowledge, skills, and capabilities needed to effectively leverage digital technologies and tools in their roles. Ensuring that the workforce is adequately prepared for technological changes not only enhances operational efficiency but also fosters a culture of continuous improvement and innovation (Ghobakhloo & Ching, 2019).

Establishing Cross-Functional Collaboration

Importance of Interdisciplinary Teams

Cross-functional teams bring together diverse skills and perspectives, fostering innovation and effective problem-solving. This interdisciplinary approach ensures that digital technologies are integrated seamlessly across various functional areas, aligning with both strategic and operational goals.

Enhancing Communication and Collaboration

Utilizing collaboration platforms and regular communication channels helps in maintaining alignment and transparency among different teams. This practice minimizes conflicts and accelerates the implementation of digital initiatives, ensuring a smoother transition to new technologies (Budde et al., 2022).

Investing in Employee Training and Skills Development

Digital Skills Training Programs

Organizations should invest in comprehensive training programs that focus on developing digital skills among employees. These programs can include workshops, online courses, and certification programs tailored to the specific needs of the organization and its technological roadmap (Leesakul et al., 2022).

Continuous Learning and Development

Creating a culture of continuous learning is essential for keeping pace with rapid technological advancements. Encouraging employees to pursue ongoing education and professional development helps in maintaining a workforce that is adaptable and proficient in the latest digital tools and technologies.

Fostering a Culture of Innovation

Encouraging Innovation and Experimentation

Organizations should create an environment that encourages innovation and experimentation. Allowing employees to test new ideas and approaches without the fear of failure can lead to significant breakthroughs and advancements in digital transformation efforts (Albukhitan, 2020).

Supporting Change Management

Effective change management practices are crucial for the successful adoption of digital technologies. This includes clear communication about the benefits of digital transformation, as well as providing support and resources to help employees transition smoothly (Björkdahl, 2020).

Leveraging Data and Analytics

Data-Driven Decision Making

Utilizing data and analytics to inform decision-making processes enhances the accuracy and effectiveness of digital transformation strategies. Organizations should invest in advanced analytics tools and technologies to harness the power of data in driving operational improvements and strategic initiatives.

Building a Robust Data Infrastructure

A strong data infrastructure is essential for supporting digital transformation efforts. This includes implementing data management systems that ensure the integrity, security, and accessibility of data across the organization. By building a robust data infrastructure, organizations can better leverage data insights to drive innovation and improve operational efficiency (Butt, 2020).

Embracing Agile Methodologies

Implementing Agile Practices

Agile methodologies can significantly enhance the flexibility and responsiveness of digital transformation initiatives. By adopting agile practices, organizations can quickly adapt to changes, iterate on solutions, and deliver value incrementally. This approach fosters a more dynamic and resilient transformation process (Zangiacomi et al., 2020).

Continuous Improvement and Feedback Loops

Regular feedback and continuous improvement are key components of successful digital transformation. Establishing feedback loops allows organizations to learn from each iteration, refine their approaches, and continuously enhance their digital strategies.

Future Directions and Opportunities

In this section, we explore future directions and opportunities in smart manufacturing, highlighting emerging trends and their implications for production management. Firstly, we examine the evolving landscape of smart manufacturing by identifying key trends. These trends hold the potential to revolutionize production management practices, enabling manufacturers to achieve greater visibility, agility, and efficiency across the entire value chain (Kang et al., 2016).

Key Emerging Trends in Smart Manufacturing

Smart manufacturing is continuously evolving with the integration of cutting-edge technologies such as artificial intelligence, machine learning, the Internet of Things, and advanced robotics. These technologies facilitate real-time data analytics, predictive maintenance, and more adaptive manufacturing processes. For example, the use of IoT and cyber-physical systems allows for seamless communication between machines and systems, leading to enhanced operational efficiency and reduced downtime (Kusiak, 2018).

Implications for Production Management

The adoption of these emerging trends can significantly impact production management. Predictive maintenance, for instance, utilizes AI and machine learning to anticipate equipment failures before they occur, thus minimizing downtime and extending the lifespan of machinery. Real-time monitoring enabled by IoT technologies provides immediate insights into production processes, allowing for swift adjustments and improvements (Phuyal et al., 2020).

Enhancing Production Efficiency

Emerging technologies contribute to enhancing production efficiency by optimizing resource utilization and streamlining workflows. AI-driven analytics can help manufacturers forecast demand more accurately, aligning production schedules with market needs and reducing waste. Furthermore, advanced robotics can automate repetitive tasks, freeing up human workers to focus on more complex and value-added activities (Zheng et al., 2018).

Cost Optimization and Competitive Advantage

Implementing smart manufacturing technologies can lead to significant cost savings by reducing operational inefficiencies and improving production speed and quality. These improvements not only lower production costs but also enhance the ability to meet customer demands swiftly, providing a competitive edge in the marketplace (Chmielarz, 2019).

Future Opportunities

The future of smart manufacturing presents numerous opportunities for innovation and growth. Advances in AI, machine learning, and IoT will continue to drive the development of more sophisticated and integrated manufacturing systems. These systems will be capable of self-optimizing and self-repairing, further enhancing efficiency and productivity. Additionally, the emphasis on sustainability will lead to the adoption of greener manufacturing practices, contributing to environmental conservation while maintaining economic viability (Rosso Jr et al., 2022).

Edge Computing and 5G Networks

Edge computing and 5G networks significantly enhance the performance of CPS and digital twins by providing faster data processing and lower latency. Edge computing allows data to be processed closer to the source, reducing the time it takes to analyze and act on information. This is particularly beneficial for applications requiring real-time responses, such as autonomous vehicles and industrial robotics. 5G networks provide the high-speed, low-latency connectivity necessary for seamless communication between CPS components and digital twins. This enables more efficient data transfer and real-time synchronization of virtual and physical systems. For example, in a smart factory, 5G can facilitate the instant transmission of sensor data to digital twins, ensuring accurate and up-to-date virtual representations of physical assets.

Expansion to Healthcare and Smart Cities

In healthcare, digital twins can be used to create virtual models of patients, allowing for personalized treatment plans and better management of chronic diseases. For instance, the Living Heart Project by Dassault Systèmes developed a digital twin of the human heart to simulate and analyze cardiovascular conditions and treatments. This digital heart model helps cardiologists plan surgeries and predict the outcomes of various interventions, improving patient care and reducing risks. In smart cities, CPS and digital twins can optimize urban infrastructure, enhance public services, and improve residents' quality of life. Singapore's Smart Nation initiative leverages digital twins to create a virtual model of the entire city. This model integrates data from various CPS to monitor and manage urban systems in real-time. For example, the digital twin of the city's transportation network helps manage traffic congestion by analyzing real-time data and predicting traffic patterns. This allows for dynamic adjustments to traffic signals and public transportation schedules, improving mobility and reducing congestion.

CONCLUSION

In conclusion, this chapter aimed to explore the important role of smart manufacturing and Industry 4.0 technologies in revolutionizing production management within supply chains. From the integration of cyber-physical systems to the adoption of AI, IoT, and robotics, each section has underscored the potential for enhancing efficiency, agility, and competitiveness in modern manufacturing environments. The implementation of cyber-physical systems and digital twins enables real-time monitoring, optimization, and control of production processes, leading to significant improvements in operational efficiency and productivity. The adoption of IoT and sensor technologies facilitates real-time production monitoring, providing valuable insights that drive proactive maintenance and quality control measures. AI and predictive analytics empower manufacturers to predict demand accurately and optimize production schedules, minimizing inventory costs and reducing the risk of stockouts or overstocking.

Robotics and automation technologies enhance production flexibility, allowing manufacturers to quickly adapt to changing demands and optimize resource utilization. The integration of collaborative robots (cobots) fosters human-robot collaboration, combining the strengths of human workers with the precision of robotic systems. Case studies have demonstrated the practical applications and benefits of these technologies, showcasing their ability to address real-world challenges and drive innovation within the manufacturing sector. Despite the numerous benefits, the adoption of these technologies also presents challenges such as cybersecurity risks, technical integration complexities, and the need for workforce adaptation and training.

To maximize the success of digital transformation initiatives, it is essential to establish cross-functional collaboration, invest in employee training, and foster a culture of continuous learning and innovation. Looking ahead, emerging trends such as advanced AI, machine learning, and IoT will continue to shape the future of smart manufacturing, offering new opportunities for enhancing production efficiency, cost optimization, and competitive advantage. By embracing these technologies and addressing the associated challenges, manufacturers can position themselves at the forefront of the next industrial revolution, driving sustained growth and success in an increasingly dynamic and interconnected global marketplace.

REFERENCES:

Abdallah, Y. O., Shehab, E., & Al-Ashaab, A. (2021). Digital Transformation Challenges in the Manufacturing Industry. In Shafik, M., & Case, K. (Eds.), *Advances in Transdisciplinary Engineering*. IOS Press., DOI: 10.3233/ATDE210004

Albukhitan, S. (2020). Developing Digital Transformation Strategy for Manufacturing. *Procedia Computer Science*, 170, 664–671. DOI: 10.1016/j.procs.2020.03.173

Bag, S., Gupta, S., & Kumar, S. (2021). Industry 4.0 adoption and 10R advance manufacturing capabilities for sustainable development. *International Journal of Production Economics*, 231, 107844. DOI: 10.1016/j.ijpe.2020.107844

Björkdahl, J. (2020). Strategies for Digitalization in Manufacturing Firms. *California Management Review*, 62(4), 17–36. DOI: 10.1177/0008125620920349

Blackburn, R., Lurz, K., Priese, B., Göb, R., & Darkow, I. (2015). A predictive analytics approach for demand forecasting in the process industry. *International Transactions in Operational Research*, 22(3), 407–428. DOI: 10.1111/itor.12122

Budde, L., Benninghaus, C., Hänggi, R., & Friedli, T. (2022). Managerial Practices for the Digital Transformation of Manufacturers. *Digital*, 2(4), 463–483. DOI: 10.3390/digital2040025

Bueno, A., Godinho Filho, M., & Frank, A. G. (2020). Smart production planning and control in the Industry 4.0 context: A systematic literature review. *Computers & Industrial Engineering*, 149, 106774. DOI: 10.1016/j.cie.2020.106774

Butt, J. (2020). A Conceptual Framework to Support Digital Transformation in Manufacturing Using an Integrated Business Process Management Approach. *Designs*, 4(3), 17. DOI: 10.3390/designs4030017

Chatterjee, S., Rana, N. P., Dwivedi, Y. K., & Baabdullah, A. M. (2021). Understanding AI adoption in manufacturing and production firms using an integrated TAM-TOE model. *Technological Forecasting and Social Change*, 170, 120880. DOI: 10.1016/j.techfore.2021.120880

Chen, W. (2020). Intelligent manufacturing production line data monitoring system for industrial internet of things. *Computer Communications*, 151, 31–41. DOI: 10.1016/j.comcom.2019.12.035

Chien, C.-F., Dauzère-Pérès, S., Huh, W. T., Jang, Y. J., & Morrison, J. R. (2020). Artificial intelligence in manufacturing and logistics systems: Algorithms, applications, and case studies. *International Journal of Production Research*, 58(9), 2730–2731. DOI: 10.1080/00207543.2020.1752488

Chmielarz, G. (2019). Present state and future application of smart technologies in manufacturing processes. *Production Engineering Archives*, 24(24), 14–19. DOI: 10.30657/pea.2019.24.04

Dean-Leon, E., Ramirez-Amaro, K., Bergner, F., Dianov, I., & Cheng, G. (2018). Integration of Robotic Technologies for Rapidly Deployable Robots. *IEEE Transactions on Industrial Informatics*, 14(4), 1691–1700. DOI: 10.1109/TII.2017.2766096

Demartini, M., Evans, S., & Tonelli, F. (2019). Digitalization Technologies for Industrial Sustainability. *Procedia Manufacturing*, 33, 264–271. DOI: 10.1016/j.promfg.2019.04.032

Garcia, C. A., Salazar, L. F., Marino, C., Villalba, W. R., & Garcia, M. V. (2018). Design of Flexible Cyber-Physical Production Systems Architecture for Industrial Robot Control. *2018 IEEE Third Ecuador Technical Chapters Meeting (ETCM)*, 1–6. DOI: 10.1109/ETCM.2018.8580338

Ghahramani, M., Qiao, Y., Zhou, M. C., O'Hagan, A., & Sweeney, J. (2020). AI-based modeling and data-driven evaluation for smart manufacturing processes. *IEEE/CAA Journal of Automatica Sinica, 7*(4), 1026–1037. DOI: 10.1109/JAS.2020.1003114

Ghobakhloo, M., & Ching, N. T. (2019). Adoption of digital technologies of smart manufacturing in SMEs. *Journal of Industrial Information Integration*, 16, 100107. DOI: 10.1016/j.jii.2019.100107

Giberti, H., Abbattista, T., Carnevale, M., Giagu, L., & Cristini, F. (2022). A Methodology for Flexible Implementation of Collaborative Robots in Smart Manufacturing Systems. *Robotics (Basel, Switzerland)*, 11(1), 9. DOI: 10.3390/robotics11010009

Graessler, I., & Poehler, A. (2017). Integration of a digital twin as human representation in a scheduling procedure of a cyber-physical production system. *2017 IEEE International Conference on Industrial Engineering and Engineering Management (IEEM)*, 289–293. DOI: 10.1109/IEEM.2017.8289898

Havard, V., Sahnoun, M., Bettayeb, B., Duval, F., & Baudry, D. (2021). Data architecture and model design for Industry 4.0 components integration in cyber-physical production systems. *Proceedings of the Institution of Mechanical Engineers. Part B, Journal of Engineering Manufacture*, 235(14), 2338–2349. DOI: 10.1177/0954405420979463

Hildebrandt, A.-C., Schuetz, C., Wahrmann, D., Wittmann, R., & Rixen, D. (2016). A Flexible Robotic Framework for Autonomous Manufacturing Processes: Report from the European Robotics Challenge Stage 1. *2016 International Conference on Autonomous Robot Systems and Competitions (ICARSC)*, 21–27. DOI: 10.1109/ICARSC.2016.15

Hrnjica, B., & Softic, S. (2020). Explainable AI in Manufacturing: A Predictive Maintenance Case Study. In Lalic, B., Majstorovic, V., Marjanovic, U., Von Cieminski, G., & Romero, D. (Eds.), *Advances in Production Management Systems. Towards Smart and Digital Manufacturing* (Vol. 592, pp. 66–73). Springer International Publishing., DOI: 10.1007/978-3-030-57997-5_8

Kang, H. S., Lee, J. Y., Choi, S., Kim, H., Park, J. H., Son, J. Y., Kim, B. H., & Noh, S. D. (2016). Smart manufacturing: Past research, present findings, and future directions. *International Journal of Precision Engineering and Manufacturing-Green Technology*, 3(1), 111–128. DOI: 10.1007/s40684-016-0015-5

Kusiak, A. (2018). Smart manufacturing. *International Journal of Production Research*, 56(1–2), 508–517. DOI: 10.1080/00207543.2017.1351644

Lade, P., Ghosh, R., & Srinivasan, S. (2017). Manufacturing Analytics and Industrial Internet of Things. *IEEE Intelligent Systems*, 32(3), 74–79. DOI: 10.1109/MIS.2017.49

Lee, J., Bagheri, B., & Kao, H.-A. (2015). A Cyber-Physical Systems architecture for Industry 4.0-based manufacturing systems. *Manufacturing Letters*, 3, 18–23. DOI: 10.1016/j.mfglet.2014.12.001

Leesakul, N., Oostveen, A.-M., Eimontaite, I., Wilson, M. L., & Hyde, R. (2022). Workplace 4.0: Exploring the Implications of Technology Adoption in Digital Manufacturing on a Sustainable Workforce. *Sustainability (Basel)*, 14(6), 3311. DOI: 10.3390/su14063311

Li, Y., Chang, Q., Brundage, M. P., Biller, S., Arinez, J., & Xiao, G. (2015). Market Demand Oriented Data-Driven Modeling for Dynamic Manufacturing System Control. *IEEE Transactions on Systems, Man, and Cybernetics. Systems*, 45(1), 109–121. DOI: 10.1109/TSMC.2014.2316268

Löfving, M., Almström, P., Jarebrant, C., Wadman, B., & Widfeldt, M. (2018). Evaluation of flexible automation for small batch production. *Procedia Manufacturing*, 25, 177–184. DOI: 10.1016/j.promfg.2018.06.072

Ma, J., Chen, H., Zhang, Y., Guo, H., Ren, Y., Mo, R., & Liu, L. (2020). A digital twin-driven production management system for production workshop. *International Journal of Advanced Manufacturing Technology*, 110(5–6), 1385–1397. DOI: 10.1007/s00170-020-05977-5

Ma, J., Kwak, M., & Kim, H. M. (2014). Demand Trend Mining for Predictive Life Cycle Design. *Journal of Cleaner Production*, 68, 189–199. DOI: 10.1016/j.jclepro.2014.01.026

Nguyen, T. N., Zeadally, S., & Vuduthala, A. B. (2022). Cyber-Physical Cloud Manufacturing Systems With Digital Twins. *IEEE Internet Computing*, 26(3), 15–21. DOI: 10.1109/MIC.2021.3058921

Pan, Z., Polden, J., Larkin, N., Van Duin, S., & Norrish, J. (2012). Recent progress on programming methods for industrial robots. *Robotics and Computer-integrated Manufacturing*, 28(2), 87–94. DOI: 10.1016/j.rcim.2011.08.004

Park, H., Easwaran, A., & Andalam, S. (2019). Challenges in Digital Twin Development for Cyber-Physical Production Systems. In R. Chamberlain, W. Taha, & M. Törngren (Eds.), *Cyber Physical Systems. Model-Based Design* (Vol. 11615, pp. 28–48). Springer International Publishing. DOI: 10.1007/978-3-030-23703-5_2

Phuyal, S., Bista, D., & Bista, R. (2020). Challenges, Opportunities and Future Directions of Smart Manufacturing: A State of Art Review. *Sustainable Futures : An Applied Journal of Technology, Environment and Society*, 2, 100023. DOI: 10.1016/j.sftr.2020.100023

Riad, M., Elgammal, A., & Elzanfaly, D. (2019). *Efficient Production Monitoring on the Basis of Domain Ontologies by Utilizing IoT*. 93–100. DOI: 10.15439/2019F228

Rosso, R. S. U.Jr, Tsuzuki, M. D. S. G., Barari, A., & Macchi, M. (2022). Transition towards Smart Factories. *International Journal of Computer Integrated Manufacturing*, 35(4–5), 341–344. DOI: 10.1080/0951192X.2022.2080451

Shahbazi, Z., & Byun, Y.-C. (2021). Smart Manufacturing Real-Time Analysis Based on Blockchain and Machine Learning Approaches. *Applied Sciences (Basel, Switzerland)*, 11(8), 3535. DOI: 10.3390/app11083535

Shangguan, D., Chen, L., & Ding, J. (2019). A Hierarchical Digital Twin Model Framework for Dynamic Cyber-Physical System Design. *Proceedings of the 5th International Conference on Mechatronics and Robotics Engineering*, 123–129. DOI: 10.1145/3314493.3314504

Syafrudin, M., Alfian, G., Fitriyani, N., & Rhee, J. (2018). Performance Analysis of IoT-Based Sensor, Big Data Processing, and Machine Learning Model for Real-Time Monitoring System in Automotive Manufacturing. *Sensors (Basel)*, 18(9), 2946. DOI: 10.3390/s18092946 PMID: 30181525

Verma, D. (2018). Analysis of Smart Manufacturing Technologies for Industry Using AI Methods. [TURCOMAT]. *Turkish Journal of Computer and Mathematics Education*, 9(2), 529–540. DOI: 10.17762/turcomat.v9i2.13857

Villalonga, A., Negri, E., Biscardo, G., Castano, F., Haber, R. E., Fumagalli, L., & Macchi, M. (2021). A decision-making framework for dynamic scheduling of cyber-physical production systems based on digital twins. *Annual Reviews in Control*, 51, 357–373. DOI: 10.1016/j.arcontrol.2021.04.008

Wiese, T., Abicht, J., Friedrich, C., Hellmich, A., & Ihlenfeldt, S. (2022). Flexible skill-based control for robot cells in manufacturing. *Frontiers in Robotics and AI*, 9, 1014476. DOI: 10.3389/frobt.2022.1014476 PMID: 36246488

Zangiacomi, A., Pessot, E., Fornasiero, R., Bertetti, M., & Sacco, M. (2020). Moving towards digitalization: A multiple case study in manufacturing. *Production Planning and Control*, 31(2–3), 143–157. DOI: 10.1080/09537287.2019.1631468

Zhang, Y., Wang, W., Wu, N., & Qian, C. (2016). IoT-Enabled Real-Time Production Performance Analysis and Exception Diagnosis Model. *IEEE Transactions on Automation Science and Engineering*, 13(3), 1318–1332. DOI: 10.1109/TASE.2015.2497800

Zheng, P., Wang, H., Sang, Z., Zhong, R. Y., Liu, Y., Liu, C., Mubarok, K., Yu, S., & Xu, X. (2018). Smart manufacturing systems for Industry 4.0: Conceptual framework, scenarios, and future perspectives. *Frontiers of Mechanical Engineering*, 13(2), 137–150. DOI: 10.1007/s11465-018-0499-5

Zhou, K., Liu, T., & Zhou, L. (2015). Industry 4.0: Towards future industrial opportunities and challenges. *2015 12th International Conference on Fuzzy Systems and Knowledge Discovery (FSKD)*, 2147–2152. DOI: 10.1109/FSKD.2015.7382284

Chapter 8

Ontology-Based Semantic Tools for Evolvable Manufacturing Systems Integration

Hafsa Labbi
ENSAM Meknès, Morocco

Souhail Sekkat
ENSAM Meknès, Morocco

El-Moukhtar Zemmouri
ENSAM Meknès, Morocco

ABSTRACT

Throughout history, manufacturing systems paradigms have evolved significantly to meet the changing needs of society, from dedicated transfer lines to evolvabe production systems (EPS). Evolvable Production Systems are designed for swift response to market changes, pose a complex integration challenge due to component heterogeneity. Ontology-based semantic tools facilitate this integration by providing a common language for components. This chapter reviews the evolution of manufacturing systems paradigms by the emergence of Industry 4.0 technologies. It also explores the ontology-based semantic tools for EPS integration and reviews the existing ontologies for manufacturing systems. It highlights representative ontology development methodologies and concludes with future trends in ontology-based evolvable manufacturing systems development.

DOI: 10.4018/979-8-3693-4427-9.ch008

INTRODUCTION

The advent of Industry 4.0 has created a paradigm shift in the manufacturing sector, with an increasing emphasis on automation, data exchange, and the Internet of Things (IoT). This new industrial revolution, characterized by the fusion of the physical and digital worlds, has transformed traditional manufacturing processes, paving the way for smart factories. This chapter delves into the realm of Ontology-based Semantic Tools for Evolvable Manufacturing Systems Integration, a critical area of study that holds the potential to revolutionize the way manufacturing systems operate and evolve. These tools, which leverage the power of ontologies and semantics, are instrumental in facilitating the integration of diverse manufacturing systems, thereby enhancing their adaptability and evolution.

Ontologies, in the context of manufacturing systems, serve as a formal representation of knowledge as a set of concepts within a domain, and the relationships between those concepts. They provide a shared and common understanding of a domain that can be communicated across people and machines. This shared understanding is crucial in a manufacturing environment where various components need to interact and collaborate. Semantic tools leverage these ontologies to enable intelligent information processing and integration in manufacturing systems. They facilitate the interpretation and understanding of data, thereby enabling machines to make sense of the information and take appropriate actions.

Evolvable Production Systems (EPS) are designed to respond swiftly to market changes through reconfiguration of their components. These systems, characterized by their flexibility and adaptability, can evolve in response to changing market demands. The integration of these systems is a complex task due to the heterogeneity of the components involved. Each component, being unique in its functionality and operation, poses a challenge to the integration process. Ontology-based semantic tools can play a pivotal role in this integration process by providing a common language for the components, thereby facilitating seamless communication and coordination.

This chapter provides a comprehensive review of the various ontology-based semantic tools available for EPS integration. First, manufacturing systems design paradigms and their evolution are presented, followed by an overview of ontology and semantic web development. Various existing ontologies for manufacturing systems are then reviewed, each with its unique contribution and domain of application. Subsequently, several most representative ontology development methodologies and approaches are highlighted, guiding the process of building, implementing, and maintaining ontologies of interoperable systems. The chapter concludes with a discussion on future trends and research directions in ontology based evolvable manufacturing systems development and presents the potential of these systems in shaping the future of manufacturing.

MANUFACTURING SYSTEMS DESIGN PARADIGMS

To answer quickly and economically the increasingly variable demands, the production system became more and more complex. The next generation manufacturing systems need to be able to change quickly, work together smoothly, and be smart about how they operate. Several enterprise engineering paradigms have been proposed to satisfy these requirements. In the following we present the evolution of manufacturing systems and their design paradigms. The first paradigm is the concept of Dedicated Transfer Lines (Mehrabi, 2000) which first goal is productivity. Flexible production system (FMS) (Kumar, 2017) is a second concept proposed to produce small and middle batches. It is based on a Computer Integrated Manufacturing (CIM) approach, which is all about using information technology to fully automate production systems. It integrates everything into one common information system, and it uses software like ERP, MES, CAD, and PLM to make sure everything runs smoothly.

The CIM Approach employs a hierarchical control architecture, which includes various control architectures and models for describing Automation Facility systems. Among these models, one of the most prominent is the NIST/AMRF (National Institute of Standard and Technology/Advanced Manufacturing Research Facility) model proposed by the National Bureau of Standards (Simpson, 1982) (Williams, 1989). The AMRF model (Figure 1), consists of a five-level hierarchy: facility, shop, cell, workstation, and Actuator/Sensor. Each level serves specific functions within the automation process. At the facility level, business functions such as cost accounting and aggregate planning are executed, typically managed by ERP software. The shop level coordinates production tasks, including resource allocation and task assignment, utilizing Manufacturing Execution Systems (MES). The cell level organizes the sequence of similar parts in batch jobs and supervises supporting tasks such as material handling and transportation, often facilitated by SCADA software. Finally, the workstation level is responsible for monitoring the execution of production tasks, incorporating elements like robots, manufacturing stations, or material storage buffers.

Figure 1. CIM Pyramid

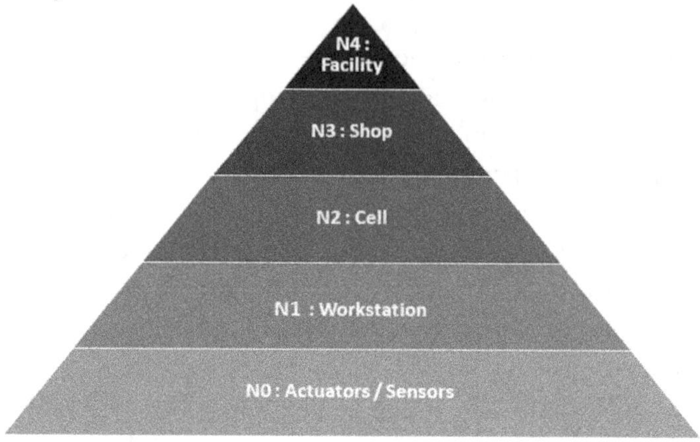

Flexible Production Systems are unable to cope with frequent changes in demand regarding diversity and volume. Reconfigurable Manufacturing Systems (RMS) emerged in response to this issue. They were introduced by Yoram Koren and his team at the University of Michigan in 1995 (Ulsoy, "Reconfigurable manufacturing systems, 1997). For instance, if a production system is designed to produce 3,000 pieces per month and the market only require s 1,500 pieces during a certain month, the factory will remain inactive for 50% of the time, resulting in significant loss. Similarly, if the market demand for another month is 4,000 pieces, again there will be substantial financial loss, equivalent to sales loss of 1,000 pieces. The RMS has a matrix-type system architecture and contains CNC machines arranged in operational stages and inline inspection machines. The significant reduction in CNC machine prices, facilitated by economic globalization during the final decade of the twentieth century, opened the door for manufacturers to look for economical replacements of the dedicated production lines. Embracing the Plug-and-Produce concept, the RMS paradigm (Figure 2) facilitates the seamless addition and removal of Manufacturing Systems components in response to fluctuations in demand. Achieving modularity in RMS necessitates the standardization of connection interfaces among modules, ensuring interoperability across the system.

Figure 2. The Evolution of Manufacturing Systems Paradigm

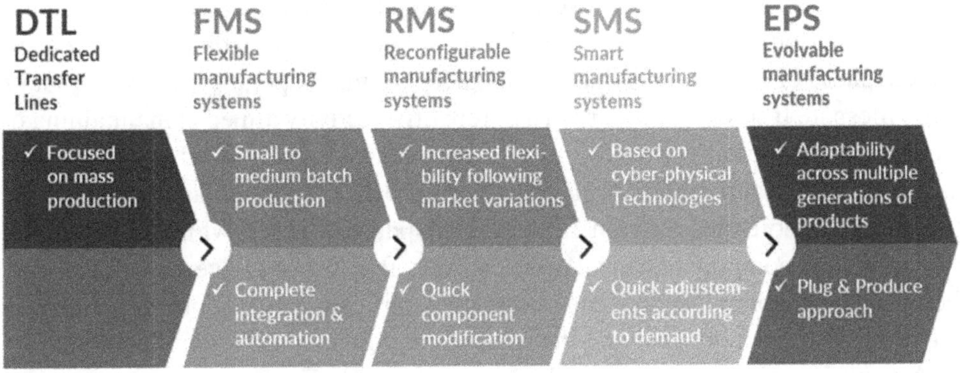

Recently, with the development of internet and web technologies, Smart Manufacturing Systems (SMS) (Zheng, 2018) based on Cyber Physical Technology was proposed. Smart Manufacturing Systems (SMS) utilize Cyber-Physical Systems (CPS), digital technology, and enhanced workforce training to swiftly adapt production levels according to demand. On the other hand, Onori et al. proposed an Evolvable Production Systems paradigm (Onori, 2009), which must be able to adapt. To deal with this, EPS should provide solutions that work for several generations of product variants and predict how Manufacturing Systems will adapt, especially at lower levels.

Production systems are supposed to operate for decades before being dismantled. These systems are too valuable, and their frequent replacement would require a very long shutdown that the industrialist cannot afford for economic reasons (Vogel-Heuser B. a., 2015).

Production systems consist of mechanical parts, electrical and electronic components, and software, all closely interconnected. These systems are typically custom-designed, meaning they are initiated only after the client has signed a contract with the supplier. Such projects usually last for several weeks to several months. The German association ZVEI (Zentral Verband Elektrotechnik- und Elektronik Industrie e.V.): Central Association of the Electrical and Electronics Industry, provides recommendations for optimizing the management of production systems, taking into account their entire lifecycle. (Birkhofer, 2010). Unlike conventional systems, which have a lifecycle comprising three stages: design, use, and decommissioning, in the lifecycle of Evolutionary Production Systems, the usage stage, which covers the majority of the lifecycle period, is replaced by an evolution stage. During this stage, there needs to be an iterative loop between usage and evolution (Rahatulain, 2015). Market requirements and regulations necessitate frequent adaptations, modernizations, or re-engineering of the production tool. These necessary changes and adaptations, referred to as "evolution," help preserve the value of the system.

The evolution of the production system must be considered from the initial development phase of the system, which is intended to remain operational throughout its entire lifespan. It should be regarded as a repetitive activity aimed at maintaining or even increasing the value of the system. Consequently, evolution must be systematically planned, executed, and documented to ensure the system remains maintainable over time. The software component should be updated weekly, while the electronic control system component can be updated every four years. However, refurbishing the mechanical components of the operational part can only be done at least every ten years, given its high cost and the need for prolonged production downtime.

A manufacturing system should be reconfigurable/Evolvable and knowledge-based (KB), in order to produce multiple products with minimum costs. To meet these requirements, intelligent data models need to enable the manufacturing systems performance prediction at an early stage of the design cycle. After achieving this in a systematic way, it will then require the design and development of ontology methods and techniques to contain semantic contents.

ONTOLOGY AND SEMANTIC WEB

Ontology and the Semantic Web (Grimm, 2011) represent a revolutionary combination of knowledge representation and web technologies, revolutionizing how information is organized, accessed, and interpreted on the internet.

Data, information, and knowledge are interconnected concepts essential in understanding the hierarchy of information processing. Data refers to the raw collected sequence of signs, symbols, and facts that have meaning within a specified representational or organizational system. When data is processed and structured into a meaningful context, it becomes information, providing insights and understanding. Knowledge is a deeper level of understanding gained through experience, context, and interpretation of information.

The DIKW pyramid (Figure 3), also known as the Data-Information-Knowledge-Wisdom pyramid, is a hierarchical model that illustrates the relationships between Data, Information, Knowledge and Wisdom. It is often used in various fields, including information science, knowledge management, and decision-making, to illustrate how data is transformed into actionable insights and wisdom through processing and interpretation.

Figure 3. DIKW Pyramid

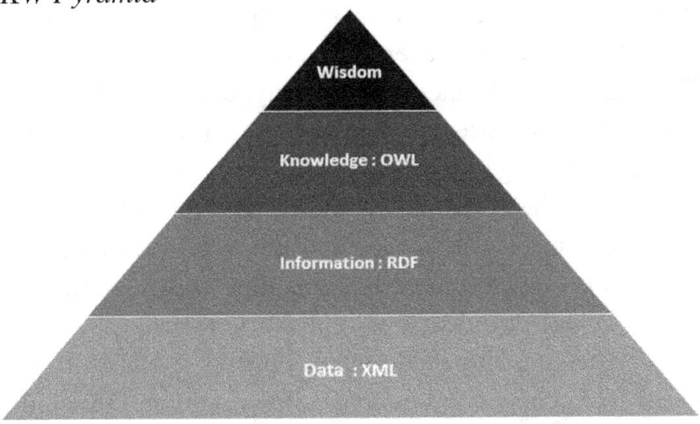

Ontology, on the other hand, provides a formal way to represent knowledge and information by defining the relationships and categories within a domain. It helps organize data and information into meaningful structures, making it easier to understand and use. So, ontology

provides a structured framework for defining concepts, entities, and their relationships within a specific domain. By capturing the semantics of a subject area in a formalized manner, ontology enables computers to understand and reason about the world in a way similar to human thinking. This structured representation facilitates enhanced search, integration, and analysis of data across diverse sources and applications. In parallel, the Semantic Web extends the capabilities of the traditional web by infusing content with machine-readable metadata, enabling automated processing and interpretation by intelligent systems. Through standards like RDF/XML (Resource Description Framework) (Decker, 2000) and OWL (Web Ontology Language) (McGuinness, 2004), the Semantic Web promotes the creation of a web of interlinked data, where information is not only accessible to humans but also comprehensible to machines.

The software tools designed to address complex problems through the utilization of specialized knowledge and reasoning capabilities are known as Knowledge-Based Systems (KBS). These systems integrate domain-specific knowledge into their operation, enabling them to analyze data, infer relationships, and make informed decisions. Typically, a KBS comprises a knowledge base, which stores relevant information about the problem domain, including an ontology which is a collection of classes and relationships between these classes that provide a structured framework for organizing knowledge. Additionally, KBS often incorporate rules that express constraints on the properties and classes within the ontology, further refining the system's understanding and reasoning capabilities. An inference engine then utilizes this structured knowledge, along with predefined rules and logical mechanisms, to generate solutions or recommendations. By merging domain expertise with computational power, KBS empower users to tackle challenging tasks across diverse fields, including healthcare, finance, engineering, and beyond.

A modern family of knowledge representation (KR) formalisms focused on organising domain knowledge into terminologies and world descriptions is represented by description logics (DLs). DLs emphasise a semantics that is logic-based, guaranteeing accuracy and lucidity in the representation of knowledge. The emphasis on reasoning in DLs is one of its core features, this allows implicit information to be deduced from explicit definitions within the knowledge base. DLs aid in the organisation and understanding of domain concepts by supporting fundamental inference patterns like concept and instance classification. Decision processes are given top priority by DL researchers to guarantee prompt answers to user inquiries. Based on networks of structured inheritance, DLs start with atomic concepts, roles, and entities as fundamental building blocks. They then add restricted constructors to create more complicated concepts and roles. These restricted constructors are designed with predefined limitations or constraints, governing how they can be combined to form more intricate concepts and roles within the knowledge representation system. DLs have inference processes that automatically infer implicit knowledge, which is important for constructing instance and subsumption links. Despite early challenges with computational complexity, DLs have proven essential in real-world applications, inspiring the development of advanced optimization approaches. The TBox (terminology) and ABox (assertions) are essential components of DL systems, and reasoning tasks include satisfiability checks, subsumption tests, and consistency checks. Description languages, such as Attributive Language (AL), provide the necessary tools for constructing intricate descriptions within knowledge representation systems. AL, in particular, serves as a foundational language due to its minimalist yet functional nature. By offering a range of constructs and operators, AL enables the formulation of complex descriptions that accurately capture the nuances of domain-specific concepts and relationships. Its simplicity facilitates ease of use while maintaining sufficient expressive power to represent diverse knowledge domains effectively. AL's practicality stems from its ability to strike a balance between simplicity and functionality, making it an appealing choice for building knowledge representation systems.

A knowledge-based approach holds significant relevance in addressing the challenge of evolvble manufacturing systems integration. This approach involves leveraging explicit knowledge representations to capture the intricate relationships between various components, processes, and configurations involved in product manufacturing. By systematically organizing and codifying this knowledge, a knowledge-based system can facilitate efficient re-configuration of production processes and systems to accommodate changes in product specifications or market demands. Through the use of ontologies, rules, and inference mechanisms, such systems can autonomously reason and make decisions regarding optimal re-configuration strategies, thereby streamlining the adaptation process and reducing time-to-market. Additionally, knowledge-based systems enable the integration of expert insights and best practices, ensuring that re-configured production systems are optimized for performance, quality, and cost-effectiveness. Overall, a knowledge-based approach offers a systematic and adaptive framework to address the dynamic challenges of product re-configurability in modern production systems.

A REVIEW OF EXISTING ONTOLOGIES FOR MANUFACTURING SYSTEMS

In the rapidly evolving field of manufacturing systems, ontologies have emerged as a critical tool for capturing, structuring, and reusing knowledge. They provide a common vocabulary for collaborators, facilitating communication and interoperability across diverse systems. To enhance communication, knowledge sharing, and shared understanding throughout the system development process, several manufacturing systems ontologies in different industrial fields have been proposed. In the microelectronics industry, Soares et al. (Soares, 2000) used ontologies in the development of a planning and control system, allowing the mediation of different perspectives and establishing a common conceptual and terminological core among project partners. Dassisti et al. (Dassisti, 2008) also introduced a custom ontology-based model designed to address information interoperability challenges by integrating two key principles: formalization (using appropriate knowledge management tools) and standardisation (using shared standards). This model aims to resolve interoperability issues within single enterprises and across collaborative networks of enterprises.Top of Form

To improve the performance of product information modelling in manufacturing, Lemaignan et al. (Lemaignan, 2006) proposed the MASON (MAnufacturing's Semantics Ontology), which emphasizes on formalization and sharing in manufacturing environments, highlighting the role of Web Ontology Language (OWL) in manufacturing systems, aims to create a common semantic net in the manufacturing field by introducing a class named Operations. This class and its subclasses are used to specify several processes, such as manufacturing, logistics and human operations. Moreover, regarding shop floor assembly, Cândido et al. (Cândido, 2007) outlined an ontology detailing two primary categories of concepts: modules and skills. Modules encapsulate physical processing units or their amalgamations, such as compositions of workstations. Workstations are composed of transforming, flow, or verification units. The relationships between these components are described using the constructs "composed-of" and "is-a" to denote compositions and specialization. Skills denote the abilities required to execute operations effectively. At the core of this ontology-based reasoning framework lies the Manufacturing Resource Agent (MRA), which utilizes the ontology to reason about objects and their interrelations.

Garetti et al. (2012) proposed a three-layer structure within their P-PSO ontology, consisting of the physical, technological, and control layers. Key classes within this ontology include part; component (representing system structures); operation; controller (a decision-making entity for production planning and control, such as a person, PLC, or software); operator; and subsystem (a service class for grouping objects of various classes). Notably, the ontology features a comprehensive taxonomy of transporter and storage subclasses. In addition to the controller class, the control aspect of the P-PSO ontology encompasses the following classes: rule (defining the logic of decision-making, including algorithms, heuristics, simple rules, or knowledge-based rules); order (representing items to be produced or purchased); production plan (a set of orders generated by the controller for a specific time frame, which can be further divided into sub-plans); batch; and task (denoting actions performed by the controller on components, parts, and operations, translating controller actions at the physical level, such as dispatching).

For Agent-Based Manufacturing Systems, Obitko et al. (Obitko, 2010)introduced an ontology comprising fundamental categories such as: (1) customer order, (2) production plan, and (3) workstation, transportation, and material handling. These categories make use of classes and properties from the Core Ontology, which distinguishes between physical and informational resources. Alsafi et al. (Alsafi, 2010) also proposed an Ontology-based reconfiguration agent for intelligent mechatronic systems in flexible manufacturing. It is an intelligent reasoning software agent that allows the manufacturing system to adapt to changes in the manufacturing requirement and/or environment by generating an alternative or a new feasible configuration. It infers facts about the manufacturing environment from the ontological knowledge model and then decides whether the current environment can support the given manufacturing requirements.

ABADI et al. explored the use of ontologies to optimize the New Product Development (NPD) Process (ABADI, 2018). They proposed an ontological model of product-related information, their production processes, and their supply chains. Indeed, they developed a new domain ontology called CPD-Onto (Collaborative Product Design Ontology). To demonstrate the applicability of this model, they conducted an industrial case study involving the implementation of SolidWorks PLM within LAMACOM. LAMACOM is a Moroccan company specializing in the manufacturing and marketing of household items, including cookware, kitchen utensils, cutlery, manual household appliances, tableware, and small appliances. The information stored in the SolidWorks PDM database comprises a set of disjointed files, with no semantics modeled, and the proposed meta-ontology has addressed these issues. Describing LAMACOM's products using an ontology provides several advantages over a simple database description (SolidWorks PDM vault). Indeed, it ensures the integration of information circulating between different departments and the exploitation of ontology reasoning potentials.

Regarding Product data, which is often managed and processed in various ways across various systems and organizations, each group of participants and stakeholders bring their own domain involvement, knowledge, and expertise. This diversity can lead to information heterogeneity, which can hinder the application system from meeting its design objectives. This challenge is a well-known issue in the research area of interoperability problems. To facilitate the sharing of product information and overcome these challenges, Vegetti et al. (Vegetti, 2005) developed PRONTO (PRoduct ONTOlogy) for managing product families and structures within manufacturing contexts. It models variations, compositions, and decompositions of products, providing support for distributed product data management and logistics planning using different levels of abstraction.

Additionnaly, OntoCAPE (Ontology for CAPE Systems) is a specialized ontology designed to enhance the integration and interoperability of Computer-Aided Process Engineering (CAPE) systems. Developed to standardize the representation of process engineering knowledge, OntoCAPE facilitates the exchange of information between different software tools and models used in process design, simulation, and optimization. By providing a common framework for representing process engineering concepts, OntoCAPE aims to bridge gaps between disparate systems and enhance the efficiency of process engineering workflows. The ontology encompasses various aspects of CAPE systems, including process modeling, simulation, and analysis, and supports the semantic integration of these elements across different platforms.

The development and application of OntoCAPE are grounded in the need for a unified approach to managing complex process engineering information. The ontology is designed to be extensible and adaptable to evolving technological and methodological advancements in the field. By leveraging semantic web technologies and formal ontological frameworks, OntoCAPE ensures that process engineering data is consistently represented and easily shareable. This promotes better collaboration among researchers and practitioners, and supports more effective decision-making in process design and optimization (Van Dongen, 2010). The ontology's development and application are discussed in the context of advancing the state of the art in CAPE systems and improving the overall efficiency of process engineering practices.

Finally, for simulating and modelling manufacturing systems, Battista et al. (Battista, 2010) proposed a standard framework that revolves around four key components: (1) product and planning data (BOM - Bill of Materials, process charts,

MPS (Master production Schedule), calendars etc.); (2) operations and equipment data; (3) production and inventory control policies; (4) distinction between physical and information layer.

A REVIEW OF ONTOLOGY DEVELOPMENT METHODOLOGIES

The main reasons for developing ontologies revolve around sharing information and reusing knowledge within particular domain (Gómez-Pérez, 2004), However, creating ontologies is not a simple task. Researchers are actively seeking effective methods for ontology development within the Semantic Web domain. Yet, due to the diverse nature of applications and requirements, there isn't a universal method that suits all scenarios. Instead, the optimal approach often involves selecting from various available methods or combining them to meet specific needs. In this context, we introduce different methods for building ontologies. No single method is ++universally the best. Each method has its own advantages, depending on the specific requirements of the application. Therefore, our discussion in this section explores various methods to grasp the challenges associated with extracting, modelling, and constructing ontologies as follows:

The Uschold and King Ontology Development Method (Uschold, 1995) involves four essential stages: firstly, identifying the purpose and scope of the ontology to determine its intended use; secondly, constructing the ontology by capturing and formalizing concepts and relationships, while considering the integration of existing ontologies; thirdly, evaluating the ontology using technical criteria and real-world validations; and finally, documenting the ontology construction process to ensure clarity and facilitate future reference. This method emphasizes the significance of clearly defining the ontology's purpose, capturing key concepts effectively, evaluating the ontology rigorously, and documenting the development process for comprehensive ontology construction.

Gruninger and Fox (1995) introduced the **Toronto Virtual Enterprise Method (TOVE)** (Grüninger, 2000) for ontology development. TOVE begins with the identification of motivating scenarios, which are real-world problems or examples not covered by existing ontologies. These scenarios guide the formulation of informal competency questions, defining what the ontology should address. The method then progresses through stages including the formal specification of ontology terms, the formulation of formal competency questions, axiom specification, and ontology completeness verification. However, relying solely on motivating scenarios to derive ontology concepts may overlook static entities, as scenarios are better suited for capturing dynamic aspects of an environment.

METHONTOLOGY (Methodology for Ontology Engineering) (Fernández-López M. a.-P., 2002) is a widely used methodology for ontology development developed by Gomez-Perez . It consists of a set of guidelines and activities divided into four main phases: specification, conceptualization, implementation, and evaluation. METHONTOLOGY emphasizes the importance of iterative refinement and stakeholder involvement throughout the ontology development process.

The SENSUS-based methodology (Fernández-López M. a.-P., 2002) is an approach that relies on a large ontology called SENSUS to construct specific ontologies and knowledge bases for use in applications. SENSUS contains over 50,000 concepts organized hierarchically based on their level of abstraction. The methodology involves the following steps: (1) Select a series of terms as seed concepts,(2) Manually link these seed terms to SENSUS, (3) Include all concepts in the path from the new terms to the root of SENSUS, (4) Add relevant terms within the domain that have not yet appeared, (5) For nodes with many paths through them, consider adding the entire subtree under the node manually, (6) Add new domain terms to complete the base obtained in the previous steps. This methodology promotes the shareability of models by using the same base ontology to develop ontologies in specific domains.

The **KACTUS Project Ontology Development Method** underscores the importance of concept reuse from existing ontologies to streamline ontology construction. The method involves stages such as specifying the application context, designing the ontology based on upper ontology evaluation, and refining the ontology structure for modularity and hierarchical organization. By promoting concept reuse, the KACTUS method aims to reduce development time, minimize risks through tested concepts, ensure vocabulary consistency, and encourage continuous updates and additions to existing ontologies. Additionally, it emphasizes the advantages of leveraging upper ontologies for information traceability, quality assurance, and fostering a user community familiar with adopted concepts, highlighting the significance of concept reuse in ontology development.

The Horrocks Ontology Development Method (Horrocks, 2003) originates from the Manchester research group, led by Ian Horrocks. Horrocks (2003) proposed a straightforward yet effective approach for creating and editing OWL ontologies. The method is outlined as follows: Firstly, defining the structure of the domain by identifying classes, properties, domains, ranges, and class characteristics, then adding individuals and relationships as needed. Iteration refines the ontology until satisfactory. Secondly, constructing the OWL ontology involves ensuring consistency and coherence of classes. This method provides a practical framework for ontology development, emphasizing clarity and effectiveness.

DISCUSSION

The landscape of ontologies for manufacturing systems is indeed diverse and continually evolving. These ontologies, which serve as structured representations of knowledge, have been instrumental in facilitating interoperability and knowledge sharing across various manufacturing systems. They provide a common language that enables different systems to understand and communicate with each other effectively. However, despite their significant benefits, there are still numerous challenges to be addressed. One of the primary challenges is the lack of standardization across these ontologies. This lack of standardization can lead to inconsistencies, which can hinder their widespread adoption. It can also result in difficulties in integrating different ontologies, which is a crucial requirement for achieving seamless interoperability.

Furthermore, the complexity of manufacturing processes often necessitates highly specialized ontologies. These specialized ontologies, while effective in their specific domains, may not be easily understood or reused by non-experts. This poses a significant barrier to their adoption, particularly in environments where there is a lack of expertise in ontology development and usage. This is why ontology development methodologies play a crucial role in the creation of effective and efficient ontologies. These methodologies provide systematic approaches to ontology development, guiding developers through the various stages of ontology creation, from concept definition and structuring to implementation and maintenance.

While some methodologies prioritize ease of use and accessibility, making them suitable for non-experts, others focus on logical rigor and formal semantics, ensuring the accuracy and consistency of the ontologies. The choice of methodology can significantly impact the ontology's applicability and effectiveness in a given context. Therefore, it is essential to carefully consider the specific requirements of the manufacturing system when selecting a methodology.

The continuous evolution of manufacturing systems necessitates ontologies that can adapt and evolve hand in hand. This adaptability will enable manufacturing systems to better respond to changing environments and requirements, enhancing their flexibility and resilience. Moreover, advancements in artificial intelligence and machine learning could further enhance the capabilities of these ontologies. These technologies can enable ontologies to learn and adapt dynamically, potentially leading to more intelligent and autonomous manufacturing systems. They can also facilitate the automation of ontology development and maintenance, reducing the burden on human experts and increasing the efficiency of ontology usage.

The integration of emerging technologies into ontology development also opens new possibilities for enhancing manufacturing systems. For instance, the use of natural language processing (NLP) can help in the automatic extraction and classification of knowledge from unstructured data sources, which can then be integrated into ontologies. This not only enriches the knowledge base of manufacturing systems but also improves their ability to process and interpret vast amounts of data. Additionally, the implementation of blockchain technology can offer solutions to some of the standardization and interoperability challenges by providing a decentralized, transparent, and secure framework for ontology management and sharing.

Finally, as manufacturing systems become increasingly globalized, the importance of multilingual and cross-cultural ontologies is becoming more apparent. Developing ontologies that can cater to diverse linguistic and cultural contexts will be critical in ensuring that these systems can operate effectively across different regions and markets. This global perspective on ontology development will require collaborative efforts across industries, academic institutions, and governments to establish frameworks that support both local and international manufacturing needs. In this context, the role of standards organizations becomes even more vital, as they can help to drive the creation of universally accepted ontological frameworks that facilitate global interoperability and innovation in manufacturing systems.

CONCLUSION

The exploration of Ontology-based Semantic Tools for Evolvable Manufacturing Systems Integration has underscored the transformative potential of these tools in the realm of Industry 4.0. By leveraging the power of ontologies, these tools facilitate the integration of diverse manufacturing systems, thereby enhancing their adaptability and evolution. The ability to provide a common language for component interaction is a significant advantage, enabling seamless communication and coordination among heterogeneous components.

The comprehensive review of various ontology-based semantic tools for EPS integration has provided valuable insights into their features, capabilities, and limitations. It has also highlighted their practical applications, equipping readers with the knowledge to understand, evaluate, and select appropriate tools for their specific manufacturing integration needs. The comparative analysis of these tools serves as a valuable resource for decision-making in the context of EPS integration.

Looking ahead, the field of Ontology-based Semantic Tools for Evolvable Manufacturing Systems Integration presents exciting opportunities for future research and development. As manufacturing systems continue to evolve and become increasingly complex, the demand for effective integration tools will only grow. The ongoing advancements in this field are expected to shape the future of manufacturing, paving the way for more efficient, adaptable, and intelligent manufacturing systems.

REFERENCES

ABADI, A. (2018). *Ontologies pour le développement collaboratif des produits industriels.* Meknes: Thése de Doctortat, Ecole Nationale Supérieure d'Arts et Métiers de Meknès, Sciences de l'ingénieur, spécialité ; Génie Industriel et Productique.

Alsafi, Y., & Vyatkin, V. (2010). Ontology-based reconfiguration agent for intelligent mechatronic systems in flexible manufacturing. *Robotics and Computer-integrated Manufacturing*, 26(4), 381–391. DOI: 10.1016/j.rcim.2009.12.001

Battista, C. a. (2010). A proposal for a standard framework for simulating and modeling manufacturing systems. In *Proceedings of the Conference on sustainable development: industrial practice, education \& research.*

Birkhofer, R. a. (2010). *Life-Cycle Management für Produkte und Systeme der Automation Ein Leitfaden des Arbeitskreises System Aspekte.* Frankfurt: ZVEI Fachverband Automation, Zentralverband Elektrotechnik und Elektronikindustrie e.V.

Cândido, G. a. (2007). A multiagent control system for shop floor assembly. In *International Conference on Industrial Applications of Holonic and Multi-Agent Systems* (pp. 293-302). DOI: 10.1007/978-3-540-74481-8_28

Dassisti, M. a. (2008). Ontology-based model for production-control systems interoperability. In *The 5th CIRP Digital Enterprise Technology Conference* (pp. 527--543).

Decker, S., Melnik, S., van Harmelen, F., Fensel, D., Klein, M., Broekstra, J., Erdmann, M., & Horrocks, I. (2000). The Semantic Web: The roles of XML and RDF. *IEEE Internet Computing*, 4(5), 63–73. DOI: 10.1109/4236.877487

Fernández-López, M. P., & Gómez-Pérez, A. (2002). Overview and analysis of methodologies for building ontologies. *The Knowledge Engineering Review*, 17(2), 129–156. DOI: 10.1017/S0269888902000462

Fernández-López, M. P., & Gómez-Pérez, A. (2002). Overview and analysis of methodologies for building ontologies. *The Knowledge Engineering Review*, 17(2), 129–156. DOI: 10.1017/S0269888902000462

Garetti, M. F. (2012). P-PSO ontology for manufacturing systems. In *Proceedings of 14th IFAC Symposium on Information Control Problems in Manufacturing* (pp. 247–254).

Gómez-Pérez, A. (2004). Ontology evaluation. In *Handbook on ontologies* (pp. 251–273). Springer. DOI: 10.1007/978-3-540-24750-0_13

Grimm, S. a. (2011). Ontologies and the semantic web. In *Handbook of semantic web technologies.* DOI: 10.1007/978-3-540-92913-0_13

Grüninger, M. K. (2000). Ontologies to support process integration in enterprise engineering. *Computational \& Mathematical Organization Theory, 6*, 381--394.

Horrocks, I. a.-S. (2003). From SHIQ and RDF to OWL: The making of a web ontology language. *1*(1), 7--26.

Khadiri, H. (2023). *Le pilotage de la production par une approche architectural digitale et holonique.* Fes: Thèse de Doctorat en Génie Industriel, Faculté des Sciences et Techniques de Fès.

Koren, Y., & Ulsoy, A. G. (1997). Reconfigurable manufacturing systems. Engineering Research Center for Reconfigurable Machining Systems. ERC/RMS report #1. Ann Arbor.

Kumar, S. a. (2017). Manufacturing Flexibility and its Effect on System Performance. *Jordan Journal of Mechanical and Industrial Engineering*, 11, 105–112.

Lemaignan, S. Y. (2006). MASON: A proposal for an ontology of manufacturing domain. In *IEEE Workshop on Distributed Intelligent Systems: Collective Intelligence and Its Applications (DIS'06)}* (pp. 195-200). DOI: 10.1109/DIS.2006.48

McGuinness, D. L. (2004). OWL web ontology language overview. (10), 10.

Mehrabi, M., Ulsoy, A. G., & Koren, Y. (2000). Reconfigurable manufacturing systems: Key to future manufacturing. *Journal of Intelligent Manufacturing*, 11(4), 403–419. DOI: 10.1023/A:1008930403506

Obitko, M. V. (2010). Applications of semantics in manufacturing systems. *Informatica (Vilnius)*, 34, 315–330.

Onori, M. a. (2009). *Evolvable systems: An approach to Self-X Production.* Digital Enterprise Technology.

Rahatulain, A. a. (2015). Towards a Model-Based Development Methodology for Evolvable Production Systems - A Domain-Specific Modeling Approach. *Proceedings of the Second International Afro-European Conference for Industrial Advancement AECIA 2015.: Springer International Publishing,427,83–92.* Warsaw, Poland.

Simpson, J., Hocken, R. J., & Albus, J. S. (1982). The automated manufacturing research facility of the National Bureau of Standards. *Journal of Manufacturing Systems*, 1(1), 17–32. DOI: 10.1016/S0278-6125(82)80064-2

Soares, A. A., Azevedo, A´. L., & de Sousa, J. P. (2000). Distributed planning and control systems for the virtual enterprise: Organizational requirements and development life-cycle. *Journal of Intelligent Manufacturing*, 11(6), 253–270. DOI: 10.1023/A:1008967209167

Ulsoy, Y. K. (1997). "Reconfigurable manufacturing systems.

Ulsoy, Y. K. (1997). Reconfigurable manufacturing systems. *Engineering Research Center for Reconfigurable Machining Systems, ERC/RMS.*

Uschold, M. a. (1995). Towards a methodology for building ontologies. In *uschold-1995towards.* Citeseer.

Van Dongen, B. e. (2010). OntoCAPE: An Ontology for Computer-Aided Process Engineering. *Journal of Process Control*, 623–638.

Vegetti, M. a. (2005). Product ontology: definition of an ontology for the complex product modelling domain. In *Proceedings of the Mercosur Congress on Process Systems Engineering.*

Vogel-Heuser, B., Fay, A., Schaefer, I., & Tichy, M. (2015). Evolution of software in automated production systems: Challenges and research directions. *Journal of Systems and Software*, 110, 54–84. DOI: 10.1016/j.jss.2015.08.026

Vogel-Heuser, B., Fay, A., Schaefer, I., & Tichy, M. (2015). Evolution of software in automated production systems: Challenges and research directions. *Journal of Systems and Software*, 110, 54–84. DOI: 10.1016/j.jss.2015.08.026

Williams, T. J. (1989). *A reference model for computer integrated manufacturing (CIM).* International Purdue Works.

Zheng, P., wang, H., Sang, Z., Zhong, R. Y., Liu, Y., Liu, C., Mubarok, K., Yu, S., & Xu, X. (2018). Smart manufacturing systems for Industry 4.0: Conceptual framework, scenarios, and future perspectives. *Frontiers of Mechanical Engineering*, 13(2), 137–150. DOI: 10.1007/s11465-018-0499-5

Chapter 9
Leveraging Blockchain Technology in Indian Agri-Food Supply Chains:
Examining the Challenges and Opportunities

Mushtaq Ahmad Shah
https://orcid.org/0000-0002-3177-9622
Lovely Professional University, India

Mihir Aggarwal
Lovely Professional University, India

ABSTRACT

Blockchain technology has been recognised for its potential to improve transparency, traceability, and security in the financial industry, prompting the RBI to push banks to implement it into their operations. Blockchain has applications outside banking and finance, including in agro-food supply chains, land record administration, intellectual property rights, voting systems, cybersecurity and healthcare management. Despite its great potential, blockchain technology is still in the early stages of adoption in India's agro-food supply chain. This study conducts a rigorous literature review and expert questionnaire survey to identify the key barriers and opportunities for blockchain implementation in agricultural supply chain management. The findings aim to improve digital strategies connected to blockchain, assisting decision-makers in overcoming considerable challenges and deciding the best course of action. By solving these issues, blockchain can empower farmers, minimize food waste and promote a more efficient, secure, and sustainable agro-food supply chain in India.

DOI: 10.4018/979-8-3693-4427-9.ch009

INTRODUCTION

The agriculture industry plays a significant role in providing food to sustain over 7 billion people globally and employs more than 40% of the global workforce (Babaniyi, 2024; Shah, 2016). However, the industry faces significant challenges, including the loss of approximately $40 billion annually due to global food fraud and the risk of farmers not receiving payment. With the worldwide population expected to rise to 8.5 billion by 2030 and 10.9 billion by 2100, concerns about the Earth's capacity to sustain this rapid population growth and the associated environmental impacts are increasing. The food industry, in particular, is highly susceptible to the effects of climate change, such as greenhouse gas emissions, which exacerbate existing challenges. As demand, consumption, and climate change pressures intensify, there is an urgent need for more efficient supply chains (Ghadge, Wurtmann & Seuring, 2020). However, supply chains are becoming more complicated as a result of advancement, regulations pertaining to the environment, and more challenging regulatory and legal requirements. These developments present challenges for supply chain partners, pushing them to adopt new tools and technologies to maintain a competitive edge. Blockchain technology is one such emerging tool that has garnered significant attention from both supply chain stakeholders and academia. By enhancing end-to-end visibility, blockchain can improve supply chain operations and has made notable progresses in deception preclusion and data security (Demirkan et al., 2020). Moreover, BT also tackles additional supply chain issues such as loss of information, precision, openness and trustworthy interaction. It is seen as a tool that may help rebuild trust between supply chain participants by offering a reliable and safe platform in transferring information, which makes it an intriguing revolutionary technological advancement for companies as well as for society (Khan et al., 2019).

Blockchain, serving as a versatile technology, has transformed how organizations operate and is supported by certain governments for its capability to reveal material and transactions that necessitate confirmation and trust (Yli-Huumo et al., 2016). Blockchain technology is a decentralised system that records and verifies transactions at different nodes. Once these nodes establish a consensus, the data is permanently saved on the blockchain, making it immutable and tamper-proof. Blockchain's key advantages include 'decentralisation, immutability, reliability, cost savings, faster speeds, automated processes and transparency with pseudonymity' (Treiblmaier, 2018). These attributes result in benefits such as heightened safety, trust, privacy, authenticity, consensus, and accountability all of which have significant managerial implications (Neisse et al., 2017). These implications are particularly beneficial for supply chain management, as overseeing blockchain-related supply chain activities can lead to transformative changes (Venkatesh et al., 2020). Contemporary supply chain managers are prioritizing reducing redundancies and maximizing productivity. Utilizing blockchain technology can potentially improve efficiencies, saving stakeholders both time and costs. Blockchain can enhance supply chain visibility by recording critical data throughout the product lifecycle. This helps reduce waste, improve transparency, and ensure product quality (Xu et al., 2019; Upadhyay et al., 2021). However, despite the numerous advantages blockchain technology offers for dynamic and volatile supply chains, its effective implementation faces several challenges. Current literature shows a scarcity of research on BT deployment, with many limitations and problems remaining unresolved, necessitating further investigation and analysis. This chapter aims to identify these barriers, develop an understanding of their interrelationships, and propose solutions to overcome these challenges in the context of SCM

Background of the Study

India's agriculture sector is a vital pillar of its economy, generating employment opportunities to more than half of the population and making a substantial contribution to the GDP (Shah, 2016). This sector not only feeds over 1.3 billion people but also provides raw materials for various industries. The food industry, in particular, plays a critical role in society by supplying essential goods necessary for sustenance and economic growth (Timmer, 2000). Despite its importance, the FSC faces numerous challenges, including issues related to traceability, transparency, and food safety (Gurrala & Hariga 2022). Fragmented landholdings, limited storage capacity, and inadequate infrastructure lead to substantial post-harvest losses. Furthermore, the opacity of the food supply chain hinders the traceability of food products, leading to worries about adulteration and equitable pricing (Brun, Karaosman & Barresi 2020). Farmers also face significant hurdles in accessing credit. Integration of world economies and the growing complication of supply chains have further exacerbated these issues, leading to heightened concerns about food security, fraud, and sustainability (King et al. 2017).

BT emerges as a promising solution to these challenges by creating a secure, shared record of transactions that offers transparency, traceability, and trust (Shah & Uddin 2023). This technology can empower farmers, enhance food safety, and boost consumer confidence in the food system. Research suggests that implementing blockchain in supply chains can enhance operational visibility and efficiency, boost trust, eliminate unnecessary mediators, and increase consumer confidence (Saurabh and Dey, 2021). In supply chain management, five major goals have been established, and blockchain's unique capabilities, including 'real-time information sharing, cybersecurity, visibility, consistency, traceability, and transparency', are needed for its effective integration. Aslam et al. (2021) explored the need to adopt blockchain and its influence on functioning of organisations and find a positive relationship between operational performance and supply chain management practices.

Definition of Blockchain

Risius and Spohrer (2017) outline BT as a decentralized system that uses cryptography to create a secure, immutable record of transactions. BT ensures transparency and consent on the validity of all transactions, making it a reliable "digital logbook." This enables secure, decentralized peer-to-peer information sharing. Blockchain has been used in a variety of sectors including IoT, smart contracts, healthcare, Industry 4.0, and digital assets. For example, Perera et al. (2020) investigated BT deployment in the building sector and discovered that the industry's cautious attitude to digitalisation and unwillingness to change impedes blockchain acceptance. Li et al. (2021) performed a review of the current studies on blockchain applications to identify key problems, possibilities, and impediments to industrial blockchain adoption. Lim et al. (2021) investigated the usage of blockchain in SCM, and stress on enlarged attention in its application for SC operations. Kamble et al. (2021) created a choice-based support system to assist officials in predicting the chances of successful blockchain adoption using machine learning approaches.

Figure 1. Blockchain in the Supply Chain Management

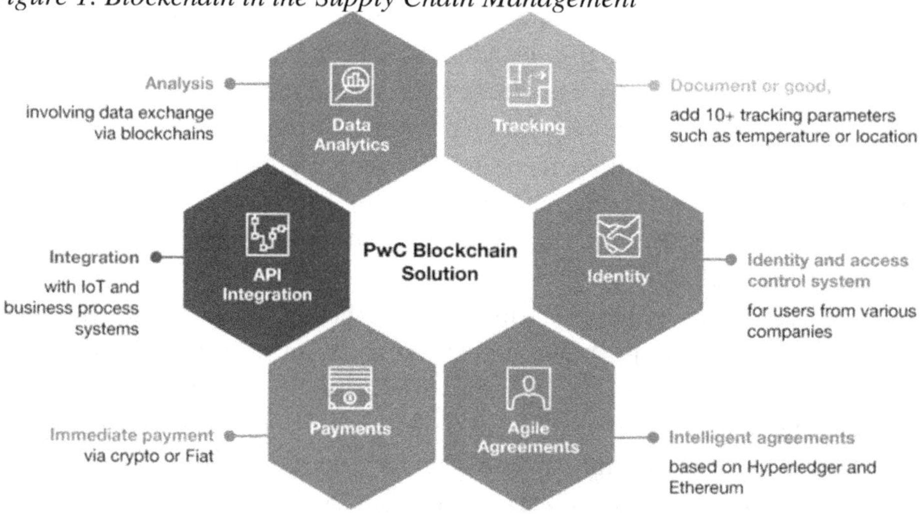

Source: PWC

While BT offers numerous advantages in navigating the complexities of ever-changing and unpredictable supply chains (see figure 1), its effective application faces several barriers. Current literature shows a scarcity of research on BT deployment, with many limitations and problems remaining unresolved, necessitating further investigation and analysis. In developing economies like India, the challenges to implementing blockchain technology are particularly significant due to factors such as limited IT infrastructure, low technological expertise, and a widespread supply chain network. To ensure the successful adoption of blockchain technology, it is crucial to address the challenges faced by developing economies like India. This research seeks to identify these barriers, understand how they are interconnected, and propose effective solutions to overcome them within the context of supply chain management.

Ranking of Challenges in Adopting Blockchain Technology

The ranking of challenges in adopting blockchain technology in the agro-food supply chain was determined through a questionnaire survey distributed to logistics and supply chain companies in India. Questionnaire was communicated through E-mail to the respondents who are involved in the development design, implementation or having knowledge of blockchain. Out of 150 questionnaires sent, 120 were deemed fit for the study after careful scrutiny. The analysis revealed that scalability and security emerged as the top challenges (see Table 1), both with a mean score of 4.1 and 4.05 indicating significant concerns among respondents about the capability of blockchain systems to handle large set of high-volume transactions and maintain robust security measures against potential threats. Privacy followed closely with a mean score of 4, reflecting apprehensions about safeguarding sensitive data within the blockchain framework.

Table 1. Major Challenges in Adopting Blockchain in Agriculture Supply Chain

S. No.	Major challenges	Mean	Std. Devation	Rank
1	Scalability	4.10	0.933	1
2	Security	4.05	0.874	2
3	Privacy	4.00	1.037	3
4	Higher Cost	3.80	0.891	4
5	Interoperability	3.80	1.071	5
6	Energy consumption	3.72	1.038	6
7	Latency	3.64	1.074	7
8	Storage	3.62	1.063	8
9	Standardization	3.52	0.802	9
10	Regulations	3.25	1.166	10

continued on following page

Table 1. Continued

S. No.	Major challenges	Mean	Std. Devation	Rank
11	Stakeholder involvement	3.28	1.063	11
12	Confidentiality	3.20	1.124	12
13	Digitalization	3.10	1.082	13
14	Technology immaturity	3.04	1.246	14
15	Data integrity	3.00	0.933	15

As evident from the above table 1, Cost and Interoperability were also highlighted as major challenges, with mean scores of 3.8 each, suggesting that the financial implications of implementing blockchain and the need for seamless integration with existing systems are critical issues. Energy consumption, with a mean score of 3.72, was ranked sixth, underscoring the environmental and operational cost concerns associated with blockchain technology. Latency, storage, and standardization, scoring 3.6, 3.5, and 3.5 respectively, further emphasize the technical and infrastructural hurdles in blockchain adoption. Regulations, stakeholder involvement, and confidentiality were ranked lower, with mean scores around 3.20, indicating that while these are significant, they may be perceived as less immediate barriers compared to the more technical and financial challenges. Digitalization and technology immaturity, with scores of 3.1, reflect the ongoing development and adaptation phase of blockchain technology in the agro-food sector. Lastly, data integrity, with a mean score of 3, although important, appears to be less of a concern compared to other challenges. These findings provide a comprehensive understanding of the key barriers to blockchain adoption in the agro-food supply chain, guiding future efforts to address these issues effectively.

Challenges in adoption and implementation of Blockchain Technology in AFSC

Despite the potential benefits of blockchain for agri-food supply chains (AFSCs), several challenges remain, including scalability, complication, lack of technical skills, high expenses, and supervisory issues (Menon & Jain 2021). While extensive research suggests that blockchain offers significant potential for agri-food supply chains, the technology is still in its early stages of development and testing. Many enterprises are currently exploring proof-of-concepts or experimenting with deployment and implementation. It is crucial to separate the hype from reality and carefully examine the inherent challenges that may hinder the adoption, deployment, and scalability of blockchain in this context. The following section discuss on various impediments in adoption of blockchain technology in agriculture food supply chain

Scalability: A recurring and significant challenge identified in the literature is the scalability problem associated with blockchain implementation in supply chains (SCs). This challenge pertains to the network's ability to handle transactions at scale without causing disruptions to business processes (Duan et al., 2020; Menon & Jain, 2021). Consensus mechanisms such as Proof-of-Work and Proof-of-Stake require substantial computational resources, making it difficult to attain both scalability and stability in systems that combine blockchain and IoT technologies. The time taken to confirm transactions in a PoW system can range from 10 to 60 minutes, which is not suitable for high-frequency transaction environments like IoT (Xu et al., 2021). From farm production to consumer purchase, every transaction and data point needs to be recorded on the blockchain, potentially overwhelming the system. Current blockchain infrastructures, particularly public ones like Bitcoin and Ethereum, struggle with high transaction volumes, leading to slower processing times and higher costs. To be effective, blockchain solutions in agriculture must handle large-scale operations efficiently, which necessitates advancements in scalability solutions such as sharding, off-chain transactions, or adopting more scalable blockchain platforms. Various decentralized storage solutions were investigated to improve the scalability of blockchain solutions. Moreover, Gai et al., (2020) recommended incorporating lightning network technology with edge computing into a blockchain-based food safety management system to boost transaction efficiency and performance. By handling transactions through an off-chain channel, they avoided the need to record data on the blockchain. To cut down on lightning network costs, they utilized a dynamic programming algorithm.

Security: Security is paramount in the agriculture food supply chain, and while blockchain technology offers enhanced security features through its decentralized and immutable ledger, it is not entirely foolproof. Potential vulnerabilities include 51% attacks, where malicious actors could gain control over the network, and smart contract bugs that could be exploited. Additionally, the security of the endpoints, such as IoT devices used in agriculture, must be ensured to prevent tampering with the data before it is recorded on the blockchain. Comprehensive security measures, regular audits, and robust encryption protocols are essential to safeguard the system against these threats (Akram et al., 2020)

Privacy: Privacy concerns arise because blockchain's transparency, while beneficial for traceability, can lead to the exposure of sensitive information (Menon & Jain 2021). When each transaction on the system is logged, validated, and examined, and users are identified by their unique hashes, issues with confidentiality arise. Striking a balance between openness and secrecy may cause both organisations and people to be hesitant in exchanging secret data on the blockchain, especially if some participants are rivals. In the agricultural food supply chain, public blockchains automatically divulge transaction information, which might pose issues for enterprises that wish to keep their competitive edge.

Cost: Employing BT in the agriculture food supply chain can be prohibitively expensive, particularly for SMEs. The costs related with developing, deploying, and maintaining blockchain systems include hardware investments, software development, transaction fees, and continuous operational expenses. Sophisticated blockchains will unavoidably lead to increased expenses, as the platform will require greater computing power. Various stakeholders are likely to face higher costs during the shift from conventional supply chain practices to blockchain-enabled agri-food supply chains. Additionally, training personnel to manage and utilize blockchain technology adds to the financial burden. To mitigate these costs, cost-sharing models, subsidies, and the development of more cost-effective blockchain solutions are necessary to make this technology accessible to all stakeholders in the agricultural sector (Ehsan et al., 2022)

Interoperability: To be effective, the use of blockchain must interact with current existing systems and allow for collaboration of data. However, the many IT infrastructure and data management platforms used by supply chain players, such as ERP and warehouse management software, limit the scope of end-to-end traceability. Interoperability in this sense refers to the capacity of several blockchains to exchange data and communicate with one another. Currently, several blockchain projects are being developed, each using different programming languages and running on distinct platforms. However, these diverse blockchain networks often cannot connect or interact due to their inability to communicate with each other, consequential in network seclusion and information asymmetry. Interoperability is critical for the seamless integration of blockchain technology within the existing systems of the agriculture food supply chain. Various participants in the supply chain, such as farmers, distributors, retailers, and regulators, often use different systems and platforms. Ensuring that these disparate systems can effectively communicate and share data with the blockchain network is challenging. Standards and protocols for interoperability must be established to enable smooth data exchange and integration, which in turn can drive broader adoption and functionality of blockchain solutions in agriculture.

***Human capital*:** The broad lack of understanding of blockchain's technological complexity is going to cause problems in human capital. Because of the platform's recent inception, there is a scarcity of people with the essential knowledge to deploy blockchain in supply chains. As a result, investment in technical training, skill development, and a thorough understanding of blockchain will be critical to its effective acceptance and widespread application. Blockchain technology (BCT) is still in its early stages, and many stakeholders are unclear of how it may affect the economy.

Many organisations are concerned about their lack of expertise and familiarity with blockchain. Implementing blockchain is a hard and time-consuming process that necessitates a certain degree of technical skill and infrastructure for organisations to thrive (Pólkowski, Łukaszewska & Borah 2018).

***Energy Consumption*:** Energy consumption is a significant concern, particularly for public blockchains that rely on proof-of-work (PoW) consensus mechanisms, which are highly energy-intensive. In agriculture, where sustainability is a priority, the high energy demands of blockchain could offset some of its environmental benefits (Song, Wang & Merveill 2020). More efficient agreement mechanisms, such as proof-of-stake (PoS) or delegated proof-of-stake (DPoS), are being explored to reduce the environmental footprint. Additionally, blockchain solutions tailored for the agriculture sector need to prioritize energy efficiency to align with sustainability goals and reduce operational costs.

Latency: Latency issues can impede the real-time processing and updating of data on the blockchain, which is crucial for the timely monitoring and management of the agriculture food supply chain. High latency can result in delays in recording transactions, verifying data, and updating the ledger, which can disrupt supply chain operations and reduce trust in the system. Addressing latency requires optimizing the blockchain infrastructure, improving network speed, and possibly incorporating off-chain solutions or layer-2 technologies to enhance transaction throughput and reduce delays (Gracy & Jeyavadhanam 2021).

Storage: The storage capacity of blockchain networks is a critical challenge, especially considering the vast amount of data generated in the agriculture food supply chain, including detailed records of farming activities, transportation logs, and product specifications. Blockchain's immutable attribute that the data once chronicled cannot be modified, leading to continuous growth in data volume. Efficient data storage solutions, such as pruning, off-chain storage, and the use of decentralized storage networks like IPFS (Inter Planetary File System), are essential to manage and sustain the increasing data load without compromising performance.

Standardization: The lack of standardization in blockchain technology presents a hurdle for its adoption in the agriculture food supply chain. Without industry-wide standards, different blockchain solutions may be incompatible, leading to fragmented systems that cannot communicate with each other (Kampan, Tsusaka & Anal, 2022). Standardization involves creating uniform protocols, data formats, and interoperability guidelines to ensure that blockchain implementations can seamlessly interact and integrate across various segments of the supply chain. Efforts from international organizations and industry consortia are crucial to developing these standards, which will facilitate broader and more effective use of blockchain technology in agriculture.

Regulations. Policy development and a supportive regulatory environment are critical components of blockchain adoption. Policymakers and technical experts frequently disagree on blockchain applications, resulting in regulatory obstacles that have hampered their wider implementation. Furthermore, there are no defined norms or regulations for using blockchain technology in financial supply chains (FSCs). To enable efficient deployment in FSCs, it is critical to create clear regulations and norms (Mohammed, et al., 2023). It is essential to examine how BCT affects governance thoroughly governing challenges are significant when implementing blockchain technology in the agriculture food supply chain. Blockchain's decentralized nature can conflict with existing regulations that require centralized control and oversight. Additionally, varying regulations across regions complicate the development of a unified blockchain solution. Compliance with data protection laws, such as GDPR, and agricultural standards must be ensured, requiring close collaboration with regulators to create frameworks that support blockchain innovation while safeguarding public and consumer interests.

Stakeholder Involvement: Engaging all stakeholders in the agriculture food supply chain is crucial for the successful adoption of blockchain technology. Farmers, suppliers, distributors, retailers, and consumers must be convinced of the benefits and trained to use the new system. Resistance to change, lack of technical expertise, and concerns about transparency and data sharing can hinder adoption. Inclusive stakeholder engagement strategies, education, and clear demonstrations of blockchain's value proposition are necessary to build trust and encourage widespread participation.

Confidentiality: Maintaining confidentiality in the blockchain-based agriculture food supply chain is a challenge due to the transparent nature of most blockchain systems. Ensuring that sensitive business information, such as pricing, supplier agreements, and personal data, is protected from unauthorized access is crucial. Solutions like permissioned blockchains, where access to data is restricted to authorized parties, and advanced cryptographic techniques can help maintain confidentiality while still benefiting from blockchain's transparency and immutability (Hayek et al., 2023).

Digitalization: The move towards digitalization is a fundamental shift required for blockchain adoption in the agriculture food supply chain. Many agricultural processes are still manual or rely on outdated digital systems, making the transition to blockchain a significant leap. This shift involves digitizing all records, adopting IoT devices for data collection, and integrating these systems with blockchain platforms (Bahn, 2021). Overcoming the challenges of digital literacy, infrastructure investment, and change management is essential for the successful digitalization of agriculture, paving the way for effective blockchain integration.

Technology Immaturity: Blockchain technology is still relatively immature, with many platforms in the early stages of development and adoption. Issues such as scalability, interoperability, and usability are still being addressed, and widespread commercial deployment in agriculture faces technical and practical hurdles (Bhusal, 2021). Continuous research and development, pilot projects, and iterative improvements are needed to mature blockchain technology. Collaboration between tech developers, agricultural experts, and policymakers can accelerate this process, ensuring that blockchain solutions are robust, reliable, and ready for large-scale implementation in the agriculture food supply chain.

Possible Solutions for mitigating the challenges of Adopting Blockchain Technology

The integration of blockchain technology into the agriculture food supply chain presents numerous challenges, each requiring targeted solutions to enhance feasibility and effectiveness. The detailed outline (see table 2) on the possible solution for Adopting Blockchain Technology in the Agro-Food Supply Chain is provided in this section

Table 2. Possible Solutions for Adopting Blockchain Technology in the Agro-Food Supply Chain

Challenges	**Possible Solutions**
Scalability	Implement sharding and off-chain transactions
	Use more scalable blockchain platforms like EOS or Hyperledger Fabric
	Develop Layer-2 solutions to handle high transaction volumes
Security	Regularly audit smart contracts and code for vulnerabilities
	Use advanced encryption protocols and multi-signature wallets
	Enhance endpoint security, especially for IoT devices
Privacy	Employ privacy-preserving techniques like zero-knowledge proofs
	Use confidential transactions and private blockchains
	Implement access control mechanisms to restrict data visibility
Cost	Develop cost-effective blockchain solutions tailored for agriculture
	Explore cost-sharing models and subsidies for small farmers
	Utilize existing blockchain-as-a-service platforms to reduce initial setup costs

continued on following page

Table 2. Continued

Challenges	Possible Solutions
Interoperability	Establish industry-wide standards and protocols for data exchange
	Develop middleware solutions that enable seamless integration with existing systems
	Encourage the use of blockchain platforms that support interoperability, like Hyperledger Fabric
Energy Consumption	Adopt energy-efficient consensus mechanisms like proof-of-stake (PoS)
	Utilize hybrid blockchain models combining public and private elements
	Implement energy-efficient hardware and renewable energy sources
Latency	Optimize blockchain network speed and infrastructure
	Incorporate off-chain solutions and layer-2 technologies to enhance transaction throughput
	Use permissioned blockchains that can offer faster transaction times
Storage	Use pruning techniques to manage blockchain data size
	Implement off-chain storage solutions like IPFS (InterPlanetary File System)
	Utilize decentralized storage networks to handle large data volumes
Standardization	Collaborate with international organizations to develop blockchain standards
	Establish uniform protocols and data formats across the industry
	Participate in industry consortia to promote standardization efforts
Regulations	Work closely with regulators to develop supportive frameworks
	Ensure compliance with data protection laws and agricultural standards
	Advocate for regulatory sandboxes to test and refine blockchain applications
Stakeholder Involvement	Conduct awareness and training programs for all stakeholders
	Demonstrate blockchain's value through pilot projects and case studies
	Develop user-friendly blockchain interfaces and applications
Confidentiality	Use permissioned blockchains to restrict access to sensitive data
	Implement advanced cryptographic techniques to protect data privacy
	Establish robust access control policies
Digitalization	Promote the adoption of IoT devices and digital record-keeping
	Provide incentives for farmers to digitize their operations
	Develop comprehensive digital infrastructure and support systems
Technology Immaturity	Invest in research and development to mature blockchain technology
	Conduct pilot projects to test and refine blockchain applications
	Foster collaboration between tech developers, agricultural experts, and policymakers

The table 2 serves as a comprehensive guide for stakeholders, offering a clear roadmap to address these issues and effectively implement blockchain technology to enhance the efficiency, transparency, and sustainability of the agriculture food supply chain.

Opportunities of Adoption of Blockchain Technology in Agriculture Food Supply Chain

The Blockchain has an immutable ledger that ensures total transparency on food products from farm to fork. Blockchain provides a solution to this problem by generating transparent, immutable ledgers of transaction data. Furthermore, combining IoT devices with blockchain for real-time monitoring and data collecting might lead to better decision-making. Furthermore, quick tracking of the source in the event of food contamination aids in faster recall, responsible customer care, and brand image. This section discusses the technical advantages of using blockchain technology in the agricultural food supply chain.

Traceability and Transparency: Blockchain technology offers significant opportunities for enhancing traceability and transparency in the agriculture food supply chain, particularly in India (Shah et al., 2022). The decentralized and immutable nature of blockchain ensures that every transaction and process step, from farm to fork, is recorded in a transparent and tamper-proof manner. This capability is crucial in a country like India, where issues such as food fraud, contamination, and supply chain inefficiencies are prevalent. By providing a reliable record of the origin, quality, and journey of agricultural products, blockchain can enhance consumer trust and ensure compliance with safety standards. Projects like the Andhra Pradesh government's collaboration with the International Crops Research Institute for the Semi-Arid Tropics (ICRISAT) demonstrate the potential of blockchain in improving the traceability of agricultural produce in India.

Farmer Empowerment: Blockchain technology can empower farmers in India by providing them with direct access to market prices, reducing the influence of intermediaries, and ensuring fair compensation for their produce. Javaid (2022) Smart contracts could streamline operations and uphold commitments without the need for middlemen, lowering costs and minimising delays. Additionally, blockchain-based platforms can facilitate access to financial services such as microloans and crop insurance, which are often challenging for small farmers to obtain through traditional means. For instance, the use of blockchain in the Electronic National Agriculture Market (e-NAM) platform can enhance transparency and efficiency in agricultural trading, leading to better price discovery and improved income for farmers.

Supply Chain Efficiency: By integrating the BT in agriculture food supply chain in India can significantly improve the efficiency of. By providing a single, immutable ledger accessible to all participants, blockchain can streamline processes, reduce paperwork, and minimize errors and fraud. Enhanced supply chain visibility allows for better inventory management, quicker response times to market demands, and reduced waste. For example, the integration of blockchain with IoT devices can enable real-time monitoring of crop conditions, storage environments, and transportation logistics, ensuring optimal conditions are maintained throughout the supply chain. This level of efficiency is crucial for a country like India, where post-harvest losses are substantial (Harini et al., 2023)

Quality Assurance: Blockchain technology can play a pivotal role in ensuring the quality and safety of agricultural products in India. By providing a transparent and verifiable record of farming practices, inputs used, and handling procedures, blockchain can help certify organic produce and adherence to agricultural standards. This is particularly beneficial for exports, as international buyers often require stringent quality certifications. The Tea Board of India's initiative to use blockchain for tracing the origin and quality of tea is an example of how this technology can help maintain quality assurance and boost the global reputation of Indian agricultural products (Prashar et al., 2020).

Consumer Trust and Brand Loyalty: In a diverse market like India, where consumers are increasingly concerned about food safety and ethical sourcing, blockchain can significantly enhance consumer trust and brand loyalty (Ali et al., 2023). Consumers may learn more about a product's journey by scanning its QR code, which includes where it was produced, how it was handled, and any certifications that it possesses. This level of transparency can differentiate brands in a competitive market, fostering loyalty among health-conscious and environmentally aware consumers. Companies like ITC have started exploring blockchain to provide detailed traceability of their food products, which can help in building a trustworthy relationship with consumers.

Sustainable Agriculture: Blockchain technology can support sustainable agriculture practices in India by enabling more efficient resource management and promoting transparency in environmental impact reporting. By tracking the use of resources such as water, fertilizers, and pesticides, blockchain can help farmers optimize their use and reduce waste, leading to more sustainable farming practices. Additionally, blockchain can facilitate the certification of sustainable and organic farming methods, making it easier for consumers to make informed choices. This aligns with India's growing emphasis on sustainability and environmental conservation in agriculture.

Collaboration and Innovation: The adoption of blockchain technology in India's agriculture sector can foster greater collaboration and innovation among stakeholders(Dubey et al., 2020). By creating a shared, transparent platform, blockchain can facilitate better cooperation between farmers, suppliers, distributors, retailers, and regulators. This collaborative environment can drive innovations in farming techniques, supply chain management, and market strategies. For instance, collaborations between tech companies and agricultural cooperatives can lead to the development of new blockchain-based applications tailored to the needs of Indian farmers, promoting innovation and improving the overall efficiency and productivity of the agricultural sector.

Financial Inclusion: Blockchain technology can enhance financial inclusion for farmers in India by providing a secure and transparent platform for transactions and financial services. With blockchain, farmers can access credit, insurance, and subsidies more easily and at lower costs. Smart contracts can automate the disbursement of loans and insurance payouts based on pre-defined conditions, reducing the risk of fraud and delays (Khan et al., 2021). This is particularly beneficial for small and marginal farmers who often face barriers in accessing traditional banking services. Initiatives like the use of blockchain for managing agricultural subsidies and loans can help in reaching out to a larger number of farmers and ensuring timely financial support. The adopting blockchain technology in India's agriculture food supply chain offers numerous opportunities to enhance transparency, efficiency, and sustainability, thereby benefiting farmers, consumers, and the entire agricultural ecosystem.

Conclusion of the study

The agriculture sector in India faces significant challenges, including supply chain inefficiencies, economic disparities, and issues related to food safety and quality. Blockchain technology emerges as a promising solution to these hurdles within the AFSM. By enhancing transparency and traceability, blockchain can help reduce losses up to 60% in yield for farmers by providing a clear view of the supply chain, thus improving inventory management and logistics (Mane, Tatane & Chihab 2024). Additionally, it fosters trust between farmers and consumers, allowing for better pricing and reducing the impact of intermediaries who inflate costs through unscrupulous practices (Mukherjee, 2022) The adoption of blockchain technology in the agriculture food supply chain presents a transformative opportunity to address many longstanding challenges in the sector. By providing a transparent, immutable record of transactions, blockchain can significantly reduce fraud, enhance the credibility of agricultural products, and ensure product authenticity. This increased transparency is crucial for building consumer trust, particularly in an era where food safety and ethical sourcing are paramount concerns. Blockchain also empowers farmers by giving them direct access to market prices, reducing the reliance on intermediaries, and ensuring they receive fair and timely compensation. Smart contracts further enhance this by automating transactions and enforcing agreements, which minimizes delays and disputes. Moreover, blockchain technology facilitates access to financial services such as microloans and crop insurance, which are often difficult for small farmers to obtain through traditional means. The integration of IoT devices with blockchain allows for real-time monitoring of crop conditions, storage environments, and transportation logistics. This capability not only improves supply chain efficiency by optimizing resource use and reducing waste but also ensures that agricultural products are maintained in optimal conditions throughout their journey, thus reducing spoilage and loss.

As blockchain technology advances, its integration with sophisticated technologies like artificial intelligence and machine learning has the ability to increase its effect by delivering predictive analytics and considerably enhancing efficiency. However, for widespread adoption, it is crucial to address challenges such as digital literacy, infrastructure, and regulatory support. By investing in these areas and fostering a conducive environment for innovation, India can harness the full potential of blockchain technology to create a more transparent, efficient, and equitable agricultural supply chain, benefiting all stakeholders involved.

Implication of the Study

This study discusses the adoption of BT in the agriculture food supply chain has significant implications for various stakeholders, including farmers, consumers, policymakers, and technology developers. For farmers, blockchain technology can be a powerful tool, providing direct access to markets, ensuring fair compensation, and reducing dependency on intermediaries, which can lead to improved incomes and economic stability. Additionally, it can facilitate access to financial services like microloans and crop insurance, enhancing financial inclusion. Consumers benefit from increased transparency and traceability, allowing them to access detailed information about the origin, quality, and journey of their food, thereby enhancing trust and enabling more informed purchasing decisions.

Establishing standards and guidelines for interoperability, data security, and privacy is crucial. Investment in digital infrastructure and education is also necessary to overcome barriers related to digital literacy and access, making blockchain technology more accessible to all farmers. For technology developers, the study highlights opportunities to innovate and tailor blockchain solutions to the specific needs of the agriculture sector, such as developing user-friendly interfaces and employing blockchain and other advanced technologies like IoT and AI to enhance its utility and adoption. Other stakeholders in the supply chain, categorised as processors, distributors, and retailers, can benefit from improved efficiency and reduced fraud through blockchain's transparent and secure nature, which can streamline operations, reduce errors, and enhance trust among all parties involved. This can lead to more reliable and efficient supply chains, ultimately benefiting the entire agricultural ecosystem.

On a broader scale, the integration of BT in food Industry can contribute to economic development by creating more efficient and transparent markets. It can also promote sustainable agricultural practices by enabling better usage of the resources and minimizing the waste. The eco-friendly benefits of reduced spoilage, optimized resource use, and support for organic farming practices align with global sustainability goals. The study demonstrates the transformative potential of BT in the agriculture food supply chain. By addressing the highlighted challenges and leveraging the opportunities, stakeholders can work together to create a collaborative more transparent and well-functioning agricultural system, suggesting a positive trajectory for the future of agriculture driven by technological innovation and collaboration.

REFERENCES

Akram, S. V., Malik, P. K., Singh, R., Anita, G., & Tanwar, S. (2020). Adoption of blockchain technology in various realms: Opportunities and challenges. *Security and Privacy*, 3(5), e109. DOI: 10.1002/spy2.109

Ali, S., Abdullah, , Armand, T. P. T., Athar, A., Hussain, A., Ali, M., Yaseen, M., Joo, M.-I., & Kim, H.-C. (2023). Metaverse in Healthcare Integrated with Explainable AI and Blockchain: Enabling Immersiveness, Ensuring Trust, and Providing Patient Data Security. *Sensors (Basel)*, 23(2), 2. Advance online publication. DOI: 10.3390/s23020565 PMID: 36679361

Aslam, J., Saleem, A., Khan, N. T., & Kim, Y. B. (2021). Factors influencing blockchain adoption in supply chain management practices: A study based on the oil industry. *Journal of Innovation & Knowledge*, 6(2), 124–134. DOI: 10.1016/j.jik.2021.01.002

Babaniyi, G. G., Ibrahim, F., Akor, U. J., & Daramola, O. E. (2024). Regenerative Agriculture for Food Security. In *Prospects for Soil Regeneration and Its Impact on Environmental Protection* (pp. 227–242). Springer Nature Switzerland. DOI: 10.1007/978-3-031-53270-2_10

Bahn, R. A., Yehya, A. A. K., & Zurayk, R. (2021). Digitalization for sustainable agri-food systems: Potential, status, and risks for the MENA region. *Sustainability (Basel)*, 13(6), 3223. DOI: 10.3390/su13063223

Bhusal, C. S. (2021). Blockchain technology in agriculture: A case study of blockchain start-up companies. [IJCSIT]. *International Journal of Computer Science and Information Technologies*, 13, •••.

Brun, A., Karaosman, H., & Barresi, T. (2020). Supply chain collaboration for transparency. *Sustainability (Basel)*, 12(11), 4429. DOI: 10.3390/su12114429

Demirkan, S., Demirkan, I., & McKee, A. (2020). Blockchain technology in the future of business cyber security and accounting. *Journal of Management Analytics*, 7(2), 189–208. DOI: 10.1080/23270012.2020.1731721

Duan, J., Zhang, C., Gong, Y., Brown, S., & Li, Z. (2020). A ContentAnalysis Based Literature Review in Blockchain Adoption within Food Supply Chain. *International Journal of Environmental Research and Public Health*, 17(5), 1784. DOI: 10.3390/ijerph17051784 PMID: 32182951

Dubey, R., Gunasekaran, A., Bryde, D. J., Dwivedi, Y. K., & Papadopoulos, T. (2020). Blockchain technology for enhancing swift-trust, collaboration and resilience within a humanitarian supply chain setting. *International Journal of Production Research*, 58(11), 3381–3398. DOI: 10.1080/00207543.2020.1722860

Ehsan, I., Irfan Khalid, M., Ricci, L., Iqbal, J., Alabrah, A., Sajid Ullah, S., & Alfakih, T. M. (2022). A conceptual model for blockchain-based agriculture food supply chain system. *Scientific Programming*, 2022, 1–15. DOI: 10.1155/2022/7358354

El Mane, A., Tatane, K., & Chihab, Y. (2024). Transforming agricultural supply chains: Leveraging blockchain-enabled java smart contracts and IoT integration. *ICT Express*.

Gai, K., Fang, Z., Wang, R., Zhu, L., Jiang, P., & Choo, K. K. R. (2020). Edge computing and lightning network empowered secure food supply management. *IEEE Internet of Things Journal*, 9(16), 14247–14259. DOI: 10.1109/JIOT.2020.3024694

Ghadge, A., Wurtmann, H., & Seuring, S. (2020). Managing climate change risks in global supply chains: A review and research agenda. *International Journal of Production Research*, 58(1), 44–64. DOI: 10.1080/00207543.2019.1629670

Gracy, M., & Jeyavadhanam, B. R. (2021, November). A systematic review of blockchain-based system: Transaction throughput latency and challenges. In *2021 International Conference on Computational Intelligence and Computing Applications (ICCICA)* (pp. 1-6). IEEE.

Gurrala, K., & Hariga, M. (2022). Key food supply chain challenges: A review of the literature and research gaps. *Operations and Supply Chain Management: An International Journal*, 15(4), 441–460. DOI: 10.31387/oscm0510358

Harini, M., Dhinakaran, D., Prabhu, D., Sankar, S. U., Pooja, V., & Sruthi, P. K. (2023, July). Leveraging Blockchain for Transparency in Agriculture Supply Chain Management Using IoT and Machine Learning. In *2023 World Conference on Communication & Computing (WCONF)* (pp. 1-6). IEEE.

Javaid, M., Haleem, A., Singh, R. P., & Suman, R. (2022). Enhancing smart farming through the applications of Agriculture 4.0 technologies. *International Journal of Intelligent Networks*, 3, 150–164. DOI: 10.1016/j.ijin.2022.09.004

Kampan, K., Tsusaka, T. W., & Anal, A. K. (2022). Adoption of blockchain technology for enhanced traceability of livestock-based products. *Sustainability (Basel)*, 14(20), 13148. DOI: 10.3390/su142013148

Khan, S., Khan, M., & Haleem, A. (2019). Blockchain enabled supply chain: An implementation perspective. *Our Heritage*, 67(5), 318–334.

Khan, S. N., Loukil, F., Ghedira-Guegan, C., Benkhelifa, E., & Bani-Hani, A. (2021). Blockchain smart contracts: Applications, challenges, and future trends. *Peer-to-Peer Networking and Applications*, 14(5), 2901–2925. DOI: 10.1007/s12083-021-01127-0 PMID: 33897937

King, T., Cole, M., Farber, J. M., Eisenbrand, G., Zabaras, D., Fox, E. M., & Hill, J. P. (2017). Food safety for food security: Relationship between global megatrends and developments in food safety. *Trends in Food Science & Technology*, 68, 160–175. DOI: 10.1016/j.tifs.2017.08.014

Kosba, A., Miller, A., Shi, E., Wen, Z., & Papamanthou, C. (2016, May). Hawk: The blockchain model of cryptography and privacy-preserving smart contracts. In *2016 IEEE symposium on security and privacy (SP)* (pp. 839-858). IEEE.

Li, Z., Zhong, R. Y., Tian, Z. G., Dai, H. N., Barenji, A. V., & Huang, G. Q. (2021). Industrial Blockchain: A state-of-the-art Survey. *Robotics and Computer-integrated Manufacturing*, 70, 102124. DOI: 10.1016/j.rcim.2021.102124

Lu, Y. (2019). The Blockchain: State-of-the-art and research challenges. *Journal of Industrial Information Integration*, 15, 80–90. DOI: 10.1016/j.jii.2019.04.002

Lu, Y. (2019). The blockchain: State-of-the-art and research challenges. *Journal of Industrial Information Integration*, 15, 80–90. DOI: 10.1016/j.jii.2019.04.002

Menon, S., & Jain, K. (2021). Blockchain technology for transparency in agri-food supply chain: Use cases, limitations, and future directions. *IEEE Transactions on Engineering Management*, 71, 106–120. DOI: 10.1109/TEM.2021.3110903

Mohammed, A., Potdar, V., Quaddus, M., & Hui, W. (2023). Blockchain adoption in food supply chains: A systematic literature review on enablers, benefits, and barriers. *IEEE Access : Practical Innovations, Open Solutions*, 11, 14236–14255. DOI: 10.1109/ACCESS.2023.3236666

Mukherjee, A. A., Singh, R. K., Mishra, R., & Bag, S. (2022). Application of blockchain technology for sustainability development in agricultural supply chain: Justification framework. *Operations Management Research : Advancing Practice Through Research*, 15(1), 46–61. DOI: 10.1007/s12063-021-00180-5

Neisse, R., Steri, G., & Nai-Fovino, I. (2017, August). A blockchain-based approach for data accountability and provenance tracking. In *Proceedings of the 12th international conference on availability, reliability and security* (pp. 1-10). DOI: 10.1145/3098954.3098958

Perera, S., Nanayakkara, S., Rodrigo, M. N. N., Senaratne, S., & Weinand, R. (2020). Blockchain technology: Is it hype or real in the construction industry? *Journal of Industrial Information Integration*, 17, 100125. DOI: 10.1016/j.jii.2020.100125

Pólkowski, Z., Nycz-Łukaszewska, M., & Borah, S. (2018). Blockchain implementation in Small and Medium Enterprises. *Scientific Bulletin–Economic Sciences, 17*(3, special).

Prashar, D., Jha, N., Jha, S., Lee, Y., & Joshi, G. P. (2020). Blockchain-based traceability and visibility for agricultural products: A decentralized way of ensuring food safety in india. *Sustainability (Basel)*, 12(8), 3497. DOI: 10.3390/su12083497

Risius, M., & Spohrer, K. (2017). A blockchain research framework: What we (don't) know, where we go from here, and how we will get there. *Business & Information Systems Engineering*, 59(6), 385–409. DOI: 10.1007/s12599-017-0506-0

Saurabh, S., & Dey, K. (2021). Blockchain technology adoption, architecture, and sustainable agri-food supply chains. *Journal of Cleaner Production*, 284, 124731. DOI: 10.1016/j.jclepro.2020.124731

Shah, K., Patel, N., Thakkar, J., & Patel, C. (2022). Exploring applications of blockchain technology for Industry 4.0. *Materials Today: Proceedings*, 62, 7238–7242. DOI: 10.1016/j.matpr.2022.03.681

Shah, M. A. (2016). Accelerating public private partnership in agricultural storage infrastructure in India. *Journal of Commerce and Management Thought*, 7(1), 9–25. DOI: 10.5958/0976-478X.2016.00001.X

Shah, M. A., & Uddin, F. (2023). Leveraging blockchain technology in the construction industry. In *Building Secure Business Models Through Blockchain Technology: Tactics, Methods, Limitations, and Performance* (pp. 50-65). IGI Global. DOI: 10.4018/978-1-6684-7808-0.ch004

Song, L., Wang, X., & Merveille, N. (2020, June). Research on blockchain for sustainable e-agriculture. In *2020 IEEE Technology & Engineering management conference (TEMSCON)* (pp. 1-5). IEEE. DOI: 10.1109/TEMSCON47658.2020.9140121

Timmer, C. P. (2000). The macro dimensions of food security: Economic growth, equitable distribution, and food price stability. *Food Policy*, 25(3), 283–295. DOI: 10.1016/S0306-9192(00)00007-5

Treiblmaier, H. (2018). The impact of the blockchain on the supply chain: A theory-based research framework and a call for action. *Supply Chain Management*, 23(6), 545–559. DOI: 10.1108/SCM-01-2018-0029

Upadhyay, A., Mukhuty, S., Kumar, V., & Kazancoglu, Y. (2021). Blockchain technology and the circular economy: Implications for sustainability and social responsibility. *Journal of Cleaner Production*, 293, 126130. DOI: 10.1016/j.jclepro.2021.126130

Venkatesh, V. G., Kang, K., Wang, B., Zhong, R. Y., & Zhang, A. (2020). System architecture for blockchain based transparency of supply chain social sustainability. *Robotics and Computer-integrated Manufacturing*, 63, 101896. DOI: 10.1016/j.rcim.2019.101896

Xu, C., Qu, Y., Luan, T. H., Eklund, P. W., Xiang, Y., & Gao, L. (2021). A lightweight and attack-proof bidirectional blockchain paradigm for internet of things. *IEEE Internet of Things Journal*, 9(6), 4371–4384. DOI: 10.1109/JIOT.2021.3103275

Xu, M., Chen, X., & Kou, G. (2019). A systematic review of blockchain. *Financial Innovation*, 5(1), 1–14. DOI: 10.1186/s40854-019-0147-z

Yli-Huumo, J., Ko, D., Choi, S., Park, S., & Smolander, K. (2016). Where is current research on blockchain technology?—A systematic review. *PLoS One*, 11(10), e0163477. DOI: 10.1371/journal.pone.0163477 PMID: 27695049

Chapter 10
Post-COVID-19 Vaccine Supply Chain:
Challenges, Disruptions, and Digital Transformation

Amit Kumar Yadav
https://orcid.org/0000-0002-4565-5284
O.P. Jindal Global University, Sonipat, India

Hewawasam Puwakpitiyage Gayan Dhanushka Wijethilaka
https://orcid.org/0009-0006-9611-5735
University of Colombo, Sri Lanka

ABSTRACT

The COVID-19 pandemic, started in late 2019, rapidly expanded into a global crisis, showing the critical importance of an effective vaccine supply chain. This unique situation prompted governments, pharmaceutical companies, and research institutions to came together for a historic effort, leading to the development and approval of vaccines within a year. The pandemic highlighted the issues of traditional vaccine supply chains, particularly in ensuring efficient and equitable distribution across developed and developing countries. It also highlighted areas of vulnerability in supply chain structures globally including storage, transport and production structures. As a result, the crisis boosted the use of modern digital technologies such as AI and Blockchain, which were instrumental in predicting the demand for vaccines and maintaining the security of records. Ahead, innovations such as the metaverse, augmented reality, and digital twins provide the prospect for redefining even further the distribution of vaccines, collaboration, learning, and even supply chain management.

DOI: 10.4018/979-8-3693-4427-9.ch010

1. INTRODUCTION

The COVID-19, novel coronavirus, started in late 2019, and the fast-evolving event quickly turned into a global health concern, which produced dire outcomes all around the globe. When the virus started spreading across the world, people realized the importance of having a vaccine for the virus, hence mobilizing governments, pharmaceutical firms, and research institutions in a historical initiative. Measures such as the development and approval of vaccines in less than a year were achieved scientifically(Botene et al., 2021; Burgos et al., 2021; Hayman et al., 2021; M. S. Kumar et al., 2020).

The pandemic especially proved that supply chains of vaccines are very sensitive in the delivery process. Each of such supply chains includes manufacturers, governments, logistics providers, and health care institutions to transport vaccines from the manufacturing companies to the distribution hub and the final destinations. Therefore, the efficiency of these supply chains played a vital role in deciding the pace and fairness of the vaccine distribution across the globe, especially in addressing the demand of the developed countries and the poor ones (Gao et al., 2023; Massinga Loembé & Nkengasong, 2021).

Additionally, the pandemic revealed some issues in the conventional supply chain models, for instance, having proper storage for perishable foods, synchronising timely global transportation, and expanding production capacities to meet the global market demands (Chowdhury et al., 2021; Pandey et al., 2021; Wouters et al., 2021). The experiences derived from these issues have provided lessons on the ways of putting effective and robust supply chain infrastructure in preparation for other diseases in future. The nature of the emergency also enhanced the deployment of advanced technologies that had the ability to shorten the supply chain starting from production to the final delivery of vaccine (Botene et al., 2021; Chowdhury et al., 2021; M. S. Kumar et al., 2020; Pandey et al., 2021; Wouters et al., 2021).

The application of digital supply chain technologies such as; Artificial Intelligence (AI), Blockchain, and others during the pandemic proved that they could be a real game-changer for traditional supply chain systems(Hu et al., 2023; Khezr et al., 2019). The role of AI was discovered handy in the analysis of diseases and the necessity of vaccines, on the other hand, Blockchain played an essential role in the Tracking and Tracing of vaccines(S. Kumar et al., 2022a).

In the future, some of the most innovative technologies that more significantly impact the distribution of vaccines include the metaverse, augmented reality, and the digital twin. The metaverse could help people from various countries work together in a virtual space to plan how to distribute vaccines, AR might help in training and informing logistics personnel, while digital twins could help model and improve the entire supply chain, so that there would be fewer problems with distributing vaccines in the future (Charles Chukwudalu Ebulue et al., 2024; Chen & Ruan, 2024).

2. LITERATURE REVIEW

The Vaccine Supply Chain (VSC) is a highly specialized and complex system which aims to ensure safe and timely delivery from inception to final delivery of the potent vaccines (Chandra & Kumar, 2020). It involves several critical components, including the production of vaccines, cold chain logistics, regulatory compliance, and distribution networks. Each of these elements plays a vital role in maintaining the integrity of vaccines, ensuring their efficacy upon administration, and meeting global health needs(Zaffran et al., 2013).

One of the fundamental characteristics of the vaccine supply chain is that it relies heavily on cold chain logistics. Vaccines are sensitive biological products stored at specific temperatures that must maintain their potency and safety(Comes et al., 2018; Pambudi et al., 2022a). From the manufacturing site, the cold chain comprises a series of refrigeration and transportation steps that extend all the way to providing injections Maintaining the cold chain is critical; any departure from these required temperatures may reduce vaccine efficacy or even lead to wastage altogether (Esmizadeh et al., 2021; Karp et al., 2015).

Cold chain logistics present significant challenges, particularly in regions with underdeveloped infrastructure. For example, in low- and middle-income countries, unreliable electricity poses challenges to refrigeration required for vaccine distribution, leading delays or losses(Kristensen et al., 2016; Santos et al., 2021). The COVID-19 pandemic brought this hurdle to the fore once more, e.g., with Pfizer-BioNTech's distribution requiring ultra-cold storage and adding complexity to logistics handling products that cannot tolerate heat (Gupta et al., 2021)

Vaccine supply chains are distinguished by strict compliance with regulations and quality control standards. Given that vaccines are given to healthy populations often including vulnerable groups like infants and the elderly, they must still meet the highest possible safety and efficacy standards. Bodies like the WHO or EMA (the European Medicines Agency) U.S.'s FDA and Europe's EEA enforce stringent rules on vaccine production, storage, transport and administration (Koshta et al., 2022; Vu et al., 2021)

These regulatory frameworks ensure that vaccines undergo rigorous testing and quality assurance procedures before they are sanctioned for use. These processes can be complex depending upon the type of vaccine as well as its target market, with differing requirements across countries making manufacturers or distributors navigate a mire of varying criteria and regulations (Plotkin et al., 2017).

Before COVID -19, supply chains were highly dependent on global sourcing. Companies often outsourced the production of goods to areas with low costs or cheap labour, especially from Asia. Naturally, this strategy is cost effective, and profits for companies. But it also meant they depended on a network of producers in these regions and so were vulnerable if those parts of the network experienced any disruptions. For instance, if key suppliers or manufacturers confronted interruptions due to natural calamities, political turmoil, or health hazards such as COVID-19, they had disastrous effects up and down the line. As the COVID-19 virus originated in China, this created an unprecedented situation in which demand for vaccines surged while supply was severely impacted. This combination of increased demand and reduced supply intensified the challenges faced by vaccine manufacturers, leading to delays and shortages worldwide[1].

Apart from global sourcing, the issue of multi-tier supply chains especially in the development of vaccines was another issue that was a threat to the supply chain. Such supply chains generally include several tier of the supply chain throughout which different parts and materials used in the creation of vaccines would be supplied (Choi & Hong, 2002). Thus, the complex environment of interconnection made the issues of risk management and overall organization's resilience to disruptions challenging. Any disruption at one point within the SC, based on logistic problems, material shortages etc, could mean cascading effects manifested through a disruption inversely affecting the entire structure in terms of delays, scarcities and most importantly, escalated cost (Ivanov, 2022; Thomas et al., 2021).

A number of studies have emphasized the critically important role played by infrastructure in global supply chain performance. The World Bank (2019) pointed out that improving infrastructure is essential not only for making supply chains more efficient and resilient, but also to guarantee it in certain areas of the world where logistical challenges are particularly severe. Besides, other scholars have dealt with consequences and causes of inadequate transportation infrastructure on a global scale. (Xu et al., 2021) focused on how delays in transit points and inefficiencies at major junctions interrupt entire supply chains with hub and spoke distribution design.

(Fawcett et al., 2011) also emphasized the importance of technological infrastructure. According to their research, advanced information systems are vital to supply chain visibility, coherence and even survival. Their study further showed that companies with strong technical infrastructure were able to manage complex supply chains better as well as effectively respond to disruptions.

3. CHALLENGES FACED IN THE COVID-19 VACCINE SUPPLY CHAIN

So before the outbreak of COVID-19, the specialized global supply chains were indeed the most efficient and cost-effective ever. They were also, however, full of vulnerabilities, especially in terms of their global sourcing situation and the hidden costs from an overly complex system. These weaknesses in regions where the physical and technological infrastructure is inadequate greatly reduced the resilience of these supply networks, making them even more vulnerable to disruption by COVID-19(Hayman et al., 2021; Shet et al., 2021; Wang & Flessa, 2020).

The pandemic of COVID-19 not only surged the demand of vaccine but also effected the production, distribution and other aspect due to dynamic nature of virus which behaviours was very unpredictable. Such problems were complex, going as far as including the issues of manufacturing, distribution, and availability of products, which also formed a part of the strategies developed for addressing the pandemic.

3.1. Manufacturing Bottlenecks

A primary issue that dogged the development of the vaccine supply chain system was the poor production output caused by yield uncertainty and other production related complexities (Arifo lu et al., 2012; Jarrett et al., 2020). It is important to note that the fast and massive global need for vaccines abruptly exceeded the manufacturing capabilities. Some of them pointed out that most of the large pharmaceutical firms were unable to ramp up manufacturing to quickly to meet demand and this caused a slow down on the number of vaccines produced[2]. The process of vaccine production is technically demanding and involves use of equipment and inputs, that are specific to the product. Another problem was quality control since even small changes in the production process could lead to production stoppage or, even worse, the destruction of the manufactured vaccines (King, 2024). Furthermore, the increasing the rate that production was being scaled has also posed a new problem for maintaining product quality across different plants when expanding operations to other facilities[3].

Besides, the complications of supply chain dependencies make things even harder for vaccine production. Specialized raw materials and components, for example, are hard to obtain in the right quality and quantities. To produce vaccines, you have to draw on a global network of suppliers that includes companies tipping in anything from adjuvants to allergens, not to mention packaging materials and many other items. These scarce inputs are not only crucial to vaccine efficacy; they are also manufactured by just a few suppliers globally, thus making supply chains clog up as each link struggles with demand (Hayman et al., 2021; Liu et al., 2023). In the

COVID-19 pandemic, this has led to even worse knots: with skyrocketing global demand for vaccines severe shortfalls emerged in some of these essential inputs, delaying vaccine production further still. The problem was exacerbated by the fact that the supply chain's interdependencies meant that time delays or breakdowns in one part of it could have knock-on effects across all stages of production, causing long waits for vaccines (Chandra & Vipin, 2021)

However, there were also many challenges confronting the scaling of vaccine production that involved both regulatory submissions and actual work. On one hand, we had to make sure that output would not fall below quality standards as it moved from one manufacturing plant to the next; while on another hand, each site had its own set of regulations which could translate into higher costs for operations. It was a matter of not just weeks or months, but also significant amounts of time and effort being invested in transferring production technology and expertise for new sites. Even small differences between equipment or processes might give rise to unpredictable results when one company tries to mimic another's products, or when what one company publishes as 'finished goods' arrives at another plant for further work.This was particularly challenging during the COVID-19 pandemic, when the urgency of deploying vaccines sometimes caused people to pay less attention than they should have done over quality control measures such as test conditions. Consequently, vaccines that fell short in quality began being produced "by accident," adding to the problems of the world as it struggled to find immunity(Filia et al., 2022; Sato et al., 2021).

3.2. Distribution Complexities

The distribution of COVID vaccines was a new form of challenge chiefly due to the fact that this was a global issue. Vaccine distribution across the borders also presented a lot of challenges arising from policies, customs, and bureaucratic measures. This made the international supply chain challenging because several countries either put in place export controls or focused on local use. The requirements of cold chain supply chain which was particularly challenging for vaccines that require ultra-cold storage was another challenge(De Boeck et al., 2020). Such conditions called for proper means of transporting the vaccines without the risk of compromise of either the vaccines or the patients who received them hitting the cold season. Challenges that include lack of proper infrastructure in some of the countries, long time taken for the vaccines to be transported, and the sheer number of persons who needed to be vaccinated also put pressure on the supply chain(Alam et al., 2021).

The unprecedented size of the global vaccination project further delayed COVID-19 vaccine allocation. Like no earlier immunization campaign, the COVID-19 vaccine needed to be widely distributed at the same time worldwide. This brought enormous logistic problems, especially as it meant coordinating supply chains across different continents with varying infrastructure and available resources. The urgency of coping with a global pandemic only heightened these logistics challenges, as there was little margin for error in getting vaccines out rapidly and safely tinkering in couriers' hands. Another major hurdle in this regard was ensuring that vaccines were distributed fairly and evenly among all countries. High-income countries frequently managed to buy up large quantities of vaccines through advance purchase contracts, whereas many low- and middle-income countries did not even have access to the necessary doses of these life-saving inoculations (Bae et al., 2020). In consequence, this unequal distribution of the vaccine widened existing inequities within a global healthcare system and raised moral objections to securing relief from it. Moreover, the infrastructure needed for vaccine storage and delivery (especially where ultra-cold storage is required) was not available to all regions equally. Lack of such facilities in poorer areas slowed down vaccine provision or even threatened to undermine its effectiveness, leading to a decline in overall vaccination results (Lee & Chen, 2021).

3.3. Supply Chain Disruptions

The pandemic also disrupted the supply globally supply chains, which influenced the accessibility of the raw materials utilizing essential components that are vital for the production of vaccines. The COVID-19 pandemic halted the operations of industries that rely on importing and exporting goods across the world by putting measures such as the lockdowns and the restrictions on travels into practice, this hindered the supply of vital necessities such as the vials, syringes, and packaging materials(De Boeck et al., 2022; Le Daré et al., 2021). The pandemic also led to distance constraints affecting some workers; many workers from the manufacturing and logistics industries got infected, or there were restrictions on their mobility in and out of work. These disruptions influenced a domino effect across the supply chain where production and delivery of vaccines got affected in their endeavours to meet the global vaccine demand.

Because of the COVID-19 pandemic, the supply or logistics networks, also disrupted overall logistics and transportation channels vitally important to vaccine delivery. That's because with global transport networks now frozen nearly to a standstill due virus-induced travel restrictions and lockdowns, so is the movement of almost everything including vaccines and all their inputs. Cargo flights were cut, and quayside handling slowed down, resulting in significant delays in transporting vaccine-related material (Ivanov; Dolgui, 2020). This was particularly troublesome for products of an urgent nature that require strict temperature control and to be kept within a given timeframe if their effectiveness is not to be destroyed(Yang et al., 2020). As a result, the transportation delays not only held up vaccine production but also spawned material stockpiles in various places, thus grinding out the whole global inoculation effort (Zhu et al., 2021). Furthermore, the pandemic has spotlighted vulnerabilities in industries reliant on the global supply chain's profits extraction as exemplified by just-in-time (JIT) inventory methods using entire multination supply networks. Most notably vaccine manufacturing turned out to be one such industry vulnerable to sudden supply chain disruption.The JIT, efficient under normal circumstances but a terrible weakness during pandemic since it offers no space for flexibility or reserves when difficulties arise. The lack of such systems was seen even more in full relief when shortages of essential items like glass vials, stoppers and syringes were made catastrophically worse by this system and it led to chokepoints in medical treatment (Shih, 2020). So, as manufacturers struggled to cope with sales volumes never seen before, the lack of these vital ingredients on hand brought about production slowdowns and delays in the release of new vaccines. This has led to a rethinking of supply chain strategies, with greater stress on stabilizing system through diversifying sources of supply, increasing storage capacity and investing in local production facilities (Hobbs, 2021).

3.4. Sustainability Challenges

The COVID-19 pandemic raised serious issues of sustainability in producing and distributing vaccines and discussed questions of environmental consequences and vaccine waste. Vaccines production at an industrial scale entails the use of large amounts of raw materials, which the world has been unable to source sustainably without emitting more carbon or using more energy (Jiang et al., 2021). A large portion of vaccines are temperature sensitive, that must be stored and transported using cold chain which is energy intensive and therefore a cause of various environmental effects(Klemeš et al., 2021).

Thus, environmental effects of producing vaccines are indeed complex. End users' premises, especially the manufacturing plants, require large proportions of energy and natural resources that lead to emission of carbon dioxide among other industrial effluents. The cold chain which is an important aspect in vaccine distribution entails refrigerator and transport equipment which needs power constantly and these are dependent on non-renewable energy. Not only does this raise the quantity of CO2 emissions but also creates additional stress on exhausted energy structures, especially in the developing countries (Jiang et al., 2021).

Apart from this, the problem of vaccine wastage, which is especially relevant in connection with carrying out large-scale immunization programmes is also critical efficient vaccine distribution (Haidari et al., 2015; Oberoi et al., 2021). There are several places where wastage can take place starting from the point of production to the store, transportation as well as administration. They also include other factors such as inadequate storage conditions, chances, and shelf doses are some of the common causes. It was revealed that some areas use as much as 30% of the vaccines, which only complicates the problem of their supply to the world market and environmental concerns (Radwan et al., 2021; Wallace et al., 2017; Yadav & Kumar, 2022).

3.5. Equity and Access Issues

Undoubtedly, one of the most significant problems that arose regarding the COVID-19 vaccines was equal distribution. Thus, the distribution of vaccines was followed by highly unequal picture in developed and developing countries. Developed countries easy accessed large quantities of vaccines, many ordering them in advance, while the majority of LMICs faced difficulties in getting adequate doses (Bae et al., 2020; Schwartz, 2020). Such an outcome was felt to be compounded by the problem of accessing people in the peripheral and rural regions since the infrastructure was relatively poor to support the vaccination campaign (Decouttere et al., 2021; Pandey et al., 2021).

Apart from issues arising from disparity between the developed and the developing countries in the distribution of vaccines, imbalances within individual countries were quite problematic. Although reduced vaccination rates in some countries might be attributed to hesitancy, in other countries access and utilization to vaccines were also impeded depending on the region and the existing status of health care facilities especially in the rural areas. The distribution networks in these regions are comparatively weaker due to less number of cold chain storage facilities, inadequate transport and scarcity of health care professionals for administering vaccines. Many of these gaps were not only a hindrance to the distribution and administration of the vaccines but also deepened existing disparities in health care and exposed the marginalised societies to higher levels of vulnerability of not only getting infected. Besides, to register for vaccination and book appointments on social media or websites, most persons left out various individuals, especially those who could not access the internet or lack any computer literacy, increase the gap of persons who could access vaccines(Bae et al., 2020; Rastegar et al., 2021; Tavana et al., 2021).

3.6. Coordination and communication challenges

The COVID 19 Vaccine management and distribution gives an account of how problems of coordination and communication in the supply chain were one of major challenge that hindered the right distribution of vaccines during pandemic(Alam et al., 2021). Industry, government, logistics partners and health care systems were multiple role-players that formed an environment filled with fragmented interactions. Lack of integrated means of communication and their decentralization without a single site resulted in time-consuming, misunderstandings and logistical problems. These challenges were exacerbated by variance in regulatory standards of the nations, making it difficult to correspond the supply chain. Also, vaccines being a cold chain commodity and scarce during pandemic, tracking and tracing was critically important for potent vaccines distribution(Yadav et al., 2023). This showed that a robust digital infrastructure is required to manage the effective vaccine distribution in such cases.

As we discussed 6 major dimensions of the vaccine distribution during pandemic, the proactive strategies must be designed to tackle this in future, and more generally the long-term strategies of the practices, must be based on an environmental, economic and social vision. Even though there are certain advances that cannot be made reversible, it is vital to invent new sorts of technologies that will consume minimum energy for storage and transport. For instance, specific vaccines stable at room temperature could basically alter the way vaccines are transported and stored especially in less developed countries. Apart from this, digital technologies like IoT, Blockchain and others have potential to fully revolutionize the vaccine distribution in coming future.

4. ADAPTATIONS AND INNOVATIONS DURING THE PANDEMIC

While analysing the major issues of immunization during the pandemic in the previous section of this chapter, this section focuses on the developments that appeared as responses to these challenges during pandemic. The COVID-19 pandemic put pressure on the stakeholders in the vaccine distribution system to introduce drastic changes that would bring efficient outcomes and deliveries of the vaccines. This was a period of a radical change in the functions of the manufacturing, stakeholders' coordination, logistics, distribution and waste management. The main goal of innovation in these was to reduce the decision-making response time with more stress on the dynamism and flexibility. AI, Blockchain, and IoT were quickly adopted throughout the supply chain management processes in an effort to continually monitor the location of vaccines, an optimal delivery routes, and confirm proper storage conditions(Gao et al., 2023). It also revealed some of the areas for the collaboration to grow and evolve in the future such as enhanced use of digital technologies, better synchronizing of multi-national actors, as well as the necessity of strengthening and increasing visibility of the supply chains. These innovations include performance of mitigation measures on the impact of the pandemic but also assisted in creating a strong vaccine supply chain that will enable future occurrence of disease outbreaks. The innovations in major areas of supply chain are explained in following sub sections.

4.1. Manufacturing Adaptations

Another major change that the pandemic brought was the focus on decentralizing and localizing production processes. To address the issues of long lead times and low manufacturing capacities of the central production hubs, most of the pharma manufacturers and governments set new production facilities at the end-consumer level. Additionally, this approach brought down the time and cost of moving vaccines over long distances in the chain and at the same time work as a tool to minimize chances of disruption of the supply chain(King, 2024).

The virus also significantly impacted the prevalence of innovative methods that would help accelerate the process of creating vaccines. For instance, the cutting-edge of mRNA business such as Pfizer-BioNTech and Moderna used the mRNA technology to come up with vaccines much faster than the normal procedure. mRNA Vaccine is faster in development because a virus needs to be cultured in a laboratory in preparing for the development of this kind of vaccine. This technological advancement shortened the duration of research on vaccines and made it easier to counter the health calamity affecting the world(King, 2024; Rosa et al., 2021).

4.2. Technological Innovations in Distribution

However, the phase that came with the launching of the vaccines also needed unique strategies on how they would be distributed. It is important to note technology integrated in the distribution and monitoring of the vaccines in realtime. They offered the exposure and this assisted the stakeholders in tracking the movement of vaccines from production facilities to depots and subsequently to the vaccination places. A further augmentation of the supply chain security and credibility was facilitated by the application of the blockchain solution, which offered proof of the transactions' occurrence and of the vaccine's intactness at the time of transportation(Gao et al., 2023).

AI and data analytics acted as a catalyst towards improving the desired supply chain objectives. AI was applied to estimate demand, manage stock and find out the critical points in the supply chain(Torky & Hassanien, 2020). Decision making could occur on the real time basis with the help of data analytics and the distribution strategies could be modified swiftly depending on the conditions for existence. Such technological means guaranteed the effective and fair distribution of vaccines despite the many difficulties that arose in this process.

These further enhanced the efficiency and reliability of the vaccine supply chain by integrating IoT into it. Some IoT devices were used for monitoring and management related to cold chain requirements, considered critical for maintaining vaccine efficacy, particularly those that needed ultra-low temperature storage (Pambudi et al., 2022a). Real-time tracking devices for temperature, humidity, and other environmental variables automatically alert if the conditions are outside the limits of required parameters. This level of monitoring will ensure the quality of vaccines all the way from the manufacturer up to the end-user and will help reduce vaccine wastage due to inappropriate storage conditions. Furthermore, smart logistics enabled through IoT facilitated much coordination among the concerned stakeholders for the delivery of vaccines efficiently and safely to even hard-to-reach areas (Mutanu et al., 2022; Pambudi et al., 2022a; Yadav et al., 2023)

Moreover, the advanced predictive analytics contributed much to optimizing vaccine distribution with regard to the forecast of possible disruptions and their implication in logistic adjustments. Predictive models, powered by machine learning algorithms, were used to analyze vast amounts of data, including weather patterns, transportation schedules, and historical shipment data, to forecast possible delays or risks in the supply chain (Choi, 2021). This proactive approach allowed supply chain managers to make informed decisions and implement contingency plans before disruptions could significantly impact vaccine distribution. Furthermore, these models helped in dynamically allocating resources, such as rerouting shipments or prioritizing deliveries to regions with the highest demand, thereby ensuring a more responsive and resilient vaccine supply chain(Golan et al., 2021b). The combined use of IoT, AI, blockchain, and predictive analytics marked a significant technological leap in managing the complex logistics of global vaccine distribution during the COVID-19 pandemic (S. Kumar et al., 2022; Pambudi et al., 2022)

4.3. Public-Private Partnerships

Due to the global and large scale of vaccine distribution the pandemic required a very complex network of distribution between the public and private domain. Thus, new public-private partnership (PPP) emerged as a key strategic approach on an international level where governments and agencies and private companies had to unite in overcoming the problems that arose in connection with the development and delivery of vaccines.

Efforts such as these were coordinated by international bodies such as the World Health Organization (WHO) as well as organizations such as the COVAX consortium. COVAX is an international initiative to address unequal distribution of COVID-19 vaccines collaborating cooperating governments, manufacturers and donors for the developing world(Storeng et al., 2021). They showed how the global health crises can be solved through cooperation and stressed that the cooperation should continue after COVID-19 is under control.

These partnerships showed that the right time for the private sector to respond was also a crucial reminder of supply chain effectiveness as a way of approaching global health crises. Due to the partnerships between governments, humanitarian and international organisations, NGOs, science and pharmaceutical companies, both the necessary components and the capable knowledge, data, technologies were not only produced and distributed, but also shared For example, pharmaceutical companies' knowledge in vaccines' formulation, production, and manufacturing processes; logistic companies' knowledge in delivery and transportation was availed to the cause(Ferreira & Marques, 2021; Pereira et al., 2021). More productive and coordinated use of resources and decreased duplication as well as overall global vaccine advancement can be attributed to such a cooperation. Moreover, these collaborations exposed the possibility of extended cooperation in managing subsequent pandemics and other illnesses attaching greater significance to a more interdependent and synergistic framework in the post COVID-19 world (Ongel et al., 2023). They serve as a valuable experience to what it takes to build international cooperation in meeting the challenges of global health governance and prevention of future catastrophic occurrences.

4.4. Flexibility and Agility

Pandemic is dynamic in nature; thus, the supply chains had to become more flexible and adaptive than ever before. It became possible for the first time to share data in real-time and thus facilitate synchronized actions among stakeholders and geographical locations. Through the ideological influence of digital media and communication technology, supply chain managers provided timely decisions in response to the change of conditions and can reroute the shipment to avoid undesirable circumstances.

The strategies also included the creation of more adaptive and flexible supply chain architectures. Companies started creating multiple but connected supply chains instead of a single and sequential supply chain. Some of the concepts conducted involved supplier diversity, enhancing local production capacity and risk management for supplier compromising . The primary aims of these adaptations were to manage the first wave and subsequent surges of the Covid-19 pandemic while preparing for future shocks to the supply chain(Storeng et al., 2021).

Apart from these strategies other approaches were undertaken that involves deployment of new technologies like the Artificial Intelligence (AI), machine learning and analytics that aims at identifying and handling risks as they occur in business. These technologies made it possible for supply chain managers to detect disruption early enough before it took place, hence preparing the supply chain for global distribution of vaccines avoiding the various complications involved . Further, the application of digital twins, near photorealistic replicas of physical supply chains allowed the experience of various situations and fine-tuning the processes, with some of the opportunities for real experimentation (Cavalcante et al., 2019; Golan et al., 2021a). These innovations include key changes toward profounder intelligent and data centred supply chains which are much more capable for future disruptions.

Such changes and reinventions in production, delivery systems, affiliations, and logistics and supply systems have not only assisted in eradicating the problems brought by the COVID-19 pandemic but also, they have created new paradigms of how future global health risks can be addressed.

5. LESSONS LEARNED FROM THE COVID-19 VACCINE SUPPLY CHAIN

In the previous section, we discussed the changes in the global supply chain of the vaccine forced by COVID-19. The main discussion of this section revolves around the fact that there is a lot depending on the world cooperation in present and future crises, as well as expanding the usage of technological solutions during the pandemic. The COVID-19 experience has underlined the need especially for more adaptive resilient and agile supply chains to deal with new shocks. It has also pointed out at proper coordination between the global actors for the increased efforts and importance of digital platforms in the management and distribution of vaccines. All these findings will prove useful when addressing the similar interference in the future pandemics and in the development of the higher level of the healthcare systems' readiness at the global level.

5.1. Importance of Collaboration

Based on the experiences of COVID-19, one of the most effective actions that countries should take is the improvement of coordination and information sharing among the stakeholders. The development and distribution of COVID-19 vaccines were carrying out at a very fast pace and vaccination was taking place across the world clearly showed how the world community can work together. In an unprecedented effort to tackle the pandemic, governments, international organizations, pharmaceutical companies, and logistical providers came together, leading to the rapid creation, approval, and delivery of vaccines on a scale never seen before. Programs like COVAX coordinated by the WHO, Gavi, and other key global partners, have successfully tackled a number of barriers to achieve one of the global targets of equal vaccine access for everyone, including the low-income countries. This highlights the role of cooperation in terms of assets, information and technology in combating health problems across the world(De Boeck et al., 2020).

Nevertheless, it has also been seen that how these collaborative frameworks can be further enhanced by learning from the pandemic. Future health contingencies are going to demand a much more comprehensive coordination than hitherto witnessed; the aspects that are most likely to be focused in the future will include aspects such as – real-time data sharing, less bureaucratic and more open-ended regulation besides a more equal representation of all the nations, developing as well as developed, in formulating the common health policies and actions. Building on these frameworks will require not only sustaining the collaborations that have been forged in the context of the COVID-19 pandemic but also broadening them to embrace more stakeholders that include innovative firms, non-governmental organisations and community-based partners. From this pandemic experience, the world can establish a new form of health system framework that is much more prepared and able to prevent and combat the next pandemic.

5.2. Creating resilience in the supply chains

The COVID-19 pandemic also emphasized the need to quickly correct vulnerabilities that had been identified during the emergency period. Staggering disarray due to lockdowns, scarce raw materials and restraint bottlenecks exposed risks of centralized supply lines. If production and distribution are concentrated in one country or a few sources, then any breakdown in that region can have widespread impacts on the standing supply chain delays, shortages and costs (Rajesh & Ravi, 2015).

This new reality has shown that improving risk management was only possible by increasing the supply chain partners network and replicating production capabilities across multiple regions. This allows companies and governments to be less dependent on a single source of production and develop more robust supply chains that are better equipped to handle shocks. One of the key strategies was to bring redundancy in supply chain (having multiple suppliers and logistics routes). This overlap in the sourcing of goods and serveries provides for a backup, so if one piece of that supply chain fails another can easily fill its place ensuring there is no break in the availability to run smoothly.

The pandemic also showed how crucial is international cooperation in reinforcing the resilience of supply chains. After all, nations and organizations globally are already considering a redesign of their supply chains focusing to make them more leaves leant or versatile able to quickly adapt amongst the uncertain states of affair that likely will become-new-norms. Providing additional geographically diverse options of supply would help to mitigate some risks, and global sharing can coordinate responses more effectively in the event that a disruption responds from pandemics, natural disasters or geopolitical tensions. Enhanced Supply Chains: This shift from Efficiency toward building more sound and diversified supply chains will prepare the world for any future crises while making global trade networks stronger, reliable, stable.

5.3. Adaptive resource Management

Another important strategy for preparing future pandemics is 'resource dynamic pooling systems'. These are flexible and responsive management methods of resources that are put into place so as not just to survive better in today's global market but also deal with changing conditions around us. In contrast to static resource allocation, dynamic pooling focuses on rapidly adjusting and reallocating resources based on real-time needs and evolving situations.

The pragmatic meaning of dynamic pooling is to establish mechanisms that can quickly mobilize and relocate resources, such as medical supplies, personnel, or capital. This involves setting up central repositories or 'hubs' from which services can be activated at any time as needed. It also means creating partnerships and networks among various stakeholders, such as governments, hospitals, private sector firms, and international organizations(Ahmad & Mondal, 2016; Emirhüseyinoğlu & Ekici, 2019; Fawcett et al., 2011). This will ensure that valuable resources can be shared among those most in need during an emergency.

Dynamic pooling of resources also requires investment in suitable technologies and infrastructure to facilitate real-time monitoring and coordination. Cutting-edge data analysis, communication platforms, and distribution systems can help to improve the capacity for keeping tabs on supply levels, predicting demand, and coordinating responses across different parts of the world or industrial sectors. By adopting this approach, decision makers can strengthen their ability to manage the impact of future pandemics on society.

5.4. Technological advancements in Supply Chain

The COVID-19 pandemic highlighted the huge importance of technology as a key driver to improving supply chain management especially in the distribution of vaccines. One of the areas most effectively digitized during the crisis was the supply chain and this process was packed full of useful tips on how to design more efficient supply chains. Some of the most effective technologies used included Artificial Intelligence (AI), Blockchain, and Internet of Things (IoT). Not only allowed these innovations help for the distribution of vaccines during the pandemic, but also offer roadmap for better management of supply chain in the future vaccines.

AI was prominently used in managing the demand and inventory for vaccines where it involves the use of complex analytical methods to estimate the needs for the vaccines. Through data analysis AI was able to predict where there was a more demand for vaccines and to avoid having large stock, they had to deliver vaccines to the areas that needed them the most. This will be particularly essential in future vaccination exercises since the accurate forecast of demand in the shortest time possible is determinative to successful public interventions.

Blockchain technology that has been used for the creation of decentralized ledgers and records proved vital in the sealing of vaccine supply chains. In addition to addressing some of the more specific concerns of global distribution networks such as fraud, counterfeiting, and theft of vaccines. Blockchain made it possible to have an accurate record of every transaction and movement of the vaccines. This level of security is very essential when it comes to vaccines for instance it is very important that vaccines are stored at the right temperature and that vaccines are not counterfeit. That is why as more and more vaccines reach the worldwide markets blockchain will remain one of the foundational technologies ensuring security and credibility of the supply chains (Botene et al., 2021).

IoT devices were also very important during the transportation of vaccines especially in monitoring factors such as temperature, humidity and light exposure. These devices gave the real time data of the environments in which vaccines were conserved and transported with a view of ensuring that the conditions were favourable and that the vaccines offered the required impacts. As to IoT in future distribution of vaccines, its application will be even more developed with application of sensors and tracking systems in all stages of distribution. This will create even more optimise possibilities for controlling and tracking the factors that are crucial for the vaccine efficiency(Hu et al., 2023).

Apart from this, there are future digital technologies which have the potential to further transform vaccine supply chain and make it more prepared for future pandemics. For instance, digital twin can be employed in designing digital environment of a supply chain where stakeholders can experiment various situations, evaluate actual constraints and proactively design the right strategies for application in the real world. This capability would allow a more efficient and accurate handling of the logistical issues associated with the distribution of the vaccine especially in diverse and unpredictable situations.

The metaverse is the intersection of Virtual Reality (VR) and Augment Reality (AR) where the actual world becomes a web of shared virtual reality space; this could aid the professionals of the supply chain in collaboration and training across the globe. Applied in the vaccination process, different country stakeholders could meet in virtual reality and develop strategies of vaccine distribution eliminating geographical and other barriers. Consequently, there is a possibility of using augmented reality (AR) in training the logistical staff in real-time, in the correct angle of packing and handling vaccines.

The optimization of logistic networks is also linked with quantum computing, as well as with solving diverse problems related to supply chains of vaccines. Quantum computing, having the potential of analysing vast data sets at very high speeds, id fitted to locations such as route optimization, inventory, and demand forecasting. This technology has the potential of transforming supply chain by being able to adapt to changes in real time so that vaccines get to reach the target population irrespective of the conditions on the ground.

Last but not least, it was found that smart automation or more specifically, robotics and self-driving cars will be quite important in the distribution of vaccines in the future. Autonomous drones and vehicles may help transport vaccines to the regions which are not easily accessible due to certain restrictions. On the flip side, the high levels of automation might be facilitated by advanced robotics technology in a number of steps of the supply chain, including warehousing, inventory, packaging and distribution to name a few.

In future, thus, the combination of these futuristic digital technologies with AI, Blockchain, and IoT will assist vaccine supply chains to be smarter, balance demands, and be more responsive to health needs of the world. The lessons learnt during the Coronavirus outbreak concerning the digitalization of supply chains reveal that what is currently being witnessed is not a temporary fix but rather the way in which the process of transporting vaccines in the future is going to work. Therefore, through the use of these technologies, future immunization exercises will be coordinated properly so that vaccines can get to the targeted population in any part of the world.

6. THE WAY FORWARD: IMPROVING SUPPLY CHAIN OF VACCINES

In the following discussion, manoeuvring through the COVID-19 pandemic sheds light on the future vaccine global supply chain. Looking to the future, it is necessary to look at risks and threats, adaptation of recommendations and conclusions, as well as the definition of the functions of governments and international organizations in the content of long-term, stable and equitable deliveries of vaccines.

6.1. Future Challenges

Though there are many opportunities in the post- pandemic scenario, vaccine supply chains are also exposed to several emerging risks that may negatively impact the delivery of vaccines to the population. Thus, the potential for new challenges will remain high as the population and the world trouble through COVID-19 consequences, it can be newly identified infectious diseases or the renewal of diseases, which were potentially controlled. Our world today has highly advanced trade and travel circuits and as such when diseases attack, they move within circuits similar to those used for business and people's movements. Such situation brings the necessity of a strong and efficient vaccine supply chain that can respond to emergent threats and deliver the vaccine in the right place, in the right time.

Climate change is a major threat to global health as well as the vaccine distribution. Natural disasters like of hurricanes, floods, and wildfires negatively impact the transportation systems hence slowing down or halting the transport of vaccines. It is also important to look at the facilitators, this includes high temperatures and evolving climate patterns may affect storage and movement of vaccines including those that utilize cold chain solutions.

The distribution of vaccines in the post-pandemic world is also hindered with another problem that is the issue of economic disparity. Geopolitical inequalities in access to and availability of resources also affect availability of vaccines with the less privileged nations not being in a position to afford or get vaccines for their people. One form of inequality that became glaringly obvious at the time of the COVID-19 pandemic is inequality in accessing vaccines with developed countries being in a position to order and distribute vaccines far much faster than the developing ones. This must be tackled in the next generation vaccine supply chains.

6.2. Strategic Recommendations

Based on the discussions of previous sections, the following strategic recommendations to enhance the reliability and effectiveness of vaccine supply chains can be suggested. First, outgoing manufacturing and suppliers are critical as it will minimize the risks due to halt of supplies originating from one source only. Another way to decrease supply chain vulnerability is to invest in production capacities within countries, especially those classified as the developing ones. Second, seeking equal vaccine distribution will be another success factor because different distribution models like decentralized production and distribution will be useful in increasing vaccine accessibility throughout the world without regard to location or economic status. This is an issue that can only be solved through the effort of all the countries in the world as well as national and international cooperation as well as standard setting that will take into consideration interests of low-income countries and further development of funding strategies which would serve for the procurement as well as distribution of vaccines in developing countries. Enhancing the healthcare system in other countries, such as distribution of vaccines, cold chain systems, and related transportation systems, also plays a big role in vaccine administration.

Due to movement of vaccines from producers to users, governments and international organizations have a critical role in matter of supply chain. Based on these findings of supply chain vulnerabilities, policy suggestions made are as follows; there needs to be enhanced guidance on the conduct of global response, there is need for rationalisation of the laid down rules and there is need to fund global health and security. The governments also need to increase expenditure on research to foster innovation in the development of new vaccines and storage solutions. The world must maintain cooperation and collaboration with international organisations such as WHO, Gavi, and, in particular, the COVAX facility to integrate resources and endeavours so that everything is ready to respond to further pandemics as soon as possible.

Overcoming such future challenges and stipulating the usefulness of particular recommendations, the global community could ensure the qualitative enhancement of the discussed vaccine chains, as well as increase the readiness of required systems to provide the world population in terms of future health crises.

7. CONCLUSION

Covid-19 highlighted several issues with regards to supply chain in the production and distribution of vaccines such as manufacturer constraints, the process of delivering vaccines to intended recipients and fairness in distribution. But it also brought about unprecedented advancements like, deployment of mRNA, application of artificial intelligence and block chain in distribution, subsequently, it also fostered strong PPP. These have been good learning points on how to address collaboration, work as a supply chain when issues arise and the role of technology in improving supply chain functionality.

Thus, focusing on the future needs for global health, important to develop lasting guarding and self-organization. The pandemic experience proves that the risks of outbreaks of new diseases are constant, and the necessity of creating versatile, reliable and fair supply chains is indisputable. It is visioned that further advancement in digital technologies, manufacturing and solid international cooperation would play significant role to ensure the supply chain of vaccines that ready to respond the emerging future challenges. All the three sectors governmental, non-governmental as well as private entities should continue to persevere to these goals to protect the international population.

REFERENCES

Ahmad, M. T., & Mondal, S. (2016). Dynamic supplier selection model under two-echelon supply network. *Expert Systems with Applications*, 65, 255–270. DOI: 10.1016/j.eswa.2016.08.043

Alam, S. T., Ahmed, S., Ali, S. M., Sarker, S., Kabir, G., & Ul-Islam, A. (2021). Challenges to COVID-19 vaccine supply chain: Implications for sustainable development goals. *International Journal of Production Economics*, 239, 108193. DOI: 10.1016/j.ijpe.2021.108193 PMID: 34121813

Arifo lu, K., Deo, S., & Iravani, S. M. R. (2012). Consumption externality and yield uncertainty in the influenza vaccine supply chain: Interventions in demand and supply sides. *Management Science*, 58(6), 1072–1091. DOI: 10.1287/mnsc.1110.1469

Bae, J., Gandhi, D., Kothari, J., Shankar, S., Bae, J., Patwa, P., Sukumaran, R., Chharia, A., Adhikesaven, S., Rathod, S., & Nandutu, I. TV, S., Yu, V., Misra, K., Murali, S., Saxena, A., Jakimowicz, K., Sharma, V., Iyer, R., … Raskar, R. (2020). *Challenges of Equitable Vaccine Distribution in the COVID-19 Pandemic*. https://web.media.mit.edu/~raskar/

Botene, P. H. R., de Azevedo, A. T., & de Arruda Ignácio, P. S. (2021). Blockchain as an enabling technology in the COVID-19 pandemic: a systematic review. In *Health and Technology* (Vol. 11, Issue 6, pp. 1369–1382). DOI: 10.1007/s12553-021-00593-z

Burgos, R. M., Badowski, M. E., Drwiega, E., Ghassemi, S., Griffith, N., Herald, F., Johnson, M., Smith, R. O., & Michienzi, S. M. (2021). The race to a COVID-19 vaccine: Opportunities and challenges in development and distribution. In *Drugs in Context* (Vol. 10). DOI: 10.7573/dic.2020-12-2

Cavalcante, I. M., Frazzon, E. M., Forcellini, F. A., & Ivanov, D. (2019). A supervised machine learning approach to data-driven simulation of resilient supplier selection in digital manufacturing. *International Journal of Information Management*, 49, 86–97. DOI: 10.1016/j.ijinfomgt.2019.03.004

Chandra, D., & Kumar, D. (2020). Prioritizing the vaccine supply chain issues of developing countries using an integrated ISM-fuzzy ANP framework. *Journal of Modelling in Management*, 15(1), 112–165. DOI: 10.1108/JM2-08-2018-0111

Chandra, D., & Vipin, B. (2021). Investigating the Vaccine Supply Chain. *RE:view*, •••, 251–268. DOI: 10.1007/978-981-16-2774-3_13

Chen, Z. S., & Ruan, J. Q. (2024). Metaverse healthcare supply chain: Conceptual framework and barrier identification. *Engineering Applications of Artificial Intelligence, 133*(PA), 108113. DOI: 10.1016/j.engappai.2024.108113

Choi, T. Y., & Hong, Y. (2002). Unveiling the structure of supply networks: Case studies in Honda, Acura, and DaimlerChrysler. *Journal of Operations Management*, 20(5), 469–493. DOI: 10.1016/S0272-6963(02)00025-6

Chowdhury, P., Paul, S. K., Kaisar, S., & Moktadir, M. A. (2021). COVID-19 pandemic related supply chain studies: A systematic review. *Transportation Research Part E, Logistics and Transportation Review*, 148, 102271. DOI: 10.1016/j.tre.2021.102271 PMID: 33613082

Comes, T., Bergtora Sandvik, K., & Van de Walle, B. (2018). Cold chains, interrupted: The use of technology and information for decisions that keep humanitarian vaccines cool. *Journal of Humanitarian Logistics and Supply Chain Management*, 8(1), 49–69. DOI: 10.1108/JHLSCM-03-2017-0006

De Boeck, K., Decouttere, C., Jónasson, J. O., & Vandaele, N. (2022). Vaccine supply chains in resource-limited settings: Mitigating the impact of rainy season disruptions. *European Journal of Operational Research*, 301(1), 300–317. DOI: 10.1016/j.ejor.2021.10.040

De Boeck, K., Decouttere, C., & Vandaele, N. (2020). Vaccine distribution chains in low- and middle-income countries: A literature review. In *Omega (United Kingdom)* (Vol. 97, p. 102097). Pergamon. DOI: 10.1016/j.omega.2019.08.004

Decouttere, C., De Boeck, K., & Vandaele, N. (2021). Advancing sustainable development goals through immunization: a literature review. In *Globalization and Health* (Vol. 17, Issue 1). DOI: 10.1186/s12992-021-00745-w

Ebulue, C. C., Ekkeh, O. V., Ebulue, O. R., & Ekesiobi, C. S. (2024). Leveraging machine learning for vaccine distribution in resource-limited settings: A synthesis of approaches. *International Medical Science Research Journal*, 4(5), 544–557.

Emirhüseyinoğlu, G., & Ekici, A. (2019). Dynamic facility location with supplier selection under quantity discount. *Computers & Industrial Engineering*, 134, 64–74. DOI: 10.1016/j.cie.2019.05.023

Esmizadeh, Y., Bashiri, M., Jahani, H., & Almada-Lobo, B. (2021). Cold chain management in hierarchical operational hub networks. *Transportation Research Part E, Logistics and Transportation Review*, 147, 102202. Advance online publication. DOI: 10.1016/j.tre.2020.102202

Fawcett, S. E., Wallin, C., Allred, C., Fawcett, A. M., & Magnan, G. M. (2011). INFORMATION TECHNOLOGY AS AN ENABLER OF SUPPLY CHAIN COLLABORATION: A DYNAMIC-CAPABILITIES PERSPECTIVE. *The Journal of Supply Chain Management*, 47(1), 38–59. DOI: 10.1111/j.1745-493X.2010.03213.x

Ferreira, D. C., & Marques, R. C. (2021). Public-private partnerships in health care services: Do they outperform public hospitals regarding quality and access? Evidence from Portugal. *Socio-Economic Planning Sciences*, 73, 100798. DOI: 10.1016/j.seps.2020.100798

Filia, A., Rota, M. C., Grossi, A., Martinelli, D., Prato, R., & Rezza, G. (2022). Are vaccine shortages a relevant public health issue in Europe? Results from a survey conducted in the framework of the EU Joint Action on Vaccination. *Vaccine*, 40(13), 1987–1995. DOI: 10.1016/j.vaccine.2022.02.041 PMID: 35190211

Gao, Y., Gao, H., Xiao, H., & Yao, F. (2023). Vaccine supply chain coordination using blockchain and artificial intelligence technologies. *Computers and Industrial Engineering, 175*(December 2022), 108885. DOI: 10.1016/j.cie.2022.108885

Golan, M. S., Trump, B. D., Cegan, J. C., & Linkov, I. (2021a). Supply chain resilience for vaccines: Review of modeling approaches in the context of the COVID-19 pandemic. *Industrial Management & Data Systems*, 121(7), 1723–1748. DOI: 10.1108/IMDS-01-2021-0022

Golan, M. S., Trump, B. D., Cegan, J. C., & Linkov, I. (2021b). *The Vaccine Supply Chain: A Call for Resilience Analytics to Support COVID-19 Vaccine Production and Distribution* (pp. 389–437). DOI: 10.1007/978-3-030-71587-8_22

Gupta, S., Starr, M. K., Farahani, R. Z., & Asgari, N. (2021). Pandemics/Epidemics: Challenges and Opportunities for Operations Management Research. *Manufacturing & Service Operations Management*. Advance online publication. DOI: 10.1287/msom.2021.0965

Haidari, L. A., Wahl, B., Brown, S. T., Privor-Dumm, L., Wallman-Stokes, C., Gorham, K., Connor, D. L., Wateska, A. R., Schreiber, B., Dicko, H., Jaillard, P., Avella, M., & Lee, B. Y. (2015). One size does not fit all: The impact of primary vaccine container size on vaccine distribution and delivery. *Vaccine*, 33(28), 3242–3247. DOI: 10.1016/j.vaccine.2015.04.018 PMID: 25889160

Hayman, B., Suri, R., & Prasad, S. D. (2021). COVID-19 vaccine capacity: Challenges and mitigation – The DCVMN perspective. *Vaccine*, 39(35), 4932–4937. DOI: 10.1016/j.vaccine.2021.07.007 PMID: 34325932

Hu, H., Xu, J., Liu, M., & Lim, M. K. (2023). Vaccine supply chain management: An intelligent system utilizing blockchain, IoT and machine learning. *Journal of Business Research, 156*(November 2022), 113480. DOI: 10.1016/j.jbusres.2022.113480

Ivanov, D. (2022). Viable supply chain model: Integrating agility, resilience and sustainability perspectives—lessons from and thinking beyond the COVID-19 pandemic. *Annals of Operations Research*, 319(1), 1411–1431. DOI: 10.1007/s10479-020-03640-6 PMID: 32836614

Jarrett, S., Yang, L., & Pagliusi, S. (2020). Roadmap for strengthening the vaccine supply chain in emerging countries: Manufacturers' perspectives. *Vaccine: X*, 5, 100068. DOI: 10.1016/j.jvacx.2020.100068 PMID: 32775997

Jiang, P., Klemeš, J. J., Van Fan, Y., Fu, X., Tan, R. R., You, S., & Foley, A. M. (2021). Energy, environmental, economic and social equity (4E) pressures of COVID-19 vaccination mismanagement: A global perspective. *Energy*, 235, 121315. DOI: 10.1016/j.energy.2021.121315 PMID: 34226789

Karp, C. L., Lans, D., Esparza, J., Edson, E. B., Owen, K. E., Wilson, C. B., Heaton, P. M., Levine, O. S., & Rao, R. (2015). Evaluating the value proposition for improving vaccine thermostability to increase vaccine impact in low and middle-income countries. *Vaccine*, 33(30), 3471–3479. DOI: 10.1016/j.vaccine.2015.05.071 PMID: 26055297

Khezr, S., Moniruzzaman, M., Yassine, A., & Benlamri, R. (2019). Blockchain Technology in Healthcare: A Comprehensive Review and Directions for Future Research. *Applied Sciences 2019, Vol. 9, Page 1736, 9*(9), 1736. DOI: 10.3390/app9091736

King, M. L. (2024). How manufacturing won or lost the COVID-19 vaccine race. *Vaccine*, 42(5), 1004–1012. DOI: 10.1016/j.vaccine.2023.12.031 PMID: 38228438

Klemeš, J. J., Jiang, P., Van Fan, Y., Bokhari, A., & Wang, X.-C. (2021). COVID-19 pandemics Stage II – Energy and environmental impacts of vaccination. *Renewable & Sustainable Energy Reviews*, 150, 111400. DOI: 10.1016/j.rser.2021.111400 PMID: 34248390

Koshta, N., Devi, Y., & Chauhan, C. (2022). Evaluating Barriers to the Adoption of Delivery Drones in Rural Healthcare Supply Chains: Preparing the Healthcare System for the Future. *IEEE Transactions on Engineering Management*, 1–13. DOI: 10.1109/TEM.2022.3210121

Kristensen, D. D., Lorenson, T., Bartholomew, K., & Villadiego, S. (2016). Can thermostable vaccines help address cold-chain challenges? Results from stakeholder interviews in six low- and middle-income countries. *Vaccine*, 34(7), 899–904. DOI: 10.1016/j.vaccine.2016.01.001 PMID: 26778422

Kumar, M. S., Raut, D. R. D., Narwane, D. V. S., & Narkhede, D. B. E. (2020). Applications of industry 4.0 to overcome the COVID-19 operational challenges. *Diabetes & Metabolic Syndrome*, 14(5), 1283–1289. DOI: 10.1016/j.dsx.2020.07.010 PMID: 32755822

Kumar, S., Raut, R. D., Priyadarshinee, P., Mangla, S. K., Awan, U., & Narkhede, B. E. (2022a). The Impact of IoT on the Performance of Vaccine Supply Chain Distribution in the COVID-19 Context. *IEEE Transactions on Engineering Management*, 1–11. DOI: 10.1109/TEM.2022.3157625

Kumar, S., Raut, R. D., Priyadarshinee, P., Mangla, S. K., Awan, U., & Narkhede, B. E. (2022b). The Impact of IoT on the Performance of Vaccine Supply Chain Distribution in the COVID-19 Context. *IEEE Transactions on Engineering Management, PP*, 1–11. DOI: 10.1109/TEM.2022.3157625

Le Daré, B., Bacle, A., Lhermitte, R., Lesourd, F., & Lurton, Y. (2021). Increasing vaccine supply with low dead-volume syringes and needles. *International Journal of Pharmaceutics*, 608, 121053. Advance online publication. DOI: 10.1016/j.ijpharm.2021.121053 PMID: 34461171

Lee, T. H., & Chen, A. H. (2021). Last-Mile Logistics of Covid Vaccination — The Role of Health Care Organizations. *The New England Journal of Medicine*, 384(8), 685–687. DOI: 10.1056/NEJMp2100574 PMID: 33503340

Liu, R., Tan, C., Wu, D. D., & Zhao, C. (2023). Strategies choice for blockchain construction and coordination in vaccine supply chain. *Computers & Industrial Engineering*, 182(May), 109346. DOI: 10.1016/j.cie.2023.109346

Massinga Loembé, M., & Nkengasong, J. N. (2021). COVID-19 vaccine access in Africa: Global distribution, vaccine platforms, and challenges ahead. *Immunity*, 54(7), 1353–1362. DOI: 10.1016/j.immuni.2021.06.017 PMID: 34260880

Mutanu, L., Gupta, K., & Gohil, J. (2022). Leveraging IoT solutions for enhanced health information exchange. *Technology in Society*, 68, 101882. DOI: 10.1016/j.techsoc.2022.101882

Oberoi, S., Mishra, P., Gupta, V. K., Patnaik, S., Garg, A., & Kaur, R. (2021). Vaccine wastage at primary, secondary, and tertiary level of healthcare system—A study from Northern India. *Journal of Family Medicine and Primary Care*, 10(2), 877–882. DOI: 10.4103/jfmpc.jfmpc_1442_20 PMID: 34041092

Ongel, B., Tanyer, A. M., & Dikmen, I. (2023). A network-based model for the assessment of success in PPP healthcare projects. *International Journal of Construction Management*, 0(0), 1–13. DOI: 10.1080/15623599.2023.2239438

Pambudi, N. A., Sarifudin, A., Gandidi, I. M., & Romadhon, R. (2022a). Vaccine cold chain management and cold storage technology to address the challenges of vaccination programs. *Energy Reports*, 8, 955–972. DOI: 10.1016/j.egyr.2021.12.039

Pambudi, N. A., Sarifudin, A., Gandidi, I. M., & Romadhon, R. (2022b). Vaccine cold chain management and cold storage technology to address the challenges of vaccination programs. *Energy Reports*, 8, 955–972. DOI: 10.1016/j.egyr.2021.12.039

Pandey, A., Sah, P., Moghadas, S. M., Mandal, S., Banerjee, S., Hotez, P. J., & Galvani, A. P. (2021). Challenges facing COVID-19 vaccination in India: Lessons from the initial vaccine rollout. *Journal of Global Health*, 11, 1–5. DOI: 10.7189/jogh.11.03083 PMID: 34221355

Pereira, M. A., Ferreira, D. C., & Marques, R. C. (2021). A critical look at the Portuguese public–private partnerships in healthcare. *The International Journal of Health Planning and Management*, 36(2), 302–315. DOI: 10.1002/hpm.3084 PMID: 33015900

Plotkin, S., Robinson, J. M., Cunningham, G., Iqbal, R., & Larsen, S. (2017). The complexity and cost of vaccine manufacturing – An overview. *Vaccine*, 35(33), 4064–4071. DOI: 10.1016/j.vaccine.2017.06.003 PMID: 28647170

Radwan, N. F., Abu-Sheasha, G. A., Bedwani, R. N., & Yassine, O. G. (2021). Vaccine wastage and cost saving after multi-dose vial policy implementation in Egypt: A success story. *Vaccine*, 39(51), 7457–7463. DOI: 10.1016/j.vaccine.2021.10.067 PMID: 34772545

Rajesh, R., & Ravi, V. (2015). Supplier selection in resilient supply chains: A grey relational analysis approach. *Journal of Cleaner Production*, 86, 343–359. DOI: 10.1016/j.jclepro.2014.08.054

Rastegar, M., Tavana, M., Meraj, A., & Mina, H. (2021). An inventory-location optimization model for equitable influenza vaccine distribution in developing countries during the COVID-19 pandemic. *Vaccine*, 39(3), 495–504. DOI: 10.1016/j.vaccine.2020.12.022 PMID: 33342632

Rosa, S. S., Prazeres, D. M. F., Azevedo, A. M., & Marques, M. P. C. (2021). mRNA vaccines manufacturing: Challenges and bottlenecks. *Vaccine*, 39(16), 2190–2200. DOI: 10.1016/j.vaccine.2021.03.038 PMID: 33771389

Santos, A. F., Gaspar, P. D., & de Souza, H. J. L. (2021). Refrigeration of COVID-19 vaccines: Ideal storage characteristics, energy efficiency and environmental impacts of various vaccine options. *Energies*, 14(7), 1849. Advance online publication. DOI: 10.3390/en14071849

Sato, R., Thompson, A., Sani, I., Metiboba, L., Giwa, A., Femi-Ojo, O., & Odezugo, V. (2021). Effect of Vaccine Direct Delivery (VDD) on vaccine stockouts and number of vaccinations: Case study from Bauchi State, Nigeria. *Vaccine*, 39(9), 1445–1451. DOI: 10.1016/j.vaccine.2021.01.037 PMID: 33541796

Schwartz, J. L. (2020). Equitable global access to coronavirus disease 2019 vaccines. In *The BMJ* (Vol. 371). BMJ Publishing Group., DOI: 10.1136/bmj.m4735

Shet, A., Dhaliwal, B., Banerjee, P., Carr, K., Deluca, A., Britto, C., Seth, R., Parekh, B., Basavaraj, G. V., Shastri, D., & Gupta, P. (2021). COVID-19-related disruptions to routine vaccination services in India: A survey of paediatric providers. *BMJ Paediatrics Open*, 5(1), 2021.01.25.21250040. Advance online publication. DOI: 10.1136/bmjpo-2021-001060 PMID: 34192200

Storeng, K. T., de Bengy Puyvallée, A., & Stein, F. (2021). COVAX and the rise of the 'super public private partnership' for global health. *Global Public Health: An International Journal for Research, Policy and Practice*, 18(1), 1987502. Advance online publication. DOI: 10.1080/17441692.2021.1987502 PMID: 34686103

Tavana, M., Govindan, K., Nasr, A. K., Heidary, M. S., & Mina, H. (2021). A mathematical programming approach for equitable COVID-19 vaccine distribution in developing countries. In *Annals of Operations Research* (Issue 0123456789). Springer US. DOI: 10.1007/s10479-021-04130-z

Thomas, R., Darby, J. L., Dobrzykowski, D., & van Hoek, R. (2021). Decomposing Social Sustainability: Signaling Theory Insights into Supplier Selection Decisions. *The Journal of Supply Chain Management*, 57(4), 117–136. DOI: 10.1111/jscm.12247

Torky, M., & Hassanien, A. E. (2020). *COVID-19 Blockchain Framework: Innovative Approach*. https://arxiv.org/abs/2004.06081v1

Vu, N., Ghadge, A., & Bourlakis, M. (2021). Blockchain adoption in food supply chains: A review and implementation framework. *Production Planning and Control*, 0(0), 1–18. DOI: 10.1080/09537287.2021.1939902

Wallace, A. S., Willis, F., Nwaze, E., Dieng, B., Sipilanyambe, N., Daniels, D., Abanida, E., Gasasira, A., Mahmud, M., & Ryman, T. K. (2017). Vaccine wastage in Nigeria: An assessment of wastage rates and related vaccinator knowledge, attitudes and practices. *Vaccine*, 35(48), 6751–6758. DOI: 10.1016/j.vaccine.2017.09.082 PMID: 29066189

Wang, M., & Flessa, S. (2020). Modelling Covid-19 under uncertainty: What can we expect? *The European Journal of Health Economics*, 21(5), 665–668. DOI: 10.1007/s10198-020-01202-y PMID: 32494911

Wouters, O. J., Shadlen, K. C., Salcher-Konrad, M., Pollard, A. J., Larson, H. J., Teerawattananon, Y., & Jit, M. (2021). Challenges in ensuring global access to COVID-19 vaccines: Production, affordability, allocation, and deployment. *Lancet*, 397(10278), 1023–1034. DOI: 10.1016/S0140-6736(21)00306-8 PMID: 33587887

Xu, X., Rodgers, M. D., & Guo, W. (2021). A hub-and-spoke design for ultra-cold COVID-19 vaccine distribution. *Vaccine*, 39(41), 6127–6136. DOI: 10.1016/j.vaccine.2021.08.069 PMID: 34509324

Yadav, A. K., & Kumar, D. (2022). A LAG-based framework to overcome the challenges of the sustainable vaccine supply chain: an integrated BWM–MARCOS approach. *Journal of Humanitarian Logistics and Supply Chain Management*. DOI: 10.1108/JHLSCM-09-2021-0091

Yadav, A. K., Shweta, , & Kumar, D. (2022, November). Shweta, & Kumar, D. (2023). Blockchain technology and vaccine supply chain: Exploration and analysis of the adoption barriers in the Indian context. *International Journal of Production Economics*, 255, 108716. DOI: 10.1016/j.ijpe.2022.108716

Yang, Y., Bidkhori, H., & Rajgopal, J. (2020). Optimizing vaccine distribution networks in low and middle-income countries. *Omega*, 99, 102197. DOI: 10.1016/j.omega.2020.102197

Zaffran, M., Vandelaer, J., Kristensen, D., Melgaard, B., Yadav, P., Antwi-Agyei, K. O., & Lasher, H. (2013). The imperative for stronger vaccine supply and logistics systems. *Vaccine*, 31(SUPPL2), B73–B80. DOI: 10.1016/j.vaccine.2012.11.036 PMID: 23598495

ENDNOTES

1 https://hbr.org/2020/09/global-supply-chains-in-a-post-pandemic-world

2 https://www.theguardian.com/society/2021/mar/19/how-are-covid-vaccines-produced-and-why-have-there-been-delays

3 https://www.who.int/news/item/25-03-2021-covax-updates-participants-on-delivery-delays-for-vaccines-from-serum-institute-of-india-(sii)-and-astrazeneca

Chapter 11
Study of the Impact of Artificial Intelligence and the Digitalization of Purchasing Practices on Economic Performance

Jouali Youssef
EMSI Rabat, Morocco

Jouali Jamila
ESTCASA, Morocco

ABSTRACT

This chapter explores the impact of technological advances on purchasing practices and their influence on the performance of Moroccan companies, focusing on crucial aspects such as the impact of information technology, machine learning techniques, and the resolution of logistical challenges. The study underlines the importance of digitization for Moroccan businesses and policymakers, highlighting the critical role of technology adoption in promoting the procurement sector. It identifies the main drivers of digitization adoption, including organizational, technological, environmental, and human aspects, while addressing ethical considerations, such as data privacy and the impact on employment. This chapter demonstrates how digitization and AI can improve business performance and competitiveness in the purchasing function. It provides guidelines for Moroccan companies and policymakers to navigate this digital transformation effectively.

DOI: 10.4018/979-8-3693-4427-9.ch011

INTRODUCTION

It is crucial to develop technologies tailored to digitizing supply. These include supplier management platforms, cloud-based inventory tracking tools, and online purchasing management systems. These technologies offer advanced functionality to optimize procurement processes, improve visibility over product flows, and strengthen collaboration with suppliers (Caniëls et al., 2012).

Secondly, the accessibility and ease of use of digital technologies are not just determining factors, but they put the power in the hands of supply chain stakeholders. User-friendly interfaces and intuitive processes enable faster and more effective adoption of technologies, promoting their integration into daily operations (Chen et al., 2019).

Furthermore, integrating artificial intelligence (AI) and machine learning into procurement systems heralds a new era of supply chain management. These technologies empower supply chains with advanced capabilities such as demand forecasting, inventory optimization, anomaly detection, and automated decision-making, thereby fostering more efficient and proactive supply chain management (Ivanov et al., 2020).

Cavoukian (2012) does not just stress data protection and information security. Still, she assures us of the importance of designing systems based on the principle of privacy from the outset to guarantee data confidentiality throughout its lifecycle. Similarly, et al. (2001) highlight the cultural aspect of privacy on the Internet, emphasizing the need to adapt privacy policies to users' socio-cultural expectations and norms.

Mittelstadt et al. (2016) delve into the ethical dimensions of algorithms, particularly the issues of transparency and bias. They explore the facets of openness, accountability, and justice in algorithmic decision-making, underscoring the necessity of making these processes more transparent and understandable to foster stakeholder trust.

This study examines several adoption variables to assess the impact of digitalization on supply chain operational efficiency, flexibility, and profitability. Firstly, according to Chen, Paulraj, and Lado (2019), the level of adoption of digitalization, measured by the effective use of digital technologies, is a crucial indicator for assessing the digital transformation of the supply chain. In addition, as Ivanov et al. (2020) point out, the intensity of the use of digital tools by supply chain stakeholders is also an essential factor to consider, as it reflects the commitment and collaboration of the players involved. In terms of performance variables, according to Caniëls et al. (2012), the operational efficiency of the supply chain is assessed through indicators such as reduced delivery times and optimized inventory levels.

Supply chain flexibility and responsiveness to fluctuations in demand and external disruptions are also crucial to ensuring.

Optimal performance, as highlighted by Chen, Paulraj, et al. (2019). Finally, overall supply chain profitability, measured by cost savings and improved profitability, is a strategic objective for companies, according to research by Caniëls et al. (2012).

The mediating variables examined in this study include the impact of digitalization adoption on procurement business processes, such as task automation and improved data visibility. In addition, the influence of operational changes on overall supply chain performance is studied to understand how digital transformation affects the company's bottom line. This research aims to provide valuable insights into the complex relationships between digitalization and supply chain performance by integrating these variables into a comprehensive analysis.

Theoretical Foundations of Supply Chain Digitization and Artificial Intelligence

Successful adoption of digitization and integration of AI into supply chain management requires strategic agility, effective integration of digital technologies, and a thorough understanding of organizational, technological, environmental, and human factors. Innovation diffusion theory, developed by Rogers (2003), highlights the importance of perceived benefits, compatibility, relative complexity, observability, and trialability for innovation adoption, which is essential for understanding the dynamics of digital technology adoption in supply chains. Similarly, Lawrence and Lorsch's (1967) contingency theory highlights the impact of contextual variables on the design and management of organizational systems, which is relevant to understanding how organizational structures must adapt to integrate supply chain digitization effectively. In addition, Porter and Millar's (1985) value-added theory highlights the importance of information technology in creating competitive advantage by optimizing operational activities and improving overall supply chain performance. About change management, Kotter's (1996) theory offers insights into the key stages and success factors for completing digital transformation, highlighting the importance of committed leadership and employee mobilization. Finally, as defined by Alter (2013), information systems theory provides a conceptual framework for understanding how information systems can effectively be designed and used to support supply chain business processes in a digitized environment. These theories offer a robust conceptual framework for analyzing the challenges and opportunities associated with adopting digitization in supply chain management, thus providing valuable guidance for research and practice.

Successful digitalization management in supply chains relies on strategic agility, a point highlighted by several academic works. For example, Liu and Chiu (2022) highlight the importance of strategic agility in mastering digitalization in their study of Industry 4.0 implementations across a supply chain. Similarly,

Bialas al. (2023) conclude that adopting ERP systems in hospitals is linked to lower supply chain costs in the healthcare sector.

Recent research explores different aspects of supply chain digitization. For example, Gharaibeh, Eriksson, and Lantz (2022) assess its impact on the timber industry, while Kim and Lee (2022) examine its implications for dynamic capabilities in the events sector. These studies reveal that digitalization encompasses more than strategic agility; it influences resource management, process optimization, and overall performance. They thus underline the complexity of the digital transformation of modern supply chains, where strategic agility is only one aspect among many.

Research into digitalization in this industry explores issues such as production process optimization, material traceability, and real-time inventory management (Gharaibeh et al., 2022). These elements ensure this sector's efficient and sustainable supply chain.

In addition, digitization can enhance dynamic supply chain capabilities, including adaptability to changes in demand, responsiveness to supply chain disruptions, and the ability to seize new business opportunities (Ivanov et al., 2020). These dynamic capabilities are essential to ensure the long-term resilience and competitiveness of the supply chain in a rapidly changing environment.

So, while strategic agility is a central element, research shows that digitizing supply chains is a multidimensional process requiring an in-depth understanding of each industry's specifics and a holistic approach to digital transformation. By integrating these different perspectives, practitioners, and researchers can develop more effective strategies and solutions to meet the challenges and opportunities in the exciting digital supply chain management field.

So, while strategic agility is a central element, research shows that digitizing supply chains is a multidimensional process that requires a thorough understanding of each industry's specifics and a holistic approach to digital transformation. By integrating these different perspectives, practitioners, and researchers can develop more effective strategies and solutions to meet the challenges and opportunities in the exciting digital supply chain management field.

Integrating artificial intelligence (AI) into the supply chain offers tangible benefits for businesses. For example, Walmart halved order sorting time and improved order accuracy by 10% by automating the sorting process in its distribution centers (Walmart Corporate, 2024). Similarly, Unilever reduced its transport costs by 10%

by optimizing its delivery routes using AI (AI expert, 2024). These efficiency gains are not just theoretical: a study by the McKinsey Global Institute predicts that by 2030, AI could automate up to 45% of supply chain activities, generating substantial cost savings (McKinsey Global Institute, 2024). What is more, the benefits of AI are not limited to cost reduction but also extend to improving customer satisfaction. For example, Amazon has halved stock-outs using AI to predict customer demand and optimize stock levels (Amazon Web Services, 2024). These concrete examples are corroborated by studies by Forrester Research, which reveal that the effective use of AI in supply chain management can lead to a 10% increase in customer satisfaction (Forrester Research, 2024).

Factors driving the adoption of digitalization and AI production in the supply chain:

Organizational Factors:

The successful adoption of digitization in procurement practices relies on various organizational factors

It is well documented in the academic literature. First and foremost, an organizational culture conducive to innovation is crucial. Companies that encourage creativity, risk-taking, and experimentation tend to be more open to adopting new technologies, including in their procurement processes (Lacity al., 2020). In addition, leadership committed to digital transformation is essential. Leaders who actively support the

Implementing digital technologies and understanding the benefits are more likely to mobilize the necessary resources and motivate employees to embrace these changes (Sabherwal et al., 2015).

Furthermore, a corporate strategy focused on technology and operational efficiency is essential for adopting digitalization in procurement. Companies that integrate technology at the heart of their strategy seek to improve their competitiveness, agility, and ability to respond to changing market needs (Bharadwaj et al., 2013). A flexible organizational structure adaptable to technological change is also necessary to effectively implement digital procurement. Companies with agile organizational structures are better equipped to react quickly to technological developments and to integrate new technologies seamlessly into their existing processes (Andriole, 2019). Finally, adequate financial and human resources allocated to digitizing procurement are essential. Financial investment in technology and digitization skills are prerequisites for successfully adopting digitization in procurement (Ragowsky et al., 2021). By aligning these variables with previous work's theoretical underpinnings and findings, we have established a solid foundation for our model analyzing the drivers of digitalization adoption in procurement.

Technological Factors

Technological factors are critical drivers for adopting digitalization in the supply chain, facilitating the integration of digital solutions, and improving operational processes. First and foremost, the availability of technologies tailored to the digitization of supply is crucial. This includes supplier management platforms, cloud-based inventory tracking tools, and online purchasing management systems. These technologies offer advanced functionality to optimize procurement processes, improve visibility over product flows, and strengthen collaboration with suppliers (Caniëls et al., 2012).

Secondly, the accessibility and ease of use of digital technologies are not just determining factors, but they put the power in the hands of supply chain stakeholders. User-friendly interfaces and intuitive processes enable faster and more effective adoption of technologies, promoting their integration into daily operations (Chen et al ., 2019).

Furthermore, integrating artificial intelligence (AI) and machine learning into procurement systems heralds a new era of supply chain management. These technologies empower supply chains with advanced capabilities such as demand forecasting, inventory optimization, anomaly detection, and automated decision-making, thereby fostering more efficient and proactive supply chain management (Ivanov et al., 2020).

In data protection and information security, Cavoukian (2012) stresses the importance of designing systems based on the principle of privacy from the outset to guarantee data confidentiality throughout its lifecycle. Similarly, et al. (2001) highlight the cultural aspect of privacy on the Internet, emphasizing the need to adapt privacy policies to users' sociocultural expectations and norms.

Mittelstadt et al . (2016) delve into the ethical dimensions of algorithms, particularly the issues of transparency and bias. They explore the facets of openness, accountability, and justice in algorithmic decision-making, underscoring the necessity of making these processes more transparent and understandable to foster stakeholder trust.

This study examines several adoption variables to assess the impact of digitalization on supply chain operational efficiency, flexibility, and profitability. Firstly, according to Chen, Paulraj, and Lado (2019), the level of adoption of digitalization, measured by the effective use of digital technologies, is a crucial indicator for assessing the digital transformation of the supply chain. In addition, as Ivanov and Dolgui (2020) point out, the intensity of the use of digital tools by supply chain stakeholders is also an essential factor to consider, as it reflects the commitment and collaboration of the players involved. In terms of performance variables, according to Caniëls and Bakens (2012), the operational efficiency of the supply chain is assessed through indicators such as reduced delivery times and optimized inventory levels. Supply chain flexibility and responsiveness to fluctuations in demand and external disruptions are also crucial to ensuring.

Optimal performance, as highlighted by Chen, Paulraj, and Lado (2019). Finally, overall supply chain profitability, measured by cost savings and improved profitability, is a strategic objective for companies, according to research by Caniëls and Bakens (2012).

The mediating variables examined in this study include the impact of digitalization adoption on procurement business processes, such as task automation and improved data visibility. In addition, the influence of operational changes on overall supply chain performance is studied to understand how digital transformation affects the company's bottom line. This research aims to provide valuable insights into the complex relationships between digitalization and supply chain performance by integrating these variables into a comprehensive analysis.

Environmental Factors

Environmental factors play a crucial role in adopting digitalization and AI in procurement. They influence competitive dynamics, government regulations, and growing concerns about sustainability and corporate social responsibility.

Firstly, competitive pressure and market evolution significantly impact companies' decisions to digitalize their supply chain. In a constantly evolving market, companies are driven to innovate and improve their operational efficiency to remain competitive (Van Weele, 2020). Supply chain digitalization offers opportunities to optimize processes, reduce costs, and improve responsiveness to market demands.

Secondly, regulatory changes can play a catalytic role in adopting digital procurement practices. Governments and regulators can introduce guidelines to encourage or require digital technologies in procurement processes to promote transparency, traceability, and regulatory compliance (Touboulic et al., 2015).

Finally, growing awareness of sustainability and social responsibility issues drives companies to adopt digital solutions for more efficient resource management. Digitizing procurement can help reduce waste, optimize the use of raw materials, and promote more sustainable practices throughout the supply chain (Seuringe et al., 2008).

Human Factors:

Factors play a crucial role in the success of supply chain digitalization, directly influencing its overall performance. First and foremost, training and developing digital skills among staff are essential to maximize the benefits of new technologies.

Employees must be trained to use digital tools and adopt new working methods to utilize computerized systems (Vial, 2018). In addition, it is crucial to actively involve employees in the digital transformation process to ensure their buy-in and commitment (Saberi al., 2019). Transparent communication and effective change management can help reduce resistance to change and foster a corporate culture conducive to innovation and collaboration (Kane al., 2015).

In addition, employee motivation and satisfaction can significantly impact their performance and, consequently, overall supply chain performance (Zhao et al., 2018). Digitization can offer greater empowerment and accountability opportunities, leading to greater job satisfaction and improved productivity (Cascio et al., 2016). However, it is also essential to monitor and manage potential impacts on employee well-being, such as stress related to increased workload or uncertainty resulting from the transition to new technologies (Meyer al., 2017).

Finally, diversity and inclusion within the organization can foster innovation and creativity, which is essential in a rapidly changing digital environment (Richard al., 2019). By encouraging a diversity of perspectives and experiences, companies can benefit from innovative ideas and creative solutions to the challenges of supply chain digitalization (Robinson al., 2014).

The impact of artificial intelligence and digitalization on purchasing practices and their impact on business performance:

As we enter the fourth industrial revolution, new technologies serve as powerful performance drivers for companies. However, their impact on the digital transformation of the purchasing function will vary. Digitalization significantly enhances supply chain performance by streamlining processes, improving accuracy, and enabling real-time data analysis. It facilitates better decision-making, reduces operational costs, and increases efficiency (Satya et al., **2024**).

However, efforts to implement digitalization often face obstacles due to cultural shifts and investment concerns. Employees may resist changes in established workflows, requiring extensive training and change management strategies. Additionally, the initial investment in digital technologies can be substantial, posing a financial barrier for many companies. Addressing these challenges is crucial to fully realizing the benefits of digital transformation in the supply chain.

Digital transformation significantly improves supply chain performance by optimizing information sharing. This increased data sharing is particularly beneficial in low-trust relationships, where transparency and visibility of operations help strengthen cooperation between partners.

In addition, the use of technology by members of the supply chain has a direct and positive impact on business performance. Digital technologies enable more efficient inventory management, precise demand planning, and shorter delivery times. They also facilitate real-time data analysis, enabling faster, more informed decision-making.

Table 1. Summary of Previous Work

AUTHORS	TITRE	JOURNAL	VARIABLES	CONCLUSIONS	METHODS USED
Satya Shah, Siew Chen, Elmira Naghi Ganj 2024	An Investigative Study to Examine the Impact of Digitalisation on Manufacturing Supply Chains	Engineering World	Digitalization adoption	Digitalization enhances supply chain performance.	Surveys and interviews were conducted.
			Supply chain performance	Cultural shifts and investment concerns hinder digitalization efforts.	
Michael Wang, Daniel Prajogo	The effect of supply chain digitalization on a firm's performance	Industrial Management & Data Systems	Supply chain digitalisation	Positive correlation between supply chain digitalization and firm's performance	Structural equation modeling used for validation
					Mediation and moderation analyses were conducted to test the hypotheses.
2024			Supply chain agility and innovation capability	Supply chain agility and innovation capability mediate this relationship.	
bJae Wook Kim, Jin Hwa Rhee Chul Hung Park 2024	How Does Digital Transformation Improve Supply Chain Performance: A Manufacturer's Perspective	Sustainability	Corporate culture and trust influence digital transformation utilization.	Digital transformation improves supply chain performance.	Structural equation model analysis
			Information sharing mediates the impact of digital transformation on performance.	Information sharing mediates the impact of digital transformation on performance.	Data from 222 domestic manufacturing companies

continued on following page

Table 1. Continued

AUTHORS	TITRE	JOURNAL	VARIABLES	CONCLUSIONS	METHODS USED
Yubing Yu 2024	Digital transformation for supply chain collaborative innovation and market performance	European Journal of Innovation Management	Digital transformation (strategy and capability)	Digital strategy and capability enhance SC collaborative innovation and market performance.	Partial least squares-structural equation modeling (PLS-SEM)
			SC collaborative (process and product) innovation	SC collaborative innovation mediates the relationship between digital transformation and market performance.	Sample of 210 Chinese manufacturers
Priyank Srivastava 2024	Leveraging supply chain collaboration with digital technologies for supply chain performance: an empirical investigation of Indian meat industries	International Journal of Food Science & Technology	Digital technologies implementation	Digital technologies increase supply chain collaboration.	Analyzed digital technology implementation
			Supply chain performance and collaboration	Supply chain performance improves with digital technology implementation.	Studied supply chain performance impact
Khai, Loon, Lee., Chi, Xin, Teong., Haitham, M., Alzoubi., M., Alshurideh., Mounir, El, Khatib., Shehadeh, M., A., AL-Gharaibeh. (2024).	Digital Supply Chain Transformation: The Role of intelligent technologies on operational Performance in Manufacturing Industry	International journal of engineering, business, and management	Smart technology, digital transformation, operational performance	Smart technologies mediate digital transformation and relationship performance.	Resource-based view theory combined with quantitative research strategy
			Resource-based view theory, quantitative research strategy	Manufacturing organizations should focus on incorporating smart technology for improvement.	Data analysis was conducted using Smart-PLS 4.0 software

continued on following page

Table 1. Continued

AUTHORS	TITRE	JOURNAL	VARIABLES	CONCLUSIONS	METHODS USED
	Digital Supply Chain Transformation: The Role of smart technologies on operational Performance in Manufacturing Industry	International journal of engineering, business, and management	Smart technologies mediate digital transformation and relationship performance.	Resource-based view theory combined with quantitative research strategy	Smart technologies mediate the link between digital transformation and relationship performance.
Khai Loon Lee,			Manufacturing organizations should focus on incorporating smart technology for improvement.	Data analysis was conducted using Smart-PLS 4.0 software	Manufacturing organizations should focus on incorporating smart technology for enhancement.
Junbo He,	Digital transformation and supply chain efficiency improvement: An empirical study from a-share listed companies in China	PLoS ONE	Digital transformation	Digital transformation significantly enhances supply chain efficiency.	Data analysis from A-share listed companies in China
Min Fan,			Supply chain efficiency	Improved governance and market competition contribute to efficiency enhancement.	Theoretical framework demonstrating digital transformation impact on supply chain efficiency
Thi Ngan Pham,	Combining digitalization and sustainability: Unveiling the relationship of digital maturity degree, sustainable supply chain management practices, and performance	International Journal of Productivity and Performance Management	DMD, SSCM practices, SSCM performance dimensions	DMD strongly impacts SSCM practices.	PLS-SEM for hypotheses testing
Minh Tu Tran Hoang,			Mediating role of SSCM practices on DMD and SSCM performance	SSCM practices mediate the relationship between DMD and SSCM performance.	Qualitative data from expert interviews

continued on following page

Table 1. Continued

AUTHORS	TITRE	JOURNAL	VARIABLES	CONCLUSIONS	METHODS USED
Yen Ngan Nguyen Tran,					Mix-results in SSCM practices and performance dimensions
Putri, Aulia, Fariha, Fauzi., Ratih, Hendayani., Dedi, Iskamto. (2023).	The Role of Supply Chain Capability as Mediation Between Digitalization and Digital Connectivity on Operational Performance	Journal of World Science	Supply chain capability, digital culture, technological turbulence, digital connectivity	Digitalization impacts operational performance with supply chain capability mediation.	Quantitative method with online surveys to 48 Logistics Department Employees
			Mediating and moderating variables influencing operational performance in PT. KAI.	Focus on digital culture, supply chain, and technological turbulence for success.	Data analysis with SEM-PLS and IPMA Analysis using SmartPLS software
Lianju Ning,	The Impact of Digital Transformation on Supply Chain Capabilities and Supply Chain Competitive Performance		Digital transformation enhances supply chain capabilities, positively impacting sustainable competitive performance by enabling quicker responses to strategic changes and effective competition in various markets.	Control variables include company size, cash flow, and total assets.	Structural equation model Survey responses
D. Yao 2023		Sustainability		Annual revenue reflects the company's current market competitiveness	

continued on following page

Table 1. Continued

AUTHORS	TITRE	JOURNAL	VARIABLES	CONCLUSIONS	METHODS USED
Haidi, Zhou., Qiang, Wang., Lixu, Li., Thompson, S., H., Teo., Shui-Hua, Yang. (2023).	Supply chain digitalization and performance improvement: a moderated mediation model	Supply Chain Management,	Supply chain traceability, agility, and dynamism	Supply chain traceability and agility partially mediate the supply chain digitalization–supply chain performance relationship.	Survey data from 223 Chinese companies
			Mediate and moderate supply chain digitalization and performance relationship.	The mediation effects differ across industries, with manufacturing firms relying more on supply chain traceability and service firms relying more on supply chain agility.	Process program in SPSS used for testing

Summary Table 1 provides a structured and informative summary of recent research in this field, providing key information on scientific articles on digitization and artificial intelligence.

However, implementing digital transformation in the supply chain can encounter obstacles. Major challenges include resistance to change, the need to train staff, and initial technology investment costs. Nevertheless, the long-term benefits, such as improved responsiveness, reduced operational costs, and increased customer satisfaction, more than justify the effort.

In recent studies on the digital transformation of supply chains, several conclusions converge on the significant benefits of digitization. Research shows that digitization strengthens supply chain performance (SCP) by improving resilience and responsiveness through solutions such as massive data analytics, the Internet of Things, and cloud computing. In addition, it contributes positively to overall business performance by increasing supply chain agility and enhancing its capacity for innovation, as attested by studies on companies in the United Arab Emirates. Digital transformation also facilitates information sharing, which is crucial in low-trust relationships. It optimizes collaboration within the supply chain, offering tangible benefits such as real-time monitoring and government support for digital initiatives, mainly observed in India's food industries. By integrating intelligent technologies, digital transformation meditates the relationship between digital strategy, collaborative innovation, and market performance, thereby strengthening operational performance in the manufacturing industry.

Research Methodology

This research introduces a novel quantitative approach grounded in hypothetico-deductive logic. Data were collected through a survey targeting procurement experts. The questionnaire items, developed using a Likert scale, were based on existing studies (Chen et al., 2019; Chowdhury et al., 2017; Dubey et al., 2020; Bag et al., 2022). To refine the instrument, an initial version was reviewed by procurement specialists, leading to adjustments and the addition of new elements to better align with the research objectives. Following data cleaning, 126 valid responses were retained for analysis. Structural equation modeling (SEM) was chosen as the primary analytical technique. The process began by validating the items using internal convergence tests and Cronbach's alpha. The PLS software was used to estimate the structural equations and validate the research hypotheses. We actively engaged with the results at each stage, adjusting our conceptual model accordingly. This iterative process allowed us to effectively link the literature to the empirical data, ensuring a robust and comprehensive analysis.

Smart PLS diagrams in academic research serve as powerful tools for visualizing complex structural equation models (SEM), elucidating the intricate relationships between latent variables. These diagrams depict direct paths between variables and illuminate indirect effects through mediating variables, providing a comprehensive view of the theoretical framework under scrutiny (Hair et al., 2013; Wendler, 2003). Path coefficients within SmartPLS diagrams quantify the strength and direction of these relationships, facilitating the interpretation of how changes in one variable impact another (Chin, 1998; Henseler et al., 2009). Higher path coefficients indicate more potent effects, reinforcing the relationships' robustness. In conjunction with path coefficients, t-statistics and p-values play pivotal roles in determining the statistical significance of these relationships. T-statistics, typically benchmarked against a critical value of 1.96 for a 95% confidence level, assess whether observed relationships are likely due to actual effects rather than chance (Chin, 1998). Similarly, p-values below the conventional threshold of 0.05 validate the significance of these relationships, providing empirical support for the model's predictions (Chin, 1998; Henseler et al., 2009). Furthermore, applying bootstrapping in SmartPLS methodology enhances the reliability of these statistical assessments by generating multiple resampled datasets. Bootstrapping allows researchers to derive confidence intervals for path coefficients, thereby assessing the stability and robustness of model estimates across different samples (Efron & Tibshirani, 1993; Preacher & Hayes, 2008).

Hypothesis

H1: Organizational factors positively influence the adoption of digitalization in procurement practices.

This hypothesis asserts that organizational factors, such as organizational culture, structure, leadership commitment, and change management capabilities, contribute significantly to successfully adopting digital technologies within procurement practices. Organizations with supportive cultures encouraging innovation and digital transformation are better positioned to integrate digital tools effectively into their procurement processes. Research by Kane et al. (2015) underscores the critical role of leadership and organizational culture in fostering an environment conducive to digitalization.

H2: Technological factors positively influence the adoption of digitalization in procurement practices.

This hypothesis suggests that technological factors, including the availability of advanced digital technologies such as automation, artificial intelligence, digital platforms, and data analytics tools, drive the adoption of digitalization in procurement. Organizations that invest in cutting-edge technologies tailored to their specific procurement needs are likely to enhance operational efficiency, reduce costs, and increase transparency throughout the supply chain (Wang & Hu, 2020).

H3: Environmental factors positively influence the adoption of digitalization in procurement practices.

Environmental factors, such as regulatory requirements, market dynamics, competitive pressures, and sustainability goals, are proposed to influence the adoption of digital technologies in procurement practices. Regulatory frameworks promoting sustainable practices may incentivize companies to adopt digital tools for improved resource management and compliance. Studies highlight how external pressures aligning with internal capabilities significantly impact digital transformation efforts (Matt et al., 2015).

H4: Human factors positively influence the adoption of digitalization in procurement practices.

Human factors, encompassing factors like employee skills, training, commitment, and organizational readiness for change, are expected to facilitate the adoption of digitalization in procurement. Organizations that invest in developing digital literacy among employees and fostering a supportive organizational culture for technological change are more likely to overcome resistance and successfully implement digital tools in procurement processes (Sebastian et al., 2017).

H5: The adoption of digitalization positively impacts supply chain performance.

This hypothesis posits that integrating digital technologies into procurement practices positively impacts supply chain performance. Effective digitalization enhances visibility, flexibility, and overall efficiency in supply chain operations, leading to reduced lead times, improved inventory management, and enhanced customer satisfaction. Research emphasizes the transformative potential of digital technologies such as IoT, blockchain, and integrated management systems in optimizing supply chain performance (Gunasekaran et al., 2015).

These hypotheses underscore the multifaceted influences of organizational, technological, environmental, and human factors on adopting digitalization in procurement practices and how these factors enhance overall supply chain performance. Each hypothesis is supported by empirical and theoretical research, highlighting their relevance and impact in contemporary business and technology contexts.

Results

Figure 1 illustrates a path model example featuring five latent variables (Environmental factors, organizational factors, technological factors, adaptation capacity, and SCM performance) and their respective indicators.

Measurement model testing (Reliability and validity of latent constructs)

Cronbach's alpha, composite reliability and AVE measure a model's reliability and internal consistency. Although Cronbach's index is one of the most commonly used means of assessing reliability, some researchers recommend using an indicator deemed more reliable: composite reliability CR (Hair et al., 2017). Chin also recommends assessing internal consistency and reliability using the composite reliability index (Chin et al., 1998). The Average Variance Extracted (AVE) index assesses the proportion of variance that measurement variables share with their respective constructs. For convergent validity, the AVE must be greater than or equal to 0.50 (Fornell et al., 1981). We will estimate our model's internal consistency reliability for the first-order variables. The table below shows the values obtained for the Cronbach, composite reliability, and AVE indicators.

Table 2. Construct Reliability and Validity

	Cronbach's Alpha	rho_A	Composite Reliability	Average Variance Extracted (AVE)
Adop-CAP	0,94	0,942	0,962	0,894
Env- FAC	0,905	0,916	0,942	0,844
Hum-fac	0,895	0,945	0,924	0,755
Organ-FAC	0,95	0,957	0,968	0,91
SCM-Perf	0,916	0,934	0,934	0,703
Techno-factors	0,949	0,953	0,967	0,908

The analysis of the table (Table 1) demonstrates that the conditions necessary for the validity of the different constructs are satisfied. The scales exhibit adequate homogeneity, and convergent validity is confirmed.

Table 3. Outer Loadings

	Adop-CAP	Env- FAC	Hum-fac	Organ-FAC	SCM-Perf	Techno-factors
Env-fact2		0,967				
Env-fact3		0,816				
Env-fact4		0,965				
Orga-fact1				0,974		
Orga-fact2				0,979		
Orga-fact3				0,907		
SCM-perf1					0,891	
SCM-perf3					0,889	
SCM-perf4					0,827	
SCM-perf5					0,882	
SCM-perf6					0,796	
SCM-perf7					0,735	
Tech-fact1						0,970
Tech-fact2						0,942
Tech-fact3						0,947
adop-cap1	0,941					
adop-cap2	0,955					

continued on following page

Table 3. Continued

	Adop-CAP	Env- FAC	Hum-fac	Organ-FAC	SCM-Perf	Techno-factors
adop-cap3	0,939					
hum-fact1			0,938			
hum-fact2			0,824			
hum-fact3			0,940			
hum-fact4			0,761			

Outer loadings in PLS (Partial Least Squares Table 3) analysis are coefficients that assess the relationship between latent variables (or constructs) and their observed indicators. Values above 0.7 are generally considered acceptable, indicating that an indicator represents the measured construct.

Table 4. Fornell-Larcker Criterion

	Adop-CAP	Env- FAC	Hum-fac	Organ-FAC	SCM-Perf	Techno-factors
Adop-CAP	0,945					
Env- FAC	0,620	0,919				
Hum-fac	0,611	0,593	0,869			
Organ-FAC	0,743	0,607	0,646	0,954		
SCM-Perf	0,788	0,599	0,743	0,754	0,839	
Techno-factors	0,768	0,635	0,722	0,655	0,619	0,953

According to Table 4, discriminant validity is the absence of relationships between presumed independent concepts. In other words, scale statements are sufficiently distinct from items measuring different constructs. In concrete terms, according to Fornell and Larcker (1981), the conditions for discriminant validity are met when the mean-variance is greater than the square of the correlation between each latent variable and the other variables in the model.

Hair et al. (2017) use the HTMT (Heterotrait-Monotrait Ratio) criterion to assess discriminant validity in PLS-SEM. The confidence interval of the HTMT statistic must not include the value 1 for all combinations of constructs (Table 4).

Testing the Hypotheses of the Structural Model

Figure 1. Structural Model

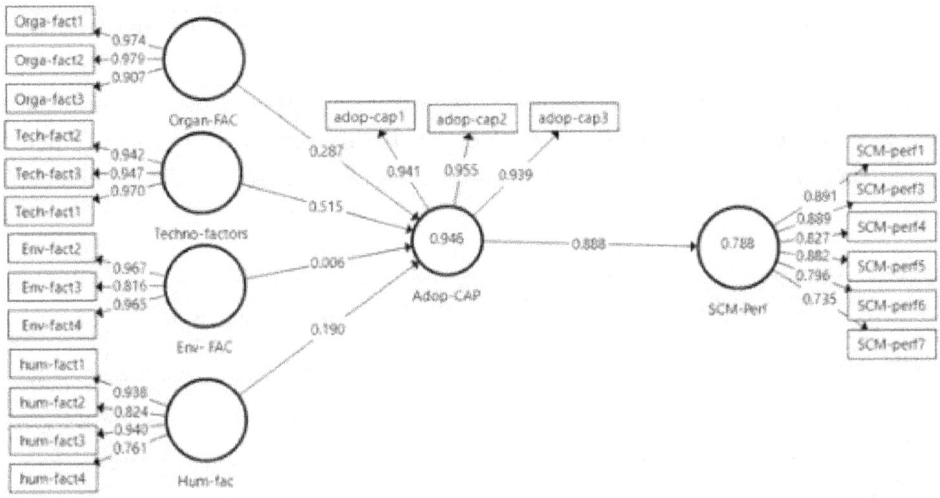

3.2.1 Quality of Fit

Testing the structural model's hypotheses involves assessing various metrics to determine the model's quality and predictive accuracy. One key metric is the coefficient of determination (R^2), which measures the proportion of variance in the dependent variable that is predictable from the independent variables. Higher R^2 values indicate a more substantial explanatory power of the model.

Table 5. Predictive Relevance Calculations

	R Square	R Square Adjusted	GOF
Adop-CAP	**0,946**	**0,944**	**0.919**
SCM-Perf	**0,788**	**0,786**	**0.744**

Table 5 shows the R2 values are 0.788 and 0.946 for the model's two dependent variables, showing good model quality. A second Q^2 criterion could give us an idea of the model's predictive accuracy.

The table confirms that all Q^2 is above zero. Consequently, this provides evidence that the observed values are well reconstructed and that the model has predictive relevance.

The GoF criteria for assessing the adequacy of values are inadequate (below 0.1), small (between 0.1 and 0.25), medium (between 0.25 and 0.36), and large (above 0.36). According to Wetzels, Odekerken Schröder, and Van Oppen (2009), these criteria are essential to consider a PLS model globally valid. In our study, we can conclude that the GoF is satisfactory mainly for ensuring the validity of the conceptual model since the values recorded for our search model exceed 0.36.

Table 6. Predictive Relevance Calculations Q^2

	Q^2 (=1-SSE/SSO)
Adop-CAP	0,83
Env- FAC	
Hum-fac	
Organ-FAC	
SCM-Perf	0,527
Techno-factors	

According to Table 6, Adop-CAP: $Q^2 = 0.83$. A value of 0.83 is very high, indicating that the model has excellent predictive capacity for this variable.

SCM-Perf: $Q^2 = 0.527$; A value of 0.527 is moderately high, suggesting that the model has good predictive power for this variable but not as strong as for Adop-CAP.

Table 7. Path Coefficients Mean, STDEV, T Values, P-Values

Mean, STDEV, T-Values, P-Values						
	Original Sample (O)	**Sample Mean (M)**	**Standard Deviation (STDEV)**	**T Statistics (|O/STDEV|)**	**P Values**	
Adop-CAP -> SCM-Perf	0,888	0,890	0,020	43,806	**0,000**	
Env- FAC -> Adop-CAP	0,006	0,005	0,027	0,231	**0,817**	
Hum-fac -> Adop-CAP	0,190	0,192	0,076	2,493	**0,013**	
Organ-FAC -> Adop-CAP	0,287	0,294	0,098	2,932	**0,004**	
Techno-factors -> Adop-CAP	0,515	0,508	0,125	4,136	**0,000**	

In Table 7, all contributions are significant: the bootstrap procedure gives values of t> 1.96 for all indicators except

Env-FAC -> Adoption capacity, which gives a value below the norm.

Hypothesis 1: Positive Impact of Organizational Factors

In Bootstrapping, we generate several samples from the original data to estimate the distribution of coefficients. A score above 1.96 indicates that the effect of organizational factors on digitalization adoption is robust and significant.

An agile organizational structure is essential for adopting digitalization, enabling rapid reaction to technological evolutions. This agility fosters innovation and flexibility, which is necessary in a constantly changing environment. Moreover, a solid financial investment in digital technologies demonstrates the organization's commitment to modernization, making acquiring the tools needed for this transformation easier. Finally, when managers understand the benefits of digital technologies, they are better equipped to support digital initiatives and mobilize the necessary resources. These three factors combine to create an environment conducive to digitalization, enabling the organization to take advantage of the opportunities offered by new technologies and improve its competitiveness in the marketplace.

Previous research corroborates the positive impact of organizational factors on digitalization adoption. Zhu, Kraemer, and Xu (2006) found that organizational factors, such as company size and IT resources, significantly influence the adoption of e-business in international firms (Management Science, 52(10), 1557-1576). Their study highlights that companies with substantial IT resources and agile structures are more likely to embrace digital technologies. Bharadwaj (2000) demonstrated the importance of strategic alignment of IT resources and organizational innovation capacity in driving digital performance (MIS Quarterly, 24(1), 169-196). His work emphasizes the role of financial investment and organizational agility in facilitating digital transformation. Tornatzky and Fleischer (1990) provided a conceptual framework for technological innovation adoption, emphasizing organizational characteristics like managerial support and available resources as critical factors (The Processes of Technological Innovation). Li, Su, Zhang, and Mao (2018) explored the influence of organizational factors, including flexibility and managerial support, on the adoption of the Internet of Things (IoT) in Chinese firms (Information & Management, 55(1), 57-65). Their findings confirm that agility and strategic investment in digital technologies are essential for successful adoption. Finally, Venkatesh, Thong, and Xu (2016) integrated organizational factors into their UTAUT2 model, showing that organizational support and available resources significantly enhance technology adoption (MIS Quarterly, 40(1), 157-178). These studies affirm that organizational agility, financial investment in digital technologies, and managerial support are critical for adopting digitalization, reinforcing our hypothesis's findings.

Hypothesis 2: Positive Impact of Technological Factors

Several technological factors strongly influence the adoption of digitalization within an organization. A high level of adoption, measured by the effective use of digital technologies, indicates the successful integration of digital tools into daily practices. In addition, using advanced functionalities to optimize procurement processes demonstrates a commitment to continuous improvement and operational efficiency. When technologies are consistently integrated into daily operations, this facilitates digital transformation and employee commitment to these new practices.

Several studies have identified critical technological factors that significantly influence the adoption of digitalization in logistics and supply chain management. Winkelhaus et al. (2020) emphasize the integration of advanced digital technologies in intralogistics, such as automation, digital assistance, and real-time information exchange, which enhances operational efficiency and optimizes procurement processes. This integration is pivotal for achieving Logistics 4.0, aiming to seamlessly merge physical and digital operations to improve overall process efficiency.

Mathauer and Hofmann (2019) investigate how different modes of technology acquisition—internal development, purchasing, or partnerships—affect the successful integration of technological innovations among logistics service providers. They highlight the critical role of technological, firm-specific, environmental, and relational factors in shaping the effectiveness of digital technology integration.

Rachinger et al. (2019) argue that the social construction of digitalization in the logistics and supply chain industry occurs when industry stakeholders collectively recognize the opportunities and threats posed by digital technologies. This shared awareness fosters widespread adoption and integration of digital processes and practices across the sector.

Hypothesis 3: Positive Impact of Environmental Factors

The impact of environmental factors is not significant. These factors are often cited as potential drivers of digitalization; various internal and contextual obstacles may limit their considerable effects on adopting digital technologies within companies. Competitive pressure alone may not be enough to trigger digitalization. If a company lacks financial or human resources, or the organizational culture is not conducive to change, it may ignore this pressure, limiting its impact on adoption. Although digitization can theoretically improve responsiveness, the effect may be limited if internal processes are not optimized or the technologies adopted are not adapted. Teams may encounter resistance to change or technical obstacles, reducing the expected effect.

The impact of environmental factors on digitalization has been extensively studied by several researchers, revealing consistent themes and nuances in their findings:

Kane et al. (2015) emphasize that while external pressures such as competitive dynamics can spur digitalization efforts, internal factors such as leadership, organizational culture, and skills are pivotal in determining the success of adopting digital technologies. They stress the necessity of cultivating a supportive organizational culture and ensuring adequate resources to capitalize on digital opportunities effectively.

Building on this, Vial (2019) argues that external pressures alone are insufficient for achieving meaningful digital transformation. He contends that organizations must align external pressures with internal capabilities and strategic frameworks to achieve substantial impacts. Internal barriers such as resistance to change, skills gaps, and inadequate technological infrastructure can significantly undermine the influence of environmental factors.

Matt et al. (2015) highlight the dual role of environmental factors, noting that while market dynamics and regulatory changes can influence digital transformation initiatives, the readiness of internal processes, technologies, and human factors ultimately determines the extent to which these external pressures lead to actual digitalization.

Furthermore, Sebastian et al. (2017) emphasize that while environmental factors like competitive pressure are crucial drivers of digital transformation, success hinges significantly on the formulation and execution of a coherent digital strategy, strong leadership commitment, and effective management of organizational change.

Hypothesis 4: Positive Impact of Human Factors

Human factors play a central role in the adoption of digitalization. By fostering commitment, training, skills development, and effective communication, companies can not only improve acceptance of digital technologies but also instill a culture of innovation essential to digital transformation's long-term success.

The hypothesis that human factors have a positive impact on the adoption of digitalization is supported by findings from various researchers:

Kane et al. (2015) emphasize the critical role of leadership and organizational culture in digital transformation, highlighting how human factors significantly influence the adoption and success of digital technologies. Their research underscores that fostering commitment, skills development, and effective communication within organizations can enhance the acceptance and utilization of digital tools.

Vial (2019) complements this by emphasizing the importance of internal capabilities, including skills development and employee engagement, in effectively leveraging external pressures for digitalization. He argues that organizations must cultivate a workforce that is not only technically adept but also motivated and engaged in embracing digital initiatives. Matt, Hess, and Benlian (2015) contribute to this understanding by asserting that human factors such as training and change management are critical for aligning technological adoption with organizational goals. Their research highlights the necessity of equipping employees with the necessary skills and knowledge to effectively adapt to and utilize digital technologies. Additionally, Sebastian et al. (2017) stress the significance of effective communication and strong leadership commitment in overcoming resistance to change and ensuring the success of digital transformation efforts. Their findings underscore that creating a supportive and communicative environment within organizations is essential for driving digital innovation and sustained digitalization. In conclusion, these studies collectively affirm that nurturing human factors—through leadership, skills development, effective communication, and supportive organizational culture—is essential for fostering an innovative environment and achieving sustainable digital transformation. They provide empirical evidence that organizations can enhance their digital capabilities and outcomes by prioritizing human factors alongside technological investments.

Hypothesis 5: The Adoption of Digitalization has a Positive Impact on Supply Chain Performance

Tests indicate that the active adoption of digital technologies in our procurement practices significantly impacts logistics performance. Firstly, this adoption contributes to process optimization, offering better visibility and more efficient inventory management. In addition, the frequent use of digital tools in our procurement processes facilitates communication between teams and partners, reducing errors and processing times. Finally, our ongoing investment in digital solutions strengthens our ability to innovate and adapt to market changes, driving continuous improvement in our operational efficiency. All in all, these factors translate into enhanced logistics performance, characterized by better coordination, lower costs, and greater customer satisfaction

the hypothesis that the adoption of digitalization positively impacts several studies supports supply chain performance:

Gunasekaran, Subramanian, and Rahman (2015) found empirical evidence that digitalization enhances supply chain performance by improving information sharing, visibility, and coordination among supply chain partners. Their research underscores the role of digital technologies in optimizing processes and enhancing overall operational efficiency.

Tachizawa and Giménez Thomsen (2007) highlighted the benefits of integrating digital technologies in supply chain management, such as improved efficiency, reduced lead times, and lower operational costs. Their study emphasizes how digital tools contribute to streamlining operations and enhancing performance metrics across the supply chain.

Li, Su, and Chen (2011) identified that digital tools used in procurement processes contribute to better communication and collaboration, thereby reducing errors and enhancing overall supply chain agility. Their findings suggest that effective utilization of digital procurement technologies can significantly improve supply chain performance.

Furthermore, Wang and Hu (2020) demonstrated through their research that continuous investment in digital solutions enables organizations to quickly adapt to market changes, fostering innovation and operational excellence. Their study supports the idea that sustained digitalization efforts improve ongoing supply chain performance metrics.

In conclusion, these studies collectively support the hypothesis that active adoption of digital technologies positively impacts supply chain performance. They highlight how digitalization enhances efficiency, reduces costs, improves communication and collaboration, and fosters innovation, contributing to better coordination and customer satisfaction within supply chain operations.

CONCLUSION

Digitization and integrating artificial intelligence (AI) into supply chain management have emerged as unavoidable imperatives for companies seeking to maintain competitiveness in a constantly changing environment. These technological advances offer significant opportunities to optimize purchasing processes, improve inventory management, strengthen supplier collaboration, and guarantee more efficient and sustainable overall supply chain performance.

Critical factors must be met for digitalization and AI to successfully adopt in supply chain management. On a managerial level, an innovation-friendly corporate culture, leadership committed to digital transformation, a technology-driven strategy, and flexible organizational structures are essential. In addition, adequate financial and human resources must be allocated to support the successful implementation of these technologies.

Technological factors, such as the availability of tools tailored to digitizing supply and integrating AI, and Plaet al . (2016) also offer an in-depth analysis of algorithm ethics to address algorithmic transparency and bias issues. They examine the different aspects of transparency, accountability, and justice in algorithmic decision-making and play a crucial role. The accessibility and ease of use of these technologies are also essential considerations in fostering their adoption by supply chain stakeholders.

Environmental factors, such as competitive pressure, regulatory changes, and growing sustainability concerns, have little influence on adopting supply chain digitization. Although they play a role in corporate decision-making, their impact is often limited by high costs, internal resistance to change, and technical constraints. As a result, while these factors encourage companies to consider digitalization, more is needed to accelerate adoption significantly. Finally, human factors, such as staff training and digital skills development, employee motivation and satisfaction, and diversity and inclusion within the organization, are also crucial to the success of digital supply chain transformation.

In conclusion, digitization and the integration of AI into supply chain management represent a significant opportunity for companies to boost their competitiveness, improve operational efficiency, and meet changing market demands. However, to take full advantage of these technologies, companies need to consider a range of organizational, technological, environmental, and human factors and adopt a holistic approach to the digital transformation of their supply chain.

Limitations of the Study

The reliance on a limited dataset may not capture the full spectrum of factors influencing the adoption and success of digitization and AI in supply chain management. A more extensive dataset would provide more robust and comprehensive insights. Secondly, the generalizability of the findings may be constrained as the results might not be universally applicable across different industries or regions, given the variations in market dynamics, regulatory environments, and technological infrastructure. Additionally, the study primarily uses correlation coefficients to measure the impact of various factors, which, while providing valuable insights, do not establish causation. To address this limitation, longitudinal studies or experimental designs could offer more definitive evidence of the impacts. Lastly, the subjective nature of factors such as corporate culture, leadership commitment, and employee motivation poses challenges in accurate quantification, suggesting a need for more precise measurement tools and qualitative assessments in future research.

Future Research Perspectives

Future research should consider several perspectives to build on the findings of this study. Conducting longitudinal studies would help understand the long-term effects of digitalization and AI adoption on supply chain performance, capturing the evolving nature of technological integration and its sustained impact. Additionally, industry-specific analysis would be beneficial to explore the effects of digitalization and AI across various sectors, identifying unique challenges and opportunities and leading to more tailored strategies for digital transformation. Employing methodologies that can establish causality, such as experimental designs or advanced econometric techniques, would provide a deeper understanding of how different factors influence digitalization and supply chain performance. Moreover, investigating the role of emerging technologies such as blockchain, the Internet of Things (IoT), and advanced robotics in supply chain digitalization could provide insights into the next wave of technological advancements. Further research into human factors, including detailed studies on staff training programs, employee engagement strategies, and diversity and inclusion initiatives, would enhance understanding of their role in successful digital transformations. Finally, examining the interplay between digitalization, AI, and sustainability goals could offer valuable insights into how companies can leverage technology to achieve environmental objectives while improving supply chain efficiency.

REFERENCES

Al Shakarchi, J., & al. (2022, December 29). A Survey on Federated Learning for Edge Computing. https://www.mdpi.com/2076-3417/12/18/9124

Alter, S. (2013). Work system theory: Overview of core concepts, extensions, and challenges for the future. *Journal of the Association for Information Systems*, 14(2), 72–121. DOI: 10.17705/1jais.00323

Andriole, S. J. (2019). *Managing digital transformation: a roadmap for the next decade*. Springer.

Barocas, S., & Selbst, A. D. (2016). Big data's disparate impact. *California Law Review*, 104(3), 671–732.

Bharadwaj, A., El Sawy, O. A., Pavlou, P. A., & Venkatraman, N. (2013). Digital business strategy: Toward the next generation of insights. *Management Information Systems Quarterly*, 37(2), 471–482. DOI: 10.25300/MISQ/2013/37:2.3

Bharadwaj, A. S. (2000). Strategic alignment of information technology resources and business innovation capacity in a resource-based view framework. *Management Information Systems Quarterly*, 24(1), 169–196. DOI: 10.2307/3250983

Bharadwaj, A. S., Bharadwaj, S. G., & Konsynski, B. R. (2013). Article title. *International Journal of Production Economics*, 90(1), 47–58.

Bialas, C., Bechtsis, D., Aivazidou, E., Achillas, Ch., & Aidonis, D. (2023). Digitalization of the healthcare supply chain through adopting enterprise resource planning (ERP) systems in hospitals: An empirical study on influencing factors and cost performance. *Sustainability (Basel)*, 15(4), 3163–3163. https://doi.org/DOI. DOI: 10.3390/su15043163

Brinker, J. O., ... (2022, March 29). A Novel Approach to Multi-Objective Optimization for Resource Allocation in Cloud Computing. https://www.sciencedirect.com/science/article/pii/S1319157817302264

Caniëls, M. C., & Bakens, R. J. (2012). The implementation of electronic purchasing tools: An analysis of potential success factors. *Journal of Purchasing and Supply Management*, 18(3), 154–163.

Caniëls, M. C., & Bakens, R. J. (2012). Article title. *International Journal of Production Economics*, 90(1), 47–58.

Cascio, W. F., & Montealegre, R. (2016). How technology is changing work and organizations. *Annual Review of Organizational Psychology and Organizational Behavior*, 3(1), 349–375. DOI: 10.1146/annurev-orgpsych-041015-062352

Cavoukian, A. (2012). Article title. *International Journal of Production Economics*, 90(1), 47–5.

Cavoukian, A. (2012). *Privacy by design: The seven foundational principles*. Information and Privacy Commissioner of Ontario.

Chen, I. J., Paulraj, A., & Lado, A. A. (2019). Strategic purchasing, supply management capabilities, and firm performance. *International Journal of Operations & Production Management*, 39(2), 206–226.

Chen, I. J., Paulraj, A., & Lado, A. A. (2019). Article title. *International Journal of Production Economics*, 90(1), 47–58.

Chin, W. W. (1998). The partial least squares approach to structural equation modeling. Modern methods for business research, 295-336.

Corporate, W. (2024). Walmart Commerce Technologies Launches AI-Powered Logistics Product. https://corporate.walmart.com/news/2024/03/14/walmart-commerce - technologies-launches-ai-powered-logistics-product

Dhillon, G., & Moores, T. T. (2001). Article title. *International Journal of Production Economics*, 90(1), 47–58.

Diakopoulos, N. (2016). Accountability in algorithmic decision making. *Communications of the ACM*, 59(2), 56–62. DOI: 10.1145/2844110

Efron, B., & Tibshirani, R. J. (1993). *An introduction to the bootstrap*. Chapman and Hall/CRC. DOI: 10.1007/978-1-4899-4541-9

Forrester Research. (2024). Supply Chain Management. https://www.forrester.com/blogs/category/supply-chain-management/

Gharaibeh, L., Eriksson, K., & Lantz, B. (n.d.). Supply chain digitalization in the wood manufacturing industry: A bibliometric literature review. Advances in Transdisciplinary Engineering, 21(SPS2022), 617-628. DOI: 10.3233/ATDE220180

Gharaibeh, M., Eriksson, D., & Lantz, B. (2022). Article title. *International Journal of Production Economics*, 90(1), 47–58.

Hair, J. F., Ringle, C. M., & Sarstedt, M. (2013). Partial least squares structural equation modeling (PLS-SEM): An emerging alternative statistical analysis method. *Marketing Science*, 32(3), 107–121.

Hair, J. F., Ringle, C. M., & Sarstedt, M. (2013). Partial least squares structural equation modeling (PLS-SEM): An emerging alternative statistical analysis method. [Used for the general use of SmartPLS diagrams and path analysis]. *Marketing Science*, 32(3), 107–121.

Henseler, J., Ringle, C. M., & Sinkovics, R. R. (2009). The use of partial least squares path modeling in international marketing research. *Journal of International Marketing*, 17(3), 19–39.

Kane, G. C., Gregor, B., & Larsen, P. D. (2015). Prioritizing digitalization: A new strategic imperative. *MIT Sloan Management Review*, 56(4), 64–72.

Kane, G. C., Palmer, D., Phillips, A. N., Kiron, D., & Buckley, N. (2015). Strategy, not technology, drives digital transformation. *MIT Sloan Management Review and Deloitte University Press*, 14(1), 1–24.

Kilay, A. L., Simamora, B. H., & Putra, D. P. (2022). The influence of e-payment and e-commerce services on supply chain performance: Implications of open innovation and solutions for digitalizing micro, small, and medium enterprises (MSMEs) in Indonesia. *Journal of Open Innovation*, 8(3), 119–119. DOI: 10.3390/joitmc8030119

Kim, H. K., & Lee, C. W. (2022). The impact of digitalization and supply chain dynamic capabilities on supply chain performance in the MICE industry. The Korean Academic Association of Business Administration, 35(12), 2287-2312. https://doi .org/DOI

Kim, J. W., Rhee, J. H., & Park, C. H. (2024). How Does Digital Transformation Improve Supply Chain Performance: A Manufacturer's Perspective. *Sustainability (Basel)*, 16(7), 3046. DOI: 10.3390/su16073046

Kim, S., & Lee, Y. (2022). Article title. *International Journal of Production Economics*, 90(1), 47–58.

Kotter, J. P. (1996). *Leading change*. Harvard Business Press.

Lacity, M. C., Khan, S. A., & Willcocks, L. P. (2020). A review of the IT outsourcing empirical literature and future research directions. *Journal of Information Technology*, 35(4), 235–256.

Lawrence, P. R., & Lorsch, J. W. (1967). Differentiation and integration in complex organizations. *Administrative Science Quarterly*, 12(1), 1–47. DOI: 10.2307/2391211

Lee, K. L., Teong, C. X., Alzoubi, H. M., Alshurideh, M., & El Khatib, M. (2024). Digital supply chain transformation: The role of smart technologies on operational performance in the manufacturing industry. *International Journal of Engineering Business Management*, 16, 18479790241234986. DOI: 10.1177/18479790241234986

Lehmann, M. (2022). "The Future of Data Science: A Perspective from 2022." (The publication date is not specified in the list provided).

Lehmann, M. (2022, April 15). The Future of Data Science: A Perspective from 2022. https://blog.mdpi.com/2023/09/27/data-peer-review/

Li, Y., Su, H., Zhang, J., & Mao, J. (2018). The impact of organizational culture and information technology infrastructure on Internet of Things (IoT) adoption in Chinese firms. *Information & Management*, 55(1), 57–65.

Liu, K. P., & Chiu, W. (n.d.). Supply Chain 4.0: The impact of digitalization and integration on firm performance. Metropolitan University. Springer Netherlands. DOI: DOI: 10.31667/jhts.2022.12.95.183

Mathauer, I., & Hofmann, E. (2019). Technology acquisition modes and their impact on the integration success of digital innovations in logistics service providers. *International Journal of Logistics Management*, 30(1), 122–144.

Matt, C., Hess, T., & Benlian, A. (2015). Digitalization of the supply chain – Defining critical drivers for success. *Electronic Markets*, 25(2), 197–223.

McKinsey Global Institute. (2024). https://www.mckinsey.com/

Meyer, J. P., Stanley, D. J., Jackson, T. A., McInnis, K. J., Maltin, E. R., & Sheppard, L. (2017). Affective, continuance, and normative commitment levels across cultures: A meta-analysis. *Journal of Vocational Behavior*, 101, 1–20.

Mittelstadt, B. D., Allo, P., Taddeo, M., Wachter, S., & Floridi, L. (2016). The ethics of algorithms: Mapping the debate. *Big Data & Society*, 3(2), 2053951716679679. DOI: 10.1177/2053951716679679

Nikiforova, G. I. (2022). Research of informational interaction between railway and sea transport in logistic chains of cargo delivery. *Proceedings of Petersburg Transport University*, 19(1), 82–89. DOI: 10.20295/1815-588X-2022-19-1-82-89

Ning, L., & Yao, D. (2023). The Impact of Digital Transformation on Supply Chain Capabilities and Competitive Performance. *Sustainability (Basel)*, 15(13), 10107. DOI: 10.3390/su151310107

Pham, T. N., Hoang, M. T. T., Tran, Y. N. N., & Phan, B. N. (2024). Combining digitalization and sustainability: Unveiling the relationship of digital maturity degree, sustainable supply chain management practices, and performance. *International Journal of Productivity and Performance Management*, 73(8), 2508–2529. DOI: 10.1108/IJPPM-06-2023-0311

Porter, M. E., & Millar, V. E. (1985). How information gives you a competitive advantage. *Harvard Business Review*, 63(4), 149–160.

Porter, M. E., & Millar, V. E. (1985). How information gives you a competitive advantage. *Harvard Business Review*, 63(4), 149–160.

Preacher, K. J., & Hayes, A. F. (2008). Asymptotic and resampling strategies for assessing and comparing indirect effects in structural equation models. *Psychological Methods*, 13(3), 181.

Putri, A. F., Fauzi, R., Hendayani, D., & Iskamto, D. (2023). The Role of Supply Chain Capability as Mediation Between Digitalization and Digital Connectivity on Operational Performance. Journal of World Science.

Rachinger, M., Riedel, R., & Davies, J. (2019). The social construction of digitalization in logistics and supply chain management. *Journal of Business Logistics*, 40(2), 223–238.

Ragowsky, A., Bearden, N., & Licker, P. (2021). Factors influencing IT investments in digital transformation: A study of US businesses. *Journal of Information Technology Management*, 32(4), 1–16.

Ragowsky, A., Mabert, V. A., & Klassen, R. D. (2021). Article title. *International Journal of Production Economics*, 90(1), 47–58.

Richard, O. C., Murthi, B. P. S., & Ismail, K. (2019). Corporate social responsibility (CSR) and firm performance: Human resource management perspective. *Human Resource Management*, 58(6), 539–548.

Rogers, E. M. (2003). *Diffusion of innovations* (5th ed.). Free Press.

Saberi, S., Kouhizadeh, M., Sarkis, J., & Shen, L. (2019). Blockchain technology and its relationships to sustainable supply chain management. *International Journal of Production Research*, 57(7), 2117–2135. DOI: 10.1080/00207543.2018.1533261

Sabherwal, R., & Sabherwal, S. (2015). Article title. *International Journal of Production Economics*, 90(1), 47–58.

Sabherwal, R., & Sabherwal, S. (2015). The impact of top management support for information systems on information systems planning effectiveness. *Information & Management*, 52(3), 351–364.

Sebastian, I. M., Morris, T., Burgess, S., & Daugherty, P. R. (2017). Making digital supply chain transformation a reality: Key challenges and a roadmap for success. *Supply Chain Management*, 22(3), 399–420.

Seuring, S., & Müller, M. (2008). Article title. *International Journal of Production Economics*, 90(1), 47–58.

Seuring, S., & Müller, M. (2008). From a literature review to a conceptual framework for sustainable supply chain management. *Journal of Cleaner Production*, 16(15), 1699–1710. DOI: 10.1016/j.jclepro.2008.04.020

Shah, S., Chen, S., & Naghi Ganj, E. (2024). An Investigative Study to Examine the Impact of Digitalisation on Manufacturing Supply Chains. Engineering World.

Solove, D. J. (2006). A taxonomy of privacy. *University of Pennsylvania Law Review*, 154(3), 477–564. DOI: 10.2307/40041279

Srivastava, P., Ansari, H., Alrasheedi, M., Sharma, R., Prakash, S., & Gupta, S. (2024). Leveraging supply chain collaboration with digital technologies for supply chain performance: An empirical investigation of Indian meat industries. *International Journal of Food Science & Technology*, 59(5), 3514–3522. DOI: 10.1111/ijfs.17052

Tornatzky, L. G., & Fleischer, M. (1990). *The processes of technological innovation*. Lexington Books.

Touboulic, A., & Walker, H. (2015). Article title. *International Journal of Production Economics*, 90(1), 47–58.

Touboulic, A., & Walker, H. (2015). Theories in sustainable supply chain management: A structured literature review. *International Journal of Physical Distribution & Logistics Management*, 45(1/2), 16–42. DOI: 10.1108/IJPDLM-05-2013-0106

Tseng, M. L., Bui, T. D., Lewi, S., Rizaldy, H., Lim, M. K., & Wu, K. J. (2022). Using qualitative information, sustainable supply chain management practices in the Indonesian coffee industry: Digitalization integration improves performance. Advanced online publication. DOI: 10.1080/13675567.2022.2155936

Van Weele, A. J. (2020). Purchasing and supply chain management: Analysis, strategy, planning and practice. Cengage Learning EMEA.

Venkatesh, V., Thong, J. Y., & Xu, X. (2016). Digitalization and performance: How organizational, cultural, and technological factors shape digital adoption and new performance creation. *Management Information Systems Quarterly*, 40(1), 157–178. DOI: 10.2307/41410412

Vial, G. (2018). Digital innovation and the fourth industrial revolution: Epochal social changes? *Journal of Innovation Economics & Management*, 26(3), 3–14.

Vial, G. (2019). Building digital capabilities for transformative performance: A dynamic capabilities perspective. *Journal of Business Research*, 101, 638–650.

Wang, M., & Prajogo, D. (2024). The effect of supply chain digitalization on a firm's performance. *Industrial Management & Data Systems*, 124(5), 1725–1745. DOI: 10.1108/IMDS-09-2023-0629

Wang, R., & Strong, D. M. (1996). Beyond accuracy: What data quality means to data consumers. *Journal of Management Information Systems*, 12(4), 5–34. DOI: 10.1080/07421222.1996.11518099

Westin, A. F. (1967). *Privacy and freedom*. Atheneum.

Winkelhaus, S., Strauss, C., & Zühlke, D. (2020). Logistics 4.0: A definition for research and practice. *Decisions*, 58(5), 1285–1300.

Yu, Y., Zeng, H., & Zhang, M. (2024). Digital transformation for supply chain collaborative innovation and market performance. *European Journal of Innovation Management*. Advance online publication. DOI: 10.1108/EJIM-09-2023-0736

Zhao, H., Wayne, S. J., Glibkowski, B. C., & Bravo, J. (2007). The impact of psychological contract breach on work-related outcomes: A meta-analysis. *Personnel Psychology*, 60(3), 647–680. DOI: 10.1111/j.1744-6570.2007.00087.x

Zhou, H., Wang, Q., Li, L., Teo, S. H. H., & Yang, S. H. (2023). Supply chain digitalization and performance improvement: A moderated mediation model. *Supply Chain Management*, 28(6), 993–1008. DOI: 10.1108/SCM-11-2022-0434

Zhu, K., Kraemer, K. L., & Xu, S. (2006). The influence of institutional factors on e-business adoption in China. *Management Science*, 52(10), 1557–1576. DOI: 10.1287/mnsc.1050.0487

APPENDIX 1: QUESTIONNAIRE

- **Organizational factors**
  - o Our organizational structure is agile and can react quickly to technological developments.
  - o Our organization invests financially in digital technologies.
  - o Our organization's leaders understand the benefits of digital technologies.
  - o Our organization has the right skills and human resources for digitalization.

    Technological factors
  - o The level of adoption of digitalization is high, as measured by the effective use of digital technologies.
  - o Advanced functionalities are used to optimize procurement processes.
  - o Technologies are integrated into daily operations.
  - o Online purchasing management systems are widely adopted.
  - o Decision-making processes are automated thanks to AI.
- **Human factors**:
  - o Actively involving employees in the digital transformation process is essential to ensure their buy-in and commitment.
  - o Training employees using digital tools is essential to maximize the benefits of new technologies.
  - o Developing employees' digital skills is crucial to fully embracing new working methods.
  - o Transparent communication and practical change management help reduce resistance to change and foster a corporate culture conducive to innovation and collaboration.
- **Digital adoption capability**
  - o Our organization actively adopts digital technologies in its procurement practices.
  - o Digital tools are commonly used in our procurement processes.
  - o We regularly invest in digital solutions to improve our procurement operations.
- **Environmental factors**
  - o Digitalization improves our company's responsiveness to market demands.
  - o Competitive pressures are driving our company to digitalize the supply chain.
  - o Growing sustainability awareness drives our company to adopt digital solutions for more efficient resource management.

- Regulatory changes catalyze the adoption of digital procurement practices in our company.

- **Supply chain logistics performance**
    - Our supply chain can adapt quickly to changing circumstances thanks to digitalization.
    - We use digital tools to share real-time information across our supply chain.
    - Adopting digitalization has led to significant savings in our supply chain.
    - Digital technologies enable us to optimize the use of our resources.
    - AI tools enable better adaptation to changes in demand and external disruptions.
    - The adoption of AI has led to an increase in the profitability of our supply chain.
    - Ordering and delivery processes have been accelerated thanks to digitalization.

We use real-time purchasing management platforms to improve our procurement practices.

Chapter 12
Transforming Supply Chains:
Exploring the Role of 5G Technology

Sinan Çıkmak
https://orcid.org/0000-0002-4704-3409
Vocational School of Social Sciences, Duzce, Turkey

ABSTRACT

The fifth-generation (5G) technology is a next-generation communication technology that enables significantly faster data transmission, lower latency, and greater connectivity compared to its predecessors. Integrating 5G technology in supply chain management offers a competitive advantage by optimizing operations, enhancing real-time monitoring, improving logistics, and enabling advanced automation through the Internet of Things (IoT). This chapter explores how 5G technology can revolutionize supply chain management by providing a detailed overview of its value propositions, such as facilitating real-time data exchange, enhancing logistics optimization through better route planning, and supporting IoT-driven automation for more efficient inventory management. Additionally, it discusses the role of 5G in enabling seamless connectivity across supply chain networks, thus improving visibility and decision-making processes. By evaluating emerging trends and potential developments, this study aims to provide valuable insights for researchers, practitioners, and industry stakeholders on the impact of 5G technology on supply chain activities, highlighting both opportunities and challenges in its implementation.

DOI: 10.4018/979-8-3693-4427-9.ch012

1. INTRODUCTION

In the modern era, technological advancements are occurring at a pace previously unseen, resulting in significant transformations in our lives. Wireless communication technologies are playing a vital role in this transformation. Among the many advancements, the fifth-generation (5G) internet technology stands out as one of the most significant innovations in recent times, with the potential to revolutionize our future even further. 5G is the next generation cellular network and wireless technology, succeeding 4G networks. With high speed, low latency, and large connection capacity, 5G technology promises to create a more connected, intelligent, and efficient world. According to a recent report, there will be 41.6 billion internet-connected devices by 2025. In smart network communication environments, 5G technology will seamlessly connect people, objects, data, applications, transportation systems, and cities (Biswas et al., 2023).

5G technology offers several advantages over previous generations (4G, 3G). One of its most significant benefits is its exceptional speed, allowing users to easily download and upload large files and stream high-quality videos. Additionally, 5G has a remarkably low latency, resulting in minimal lag time when accessing the internet. Moreover, 5G has the possibility to support a vast number of connected devices, rendering it an indispensable technology as more and more devices become interconnected. As such, the adoption of 5G technology is rapidly increasing across various industries, from healthcare and education to transportation and finance, all of which are poised to benefit from the technology's speed, low latency, and high device density.

The 5G network's high bandwidth and low latency have the potential to provide an integrated platform for real-time device connections. Bandwidth is the maximum frequency signal transmitted through a communication channel, determining how much data can be transferred. 5G technology's higher bandwidth accelerates user data traffic. The high speed and reliability of 5G technology will significantly contribute to digital transformation by increasing the effectiveness of new technologies such as robotics and the Internet of Things (IoT). The advent of 5G technology holds significant potential for advancing the development and utilization of various technologies, including virtual reality (VR), IoT, autonomous vehicles, metaverse universes, and artificial intelligence (AI)-supported assistants. 5G's speed and capacity can enhance the capabilities of these technologies, enabling faster and more efficient data processing, greater connectivity, and seamless integration. This advancement is expected to revolutionize the way businesses and industries operate, allowing them to deliver better products and services and enhance overall productivity.

In today's business landscape, competition between enterprises is no longer limited to the companies themselves but extends to their respective supply chains. As a result, supply chain management has emerged as a crucial factor in determining a company's competitiveness. Supply chain operations require advanced data and information systems for more accurate and timely decision-making, resulting in increased productivity and customer satisfaction. In the era of Industry 4.0, supply chains must remain up-to-date with the latest technological advancements to stay competitive. The 5G technology helps supply chains to keep competitive in Industry 4.0. Organizations can improve communication and collaboration throughout the supply chain with 5G technology, which provides faster and more secure connectivity. Implementing 5G technology in supply chain operations is beneficial in ensuring visibility throughout the process.

Automation plays a vital role in enhancing supply chain processes. IoT technology is utilized to achieve automation. In this regard, 5G technology enables the efficient utilization of IoT to access data that will help all stakeholders in the supply chain to track goods, assess supply chain performance, and build better predictive models. Smart devices generate a large amount of data. When analyzed, this data can provide visibility into the supply chain, offer early warnings of internal and external issues, and help improve efficiency. The time lag between data collection and action has been a problem. The IoT enables real-time responses, remote control of supply chains, better partner collaboration, and more accurate data for more practical decision-making (Biswas et al., 2023). Therefore, the advent of 5G technology and IoT ecosystems has ushered in a new era of organizational capability. The integration of these two technologies has enabled the creation of a unified database that supports a range of functions, including procurement and purchasing, production and sales, distribution and storage, retail operations, and services after the sale. According to the theory of organizational capability, 5G technology can significantly improve an organization's capacity to integrate internal logistical processes, vendors, and clients (Taboada & Shee, 2021; Biswas et al., 2023).

There is not enough literature on 5G-enabled supply chain management despite the benefits 5G technology offers (Taboada & Shee, 2021). This section aims to provide insights into the various impacts and practical uses of the advanced 5G technology in the domain of supply chain operations. To achieve this goal, a thorough analysis was conducted on academic studies, reports, and reliable internet sources that discuss the applications of 5G technology in supply chain operations. The findings are expected to guide researchers and practitioners. The remaining sections of the study are structured as follows: Section 2 presents a brief but informative overview, showcasing the key features and capabilities of 5G technology. Section 3 offers insights into applying 5G technology in supply chain operations. It covers how 5G can be used in manufacturing, warehouse management, logistics optimization, and real-time monitoring, with explanations and case studies demonstrating its contributions to supply chain applications. Section 4 discusses the challenges to the widespread adoption of 5G in supply chain processes despite its immense potential. Finally, Section 5 offers an overall evaluation and a perspective on the future of 5G technology in the context of supply chain management.

Overall, the study aims to provide a comprehensive understanding of the potential impact of 5G technology on the supply chain, and to identify opportunities for businesses to leverage this technology to improve their operations and gain a competitive advantage.

2. OVERVIEW OF 5G TECHNOLOGY

Information technology (IT) has progressed quickly in recent years. 5G mobile communication technology has been the main force behind the industrial change and technological revolution (Cheng et al., 2022). The emergence of 5G networks lays the groundwork for industrial transformation through digitalization and advanced communication. It promises reliable services at ultra-high speeds with very low latency (Dogra et al., 2020).

Over the past 30 years, cellular wireless networks have advanced through 1G, 2G, 3G, 4G, and now 5G, each bringing significant improvements to mobile communication technologies, as illustrated in Figure 1. (Attaran, 2023). 1G introduced mass-market mobile telephony, 2G enabled global interoperability and SMS text messaging, 3G provided high-speed data transfer for internet access, and 4G brought enhanced data capabilities and speeds, making high-speed mobile internet widely accessible. Now, 5G technology is poised to offer the most powerful cellular wireless network with extraordinary data capabilities, unlimited call volumes, and infinite data broadcasts (Attaran, 2023).

5G represents an innovative networking solution designed to meet the challenges of upcoming communication demands. It allows a vast array of smart devices to connect and communicate with each other from any location at any time (Taboada & Shee, 2021). The previous generation of wireless networks, such as 4G LTE-A, faced challenges related to data rates, connectivity, and latency. For instance, 4G LTE-A could support a maximum download data rate of up to 3 Gb/s and an upload data rate of up to 1.5 Gb/s, with connectivity for approximately 600 users per cell and latency of around 30–50 milliseconds. These limitations made 4G networks inadequate for applications such as VR, augmented reality (AR), HD streaming, video conferencing, and 360° video. However, 5G networks have addressed these challenges by introducing new features, services, and technologies (Dogra et al., 2020).

Figure 1. The Evolution of Cellular Wireless Networks

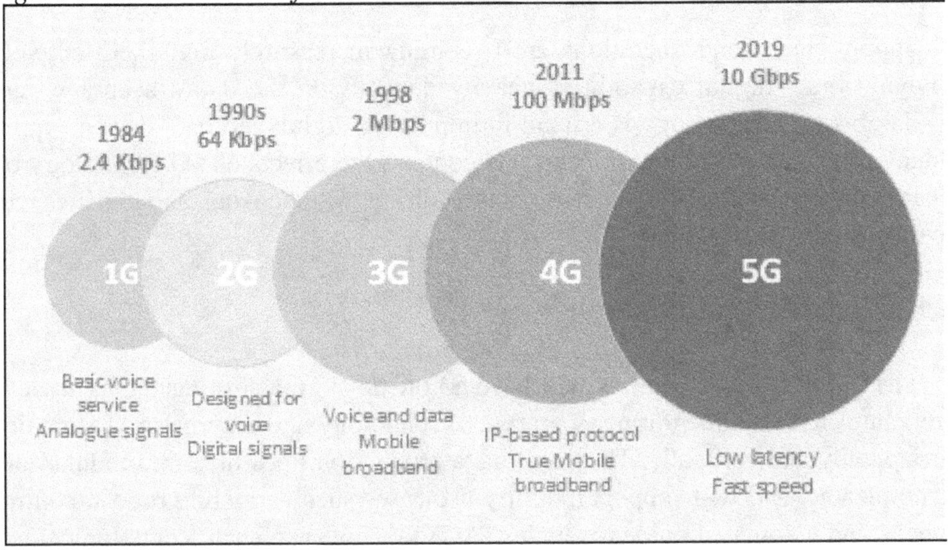

The key characteristics of 5G technology can be summarized as follows (Attaran, 2023; Lagorio et al., 2023):

- The theoretical maximum speed is 10 Gbps, allowing for the transfer and handling of a large amount of data simultaneously.
- Lower power consumption compared to earlier technologies, with stand-by modes capable of reducing energy usage by up to 50%, significantly surpassing the up to 20% energy savings offered by 4G technology.
- The density of connections, defined as the simultaneous connection of devices and their data handling capacity, reaches roughly one million connections per square kilometer.
- 5G frequencies utilize expanded spectrum bands, with potential frequency bands ranging from 30 GHz to 300 GHz.

Given these innovative features, 5G is a vital enterprise instrument to accelerate digital transformation across sectors, especially in their supply chain management initiatives.

3. IMPACTS OF 5G ON SUPPLY CHAIN ACTIVITIES

Supply chains and operations are becoming increasingly digital. Effectively applying these digital capabilities heavily depends on the data's accuracy, and availability. 5G technology is crucial in improving digital and data-driven supply chains (Dolgui & Ivanov, 2022). In this context, the effects of 5G technology on basic supply chain activities such as manufacturing, warehousing, and logistics will be discussed in this section.

3.1. 5G in Manufacturing

The future's smart factories will have a holistic approach to managing the entire value chain by integrating operational technology and enterprise IT domains horizontally and vertically. They will have production lines that are modular and customizable, and will support mobility use cases such as mobile robots, control panels, and automated guided vehicles (AGVs). However, such technological advances need the seamless connection of people, machines, and computing resources in production processes. (Mahmood et al., 2022). Advancements in digital manufacturing have led to new applications that demand sophisticated communication technologies. To fully leverage these applications, it is imperative to employ advanced communication systems. Currently, most smart factories use wired connections to communicate between systems and equipment. However, setting up hardware for wired connections is a complex and time-consuming process. Additionally, the hardware deteriorates over time, making troubleshooting, maintenance, and equipment replacement difficult. Wired connections also limit the ability to adjust the production line, which is problematic in an increasingly intelligent and flexible manufacturing industry (Ling, 2021). The development model of smart manufacturing necessitates increasing machine-to-machine, machine-to-man, and man-to-machine communication requirements (Cheng et al., 2022).

Manufacturing processes require real-time monitoring of production factors, worker training, maintenance, and communication of industrial data. Interconnecting all production equipment, materials, tools, workers, and processes is necessary for "ubiquitous communication." Unmanned factories, man-machine collaboration, machine-machine collaboration, and remote real-time control demand accurate and reliable data communication, making industrial data communication crucial to intelligent manufacturing (Cheng et al., 2022). However, transmitting this data through wired systems can be costly compared to wireless networks. This is where 5G technology comes in, providing an ideal solution for managing data on a large scale with up-to-date information (O'Connell et al., 2020).

The process of collecting and utilizing data necessitates seamless connectivity to bridge the physical and digital worlds, enabling the development of novel revenue streams and cost-saving opportunities (Mahmood et al., 2022). Given the critical role of data in driving modern-day business operations, establishing a robust and reliable digital infrastructure is essential. Therefore, organizations must prioritize investing in high-quality connectivity solutions to ensure optimal data utilization for growth and profitability. 5G technology provides low latency, high data rates, and high reliability to meet the connectivity requirements of digitalized manufacturing (Lundgren et al., 2022). By incorporating 5G technology, businesses can streamline their data collection process, making gathering information from various sources easier. It enables companies to retrofit old machines with sensors to collect and analyze data (Lundgren et al., 2022). This means that even outdated equipment can be upgraded with the latest technology, improving efficiency and productivity.

Deploying 5G has sparked expectations of new opportunities for manufacturing business models, with increased data requirements ranging from critical missions to massive machine connectivity (O'Connell et al., 2020). Manufacturing facilities are increasingly capable of incorporating 5G technology into their smart devices, enhancing communication capabilities between devices and resulting in a more streamlined production process. Examples of successful 5G implementations include MTU Aero Engines, a German aircraft engine manufacturer, which tested 5G-based production technology on blade-integrated disks used in jet engines. The implementation of 5G-enabled production technology reduced the process design phase by 75% (Tomás, 2021a). Similarly, Worcester Bosch launched the UK's first 5G factory, utilizing a 5G private network and mobile edge computing infrastructure provided by Ericsson. The factory uses 5G technology to optimize machine performance, increase output by up to 2%, and enhance safety for employees through real-time machine sensors and collision detection technology (Tomás, 2021a). In another instance, e.GO, a German electric vehicle manufacturer has incorporated 5G technology into its car production process. The company uses multi-access edge computing (MEC) to enhance the processing power of its AGVs. These vehicles transport the chassis from one station to another, replacing the traditional production line. By employing this technology, the AGVs analyze environmental data in real-time, such as detecting any obstacles in their path, and adjust their operations accordingly with minimal delay (less than ten milliseconds), ensuring efficient and safe operation of all the machines in the plant (O'Connell et al., 2020; Rose, 2019). Since 2018, Audi has partnered with Ericsson to explore 5G in car manufacturing. This technology enables real-time, wireless human-machine interactions, which is critical for safely operating industrial robots. The low latency of 5G allows for the quick response times needed for these applications (Jablonski, 2020).

Private 5G networks are likely to become the go-to choose for numerous businesses worldwide, especially in industrial settings such as manufacturing plants, logistics centers, and ports. Essentially, a mobile private 5G network is a local area network that uses 5G technology to create a secure and private network controlled by the user, such as an industrial company, and can be customized to meet specific requirements (O'Connell et al., 2020). The combination of 5G, cloud computing, sensor technology, and IoT is expected to revolutionize factory floors. In addition to reducing costs and minimizing downtime through predictive maintenance, factories will be able to utilize 5G technology to precisely control and analyze industrial processes at an unprecedented level of accuracy. For instance, Valin Xiangtan Iron & Steel, a factory in China's Hunan Province, has successfully implemented 5G and cloud computing technology to control their bridge cranes remotely. Previously, maintaining the equipment was dangerous, making finding people to work in the small control room difficult. However, with 5G and cloud computing, operators can now control the equipment from a more comfortable and safer environment (Ling, 2021). With support from Huawei and China Mobile, Haier has implemented innovative manufacturing solutions combining 5G and mobile edge computing in its smart factories. By using a 500W industrial camera mounted on a robotic arm with high-intensity lighting, the factory can scan refrigerators as they come off the production line. The local application, powered by a trained algorithm, identifies any damage to the refrigerator's exterior that requires replacement. This solution has significantly reduced the time it takes to manually check refrigerators, ensuring no delays in the production line (Tomás, 2021b).

To fully digitalize the manufacturing industry, it is essential to have wide-ranging and fine-grained connectivity (Mahmood et al., 2022). Valin Xiangtan Iron & Steel uses advanced technology to detect defects in steel. They take pictures of the steel surfaces with industrial cameras and then send these images to the cloud using the 5G network. An AI-based machine vision technology then automatically identifies any defects in the photos. This method is more precise than manual detection since it can detect even subtle defects and objects in motion (Ling, 2021). The adoption of 5G technology is likely to result in increased operational efficiency, improved maintenance processes, and a more agile and adaptable business environment. These benefits are expected to provide a competitive advantage to companies that leverage 5G technology effectively.

3.2. 5G in Warehousing

Warehouses are complex environments with numerous operations and processes running simultaneously. Automating these workflows can bring many benefits, including enhanced efficiency and increased productivity. Additionally, automation can help reduce errors and increase accuracy, resulting in fewer delays and higher customer satisfaction. Implementing automation technology can significantly enhance warehouse operations and improve the bottom line. The advancement of Industry 4.0 will rely heavily upon connectivity, as machines and production assets must be linked to transmit data. Therefore, to fully leverage the benefits of automation and digitization in warehouse operations, it is essential to establish a comprehensive network that interconnects all the various systems (Gergs & Mavrakis, 2022). To effectively handle the requirements of smart warehousing, it is crucial to have network connectivity that surpasses the limitations of Wi-Fi. The current setup of warehouses that rely on Radio Frequency Identification (RFID) and Wi-Fi connectivity often leads to inconsistent data and unreliable network coverage (Gergs & Mavrakis, 2022). The integration of 5G technology in warehousing operations has the potential to bring about a significant transformation. This is primarily due to the capability of 5G to facilitate the real-time integration of data and analytics with warehouse systems (George et al., 2023).

The use of digital technologies inside warehouses is rapidly gaining momentum. This trend is expected to continue, particularly with the growth of e-commerce warehousing and fulfillment centers. Implementing 5G technology can play a vital role in further supporting this progress. With faster data transfer speeds and lower latency, 5G technology enables the warehousing and storage industries to deploy robotics, utilize automated systems, and operate sensor-based controls more effectively. The benefits of 5G adoption are most likely to have a significant impact on the operational efficiency and functions of warehouses.

Some forward-thinking companies have started researching 5G technology and integrating it into their business processes. Furthermore, the number of pilot schemes using 5G technology is increasing every day. Teltech Group, a U.S.-based company, is an example of the advantages of implementing a private 5G network for smart warehousing and logistics purposes. In 2022, the company launched a private network in one of its warehouses, which spans an area of 200,000 sq. ft. Out of the total area, two-thirds are racks, which creates 15,000 possible pallet positions. As Wi-Fi-based connectivity increases the risk of unwanted interference and dead zones, the company opted for private 5G connectivity to support smart warehouse applications (Gergs & Mavrakis, 2022). GE Research, the technology development division of the General Electric Company (GE), has officially launched two projects as part of the U.S. Department of Defense's recently announced 5G initiative. The projects aim to create "smart warehouse" facilities at two military bases. The projects will involve utilizing digital twin technology, autonomous robots, and real-time tracking of thousands of warehouse assets and components, which will be made possible by the power of a 5G network (GE Research, 2021). In October 2023, CelcomDigi and DHL Supply Chain Malaysia collaborated to launch 5G technology and AI solutions for robotic inventory management systems. With the help of drones equipped with high-resolution cameras and robots, DHL can independently conduct daily inventory management with automated stock-taking solutions and computer vision technologies without human errors. The 5G-powered solution offers many benefits, including greater efficiency, time savings, and reduced electricity consumption for inventory management (CelcomDigi, 2023).

Kollmorgen Automation AB is a provider of hardware and software solutions that simplify the precise, safe, and efficient navigation and control of AGVs and mobile robots. With the cooperation of Ericsson and Kollmorgen, the advantages of 5G network connectivity have been expanded to factory AGVs. As a result, 5G networks will facilitate the automation of intralogistics operations by supporting an increased number of AGVs and connected devices (Ericsson, 2022). The implementation of 5G technology is expected to have a major impact on warehousing operations. This will significantly affect various areas such as robotic operations involving AGVs, AR devices for picking, training, and maintenance, inventory management through real-time asset tracking, the equipment's battery life from network slicing, and data security (George et al., 2023). As part of a strategic alliance, Huawei and local carriers have established a 5G-enabled smart warehousing center in south Dubai. This innovative facility is poised to revolutionize cargo management by implementing adaptable AGVs empowered by the capabilities of 5G technology (Huawei, 2023).

A recent investigation conducted by ABI Research shows that implementing a dedicated 5G network within warehousing facilities in the United States is projected to yield substantial economic advantages over five years. The study posits that warehouses with such a network can anticipate an 11.9% increase in gross profit margin. Furthermore, the expected return on investment (ROI) is estimated at US$13.80 for every US$1 invested (Gergs & Mavrakis, 2022). Warehouse operators are increasingly recognizing the benefits of implementing 5G cellular networks as they introduce more autonomous mobile robots (AMRs) into their operations. With the capabilities of 5G, a larger number of AMRs can autonomously and safely transport pallets from the receiving area to specific destinations within the warehouse. This advancement allows operators to allocate their time to more important tasks, rather than manually moving through the vast spaces of the warehouse (Hunt & Bennett, 2022). The sensor systems and asset tracking, enabled by integrated 5G, deliver instantaneous location tracking and precise inventory information for several thousand items. The inventory data is always up-to-date, and the location tracking system can track items wherever they are in the warehouse. This system helps increase the accuracy of item picking and reduces human errors and cycle times for inventory audits (Hunt & Bennett, 2022: 2).

In order to establish a stable intralogistics solution that is in keeping with Industry 4.0 standards, it is imperative to have autonomous material handling that is supported by secure connectivity and a robust ecosystem of application providers (Ericsson, 2022). 5G technology allows for more precise warehouse management systems, which offer accurate inventory tracking. For instance, it can utilize 'smart shelves' that use IoT sensors to provide real-time visibility. These sensors alert when a product runs low and needs reordering, ensuring constant availability without overstocking (Hofman, 2023). To fully automate and digitize warehouses, AGVs, AMRs, collaborative robots, and autonomous forklifts will play a crucial role. According to ABI Research, the United States is expected to have over 3,700 robotic warehouses by 2025 (Gergs & Mavrakis, 2022). AGVs and AMRs need to be able to move freely across the entire warehouse floor. However, current wireless technologies are not able to ensure strong signal hand-offs between Access Points, which results in AGVs having to operate at lower speeds. By using private 5G, low latencies can be consistently guaranteed, allowing warehouse managers to operate AGVs at 30% higher speed (Gergs & Mavrakis, 2022).

The utilization of 5G technology in warehouse management is contributing significantly to sustainability efforts. As this technology continues to mature and be increasingly adopted, there will be gradual improvements in energy efficiency. According to research conducted by ABI Research, by 2030, each warehouse operator can reduce energy consumption by 2,000 megawatts per year thanks to 5G. This will enhance the sector's sustainability, leading to a decrease in Carbon Dioxide (CO_2) emissions by almost 700 tons annually for each warehouse (Gergs & Mavrakis, 2022). Warehouses and other facilities can experience significant improvements in their operations with the use of 5G technology. The low latencies and extensive coverage of 5G will enable warehousing processes to become more efficient than ever before, opening up new possibilities for capabilities and technologies that were previously difficult to implement (George et al., 2023).

3.3. 5G in Logistics

There are significant and robust links between 5G technology and leading Industry 4.0 technologies that will impact logistics activities (Lagorio et al., 2023). Therefore, it is necessary to understand the critical role of 5G in revolutionizing the logistics industry and improving the efficiency and effectiveness of business operations. 5G technology has the potential to enhance every stage of the supply chain, including inventory management and intelligent transportation systems. In warehouses, 5G addresses the challenge of connecting multiple wireless devices across large spaces that can span hundreds or thousands of square meters. This capability allows for an interconnected system of wireless cranes, forklifts, handheld devices, and other equipment, ultimately boosting speed and efficiency (Hofman, 2023).

One of the most significant challenges facing the logistics industry today is improving supply chain visibility. The implementation of 5G can facilitate end-to-end communication between sensors, greatly enhancing the efficiency and effectiveness of logistics operations (Apruzzese et al., 2023). The benefits of implementing 5G-supported automation in logistics operations can lead to reduced labor costs, decreased transportation costs, better resource utilization, and lower carbon emissions. These benefits can be realized in the mid to long term, resulting in a more sustainable and efficient logistics management system (Lagorio et al., 2023).

The technologies associated with 5G are evaluated in two main categories (Lagorio et al., 2023). These are technologies related to information flow and technologies related to material flow. Technologies related to information flow include IoT, big data, smart sensors, microprocessors, RFID, edge/ cloud computing, blockchain, AI, AR, and simulation. Technologies in this category include all stages of the data value chain (i.e., data creation, acquisition, transportation, pre-processing, storage, and analytics). Technologies related to material flow are unmanned aerial vehicles, AGVs, and intelligent robotics that automatically handle and transport materials within and outside the facility boundaries. The seamless integration of 5G technology with IoT is a crucial factor driving the growth of the new generation of logistics. The widespread adoption of 5G allows logistics centers to efficiently monitor and track every node in the industry, thereby improving the overall efficiency of the logistics process (Liu, 2021).

A notable feature of 5G technology is its low latency, making it ideal for highly reliable communication scenarios, such as unmanned vehicle driving and industrial automation. Logistics companies have long pursued unmanned vehicle operations and automatic distribution projects. The advent of 5G technology has made many advanced smart initiatives possible, particularly within the realm of unmanned vehicles and distribution (Liu, 2021). 5G technology also represents a significant advancement for autonomous vehicles. Through a network connection, sensors, cameras, and other devices can communicate with each other and send instructions to the vehicles. When this network is powered by 5G, self-driving systems become more reliable, accurate, and safer. Currently, autonomous vehicles are limited to restricted environments such as warehouses. However, with the help of 5G technology, it might be possible for autonomous trucks to operate on public roads (Hofman, 2023). The deployment of 5G networks in warehouses provides the potential for the automation of inventory management and tracking processes. This technology fosters seamless connections between devices and sensors, enabling real-time inventory tracking and automated management. Consequently, it streamlines logistics operations, minimizes errors, and enhances overall efficiency (An, 2023).

The logistics industry today is complex and requires a variety of different terminal devices, each with its own specific network communication needs. For instance, smart driverless vehicles require networks with low latency, whereas logistics AR equipment needs high-bandwidth communication networks. Additionally, IoT logistics systems require the ability to access numerous embedded devices, such as sensors. Fortunately, 5G technology offers a network-slicing function that can meet the various business needs of the new-generation logistics industry (Liu, 2021). 5G technology enables smart devices to communicate at nearly real-time speeds, making it ideal for supporting emerging applications like VR and AR. For instance, an AR application can provide warehouse workers with visual or textual cues to help them quickly select the correct product or part in the appropriate quantity. Once the correct item is selected, the device can guide the worker to the corresponding box for placement, thereby reducing operator errors and minimizing the time required to complete tasks (Hofman, 2023). The integration of 5G-powered AR technology outside the warehouse can significantly enhance the efficiency and safety of employees who are involved in loading vans. With AR assistance, employees can receive real-time guidance, ensuring that heavy or potentially dangerous items are flagged before handling. Efficiently loading goods in the correct order is vital, and digital technology simplifies this process by clearly indicating which packages should be loaded onto the vehicle and in what sequence (Simmons, 2023).

5G technology is designed with security as a priority. Unlike previous wireless communication technologies, which were hardware-based, 5G operates primarily on software and servers, offering a more secure infrastructure compared to 4G technologies. Furthermore, 5G supports end-to-end encryption, ensuring that data is encrypted from its source to its destination, significantly reducing the risk of interception or tampering during transmission (Simmons, 2023). With enhanced cloud computing capabilities and RFID tracking, 5G technology is poised to revolutionize communication across the entire supply chain, paving the way for large-scale smart logistics. This concept involves integrating technology to achieve advanced supply chain monitoring and tracking. The computing power and machine-to-machine communication enabled by 5G will facilitate cloud computing for efficient supply chain inventory management (George et al., 2023).

In conclusion, the implementation of 5G technology can significantly enhance logistics processes by improving the management and coordination of material flows. Additionally, it can increase visibility and transparency, leading to better control of logistics and supply chain operations (Lagorio et al., 2023).

4. CHALLENGES IN ADOPTING 5G TECHNOLOGY

The 5th generation mobile communication technology, considered a disruptive technology, promises to improve activities in many areas with faster data transfer and more reliable connection opportunities. However, there are some challenges in implementing 5G technology in supply chain processes that hinder its widespread adoption. There are still challenges that prevent companies from investing in 5G despite the potential for optimizing supply chain processes. These challenges range from technological maturity to global standardization, government regulations, and cost considerations (Attaran, 2023).

A major challenge lies in the infrastructure required for 5G networks. Establishing the necessary base stations, antennas, and fiber optic cabling across a supply chain network is particularly daunting in remote locations or areas with poor connectivity. The expenses and time involved in deploying this infrastructure can be substantial obstacles (Kadena & Rajnai, 2024; O'Connell et al., 2020; Biswas et al., 2023). Additionally, high-speed, low-latency connectivity is offered by 5G networks. However, maintaining reliable network coverage and consistency throughout the supply chain may be difficult due to signal strength, network congestion, and potential interference from physical obstacles, which can affect connectivity quality (Kadena & Rajnai, 2024).

Another key challenge to 5G adoption is the difficulty of integrating it with existing technologies (Lagorio et al., 2023). Supply chains are complex, involving multiple stakeholders, systems, and devices that must be compatible with 5G-enabled technologies. Achieving this level of interoperability requires standardized communication protocols and significant investments in upgrading existing infrastructure (Kadena & Rajnai, 2024). For instance, the integration of 5G with AGVs, RFID sensors, and Blockchain technology poses significant technical and financial hurdles (Ding et al., 2021; O'Connell et al., 2020). Addressing these integration issues demands additional investment in ancillary technologies and employee training, further increasing the costs of upgrading to 5G (Lagorio et al., 2023; Cimini et al., 2020). In the manufacturing sector, cost concerns are particularly pressing. Businesses are often reluctant to invest in new technologies unless they can clearly demonstrate cost-saving benefits. Small and medium-sized enterprises (SMEs), in particular, may struggle with the financial and technical resources needed for a smooth transition to 5G (O'Connell et al., 2020). Moreover, the technological maturity of 5G is still a concern. The lack of a clear roadmap for its deployment in industries like manufacturing and logistics complicates planning and investment decisions. The early stage of 5G technology makes it difficult to predict its business viability, leading to uncertainties for vendors and operators.

Beyond the technical and financial challenges, security and privacy issues are also major concerns in the adoption of 5G technology. The increased connectivity and reliance on open-source designs inherent in 5G networks can introduce potential security vulnerabilities (Attaran, 2023). Ensuring the confidentiality, integrity, and availability of sensitive data across a highly interconnected supply chain is a daunting task. Companies must carefully evaluate the risks associated with privacy and security to prevent potential breaches that could compromise their operations.

In conclusion, while 5G technology offers significant potential for optimizing supply chain processes, its implementation is not without challenges. The complexities of integrating 5G with existing technologies, the high costs of infrastructure and device upgrades, and the concerns over security and privacy are key barriers that need to be addressed. For companies to fully realize the benefits of 5G, a comprehensive and strategic approach is required, one that considers the technological, financial, and security implications of this transformative technology.

5. CONCLUSION

The emergence of 5G technology represents a significant milestone in the progression of global supply chains, presenting transformative opportunities across many sectors. With its capacity for enabling lightning-fast data transmission, ultra-low latency, and the ability to interconnect a vast array of devices simultaneously, 5G has the potential to revolutionize the functioning of supply chains at every level. Integrating this technology into supply chain processes is poised to usher in a new era of more streamlined manufacturing, optimized logistics, and intelligent warehousing, thereby steering the industries towards a future where automation and real-time data analytics are integral components of everyday operations.

The benefits of 5G are particularly evident in its support for advanced technologies such as the Industrial Internet of Things (IIoT), AI, VR, AR, and robotics. These technologies benefit from the high-speed, low-latency connectivity that 5G offers, allowing for predictive maintenance, efficient inventory management, and improved production efficiency. Additionally, the improved connectivity provided by 5G allows for the smooth flow of information across various points of the supply chain, promoting better collaboration and transparency between suppliers, manufacturers, and distributors.

With its unparalleled ability to gather extensive data from remote sensors and various interconnected devices, 5G provides businesses access to valuable information previously beyond their reach. This data can then be transferred to secure data centers, where state-of-the-art AI and machine learning algorithms can be applied to extract insights and patterns that can help businesses make informed decisions.

The combination of 5G and AI has the potential to supercharge businesses by providing them with real-time, actionable insights that can drive innovation, efficiency, and growth. The advanced connectivity features of 5G make it easier to integrate IIoT devices. By improving communication between machines and other devices, factory sensors can make production processes more efficient. This technology also enables the development of innovative applications, such as data analytics and predictive maintenance. AMRs are revolutionizing material handling activities within warehouses by efficiently streamlining logistics processes. Their ability to autonomously navigate through warehouse environments and perform tasks such as picking, packing, and product inspections is made possible by the low-latency wireless connectivity provided by 5G technology. This seamless integration of 5G with AMRs allows for enhanced automation, leading to increased efficiency and productivity within warehouse operations. The implementation of 5G technology in logistics brings about significant advantages, notably in the realm of enhanced monitoring and control. With 5G, there is the potential to vastly improve the real-time tracking and oversight of materials, logistics vehicles, personnel, and routes. This high-speed, low-latency connectivity enables more efficient and precise management of the entire logistics operation, leading to improved productivity, safety, and overall performance.

In addition, 5G technology represents a significant advancement with the potential for supply chain sustainability. By facilitating precise resource management and implementing enhanced monitoring and control systems, 5G has the capability to minimize waste and support environmentally conscious business practices. This aligns with the growing demand for corporate sustainability, enabling companies to comply with regulations and meet the expectations of an increasingly environmentally aware consumer base.

There are numerous challenges hindering the widespread adoption of 5G technology. The initial investment required for 5G infrastructure is substantial, often involving costly equipment and infrastructure development. Supply chains can be complex, involving various stakeholders, systems, and devices that need to be compatible with 5G-enabled technologies. This level of interoperability necessitates the implementation of standardized communication protocols and substantial investments in upgrading pre-existing infrastructure. Furthermore, the implementation of 5G technology demands a thorough overhaul of existing systems, which is not only time-consuming but also resource-intensive. Another critical consideration is the potential security risks associated with 5G, such as heightened vulnerability to cyberattacks, which must be addressed proactively by businesses to ensure a secure transition to this advanced technology.

In summary, the impact of 5G on supply chains is significant and wide-ranging. Although the shift to this new era of connectivity poses challenges, the opportunities it offers are immense. As industries continue to adjust to the digital age, 5G will play a crucial role in fostering innovation, efficiency, and resilience. Companies that invest in 5G technology and align their strategies with its capabilities will not only thrive in the present but also establish the groundwork for sustained success in the future.

REFERENCES

An, N. (2023). How Private 5G is Reshaping the Future of Logistics. *HFCL*. https://www.hfcl.com/blog/private-5G-in-logistics

Apruzzese, M., Bruni, M. E., Musso, S., & Perboli, G. (2023). 5G and companion technologies as a boost in new business models for logistics and supply chain. *Sustainability (Basel)*, 15(15), 11846. DOI: 10.3390/su151511846

Attaran, M. (2023). The impact of 5G on the evolution of intelligent automation and industry digitization. *Journal of Ambient Intelligence and Humanized Computing*, 14(5), 5977–5993. DOI: 10.1007/s12652-020-02521-x PMID: 33643481

Biswas, S., Sanyal, A., Božanić, D., Puška, A., & Marinković, D. (2023). Critical success factors for 5G technology adaptation in supply chains. *Sustainability (Basel)*, 15(6), 5539. DOI: 10.3390/su15065539

CelcomDigi. (2023). *CelcomDigi and DHL supply chain reimagine logistics with Malaysia's first 5G-Powered AI autonomous warehouse*. https://corporate.celcomdigi.com/news/celcomdigi-and-dhl-supply-chain-reimagine-logistics-with-malaysias-first-5g-powered-ai-autonomous-warehouse

Cheng, J., Yang, Y., Zou, X., & Zuo, Y. (2022). 5G in manufacturing: A literature review and future research. *International Journal of Advanced Manufacturing Technology*, •••, 1–23.

Cimini, C., Lagorio, A., Romero, D., Cavalieri, S., & Stahre, J. (2020). Smart logistics and the logistics operator 4.0. *IFAC-PapersOnLine*, 53(2), 10615–10620. DOI: 10.1016/j.ifacol.2020.12.2818

Ding, Y., Jin, M., Li, S., & Feng, D. (2021). Smart logistics based on the internet of things technology: An overview. *International Journal of Logistics*, 24(4), 323–345. DOI: 10.1080/13675567.2020.1757053

Dogra, A., Jha, R. K., & Jain, S. (2020). A survey on beyond 5G network with the advent of 6G: Architecture and emerging technologies. *IEEE Access : Practical Innovations, Open Solutions*, 9, 67512–67547. DOI: 10.1109/ACCESS.2020.3031234

Dolgui, A., & Ivanov, D. (2022). 5G in digital supply chain and operations management: Fostering flexibility, end-to-end connectivity and real-time visibility through internet-of-everything. *International Journal of Production Research*, 60(2), 442–451. DOI: 10.1080/00207543.2021.2002969

Ericsson (2022). *Ericsson Private 5G, together with Kollmorgen's NDC Solutions Platform.*https://www.ericsson.com/4ad55c/assets/local/industries/manufacturing/ericsson-and-kollmorgen.pdf

Ericsson (2022). *Ericsson Private 5G, together with Kollmorgen's NDC solutions platform.*https://www.ericsson.com/4ad55c/assets/local/industries/manufacturing/ericsson-and-kollmorgen.pdf

George, R., Cherbaka, N. S., & Ellis, K. (2023). 5G opportunities in warehousing. In *16th Proceedings (Dresden, Germany- 2023).* 14. https://digitalcommons.georgiasouthern.edu/pmhr_2023/14

Gergs, L., & Mavrakis, D. (2022). Private 5G in Warehousing. *ABI research.* https://go.abiresearch.com/lp-private-5g-in-warehousing

Hofman, H. (2023). The game-changing potential of 5G in logistics. *Maersk,*https://www.maersk.com/insights/growth/2023/01/17/the-potential-of-5g-in-logistics

Huawei (2023). *Dubai South Welcomes 5G-Powered Smart Warehousing Center.* https://www.huawei.com/en/media-center/multimedia/videos/2023/dubai-5g-smart-warehouse?utm_medium=sm&utm_source=youtube&utm_campaign=media-center

Hunt, B., & Bennett, C. (2022). Case Study: Building a private 5G network to support smart warehouse applications. *Deloitte.*https://www2.deloitte.com/content/dam/Deloitte/us/Documents/consulting/us-deloitte-building-5G-private-network.pdf

Jablonski, F. (2020). 5G in production: Audi and Ericsson take the next step. https://fuenf-g.de/en/2020/11/14/5g-in-production-audi-and-ericsson-take-the-next-step/

Kadena, E., & Rajnai, Z. (2024, January). 5G Supply Chain: An overview of applications and challenges. In *2024 IEEE 22nd World Symposium on Applied Machine Intelligence and Informatics (SAMI)* (pp. 57-162). IEEE.

Lagorio, A., Cimini, C., Pinto, R., & Cavalieri, S. (2023). 5G in Logistics 4.0: Potential applications and challenges. *Procedia Computer Science*, 217, 650–659. DOI: 10.1016/j.procs.2022.12.261

Ling, X. (2021). How 5G will Revolutionize Manufacturing. *HuaweiTech.* https://www.huawei.com/en/huaweitech/publication/winwin/38/5g-revolutionize-manufacturing

Liu, M. (2021). Research on the development of intelligent logistics based on 5g technology. In *2021 2nd International Conference on Urban Engineering and Management Science (ICUEMS)* (pp. 107-110). IEEE.

Lundgren, C., Turanoglu Bekar, E., Bärring, M., Stahre, J., Skoogh, A., Johansson, B., & Hedman, R. (2022). Determining the impact of 5G-technology on manufacturing performance using a modified TOPSIS method. *International Journal of Computer Integrated Manufacturing*, 35(1), 69–90. DOI: 10.1080/0951192X.2021.1972465

Mahmood, A., Abedin, S. F., Sauter, T., Gidlund, M., & Landernäs, K. (2022). Factory 5G: A review of industry-centric features and deployment options. *IEEE Industrial Electronics Magazine*, 16(2), 24–34. DOI: 10.1109/MIE.2022.3149209

O'Connell, E., Moore, D., & Newe, T. (2020). Challenges Associated with Implementing 5G in Manufacturing. *Telecom*, 1(1), 48–67. DOI: 10.3390/telecom1010005

Rao, S. K., & Prasad, R. (2018). Impact of 5G technologies on industry 4.0. *Wireless Personal Communications*, 100(1), 145–159. DOI: 10.1007/s11277-018-5615-7

Research, G. E. (2021). *GE Research and the US Department of Defense Partner on 5G Initiative to Create Smart Warehouses*. https://www.ge.com/research/newsroom/ge-research-and-us-department-defense-partner-5g-initiative-create-smart-warehouses

Rose, D. (2019). Factory of the Future Shows Mobile Model for Small Manufacturers. https://iot-automotive.news/vodafone-e-go-smart-5g-factory

Simmons, R. (2023). The big benefits of 5g technology in logistics. *DHL*. https://www.dhl.com/discover/en-global/logistics-advice/logistics-insights/5g-and-logistics

Taboada, I., & Shee, H. (2021). Understanding 5G technology for future supply chain management. *International Journal of Logistics*, 24(4), 392–406. DOI: 10.1080/13675567.2020.1762850

Tomás, J. P. (2021a). 5G manufacturing use case spotlight: Industrial automation. *RCR Wireless News*. https://www.rcrwireless.com/20210831/5g/5g-manufacturing-use-case-spotlight-industrial-automation

Tomás, J. P. (2021b). Three 5G manufacturing case studies: Audi, Haier, Bosch. *RCR Wireless News*. https://www.rcrwireless.com/20210726/5g/three-5g-manufacturing-case-studies

Chapter 13
Managing Waste Within Supply Chain:
From Lean Manufacturing to Lean Digital 4.0

Yousra El Krami
University Mohammed V of Rabat, Morocco

ABSTRACT

The focus of our chapter is to determine the extent to which lean manufacturing and lean digital 4.0 are complementary when it comes to reducing waste in the production chain. Indeed, Industry 4.0 is increasingly presented as a must for improving productivity and ensuring economic growth in manufacturing companies. On the other hand, many companies have already partially or fully implemented Lean principles and tools. A number of aspects remain to be clarified regarding the existing links between Industry 4.0 and the Lean approach: is there a hierarchy, improvement or complementarity between the two approaches? What are the links between the two approaches? This chapter seeks to highlight the links that exist between the two approaches in terms of continuous improvement and operational performance. To this end, we have highlighted the principles and technologies proposed by lean manufacturing and Industry 4.0 respectively. We have also discussed the theory of constraints, which has been applied in lean manufacturing circles.

INTRODUCTION

Industry and logistics increasingly dominate professional, scientific, and academic thinking. Several studies have shown that productivity gains primarily reside in the management of flows and internal and/or external logistics interfaces. Faced

DOI: 10.4018/979-8-3693-4427-9.ch013

with competitiveness constraints, companies have developed strategies to digitalize innovative methods and processes to ensure continuous improvement. Companies ensure their sustainability by innovating further and reducing non-quality costs while increasing their On Time Delivery (OTD) efficiency. This is how "Lean Manufacturing" emerged; this streamlined production system is based on eliminating waste or "Muda" in Japanese within production processes, it means production with fewer resources. The contributions of Lean include reducing stocks and production times as well as improving quality, reducing damage and obsolescence, and increasing flexibility through process-oriented organization.

Indeed, consumption patterns are changing, customers are becoming increasingly demanding, and market prices compel companies to make more efforts to streamline the production process and adopt a leaner management system because the customer only pays for the real added value to the product. In other words, what contributed to transforming the product. Companies want to increasingly reduce non-productive cost times. Thus, the Lean concept aims to satisfy its customers by reducing production costs and investment, maximizing resource utilization, and reducing inventory and production cycles. It relies on understanding customer needs. The authors of the book "The Lean System," Womack and Jones, define Lean thinking as a management method that allows the company to be closest to customer demand and eliminate all waste. Lean contributes to better productivity (Quality, Cost, Delivery (QCD)), transforming the company to make it competitive and sustainable.

In an optimization and margin-increasing perspective, companies have to align with the evolution that the industrial sector has experienced, notably Industry 4.0, where lean 4.0 is evolving from lean manufacturing. This new concept is seen as the fusion of Industry 4.0 with lean manufacturing. These approaches have a strong correlation and can mutually support each other. With the rise of this innovative concept, companies have found themselves obliged to redirect their strategy towards process digitalization to be ready to meet customer requirements. Subsequently, clarifying the real need by implementing concrete improvement proposals for the future situation.

Because it was being implemented at the time, lean seemed quite promising when it initially entered the industry. Even if this method has lost some of its appeal over time, the innovations it brought about in a variety of business sectors made it possible to achieve extremely exciting levels of quality and efficiency. Its use has often not kept up with the advances in administration, communication, and manufacturing that come from the introduction of new digital tools and procedures. The internal and external environments that industrial organizations operate in have undergone substantial changes as a result of dematerialization and pervasive digitalization. Lean developed Lean digital 4.0, or continuous process improvement, as a response to this trend of digital transformation.

The practice of monitoring machine functioning has changed in the sector in the last few years. Big Data has proliferated, enabling businesses to manage enormous volumes of data and use them to execute a range of activities, including Total Productive Maintenance (TPM) via in-depth data analysis. Strong software tools enable improved operations planning and execution, as well as better failure prediction. Additionally, business digitization interferes with process development by facilitating modeling and simulation through the creation of numerous scenarios. This makes it possible to apply the proper corrective actions, particularly by getting rid of non-conformities, delays, and waste. Processes ultimately become even more capable of sustaining competitiveness and productivity, which connects to one of the core tenets of Lean improving the production process.

Client relationships are also boosted by digital transformation ; the Lean approach also involves ensuring the improvement of the customer experience, firstly by providing them with a quality product that meets their expectations, and secondly by strengthening the connection with them through digital means. Lean 4.0 seeks to maximize the quality improvement potential of digital tools by streamlining procedures and lowering the possibility of producing a subpar or non-conforming product. Simultaneously, communications between the producer and the consumer become much more intense because of the closer connection made possible by the Internet and mobile apps. Businesses can gather vital data regarding consumer trends, expectations, purchasing patterns, and preferences.

Dematerialization of visual management, with in-depth analysis and real-time display of key performance indicators (KPIs) on dynamic display systems, is another aspect of the digitization of lean manufacturing. To summarize, Lean Digital integrates the fundamental principles of traditional Lean by facilitating ongoing enhancements across all domains and capitalizing on the novel opportunities presented by technology.

To carry out our analysis successfully, our chapter will be divided into two parts. The first part will highlight the theoretical aspect, including a literature review of the emergence of the lean manufacturing concept and its close link with the company's logistics performance. It will be necessary to demonstrate the degree of necessity of this approach and to what extent lean manufacturing has developed with the integration of the digital dimension, transitioning from Lean Manufacturing to Lean Digital 4.0. The second part of our chapter will focus mainly on evaluating the impact of this transition on the company's logistics performance. To do this, we will rely on the study of existing works analyzing efforts in this direction while mobilizing the Theory of Constraints (TOC), which extensively deals with this issue of continuous improvement of production processes. TOC is based on several steps, including identifying the constraint, deciding how to maximize the use of the constraint to try to solve or alleviate it. The advantages of the Theory of Constraints are to improve overall production capacity quickly and economically.

The interest of our research is to present a comprehensive and detailed interpretation of the evolution of the lean manufacturing concept, which has accompanied the four revolutions that the industrial world has experienced and has had a positive impact on the global economy. Indeed, the fourth and final stage concerns Lean 4.0, which is a combination of lean manufacturing and Industry 4.0.

1. THE SEVEN WASTES OF LEAN MANUFACTURING

The main cause of non-value added in a goods production system is waste. Waste is anything but the minimum amount of equipment, materials, components and labor time that are absolutely essential to production (Taj & Morosan, 2011).

Lean manufacturing is the term used to describe lean production. Lean means « skinny ». In lean and economical companies, "fat" refers to operations that do not add value from the customer's point of view (E. L. Zajkowska, 2013). The origin of "fat" in a goods production system is waste. Waste is anything but the minimum amount of equipment, materials, components and labor time that are absolutely essential to production (Taj & Morosan, 2011). Traditionally, there are 7 types of waste that can occur during the operation of a production system. These were identified and defined by Ohno (1988) and Shingo (1989) who are the precursors of lean production have identified 7 types of waste that can occur in a production system. These are identified in the figure below (figure 1): overproduction, unnecessary transport, waiting times, excessive processing operations, unnecessary stocks, unnecessary movements, defects.

Figure 1. Seven Wastes of Lean Manufacturing

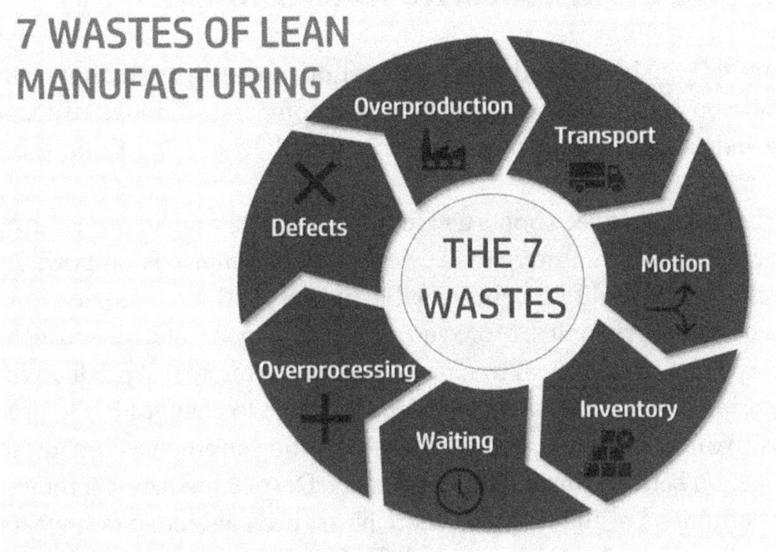

Source: *James M. Cerra & Tanya Menendez, 2021*

A synthesis of their definitions allows us to present each of the 7 wastes in very practical terms, as follows:

- **Overproduction:** Producing more than is required, or before customers demand it.
- **Unnecessary transport:** unnecessary movement of components or materials during operations.
- **Waiting time:** time spent doing nothing while waiting for an operation to be carried out, tool, etc.
- **Excessive processing:** additional processing operations, operations that produce products of higher quality than required.
- **Unnecessary movement:** movement of people in the production environment without contributing to production.
- **Defects:** manufacture of products that do not meet customer requirements.
- **Overstocking:** excess of raw material, finished product or work-in-progress over a given period.

Given these definitions, it's reasonable to assume that for a company to operate at optimum efficiency, it must be completely free of such waste. Lean manufacturing is an integrated system of principles, practices, tools and techniques that can be used to this end (R. Ciarnienė and M. Vienazindienė, 2015).

2. INDUSTRY 4.0 TECHNOLOGIES APPLICABLE TO ELIMINATING LEAN MANUFACTURING WASTE

Industry 4.0 can be defined as the integration of intelligent digital technologies into production and industrial processes. It encompasses a range of technologies including industrial IoT networks, Artificial Intelligence, Big Data, robotics and automation.

The relationship between important Industry 4.0 technologies and Lean principles was first emphasized in a literature review, with an emphasis on how, depending on the technical capability levels, specific Industry 4.0 technologies improve the application of Lean principles. More and more, Industry 4.0 and related technologies are being positioned as critical to raising manufacturing firms' productivity levels. Manufacturing systems can become more adaptable to changes in the product and more sensitive to unforeseen circumstances by putting an emphasis on instantaneous communication between machines and objects. Despite the fact that there are more than 100 definitions of Industry 4.0, there hasn't been agreement on what the term means yet (Moeuf et al., 2017), some definitions have been proposed. According to CEFRIO (Beaudoin et al., 2016), Industry 4.0 is a collection of activities meant to enhance procedures, goods, and services so that decentralized decision-making based on real-time data collection is possible. Industry 4.0, according to (Buer et al., 2018), is defined by the use of intelligent processes and products that allow for autonomous data collection and analysis as well as online interaction between suppliers, customers, and goods. Industry 4.0, according to Kohler & Weisz (2016), is a novel method to production control that makes unitary and customized production possible as well as real-time flow synchronization. According to the National Institute of Standards and Technology (NIST), Lu et al., (2016) asserts asserts that smart manufacturing is a collaborative and completely integrated process that reacts instantly to changes in the plant and supply network, all while meeting the needs of the customers. The most often used terms across all definitions are real-time, adaptability, and communication. Industry 4.0 technologies are the tools for putting the ideas of real-time, flexibility, and communication into practice.

First of all, it's worth remembering that Industry 4.0 was first announced in 2011 at the Hannover Industrial Fair in Germany to mark the advent of the 4th industrial revolution. As such, the Internet of Things can be seen as a precursor to Industry 4.0. The German telecommunications association BITKOM reveals that there are at least 104 different definitions of Industry 4.0. From our point of view, Industry 4.0 can simply be seen as a grouping of several digital technologies aimed at improving, if not optimizing, the design, manufacture and distribution of manufacturing products. What Industry 4.0 technologies have in common is digital data. Since information, and therefore data, is omnipresent in classic industry, Industry 4.0

has a very broad field of application. Each technology has its own specific field of application, but they can be combined to solve specific problems. Given the number of digital technologies mentioned in the literature, it can be rather confusing to say which technology belongs to the Industry 4.0 group. Thus, according to a synthesis elaborated by Dombrowski (2017), Cefrio (2016), Gerbert (2015), Shahin (2020), Pagliosa (2019), Mayr (2018), Wagner (2017), Rossini (2019), Kamble (2020). The most frequently identified Industry 4.0 technology group is made up of nine main technologies:

- massive big data (BD),
- cloud computing (CC),
- internet of things (IoT),
- cyber physical systems (CPS),
- autonomous machines or robots (AM),
- augmented reality (AR),
- simulation systems (SS),
- additive manufacturing (AM),
- cyber security (CS).

Indeed, the empirical frequency of each is over 50% (D. Tadja et al. 2021). The other technology groups are not sufficiently representative in the circle of Industry 4.0 technologies, namely machine-to-machine communication (M2M), artificial intelligence (AI) and then horizontal and vertical integration (HVI), however they can be considered an integral part of Industry 4.0. The nine principles technologies are mentionned in the figure below (fig. 2):

Figure 2. The Main Technologies of Industry 4.0

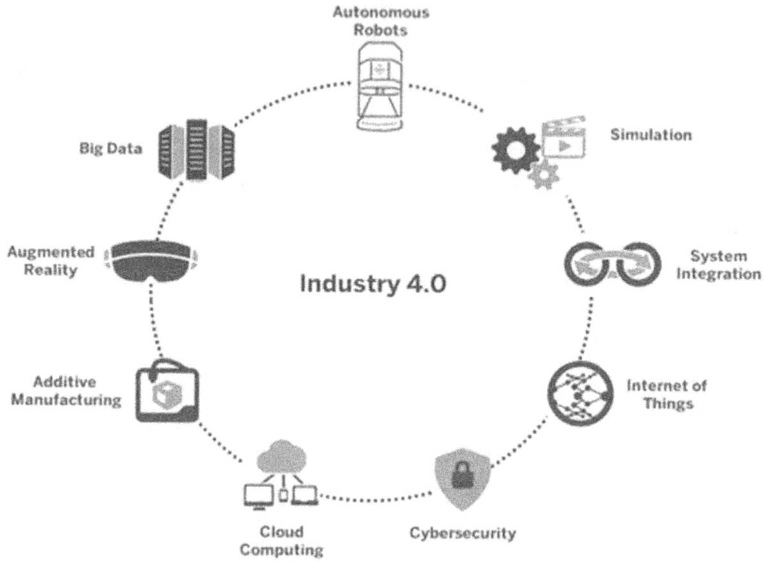

Source: *Top 9 Technology Trends Driving Industry 4.0, Shalini Sreekanth, 2019.*

2.1 Big data » (BD)

Massive data, commonly referred to as megadata, and its analysis, aims to process huge volumes of data from a variety of sources and formats in order to derive meaning and make better decisions. For example, data collected in real time from smartphone GPS, cameras and traffic lights, weather reports and even social media, provide a diverse set of data for predicting traffic jams and proposing the best route.

In the Industry 4.0 paradigm, this data can come from the process, the product or customer information. We can draw on a variety of technologies, including HPC (High-Performance Computing), HPCC (High-Performance Computing Cluster) and the HADOOP-YARN platform.

2.2 Cloud Computing

A paradigm known as "cloud computing" makes it possible for everyone to have access to shared computer resources such as servers, networks, storage, apps, and services (Nist, 2011). Cost-saving outsourcing of IT infrastructure management is made possible by cloud computing. Cloud computing enables data sharing between sites or systems in the context of Industry 4.0. Cloud deployment is possible for data and features related to production, monitoring, and process control.

Infrastructures are becoming virtualized due to a variety of resources, including platform as a service (PaaS), software as a service (SaaS), infrastructure as a service (IaaS), and data centers.

2.3 Internet of things (IOT)

The Internet of Things is defined by the ISO/IEC 30141 draft standard as an infrastructure for interconnecting physical entities, systems, information sources and intelligent services, capable of processing information from the physical and virtual worlds, and influencing activities in the physical world. IoT makes it possible to connect a vast array of physical and digital resources, embedded or not, for Industry 4.0. Decentralized decision-making and real-time response at the level of cyber-physical systems (CPS) are made possible by the resulting network. IoT makes use of technology including RFID chips, software, middleware, and networks (WSN, RSN)..

2.4 « Cyber-physical systems » (CPS)

Cyber-physical systems are mechanisms capable of autonomously exchanging information, triggering actions and controlling each other (Kagermann et al., 2013). CPSs are nodes networked by the IoT. For Industry 4.0, CPSs integrate sensors, software and communication elements, as well as actuators, enabling real-time monitoring and action on the physical world.

2.5 Autonomous robots

Production has always relied on machines to carry out intricately planned activities. Within the Industry 4.0 framework, machines are outfitted with novel networking technologies, thereby enhancing their autonomy, adaptability, and collaboration. Cobotics are those that communicate with one another and can even work securely with people.

2.6 Augmented reality

Augmented reality systems superimpose information on the surrounding reality in real time. For example, you can add and view furniture or fittings to your home virtually only via a tablet. For Industry 4.0, augmented reality helps provide assembly or repair instructions based on the current situation, or guide forklift operators inside a warehouse, in real time, to the pallet they need to retrieve.

2.7 Simulation (SS)

Although simulation already exists in various spheres of engineering, for Industry 4.0 it involves simulating the entirety of production operations. Digital twins thus constitute the virtual mirror of the physical world, including machines and associated measurements (speeds, forces...) (Grieves, 2014) products and humans. Simulation then aims to test and optimize, in particular, machine settings and flows before transposing these changes into the real world. This reduces set-up times and increases performance.

2.8 Additive manufacturing

In Industry 4.0, additive manufacturing (AM), also referred to as 3D printing, is currently viewed as a true revolution. It expands the potential for innovation by overcoming the limitations of traditional manufacturing (injection molding, machining, shaping, and assembly) and providing the ability to manufacture things of tremendous complexity that are not attainable with current processes. The use of additive manufacturing has grown steadily, and in certain industries, prototype operations have moved to the direct production of functioning parts due to equipment advancements (Abdellatif Bouzid & Maurice Duval, 2017).

2.9 Cybersecurity

The connectivity at the heart of Industry 4.0 brings with it a critical cybersecurity risk. Indeed, the exchange of industrial data and the remote control of production systems call for increased security measures. To achieve this, reliable and proven communications protocols can be used to control access to machine control systems. Supporting technologies include VPN, P2P, PIR, TLS, DNSSEC and RFID tags (Weber & Weber, 2010).

We will also review the other technology groups mentioned above:

2.10 Inter-machine communication (M2M)

With the increaing number of autonomous systems and machines, inter-machine communications technologies are on the rise. Unlike IoT, which is associated with a global network, M2M technologies create local networks of autonomous machines.

M2M relies on protocols and standards such as TCP/IP, IGRS, UPnP, DLNA and OPC-UA.

2.11 Artificial intelligence

Artificial intelligence is defined by Minsky as "the construction of computer programs that perform tasks that are, for the time being, more satisfactorily accomplished by human beings, because they require high-level mental processes such as perceptual learning, memory organization and critical reasoning". In the context of Industry 4.0, artificial intelligence can be applied to decision-making, and promises, for example, to take over the control of machines in the production process. Various resources can be evoked, such as neural networks, machine learning and Bayesian networks.

2.12 Horizontal and vertical integration (HVI)

Industry 4.0 technologies operate on the principle of horizontal and vertical integration of manufacturing systems, and are based on real-time data exchange between the varied partners in the value chain (Kamble et al., 2020). This ability to exchange and process data in real time, and the interconnectivity of all value chain players offered by Industry 4.0 technologies, have a leverage effect on existing lean manufacturing practices.

3. THEORY OF CONSTRAINTS (TOC) IN LEAN MANIFACTURING

The Theory of Constraints has been tried and tested in lean manufacturing circles. It is similar to other project management methods such as Agile and Kanban. Every process contains at least 1 bottleneck. However, any improvements made outside the constraint will be lost until the bottleneck is eliminated.

The aim of TOC is to identify constraints and maximize their use. Identifying constraints enables management to take action to alleviate constraints in the future. It also enables current production capacity to be precisely defined, and the necessary measures to be taken if capacity needs to be increased. Thus, TOC is broken down into several stages: identifying the constraint, deciding how to maximize the use of the constraint in an attempt to resolve or alleviate it. The advantages of the theory of constraints are to improve overall production capacity, in a general, rapid and economical way, to avoid the accumulation of "Work In Progress (WIP)", to avoid small, unhelpful local improvements, to improve communication between departments and to clarify the manufacturing process. The theory of constraints can be deployed in a wide range of production lines. It can be adapted to any system to detect possible constraints and mobilize the necessary levers to achieve the set objectives. Like lean manufacturing, it is applied with a view to continuous improvement.

4. INDUSTRY 4.0 AND OPERATIONAL PERFORMANCE

Presented as essential for surviving in the new economy and carrying promises of increased productivity, profitability and mass customization, Industry 4.0 requires advanced knowledge and skills to adapt or replace existing manufacturing models in the companies. In addition, the operational excellence approach, or Lean approach, and its associated principles, summarized by Liker (2004) in his House of Lean as it's represented in the figure below (fig.3), also present promises of increasing productivity and profitability for companies. The goals of quality, prices, cycle time reduction, safety, and employee motivation must all be met, and this calls for a combination of just-in-time, jidoka, workers, and work principles. Teamwork, cutting waste, and ongoing development.

Figure 3. House of Lean

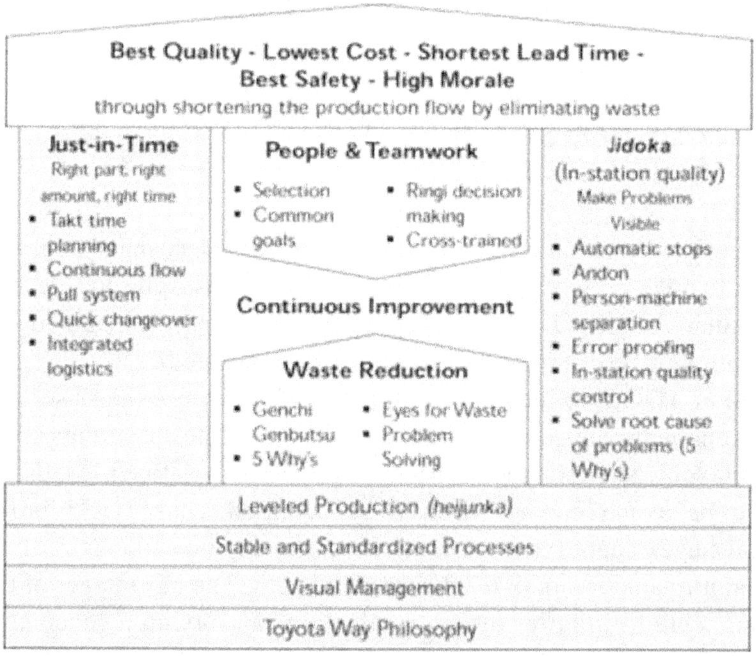

Source: *Liker (2004)*

Various authors suggest that the Lean approach can be seen as a necessary foundation for Industry 4.0 and should therefore be implemented before Industry 4.0 technologies. According to Bill Gates, visionary and co-founder of Microsoft, automating inefficient processes amplifies their inefficiency (quoted by Krishnan, 2013). Following the same idea and according to Mayr et al. (2018), the introduction of Industrie 4.0 is largely dependent on the removal of waste, standardization of processes, and a continuous focus on customer value. The Lean strategy, according to the same authors, reduces product and process complexity, which makes it possible to deploy Industrie 4.0 technology economically and effectively. For their part, Prinz et al. (2018) claim that a business using Industrie 4.0 will not be successful if they don't have standardized, continuous-flow procedures. They contend that a 4.0 implementation can only be successful if the production organization has already undergone Lean optimization and all employees are involved in establishing the principles of Lean production.

Industry 4.0 and Lean complement each other and reflect a true synergy. According to Mayr et al. (2018), Industrie 4.0 and Lean can coexist and support each other by adding tools and principles that do not exist in either. Moeuf et al. (2017) point out that since Industrie 4.0 aims to accelerate the flow of information and the Lean approach focuses on eliminating waste to speed up physical flows: the synergy of the two methods should be considered to aim for operational excellence. According to Ruessmann et al (2015) of the Boston Consulting Group, the use of technologies from their 9 pillars of Industry 4.0 can improve certain aspects of manufacturing production, hitherto unattainable by following Lean principles alone. In this vein, Rüttimann and Stöckli (2016) point out that while Industry 4.0 aims to increase the flexibility of production systems by enabling a wide variety of products and capacities to be produced, the Lean approach aims instead to smooth out the load to maximize productivity, and does so with reference to the heijuka principle. Indeed, Heijunka is a Japanese term meaning leveling, smoothing out customer production, reducing differences by equalizing and scheduling activity according to demand. It is a Lean Manufacturing tool and is used to implement the JIT method. In this way, the Lean approach would take advantage of Industry 4.0 by remaining productive even when varying the load.

CONCLUSION

In today's industry, monitoring machine operation is nothing like it was in the relatively recent past. Big Data has become widespread, enabling companies to collect massive amounts of data and use it to carry out a variety of processes, such as total productive maintenance, thanks to advanced data analysis. High-performance software resources help to better anticipate failures and better plan and carry out activities. Process improvement is also a component of lean digital 4.0, which allows for the modeling and simulation of processes through the creation of several scenarios. This enables the implementation of suitable remedial actions, such as the removal of waste, slowness, and non-conformities. Processes ultimately become even more capable of sustaining competitiveness and productivity, which returns to one of the core tenets of Lean improving the manufacturing process.

Lean manufacturing is evolving into lean 4.0 in the context of Industry 4.0. This new idea is thought to be an amalgam of Industry 4.0 and lean manufacturing. These methods can complement one another and have a favorable correlation. This indicates that by attaining more effective production and logistics processes and increasing the flexibility of the lean production system, the deployment of current ICT can improve the performance of the production system (Dombrowski, 2017).

Based on existing literature several avenues of comparison between Industry 4.0 and the Lean approach have been considered (Dombrowski et al., 2017; Buer et al., 2018). Lean is a necessary foundation for Industry 4.0, which enhances the effectiveness of Lean whose principles may change as Industry 4.0 develops. To put it succinctly, Digital Lean builds upon the foundations of conventional Lean, utilizing the additional opportunities presented by technology and promoting continuous improvement at all levels.

REFERENCES

Bidet-Mayer, T. (2016). *L'industrie du futur: une compétition mondiale*. Presses des Mines.

Bouzid, A., & Duval, M. (2017). La fabrication additive.

Buer, S. V., Strandhagen, J. O., & Chan, F. T. S. (2018). The link between Industry 4.0 and lean manufacturing: Mapping current research and establishing a research agenda. *International Journal of Production Research*, 56(8), 2924–2940. DOI: 10.1080/00207543.2018.1442945

Čiarnienė, R., & Vienažindienė, M. (2015). An empirical study of lean concept manifestation. *Procedia: Social and Behavioral Sciences*, 207, 225–233. DOI: 10.1016/j.sbspro.2015.10.091

Cloud, H. (2011). The nist definition of cloud computing. National institute of science and technology, special publication, 800(2011), 145.

Danjou, C., Rivest, L., & Pellerin, R. (2017). *PME 2.0 Le passage au numérique Industrie 4.0: des pistes pour aborder l'ère du numérique et de la connectivité*. Ceferio.

Dombrowski, U., Richter, T., & Krenkel, P. (2017). Interdependencies of industry 4.0 and lean production systems-a use cases analysis-27th international conference on flexible automation and intelligent manufacturing. *Procedia Manufacturing*, 11, 1061–1068. DOI: 10.1016/j.promfg.2017.07.217

Drath, R., & Horch, A. (2014). Industrie 4.0: Hit or hype? [Industry Forum]. *IEEE Industrial Electronics Magazine*, 8(2), 56–58. DOI: 10.1109/MIE.2014.2312079

Grieves, M. (2014), Digital Twin: Manufacturing Excellence through Virtual Factory Replication, White paper.

Kagermann, H., Wahlster, W., & Helbig, J. (2013), Recommendations for implementing the strategic initiative INDUSTRIE 4.0. Final report of the Industrie 4.

Kamble, S., Gunasekaran, A., & Dhone, N. C. (2020). Industry 4.0 and lean manufacturing practices for sustainable organisational performance in Indian manufacturing companies. *International Journal of Production Research*, 58(5), 1319–1337. DOI: 10.1080/00207543.2019.1630772

Krishnan, K. (2013). *Data Warehousing in the Age of Big Data*. Morgan Kaufmann.

Leseure-Zajkowska, E. Z. (2012). Contribution à l'implantation de la méthode Lean Six Sigma dans les Petites et Moyennes Entreprises pour l'amélioration des processus (Doctoral dissertation, Ecole Centrale de Lille).

Liker, J. (2004). *The Toyota way : 14 management principles from the world's greatest manufacturer*. McGraw-Hill Education.

Mayr, A., Weigelt, M., Kuhl, A., Grimm, S., Erll, A., Potzel, M., & Franke, J. (2018). Lean 4.0 - A conceptual conjunction of lean management and Industry 4.0. 51st CIRP Conference on Manufacturing Systems. *Procedia CIRP*, 72, 622–628. DOI: 10.1016/j.procir.2018.03.292

Moeuf, A., Tamayo, S., Lamouri, S., Pellerin, R., & Lelièvre, A. (2016). Strengths and weaknesses of small and medium sized enterprises regarding the implementation of lean manufacturing. *IFAC-PapersOnLine*, 49(12), 71–76. DOI: 10.1016/j.ifacol.2016.07.552

Nemati, A., Nadeau, S., & Ateme-Nguema, B. (2019). Lean mining, productivity and occupational health and safety: An expert-elicitation study. *American Journal of Industrial and Business Management*, 9(11), 2034–2049.

Prinz, C., Kreggenfeld, N., & Kuhlenkotter, B. (2018). Lean meets Industrie 4.0 – a practical approach to interlink the method world and cyber-physical world. 8th Conference on Learning Factories 2018 - Advanced Engineering Education & Training for Manufacturing Innovation. *Procedia Manufacturing*, 23, 21–26. DOI: 10.1016/j.promfg.2018.03.155

Rosin, F. (2022), Vers le Lean 4.0: Renforcement du processus décisionnel par les technologies de l'Industrie 4.0, thèse de doctorat, Hal open sciences.

Rosin, F., Forget, P., Lamouri, S., & Pellerin, R. (2019), Industrie 4.0 et Lean: Hiérarchie, amélioration ou complémentarité? Conference: CIGI QUALITA 2019, "Le numérique et l'intelligence industrielle: défis et opportunités" Montréal Canada.

Ruessmann, M., Lorenz, M., Gerbert, P., Waldner, M., Justus, J., Engel, P., Harnisch M., (2015) Industry 4.0: The Future of Productivity and Growth in Manufacturing Industries. Boston Consulting Group, avril.

Rüttimann, B. G., & Stöckli, M. T. (2016). Lean and Industry 4.0 - Twins, Partners, or Contenders? A Due Clarification Regarding the Supposed Clash of Two Production Systems. *Journal of Service Science and Management*, 9(6), 485–500. DOI: 10.4236/jssm.2016.96051

Tadja, D., Bassetto, S., Wong, T., & Tollenaere, M. (2021). *Les objets connectés pour améliorer la culture de la production épurée : revue de littérature et esquisse de solution applicable aux entreprises manufacturières*. ISTE OpenScience.

Tadja, D., Nadeau, V., Mercier, A., & Wong, T. (2023, April). Technologies de l'industrie 4.0 applicables à la chasse aux gaspillages du lean manufacturing. In 18ème colloque national S. mart.

Taj, S., & Morosan, C. (2011). The impact of lean operations on the Chinese manufacturing performance. *Journal of Manufacturing Technology Management*, 22(2), 223–240. DOI: 10.1108/17410381111102234

Chapter 14
Towards Decarbonized Transportation:
A Comprehensive Review of Global Challenges and Digital Transformation

Faissal Jelti
Laboratory of Advanced Materials Studies and Applications, Moulay Ismail University, Meknes, Morocco

Rachid Saadani
Laboratory of Advanced Materials Studies and Applications, Moulay Ismail University, Meknes, Morocco

ABSTRACT

This chapter provides an in-depth review of the transport sector, it begins with a detailed assessment of the barriers to global transport expansion, including economic, infrastructural, regulatory, and technological issues. Beyond identifying barriers, it proposes practical approaches and recommended actions to overcome them. The second part examines Morocco's transport sector, highlighting its progress and future prospects in decarbonization. It highlights the successes and challenges faced by developing countries in their quest for sustainable transport by examining specific initiatives, policies and technological advances. This provides valuable insights into Morocco's journey towards a greener transport system. Finally, the third section discusses how digital transformation can revolutionize transport systems. It explores how digital technologies such as big data analytics, Internet of Things, and smart infrastructure can make transport systems more efficient, sustainable, and resilient to significantly reduce emissions, optimize operations, and improve the user experience.

DOI: 10.4018/979-8-3693-4427-9.ch014

1. INTRODUCTION

Rapid growth in energy demand, increased reliance on fossil fuels subject to price volatility, and environmental concerns have led countries around the world to prioritize the identification of energy efficiency opportunities. In this way, consumers can meet their energy needs economically, while improving overall energy management and addressing environmental concerns (Chu & Majumdar, 2012). According to REN21[1], **Figure 1** (a) shows that buildings and industry are the largest energy consumers in 2020, accounting for 33% of total final energy use, followed closely by transportation at 30% and agriculture at 3%. Renewable energy use varies by sector, with industry leading with 16.8%, followed by buildings and agriculture with 15.5%. In contrast, transportation uses significantly less renewable energy at 4.1%, despite being the fastest growing sector in terms of energy consumption, dominated primarily by road transport, which accounts for about 78% in 2021, with rail accounting for just 3% (see **Figure 1** (b)). Overall, the global focus remains on advancing sustainable technologies and increasing the integration of renewable energy technologies and digital solutions across sectors to mitigate greenhouse gas (GHG) emissions and promote energy efficiency in buildings, industry, transportation, and agriculture.

Figure 1. (a) Share of total final energy consumption by sector, 2020; (b) Breakdown of transport demand in 2021

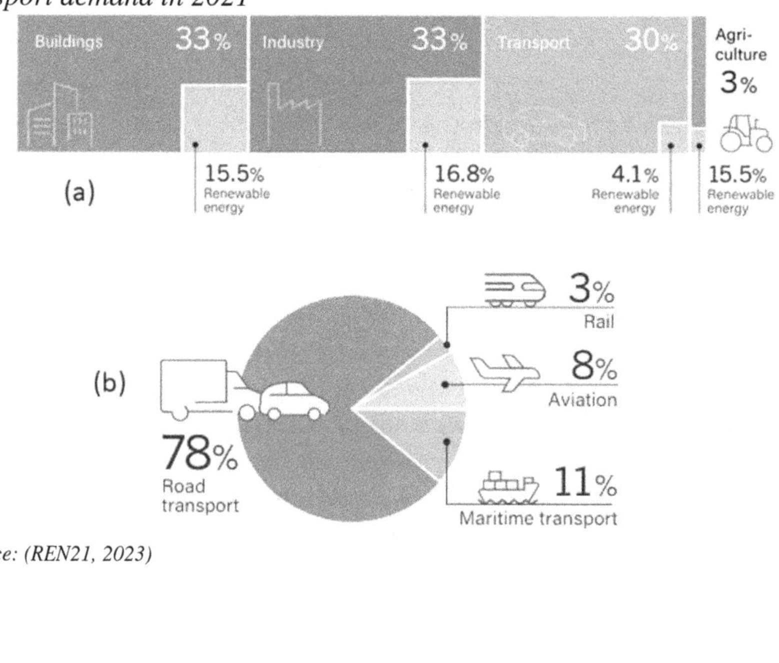

Source: (REN21, 2023)

Table 1. Classification of the cleaner transportation system

Category	Mode	Examples
Motorized - Passenger	Electric Vehicles (EVs)	Cars, Buses, Trains, Trams
	Hybrid Vehicles	Cars, Buses
	Hydrogen Fuel Cell Vehicles	Cars, Buses
	Biogas/Natural Gas Vehicles	Buses, Trucks (for short distances)
Non-Motorized - Passenger	Bicycles	Regular bikes, E-bikes
	Walking	Walking, Hiking
	Micromobility	Scooters, E-scooters
Motorized - Freight	Electric Trucks	Short-haul deliveries
	Hydrogen Fuel Cell Trucks	Long-haul deliveries (future potential)
	Electric Trains	Long-haul freight
	Biogas/Natural Gas Trucks	Short-haul deliveries
Non-Motorized - Freight	Cargo Bikes	Urban deliveries
	E-Cargo Bikes	Urban deliveries with increased capacity

Source : (Velazquez et al., 2015)

Additionally, most researchers, stakeholders, and policymakers are aware that a shift to a low-carbon energy system for the transportation sector is necessary but not enough to meet climate change challenges. It, therefore, requires significant development in current technologies, infrastructure, lifestyles, and business models (Boons et al., 2013). The accelerated deployment of these technologies and their diffusion across diverse socio-economic landscapes are especially considered fundamental components for achieving sustainability in transportation (Rennings, 2014). For example, the use of Intelligent Transportation Systems (ITS), as an innovative approach that is leading to a rapid transition to the era of smart and green cities, which combines Information and Communication Technologies (ICT) and transportation solutions in ITS. It will involve new ICT solutions, such as profitable transportation management solutions that can secure the reduction of energy consumption. It also aims to increase the efficiency and safety of the transportation network, minimize travel time and fuel consumption while reducing the environmental impact (Collotta et al., 2018). The various modes of freight and passenger transportation, both motorized and non-motorized are classified as different types of green transportation systems (Velazquez et al., 2015) (see **Table 1**). However, this chapter focuses exclusively on motorized green transportation systems from a carbon-neutral perspective. It addresses the critical issue of decarbonizing freight and passenger transport by exploring the potential of integrating renewable energy and digital technologies to significantly reduce their environmental footprint. It also examines the specific barriers to decarbonizing different transport modes, including infrastructure limitations, technological barriers and regulatory barriers. As well, comprehensive recommendations and strategies to overcome these barriers are outlined, such as promoting innovative technologies, improving cross-sector collaboration and implementing supportive policy frameworks. This multifaceted analysis aims to promote sustainable and resilient transport systems that can effectively respond to future energy and environmental challenges.

As a reminder, this chapter takes a structured approach to exploring sustainable transportation: First, an in-depth analysis of the barriers for each mode of transportation is assessed along with appropriate measures to overcome them, to provide a nuanced understanding and practical solutions. Second, the assessment of Morocco's transportation sector is conducted from a sustainability perspective, providing insights into regional challenges and opportunities. Finally, the potential of digital transformation to improve efficiency and reduce emissions across transportation modes is highlighted.

2. METHODOLOGY

In this chapter, we adopted a systematic literature review method, as it is a rigorous research method that is suitable for dealing with challenging research areas such as sustainable transport, for which there is a large and varied literature, taking into account three stages: Planning, Conducting, and Reporting (see **Table 2**) (Hempel et al., 2016; Juntunen & Lehenkari, 2021; Okoli, 2015; Uman, 2011). In the planning stage, a research question was formulated to ensure a careful focus of the research: "What is the impact of the integration of renewable energy and digital transformation on the decarbonization of transport within the supply chain, and what are the main barriers across all modes of transport, as well as recommended actions to overcome them?". In addition to the formulation of the research question, the following hypotheses were developed: H1 (Integration Hypothesis), which proposes that significant carbon reductions can be achieved through the integration of renewable energy and digital transformation in traffic; H2 (Efficiency Hypothesis), which proposes that traffic efficiency, consumption and carbon emissions can be improved by implementing digital technologies alongside renewable energy; and H3 (Cost Efficiency Hypothesis), which proposes that despite initial investment costs, the adoption of renewable energy and digital transformation can result in long-term cost savings for carriers through reduced fuel costs and operational efficiencies. Another important aspect of this stage was the definition of the following search terms: "sustainability" AND "air transportation"; "sustainability" AND "maritime transportation"; "sustainability" AND "rail transportation"; "sustainability" AND "road transportation"; "sustainable transportation" AND "digitalization", to identify relevant studies published within a specified timeframe (between 2010 and March 2024). The second stage involved a comprehensive search of multiple databases (ScienceDirect, Web of Science, Scopus, Springer, Taylor, and Francis), including scholarly journals and books. The search results were filtered using predefined criteria to select studies to be included in the review. The data from the selected studies were then extracted and further refined in response to the research question. The third stage concluded with an analysis and discussion of the results of the selected literature. They were then organized thematically to examine key strategies, technologies, policies, and challenges related to decarbonizing the transportation sector. The methodology used in this chapter was intended to feed into future research, policies and practices in this critical area of sustainability through a complete overview of the current state of decarbonization efforts in the transport sector worldwide.

Table 2. Stages of the systematic literature review (SRL) approach

<table>
<tr><th>Planning Stage</th><th>Conducting Stage</th><th>Reporting Stage</th></tr>
<tr><td>Research question:
What is the impact of the integration of renewable energy and digital transformation on the decarbonization of transport within the supply chain, and what are the main barriers across all modes of transport, as well as recommended actions to overcome them?</td><td>Scientific databases:
ScienceDirect.
Web of science.
Scopus; Springer.
Taylor and Francis.</td><td rowspan="3">Assignment selected papers
Discuss deeply all selected papers, then identify relevant conclusions and finally report extensively on results.</td></tr>
<tr><td>Hypotheses:
H1 (integration hypothesis): Significant carbon reductions will be achieved through the integration of renewable energy and digital transformation in transport.
H2 (efficiency hypothesis): Transport efficiency, consumption and carbon emissions can be improved by implementing digitalization technologies alongside renewable energy.
H3 (Cost-effectiveness hypothesis): Despite initial investment costs, the adoption of renewable energy and digital transformation can deliver long-term cost savings to carriers in reduced fuel costs and operational efficiencies.</td><td rowspan="2">Inclusion/Exclusion criteria:
Journals; Books;
Period: Between 2010 and March 2024;
Excluding proceeding conferences</td></tr>
<tr><td>Keywords
"sustainability" AND "air transportation";
"sustainability" AND "maritime transportation";
"sustainability" AND "rail transportation";
"sustainability" AND "road transportation";
"sustainable transportation" AND "digitalization"</td></tr>
</table>

Source : (Hempel et al., 2016; Juntunen & Lehenkari, 2021; Okoli, 2015; Uman, 2011)

3. BARRIERS TO ACHIEVING A FURTHER EXPANSION OF THE TRANSPORTATION SECTOR AT A WORLDWIDE LEVEL AND THEIR KEY ACTIONS

After a detailed analysis of various studies on the decarbonization of the transport sector, this section addresses the barriers to the development of decarbonized technologies in different transport modes and offers recommendations for overcoming these barriers.

3.1. Air Transportation

Air transportation has become a major component of the tourism industry, accounting for about 40% of worldwide tourists using air travel, contributing to 10% of the world's Gross Domestic Product (GDP), and generating employment for about 80 million people (Abeyratne, 2012). It also affects trade as a service that directly transports people and goods and contributes to other areas of trade, primarily tourism and hospitality (Abeyratne, 2012). However, one of the major issues facing airport authorities is the expansion of air transportation infrastructure to meet future demands, due to complicated financial systems for airports and the insecure economic conditions, which result in challenges to making decisions on new infrastructure project investments (Dimitriou & Sartzetaki, 2018). On the other hand, the environmental impacts of air transportation can be characterized by an increase in GHGs leading to air pollution, namely carbon dioxide (CO_2), nitrogen dioxide (NO_2), carbon monoxide (CO), sulfur oxide (SO_x), and Volatile Organic Compounds (VOCs). Another serious problem is aircraft noise, which has widespread impacts on the environment (Dimitriou, 2016; Maurya, 2013).

Overall, this sector provides access to global connectivity to succeed in a competitive global economy and further connects markets that make regions more competitive and promote the country's socio-economic development (Wiltshire & Jaimurzina, 2017). From this perspective, sustainable tourism should take into account the triple dimensions (social, economic and environmental) (Chèze et al., 2012; Dimitriou, 2016; Dimitriou & Sartzetaki, 2018):

- From an economic point of view, air transport is an important driver for the development of tourism. It generates employment, income and capital investment, which are mainly the result of the increase in productivity in terms of air transport services.

- Environmentally, air transport plays an important role in developing tourism, but the environmental problems caused by operating aircraft, which are important aspects of developing aviation, need to be addressed. One of the most practical and affordable ways to address such challenges is to improve aircraft fuel efficiency through technological innovation in energy use.
- Aviation's impact on society can be best measured by developing advanced approaches to assessing its social effects. The efficient functioning and safety of aviation systems make a significant contribution to access to markets, employment opportunities and services, which is vital to reducing social exclusion.

3.2. Maritime Transportation

Maritime transportation is one of the most efficient modes of freight transportation, as compared to aircraft or trucks. However, it contributes significantly to the degradation of air quality in coastal areas, such as the release of Particulate Matter 2.5 ($PM_{2.5}$), Black Carbon (BC), Sulfur Dioxide (SO_2), Nitrogen Oxide (NO_x), VOC, and CO_2 (Eyring et al., 2010; Fridell, 2019; Karl et al., 2019). According to Newell et al., maritime transportation has significant emissions of NO_x and SO_x, respectively 10-15% and 4-9% at a worldwide level.

Other factors have a major impact on the development of maritime transportation, such as the risk of natural disasters and climate change (Nuttall et al., 2014). As well, the development of maritime transportation depends largely on the mobilization of private investment, while government involvement is limited to infrastructure (mainly ports), policies, and regulations, as well as limited policies and incentive programs regarding the use of renewable propulsion, limited coordination between the different stakeholders involved in this sector, and restrictive regulatory approaches in the maritime industry (Newell et al., 2015; Nuttall et al., 2014). So, the considerable efforts by national and international authorities to further investigate alternative options for reducing GHG emissions from vessels, including renewables such as wind, solar, and Liquefied Natural Gas (LNG) (Carlton et al., 2013; Mofor et al., 2015; Newell et al., 2015). Additionally, hybrid technology for ships is used, along with their potential for custom designs that use renewable fuels. These alternatives are characterized by their advantages and limitations in how they can be deployed. As a result, further development of these innovative shipping solutions is expected to continue to be a priority for many researchers, but they require increased investments to modernize current ship designs (Nuttall et al., 2014).

3.3. Rail Transportation

Rail transportation is one of the most popular and viable modes of transportation for the movement of passengers and goods for both long and short distances. However, it suffers from significant noise and vibration problems, due to several factors, including rail route, traction type, track design, and traffic volume. The main sources of noise in rail transportation include rolling noise (caused by the interaction between wheels and rails), electrical noise (generated by locomotive engines, exhaust systems, traction motors, gears, and fans), and aerodynamic noise (caused by air flowing along the surface of the train) (Kumar & Chowdary, 2023; Yoon & Pyo, 2019). To overcome these barriers, the government and their partners should significantly invest in urban rail transportation infrastructure, including track construction and traffic management systems, to shift toward cleaner and more efficient modes of transportation like light rail, metro, and high-speed rail (Babatunde, 2019; Opeyemi & Dela Cruz, 2018).

On the other hand, the trains, especially those used for goods transport, generate noise that affects nearby residents. Therefore, measures such as building insulation, urban design and land use planning, and installing structured railroads and noise walls are necessary to mitigate these noise levels (Kumar & Chowdary, 2023).

3.4. Road Transportation

The road transportation system is considered the main driver of socio-economic development but mainly depends on fossil fuels, which are one of the main sources of air pollutants, GHGs, and other environmental impacts (congestion, traffic accidents, and the economic and environmental effects of fuel consumption) (Luoma & Sivak, 2012; Xoliswa et al., 2016). For example, internal combustion engines (IGEs) emit CO that interferes with oxygen flow in the bloodstream, while hydrocarbons (HCs) from vehicle fuel systems contribute to health problems such as headaches and cancer. As well, particulate matter (PM) emissions from IGEs and industrial sources pose serious health risks such as lung cancer, heart disease, and asthma (Salvi & Subramanian, 2015).

A classification of policies to achieve environmental benefits in road transportation is outlined as follows (Luoma & Sivak, 2012; National_Research_Council, 2013; Touzi et al., 2015):

- On the vehicle side, the initiative involves programs to encourage the adoption of low-carbon vehicles, funding Research and Development (R&D) activities, and improving vehicle performance to drive the transition towards greener vehicles.

- On the fuel side, there are alternative fuel options that can be considered in road transportation, such as renewable fuel standards and additional requirements to fight GHG emissions caused by fossil fuels (Euro VI standards).

Furthermore, the question of how to shift to low-carbon road transportation in terms of energy use and infrastructure trends, through both physical and soft measures that can provide valuable road transportation assets, needs to be addressed. The physical policies include improvements to road transportation infrastructure, particularly public transportation and land-use planning, while soft measures can be seen as initiatives to further change behavior by informing the public of the options and consequences of their transportation choices (Offer et al., 2011; Santos et al., 2010).

On the other hand, a significant potential for the implementation of ITS approaches as a means to achieve more efficient road traffic management, which aims at improving road traffic control, reducing congestion, and improving traffic operations via the application of technologies such as dynamic message signs or traffic information radio (Al-Anbari & Alkaissi, 2017).

To sum up, further expansion and decarbonization of global transport require addressing complex economic, environmental and regulatory challenges in aviation, maritime, rail and road transport. Critical actions are needed to support the expansion of the transport sector. These include increased infrastructure investment to meet future demand and the integration of sustainable practices and technologies, such as improved fuel efficiency in aviation, alternative fuels and hybrid technologies in maritime and road transport, and noise abatement measures in rail transport. In this way, we can overcome barriers and develop more sustainable and efficient transport that meets economic and environmental objectives.

4. ANALYSIS OF THE CURRENT STATUS OF THE TRANSPORTATION SECTOR IN MOROCCO IN TERMS OF THE DECARBONIZATION PERSPECTIVE

The transportation sector for both goods and passengers is the main driver of economic development in Morocco, where the World Bank[2] has ranked Morocco fifth among African countries on the economic growth index. More especially, freight transportation is a major determinant for industrial activities, but also for the logistics field (Michel et al., 2017; Rucińska & Kędzior-Laskowska, 2019). Similarly, passenger transport contributes to an increase in tourism and other services including employment, education, and health services.

According to the United Nations Framework Convention on Climate Change (UNFCCC)[3], the transportation sector in Morocco generated about 15% of total CO_2 emissions in 2012. In fact, the Organization for Economic Co-operation and Development (OECD)[4] reports that this sector is expected as a share of total GHG emissions to grow twofold between 2015 and 2050, from about 15 million tons of CO_2 equivalent (tCO_{2eq}) in 2015 to over 35 million tCO_{2eq} in 2050, due to the growth in both intercity freight and passenger traffic. To address this challenge, the implementation of national strategies for sustainable mobility in Morocco, led by the Ministry of Transport and Logistics[5], is driving the development of national plans, notably the Roadmap for Sustainable Mobility in Morocco, which will provide a long-term vision for sustainable mobility, in line with the public and private actors involved in decarbonized transportation in Morocco.

In terms of air transportation, air passenger traffic in Morocco has grown considerably in recent years, it has increased almost fourfold, reaching more than 25 million passengers in 2019, compared to 7 million passengers in 1999, as reported by the National Office of Airports (ONDA)[6]. Similarly, the largest market in terms of international flights during 2019 accounted for approximately 80% of flights to and from Europe. On the other hand, the Moroccan government is committed to boosting air cargo transportation, whose traffic has almost doubled between 2010 and 2019, via the adoption of national plans to upgrade the capacity of national terminals. According to the Moroccan Ministry of Transportation and Logistics[7], it aims to reach a total air cargo volume of 182,000 tons in 2035, compared to 96,000 tons in 2019. Moreover, the two operators (Royal Air Maroc Cargo and PortNet) have signed a new agreement to improve the exchange of digital information between all Moroccan airports.

In terms of maritime transportation, the Maritime Services Development Strategy to 2030 represents an important step forward for Morocco, which aims to build a sustainable and competitive seaport to meet increased demand for maritime services as well as to attract a larger market share of international maritime trade. It includes some key measures, such as the construction of new seaport infrastructure in the different regions of Morocco, as they provide a critical gateway for imports and exports and thus represent an extremely important factor affecting the national economy. In parallel, maritime container traffic in the world is increasing in volume on all routes. As an example, container traffic in Morocco has increased by an average of about 10% over the last ten years, as reported by the Ministry of Transportation and Logistics[8]. As maritime transportation emits fewer greenhouse gases than road and air transportation, introducing maritime freight transportation to replace road transportation and maritime passenger transportation to replace air transportation will contribute to the decarbonization of Morocco's transportation system. But the Ministry of Transportation and Logistics[9] reports that some of Morocco's seaports face limited constraints for their expansion owing to the inadequacy of regulations governing maritime activities. Maritime transportation for goods also represents a major activity in terms of international freight, accounting for 98% of Morocco's total foreign trade by sea, including the transportation of raw materials. According to the Ministry of Transportation and Logistics[10], the volume of container traffic has increased significantly in recent years, thanks to the introduction of cross-docking activities at Morocco's Tangier-Med hub. On the other hand, as claimed by the Moroccan Ministry of Transportation and Logistics[11], a significant part of the international passenger transportation in Morocco is provided by the maritime sector, which accounts for about 5 million people travelling, annually, to and from Morocco and the nearby countries, including France, Spain, and Italy. However, a real decline in maritime passenger traffic has resulted from the launch of the Open Sky program for air travel with the European Union, which has reduced the cost of air travel to and from Morocco. Following the launch of the Tangier-Med port, an improvement was noted, making it Morocco's leading passenger port in 2013.

In terms of rail transportation, the second largest rail network in Africa is that of Morocco, offering a network of more than 3,815 km of track, of which 2,300 km is an operating track, and 800 km is a double-track, as reported by the National office of Railways (ONCF)[12]. Moreover, more than 64% of the network operating in this country is powered by electricity. It includes 250 locomotives, of which more than 50% are electric, as well as a fleet of 680 passenger wagons and 5,498 freight wagons. According to the World bank[13], the National office of Railways, a state-owned organization, is responsible for managing the national railway infrastructure. In the context of passenger rail traffic, Morocco continues to grow rapidly supported by the government, with an increase in passenger traffic from nearly 4,400 million passenger kilometers in 2010 to more than 4,800 million passenger kilometers in 2019, as stated by OECD[14]. The government authorities have developed the Moroccan Rail Plan, which addresses the long-term strategy for the development of the Moroccan rail network by 2040, which includes an investment of about 375 billion dirhams to develop 1,100 km of high-speed tracks[15]. On the other hand, the ONCF[16] reports that the amount of rail freight traffic in Morocco is decreased by almost 10% between 2012 and 2014, unlike passenger traffic, due to the establishment of the pipeline from Khouribga to Jorf Lasfar in 2014, which is the current longest phosphate pipeline in the world.

To sum up, a real opportunity to decarbonize passenger and freight transportation in Morocco can be achieved by setting up measures on rail transportation, because it accounts for about 3% of CO_2 emissions while road transportation accounts for 60% of CO_2 emissions, as stated by the ONCF[17]. So, the public institutions will establish their goals to increase the benefits of rail decarbonization through increasing efforts to achieve 50% of the electricity for rail transportation from renewable sources in the future[18]. In turn, this will help achieve a reduction of 10% of GHG emissions from rail transportation in 2030 compared to 2016.

For road passenger transportation, the renewal of private vehicles and the promotion of public transportation are important avenues for decarbonizing road transportation. However, Flanders Investment & Trade[19] points out that the issue of private fleet replacement faces challenges because of limited financial affordability, which leads to a tendency to opt for used vehicles at low prices. In this context, it is important to encourage the adoption of low-carbon private vehicles through the setting up of financial incentive programs by government authorities. Similarly, simplified administrative procedures for the delivery of operating authorizations can contribute to the expansion of intercity public transportation (Blanco & Jeannière, 2021). In the case of freight transportation, the expansion of road transportation in Morocco is a major concern, because 75% of freight traffic uses the road network. Many initiatives have been introduced, by the Moroccan Ministry of Economy, Finance and Administration Reform[20], to facilitate the renewal of the vehicle fleet for vehicles older than 20 years, to reduce GHG emissions, including incentive schemes for vehicle recycling to encourage the purchase of new vehicles. Moreover, Morocco should adopt policies for sustainable road transportation to ensure economic growth with lower exposure to environmental issues (Elhasbi et al., 2015): first, better upgrading of the traffic control system and technical inspection to achieve better control of polluting emissions and engine performance. Second, managing the freight transportation operations efficiently via the introduction of highly qualified truck drivers to fulfil demands sustainably and make savings on fuel consumption.

In summary, Morocco's transport sector faces a dual challenge: balancing economic growth, driven primarily by road transport, with the need to reduce CO_2 emissions. Road transport dominates passenger and freight transport, with a significant impact on CO_2 emissions. Efforts to promote sustainable transport include encouraging the adoption of low-carbon vehicles and improving public transport infrastructure. At the same time, significant investments in rail, aviation and maritime transport are aimed at modernizing infrastructure and improving efficiency, which is essential to reduce environmental impact and promote economic development. Government-led strategies such as Sustainable Transport Roadmap, Rail Strategy 2040 and Port Strategy 2030 highlight Morocco's commitment to integrating sustainable practices into all modes of transport and demonstrate a proactive approach to achieving long-term environmental goals in the face of growing transport demand.

5. MOVING FORWARD: DIGITAL TRANSFORMATION FOR SUSTAINABLE TRANSPORTATION

Decarbonized transport and digitization are symbiotically reshaping mobility worldwide, as Morocco stands to benefit significantly from this transformative synergy. There is an urgent need to combat climate change by reducing carbon emissions, particularly from transport, a major contributor to global GHG emissions. This need has led to widespread efforts both to shift from traditional fossil-fueled vehicles to cleaner alternatives such as electric vehicles and to use digital technologies in optimizing transportation systems (see **Figure 2** (Noussan et al., 2020). These global trends in decarbonizing transport are of particular importance in Morocco, given our commitment to sustainability and our vulnerability to climate change. Morocco stands to benefit from integrating digital solutions into its transport infrastructure, given its ambitious renewable energy targets and growing interest in electric mobility. Digitalization is making it possible to introduce electric cars more quickly, to make public transport more efficient and to make the best use of existing infrastructure.

Figure 2. Digital solutions for sustainable transportation

Source: (Noussan et al., 2020)

The key driver of these synergies is policy alignment at both worldwide and regional levels

(Jelti et al., 2023). Internationally, countries are implementing policies and incentives to promote cleaner transport technologies through initiatives such as the Paris Agreement, which sets targets for reducing carbon emissions. In Morocco, for example, the government has demonstrated its commitment to sustainability through initiatives such as the National Strategy for Sustainable Development and the promotion of renewable energy. By aligning its transport policy with broader sustainability goals, Morocco will be able to leverage digitalization to deliver more efficient and environmentally friendly mobility solutions.

In addition, to enable decarbonization and digitalization efforts, technological innovation plays a crucial role (see **Figure 3** (Noussan et al., 2020; Tsakalidis et al., 2020). In the area of electric vehicles, the cost and performance of electric vehicles are being reduced and improved through advances in battery technology, charging infrastructure and vehicle-to-grid integration. Digitalization is also making it possible to develop smart charging networks, anticipatory maintenance systems and integrated mobility platforms to enhance user experience and optimize resource use.

Figure 3. Some examples of digitised technological innovations applied to the transportation industry

Source: (Noussan et al., 2020; Tsakalidis et al., 2020)

Figure 4. Advanced traffic management via secure data collection

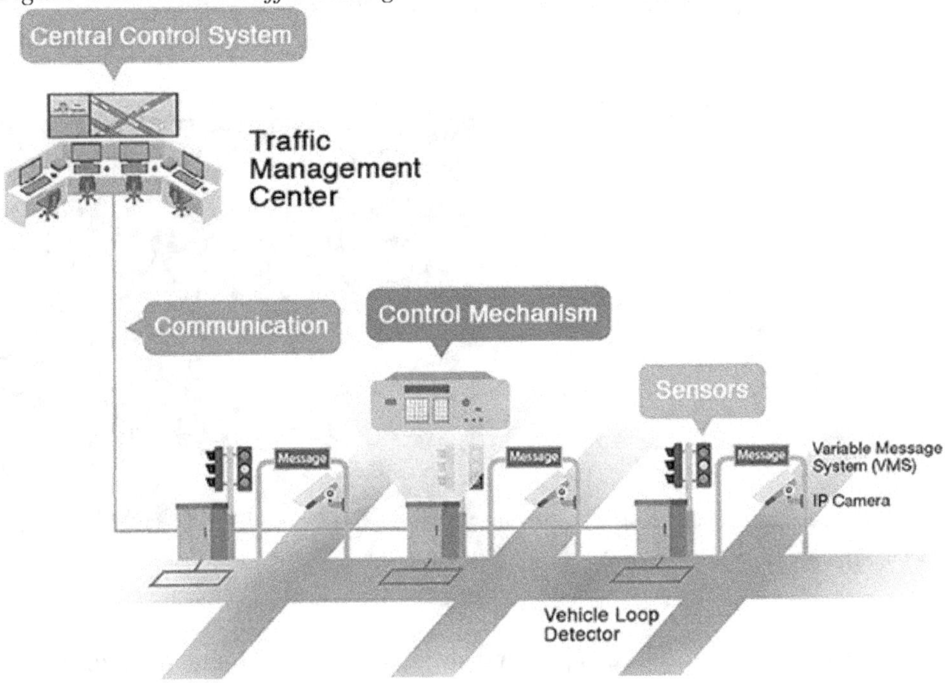

Source: (Bishop, 2022)

Another key aspect of the link between decarbonized transport and digitization is data-driven decision-making (Bishop, 2022). The huge amounts of data generated by digitized transport systems can provide invaluable information on travel patterns, congestion and environmental impacts (see **Figure 4**. By making effective use of such data through analytics and predictive modelling, policy-makers can make informed decisions on infrastructure investment, transport planning, and policy development.

Similarly, infrastructure development is essential to support efforts to decarbonize transport and drive digitalization on a global level (Kuznetsova & Podbiralina, 2023). This includes providing charging points for electric vehicles, expanding public transport networks and implementing intelligent transport systems (see **Figure 5**. Digitization is key in ensuring that this infrastructure is deployed efficiently and effectively and that it meets evolving user needs.

Alongside the environmental benefits, the transition toward decarbonized and digitized transportation offers significant socio-economic opportunities at the international and regional levels (Kwilinski et al., 2023). By investing in renewable energies and e-mobility, Morocco, for example, can create jobs in emerging sectors such as clean energy, electric vehicles and software development. It can also reduce its dependence on fossil fuels, improve energy security, and reduce air pollution, thereby improving public health and the quality of life for its citizens.

Figure 5. Infrastructures to Drive Sustainable and Connected Transportation

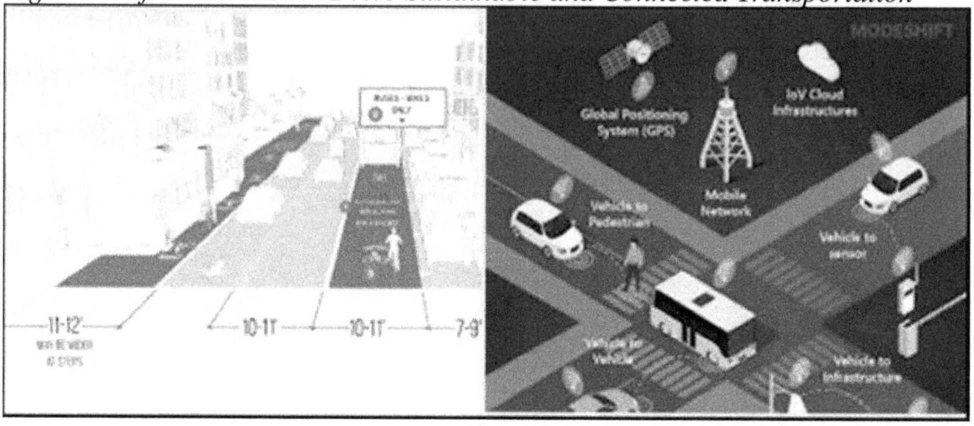

Source: (Kuznetsova & Podbiralina, 2023)

The decarbonization of transport and digitalization are mutually reinforcing global efforts to transform mobility, and offer significant opportunities for Morocco. Integrating digital solutions into transport infrastructure can enable Morocco to accelerate the adoption of electric vehicles, optimize public transport, and make more efficient use of existing infrastructure. These efforts will proceed by aligning transport policies with the Sustainable Development Goals and leveraging technological innovations in electric vehicle technology, smart charging networks, and predictive analytics. In addition, support for infrastructure development and the use of data-driven decision making will be essential for smart policy making and planning. In this way, the transition to decarbonization and digitalization of transport also offers socio-economic benefits, including job creation in the clean energy sector, improved energy security, and better public health, thus underscoring Morocco's commitment to sustainable development.

6. CONCLUSION

This chapter examines the importance of digital transformation and the integration of renewable energy into the supply chain for decarbonizing transport. The use of smart sensors, artificial intelligence, data analytics, and other digital technologies can increase the efficiency and sustainability of transportation by monitoring and managing renewable energy infrastructure in real time, as well as facilitate the increased use of renewable energy technologies such as biofuels, hydrogen and electric vehicles. Digital platforms can also improve the integration and coordination of multimodal transportation networks, promoting seamless connectivity and accessibility while reducing carbon emissions. However, the protection of critical infrastructure and sensitive data is critical to the success of these digital initiatives. Additional policies and financial incentives are essential to encourage investment in renewable energy technologies and digital transformation towards decarbonized transport, and support collaboration between the public and private sectors. By driving digital transformation and integrating renewable energy into decarbonized transport across supply chains, society will be able to combat climate change, improve mobility, and increase overall well-being.

Looking ahead, the continued development and integration of digital technologies and renewable energy in the transportation sector has great potential to further reduce CO2 emissions and improve sustainability. For example, artificial intelligence, the Internet of Things, and advanced data analytics can help manage traffic more accurately and efficiently. Transportation's dependence on fossil fuels will be further reduced by innovations in electric and autonomous vehicles and the expansion of renewable energy infrastructure. But their success hinges on their ability to manage cyber risks, foster strong cooperation between public and private sectors, and put in place supportive policies and financial incentives. These advances offer the promise of a more sustainable, resilient, and efficient transportation system that can make a significant contribution to global climate goals.

REFERENCES

Abeyratne, R. (2012). Sustainable development of air transport. In *Strategic Issues in Air Transport* (pp. 319–394). Springer., https://doi.org/https://doi.org/10.1007/978-3-642-21960-3_5 DOI: 10.1007/978-3-642-21960-3_5

Al-Anbari, M., & Alkaissi, Z. (2017). Assessment of Sustainable Indicators for Road Transportation: A Case Study of Palestine Arterial Street. *International Journal of Scientific Research*, 6, 270–279. DOI: 10.21275/ART20172243

Babatunde, A. I. (2019). Efficiency of Railway Transport as a Sustainable Mode of Transport in Nigeria: A Study of Rail Mass Transit in Lagos and its Environs. *SSRN*, 1. Advance online publication. DOI: 10.2139/ssrn.3576072

Bishop, J. D. K. (2022). Decarbonising Transport with Intelligent Mobility. In Inderwildi, O., & Kraft, M. (Eds.), *Intelligent Decarbonisation: Can Artificial Intelligence and Cyber-Physical Systems Help Achieve Climate Mitigation Targets?* (pp. 163–172). Springer International Publishing., DOI: 10.1007/978-3-030-86215-2_18

Blanco, J. A., & Jeannière, E. (2021). Decarbonising Morocco's transport system: charting the way forward. (https://www.itf-oecd.org/sites/default/files/docs/decarbonising-morocco-transport-system.pdf)

Boons, F., Montalvo, C., Quist, J., & Wagner, M. (2013). Sustainable innovation, business models and economic performance: An overview. *Journal of Cleaner Production*, 45, 1–8. https://doi.org/https://doi.org/10.1016/j.jclepro.2012.08.013. DOI: 10.1016/j.jclepro.2012.08.013

Carlton, J., Aldwinkle, J., & Anderson, J. (2013). *Future ship powering options: exploring alternative methods of ship propulsion*. Royal Academy of Engineering., https://wwwcdn.imo.org/localresources/en/OurWork/Environment/Documents/Air%20pollution/Future_ship_powering_options_report.pdf

Chu, S., & Majumdar, A. (2012). Opportunities and challenges for a sustainable energy future. *Nature*, 488(7411), 294–303. DOI: 10.1038/nature11475 PMID: 22895334

Chèze, B., Chevallier, J., & Gastineau, P. (2012). *Will technological progress be sufficient to effectively lead the air transport to a sustainable development in the mid-term (2025)?*https://ideas.repec.org/p/cec/wpaper/1207.html

Collotta, M., Sun, Y., Di Persio, L., Ebeid, E. S. M., & Muradore, R. (2018). Smart Green Applications: From Renewable Energy Management to Intelligent Transportation Systems. *Energies*, 11(5), 1317. DOI: 10.3390/en11051317

Dimitriou, D. (2016). Climate Change Implications in Aviation and Tourism Market Equilibrium. In (pp. 409-424). https://doi.org/DOI: 10.1007/978-3-319-39880-8_25

Dimitriou, D. J., & Sartzetaki, M. F. (2018). Social Dimension of Air Transport Sustainable Development. *International Journal of Industrial and Systems Engineering*, 12(4), 573–576. DOI: 10.1007/978-3-030-28661-3_9

Elhasbi, A., Jami, J., & Kammas, S. (2015). Sustainable transport in Morocco: What contingency factors for which maturity level? case of road haulage "RH" service providers in the region of Casablanca metropolis. *European Scientific Journal*, 11, •••. https://eujournal.org/index.php/esj/article/view/6345

Eyring, V., Isaksen, I. S. A., Berntsen, T., Collins, W. J., Corbett, J. J., Endresen, O., Grainger, R. G., Moldanova, J., Schlager, H., & Stevenson, D. S. (2010). Transport impacts on atmosphere and climate: Shipping. *Atmospheric Environment*, 44(37), 4735–4771. https://doi.org/https://doi.org/10.1016/j.atmosenv.2009.04.059. DOI: 10.1016/j.atmosenv.2009.04.059

Fridell, E. (2019). Emissions and Fuel Use in the Shipping Sector. In Bergqvist, R., & Monios, J. (Eds.), *Green Ports* (pp. 19–33). Elsevier., https://doi.org/https://doi.org/10.1016/B978-0-12-814054-3.00002-5 DOI: 10.1016/B978-0-12-814054-3.00002-5

Hempel, S., Xenakis, L., & Danz, M. (2016). *Systematic reviews for occupational safety and health questions*. RAND Corporation., https://www.rand.org/pubs/research_reports/RR1463.html

Jelti, F., Allouhi, A., & Tabet Aoul, K. A. (2023). Transition Paths towards a Sustainable Transportation System: A Literature Review. *Sustainability (Basel)*, 15(21), 15457. DOI: 10.3390/su152115457

Juntunen, M., & Lehenkari, M. (2021). A narrative literature review process for an academic business research thesis. *Studies in Higher Education, 46*(2), 330-342. https://doi.org/DOI: 10.1080/03075079.2019.1630813

Karl, M., Jonson, J., Uppstu, A., Aulinger, A., Prank, M., Sofiev, M., Jalkanen, J.-P., Johansson, L., Quante, M., & Matthias, V. (2019). Effects of ship emissions on air quality in the Baltic Sea region simulated with three different chemistry transport models. *Atmospheric Chemistry and Physics*, 19(10), 7019–7053. DOI: 10.5194/acp-19-7019-2019

Kumar, B. S., & Chowdary, V. (2023). Railway Noise Pollution in Urban Environments: Sources, Effects, and Control Strategies. In (pp. 1–38). https://doi.org/DOI: 10.1007/978-981-99-4638-9_2-1

Kuznetsova, G. V., & Podbiralina, G. V. (2023). Transport Digitalization. In Kahraman, C., & Haktanır, E. (Eds.), *Intelligent Systems in Digital Transformation: Theory and Applications* (pp. 579–608). Springer International Publishing., DOI: 10.1007/978-3-031-16598-6_25

Kwilinski, A., Lyulyov, O., & Pimonenko, T. (2023). Environmental Sustainability within Attaining Sustainable Development Goals: The Role of Digitalization and the Transport Sector. *Sustainability (Basel)*, 15(14), 11282. DOI: 10.3390/su151411282

Luoma, J., & Sivak, M. (2012). Interactions of environmental and safety measures for sustainable road transportation. *European Transport Research Review*, 4(4), 189–199. DOI: 10.1007/s12544-012-0078-5

Maurya, A. (2013). Environmental Impact of the Flying Scenario: An Approach Towards Sustainable Air Transportation: A Case Study of India. *OIDA International Journal of Sustainable Development, 5*(12), 107-118. (https://papers.ssrn.com/sol3/papers.cfm?abstract_id=2333269)

Michel, G., Yves, C., & Béatrice, M. (2017). *Morocco, a logistics hub between Europe and Africa?*https://www.ipemed.coop/adminIpemed/media/fich_article/1536838899_ipemedmaroc-hub-logistiquevf.pdf

Mofor, L., Nuttall, P., & Newell, A. (2015). Renewable Energy Options for Shipping. *International renewable energy agency*. (https://www.irena.org/-/media/Files/IRENA/Agency/Publication/2015/IRENA_Tech_Brief_RE_for-Shipping_2015.pdf)

National_Research_Council. (2013). *Transitions to Alternative Vehicles and Fuels*. The National Academies Press. https://doi.org/DOI: 10.17226/18264

Newell, A., Nuttall, P. M., & Holland, E. (2015). Sustainable sea transport for the Pacific Islands: the obvious way forward. (https://sustainabledevelopment.un.org/content/documents/591456-AlisonNewell-Sustainable%20sea%20transport%20for%20the%20Pacific.pdf)

Noussan, M., Hafner, M., & Tagliapietra, S. (2020). *The future of transport between digitalization and decarbonization: trends, strategies and effects on energy consumption*. Springer Nature., DOI: 10.1007/978-3-030-37966-7

Nuttall, P., Newell, A., Prasad, B., Veitayaki, J., & Holland, E. (2014). A review of sustainable sea-transport for Oceania: Providing context for renewable energy shipping for the Pacific. *Marine Policy*, 43, 283–287. https://doi.org/https://doi.org/10.1016/j.marpol.2013.06.009. DOI: 10.1016/j.marpol.2013.06.009

Offer, G. J., Contestabile, M., Howey, D. A., Clague, R., & Brandon, N. P. (2011). Techno-economic and behavioural analysis of battery electric, hydrogen fuel cell and hybrid vehicles in a future sustainable road transport system in the UK. *Energy Policy*, 39(4), 1939–1950. https://doi.org/https://doi.org/10.1016/j.enpol.2011.01.006. DOI: 10.1016/j.enpol.2011.01.006

Okoli, C. (2015). A Guide to Conducting a Standalone Systematic Literature Review. *Communications of the Association for Information Systems*, 37. Advance online publication. DOI: 10.17705/1CAIS.03743

Opeyemi, A., & Dela Cruz, M. (2018). Green Sustainability Development for Industry Internet of Things in Railway Transportation Industry. *International Journal of Trend in Scientific Research and Development*, (Special Issue), 203–208. DOI: 10.31142/ijtsrd19140

Rennings, K. (2014). Introduction: Global diffusion of environmental innovations. *Environmental Innovation and Societal Transitions*, 10, 1–3. https://doi.org/https://doi.org/10.1016/j.eist.2013.12.005. DOI: 10.1016/j.eist.2013.12.005

Rucińska, D., & Kędzior-Laskowska, M. (2019). Sustainable transport development and the quality of road freight transport. *Transport Economics and Logistics*, 76, 33–47. DOI: 10.26881/etil.2018.76.03

Salvi, B. L., & Subramanian, K. A. (2015). Sustainable development of road transportation sector using hydrogen energy system. *Renewable & Sustainable Energy Reviews*, 51, 1132–1155. https://doi.org/https://doi.org/10.1016/j.rser.2015.07.030. DOI: 10.1016/j.rser.2015.07.030

Santos, G., Behrendt, H., & Teytelboym, A. (2010). Part II: Policy instruments for sustainable road transport. *Research in Transportation Economics*, 28(1), 46–91. https://doi.org/https://doi.org/10.1016/j.retrec.2010.03.002. DOI: 10.1016/j.retrec.2010.03.002

Touzi, B., Mabrouki, C., & Farchi, A. (2015). Sustainable Road Transport in Developed and Developing Countries: Framework and Future Research. *International Journal of Engineering and Technical Research*, 4, 373. https://www.ijert.org/research/sustainable-road-transport-in-developed-and-developing-countries-framework-and-future-research-IJERTV4IS080322.pdf

Tsakalidis, A., Gkoumas, K., & Pekár, F. (2020). Digital Transformation Supporting Transport Decarbonisation: Technological Developments in EU-Funded Research and Innovation. *Sustainability (Basel)*, 12(9), 3762. DOI: 10.3390/su12093762

Uman, L. S. (2011). Systematic reviews and meta-analyses. *Journal of the Canadian Academy of Child and Adolescent Psychiatry*, 20(1), 57. https://www.ncbi.nlm.nih.gov/pmc/articles/PMC3024725/ PMID: 21286370

Velazquez, L., Munguia, N. E., Will, M., Zavala, A. G., Verdugo, S. P., Delakowitz, B., & Giannetti, B. (2015). Sustainable transportation strategies for decoupling road vehicle transport and carbon dioxide emissions. *Management of Environmental Quality*, 26(3), 373–388. DOI: 10.1108/MEQ-07-2014-0120

Wiltshire, J., & Jaimurzina, A. (2017). Air transport as a driver of sustainable development in Latin America and the Caribbean: challenges and policy proposals. *Natural Resources and Infrastructure Division*. (https://hdl.handle.net/11362/43412)

Xoliswa, F., Das, D. K., & Hassan, M. M. (2016). Sustainable road transportation: a critical reflection. *Interim: Interdisciplinary Journal, 15*(1), 87-96. (https://hdl.handle.net/10520/EJC-6cef893b3)

Yoon, J., & Pyo, S. (2019). A Review of Mitigation Measures for Reducing Railway Rolling Noise from an Infrastructure Point of View. *International Journal of Railway*, 12(1), 1–9. DOI: 10.7782/IJR.2019.12.1.001

ENDNOTES

1. REN21. (2023). Renewables 2023 Global Status Report Collection, Renewables in Energy Demand. https://www.ren21.net/gsr-2023/modules/energy_demand/03_transport_in_focus/

2. World-Bank. (2020). GDP, PPP (current international $) - Middle East & North Africa, Sub-Saharan Africa, South Africa. Retrieved 05 April 2021 from https://data.worldbank.org/indicator/%0bNY.GDP.MKTP.PP.CD?locations=ZQ-ZG-ZA&most_recent_value_desc=true

3. UNFCCC. (2020). Greenhouse gas inventory data-Detailed data by Party. Retrieved 20 February 2021 from https://di.unfccc.int/detailed_data_by_party

4. OECD. (2020). ITF Transport Outlook 2019. https://doi.org/doi:https://doi.org/10.1787/e4367294-fr

5. MMTL. (2018). Roadmap for Sustainable Mobility in Morocco - Moroccan Ministry of Transportation and Logistics.

6 ONDA. (2020). Moroccan Airports: Air traffic 2019 A new record of passenger traffic with more than 25 million passengers - National Office of Airports. Retrieved 20 March 2021 from http://www.onda.ma/content/download/11643/104317/version/1/fichier/Communiqu%C3%A9+stat+2019.pdf

7 National Strategy of Civil Aviation "AJWAE" - Moroccan Ministry of Transportation and Logistics-https://www.blogtrotter.ma/fr/wp-content/uploads/2017/04/AJWAE-1.pdf

8 MMTL. (2019). Moroccan ports activity in 2018 - Moroccan Ministry of Transportation and Logistics. https://www.equipement.gov.ma/DocumentsActualites/Note-de-Synthese-fr-Activites-des-Ports-2018-20022019.pdf

9 MMTL. (2013). Study on the Strategy of the Moroccan Maritime Transport Sector and the Development of the National Flag in Morocco - Moroccan Ministry of Transportation and Logistics. https://www.challenge.ma/wp-content/uploads/2013/07/ETUDE-1-ALG-Maritime-2013.pdf

10 MMTL. (2019). Maritime Transport data in 2018 - Moroccan Ministry of Transportation and Logistics. https://www.transport.gov.ma/maritime/Chiffes-cles/Pages/Marine-Marchande-en-Chiffres.aspx

11 Moroccan Ministry of Transportation and Logistics - https://www.transport.gov.ma/maritime/Strategie/Pages/Strategie-Marine-Marchande.aspx

12 ONCF. (2019). Rail transport data 2018 in Morocco - National Office of Railways. Retrieved 12 March 2021 from https://www.oncf.ma/en/Company/Oncf-profile/Key-figures-2018

13 World-Bank. (2017). Railroad Reform: A Handbook for Improving Railway Sector Performance.

14 OECD. (2020). ITF Transport Outlook 2019. https://doi.org/doi:https://doi.org/10.1787/e4367294-fr

15 Morroco's 2040 Rail Strategy - National Office of Railways https://www.oncf.ma/en/Development/Strategy/Morroco-s-2040-rail-strategy

16 ONCF. (2015). Prospectus Summary- Bond Issue of the National Office of Railways. http://www.casablanca-bourse.com/BourseWeb/UserFiles/File/ONCF_ENG.pdf?csrt=16242642700587357458

17 ONCF. (2019). Rail transport data 2018 in Morocco - National Office of Railways. Retrieved 12 March 2021 from https://www.oncf.ma/en/Company/Oncf-profile/Key-figures-2018

18 ONCF - Key facts about carbon footprint - https://www.oncf.ma/fr/content/download/37190/850709/file/Plaquette%20Bilan%20carbone%202016.pdf

19 Flanders-Investment&Trade. (2015). The automotive sector in Morocco - Flanders Investment & Trade. https://www.flandersinvestmentandtrade.com/export/sites/trade/files/market_studies/685150910151411/685150910151411_2.pdf

20 MMEFAR. (2013). The Freight Transport Sector: Constraints and Reform Paths - Moroccan Ministry of Economy, Finance and Administration Reform. https://www.finances.gov.ma/Publication/depf/2013/4193_secteur_transport_mdises_03_2013.pdf

Compilation of References

Aazam, M., & Huh, E. N. (2014). "Fog computing and smart gateway based communication for cloud of things," in Proceedings of the 2nd IEEE International Conference on Future Internet of Things and Cloud (FiCloud' 14), 464–470, Barcelona, Spain, August 2014. DOI: 10.1109/FiCloud.2014.83

ABADI, A. (2018). *Ontologies pour le développement collaboratif des produits industriels.* Meknes: Thése de Doctortat, Ecole Nationale Supérieure d'Arts et Métiers de Meknès, Sciences de l'ingénieur, spécialité ; Génie Industriel et Productique.

Abdallah, Y. O., Shehab, E., & Al-Ashaab, A. (2021). Digital Transformation Challenges in the Manufacturing Industry. In Shafik, M., & Case, K. (Eds.), *Advances in Transdisciplinary Engineering*. IOS Press., DOI: 10.3233/ATDE210004

Abeyratne, R. (2012). Sustainable development of air transport. In *Strategic Issues in Air Transport* (pp. 319–394). Springer., https://doi.org/https://doi.org/10.1007/978-3-642-21960-3_5 DOI: 10.1007/978-3-642-21960-3_5

Aday, S., & Aday, M. (2020, December 01). Impact of COVID-19 on the food supply chain. *Food Quality and Safety*, 04(04), 167–180. DOI: 10.1093/fqsafe/fyaa024

Adeel, A., Gogate, M., Farooq, S., Ieracitano, C., Dashtipour, K., Larijani, H., & Hussain, A. (2019). *A Survey on the Role of Wireless Sensor Networks and IoT in Disaster Management*. DOI: 10.1007/978-981-13-0992-2_5

Adeusi, K. B., Adegbola, A. E., Amajuoyi, P., Adegbola, M. D., & Benjamin, L. B. (2024). The potential of IoT to transform supply chain management through enhanced connectivity and real-time data. *World Journal of Advanced Engineering Technology and Sciences*, 12(1), 145–151. DOI: 10.30574/wjaets.2024.12.1.0202

Ahmad, M. T., & Mondal, S. (2016). Dynamic supplier selection model under two-echelon supply network. *Expert Systems with Applications*, 65, 255–270. DOI: 10.1016/j.eswa.2016.08.043

Ahmed, E., Yaqoob, I., Hashem, I. A. T., Khan, I., Ahmed, A. I. A., Imran, M., & Vasilakos, A. V. (2017). The role of big data analytics in Internet of Things. *Computer Networks*, 129, 459–471. DOI: 10.1016/j.comnet.2017.06.013

Ahmed, M., Abdou, M. Y. K., & Elnagar, A. M. (2022). The Impact of Implementing the Internet of Things (IoT) on Customer Satisfaction: Evidence from Egypt. [JA-AUTH]. *Journal of Association of Arab Universities For Tourism and Hospitality*, 22(2), 365–380. DOI: 10.21608/jaauth.2022.123022.1304

Ahmed, S., Kalsoom, T., Ramzan, N., Pervez, Z., Azmat, M., Zeb, B., & Ur Rehman, M. (2021). Towards Supply Chain Visibility Using Internet of Things: A Dyadic Analysis Review. *Sensors (Basel)*, 21(12), 4158. DOI: 10.3390/s21124158 PMID: 34204434

Ajay Guru Dev, C., & Senthil Kumar, V. S. (2016). Analysis on critical success factors for agile manufacturing evaluation in original equipment manufacturing industry-an AHP approach. *Chinese Journal of Mechanical Engineering*, 29(5), 880–888.

Akram, S. V., Malik, P. K., Singh, R., Anita, G., & Tanwar, S. (2020). Adoption of blockchain technology in various realms: Opportunities and challenges. *Security and Privacy*, 3(5), e109. DOI: 10.1002/spy2.109

Al Shakarchi, J., & al. (2022, December 29). A Survey on Federated Learning for Edge Computing. https://www.mdpi.com/2076-3417/12/18/9124

Alam, S. T., Ahmed, S., Ali, S. M., Sarker, S., Kabir, G., & Ul-Islam, A. (2021). Challenges to COVID-19 vaccine supply chain: Implications for sustainable development goals. *International Journal of Production Economics*, 239, 108193. DOI: 10.1016/j.ijpe.2021.108193 PMID: 34121813

Al-Anbari, M., & Alkaissi, Z. (2017). Assessment of Sustainable Indicators for Road Transportation: A Case Study of Palestine Arterial Street. *International Journal of Scientific Research*, 6, 270–279. DOI: 10.21275/ART20172243

Al-Banna, A., Franzoi, R. E., Menezes, B. C., Al-Enazi, A., Rogers, S., & Kelly, J. D. (2022, January). Roadmap to digital supply chain resilience. *Computer-Aided Chemical Engineering*, 49, 571–576. DOI: 10.1016/B978-0-323-85159-6.50095-6

Albukhitan, S. (2020). Developing Digital Transformation Strategy for Manufacturing. *Procedia Computer Science*, 170, 664–671. DOI: 10.1016/j.procs.2020.03.173

Ali, S., Abdullah, , Armand, T. P. T., Athar, A., Hussain, A., Ali, M., Yaseen, M., Joo, M.-I., & Kim, H.-C. (2023). Metaverse in Healthcare Integrated with Explainable AI and Blockchain: Enabling Immersiveness, Ensuring Trust, and Providing Patient Data Security. *Sensors (Basel)*, 23(2), 2. Advance online publication. DOI: 10.3390/s23020565 PMID: 36679361

Alsafi, Y., & Vyatkin, V. (2010). Ontology-based reconfiguration agent for intelligent mechatronic systems in flexible manufacturing. *Robotics and Computer-integrated Manufacturing*, 26(4), 381–391. DOI: 10.1016/j.rcim.2009.12.001

Al-Shorman, H., Eldahamsheh, M., Attiany, M., Al-Azzam, M., & Al-Quran, A. (2023). Potential effects of smart innovative solutions for supply chain performance. *Uncertain Supply Chain Management*, 11(1), 103–110. DOI: 10.5267/j.uscm.2022.11.005

Alter, S. (2013). Work system theory: Overview of core concepts, extensions, and challenges for the future. *Journal of the Association for Information Systems*, 14(2), 72–121. DOI: 10.17705/1jais.00323

Alvarez-Rodriguez, U., Sanz, M., Lamata, L., & Solano, E. (2018). Quantum artificial life in an ibm quantum computer. *Scientific Reports*, 8(1), 14793. Advance online publication. DOI: 10.1038/s41598-018-33125-3 PMID: 30287854

An, N. (2023). How Private 5G is Reshaping the Future of Logistics. *HFCL*. https://www.hfcl.com/blog/private-5G-in-logistics

Anand, D. (2023, January 10). *IOT in Tesla (Automotive industry)*. Medium. https://medium.com/aictespices-iot-club-blog-contest-2023/iot-in-tesla-automotive-industry-b1d0871e3363

Andaloussi, M. B. (2024). A bibliometric literature review of digital supply chain: Trends, insights, and future directions. *SAGE Open*, 14(2), 1–20. DOI: 10.1177/21582440241240340

Andriole, S. J. (2019). *Managing digital transformation: a roadmap for the next decade*. Springer.

Antai, I., & Olson, H. (2013). Interaction: A new focus for supply chain vs supply chain competition. *International Journal of Physical Distribution & Logistics Management*, 43(7), 511–528. DOI: 10.1108/IJPDLM-06-2012-0195

Anupam, G. (2015). Role of responsiveness and process integration in supply chain coordination. *Advances in Management Accounting, 08*(02), 01-08. Retrieved Apr 15, 2024, from https://www.scopus.com/record/display.uri?eid=2-s2.0-84923867319&origin=scopusAI

APICS (2017). Supply Chain Operations Reference Model, v12.0, Supply Chain Operations Management.

Apruzzese, M., Bruni, M. E., Musso, S., & Perboli, G. (2023). 5G and companion technologies as a boost in new business models for logistics and supply chain. *Sustainability (Basel)*, 15(15), 11846. DOI: 10.3390/su151511846

Arifo lu, K., Deo, S., & Iravani, S. M. R. (2012). Consumption externality and yield uncertainty in the influenza vaccine supply chain: Interventions in demand and supply sides. *Management Science*, 58(6), 1072–1091. DOI: 10.1287/mnsc.1110.1469

Arunachalam, D., Kumar, N., & Kawalek, J. P. (2017). Understanding big data analytics capabilities in supply chain management: Unravelling the issues, challenges and implications for practice. *Transportation Research Part E, Logistics and Transportation Review*. Advance online publication. DOI: 10.1016/j.tre.2017.04.001

Ashton, K. (2009). That "internet of things" thing. *RFID Journal*, 22(7), 97–114.

Aslam, J., Saleem, A., Khan, N. T., & Kim, Y. B. (2021). Factors influencing blockchain adoption in supply chain management practices: A study based on the oil industry. *Journal of Innovation & Knowledge*, 6(2), 124–134. DOI: 10.1016/j.jik.2021.01.002

Attaran, M. (2023). The impact of 5G on the evolution of intelligent automation and industry digitization. *Journal of Ambient Intelligence and Humanized Computing*, 14(5), 5977–5993. DOI: 10.1007/s12652-020-02521-x PMID: 33643481

Atzori, L., Iera, A., & Morabito, G. (2011). IoT: Giving a social structure to the internet of things. *IEEE Communications Letters*, 15(11), 1193–1195. DOI: 10.1109/LCOMM.2011.090911.111340

AumRaj. (2022). *Challenges of IoT in Smart Home Automation*. AumRaj. https://aumraj.com/challenges-of-iot-in-smart-home-automation/#:~:text=The%20home%20appliances%20are%20connected,issues%20in%20smart%20home%20automation

AutoPi. (2024). *Device to Cloud Communication*. Autopi.Io. https://www.autopi.io/glossary/device-to-cloud-communication/

Awwad, M., & Pazour, J. (2018). Search Plan for a Single Item in an Inverted T k-Deep Storage System. *Military Operations Research*, 23(1), 5–22.

Azzi, R., Chamoun, R. K., & Sokhn, M. (2019). The power of a blockchain-based supply chain. *Computers & Industrial Engineering*, 135, 582–592. DOI: 10.1016/j.cie.2019.06.042

Baader, F., Calvanese, D., McGuinness, D., Nardi, D., & Patel-Schneider, P. (Eds.). (2002). *The Description Logic Handbook*. Cambridge University Press.

Babaniyi, G. G., Ibrahim, F., Akor, U. J., & Daramola, O. E. (2024). Regenerative Agriculture for Food Security. In *Prospects for Soil Regeneration and Its Impact on Environmental Protection* (pp. 227–242). Springer Nature Switzerland. DOI: 10.1007/978-3-031-53270-2_10

Babatunde, A. I. (2019). Efficiency of Railway Transport as a Sustainable Mode of Transport in Nigeria: A Study of Rail Mass Transit in Lagos and its Environs. *SSRN*, 1. Advance online publication. DOI: 10.2139/ssrn.3576072

Babatunde, F. O., Omotayo, A. B., Oluwole, O. I., & Ukoba, K. (2021, April). A Review on Waste-wood Reinforced Polymer Matrix Composites for Sustainable Development. []). IOP Publishing.]. *IOP Conference Series. Materials Science and Engineering*, 1107(1), 012057. DOI: 10.1088/1757-899X/1107/1/012057

Babu, B. S., Srikanth, K., Ramanjaneyulu, T., & Narayana, I. L. (2013). IoT for Healthcare. [IJSR]. *International Journal of Scientific Research*, 5(2), 322–326.

Bae, J., Gandhi, D., Kothari, J., Shankar, S., Bae, J., Patwa, P., Sukumaran, R., Chharia, A., Adhikesaven, S., Rathod, S., & Nandutu, I. TV, S., Yu, V., Misra, K., Murali, S., Saxena, A., Jakimowicz, K., Sharma, V., Iyer, R., … Raskar, R. (2020). *Challenges of Equitable Vaccine Distribution in the COVID-19 Pandemic*. https://web.media.mit.edu/~raskar/

Bag, S., Gupta, S., & Kumar, S. (2021). Industry 4.0 adoption and 10R advance manufacturing capabilities for sustainable development. *International Journal of Production Economics*, 231, 107844. DOI: 10.1016/j.ijpe.2020.107844

Bahn, R. A., Yehya, A. A. K., & Zurayk, R. (2021). Digitalization for sustainable agri-food systems: Potential, status, and risks for the MENA region. *Sustainability (Basel)*, 13(6), 3223. DOI: 10.3390/su13063223

Bansal, P., Gualandris, J., & Kim, N. (2020). Theorizing supply chains with qualitative big data and topic modeling. *The Journal of Supply Chain Management*, 56(2), 7–18. DOI: 10.1111/jscm.12224

Barbosa, M. W., Vicente, A. C., Ladeira, M. B., & Oliveira, M. P. V. (2018). Managing supply chain resources with big data analytics: A systematic review. *International Journal of Logistics*, 21(3), 177–200. DOI: 10.1080/13675567.2017.1369501

Bardhan, P. (2003). *International Trade Growth and Development: Essays*. Wiley-Blackwell. DOI: 10.1002/9780470752777

Barnaghi, P., Presser, M., & Moessner, K. (2010). "Publishing Linked Sensor Data", in *Proceedings of the 3rd International Workshop on Semantic Sensor Networks.*

Barney, J. (1991). Firm resources and sustained competitive advantage. *Journal of Management*, 17(1), 99–120. DOI: 10.1177/014920639101700108

Barocas, S., & Selbst, A. D. (2016). Big data's disparate impact. *California Law Review*, 104(3), 671–732.

Barpagga, M. (2023, Aug 17). *Case Study Analysis: The Rise of Plant-Based Meat Alternatives in the Food Industry*. Retrieved May 08, 2024, from https://www.linkedin.com/pulse/case-study-analysis-rise-plant-based-meat-food-mukul-barpagga/: https://www.linkedin.com/pulse/case-study-analysis-rise-plant-based-meat-food-mukul-barpagga/

Barratt, M., & Oke, A. (2007). Antecedents of supply chain visibility in retail supply chains: A resource-based theory perspective. *Journal of Operations Management*, 25(6), 1217–1233. DOI: 10.1016/j.jom.2007.01.003

Baryannis, G., Dani, S., & Antoniou, G. (2019). Supply chain risk management and artificial intelligence: State of the art and future directions. *Computers & Industrial Engineering*, 137, 106024.

Batra, T. (2023, Aug 30). *Evolving Tastes: Coca-Cola's Health-Conscious Approach to Beverage Innovation.* Retrieved May 08, 2024, from https://www.linkedin.com: https://www.linkedin.com/pulse/evolving-tastes-coca-colas-health-conscious-approach-beverage-batra/

Battista, C. a. (2010). A proposal for a standard framework for simulating and modeling manufacturing systems. In *Proceedings of the Conference on sustainable development: industrial practice, education \& research.*

Bello, O., & Zeadally, S. (2016). Intelligent Device-to-Device Communication in the Internet of Things. *IEEE Systems Journal*, 10(3), 1172–1182. DOI: 10.1109/JSYST.2014.2298837

Benabdellah, A. C., Benghabrit, A., Bouhaddou, I., & Zemmouri, E. M. (2016, Nov. 29 2016-Dec. 2 2016). *Big data for supply chain management: Opportunities and challenges.* Paper presented at the 2016 IEEE/ACS 13th International Conference of Computer Systems and Applications (AICCSA).

Berisha, B., Meziu, E., & Shabani, I. (2022). Big data analytics in cloud computing: An Overview. *Journal of Cloud Computing (Heidelberg, Germany)*, 11(24), 24. DOI: 10.1186/s13677-022-00301-w PMID: 35966392

Berners-Lee, T. (2000). *Weaving the Web: The Original Design and Ultimate Design of the World Wide Web by its inventor*. Harper Business.

Bettiga, D., & Ciccullo, F. (2019, March 19). Co-creation with customers and suppliers: An exploratory study. *Business Process Management Journal*, 25(02), 250–270. DOI: 10.1108/BPMJ-12-2016-0246

Bharadwaj, A. S. (2000). Strategic alignment of information technology resources and business innovation capacity in a resource-based view framework. *Management Information Systems Quarterly*, 24(1), 169–196. DOI: 10.2307/3250983

Bharadwaj, A. S., Bharadwaj, S. G., & Konsynski, B. R. (2013). Article title. *International Journal of Production Economics*, 90(1), 47–58.

Bharadwaj, A., El Sawy, O. A., Pavlou, P. A., & Venkatraman, N. (2013). Digital business strategy: Toward the next generation of insights. *Management Information Systems Quarterly*, 37(2), 471–482. DOI: 10.25300/MISQ/2013/37:2.3

Bhattacharjya, J., Ellison, A., & Tripathi, S. (2016). An Exploration of Logistics-Related Customer Service Provision on Twitter: The Case of e-Retailers. *International Journal of Physical Distribution & Logistics Management*, 45(9/10), 979–1006.

Bhoir, H., & Principal, R. P. (2014). Cloud Computing For Supply Chain Management. *INTERNATIONAL JOURNAL OF INNOVATIONS IN ENGINEERING RESEARCH AND TECHNOLOGY [IJIERT], 1*(2).

Bhusal, C. S. (2021). Blockchain technology in agriculture: A case study of blockchain start-up companies. [IJCSIT]. *International Journal of Computer Science and Information Technologies*, 13, •••.

Bialas, C., Bechtsis, D., Aivazidou, E., Achillas, Ch., & Aidonis, D. (2023). Digitalization of the healthcare supply chain through adopting enterprise resource planning (ERP) systems in hospitals: An empirical study on influencing factors and cost performance. *Sustainability (Basel)*, 15(4), 3163–3163. https://doi.org/DOI. DOI: 10.3390/su15043163

Bian, W., Shang, J., & Zhang, J. (2016). Two-way information sharing under supply chain competition. *International Journal of Production Economics*, 178, 82–94. DOI: 10.1016/j.ijpe.2016.04.025

Bidet-Mayer, T. (2016). *L'industrie du futur: une compétition mondiale*. Presses des Mines.

Birkhofer, R. a. (2010). *Life-Cycle Management für Produkte und Systeme der Automation Ein Leitfaden des Arbeitskreises System Aspekte.* Frankfurt: ZVEI Fachverband Automation, Zentralverband Elektrotechnik und Elektronikindustrie e.V.

Bishop, J. D. K. (2022). Decarbonising Transport with Intelligent Mobility. In Inderwildi, O., & Kraft, M. (Eds.), *Intelligent Decarbonisation: Can Artificial Intelligence and Cyber-Physical Systems Help Achieve Climate Mitigation Targets?* (pp. 163–172). Springer International Publishing., DOI: 10.1007/978-3-030-86215-2_18

Biswas, S., Sanyal, A., Božanić, D., Puška, A., & Marinković, D. (2023). Critical success factors for 5G technology adaptation in supply chains. *Sustainability (Basel)*, 15(6), 5539. DOI: 10.3390/su15065539

Bjerkenes, M., & Haddara, M. (2019). Blockchain Technology Solutions for Supply Chains. *4th Future Technologies Conference, FTC 2019. 1069*, pp. 909-918. San Francisco: Springer. DOI: 10.1007/978-3-030-32520-6_65

Björkdahl, J. (2020). Strategies for Digitalization in Manufacturing Firms. *California Management Review*, 62(4), 17–36. DOI: 10.1177/0008125620920349

Blackburn, R., Lurz, K., Priese, B., Göb, R., & Darkow, I. (2015). A predictive analytics approach for demand forecasting in the process industry. *International Transactions in Operational Research*, 22(3), 407–428. DOI: 10.1111/itor.12122

Blanco, J. A., & Jeannière, E. (2021). Decarbonising Morocco's transport system: charting the way forward. (https://www.itf-oecd.org/sites/default/files/docs/decarbonising-morocco-transport-system.pdf)

Bondi, A. B. (2000). Characteristics of scalability and their impact on performance. *2nd International Workshop on Software and Performance*, 195–203. DOI: 10.1145/350391.350432

Bonomi, F., Milito, R., Natarajan, P., & Zhu, J. (2014). *"Fog computing: a platform for internet of things and analytics," in Big Data and Internet ofThings: A Road Map for Smart Environments*. Springer.

Bonomi, F., Milito, R., Zhu, J., & Addepalli, S. (2012). "Fog computing and its role in the internet of things," in *Proceedings of the 1st ACM MCC Workshop on Mobile Cloud Computing*, 13–16, 2012. DOI: 10.1145/2342509.2342513

Boons, F., Montalvo, C., Quist, J., & Wagner, M. (2013). Sustainable innovation, business models and economic performance: An overview. *Journal of Cleaner Production*, 45, 1–8. https://doi.org/https://doi.org/10.1016/j.jclepro.2012.08.013. DOI: 10.1016/j.jclepro.2012.08.013

Bordel Sánchez, B., Alcarria, R., Sánchez de Rivera, D., & Robles, T. (2018). Process execution in CyberPhysical Systems using cloud and Cyber-Physical Internet services. *The Journal of Supercomputing*, 74(8), 4127–4169. DOI: 10.1007/s11227-018-2416-4

Borucka, A. (2023, May). Seasonal Methods of Demand Forecasting in the Supply Chain as Support for the Company's Sustainable Growth. *Sustainability (Basel)*, 15(09), 7399. Advance online publication. DOI: 10.3390/su15097399

Botene, P. H. R., de Azevedo, A. T., & de Arruda Ignácio, P. S. (2021). Blockchain as an enabling technology in the COVID-19 pandemic: a systematic review. In *Health and Technology* (Vol. 11, Issue 6, pp. 1369–1382). DOI: 10.1007/s12553-021-00593-z

Botín-Sanabria, D. M., Mihaita, A.-S., Peimbert-García, R. E., Ramírez-Moreno, M. A., Ramírez-Mendoza, R. A., & Lozoya-Santos, J. de J. (2022). Digital Twin Technology Challenges and Applications: A Comprehensive Review. *Remote Sensing (Basel)*, 14(6), 1335. DOI: 10.3390/rs14061335

Bouzid, A., & Duval, M. (2017). La fabrication additive.

Brandau, A., & Tolujevs, J. (2013). Modelling and Analysis of Logistical State Data. *Transport and Telecommunication Journal*, 14(2), 102–115. DOI: 10.2478/ttj-2013-0009

Breivold, H. P., & Sandstrom, K. (2015). Internet of Things for Industrial Automation — Challenges and Technical Solutions. *2015 IEEE International Conference on Data Science and Data Intensive Systems*, 532–539. DOI: 10.1109/DSDIS.2015.11

Brinch, M. (2018). Understanding the value of big data in supply chain management and its business processes. *International Journal of Operations & Production Management*, 38(7), 1589–1614. DOI: 10.1108/IJOPM-05-2017-0268

Brinch, M., Stentoft, J., Jensen, J. K., & Rajkumar, C. (2018). Practitioners understanding of big data and its applications in supply chain management. *International Journal of Logistics Management*, 29(2), 555–574. DOI: 10.1108/IJLM-05-2017-0115

Brinker, J. O., ... (2022, March 29). A Novel Approach to Multi-Objective Optimization for Resource Allocation in Cloud Computing. https://www.sciencedirect.com/science/article/pii/S1319157817302264

Brou, P., & Janssen, M. (2015). Effects Of The Internet Of Things (IoT): A Systematic Review Of The Benefits And Risks. *The Fifteenth International Conference on Electronic Business*, 217–222.

Broy, M., Cengarle, M. V., & Geisberger, E. (2012). Cyber-Physical Systems: Imminent Challenges. In Large-Scale Complex IT Syst. Dev., Operat. and Manag. - 17th Monterey Workshop, volume 7539 of LNCS, 1–28.

Brun, A., Karaosman, H., & Barresi, T. (2020). Supply chain collaboration for transparency. *Sustainability (Basel)*, 12(11), 4429. DOI: 10.3390/su12114429

Brynjolfsson, E., & McAfee, A. (2014). *The second machine age: Work, progress, and prosperity in a time of brilliant technologies*. WW Norton & Company.

Budde, L., Benninghaus, C., Hänggi, R., & Friedli, T. (2022). Managerial Practices for the Digital Transformation of Manufacturers. *Digital*, 2(4), 463–483. DOI: 10.3390/digital2040025

Bueno, A., Godinho Filho, M., & Frank, A. G. (2020). Smart production planning and control in the Industry 4.0 context: A systematic literature review. *Computers & Industrial Engineering*, 149, 106774. DOI: 10.1016/j.cie.2020.106774

Buer, S. V., Strandhagen, J. O., & Chan, F. T. S. (2018). The link between Industry 4.0 and lean manufacturing: Mapping current research and establishing a research agenda. *International Journal of Production Research*, 56(8), 2924–2940. DOI: 10.1080/00207543.2018.1442945

Bughin, J. (2016) "Big data, Big bang?," Journal of Big Data, pp. 3(1), 2.

-Bughin, J., Hazan, E., Ramaswamy, S., Chui, M., Allas, T., Dahlström, P., ... & Henke, N. (2017). Artificial intelligence: The next digital frontier?. McKinsey Global Institute, 1-118.

Bujak, A., Topolski, M., & Miler, R. K. (2015). Telematics as a tool of efficient supply chain management. *Archives of Transport System Telematics*, 8(2), 8–12.

Bumblauskas, D., Gemmill, D., Igou, A., & Anzengruber, J. (2017). Smart Maintenance Decision Support Systems (SMDSS) Based on Corporate Big Data Analytics. *Expert Systems with Applications*, 90, 303–317. DOI: 10.1016/j.eswa.2017.08.025

Buntain, M. (2021, Apr). Process Manufacturers Leverage Cloud Computing for Advanced Analytics. *InTech, 68*(02), 01-09. Retrieved May 15, 2024, from https://www.scopus.com/record/display.uri?eid=2-s2.0-85159211081&origin=scopusAI

Burgos, R. M., Badowski, M. E., Drwiega, E., Ghassemi, S., Griffith, N., Herald, F., Johnson, M., Smith, R. O., & Michienzi, S. M. (2021). The race to a COVID-19 vaccine: Opportunities and challenges in development and distribution. In *Drugs in Context* (Vol. 10). DOI: 10.7573/dic.2020-12-2

Burkhart, D., & Bode, C. (2022). TRANSPARENCY IN BUYER-SUPPLIER RELATIONSHIPS: THE WHAT AND WHEN OF SENSITIVE INFORMATION EXCHANGES. *82nd Annual Meeting of the Academy of Management, AOM 2022.* 2022. Seattle: Academy of Management. DOI: 10.5465/AMBPP.2022.37

Butt, J. (2020). A Conceptual Framework to Support Digital Transformation in Manufacturing Using an Integrated Business Process Management Approach. *Designs*, 4(3), 17. DOI: 10.3390/designs4030017

Cameron, L. (2018). Internet of Things Meets the Military and Battlefield: Connecting Gear and Biometric Wearables for an IoMT and IoBT. *IEEE Computer Society*. https://www.computer.org/publications/tech-news/research/internet-of-military-battlefield-things-iomt-iobt

Cândido, G. a. (2007). A multiagent control system for shop floor assembly. In *International Conference on Industrial Applications of Holonic and Multi-Agent Systems* (pp. 293-302). DOI: 10.1007/978-3-540-74481-8_28

Caniëls, M. C., & Bakens, R. J. (2012). The implementation of electronic purchasing tools: An analysis of potential success factors. *Journal of Purchasing and Supply Management*, 18(3), 154–163.

Carbonneau, R., Laframboise, K., & Vahidov, R. (2008). Application of machine learning techniques for supply chain demand forecasting. *European Journal of Operational Research*, 184(3), 1140–1154. DOI: 10.1016/j.ejor.2006.12.004

Cardoso, J., Sheth, A., Miller, J., Arnold, J., & Kochut, K. (2004). Quality of service for workflows and web service processes. *Journal of Web Semantics*, 1(3), 281–308. DOI: 10.1016/j.websem.2004.03.001

Carlton, J., Aldwinkle, J., & Anderson, J. (2013). *Future ship powering options: exploring alternative methods of ship propulsion*. Royal Academy of Engineering., https://wwwcdn.imo.org/localresources/en/OurWork/Environment/Documents/Air%20pollution/Future_ship_powering_options_report.pdf

Cascio, W. F., & Montealegre, R. (2016). How technology is changing work and organizations. *Annual Review of Organizational Psychology and Organizational Behavior*, 3(1), 349–375. DOI: 10.1146/annurev-orgpsych-041015-062352

Castiglione, A., Choo, K.-K. R., Nappi, M., & Ricciardi, S. (2017). Context Aware Ubiquitous Biometrics in Edge of Military Things. *IEEE Cloud Computing*, 4(6), 16–20. DOI: 10.1109/MCC.2018.1081072

Cavalcante, I. M., Frazzon, E. M., Forcellini, F. A., & Ivanov, D. (2019). A supervised machine learning approach to data-driven simulation of resilient supplier selection in digital manufacturing. *International Journal of Information Management*, 49, 86–97. DOI: 10.1016/j.ijinfomgt.2019.03.004

-Cavelius, F., Endenich, C., & Zicari, A. (2018, May). L'impact de la digitalisation sur le role du controleur de gestion. In *Transitions numériques et informations comptables* (pp. cd-rom)

Cavoukian, A. (2012). *Privacy by design: The seven foundational principles*. Information and Privacy Commissioner of Ontario.

CelcomDigi. (2023). *CelcomDigi and DHL supply chain reimagine logistics with Malaysia's first 5G-Powered AI autonomous warehouse*. https://corporate.celcomdigi.com/news/celcomdigi-and-dhl-supply-chain-reimagine-logistics-with-malaysias-first-5g-powered-ai-autonomous-warehouse

certain investigations for research and applications. International Journal of Production Economics, 176, 98-110. .DOI: 10.1016/j.ijpe.2016.03.014

Chandra, D., & Kumar, D. (2020). Prioritizing the vaccine supply chain issues of developing countries using an integrated ISM-fuzzy ANP framework. *Journal of Modelling in Management*, 15(1), 112–165. DOI: 10.1108/JM2-08-2018-0111

Chandra, D., & Vipin, B. (2021). Investigating the Vaccine Supply Chain. *RE:view*, •••, 251–268. DOI: 10.1007/978-981-16-2774-3_13

Chatterjee, S., Rana, N. P., Dwivedi, Y. K., & Baabdullah, A. M. (2021). Understanding AI adoption in manufacturing and production firms using an integrated TAM-TOE model. *Technological Forecasting and Social Change*, 170, 120880. DOI: 10.1016/j.techfore.2021.120880

Chavez, R., Yu, W., Jacobs, M. A., & Feng, M. (2017). Data-Driven Supply Chains, Manufacturing Capability and Customer Satisfaction. *Production Planning and Control*, 28(11–12), 906–918. DOI: 10.1080/09537287.2017.1336788

Chen, Z. S., & Ruan, J. Q. (2024). Metaverse healthcare supply chain: Conceptual framework and barrier identification. *Engineering Applications of Artificial Intelligence, 133*(PA), 108113. DOI: 10.1016/j.engappai.2024.108113

Cheng, H., Xue, L., Wang, P., Zeng, P., & Yu, H. (2017). Ontology-based web service integration for flexible manufacturing systems. In 15th Int. Conf. on Ind. Inf., pages 351–356. IEEE. DOI: 10.1109/INDIN.2017.8104797

Cheng, J., Chen, W., & Luo, C. (2015). Cloud computing in manufacturing: A review of the state-of-the-art. *Enterprise Information Systems*, 9(5–6), 606–625.

Cheng, J., Yang, Y., Zou, X., & Zuo, Y. (2022). 5G in manufacturing: A literature review and future research. *International Journal of Advanced Manufacturing Technology*, •••, 1–23.

Chen, I. J., Paulraj, A., & Lado, A. A. (2019). Strategic purchasing, supply management capabilities, and firm performance. *International Journal of Operations & Production Management*, 39(2), 206–226.

Chen, J., Chiu, M. L., & Petrescu, M. (2018). Customized product recommendation in e-commerce. *Information & Management*, 55(7), 833–851.

Chen, M., Mao, S., Zhang, Y., & Leung, V. C. (2014). *Big data: related technologies, challenges and future prospects*. Springer International Publishing. DOI: 10.1007/978-3-319-06245-7

Chen, P. C., & Kezunovic, M. (2016). Fuzzy Logic Approach to Predictive Risk Analysis in Distribution Outage Management. *IEEE Transactions on Smart Grid*, 7(6), 2827–2836. DOI: 10.1109/TSG.2016.2576282

Chen, W. (2020). Intelligent manufacturing production line data monitoring system for industrial internet of things. *Computer Communications*, 151, 31–41. DOI: 10.1016/j.comcom.2019.12.035

Chen, Y., Chen, N., & Wen, Y. (2019). The Spotify business model: Redefining the music streaming industry. *Information Systems Management*, 36(2), 116–132.

Chesbrough, H., Vanhaverbeke, W., & West, J. (Eds.). (2018). *New frontiers in open innovation*. Oxford University Press.

Chèze, B., Chevallier, J., & Gastineau, P. (2012). *Will technological progress be sufficient to effectively lead the air transport to a sustainable development in the mid-term (2025)?*https://ideas.repec.org/p/cec/wpaper/1207.html

Chien, C.-F., Dauzère-Pérès, S., Huh, W. T., Jang, Y. J., & Morrison, J. R. (2020). Artificial intelligence in manufacturing and logistics systems: Algorithms, applications, and case studies. *International Journal of Production Research*, 58(9), 2730–2731. DOI: 10.1080/00207543.2020.1752488

Chin, W. W. (1998). The partial least squares approach to structural equation modeling. Modern methods for business research, 295-336.

Chmielarz, G. (2019). Present state and future application of smart technologies in manufacturing processes. *Production Engineering Archives*, 24(24), 14–19. DOI: 10.30657/pea.2019.24.04

Choi, D.-H. (2019). Impact of Internet of Things (IoT)'s Service Quality on the Hotel Customer Satisfaction. *International Journal of Recent Technology and Engineering, 8*(2S6), 362–366. DOI: 10.35940/ijrte.B1069.0782S619

Choi, T. M., Chan, H. K., & Yue, X. (2021). Recent development in big data analytics for business operations and risk management. *IEEE Transactions on Cybernetics*, 51(5), 2518–2534. PMID: 31329572

Choi, T. M., Wallace, S. W., & Wang, Y. (2017). Big data analytics in operations management. *Production and Operations Management*. Advance online publication. DOI: 10.1111/poms.12838 PMID: 26766385

Choi, T. Y., & Hong, Y. (2002). Unveiling the structure of supply networks: Case studies in Honda, Acura, and DaimlerChrysler. *Journal of Operations Management*, 20(5), 469–493. DOI: 10.1016/S0272-6963(02)00025-6

Choi, Y., Lee, H., & Irani, Z. (2018). Big data-driven fuzzy cognitive map for prioritising IT service procurement in the public sector. *Annals of Operations Research*, 270(1–2), 75–104. DOI: 10.1007/s10479-016-2281-6

Chopra, S., & Meindl, P. (2020). *Supply chain management: Strategy, planning, and operation* (7th ed.). Pearson Education.

Choudhury, M. M., & Harrigan, P. (2014). CRM to social CRM: The integration of new technologies into customer relationship management. *Journal of Strategic Marketing*, 22(2), 149–176. DOI: 10.1080/0965254X.2013.876069

Chowdhury, P., Paul, S. K., Kaisar, S., & Moktadir, M. A. (2021). COVID-19 pandemic related supply chain studies: A systematic review. *Transportation Research Part E, Logistics and Transportation Review*, 148, 102271. DOI: 10.1016/j.tre.2021.102271 PMID: 33613082

Christopher, M. (1992). *Logistics and Supply Chain Management: Strategies for Reducing Costs and Improving Services*. Financial Times.

Christopher, M. (2011). *Logistics & Supply Chain Management* (4th ed.). Pearson Education Limited.

Christopher, M. (2016). *Logistics & supply chain management* (5th ed.). Pearson Education.

Chu, S., & Majumdar, A. (2012). Opportunities and challenges for a sustainable energy future. *Nature*, 488(7411), 294–303. DOI: 10.1038/nature11475 PMID: 22895334

Čiarnienė, R., & Vienažindienė, M. (2015). An empirical study of lean concept manifestation. *Procedia: Social and Behavioral Sciences*, 207, 225–233. DOI: 10.1016/j.sbspro.2015.10.091

Cimini, C., Lagorio, A., Romero, D., Cavalieri, S., & Stahre, J. (2020). Smart logistics and the logistics operator 4.0. *IFAC-PapersOnLine*, 53(2), 10615–10620. DOI: 10.1016/j.ifacol.2020.12.2818

Ciortea, A., Mayer, S., & Michahelles, F. (2018). Repurposing Manufacturing Lines on the Fly with Multi-agent Systems for the Web of Things. In Proc. of the 17th Int. Conf. on Autonomous Agents and Multi-Agent Systems, pages 813–822. Int. Found. for Autonomous Agents and Multiagent Systems / ACM.

Cloud, H. (2011). The nist definition of cloud computing. National institute of science and technology, special publication, 800(2011), 145.

-Coase, R. H. (1972). Industrial organization: a proposal for research. In *Economic research: Retrospect and prospect, Volume 3, policy issues and research opportunities in industrial organization* (pp. 59-73). NBER.

Cocolin, N., DeVarney, A., & Aqlan, F. (2018). Analysis of soft skills requirements for manufacturing jobs. *3rd North American IEOM Conference. IEOM 2018. 2018*, pp. 1443-1451. IEOM Society. Retrieved May 15, 2024, from https://www.scopus.com/record/display.uri?eid=2-s2.0-85066977758&origin=scopusAI

Cohen, M. A. (2015). Inventory management in the age of big data. *Harvard Business Review*.

Colitti, W., Steenhaut, K., Caro, N. De., (2011). "Integrating Wireless Sensor Networks with the Web", Extending the Internet to Low power and Lossy Networks (IP+SN).

Collotta, M., Sun, Y., Di Persio, L., Ebeid, E. S. M., & Muradore, R. (2018). Smart Green Applications: From Renewable Energy Management to Intelligent Transportation Systems. *Energies*, 11(5), 1317. DOI: 10.3390/en11051317

Colucci, S., Di Noia, T., Pinto, A., Ruta, M., Ragone, A., & Tinelli, E. (2007). A Nonmonotonic Approach to Semantic Matchmaking and Request Refinement in E-Marketplaces. *International Journal of Electronic Commerce*, 12(2), 127–154. DOI: 10.2753/JEC1086-4415120205

Comes, T., Bergtora Sandvik, K., & Van de Walle, B. (2018). Cold chains, interrupted: The use of technology and information for decisions that keep humanitarian vaccines cool. *Journal of Humanitarian Logistics and Supply Chain Management*, 8(1), 49–69. DOI: 10.1108/JHLSCM-03-2017-0006

ComputerWorld. (2018). *Overcoming 5 Major Supply Chain Challenges with Big Data Analytics.*

Constante, F., Silva, F., & Pereira, A. (2019) DataCo smart supply chain for big data analysis. Mendeley Data. vg2k6. 5.DOI: <ALIGNMENT.qj></ALIGNMENT>10.17632 /8gx2f

Copacino, W. C. (1997). *Supply Chain Management: The Basics and Beyond. APICS Series onResource Management*. St. Lucie Press.

Corporate, W. (2024). Walmart Commerce Technologies Launches AI-Powered Logistics Product. https://corporate.walmart.com/news/2024/03/14/walmart-commerce - technologies-launches-ai-powered-logistics-product

Cory, A., Henson, J., Pschorr, K., Sheth, A. P., & Thirunarayan, K. (2009). "SemSOS: Semantic sensor Observation Service", in *Proceedings of the International Symposium on Collaborative Technologies and Systems.*

Costello, T., & Prohaska, B. (2013). Trends and strategies. *IT Professional*, 15(1), 64. DOI: 10.1109/MITP.2013.5

Courbis, C., & Finkelstein, A. (2005). Weaving Aspects into Web Service Orchestrations, in *Proceeding of International Conference of Web Services (ICWS '05)*, July 2005. DOI: 10.1109/ICWS.2005.129

Cui, J., Liu, F., Hu, J., Janssens, D., Wets, G., & Cools, M. (2016). Identifying mismatch between urban travel demand and transport network services using GPS data: A case study in the fast growing Chinese city of Harbin. *Neurocomputing*, 181, 4–18. DOI: 10.1016/j.neucom.2015.08.100

Dallasega, P., Rojas, R. A., Rauch, E., & Matt, D. T. (2017). Simulation Based Validation of Supply Chain Effects through ICT enabled Real-time-capability in ETO Production Planning. *Procedia Manufacturing*, 11, 846–853. DOI: 10.1016/j.promfg.2017.07.187

Danjou, C., Rivest, L., & Pellerin, R. (2017). *PME 2.0 Le passage au numérique Industrie 4.0: des pistes pour aborder l'ère du numérique et de la connectivité.* Ceferio.

Darvazeh, S. S., Vanani, I. R., and Musolu, F. M. (2020) Big data analytics and its application in supply chain management. New Trends in the use of Artificial Intelligence for the Industry 4.0.

Dassisti, M. a. (2008). Ontology-based model for production-control systems interoperability. In *The 5th CIRP Digital Enterprise Technology Conference* (pp. 527--543).

Dave, E. (2011). How the next evolution of the internet is changing everything. *Internet of Things : Engineering Cyber Physical Human Systems*.

Davenport, T. H. (2014). How Strategists Use "Big Data" to Support Internal Business Decisions, Discovery and Production. *Strategy and Leadership*, 42(4), 45–50. DOI: 10.1108/SL-05-2014-0034

Davenport, T. H., & Harris, J. (2007). *Competing on analytics: The new science of winning*. Harvard Business Press.

Davenport, T. H., & Ronanki, R. (2018). Artificial intelligence for the real world. *Harvard Business Review*, 96(1), 108–116.

De Boeck, K., Decouttere, C., & Vandaele, N. (2020). Vaccine distribution chains in low- and middle-income countries: A literature review. In *Omega (United Kingdom)* (Vol. 97, p. 102097). Pergamon. DOI: 10.1016/j.omega.2019.08.004

De Boeck, K., Decouttere, C., Jónasson, J. O., & Vandaele, N. (2022). Vaccine supply chains in resource-limited settings: Mitigating the impact of rainy season disruptions. *European Journal of Operational Research*, 301(1), 300–317. DOI: 10.1016/j.ejor.2021.10.040

De Matta, R., & Miller, T. (2018). *A Strategic Manufacturing Capacity and Supply Chain Network Design Contingency Planning Approach. 2018 IEEE Technology and Engineering Management Conference, TEMSCON 2018*. Institute of Electrical and Electronics Engineers Inc., DOI: 10.1109/TEMSCON.2018.8488401

de Vass, T., Shee, H., & Miah, S. (2021). IoT in Supply Chain Management: Opportunities and Challenges for Businesses in Early Industry 4.0 Context. *Operations and Supply Chain Management: An International Journal*, 148–161. DOI: 10.31387/oscm0450293

De Virgilio, R., Di Sciascio, E., Ruta, M., Scioscia, F., & Torlone, R. (2011). Semantic-based rfid data management. In *Unique Radio Innovation for the 21st Century* (pp. 111–141). Springer. DOI: 10.1007/978-3-642-03462-6_6

De Vries, L., Gensler, S., & Leeflang, P. S. (2017). Popularity of brand posts on brand fan pages: An investigation of the effects of social media marketing. *Journal of Interactive Marketing*, 31, 89–100.

Dean-Leon, E., Ramirez-Amaro, K., Bergner, F., Dianov, I., & Cheng, G. (2018). Integration of Robotic Technologies for Rapidly Deployable Robots. *IEEE Transactions on Industrial Informatics*, 14(4), 1691–1700. DOI: 10.1109/TII.2017.2766096

Decker, S., Melnik, S., van Harmelen, F., Fensel, D., Klein, M., Broekstra, J., Erdmann, M., & Horrocks, I. (2000). The Semantic Web: The roles of XML and RDF. *IEEE Internet Computing*, 4(5), 63–73. DOI: 10.1109/4236.877487

Decouttere, C., De Boeck, K., & Vandaele, N. (2021). Advancing sustainable development goals through immunization: a literature review. In *Globalization and Health* (Vol. 17, Issue 1). DOI: 10.1186/s12992-021-00745-w

Demartini, M., Evans, S., & Tonelli, F. (2019). Digitalization Technologies for Industrial Sustainability. *Procedia Manufacturing*, 33, 264–271. DOI: 10.1016/j.promfg.2019.04.032

Demey, Y. T., & Wolff, M. (2016). SIMISS: A Model Based Searching Strategy for Inventory Management Systems. *IEEE Internet of Things Journal*, 4(1), 1–1. DOI: 10.1109/JIOT.2016.2638023

Demirkan, S., Demirkan, I., & McKee, A. (2020). Blockchain technology in the future of business cyber security and accounting. *Journal of Management Analytics*, 7(2), 189–208. DOI: 10.1080/23270012.2020.1731721

Despoudi, S. (2020, Jan 01). Green supply chain. In *The Interaction of Food Industry and Environment* (pp. 35–61). Elsevier., DOI: 10.1016/B978-0-12-816449-5.00002-3

Devadharshini, R., Praniis, R., Nishanth, B., & Jayapal, C. (2023). Enhancing Fleet Operations with a Vehicle Route Management Solution. *2nd International Conference on Advancements in Electrical, Electronics, Communication, Computing and Automation, ICAECA 2023.* Virtual, Online: Institute of Electrical and Electronics Engineers Inc. DOI: 10.1109/ICAECA56562.2023.10199496

Dhirani, L. L., Armstrong, E., & Newe, T. (2021). Industrial IoT, Cyber Threats, and Standards Landscape: Evaluation and Roadmap. *Sensors (Basel)*, 21(11), 3901. DOI: 10.3390/s21113901 PMID: 34198727

Diakopoulos, N. (2016). Accountability in algorithmic decision making. *Communications of the ACM*, 59(2), 56–62. DOI: 10.1145/2844110

Dimitriou, D. (2016). Climate Change Implications in Aviation and Tourism Market Equilibrium. In (pp. 409-424). https://doi.org/DOI: 10.1007/978-3-319-39880-8_25

Dimitriou, D. J., & Sartzetaki, M. F. (2018). Social Dimension of Air Transport Sustainable Development. *International Journal of Industrial and Systems Engineering*, 12(4), 573–576. DOI: 10.1007/978-3-030-28661-3_9

Ding, Y., Jin, M., Li, S., & Feng, D. (2021). Smart logistics based on the internet of things technology: An overview. *International Journal of Logistics*, 24(4), 323–345. DOI: 10.1080/13675567.2020.1757053

Divyeshkumar, V. (2024). An Analysis of the Impact of Human-Computer Interaction on Artificial Intelligence in Healthcare. *NeuroQuantology : An Interdisciplinary Journal of Neuroscience and Quantum Physics*, 22(3), 95.

Divyeshkumar, V. (2024). Balancing Safety and Decision-Making Algorithms in AI-Driven Autonomous Vehicles. *NeuroQuantology : An Interdisciplinary Journal of Neuroscience and Quantum Physics*, 22(3), 112.

Divyeshkumar, V. (2024). Block-chain based data provenance and integrity verification. *International Journal of Science and Research Archive*, 12(1), 2516–2533.

Divyeshkumar, V. (2024). Leveraging Electronic Health Records (EHR) for Enhanced Patient Care. *International Journal of Current Science Research and Review*, 7(5), 2963–2971.

Dogra, A., Jha, R. K., & Jain, S. (2020). A survey on beyond 5G network with the advent of 6G: Architecture and emerging technologies. *IEEE Access : Practical Innovations, Open Solutions*, 9, 67512–67547. DOI: 10.1109/ACCESS.2020.3031234

Dolgui, A., & Ivanov, D. (2022). 5G in digital supply chain and operations management: Fostering flexibility, end-to-end connectivity and real-time visibility through internet-of-everything. *International Journal of Production Research*, 60(2), 442–451. DOI: 10.1080/00207543.2021.2002969

Dombrowski, U., Richter, T., & Krenkel, P. (2017). Interdependencies of industry 4.0 and lean production systems-a use cases analysis-27th international conference on flexible automation and intelligent manufacturing. *Procedia Manufacturing*, 11, 1061–1068. DOI: 10.1016/j.promfg.2017.07.217

Drath, R., & Horch, A. (2014). Industrie 4.0: Hit or hype? [Industry Forum]. *IEEE Industrial Electronics Magazine*, 8(2), 56–58. DOI: 10.1109/MIE.2014.2312079

Duan, J., Zhang, C., Gong, Y., Brown, S., & Li, Z. (2020). A ContentAnalysis Based Literature Review in Blockchain Adoption within Food Supply Chain. *International Journal of Environmental Research and Public Health*, 17(5), 1784. DOI: 10.3390/ijerph17051784 PMID: 32182951

Duarte, A. Y. S., Sanches, R. A., & Dedini, F. G. (2018). Assessment and technological forecasting in the textile industry: From first industrial revolution to the Industry 4.0. *Strategic Design Research Journal*, 11(3). Advance online publication. DOI: 10.4013/sdrj.2018.113.03

Dubey, R., Gunasekaran, A., Bryde, D. J., Dwivedi, Y. K., & Papadopoulos, T. (2020). Blockchain technology for enhancing swift-trust, collaboration and resilience within a humanitarian supply chain setting. *International Journal of Production Research*, 58(11), 3381–3398. DOI: 10.1080/00207543.2020.1722860

Dubey, R., Gunasekaran, A., Childe, S. J., Blome, C., Papadopoulos, T., & Luo, Z. (2017). Big data and predictive analytics and manufacturing performance: Integrating institutional theory, resource-based view, and big data culture. *British Journal of Management*, 30(2), 341–361. DOI: 10.1111/1467-8551.12355

Dubey, R., Gunasekaran, A., Childe, S. J., Luo, Z., Fosso Wamba, S., Roubaud, D., & Foropon, C. (2018). Examining the role of big data and predictive analytics on collaborative performance in context to sustainable consumption and production behaviour. *Journal of Cleaner Production*, 196, 1508–1521. DOI: 10.1016/j.jclepro.2018.06.097

Dutta, B. (2021) Big data in supply chain management: Impacts and applications. https://www.analyticssteps.com/blogs/big-data-supply-chain-management-impacts-and-applications

Ebulue, C. C., Ekkeh, O. V., Ebulue, O. R., & Ekesiobi, C. S. (2024). Leveraging machine learning for vaccine distribution in resource-limited settings: A synthesis of approaches. *International Medical Science Research Journal*, 4(5), 544–557.

Efron, B., & Tibshirani, R. J. (1993). *An introduction to the bootstrap*. Chapman and Hall/CRC. DOI: 10.1007/978-1-4899-4541-9

Ehsan, I., Irfan Khalid, M., Ricci, L., Iqbal, J., Alabrah, A., Sajid Ullah, S., & Alfakih, T. M. (2022). A conceptual model for blockchain-based agriculture food supply chain system. *Scientific Programming*, 2022, 1–15. DOI: 10.1155/2022/7358354

El Mane, A., Tatane, K., & Chihab, Y. (2024). Transforming agricultural supply chains: Leveraging blockchain-enabled java smart contracts and IoT integration. *ICT Express*.

Elhasbi, A., Jami, J., & Kammas, S. (2015). Sustainable transport in Morocco: What contingency factors for which maturity level? case of road haulage "RH" service providers in the region of Casablanca metropolis. *European Scientific Journal*, 11, •••. https://eujournal.org/index.php/esj/article/view/6345

Elragal, A., & Klischewski, R. (2017). Theory-driven or process-driven prediction? Epistemological challenges of big data analytics. *Journal of Big Data*, 4(19), 19. DOI: 10.1186/s40537-017-0079-2

EM-DAT. (2024). *Inventorying hazards & disasters worldwide since 1988*. https://www.emdat.be/

Emirhüseyinoğlu, G., & Ekici, A. (2019). Dynamic facility location with supplier selection under quantity discount. *Computers & Industrial Engineering*, 134, 64–74. DOI: 10.1016/j.cie.2019.05.023

Ericsson (2022). *Ericsson Private 5G, together with Kollmorgen's NDC solutions platform*.https://www.ericsson.com/4ad55c/assets/local/industries/manufacturing/ericsson-and-kollmorgen.pdf

Ericsson (2022). *Ericsson Private 5G, together with Kollmorgen's NDC Solutions Platform*.https://www.ericsson.com/4ad55c/assets/local/industries/manufacturing/ericsson-and-kollmorgen.pdf

Esmizadeh, Y., Bashiri, M., Jahani, H., & Almada-Lobo, B. (2021). Cold chain management in hierarchical operational hub networks. *Transportation Research Part E, Logistics and Transportation Review*, 147, 102202. Advance online publication. DOI: 10.1016/j.tre.2020.102202

Evans, D. S. (2016). *Matchmakers: The new economics of multisided platforms*. Harvard Business Review Press.

Eyring, V., Isaksen, I. S. A., Berntsen, T., Collins, W. J., Corbett, J. J., Endresen, O., Grainger, R. G., Moldanova, J., Schlager, H., & Stevenson, D. S. (2010). Transport impacts on atmosphere and climate: Shipping. *Atmospheric Environment*, 44(37), 4735–4771. https://doi.org/https://doi.org/10.1016/j.atmosenv.2009.04.059. DOI: 10.1016/j.atmosenv.2009.04.059

Ezeigweneme, C. A., Umoh, A. A., Ilojianya, V. I., & Adegbite, A. O.Chinedu Alex EzeigwenemeAniekan Akpan UmohValentine Ikenna IlojianyaAbimbola Oluwatoyin Adegbite. (2024). Review Of Telecommunication Regulation And Policy: Comparative Analysis USA AND AFRICA. *Computer Science & IT Research Journal*, 5(1), 81–99. DOI: 10.51594/csitrj.v5i1.703

Farooq, M. S., Riaz, S., Abid, A., Umer, T., & Zikria, Y. (2020). Role of IoT Technology in Agriculture: A Systematic Literature Review. *Electronics (Basel)*, 9(2), 319. DOI: 10.3390/electronics9020319

Fawcett, S. E., Wallin, C., Allred, C., Fawcett, A. M., & Magnan, G. M. (2011). INFORMATION TECHNOLOGY AS AN ENABLER OF SUPPLY CHAIN COLLABORATION: A DYNAMIC-CAPABILITIES PERSPECTIVE. *The Journal of Supply Chain Management*, 47(1), 38–59. DOI: 10.1111/j.1745-493X.2010.03213.x

Feng, Q., & Shanthikumar, J. G. (2018). How research in production and operations management may evolve in the era of big data. *Production and Operations Management*, 27(9), 1670–1684. DOI: 10.1111/poms.12836

Feng, T., Huang, X., & Liu, G. (2017). Social commerce research: Definition, research themes and improvement measures. *Information Systems Frontiers*, 19(3), 447–458.

Fernández-López, M. P., & Gómez-Pérez, A. (2002). Overview and analysis of methodologies for building ontologies. *The Knowledge Engineering Review*, 17(2), 129–156. DOI: 10.1017/S0269888902000462

Ferreira, D. C., & Marques, R. C. (2021). Public-private partnerships in health care services: Do they outperform public hospitals regarding quality and access? Evidence from Portugal. *Socio-Economic Planning Sciences*, 73, 100798. DOI: 10.1016/j.seps.2020.100798

Filia, A., Rota, M. C., Grossi, A., Martinelli, D., Prato, R., & Rezza, G. (2022). Are vaccine shortages a relevant public health issue in Europe? Results from a survey conducted in the framework of the EU Joint Action on Vaccination. *Vaccine*, 40(13), 1987–1995. DOI: 10.1016/j.vaccine.2022.02.041 PMID: 35190211

Firican, G. (2017). *The 10 Vs of Big Data.*

Florek-Paszkowska, A., Ujwary-Gil, A., & Godlewska-Dzioboń, B. (2021). Business innovation and critical success factors in the era of digital transformation and turbulent times.

Forrester Research. (2024). Supply Chain Management. https://www.forrester.com/blogs/category/supply-chain-management/

Fosso Wamba, S., Akter, S., Edwards, A., Chopin, G., & Gnanzou, D. (2015). How 'big data' can make big impact: Findings from a systematic review and a longitudinal case study. *International Journal of Production Economics*, 165, 234–246. DOI: 10.1016/j.ijpe.2014.12.031

Frank, M. J., Allen, J. J., Cavanagh, J. F., & Bismark, A. W. (2019). Multiple dissociations between comorbid depression and anxiety on reward and punishment processing: Evidence from computationally informed EEG. *Computational Psychiatry (Cambridge, Mass.)*, 3, 1. PMID: 31149639

Fridell, E. (2019). Emissions and Fuel Use in the Shipping Sector. In Bergqvist, R., & Monios, J. (Eds.), *Green Ports* (pp. 19–33). Elsevier., https://doi.org/https://doi.org/10.1016/B978-0-12-814054-3.00002-5 DOI: 10.1016/B978-0-12-814054-3.00002-5

Gai, K., Fang, Z., Wang, R., Zhu, L., Jiang, P., & Choo, K. K. R. (2020). Edge computing and lightning network empowered secure food supply management. *IEEE Internet of Things Journal*, 9(16), 14247–14259. DOI: 10.1109/JIOT.2020.3024694

Galbraith, J. R. (2014). Organization design challenges resulting from big data. *Journal of Organizational Design*, 3(1), 2–13. DOI: 10.7146/jod.8856

Gandomi, A., & Haider, M. (2015). Beyond the Hype: Big Data Concepts, Methods, and Analytics. *International Journal of Information Management*, 35(2), 137–144. DOI: 10.1016/j.ijinfomgt.2014.10.007

Gan, G., Jiang, H., & Li, T. (2018). Trading bots and institutional traders on cryptocurrency exchanges. *Journal of Management Information Systems*, 35(1), 333–355.

Gangaraju, P. K., Raj, R., Kumar, V., Akhil, N., De, T., & Kaswan, M. S. (2023). Financial performance in Industry 4.0 agile supply chains: Evidence from manufacturing companies. *The TQM Journal*. Advance online publication. DOI: 10.1108/TQM-07-2023-0214

Gao, Y., Gao, H., Xiao, H., & Yao, F. (2023). Vaccine supply chain coordination using blockchain and artificial intelligence technologies. *Computers and Industrial Engineering, 175*(December 2022), 108885. DOI: 10.1016/j.cie.2022.108885

Garcia, C. A., Salazar, L. F., Marino, C., Villalba, W. R., & Garcia, M. V. (2018). Design of Flexible Cyber-Physical Production Systems Architecture for Industrial Robot Control. *2018 IEEE Third Ecuador Technical Chapters Meeting (ETCM)*, 1–6. DOI: 10.1109/ETCM.2018.8580338

Garetti, M. F. (2012). P-PSO ontology for manufacturing systems. In *Proceedings of 14th IFAC Symposium on Information Control Problems in Manufacturing* (pp. 247–254).

Garrigós, J. A., & Molina, M. (2020, May 03). Integrating Customers and Suppliers in Retail Co-innovation: Mercadona, the Spanish grocery retailer, uses a co-innovation approach in which customers and suppliers collaborate to create new products. *Research Technology Management*, 63(03), 33–41. DOI: 10.1080/08956308.2020.1733887

Gartner. (2012). What Is Big Data? Ghosh, D. (2015, 14-15 Sept. 2015). *Big Data in Logistics and Supply Chain management - a rethinking step.* Paper presented at the 2015 International Symposium on Advanced Computing and Communication (ISACC).

Gawer, A. (2014). The Business Model of Platforms: A Research Overview. *Journal of Management Studies.*

Geeksforgeeks. (2023). *Characteristics of Internet of Things.* Geeksforgeeks.Org. https://www.geeksforgeeks.org/characteristics-of-internet-of-things/

George, R., Cherbaka, N. S., & Ellis, K. (2023). 5G opportunities in warehousing. In *16th Proceedings (Dresden, Germany- 2023).* 14. https://digitalcommons.georgiasouthern.edu/pmhr_2023/14

GEP. (2021). *WHAT IS SUPPLY CHAIN AGILITY?* Retrieved May 08, 2024, from www.gep.com: https://www.gep.com/knowledge-bank/glossary/what-is-supply-chain-agility

Gergs, L., & Mavrakis, D. (2022). Private 5G in Warehousing. *ABI research.* https://go.abiresearch.com/lp-private-5g-in-warehousing

Ghadge, A., Wurtmann, H., & Seuring, S. (2020). Managing climate change risks in global supply chains: A review and research agenda. *International Journal of Production Research*, 58(1), 44–64. DOI: 10.1080/00207543.2019.1629670

Ghahramani, M., Qiao, Y., Zhou, M. C., O'Hagan, A., & Sweeney, J. (2020). AI-based modeling and data-driven evaluation for smart manufacturing processes. *IEEE/CAA Journal of Automatica Sinica, 7*(4), 1026–1037. DOI: 10.1109/JAS.2020.1003114

Gharaibeh, L., Eriksson, K., & Lantz, B. (n.d.). Supply chain digitalization in the wood manufacturing industry: A bibliometric literature review. Advances in Transdisciplinary Engineering, 21(SPS2022), 617-628. DOI: 10.3233/ATDE220180

Ghobakhloo, M., & Ching, N. T. (2019). Adoption of digital technologies of smart manufacturing in SMEs. *Journal of Industrial Information Integration*, 16, 100107. DOI: 10.1016/j.jii.2019.100107

Giberti, H., Abbattista, T., Carnevale, M., Giagu, L., & Cristini, F. (2022). A Methodology for Flexible Implementation of Collaborative Robots in Smart Manufacturing Systems. *Robotics (Basel, Switzerland)*, 11(1), 9. DOI: 10.3390/robotics11010009

Golan, M. S., Trump, B. D., Cegan, J. C., & Linkov, I. (2021b). *The Vaccine Supply Chain: A Call for Resilience Analytics to Support COVID-19 Vaccine Production and Distribution* (pp. 389–437). DOI: 10.1007/978-3-030-71587-8_22

Golan, M. S., Trump, B. D., Cegan, J. C., & Linkov, I. (2021a). Supply chain resilience for vaccines: Review of modeling approaches in the context of the COVID-19 pandemic. *Industrial Management & Data Systems*, 121(7), 1723–1748. DOI: 10.1108/IMDS-01-2021-0022

Gómez-Pérez, A. (2004). Ontology evaluation. In *Handbook on ontologies* (pp. 251–273). Springer. DOI: 10.1007/978-3-540-24750-0_13

Gong, C., Liu, J., Zhang, Q., Chen, H., & Gong, Z. (2010). The Characteristics of Cloud Computing. *2010 39th International Conference on Parallel Processing Workshops*.

Govindan, K., Cheng, T., Mishra, N., & Shukla, N. (2018). Big data analytics and application for logistics and supply chain management. *Transportation Research Part E, Logistics and Transportation Review*, 114, 343–349. DOI: 10.1016/j.tre.2018.03.011

Gracy, M., & Jeyavadhanam, B. R. (2021, November). A systematic review of blockchain-based system: Transaction throughput latency and challenges. In *2021 International Conference on Computational Intelligence and Computing Applications (ICCICA)* (pp. 1-6). IEEE.

Graessler, I., & Poehler, A. (2017). Integration of a digital twin as human representation in a scheduling procedure of a cyber-physical production system. *2017 IEEE International Conference on Industrial Engineering and Engineering Management (IEEM)*, 289–293. DOI: 10.1109/IEEM.2017.8289898

Greasley, A., & Assanova, M. (2022). Robotics and automation in supply chain management. *The Journal of Supply Chain Management*, 58(3), 234–247.

Grieves, M. (2014), Digital Twin: Manufacturing Excellence through Virtual Factory Replication, White paper.

Grimm, S. a. (2011). Ontologies and the semantic web. In *Handbook of semantic web technologies*. DOI: 10.1007/978-3-540-92913-0_13

Grüninger, M. K. (2000). Ontologies to support process integration in enterprise engineering. *Computational \& Mathematical Organization Theory, 6*, 381--394.

Gulia, P., & Chahal, A. (2020). Big Data Analytics for IoT. [IJARET]. *International Journal of Advanced Research in Engineering and Technology*, 11(6), 593–603. DOI: 10.34218/IJARET.11.6.2020.054

Gunasekaran, A., Papadopoulos, T., Dubey, R., Wamba, S. F., Childe, S. J., Hazen, B., & Akter, S. (2017). Big data and predictive analytics for supply chain and organizational performance. Journal of Business Research, 70, 308-317. http://dx.doi .org/. jbusres.2016.08.004.DOI: 10.1016/j

Guo, S. Y., Ding, L. Y., Luo, H. B., & Jiang, X. Y. (2016). A Big-Data-based platform of workers' behavior: Observations from the field. *Accident; Analysis and Prevention*, 93, 299–309. DOI: 10.1016/j.aap.2015.09.024 PMID: 26614050

Gupta, S., Starr, M. K., Farahani, R. Z., & Asgari, N. (2021). Pandemics/Epidemics: Challenges and Opportunities for Operations Management Research. *Manufacturing & Service Operations Management*. Advance online publication. DOI: 10.1287/msom.2021.0965

Gurrala, K., & Hariga, M. (2022). Key food supply chain challenges: A review of the literature and research gaps. *Operations and Supply Chain Management: An International Journal*, 15(4), 441–460. DOI: 10.31387/oscm0510358

Hahn, G. J., & Packowski, J. (2015). A perspective on applications of in-memory analytics in supply chainmanagement. *Decision Support Systems*, 76, 45–52. DOI: 10.1016/j.dss.2015.01.003

Haidari, L. A., Wahl, B., Brown, S. T., Privor-Dumm, L., Wallman-Stokes, C., Gorham, K., Connor, D. L., Wateska, A. R., Schreiber, B., Dicko, H., Jaillard, P., Avella, M., & Lee, B. Y. (2015). One size does not fit all: The impact of primary vaccine container size on vaccine distribution and delivery. *Vaccine*, 33(28), 3242–3247. DOI: 10.1016/j.vaccine.2015.04.018 PMID: 25889160

Hair, J. F., Ringle, C. M., & Sarstedt, M. (2013). Partial least squares structural equation modeling (PLS-SEM): An emerging alternative statistical analysis method. *Marketing Science*, 32(3), 107–121.

Handfield, R. B., & Nichols, E. L. (1999). *Introduction to Supply Chain Management*. Prentice Hall.

Haq, A. N., & Boddu, V. (2015, January). Analysis of agile supply chain enablers for Indian food processing industries using analytical hierarchy process. *International Journal of Manufacturing Technology and Management*, 29(1-2), 30–47. DOI: 10.1504/IJMTM.2015.066780

Harini, M., Dhinakaran, D., Prabhu, D., Sankar, S. U., Pooja, V., & Sruthi, P. K. (2023, July). Leveraging Blockchain for Transparency in Agriculture Supply Chain Management Using IoT and Machine Learning. In *2023 World Conference on Communication & Computing (WCONF)* (pp. 1-6). IEEE.

Hassan, A. O., Ewuga, S. K., Abdul, A. A., Abrahams, T. O., Oladeinde, M., & Dawodu, S. O. (2024). Cybersecurity In Banking: A Global Perspective With A Focus On Nigerian Practices. *Computer Science & IT Research Journal*, 5(1), 41–59. DOI: 10.51594/csitrj.v5i1.701

Havard, V., Sahnoun, M., Bettayeb, B., Duval, F., & Baudry, D. (2021). Data architecture and model design for Industry 4.0 components integration in cyber-physical production systems. *Proceedings of the Institution of Mechanical Engineers. Part B, Journal of Engineering Manufacture*, 235(14), 2338–2349. DOI: 10.1177/0954405420979463

Hayman, B., Suri, R., & Prasad, S. D. (2021). COVID-19 vaccine capacity: Challenges and mitigation – The DCVMN perspective. *Vaccine*, 39(35), 4932–4937. DOI: 10.1016/j.vaccine.2021.07.007 PMID: 34325932

Hazen, B. T., Boone, C. A., Ezell, J. D., & Jones-Farmer, L. A. (2014). Data quality for data science, predictive analytics, and big data in supply chain management: An introduction to the problem and suggestions for research and applications. *International Journal of Production Economics*, 154, 72–80. DOI: 10.1016/j.ijpe.2014.04.018

HBC. (2023). *SUPPLY CHAIN OVERVIEW*. Retrieved May 10, 2024, from https://www.coca-colahellenic.com: https://www.coca-colahellenic.com/en/about-us/what-we-do/supply-chain

He, J., Lei, Y., & Fu, X. (2019, December 02). Do consumer's green preference and the reference price effect improve green innovation? A theoretical model using the food supply chain as a case. *International Journal of Environmental Research and Public Health*, 16(24), 5007. Advance online publication. DOI: 10.3390/ijerph16245007 PMID: 31835416

Heller, F. (2017) "Technological innovation applied to walmart and tesco's supply chain," Doctoral dissertation, Lisboa, Portugal.

Hempel, S., Xenakis, L., & Danz, M. (2016). *Systematic reviews for occupational safety and health questions*. RAND Corporation., https://www.rand.org/pubs/research_reports/RR1463.html

Henseler, J., Ringle, C. M., & Sinkovics, R. R. (2009). The use of partial least squares path modeling in international marketing research. *Journal of International Marketing*, 17(3), 19–39.

Hernandez, M. (2019). *IoT: Consumer & Commercial vs. Industrial - Main overview*. Ubidots.

He, W., Wu, H., Yan, G., Akula, V., & Shen, J. (2015). A novel social media competitive analytics framework with sentiment benchmarks. *Information & Management*, 52(7), 801–812. DOI: 10.1016/j.im.2015.04.006

Hildebrandt, A.-C., Schuetz, C., Wahrmann, D., Wittmann, R., & Rixen, D. (2016). A Flexible Robotic Framework for Autonomous Manufacturing Processes: Report from the European Robotics Challenge Stage 1. *2016 International Conference on Autonomous Robot Systems and Competitions (ICARSC)*, 21–27. DOI: 10.1109/ICARSC.2016.15

Hofman, H. (2023). The game-changing potential of 5G in logistics. *Maersk,* https://www.maersk.com/insights/growth/2023/01/17/the-potential-of-5g-in-logistics

Hofmann, E., & Rutschmann, E. (2018). Big data analytics and demand forecasting in supply chains: A conceptual analysis. *International Journal of Logistics Management*, 29(2), 739–766. DOI: 10.1108/IJLM-04-2017-0088

Hopkins, J., & Hawking, P. (2018). Big data analytics and IoT in logistics: A case study. *International Journal of Logistics Management*, 29(2), 575–591. DOI: 10.1108/IJLM-05-2017-0109

Horrocks, I. a.-S. (2003). From SHIQ and RDF to OWL: The making of a web ontology language. *1*(1), 7--26.

Howe, J. (2008). *Crowdsourcing: Why the power of the crowd is driving the future of business*. Crown Business.

Hrnjica, B., & Softic, S. (2020). Explainable AI in Manufacturing: A Predictive Maintenance Case Study. In Lalic, B., Majstorovic, V., Marjanovic, U., Von Cieminski, G., & Romero, D. (Eds.), *Advances in Production Management Systems. Towards Smart and Digital Manufacturing* (Vol. 592, pp. 66–73). Springer International Publishing., DOI: 10.1007/978-3-030-57997-5_8

Hu, H., Xu, J., Liu, M., & Lim, M. K. (2023). Vaccine supply chain management: An intelligent system utilizing blockchain, IoT and machine learning. *Journal of Business Research, 156*(November 2022), 113480. DOI: 10.1016/j.jbusres.2022.113480

Huang, Y. Y., & Handfield, R. B. (2015). Measuring the benefits of erp on supply management maturity model: A "big data" method. *International Journal of Operations & Production Management*, 35(1), 2–25. DOI: 10.1108/IJOPM-07-2013-0341

Huawei (2023). *Dubai South Welcomes 5G-Powered Smart Warehousing Center.* https://www.huawei.com/en/media-center/multimedia/videos/2023/dubai-5g-smart-warehouse?utm_medium=sm&utm_source=youtube&utm_campaign=media-center

Hunt, B., & Bennett, C. (2022). Case Study: Building a private 5G network to support smart warehouse applications. *Deloitte*.https://www2.deloitte.com/content/dam/Deloitte/us/Documents/consulting/us-deloitte-building-5G-private-network.pdf

Iheukwumere, O. C., Eze, U. F., Otuonye, A. I., & Ikerionwu, C. O. (2024). Big Data Analytics in Supply Chain Management: Applications and Challenges. *International Journal of Novel Research in Computer Science and Software Engineering*, 11(1), 3–6.

Ikegwu, A. C., Nweke, H. F., Arukwe, C. V., Alo, U. R., & Okonkwo, O. R. (2022). Big data for data-driven industry: A review of data sources, tools, challenges, solutions, and research directions. *Cluster Computing*, 25(5), 3343–3387. DOI: 10.1007/s10586-022-03568-5

Ittmann, H. W. (1999). Introduction to Supply Chain Management by Robert B. Handfield and Ernest L. Nichols. *Informs*, 111–114.

Ivankova, G. V., Mochalina, E. P., & Goncharova, N. L. (2020). Internet of Things (IoT) in logistics. *IOP Conference Series. Materials Science and Engineering*, 940(1), 012033. DOI: 10.1088/1757-899X/940/1/012033

Ivanov, D. (2022). Viable supply chain model: Integrating agility, resilience and sustainability perspectives—lessons from and thinking beyond the COVID-19 pandemic. *Annals of Operations Research*, 319(1), 1411–1431. DOI: 10.1007/s10479-020-03640-6 PMID: 32836614

Ivanov, D., & Dolgui, A. (2020). A digital supply chain twin for managing the disruption risks and resilience in the era of Industry 4.0. *Production Planning and Control*, 31(10), 775–788.

Ivanov, D., & Dolgui, A. (2021). Simulation-based approaches for supply chain resilience and risk management: Recent advances and future perspectives. *European Journal of Operational Research*, 291(2), 482–495.

Ivanov, D., Dolgui, A., & Sokolov, B. (2019). The impact of digital technology and Industry 4.0 on the ripple effect and supply chain risk analytics. *International Journal of Production Research*, 57(3), 829–846. DOI: 10.1080/00207543.2018.1488086

Jablonski, F. (2020). 5G in production: Audi and Ericsson take the next step. https://fuenf-g.de/en/2020/11/14/5g-in-production-audi-and-ericsson-take-the-next-step/

Jakl, A., Schoffer, L., Husinsky, M., & Wagner, M. (2018), Augmented Reality for Industry 4.0: Architecture and User Experience, In Proceeding of the 11th Forum Media Technology, CER-WS, 38-42.

Jandl, C., Nurgazina, J., Schoffer, L., Reichl, C., Wagner, M., & Moser, T. (2019). SensiTrack – A Privacy by Design Concept for Industrial IoT Applications, In *Proceeding of the 24th IEEE International Conference on Emerging Technologies and Factory Automation*, 10-13 September, Zaragoza, Spain, 1782-1789. DOI: 10.1109/ETFA.2019.8869186

Jarrett, S., Yang, L., & Pagliusi, S. (2020). Roadmap for strengthening the vaccine supply chain in emerging countries: Manufacturers' perspectives. *Vaccine: X*, 5, 100068. DOI: 10.1016/j.jvacx.2020.100068 PMID: 32775997

Javaid, M., Haleem, A., Singh, R. P., & Suman, R. (2022). Enhancing smart farming through the applications of Agriculture 4.0 technologies. *International Journal of Intelligent Networks*, 3, 150–164. DOI: 10.1016/j.ijin.2022.09.004

Jayanth, S., Poorvi, M. B., & Sunil, M. P. (2017). *Inventory Management System Using IOT.*, DOI: 10.1007/978-981-10-2471-9_20

Jelti, F., Allouhi, A., & Tabet Aoul, K. A. (2023). Transition Paths towards a Sustainable Transportation System: A Literature Review. *Sustainability (Basel)*, 15(21), 15457. DOI: 10.3390/su152115457

Jeschke, S., Brecher, C., Meisen, T., Ozdemir, D., & Eschert, T. (2017), Industrial Internet of Things and Cyber Manufacturing Systems, In Industrial Internet of Things, Springer, 3-19.

Jiang, P., Klemeš, J. J., Van Fan, Y., Fu, X., Tan, R. R., You, S., & Foley, A. M. (2021). Energy, environmental, economic and social equity (4E) pressures of COVID-19 vaccination mismanagement: A global perspective. *Energy*, 235, 121315. DOI: 10.1016/j.energy.2021.121315 PMID: 34226789

Jollivet, A. (2020, May 07). *Amazon & COVID-19: A paradigm shift in grocery shopping behavior and how grocery brands should adapt.* Retrieved May 01, 2024, from https://www.linkedin.com: https://www.linkedin.com/pulse/amazon-covid-19-paradigm-shift-grocery-shopping-how-brands-jollivet/

Jun S-P, Park D-H, Yeom J. (2014) The possibility of using search traffic information to explore consumer product attitudes and forecast consumer preference. Technol Forecast Soc Chang. 86:237–53. ORE.2013.10.021.DOI: <ALIGNMENT.qj></ ALIGNMENT>10.1016/J.TECHF

Juntunen, M., & Lehenkari, M. (2021). A narrative literature review process for an academic business research thesis. *Studies in Higher Education, 46*(2), 330-342. https://doi.org/DOI: 10.1080/03075079.2019.1630813

Kache, F., & Seuring, S. (2017). Challenges and opportunities of digital information at the intersection of Big Data Analytics and supply chain management. *International Journal of Operations & Production Management*, 37(1), 10–36. DOI: 10.1108/IJOPM-02-2015-0078

Kadena, E., & Rajnai, Z. (2024, January). 5G Supply Chain: An overview of applications and challenges. In *2024 IEEE 22nd World Symposium on Applied Machine Intelligence and Informatics (SAMI)* (pp. 57-162). IEEE.

Kagermann, H., Wahlster, W., & Helbig, J. (2013), Recommendations for implementing the strategic initiative INDUSTRIE 4.0. Final report of the Industrie 4.

Kaisler, S., ... (2013) Big data: issues and challenges moving forward. In: 2013 46th Hawaii International Conference on System Sciences (HICSS), Wailea, Maui, HI, 7–10 January, pp. 995–1004. IEEE. DOI: 10.1109/HICSS.2013.645

Kamble, S., Gunasekaran, A., & Dhone, N. C. (2020). Industry 4.0 and lean manufacturing practices for sustainable organisational performance in Indian manufacturing companies. *International Journal of Production Research*, 58(5), 1319–1337. DOI: 10.1080/00207543.2019.1630772

Kampan, K., Tsusaka, T. W., & Anal, A. K. (2022). Adoption of blockchain technology for enhanced traceability of livestock-based products. *Sustainability (Basel)*, 14(20), 13148. DOI: 10.3390/su142013148

Kane, G. C., Gregor, B., & Larsen, P. D. (2015). Prioritizing digitalization: A new strategic imperative. *MIT Sloan Management Review*, 56(4), 64–72.

Kane, G. C., Palmer, D., Phillips, A. N., Kiron, D., & Buckley, N. (2015). Strategy, not technology, drives digital transformation. *MIT Sloan Management Review and Deloitte University Press*, 14(1), 1–24.

Kang, H. S., Lee, J. Y., Choi, S., Kim, H., Park, J. H., Son, J. Y., Kim, B. H., & Noh, S. D. (2016). Smart manufacturing: Past research, present findings, and future directions. *International Journal of Precision Engineering and Manufacturing-Green Technology*, 3(1), 111–128. DOI: 10.1007/s40684-016-0015-5

Kannan, P. K., & Li, H. A. (2017). Digital marketing: A framework, review and research agenda. *International Journal of Research in Marketing*, 34(1), 22–45. DOI: 10.1016/j.ijresmar.2016.11.006

Karl, M., Jonson, J., Uppstu, A., Aulinger, A., Prank, M., Sofiev, M., Jalkanen, J.-P., Johansson, L., Quante, M., & Matthias, V. (2019). Effects of ship emissions on air quality in the Baltic Sea region simulated with three different chemistry transport models. *Atmospheric Chemistry and Physics*, 19(10), 7019–7053. DOI: 10.5194/acp-19-7019-2019

Karp, C. L., Lans, D., Esparza, J., Edson, E. B., Owen, K. E., Wilson, C. B., Heaton, P. M., Levine, O. S., & Rao, R. (2015). Evaluating the value proposition for improving vaccine thermostability to increase vaccine impact in low and middle-income countries. *Vaccine*, 33(30), 3471–3479. DOI: 10.1016/j.vaccine.2015.05.071 PMID: 26055297

Kato, T., & Kamoshida, R. (2020). Multi-Agent Simulation Environment for Logistics Warehouse Design Based on Self-Contained Agents. *Applied Sciences (Basel, Switzerland)*, 10(21), 7552. DOI: 10.3390/app10217552

Katz, M., Paso, T., Mikhaylov, K., Pessoa, L., Fontes, H., Hakola, L., Leppäniemi, J., Carlos, E., Dolmans, G., Rufo, J., Drzewiecki, M., Sallouha, H., Napier, B., Branquinho, A., & Eder, K. (2024). Towards truly sustainable IoT systems: The SUPERIOT project. *JPhys Photonics*, 6(1), 011001. DOI: 10.1088/2515-7647/ad1c6a

Kauppila, O., Valikangas, K., & Majava, J. (2020). Improving supply chain transparency between a manufacturer and suppliers: A triadic case study. *Management and Production Engineering Review, 11*(03), 84-91. doi:DOI: 10.24425/mper.2020.134935

Kayikci, Y. and Subramanian, N. (2022). Blockchain interoperability issues in supply chain: exploration of mass adoption procedures., 309-328. DOI: 10.1007/978-3-030-87304-2_13

Keskinock, P., & Tayur, S. (2001). Quantitative analysis of Internet-enabled supply chain. *Interfaces*, 31(2), 70–89. DOI: 10.1287/inte.31.2.70.10626

Khadiri, H. (2023). *Le pilotage de la production par une approche architectural digitale et holonique.* Fes: Thèse de Doctorat en Génie Industriel, Faculté des Sciences et Techniques de Fès.

Khan, S. N., Loukil, F., Ghedira-Guegan, C., Benkhelifa, E., & Bani-Hani, A. (2021). Blockchain smart contracts: Applications, challenges, and future trends. *Peer-to-Peer Networking and Applications*, 14(5), 2901–2925. DOI: 10.1007/s12083-021-01127-0 PMID: 33897937

Khan, S., Khan, M., & Haleem, A. (2019). Blockchain enabled supply chain: An implementation perspective. *Our Heritage*, 67(5), 318–334.

Khayyam, H., Javadi, B., Jalili, M., & Jazar, R. N. (2020). Artificial Intelligence and Internet of Things for Autonomous Vehicles. In *Nonlinear Approaches in Engineering Applications* (pp. 39–68). Springer International Publishing., DOI: 10.1007/978-3-030-18963-1_2

Khezr, S., Moniruzzaman, M., Yassine, A., & Benlamri, R. (2019). Blockchain Technology in Healthcare: A Comprehensive Review and Directions for Future Research. *Applied Sciences 2019, Vol. 9, Page 1736, 9*(9), 1736. DOI: 10.3390/app9091736

Kilay, A. L., Simamora, B. H., & Putra, D. P. (2022). The influence of e-payment and e-commerce services on supply chain performance: Implications of open innovation and solutions for digitalizing micro, small, and medium enterprises (MSMEs) in Indonesia. *Journal of Open Innovation*, 8(3), 119–119. DOI: 10.3390/joitmc8030119

Kilpatrick, J., Delesalle, P., & Mussomeli, A. (2022, Apr 01). *The new supply chain equilibrium*. Retrieved May 04, 2024, from www2.deloitte.com: https://www2.deloitte.com/xe/en/insights/focus/supply-chain/supply-chain-agility-efficiency.html

Kim, H. K., & Lee, C. W. (2022). The impact of digitalization and supply chain dynamic capabilities on supply chain performance in the MICE industry. The Korean Academic Association of Business Administration, 35(12), 2287-2312. https://doi.org/DOI

Kim, J. W., Rhee, J. H., & Park, C. H. (2024). How Does Digital Transformation Improve Supply Chain Performance: A Manufacturer's Perspective. *Sustainability (Basel)*, 16(7), 3046. DOI: 10.3390/su16073046

King, M. L. (2024). How manufacturing won or lost the COVID-19 vaccine race. *Vaccine*, 42(5), 1004–1012. DOI: 10.1016/j.vaccine.2023.12.031 PMID: 38228438

King, T., Cole, M., Farber, J. M., Eisenbrand, G., Zabaras, D., Fox, E. M., & Hill, J. P. (2017). Food safety for food security: Relationship between global megatrends and developments in food safety. *Trends in Food Science & Technology*, 68, 160–175. DOI: 10.1016/j.tifs.2017.08.014

Kiritsis, D. (2011). Closed-loop PLM for intelligent products in the era of the Internet of things. *Computer Aided Design*, 43(5), 479–501. DOI: 10.1016/j.cad.2010.03.002

Kiron, D., Prentice, P. K., & Ferguson, R. B. (2014). The analytics mandate. *MIT Sloan Management Review*, 55(4), 1–25.

KKol, A., & Pinkse, J. (2020). The role of digitalization in sustainable supply chain management: Insights from the global fashion industry. *Business Strategy and the Environment*, 29(5), 1832–1844.

Klemeš, J. J., Jiang, P., Van Fan, Y., Bokhari, A., & Wang, X.-C. (2021). COVID-19 pandemics Stage II – Energy and environmental impacts of vaccination. *Renewable & Sustainable Energy Reviews*, 150, 111400. DOI: 10.1016/j.rser.2021.111400 PMID: 34248390

Knight, W. (2015, September-October). Inside amazon. *Technology Review*, 118(05), 62–69. Retrieved May 01, 2024, from https://www.scopus.com/record/display.uri?eid=2-s2.0-85022335891&origin=scopusAI

Kodali, R. K., Swamy, G., & Lakshmi, B. (2015). An implementation of IoT for healthcare. *2015 IEEE Recent Advances in Intelligent Computational Systems (RAICS)*, 411–416. DOI: 10.1109/RAICS.2015.7488451

Kohl, M., Habl, A., Kallali, K., Puff, J., Fottner, J., Oger, R., Lauras, M., & Li, J. (2022, October). Managing supply chains during the Covid-19 crisis: Synthesis of academic and practitioner visions and recommendations for the future. *International Journal of Logistics Management*, 33(04), 1386–1407. DOI: 10.1108/IJLM-07-2021-0375

Kontopanou, M., & Tsoulfas, G. (2022). ANALYZING NEW WAYS TO ADAPT THE TRIPLE-A SUPPLY CHAIN MODEL AND ITS EXTENSIONS IN AGRI-FOOD SUPPLY CHAINS. *Logforum*, 18(03), 285–295. DOI: 10.17270/J.LOG.2022.735

Kontopanou, M., Tsoulfas, G. T., & Rachaniotis, N. P. (2021, November). The compatibility of the triple-a agri-food supply chain with the United Nations Sustainable Development Goals. [). IOP Publishing.]. *IOP Conference Series. Earth and Environmental Science*, 899(1), 012002.

Koot, M., Mes, M. R. K., & Iacob, M. E. (2021). A systematic literature review of supply chain decision making supported by the Internet of Things and Big Data Analytics. *Computers & Industrial Engineering*, 154, 107076. DOI: 10.1016/j.cie.2020.107076

Koren, Y., & Ulsoy, A. G. (1997). Reconfigurable manufacturing systems. Engineering Research Center for Reconfigurable Machining Systems. ERC/RMS report #1. Ann Arbor.

Kosba, A., Miller, A., Shi, E., Wen, Z., & Papamanthou, C. (2016, May). Hawk: The blockchain model of cryptography and privacy-preserving smart contracts. In *2016 IEEE symposium on security and privacy (SP)* (pp. 839-858). IEEE.

Koshta, N., Devi, Y., & Chauhan, C. (2022). Evaluating Barriers to the Adoption of Delivery Drones in Rural Healthcare Supply Chains: Preparing the Healthcare System for the Future. *IEEE Transactions on Engineering Management*, 1–13. DOI: 10.1109/TEM.2022.3210121

Kott, A., Swami, A., & West, B. J. (2016). The Internet of Battle Things. *Computer*, 49(12), 70–75. DOI: 10.1109/MC.2016.355

Kotter, J. P. (1996). *Leading change*. Harvard Business Press.

Kouhizadeh, M., Sarkis, J., & Zhu, Q. (2020). Blockchain technology and the sustainable supply chain: Theoretically exploring adoption barriers. *International Journal of Production Economics*, 231, 107831. DOI: 10.1016/j.ijpe.2020.107831

Krishnan, K. (2013). *Data Warehousing in the Age of Big Data*. Morgan Kaufmann.

Kristensen, D. D., Lorenson, T., Bartholomew, K., & Villadiego, S. (2016). Can thermostable vaccines help address cold-chain challenges? Results from stakeholder interviews in six low- and middle-income countries. *Vaccine*, 34(7), 899–904. DOI: 10.1016/j.vaccine.2016.01.001 PMID: 26778422

Krumeich, J., Werth, D., & Loos, P. (2016). Prescriptive Control of Business Processes. *Business & Information Systems Engineering*, 58(4), 261–280. DOI: 10.1007/s12599-015-0412-2

Kumar, B. S., & Chowdary, V. (2023). Railway Noise Pollution in Urban Environments: Sources, Effects, and Control Strategies. In (pp. 1–38). https://doi.org/DOI: 10.1007/978-981-99-4638-9_2-1

Kumar, M. (2016). *Applied big data analytics in operations management*. Appl Big Data Anal Oper Manage., DOI: 10.4018/978-1-5225-0886-1

Kumar, M. S., Raut, D. R. D., Narwane, D. V. S., & Narkhede, D. B. E. (2020). Applications of industry 4.0 to overcome the COVID-19 operational challenges. *Diabetes & Metabolic Syndrome*, 14(5), 1283–1289. DOI: 10.1016/j.dsx.2020.07.010 PMID: 32755822

Kumar, S. a. (2017). Manufacturing Flexibility and its Effect on System Performance. *Jordan Journal of Mechanical and Industrial Engineering*, 11, 105–112.

Kumar, S., & Nair, A. (2021). Sustainability in supply chains: An overview of recent trends and future directions. *Journal of Cleaner Production*, 290, 125260.

Kumar, S., Raut, R. D., Priyadarshinee, P., Mangla, S. K., Awan, U., & Narkhede, B. E. (2022a). The Impact of IoT on the Performance of Vaccine Supply Chain Distribution in the COVID-19 Context. *IEEE Transactions on Engineering Management*, 1–11. DOI: 10.1109/TEM.2022.3157625

Kumar, V., & Reinartz, W. (2018). Creating enduring customer value. *Journal of Marketing*, 80(6), 36–68.

Kusiak, A. (2018). Smart manufacturing. *International Journal of Production Research*, 56(1–2), 508–517. DOI: 10.1080/00207543.2017.1351644

Kuznetsova, G. V., & Podbiralina, G. V. (2023). Transport Digitalization. In Kahraman, C., & Haktanır, E. (Eds.), *Intelligent Systems in Digital Transformation: Theory and Applications* (pp. 579–608). Springer International Publishing., DOI: 10.1007/978-3-031-16598-6_25

Kwilinski, A., Lyulyov, O., & Pimonenko, T. (2023). Environmental Sustainability within Attaining Sustainable Development Goals: The Role of Digitalization and the Transport Sector. *Sustainability (Basel)*, 15(14), 11282. DOI: 10.3390/su151411282

Lacity, M. C., Khan, S. A., & Willcocks, L. P. (2020). A review of the IT outsourcing empirical literature and future research directions. *Journal of Information Technology*, 35(4), 235–256.

Lade, P., Ghosh, R., & Srinivasan, S. (2017). Manufacturing Analytics and Industrial Internet of Things. *IEEE Intelligent Systems*, 32(3), 74–79. DOI: 10.1109/MIS.2017.49

Lagorio, A., Cimini, C., Pinto, R., & Cavalieri, S. (2023). 5G in Logistics 4.0: Potential applications and challenges. *Procedia Computer Science*, 217, 650–659. DOI: 10.1016/j.procs.2022.12.261

Lai, Y., Sun, H., & Ren, J. (2018). Understanding the determinants of big data analytics (BDA) adoption in logistics and supply chain management: An empirical investigation. *International Journal of Logistics Management*, 29(2), 676–703. DOI: 10.1108/IJLM-06-2017-0153

Lamba, K., & Singh, S. P. (2017). Big data in operations and supply chain management: Current trends and future perspectives. *Production Planning and Control*, 28(11-12), 877–890. DOI: 10.1080/09537287.2017.1336787

Laney, D. (2001). *3 D Data Management: Controlling Data Volume*. Velocity and Variety.

Lasi, H., Fettke, P., Kemper, H.-G., Feld, T., & Hoffmann, M. (2014). Industry 4.0. BISE, 6(4):239–242. Lastra, J. L. M. and Delamer, I. M. (2006). Semantic Web Services in Factory Automation: Fundamental Insights and Research Roadmap. *IEEE Transactions on Industrial Informatics*, 2(1), 1–11.

Lau, R. Y. K., Zhang, W., & Xu, W. (2017). Parallel Aspect-Oriented Sentiment Analysis for Sales Forecasting with Big Data. *Production and Operations Management*, 27(10), 1–20.

Lauras, M., Lamothe, J., Benaben, F., Andres, B., & Pol Er, R. (2015). Towards an agile and collaborative platform for managing supply chain uncertainties. *6th International IFIP Working Conference on Enterprise Interoperability, IWEI 2015.* 213, pp. 64-72. Nimes: Springer Verlag. DOI: 10.1007/978-3-662-47157-9_6

LaValle, S., Lesser, E., Shockley, R., Hopkins, M. S., & Kruschwitz, N. (2011). Big data, analytics and the path from insights to value. *MIT Sloan Management Review*, 52(2), 21–32.

Lawrence, P. R., & Lorsch, J. W. (1967). Differentiation and integration in complex organizations. *Administrative Science Quarterly*, 12(1), 1–47. DOI: 10.2307/2391211

Le Daré, B., Bacle, A., Lhermitte, R., Lesourd, F., & Lurton, Y. (2021). Increasing vaccine supply with low dead-volume syringes and needles. *International Journal of Pharmaceutics*, 608, 121053. Advance online publication. DOI: 10.1016/j.ijpharm.2021.121053 PMID: 34461171

Lee, H. L., & Billington, C. (1992). Managing supply chain inventories: Pitfalls and opportunities. *Sloan Management Review*, 33(3), 65–77.

Lee, I., & Mangalaraj, G. (2022). Big data analytics in supply chain management: A systematic Literature Review and Research directions. Big Data Cognitive. *Computing*, 6(17).

Lee, J., Bagheri, B., & Kao, H.-A. (2015). A Cyber-Physical Systems architecture for Industry 4.0-based manufacturing systems. *Manufacturing Letters*, 3, 18–23. DOI: 10.1016/j.mfglet.2014.12.001

Lee, J., Kao, H.-A., & Yang, S. (2014). Service Innovation and Smart Analytics for Industry 4.0 and Big Data Environment. *Procedia CIRP*, 16, 3–8. DOI: 10.1016/j.procir.2014.02.001

Lee, K. L., Teong, C. X., Alzoubi, H. M., Alshurideh, M., & El Khatib, M. (2024). Digital supply chain transformation: The role of smart technologies on operational performance in the manufacturing industry. *International Journal of Engineering Business Management*, 16, 18479790241234986. DOI: 10.1177/18479790241234986

Leesakul, N., Oostveen, A.-M., Eimontaite, I., Wilson, M. L., & Hyde, R. (2022). Workplace 4.0: Exploring the Implications of Technology Adoption in Digital Manufacturing on a Sustainable Workforce. *Sustainability (Basel)*, 14(6), 3311. DOI: 10.3390/su14063311

Lee, T. H., & Chen, A. H. (2021). Last-Mile Logistics of Covid Vaccination — The Role of Health Care Organizations. *The New England Journal of Medicine*, 384(8), 685–687. DOI: 10.1056/NEJMp2100574 PMID: 33503340

Lefort, L., Henson, C., Taylor, K., Barnaghi, P., Compton, M., Corcho, O., Garcia-Castro, R., Graybeal, J., Herzog, A., Janowicz, K., ... (2005). "Semantic Sensor Network XG Final Report", 2011, W3C Incubator Group Report, https://www.w3.org/2005/Incubator/ssn/XGR-ssn/

Lehmann, M. (2022). "The Future of Data Science: A Perspective from 2022." (The publication date is not specified in the list provided).

Lehmann, M. (2022, April 15). The Future of Data Science: A Perspective from 2022. https://blog.mdpi.com/2023/09/27/data-peer-review/

Lei, Y., Qiaoming, H., & Zhao, T. (2023). Research on supply chain financial risk prevention based on machine learning. *Computational Intelligence and Neuroscience*, 2023(1), 1–15. DOI: 10.1155/2023/6531154 PMID: 36923907

Lemaignan, S. Y. (2006). MASON: A proposal for an ontology of manufacturing domain. In *IEEE Workshop on Distributed Intelligent Systems: Collective Intelligence and Its Applications (DIS'06)}* (pp. 195-200). DOI: 10.1109/DIS.2006.48

León-Bravo, V., Moretto, A., Cagliano, R., & Caniato, F. (2019, September 01). Innovation for sustainable development in the food industry: Retro and forward-looking innovation approaches to improve quality and healthiness. *Corporate Social Responsibility and Environmental Management*, 26(05), 1049–1062. DOI: 10.1002/csr.1785

Leseure-Zajkowska, E. Z. (2012). Contribution à l'implantation de la méthode Lean Six Sigma dans les Petites et Moyennes Entreprises pour l'amélioration des processus (Doctoral dissertation, Ecole Centrale de Lille).

Liker, J. (2004). *The Toyota way : 14 management principles from the world's greatest manufacturer*. McGraw-Hill Education.

Li, L., & Horrocks, I. (2004). A software framework for matchmaking based on semantic web technology. *International Journal of Electronic Commerce*, 8(4), 39–60. DOI: 10.1080/10864415.2004.11044307

Ling, X. (2021). How 5G will Revolutionize Manufacturing. *HuaweiTech*. https://www.huawei.com/en/huaweitech/publication/winwin/38/5g-revolutionize-manufacturing

Liu, K. P., & Chiu, W. (n.d.). Supply Chain 4.0: The impact of digitalization and integration on firm performance. Metropolitan University. Springer Netherlands. DOI: DOI: 10.31667/jhts.2022.12.95.183

Liu, M. (2021). Research on the development of intelligent logistics based on 5g technology. In *2021 2nd International Conference on Urban Engineering and Management Science (ICUEMS)* (pp. 107-110). IEEE.

Liu, P., & Yi, S. (2016). Investment decision-making and coordination of supply chain: A new research in the big data era. *Discrete Dynamics in Nature and Society*, 2016, 1–10. DOI: 10.1155/2016/2026715

Liu, R., Tan, C., Wu, D. D., & Zhao, C. (2023). Strategies choice for blockchain construction and coordination in vaccine supply chain. *Computers & Industrial Engineering*, 182(May), 109346. DOI: 10.1016/j.cie.2023.109346

Liu, Z., Wang, Y., Cai, L., Cheng, Q., & Zhang, H. (2016). Design and Manufacturing Model of Customized Hydrostatic Bearing System Based on Cloud and Big Data Technology. *International Journal of Advanced Manufacturing Technology*, 84(1–4), 261–273. DOI: 10.1007/s00170-015-8066-2

Li, Y., Chang, Q., Brundage, M. P., Biller, S., Arinez, J., & Xiao, G. (2015). Market Demand Oriented Data-Driven Modeling for Dynamic Manufacturing System Control. *IEEE Transactions on Systems, Man, and Cybernetics. Systems*, 45(1), 109–121. DOI: 10.1109/TSMC.2014.2316268

Li, Y., Hou, M., Liu, H., & Liu, Y. (2012). Towards a theoretical framework of strategic decision, supporting capability and information sharing under the context of Internet of Things. *Information Technology and Management*, 13(4), 205–216. DOI: 10.1007/s10799-012-0121-1

Li, Y., Su, H., Zhang, J., & Mao, J. (2018). The impact of organizational culture and information technology infrastructure on Internet of Things (IoT) adoption in Chinese firms. *Information & Management*, 55(1), 57–65.

Li, Z., Zhong, R. Y., Tian, Z. G., Dai, H. N., Barenji, A. V., & Huang, G. Q. (2021). Industrial Blockchain: A state-of-the-art Survey. *Robotics and Computer-integrated Manufacturing*, 70, 102124. DOI: 10.1016/j.rcim.2021.102124

Lobov, A., Lopez, F. U., Herrera, V. V., Puttonen, J., & Lastra, J. L. M. (2008). Semantic Web Services framework for manufacturing industries. In Int. Conf. on Rob. and Biomim., pages 2104–2108. IEEE.

Löfving, M., Almström, P., Jarebrant, C., Wadman, B., & Widfeldt, M. (2018). Evaluation of flexible automation for small batch production. *Procedia Manufacturing*, 25, 177–184. DOI: 10.1016/j.promfg.2018.06.072

Loi, F., Sivanathan, A., Gharakheili, H. H., Radford, A., & Sivaraman, V. (2017). Systematically Evaluating Security and Privacy for Consumer IoT Devices. *Proceedings of the 2017 Workshop on Internet of Things Security and Privacy*, 1–6. DOI: 10.1145/3139937.3139938

Lopienski, K. (2023, Aug 14). *Supply Chain Agility: 6 Strategies to Improve Agility.* Retrieved May 08, 2024, from https://www.shipbob.com/blog/supply-chain-agility/ : https://www.shipbob.com/blog/supply-chain-agility/

Lukong, V. T., Ukoba, K., Yoro, K. O., & Jen, T. C. (2022). Annealing temperature variation and its influence on the self-cleaning properties of TiO2 thin films. *Heliyon*, 8(5), e09460. DOI: 10.1016/j.heliyon.2022.e09460 PMID: 35647349

Lundgren, C., Turanoglu Bekar, E., Bärring, M., Stahre, J., Skoogh, A., Johansson, B., & Hedman, R. (2022). Determining the impact of 5G-technology on manufacturing performance using a modified TOPSIS method. *International Journal of Computer Integrated Manufacturing*, 35(1), 69–90. DOI: 10.1080/0951192X.2021.1972465

Luoma, J., & Sivak, M. (2012). Interactions of environmental and safety measures for sustainable road transportation. *European Transport Research Review*, 4(4), 189–199. DOI: 10.1007/s12544-012-0078-5

Luo, S., Min, X., & Zhao, J. (2022). Construction of artificial intelligence application model for supply chain financial risk assessment. *Scientific Programming*, 2022, 1–8. DOI: 10.1155/2022/4194576

Lu, Y. (2019). The Blockchain: State-of-the-art and research challenges. *Journal of Industrial Information Integration*, 15, 80–90. DOI: 10.1016/j.jii.2019.04.002

M. Jeseke, M. Grüner, F. Weiß (2013) "BIG DATA IN LOGISTICS: A DHL perspective on how to move beyond the hype", DHL Customer Solutions & Innovation, 12.

Maass, W., Filler, A. (2006). Towards an infrastructure for semantically annotated physical products. INFORMATIK 2006–Informatik für Menschen–Band 2, Beiträge der 36. Jahrestagung der Gesellschaft für Informatik eV (GI).

Mahmood, A., Abedin, S. F., Sauter, T., Gidlund, M., & Landernäs, K. (2022). Factory 5G: A review of industry-centric features and deployment options. *IEEE Industrial Electronics Magazine*, 16(2), 24–34. DOI: 10.1109/MIE.2022.3149209

Ma, J., Chen, H., Zhang, Y., Guo, H., Ren, Y., Mo, R., & Liu, L. (2020). A digital twin-driven production management system for production workshop. *International Journal of Advanced Manufacturing Technology*, 110(5–6), 1385–1397. DOI: 10.1007/s00170-020-05977-5

Ma, J., Kwak, M., & Kim, H. M. (2014). Demand Trend Mining for Predictive Life Cycle Design. *Journal of Cleaner Production*, 68, 189–199. DOI: 10.1016/j.jclepro.2014.01.026

Malche, T., & Maheshwary, P. (2017). Internet of Things (IoT) for building smart home system. *2017 International Conference on I-SMAC (IoT in Social, Mobile, Analytics and Cloud) (I-SMAC)*, 65–70. DOI: 10.1109/I-SMAC.2017.8058258

Mandal, S. (2015). Exploring the influences of relational competencies on supply chain agility. *International Journal of Applied Engineering Research: IJAER*, 10(19), 40566–40577. Retrieved April 15, 2024, from https://www.scopus.com/record/display.uri?eid=2-s2.0-84945953275&origin=scopusAI

Mann, H., Kumar, V., Kumar, U., & Mann, I. J. (2016, June). Perishable product supply chains: A fifteen year profile. *Change Management*, 16(02), 11–32. DOI: 10.18848/2327-798X/CGP/v16i02/11-32

Manyika, J., Chui, M., Brown, B., Bughin, J., Dobbs, R., Roxburgh, C., & Byers, A. H. (2011). "Big Data: The Next Frontier for Innovation, Competition, and Productivity." Accessed on January 2, 2019. Available at https://www.mckinsey.com/insights/business_technology/ big_data_the_next_frontier_for_innovation.

Manyika, J., Chui, M., Bughin, J., Dobbs, R., Bisson, P., & Marrs, A. (2017). *A future that works: Automation, employment, and productivity*. McKinsey Global Institute.

Mardenli, A., Sackmann, D., & Rhein, S. (2023). Current challenges in agricultural supply chains: an empirical assessment based on expert perspectives. *2023 International Scientific Conference on The Science and Development of Transport - Znanost i razvitak prometa, ZIRP 2023. 73*, pp. 66-76. Zagreb: Elsevier B.V. DOI: 10.1016/j.trpro.2023.11.893

Marine-Roig, E., & Anton Clavé, S. (2015). Tourism analytics with massive user-generated content: A case study of Barcelona. *Journal of Destination Marketing & Management*, 4(3), 162–172. DOI: 10.1016/j.jdmm.2015.06.004

Marrella, A. (2018). Automated Planning for Business Process Management.

Mashayekhy, Y., Babaei, A., Yuan, X.-M., & Xue, A. (2022). Impact of Internet of Things (IoT) on Inventory Management: A Literature Survey. *Logistics (Basel)*, 6(2), 33. DOI: 10.3390/logistics6020033

Massinga Loembé, M., & Nkengasong, J. N. (2021). COVID-19 vaccine access in Africa: Global distribution, vaccine platforms, and challenges ahead. *Immunity*, 54(7), 1353–1362. DOI: 10.1016/j.immuni.2021.06.017 PMID: 34260880

Mathauer, I., & Hofmann, E. (2019). Technology acquisition modes and their impact on the integration success of digital innovations in logistics service providers. *International Journal of Logistics Management*, 30(1), 122–144.

Matt, C., Hess, T., & Benlian, A. (2015). Digitalization of the supply chain – Defining critical drivers for success. *Electronic Markets*, 25(2), 197–223.

Maurya, A. (2013). Environmental Impact of the Flying Scenario: An Approach Towards Sustainable Air Transportation: A Case Study of India. *OIDA International Journal of Sustainable Development, 5*(12), 107-118. (https://papers.ssrn.com/sol3/papers.cfm?abstract_id=2333269)

Mayer-Schönberger, V., & Cukier, K. (2013). *Big data: A revolution that will transform how we live, work, and think.* Houghton Mifflin Harcourt.

Mayr, A., Weigelt, M., Kuhl, A., Grimm, S., Erll, A., Potzel, M., & Franke, J. (2018). Lean 4.0 - A conceptual conjunction of lean management and Industry 4.0. 51st CIRP Conference on Manufacturing Systems. *Procedia CIRP*, 72, 622–628. DOI: 10.1016/j.procir.2018.03.292

McAfee, A. (2011, November). What Every CEO Needs to Know About the Cloud. *Harvard Business Review*, 124–132.

McAfee, A., & Brynjolfsson, E. (2012). Big Data: The Management Revolution. *Harvard Business Review*. PMID: 23074865

McGuinness, D. L. (2004). OWL web ontology language overview. (10), 10.

McKinsey Global Institute. (2024). https://www.mckinsey.com/

Mehmood, R., & Graham, G. (2015). Big data logistics: A health-care transport capacity sharing model. *Procedia Computer Science*, 64, 1107–1114. DOI: 10.1016/j.procs.2015.08.566

Mehrabi, M., Ulsoy, A. G., & Koren, Y. (2000). Reconfigurable manufacturing systems: Key to future manufacturing. *Journal of Intelligent Manufacturing*, 11(4), 403–419. DOI: 10.1023/A:1008930403506

Mejri, I., Bouzid, A., Bacha, S., & Layed, S. B. (2021) Forecasting demand using ARIMA model and LSTM neural network: a case of detergent manufacturing industry. International Conference on Innovation and Intelligence for Informatics, Computing, and Technologies (3ICT), 346-353. DOI: 10.1109/3ICT53449.2021.9581762

Menéndez Molist, A., Kallas, Z., & Guadarrama Fuentes, O. V. (2024, March). Assessing the Downstream and Upstream Preferences of Stakeholders for Sustainability Attributes in the Tomato Value Chain. *Sustainability (Basel)*, 16(06), 2505. Advance online publication. DOI: 10.3390/su16062505

Meng, L. (2021). Using IoT in Supply Chain Risk Management, to Enable Collaboration between Business, Community, and Government. *Smart Cities*, 4(3), 995–1003. DOI: 10.3390/smartcities4030052

Meng, Y., Zhang, W., Zhu, H., & Shen, X. S. (2018). Securing Consumer IoT in the Smart Home: Architecture, Challenges, and Countermeasures. *IEEE Wireless Communications*, 25(6), 53–59. DOI: 10.1109/MWC.2017.1800100

Menon, S., & Jain, K. (2021). Blockchain technology for transparency in agri-food supply chain: Use cases, limitations, and future directions. *IEEE Transactions on Engineering Management*, 71, 106–120. DOI: 10.1109/TEM.2021.3110903

Meyer, J. P., Stanley, D. J., Jackson, T. A., McInnis, K. J., Maltin, E. R., & Sheppard, L. (2017). Affective, continuance, and normative commitment levels across cultures: A meta-analysis. *Journal of Vocational Behavior*, 101, 1–20.

Michel, G., Yves, C., & Béatrice, M. (2017). *Morocco, a logistics hub between Europe and Africa?*https://www.ipemed.coop/adminIpemed/media/fich_article/1536838899_ipemedmaroc-hub-logistiquevf.pdf

Minelli, M., Chambers, M., & Dhiraj, A. (2013). *Big Data*. Big Analytics, Big Data, Big Analytics.

Min, H., Zacharia, Z. G., & Smith, C. D. (2019). Artificial intelligence and its impact on supply chain management. *Journal of Business Logistics*, 40(1), 29–37.

Minor, M., Montani, S., & Recio-García, J. A. (2014). Process-oriented Case-based Reasoning. *Information Systems*, 40, 103–105. DOI: 10.1016/j.is.2013.06.004

Min, S., Zacharia, Z. G., & Smith, C. D. (2019). Defining Supply Chain Management: In the Past, Present, and Future. *Journal of Business Logistics*, 40(1), 44–55. DOI: 10.1111/jbl.12201

Miroslav M, Miloš M, Velimir Š, Božo D, Đorđe L. (2014) Semantic technologies on the mission: preventing corruption in public procurement. Comput Ind. 65(5):878–90. ND.2014.02.003.DOI: <ALIGNMENT.qj></ALIGNMENT>10.1016/J.COMPI

Mishra, N. K., Pande Sharma, P., & Chaudhary, S. K. (2024). xRedefining agile supply chain practices in the disruptive era: a case study identifying vital dimensions and factors. *Journal of Global Operations and Strategic Sourcing*. DOI: 10.1108/JGOSS-04-2023-0031

Mishra, N., & Silakari, S. (2012). Predictive Analytics: A Survey, Trends, Applications, Oppurtunities & Challenges. [IJCSIT]. *International Journal of Computer Science and Information Technologies*, 3(3), 4434–4438.

Mittelstadt, B. D., Allo, P., Taddeo, M., Wachter, S., & Floridi, L. (2016). The ethics of algorithms: Mapping the debate. *Big Data & Society*, 3(2), 2053951716679679. DOI: 10.1177/2053951716679679

Modgil, S., Singh, R. K., & Agrawal, S. (2023, March 03). Developing human capabilities for supply chains: An industry 5.0 perspective. *Annals of Operations Research*, 336(03). Advance online publication. DOI: 10.1007/s10479-023-05245-1

Moeuf, A., Tamayo, S., Lamouri, S., Pellerin, R., & Lelièvre, A. (2016). Strengths and weaknesses of small and medium sized enterprises regarding the implementation of lean manufacturing. *IFAC-PapersOnLine*, 49(12), 71–76. DOI: 10.1016/j.ifacol.2016.07.552

Mofor, L., Nuttall, P., & Newell, A. (2015). Renewable Energy Options for Shipping. *International renewable energy agency*. (https://www.irena.org/-/media/Files/IRENA/Agency/Publication/2015/IRENA_Tech_Brief_RE_for-Shipping_2015.pdf)

Mohajan, H. K. (2019). The First Industrial Revolution: Creation of a New Global Human Era. *Journal of Social Sciences and Humanities*, 5(4), 377–387.

Mohammed, A., Potdar, V., Quaddus, M., & Hui, W. (2023). Blockchain adoption in food supply chains: A systematic literature review on enablers, benefits, and barriers. *IEEE Access : Practical Innovations, Open Solutions*, 11, 14236–14255. DOI: 10.1109/ACCESS.2023.3236666

Monostori, L. (2014). Cyber-physical Production Systems: Roots, Expectations and R&D Challenges. *Procedia CIRP*, 17, 9–13. DOI: 10.1016/j.procir.2014.03.115

Monroe, R. (2019). Developing resilience in supply management. In *Mathematical Modelling of System Resilience* (pp. 01-30). River Publishers. Retrieved May 01, 2024, from https://www.scopus.com/record/display.uri?eid=2-s2.0-85106606876&origin=scopusAI

Montazerolghaem, A., Yaghmaee, M. H., & Leon-Garcia, A. (2020). Green Cloud Multimedia Networking: NFV/SDN Based Energy-Efficient Resource Allocation. *IEEE Transactions on Green Communications and Networking*, 4(3), 873–889. DOI: 10.1109/TGCN.2020.2982821

Montenegro, G., Kushalnagar, N., Hui, J., & Culler, D. (2007). "Transmission of IPv6 packets over IEEE 802.15.4 networks," Internet proposed standard RFC, vol. 4944.

Mukherjee, A. A., Singh, R. K., Mishra, R., & Bag, S. (2022). Application of blockchain technology for sustainability development in agricultural supply chain: Justification framework. *Operations Management Research : Advancing Practice Through Research*, 15(1), 46–61. DOI: 10.1007/s12063-021-00180-5

Mukhopadhyay, S. C., & Suryadevara, N. K. (2014). *Internet of Things: Challenges and Opportunities* (pp. 1–17). DOI: 10.1007/978-3-319-04223-7_1

Müller, G. (2018). Workflow Modeling Assistance by Casebased Reasoning. Springer Fachmedien, Wiesbaden. Ocker, F., Kovalenko, I., Barton, K., Tilbury, D., and VogelHeuser, B. (2019). A Framework for Automatic Initialization of Multi-Agent Production Systems Using Semantic Web Technologies. *IEEE Robotics and Automation Letters*, 4(4), 4330–4337.

Munir, K. (2019). *Cloud computing and big data: technologies, applications and security* (Vol. 49). Springer.

Mutanu, L., Gupta, K., & Gohil, J. (2022). Leveraging IoT solutions for enhanced health information exchange. *Technology in Society*, 68, 101882. DOI: 10.1016/j.techsoc.2022.101882

Nain, G., Pattanaik, K. K., & Sharma, G. K. (2022). Towards edge computing in intelligent manufacturing: Past, present and future. *Journal of Manufacturing Systems*, 62, 588–611. DOI: 10.1016/j.jmsy.2022.01.010

Nandan, A. S., Singh, S., Malik, A., & Kumar, R. (2021). A Green Data Collection & Transmission Method for IoT-Based WSN in Disaster Management. *IEEE Sensors Journal*, 21(22), 25912–25921. DOI: 10.1109/JSEN.2021.3117995

Nassibi, N., Fasihuddin, H., & Hsairi, L. (2022). A Proposed Demand Forecasting Model by Using Machine Learning for Food Industry. *6th International Conference on Future Networks and Distributed Systems, ICFNDS 2022* (pp. 690-694). Tashkent: Association for Computing Machinery. DOI: 10.1145/3584202.3584307

National_Research_Council. (2013). *Transitions to Alternative Vehicles and Fuels*. The National Academies Press. https://doi.org/DOI: 10.17226/18264

Naved, M. (2022). A review of the use of machine learning and artificial intelligence in various sectors. *Multimedia Research*, 5(4), 26–31. DOI: 10.46253/j.mr.v5i4.a3

Neisse, R., Steri, G., & Nai-Fovino, I. (2017, August). A blockchain-based approach for data accountability and provenance tracking. In *Proceedings of the 12th international conference on availability, reliability and security* (pp. 1-10). DOI: 10.1145/3098954.3098958

Nemati, A., Nadeau, S., & Ateme-Nguema, B. (2019). Lean mining, productivity and occupational health and safety: An expert-elicitation study. *American Journal of Industrial and Business Management*, 9(11), 2034–2049.

Newell, A., Nuttall, P. M., & Holland, E. (2015). Sustainable sea transport for the Pacific Islands: the obvious way forward. (https://sustainabledevelopment.un.org/content/documents/591456-AlisonNewell-Sustainable%20sea%20transport%20for%20the%20Pacific.pdf)

Nguyen, T. H., & Vu, H. L. (2020). Hyper-personalization in the digital age: Trends and challenges. *Journal of Retailing and Consumer Services*, 55, 102077.

Nguyen, T. N., Zeadally, S., & Vuduthala, A. B. (2022). Cyber-Physical Cloud Manufacturing Systems With Digital Twins. *IEEE Internet Computing*, 26(3), 15–21. DOI: 10.1109/MIC.2021.3058921

Nguyen, T., Zhou, L., Spiegler, V., Ieromonachou, P., & Lin, Y. (2017). Big data analytics in supply chain management: A state-of-the-art literature review. *Computers & Operations Research*. Advance online publication. DOI: 10.1016/j.cor.2017.07.004

Nikiforova, G. I. (2022). Research of informational interaction between railway and sea transport in logistic chains of cargo delivery. *Proceedings of Petersburg Transport University*, 19(1), 82–89. DOI: 10.20295/1815-588X-2022-19-1-82-89

Ning, L., & Yao, D. (2023). The Impact of Digital Transformation on Supply Chain Capabilities and Competitive Performance. *Sustainability (Basel)*, 15(13), 10107. DOI: 10.3390/su151310107

Normann, R., & Ramirez, R. (1993). From value chain to value constellation: Designing interactive strategy. *Harvard Business Review*, 71(4), 65–77. PMID: 10127040

Noussan, M., Hafner, M., & Tagliapietra, S. (2020). *The future of transport between digitalization and decarbonization: trends, strategies and effects on energy consumption*. Springer Nature., DOI: 10.1007/978-3-030-37966-7

Novijanti, E., Siagian, H., & Tarigan, Z. J. (2023). The effect of supply chain collaboration on supply chain performance through production technology, new product development and product knowledge. *Uncertain Supply Chain Management*, 11(02), 637–650. DOI: 10.5267/j.uscm.2023.2.001

Nuttall, P., Newell, A., Prasad, B., Veitayaki, J., & Holland, E. (2014). A review of sustainable sea-transport for Oceania: Providing context for renewable energy shipping for the Pacific. *Marine Policy*, 43, 283–287. https://doi.org/https://doi.org/10.1016/j.marpol.2013.06.009. DOI: 10.1016/j.marpol.2013.06.009

O'Connell, E., Moore, D., & Newe, T. (2020). Challenges Associated with Implementing 5G in Manufacturing. *Telecom*, 1(1), 48–67. DOI: 10.3390/telecom1010005

Oberoi, S., Mishra, P., Gupta, V. K., Patnaik, S., Garg, A., & Kaur, R. (2021). Vaccine wastage at primary, secondary, and tertiary level of healthcare system—A study from Northern India. *Journal of Family Medicine and Primary Care*, 10(2), 877–882. DOI: 10.4103/jfmpc.jfmpc_1442_20 PMID: 34041092

Obitko, M. V. (2010). Applications of semantics in manufacturing systems. *Informatica (Vilnius)*, 34, 315–330.

Offer, G. J., Contestabile, M., Howey, D. A., Clague, R., & Brandon, N. P. (2011). Techno-economic and behavioural analysis of battery electric, hydrogen fuel cell and hybrid vehicles in a future sustainable road transport system in the UK. *Energy Policy*, 39(4), 1939–1950. https://doi.org/https://doi.org/10.1016/j.enpol.2011.01.006. DOI: 10.1016/j.enpol.2011.01.006

Ok, K., Coskun, V., Aydin, M. N., & Ozdenizci, B. (2010). Current benefits and future directions of NFC services. *2010 International Conference on Education and Management Technology*, 334–338. DOI: 10.1109/ICEMT.2010.5657642

Okoli, C. (2015). A Guide to Conducting a Standalone Systematic Literature Review. *Communications of the Association for Information Systems*, 37. Advance online publication. DOI: 10.17705/1CAIS.03743

Oncioiu, I., Bunget, O., Turkes, M., Capusneanu, S., Topor, D., Tama , A., Rako , I.-S., & Hint, M. (2019). The impact of big data analytics on company performance in supply chain management. *Sustainability (Basel)*, 11(18), 4864. DOI: 10.3390/su11184864

Ongel, B., Tanyer, A. M., & Dikmen, I. (2023). A network-based model for the assessment of success in PPP healthcare projects. *International Journal of Construction Management*, 0(0), 1–13. DOI: 10.1080/15623599.2023.2239438

Onori, M. a. (2009). *Evolvable systems: An approach to Self-X Production*. Digital Enterprise Technology.

Opeyemi, A., & Dela Cruz, M. (2018). Green Sustainability Development for Industry Internet of Things in Railway Transportation Industry. *International Journal of Trend in Scientific Research and Development*, (Special Issue), 203–208. DOI: 10.31142/ijtsrd19140

Optimization, G. "The Power of Analytics," accessed September 8, 2019. http://www.gurobi.com/resources/prescriptive-analytics

Orieno, O. H., Ndubuisi, N. L., Ilojianya, V. I., Biu, P. W., & Odonkor, B. (2024). The Future Of Autonomous Vehicles In The US Urban Landscape: A Review: Analyzing Implications For Traffic, Urban Planning, And The Environment. *Engineering Science & Technology Journal*, 5(1), 43–64. DOI: 10.51594/estj.v5i1.721

Osińska, M., & Zalewski, W. (2020). Determinants of Using Telematics Systems in Road Transport Companies. *European Research Studies*, 28(2), 474–487. DOI: 10.35808/ersj/1604

Osterwalder, A., & Pigneur, Y. (2010). *Business model generation: a handbook for visionaries, game changers, and challengers* (Vol. 1). John Wiley & Sons.

Oyewole, A. T., Okoye, C. C., Ofodile, O. C., & Ejairu, E. (2024). Reviewing predictive analytics in supply chain management: Applications and benefits. *World Journal of Advanced Research and Reviews*, 21(3), 568–574. DOI: 10.30574/wjarr.2024.21.3.0673

Pal, K. (2017b). "A Semantic Web Service Architecture for Supply Chain Management", In 8th International Conference on Ambient Systems, Networks and Technologies (ANT 2017), 999-1004, Procedia Computer Science 109C. DOI: 10.1016/j.procs.2017.05.442

Pal, K. (2018a). "Ontology-Based Web Service Architecture for Retail Supply Chain Management", In 9th International Conference on Ambient Systems, Networks and Technologies (ANT 2018), 985-990, Procedia Computer Science 130. DOI: 10.1016/j.procs.2018.04.101

Pal, K. (2018b). *"A Big Data Framework for Decision Making in Supply Chain"*, In M. V Kumar, G. D. Putnik, J. Javakrishna, V. M. Pillai, L. Varela (Edited); IGI Publication, September 2018, USA, Chapter 1, IGI Global Publication, Hershey PA, USA.

Pal, K. (2020). "Information Sharing for Manufacturing Supply Chain Management Based on Blockchain Technology", in Dr Idongesit Williams (Eds.), Cross-Industry Use of Blockchain Technology and Opportunities for the Future, Chapter 1, May, IGI Global Publication, Hershey PA, USA. DOI: 10.4018/978-1-7998-3632-2.ch001

Pal, K., & Ul-Haque, A. (2000). "*Internet of Things and Blockchain Technology in Apparel Manufacturing Supply Chain Data Management*", In the proceeding of 11th International Conference on Ambient Systems, Networks and Technologies (ANT-2020), Procedia Computer Science, pp. 450- 457, April 6-9, Warsaw, Poland.

Pal, K., & Ul-Haque, A. (2023). "*Internet of Things Impact on Supply Chain Management*", In the proceeding of 14th International Conference on Ambient Systems, Networks and Technologies (ANT-2023), Procedia Computer Science, 478-485. DOI: 10.1016/j.procs.2023.03.061

Pal, K., Ul-Haque, A., & Shakshuki, E. (2024). "*Supply Chain Transport Management, Use of Electric Vehicles, Review of Security and Privacy for Cyber-Physical Transportation Ecosystem and Related solutions*", In the proceeding of 15th International Conference on Ambient Systems, Networks and Technologies (ANT-2020), Procedia Computer Science, 135-142, April 23-25, Hasselt, Belgium. DOI: 10.1016/j.procs.2024.06.008

Pal, A., & Kant, K. (2018, February). IoT-Based Sensing and Communications Infrastructure for the Fresh Food Supply Chain. *Computer*, 51(02), 76–80. DOI: 10.1109/MC.2018.1451665

Pal, K. (2017a). Supply Chain Coordination Based on Web Services. In Chan, H. K., Subramanian, N., & Abdulrahman, M. D. (Eds.), *Supply Chain Management in the Big Data Era* (pp. 137–171). IGI Global Publication. DOI: 10.4018/978-1-5225-0956-1.ch009

Pal, K., & Karakostas, B. (2014). A Multi Agent-Based Service Framework for Supply Chain Management, In the proceeding of International Conference on Ambient Systems, Networks and Technology. *Procedia Computer Science*, 32, 53–60. DOI: 10.1016/j.procs.2014.05.397

Pambudi, N. A., Sarifudin, A., Gandidi, I. M., & Romadhon, R. (2022a). Vaccine cold chain management and cold storage technology to address the challenges of vaccination programs. *Energy Reports*, 8, 955–972. DOI: 10.1016/j.egyr.2021.12.039

Pandey, A., Sah, P., Moghadas, S. M., Mandal, S., Banerjee, S., Hotez, P. J., & Galvani, A. P. (2021). Challenges facing COVID-19 vaccination in India: Lessons from the initial vaccine rollout. *Journal of Global Health*, 11, 1–5. DOI: 10.7189/jogh.11.03083 PMID: 34221355

Pang, J., Zhang, N., Xiao, Q., Qi, F., & Xue, X. (2021). A New Intelligent and Data-Driven Product Quality Control System of Industrial Valve Manufacturing Process in CPS. *Computer Communications*, 175, 25–34. DOI: 10.1016/j.comcom.2021.04.022

Pan, Z., Polden, J., Larkin, N., Van Duin, S., & Norrish, J. (2012). Recent progress on programming methods for industrial robots. *Robotics and Computer-integrated Manufacturing*, 28(2), 87–94. DOI: 10.1016/j.rcim.2011.08.004

Papadopoulos, T. Gunasekaran, A. Dubey, R. Altay, N. Childe, S. J. and Fosso-Wamba, S. (2017) "The role of Big Data in explaining disaster resilience in supply chains for sustainability," Journal of Cleaner Production, pp. 142, 11081118.

Parast, M. M. (2022, August). Toward a contingency perspective of organizational and supply chain resilience. *International Journal of Production Economics*, 250, 108667. Advance online publication. DOI: 10.1016/j.ijpe.2022.108667

Park, H., Easwaran, A., & Andalam, S. (2019). Challenges in Digital Twin Development for Cyber-Physical Production Systems. In R. Chamberlain, W. Taha, & M. Törngren (Eds.), *Cyber Physical Systems. Model-Based Design* (Vol. 11615, pp. 28–48). Springer International Publishing. DOI: 10.1007/978-3-030-23703-5_2

Parker, G. G., & Van Alstyne, M. W. (2019). Innovation, ecosystems, and platforms: A multilevel theory of digital technology. *Journal of Management Information Systems*, 36(2), 354–389.

Park, H., & Park, S. (2024). Emerging Trends and Challenges in IoT Networks. *Electronics (Basel)*, 13(3), 513. DOI: 10.3390/electronics13030513

Patel, K. K., & Patel, S. M. (2016). Internet of Things-IOT: Definition, Characteristics, Architecture, Enabling Technologies, Application & Future Challenges. *International Journal of Engineering Science and Computing,* 6122–6131.

Patrick, W., Anselemo, P., Ronoh, R., & Mbugua, P. (2022). Impact of predictive analytics of big data in supply chain management on decision-making. International Journal of Scientific Research in Computer Science Engineering and Information Technology, 225-238. DOI: 10.32628/CSEIT228423

Pawar, P., & Trivedi, A. (2019). Device-to-Device Communication Based IoT System: Benefits and Challenges. *IETE Technical Review*, 36(4), 362–374. DOI: 10.1080/02564602.2018.1476191

Pearson, M. (2011b). Predictive Analytics: Looking forward to better supply chain decisions. *Logistics Management*, 50(9), 22.

Pereira, E. T., & Shafique, M. N. (2023). The Implementation of Artificial Intelligence in Supply Chain. *6th International Conference on Innovative Computing and Communication, ICICC 2023.* 703, pp. 497-504. Delhi: Springer Science and Business Media Deutschland GmbH. DOI: 10.1007/978-981-99-3315-0_37

Pereira, M. A., Ferreira, D. C., & Marques, R. C. (2021). A critical look at the Portuguese public–private partnerships in healthcare. *The International Journal of Health Planning and Management*, 36(2), 302–315. DOI: 10.1002/hpm.3084 PMID: 33015900

Perera, S., Nanayakkara, S., Rodrigo, M. N. N., Senaratne, S., & Weinand, R. (2020). Blockchain technology: Is it hype or real in the construction industry? *Journal of Industrial Information Integration*, 17, 100125. DOI: 10.1016/j.jii.2020.100125

Pham, T. N., Hoang, M. T. T., Tran, Y. N. N., & Phan, B. N. (2024). Combining digitalization and sustainability: Unveiling the relationship of digital maturity degree, sustainable supply chain management practices, and performance. *International Journal of Productivity and Performance Management*, 73(8), 2508–2529. DOI: 10.1108/IJPPM-06-2023-0311

Phuyal, S., Bista, D., & Bista, R. (2020). Challenges, Opportunities and Future Directions of Smart Manufacturing: A State of Art Review. *Sustainable Futures : An Applied Journal of Technology, Environment and Society*, 2, 100023. DOI: 10.1016/j.sftr.2020.100023

Pine, B. J., & Gilmore, J. H. (1998). Welcome to the experience economy. *Harvard Business Review*, 76(4), 97–105. PMID: 10181589

Placek, M. (2023). *Autonomous vehicles worldwide - statistics & facts*. Statista.

Plotkin, S., Robinson, J. M., Cunningham, G., Iqbal, R., & Larsen, S. (2017). The complexity and cost of vaccine manufacturing – An overview. *Vaccine*, 35(33), 4064–4071. DOI: 10.1016/j.vaccine.2017.06.003 PMID: 28647170

Pólkowski, Z., Nycz-Łukaszewska, M., & Borah, S. (2018). Blockchain implementation in Small and Medium Enterprises. *Scientific Bulletin–Economic Sciences, 17*(3, special).

Porter, M. E., & Millar, V. E. (1985). How information gives you a competitive advantage. *Harvard Business Review*, 63(4), 149–160.

Pradeepa, K., & Praveen, M. (2020). A Survey on Routing Protocols With Security in Internet of Things. *Solid State Technology*, 63(4).

Prahalad, C. K., & Ramaswamy, V. (2004). Co-creation experiences: The next practice in value creation. *Journal of Interactive Marketing*, 18(3), 5–14. DOI: 10.1002/dir.20015

Prashar, D., Jha, N., Jha, S., Lee, Y., & Joshi, G. P. (2020). Blockchain-based traceability and visibility for agricultural products: A decentralized way of ensuring food safety in india. *Sustainability (Basel)*, 12(8), 3497. DOI: 10.3390/su12083497

Preacher, K. J., & Hayes, A. F. (2008). Asymptotic and resampling strategies for assessing and comparing indirect effects in structural equation models. *Psychological Methods*, 13(3), 181.

Prinz, C., Kreggenfeld, N., & Kuhlenkotter, B. (2018). Lean meets Industrie 4.0 – a practical approach to interlink the method world and cyber-physical world. 8th Conference on Learning Factories 2018 - Advanced Engineering Education & Training for Manufacturing Innovation. *Procedia Manufacturing*, 23, 21–26. DOI: 10.1016/j.promfg.2018.03.155

Provost, F., & Fawcett, T. (2013). *Data science for business: What you need to know about data mining and data-analytic thinking*. O'Reilly Media, Inc.

Putri, A. F., Fauzi, R., Hendayani, D., & Iskamto, D. (2023). The Role of Supply Chain Capability as Mediation Between Digitalization and Digital Connectivity on Operational Performance. Journal of World Science.

Puttonen, J., Lobov, A., & Lastra, J. L. M. (2013). Semantics-Based Composition of Factory Automation Processes Encapsulated by Web Services. *IEEE Transactions on Industrial Informatics*, 9(4), 2349–2359. DOI: 10.1109/TII.2012.2220554

Puttonen, J., Lobov, A., Soto, M. A. C., & Lastra, J. L. M. (2010). A Semantic Web Services-based approach for production systems control. *Advanced Engineering Informatics*, 24(3), 285–299. DOI: 10.1016/j.aei.2010.05.012

Qi, Q., & Tao, F. (2019). A Smart Manufacturing Service System Based on Edge Computing, Fog Computing, and Cloud Computing. *IEEE Access : Practical Innovations, Open Solutions*, 7, 86769–86777. DOI: 10.1109/ACCESS.2019.2923610

Rachinger, M., Riedel, R., & Davies, J. (2019). The social construction of digitalization in logistics and supply chain management. *Journal of Business Logistics*, 40(2), 223–238.

Radwan, N. F., Abu-Sheasha, G. A., Bedwani, R. N., & Yassine, O. G. (2021). Vaccine wastage and cost saving after multi-dose vial policy implementation in Egypt: A success story. *Vaccine*, 39(51), 7457–7463. DOI: 10.1016/j.vaccine.2021.10.067 PMID: 34772545

Ragowsky, A., Bearden, N., & Licker, P. (2021). Factors influencing IT investments in digital transformation: A study of US businesses. *Journal of Information Technology Management*, 32(4), 1–16.

Rahatulain, A. a. (2015). Towards a Model-Based Development Methodology for Evolvable Production Systems - A Domain-Specific Modeling Approach. *Proceedings of the Second International Afro-European Conference for Industrial Advancement AECIA 2015.: Springer International Publishing,427,83–92.* Warsaw, Poland.

Rahimi, I., Gandomi, A. H., Fong, S. J., & Ulku, M. A. (2021) *Big Data Analytics in Supply Chain Management: Theory and Applications*. CRS Press: Taylor and Francis Group, London, New York. First edition.

Rajesh, R., & Ravi, V. (2015). Supplier selection in resilient supply chains: A grey relational analysis approach. *Journal of Cleaner Production*, 86, 343–359. DOI: 10.1016/j.jclepro.2014.08.054

Rao, S. K., & Prasad, R. (2018). Impact of 5G technologies on industry 4.0. *Wireless Personal Communications*, 100(1), 145–159. DOI: 10.1007/s11277-018-5615-7

Rastegar, M., Tavana, M., Meraj, A., & Mina, H. (2021). An inventory-location optimization model for equitable influenza vaccine distribution in developing countries during the COVID-19 pandemic. *Vaccine*, 39(3), 495–504. DOI: 10.1016/j.vaccine.2020.12.022 PMID: 33342632

Rastogi, H. (2022, May 5). *IoT in Tesla: Applications, Benefits and Potential Risks*. Analytic Steps. https://analyticssteps.com/blogs/iot-tesla-applications-benefits-and-potential-risks

Ray, P. P., Mukherjee, M., & Shu, L. (2017). Internet of Things for Disaster Management: State-of-the-Art and Prospects. *IEEE Access : Practical Innovations, Open Solutions*, 5, 18818–18835. DOI: 10.1109/ACCESS.2017.2752174

Reddy, A. M. (2021). A Review on Iot Enabling Technologies and Back-End Data-Sharing Model. *Journal of Electronics. Computer Networking and Applied Mathematics*, 11(11), 41–47. DOI: 10.55529/jecnam11.41.47

Rejeb, A., Simske, S., Rejeb, K., Treiblmaier, H., & Zailani, S. (2020). Internet of Things research in supply chain management and logistics: A bibliometric analysis. *Internet of Things : Engineering Cyber Physical Human Systems*, 12, 100318. DOI: 10.1016/j.iot.2020.100318

Rennings, K. (2014). Introduction: Global diffusion of environmental innovations. *Environmental Innovation and Societal Transitions*, 10, 1–3. https://doi.org/https://doi.org/10.1016/j.eist.2013.12.005. DOI: 10.1016/j.eist.2013.12.005

Ren, S., Zhang, Y., Liu, Y., Sakao, T., Huisingh, D., & Almeida, C. M. (2019). A comprehensive review of big data analytics throughout product lifecycle to support sustainable smart manufacturing: A framework, challenges and future research directions. *Journal of Cleaner Production*, 210, 1343–1365. DOI: 10.1016/j.jclepro.2018.11.025

Research, G. E. (2021). *GE Research and the US Department of Defense Partner on 5G Initiative to Create Smart Warehouses*. https://www.ge.com/research/newsroom/ge-research-and-us-department-defense-partner-5g-initiative-create-smart-warehouses

Retailer, I. (2023, Sep 21). *India's Changing Food Palette: Embracing Plant-Based Meat*. Retrieved May 08, 2024, from https://www.indianretailer.com: https://www.indianretailer.com/article/retail-business/retail/indias-changing-food-palette-embracing-plant-based-meat

Riad, M., Elgammal, A., & Elzanfaly, D. (2019). *Efficient Production Monitoring on the Basis of Domain Ontologies by Utilizing IoT*. 93–100. DOI: 10.15439/2019F228

Rialti, R., Marzi, G., Ciappei, C., & Busso, D. (2019). Big data and dynamic capabilities: A bibliometric analysis and systematic literature review. *Management Decision*, 57(8), 2052–2068. DOI: 10.1108/MD-07-2018-0821

Ribeiro, A., Silva, A., & Rodrigues, A. (2015). Data modeling and data analytics : A Survey from a big data perspective. *Journal of Software Engineering and Applications*, 8(December), 617–634. DOI: 10.4236/jsea.2015.812058

Richard, O. C., Murthi, B. P. S., & Ismail, K. (2019). Corporate social responsibility (CSR) and firm performance: Human resource management perspective. *Human Resource Management*, 58(6), 539–548.

Rifkin, S. B. (2014). Examining the links between community participation and health outcomes: A review of the literature. *Health Policy and Planning*, 29(suppl_2), ii98–ii106. DOI: 10.1093/heapol/czu076 PMID: 25274645

Risius, M., & Spohrer, K. (2017). A blockchain research framework: What we (don't) know, where we go from here, and how we will get there. *Business & Information Systems Engineering*, 59(6), 385–409. DOI: 10.1007/s12599-017-0506-0

Rogers, E. M. (2003). *Diffusion of innovations* (5th ed.). Free Press.

Rojko, A. (2017). Industry 4.0 Concept: Background and Overview. [IJIM]. *International Journal of Interactive Mobile Technologies*, 11(5), 77. DOI: 10.3991/ijim.v11i5.7072

Romig, T. (2021). A collaborative approach to business continuity and organisational resilience when dealing with a major crisis, such as covid-19. *Journal of Airport Management*, 15(03), 226–234. Retrieved May 07, 2024, from https://www.scopus.com/record/display.uri?eid=2-s2.0-85113147420&origin=scopusAI. DOI: 10.69554/XGNV5295

Rosa, S. S., Prazeres, D. M. F., Azevedo, A. M., & Marques, M. P. C. (2021). mRNA vaccines manufacturing: Challenges and bottlenecks. *Vaccine*, 39(16), 2190–2200. DOI: 10.1016/j.vaccine.2021.03.038 PMID: 33771389

Rose, D. (2019). Factory of the Future Shows Mobile Model for Small Manufacturers. https://iot-automotive.news/vodafone-e-go-smart-5g-factory

Rose, K., Eldridge, S., & Chapin, L. (2015). The internet of things: An overview. [ISOC]. *The Internet Society*, 80(15), 1–53.

Rosin, F. (2022), Vers le Lean 4.0: Renforcement du processus décisionnel par les technologies de l'Industrie 4.0, thèse de doctorat, Hal open sciences.

Rosin, F., Forget, P., Lamouri, S., & Pellerin, R. (2019), Industrie 4.0 et Lean: Hiérarchie, amélioration ou complémentarité? Conference: CIGI QUALITA 2019, "Le numérique et l'intelligence industrielle: défis et opportunités" Montréal Canada.

Roßmann, B., Canzaniello, A., von der Gracht, H., & Hartmann, E. (2018). The future and social impact of big data analytics in supply chain management: Results from a Delphi study. *Technological Forecasting and Social Change*, 130, 135–149. DOI: 10.1016/j.techfore.2017.10.005

Rosso, R. S. U.Jr, Tsuzuki, M. D. S. G., Barari, A., & Macchi, M. (2022). Transition towards Smart Factories. *International Journal of Computer Integrated Manufacturing*, 35(4–5), 341–344. DOI: 10.1080/0951192X.2022.2080451

Rostami-Tabar, B., Babai, M. Z., Ali, M., & Boylan, J. E. (2019). The impact of temporal aggregation on supply chains with ARMA(1,1) demand processes. *European Journal of Operational Research*, 273(3), 920–932. DOI: 10.1016/j.ejor.2018.09.010

Routroy, S., & Shankar, A. (2015). Performance analysis of agile supply chain. *International Journal of Manufacturing Technology and Management*, 29(3-4), 180–210. DOI: 10.1504/IJMTM.2015.069255

Rozados, I. V., & Tjahjono, B. (2014). Big data analytics in supply chain management: trends and related research. In: *6th International Conference on Operations and Supply Chain Management*, pp. 2013–2014.

Rucińska, D., & Kędzior-Laskowska, M. (2019). Sustainable transport development and the quality of road freight transport. *Transport Economics and Logistics*, 76, 33–47. DOI: 10.26881/etil.2018.76.03

Ruessmann, M., Lorenz, M., Gerbert, P., Waldner, M., Justus, J., Engel, P., Harnisch M., (2015) Industry 4.0: The Future of Productivity and Growth in Manufacturing Industries. Boston Consulting Group, avril.

Rushton, A., Croucher, P., & Baker, P. (2017). *The handbook of logistics and distribution management* (6th ed.). Kogan Page Publishers.

Rußmann, M., Lorenz, M., Gerbert, P., Waldner, M., Justus, J., Engel, P., & Harnisch, M. (2015). *Industry 4.0: The Future of Productivity and Growth in Manufacturing Industries*. Boston Consulting Group.

Russomanno, D. J., Kothari, C. R., & Thomas, O. A. (2005). "Building a Sensor Ontology: A Practical Approach Leveraging ISO and OGC Models", in the 2005 International Conference on Artificial Intelligence, 637-643.

Rust, R. T., Kannan, P. K., & Peng, X. (2018). *The customer economy: Why customer lifetime value is the key to unlocking great business performance*. Routledge.

Ruta, M., Colucci, S., Scioscia, F., Di Sciascio, E., & Donini, F. M. (2011). Finding commonalities in RFID semantic streams. *Procedia Computer Science*, 5, 857–864. DOI: 10.1016/j.procs.2011.07.118

Rüttimann, B. G., & Stöckli, M. T. (2016). Lean and Industry 4.0 - Twins, Partners, or Contenders? A Due Clarification Regarding the Supposed Clash of Two Production Systems. *Journal of Service Science and Management*, 9(6), 485–500. DOI: 10.4236/jssm.2016.96051

Saberi, S., Kouhizadeh, M., Sarkis, J., & Shen, L. (2019). Blockchain technology and its relationships to sustainable supply chain management. *International Journal of Production Research*, 57(7), 2117–2135. DOI: 10.1080/00207543.2018.1533261

Sabherwal, R., & Sabherwal, S. (2015). The impact of top management support for information systems on information systems planning effectiveness. *Information & Management*, 52(3), 351–364.

Sabri, E. (2015). Optimization of supply chain management in contemporary organizations. In *Optimization of Supply Chain Management in Contemporary Organizations* (pp. 01-337). IGI Global. DOI: 10.4018/978-1-4666-8228-3

Sabri, E., & Verma, L. (2015). Mastering change management for successful supply chain transformation. In *Optimization of Supply Chain Management in Contemporary Organizations* (pp. 117–147). IGI Global., DOI: 10.4018/978-1-4666-8228-3.ch005

Saeid, S. D., Iman, R. V. and Farzaneh, M. M. (2020) Big Data Analytics and its Applications in Supply Chain Management. New Trends in the use of Artificial Intelligence for the Industry 4.0.

Sakib, S. (2021). Usage of data analytics in improving sourcing of supply chain inputs. DOI: 10.20944/preprints202110.0103.v1

Salam, A. (2020). *Internet of Things for Sustainability: Perspectives in Privacy.* Cybersecurity, and Future Trends., DOI: 10.1007/978-3-030-35291-2_10

Salvi, B. L., & Subramanian, K. A. (2015). Sustainable development of road transportation sector using hydrogen energy system. *Renewable & Sustainable Energy Reviews*, 51, 1132–1155. https://doi.org/https://doi.org/10.1016/j.rser.2015.07.030. DOI: 10.1016/j.rser.2015.07.030

Sanders, N. R. (2016). How to use big data to drive your supply chain. *California Management Review*, 58(3), 26–48. DOI: 10.1525/cmr.2016.58.3.26

Santos, A. F., Gaspar, P. D., & de Souza, H. J. L. (2021). Refrigeration of COVID-19 vaccines: Ideal storage characteristics, energy efficiency and environmental impacts of various vaccine options. *Energies*, 14(7), 1849. Advance online publication. DOI: 10.3390/en14071849

Santos, G., Behrendt, H., & Teytelboym, A. (2010). Part II: Policy instruments for sustainable road transport. *Research in Transportation Economics*, 28(1), 46–91. https://doi.org/https://doi.org/10.1016/j.retrec.2010.03.002. DOI: 10.1016/j.retrec.2010.03.002

Sardjono, W., Arum, I. R. M., Rahmasari, A., & Lusia, E. (2023). Impact of Track and Trace (T&T) in Industrial Revolution 4.0 of the Pharmaceutical Industry (Pharma 4.0). *E3S Web of Conferences, 388*, 03014. DOI: 10.1051/e3sconf/202338803014

Sarmah, S. S. (2018). Understanding Blockchain Technology. *Computing in Science & Engineering*, 8(2), 23–29.

SAS Institute. What is big data. http://www.sas.com/en_us/insights/big-data/what-is-big-data. html

Sato, R., Thompson, A., Sani, I., Metiboba, L., Giwa, A., Femi-Ojo, O., & Odezugo, V. (2021). Effect of Vaccine Direct Delivery (VDD) on vaccine stockouts and number of vaccinations: Case study from Bauchi State, Nigeria. *Vaccine*, 39(9), 1445–1451. DOI: 10.1016/j.vaccine.2021.01.037 PMID: 33541796

Saurabh, S., & Dey, K. (2021). Blockchain technology adoption, architecture, and sustainable agri-food supply chains. *Journal of Cleaner Production*, 284, 124731. DOI: 10.1016/j.jclepro.2020.124731

Schoenherr, T., & Speier-Pero, C. (2015). Data science, predictive analytics, and big data in supply chain management: Current state and future potential. *Journal of Business Logistics*, 36(1), 120–132. DOI: 10.1111/jbl.12082

-Schwab, K. (2018). The Impact of Digital Transformation on Business Models: Evidence from a Global Survey.

Schwartz, J. L. (2020). Equitable global access to coronavirus disease 2019 vaccines. In *The BMJ* (Vol. 371). BMJ Publishing Group., DOI: 10.1136/bmj.m4735

Sebastian, I. M., Morris, T., Burgess, S., & Daugherty, P. R. (2017). Making digital supply chain transformation a reality: Key challenges and a roadmap for success. *Supply Chain Management*, 22(3), 399–420.

Seiger, R., Huber, S., & Schlegel, T. (2018). Toward an execution system for self-healing workflows in cyber-physical systems. *Software & Systems Modeling*, 17(2), 551–572. DOI: 10.1007/s10270-016-0551-z

Selvaraj, S., & Sundaravaradhan, S. (2020). Challenges and opportunities in IoT healthcare systems: A systematic review. *SN Applied Sciences*, 2(1), 139. DOI: 10.1007/s42452-019-1925-y

Seuring, S., & Müller, M. (2008). From a literature review to a conceptual framework for sustainable supply chain management. *Journal of Cleaner Production*, 16(15), 1699–1710. DOI: 10.1016/j.jclepro.2008.04.020

Seyedan, S., & Mafakheri, F. (2020). Predictive big data analytics for supply chain demand forecasting: Methods, applications, and research opportunities. *Journal of Big Data*, 7(1), 53. Advance online publication. DOI: 10.1186/s40537-020-00329-2

Shah, M. A., & Uddin, F. (2023). Leveraging blockchain technology in the construction industry. In *Building Secure Business Models Through Blockchain Technology: Tactics, Methods, Limitations, and Performance* (pp. 50-65). IGI Global. DOI: 10.4018/978-1-6684-7808-0.ch004

Shah, S., Chen, S., & Naghi Ganj, E. (2024). An Investigative Study to Examine the Impact of Digitalisation on Manufacturing Supply Chains. Engineering World.

Shahbazi, Z., & Byun, Y.-C. (2021). Smart Manufacturing Real-Time Analysis Based on Blockchain and Machine Learning Approaches. *Applied Sciences (Basel, Switzerland)*, 11(8), 3535. DOI: 10.3390/app11083535

Shah, K., Patel, N., Thakkar, J., & Patel, C. (2022). Exploring applications of blockchain technology for Industry 4.0. *Materials Today: Proceedings*, 62, 7238–7242. DOI: 10.1016/j.matpr.2022.03.681

Shah, M. A. (2016). Accelerating public private partnership in agricultural storage infrastructure in India. *Journal of Commerce and Management Thought*, 7(1), 9–25. DOI: 10.5958/0976-478X.2016.00001.X

Shah, S. A., Seker, D. Z., Hameed, S., & Draheim, D. (2019). The Rising Role of Big Data Analytics and IoT in Disaster Management: Recent Advances, Taxonomy and Prospects. *IEEE Access : Practical Innovations, Open Solutions*, 7, 54595–54614. DOI: 10.1109/ACCESS.2019.2913340

Shahzad, A., Zhang, K., & Gherbi, A. (2020). Intuitive development to examine collaborative iot supply chain system underlying privacy and security levels and perspective powering through proactive blockchain. *Sensors (Basel)*, 20(13), 3760. DOI: 10.3390/s20133760 PMID: 32635589

Shamsuddoha, M., & Nasir, T. (2023). Principal Lessons Learned from COVID-19: Prescriptive and Long-Lasting Strategies for Sustainable Supply Chain Improvement. *Understanding Complex Systems*, F1776, 81–105. DOI: 10.1007/978-3-031-45229-1_5

Shan Z, Zhu Q. (2015) Camera location for real-time traffic state estimation in urban road network using big GPS data. Neurocomputing. 169:134–43. https://doi .org/ M.2014.11.093.DOI: 10.1016/J.NEUCO

Shangguan, D., Chen, L., & Ding, J. (2019). A Hierarchical Digital Twin Model Framework for Dynamic Cyber-Physical System Design. *Proceedings of the 5th International Conference on Mechatronics and Robotics Engineering*, 123–129. DOI: 10.1145/3314493.3314504

Shapiro, C., & Varian, H. R. (1999). The art of standards wars. *California Management Review*, 41(2), 8–32. DOI: 10.2307/41165984

Shet, A., Dhaliwal, B., Banerjee, P., Carr, K., Deluca, A., Britto, C., Seth, R., Parekh, B., Basavaraj, G. V., Shastri, D., & Gupta, P. (2021). COVID-19-related disruptions to routine vaccination services in India: A survey of paediatric providers. *BMJ Paediatrics Open*, 5(1), 2021.01.25.21250040. Advance online publication. DOI: 10.1136/bmjpo-2021-001060 PMID: 34192200

Sial, Q. A., Safder, U., Iqbal, S., & Ali, R. B. (2024). Advancement in Supercapacitors for IoT Applications by Using Machine Learning: Current Trends and Future Technology. *Sustainability (Basel)*, 16(4), 1516. DOI: 10.3390/su16041516

Siegel, E. (2013). Predictive Analytics: The Power to Predict Who Will Click, Buy, Lie, or Die, Wiley Publishing Smart Service Welt Working Group (2014) "Smart Service Welt: Recommendations for the Strategic Initiative Web-based Services for Businesses", acatech, Berlin.

Simmons, R. (2023). The big benefits of 5g technology in logistics. *DHL*. https://www.dhl.com/discover/en-global/logistics-advice/logistics-insights/5g-and-logistics

Simpson, J., Hocken, R. J., & Albus, J. S. (1982). The automated manufacturing research facility of the National Bureau of Standards. *Journal of Manufacturing Systems*, 1(1), 17–32. DOI: 10.1016/S0278-6125(82)80064-2

Smith, A. D. (2016). Exploring strategic partnering in supply chain management: Case study of successful practices. In *Supply Chain Management: Practices, Applications and Challenges* (pp. 01-19). Nova Science Publishers, Inc. Retrieved May 08, 2024, from https://www.scopus.com/record/display.uri?eid=2-s2.0-85060522719&origin=scopusAI

Smith, B. J., & Lim, M. H. (2020). How the COVID-19 pandemic is focusing attention on loneliness and social isolation. *Public Health Research & Practice*, 30(2), 3022008. PMID: 32601651

Soares, A. A., Azevedo, A´. L., & de Sousa, J. P. (2000). Distributed planning and control systems for the virtual enterprise: Organizational requirements and development life-cycle. *Journal of Intelligent Manufacturing*, 11(6), 253–270. DOI: 10.1023/A:1008967209167

Sodhi, M. S., Tang, C. S., & Willenson, E. T. (2023). Research opportunities in preparing supply chains of essential goods for future pandemics. *International Journal of Production Research*, 16(08), 2416–2431. DOI: 10.1080/00207543.2021.1884310

Solove, D. J. (2006). A taxonomy of privacy. *University of Pennsylvania Law Review*, 154(3), 477–564. DOI: 10.2307/40041279

Song, L., Wang, X., & Merveille, N. (2020, June). Research on blockchain for sustainable e-agriculture. In *2020 IEEE Technology & Engineering management conference (TEMSCON)* (pp. 1-5). IEEE. DOI: 10.1109/TEMSCON47658.2020.9140121

Sourabhi, S. (2023, Nov 09). *Supply Chain Agility: Benefits and Strategies*. Retrieved May 09, 2024, from www.oracle.com: https://www.oracle.com/in/scm/supply-chain-agility/#:~:text=Supply%20chain%20agility%20is%20a,materials%2C%20and%20acts%20of%20nature

Souza, G. C. (2014). Supply chain analytics. *Business Horizons*, 57(5), 595–605. DOI: 10.1016/j.bushor.2014.06.004

Srinivasan, R., & Swink, M. (2018). An investigation of visibility and flexibility as complements to supply chain analytics: An organizational information processing theory perspective. *Production and Operations Management*, 27(10), 1842–1862. DOI: 10.1111/poms.12746

Srivastava, P., Ansari, H., Alrasheedi, M., Sharma, R., Prakash, S., & Gupta, S. (2024). Leveraging supply chain collaboration with digital technologies for supply chain performance: An empirical investigation of Indian meat industries. *International Journal of Food Science & Technology*, 59(5), 3514–3522. DOI: 10.1111/ijfs.17052

Stank, T. P., Keller, S. B., & Daugherty, P. J. (2001). Supply chain collaboration and logistical service performance. *Journal of Business Logistics*, 22(1), 29–48. DOI: 10.1002/j.2158-1592.2001.tb00158.x

Stefanovic, N., & Milosevic, D. (2017) Model for big data analytics and management. *7th International Conference of Information Society and Technology (ICIST)*, 163-168.

Stein, M., & Voehl, F. (1998). *Macrologistics Management*. St. Lucie Press.

Stiglitz, J. (2017). Globalization and its Discontents Revisited: Anti-Globalization in the Era of Trump,Penguin.

Storeng, K. T., de Bengy Puyvallée, A., & Stein, F. (2021). COVAX and the rise of the 'super public private partnership' for global health. *Global Public Health: An International Journal for Research, Policy and Practice*, 18(1), 1987502. Advance online publication. DOI: 10.1080/17441692.2021.1987502 PMID: 34686103

Storey, V. C. and Song, I. Y. (2017) "Big data technologies and management: What conceptual modeling can do," Data & Knowledge Engineering, pp. 108, 50-67.

Sugrue, D., and P. Adriaens. (2021). "A Data Fusion Approach to Predict Shipping Efficiency for Bulk Carriers." Transportation Research Part E: Logistics and Transportation Review 149: 102326. doi:. 2021.102326.DOI: 10.1016/j.tre

Sun, E. W., Chen, Y. T., & Yu, M. T. (2015). Generalized optimal wavelet decomposing algorithm for big financial data. *International Journal of Production Economics*, 2015(165), 194–214. DOI: 10.1016/j.ijpe.2014.12.033

Supply Chain Council (2012). Supply Chain Operations Reference Model. Revision 11.0,. Supply Chain Operations Management.

Swaminathan, J. M. (2000). *Supply chain management.* International Encyclopedia of the Social and Behavioural Sciences, Elsevier Sciences.

Swamy, N., & Nayak, S., & M N, V. (2016). Analysis on IoT Challenges, Opportunities, Applications and Communication Models. *International Journal of Advanced Engineering* [IJAEMS]. *Management Science*, 2(4), 75–78.

Syafrudin, M., Alfian, G., Fitriyani, N., & Rhee, J. (2018). Performance Analysis of IoT-Based Sensor, Big Data Processing, and Machine Learning Model for Real-Time Monitoring System in Automotive Manufacturing. *Sensors (Basel)*, 18(9), 2946. DOI: 10.3390/s18092946 PMID: 30181525

Taboada, I., & Shee, H. (2021). Understanding 5G technology for future supply chain management. *International Journal of Logistics*, 24(4), 392–406. DOI: 10.1080/13675567.2020.1762850

Tadja, D., Nadeau, V., Mercier, A., & Wong, T. (2023, April). Technologies de l'industrie 4.0 applicables à la chasse aux gaspillages du lean manufacturing. In 18ème colloque national S. mart.

Tadja, D., Bassetto, S., Wong, T., & Tollenaere, M. (2021). *Les objets connectés pour améliorer la culture de la production épurée : revue de littérature et esquisse de solution applicable aux entreprises manufacturières.* ISTE OpenScience.

Taj, S., & Morosan, C. (2011). The impact of lean operations on the Chinese manufacturing performance. *Journal of Manufacturing Technology Management*, 22(2), 223–240. DOI: 10.1108/17410381111102234

Talwar, S., Kaur, P., Fosso Wamba, S., & Dhir, A. (2021). Big data in operations and supply chain management: A systematic literature review and future research agenda. *International Journal of Production Research*, 59(11), 3509–3534. DOI: 10.1080/00207543.2020.1868599

Tamilsevi, K., Sumithra, V., & Dhanapriadharsini, K. (2018). Big data analytics using hadoop technology. *IACSIT International Journal of Engineering and Technology*, 5(1), 1507–1511.

Tang, F., Lin, J., Xing, L., Yang, X., He, H., Ma, S., … & Huang, D. (2023). Privacy protection and data coordination mechanism of supply chain based on blockchain.. DOI: 10.1117/12.2685950

-Tapscott, D., & Tapscott, A. (2016). *Blockchain Technology and Digital Transformation: A Comparative Study.

Tapscott, D., & Tapscott, A. (2020). *Blockchain revolution: How the technology behind bitcoin is changing money, business, and the world*. Penguin Books.

Taranya, R. T., Rama Devi, Y., & Kavita, G. (2023). Logistics, traceability in food supply chain management. *4th International Conference on Design and Manufacturing Aspects for Sustainable Energy, ICMED-ICMPC 2023. 391*. Hyderabad: EDP Sciences. DOI: 10.1051/e3sconf/202339101075

Taseen, M., Wangyongli, & Ali, E. (2023). Integration of Artificial Intelligence for Demand Forecasting and Resource Allocation in Renewable Energy Supply Chains. *25th International Multi Topic Conference, INMIC 2023*. Lahore: Institute of Electrical and Electronics Engineers Inc. DOI: 10.1109/INMIC60434.2023.10465757

Tavana, M., Govindan, K., Nasr, A. K., Heidary, M. S., & Mina, H. (2021). A mathematical programming approach for equitable COVID-19 vaccine distribution in developing countries. In *Annals of Operations Research* (Issue 0123456789). Springer US. DOI: 10.1007/s10479-021-04130-z

Technology, N. J. I. o. (2018). *Why Data is the Next Frontier of Innovation*.

Thomas, C., Maître, I., & Symoneaux, R. (2021). Consumer-led eco-development of food products: A case study to propose a framework. *British Food Journal*, 123(07), 2430–2448. DOI: 10.1108/BFJ-11-2020-1050

Thomas, R., Darby, J. L., Dobrzykowski, D., & van Hoek, R. (2021). Decomposing Social Sustainability: Signaling Theory Insights into Supplier Selection Decisions. *The Journal of Supply Chain Management*, 57(4), 117–136. DOI: 10.1111/jscm.12247

Thrun, S., Montemerlo, M., Dahlkamp, H., Stavens, D., Aron, A., Diebel, J., Fong, P., Gale, J., Halpenny, M., Hoffmann, G., Lau, K., Oakley, C., Palatucci, M., Pratt, V., Stang, P., Strohband, S., Dupont, C., Jendrossek, L.-E., Koelen, C., & Mahoney, P. (2006). Stanley: The robot that won the DARPA Grand Challenge. *Journal of Field Robotics*, 23(9), 661–692. DOI: 10.1002/rob.20147

Timmer, C. P. (2000). The macro dimensions of food security: Economic growth, equitable distribution, and food price stability. *Food Policy*, 25(3), 283–295. DOI: 10.1016/S0306-9192(00)00007-5

Tiwari, S., Wee, H. M., & Daryanto, Y. (2018). Big data analytics in supply chain management between 2010 and 2016: Insights to industries. *Computers & Industrial Engineering*, 115, 319–330. DOI: 10.1016/j.cie.2017.11.017

Tjahjono, B., Esplugues, C., Ares, E., & Pelaez, G. (2017). What does Industry 4.0 mean to supply chain? *Procedia Manufacturing*, 13, 1175–1182. DOI: 10.1016/j.promfg.2017.09.191

Tomás, J. P. (2021a). 5G manufacturing use case spotlight: Industrial automation. *RCR Wireless News*.https://www.rcrwireless.com/20210831/5g/5g-manufacturing-use-case-spotlight-industrial-automation

Tomás, J. P. (2021b). Three 5G manufacturing case studies: Audi, Haier, Bosch. *RCR Wireless News*.https://www.rcrwireless.com/20210726/5g/three-5g-manufacturing-case-studies

Tonidandel, S. King, E. B. and Cortina, J. M. (2018) "Big data methods: Leveraging modern data analytic techniques to build organizational science," Organizational Research Methods, pp. 21(3), 525-547.

Torky, M., & Hassanien, A. E. (2020). *COVID-19 Blockchain Framework: Innovative Approach*. https://arxiv.org/abs/2004.06081v1

Tornatzky, L. G., & Fleischer, M. (1990). *The processes of technological innovation*. Lexington Books.

Touboulic, A., & Walker, H. (2015). Theories in sustainable supply chain management: A structured literature review. *International Journal of Physical Distribution & Logistics Management*, 45(1/2), 16–42. DOI: 10.1108/IJPDLM-05-2013-0106

Touzi, B., Mabrouki, C., & Farchi, A. (2015). Sustainable Road Transport in Developed and Developing Countries: Framework and Future Research. *International Journal of Engineering and Technical Research*, 4, 373. https://www.ijert.org/research/sustainable-road-transport-in-developed-and-developing-countries-framework-and-future-research-IJERTV4IS080322.pdf

Treiblmaier, H. (2018). The impact of the blockchain on the supply chain: A theory-based research framework and a call for action. *Supply Chain Management*, 23(6), 545–559. DOI: 10.1108/SCM-01-2018-0029

Tsakalidis, A., Gkoumas, K., & Pekár, F. (2020). Digital Transformation Supporting Transport Decarbonisation: Technological Developments in EU-Funded Research and Innovation. *Sustainability (Basel)*, 12(9), 3762. DOI: 10.3390/su12093762

Tseng, M. L., Bui, T. D., Lewi, S., Rizaldy, H., Lim, M. K., & Wu, K. J. (2022). Using qualitative information, sustainable supply chain management practices in the Indonesian coffee industry: Digitalization integration improves performance. Advanced online publication. DOI: 10.1080/13675567.2022.2155936

Ulsoy, Y. K. (1997). "Reconfigurable manufacturing systems.

Ulsoy, Y. K. (1997). Reconfigurable manufacturing systems. *Engineering Research Center for Reconfigurable Machining Systems, ERC/RMS.*

Uman, L. S. (2011). Systematic reviews and meta-analyses. *Journal of the Canadian Academy of Child and Adolescent Psychiatry*, 20(1), 57. https://www.ncbi.nlm.nih.gov/pmc/articles/PMC3024725/ PMID: 21286370

Untari, D. T., & Satria, B. (2021). Integration of supply chain management to business performance and business competitiveness of food micro industry. *Uncertain Supply Chain Management*, 9(03), 705–710. DOI: 10.5267/j.uscm.2021.4.008

Upadhyay, A., Mukhuty, S., Kumar, V., & Kazancoglu, Y. (2021). Blockchain technology and the circular economy: Implications for sustainability and social responsibility. *Journal of Cleaner Production*, 293, 126130. DOI: 10.1016/j.jclepro.2021.126130

Uschold, M. a. (1995). Towards a methodology for building ontologies. In *uschold-1995towards.* Citeseer.

Vachter, D., & Bányai, T. (2022). LEAN AND SIMULATION-BASED POTENTIALS IN THE MANUFACTURING PROCESSES OF FOOD INDUSTRY. *Academic Journal of Manufacturing Engineering, 20*(03), 67-73. Retrieved May 08, 2024, from https://www.scopus.com/record/display.uri?eid=2-s2.0-85145951190&origin=scopusAI

Van Alstyne, M. W., Parker, G. G., & Choudary, S. P. (2016). Pipelines, platforms, and the new rules of strategy. *Harvard Business Review*, 94(4), 54–62.

Van der Aalst, W. M. (2012). A decade of business process management conferences: personal reflections on a developing discipline. In *Proceedings of the International Conference on Business Process Management* (pp. 1-16). Berlin: Springer. DOI: 10.1007/978-3-642-32885-5_1

Van Dongen, B. e. (2010). OntoCAPE: An Ontology for Computer-Aided Process Engineering. *Journal of Process Control*, 623–638.

Van Weele, A. J. (2020). Purchasing and supply chain management: Analysis, strategy, planning and practice. Cengage Learning EMEA.

Vegetti, M. a. (2005). Product ontology: definition of an ontology for the complex product modelling domain. In *Proceedings of the Mercosur Congress on Process Systems Engineering*.

Velazquez, L., Munguia, N. E., Will, M., Zavala, A. G., Verdugo, S. P., Delakowitz, B., & Giannetti, B. (2015). Sustainable transportation strategies for decoupling road vehicle transport and carbon dioxide emissions. *Management of Environmental Quality*, 26(3), 373–388. DOI: 10.1108/MEQ-07-2014-0120

Vempati, L., Crapanzano, R., Woodyard, C., & Trunkhill, C. (2017). Linear program and simulation model for aerial package delivery: A case study of Amazon prime air in Phoenix, AZ. *17th AIAA Aviation Technology, Integration, and Operations Conference, 2017*. Denver: American Institute of Aeronautics and Astronautics Inc, AIAA. DOI: 10.2514/6.2017-3936

Venkatesh, V. G., Kang, K., Wang, B., Zhong, R. Y., & Zhang, A. (2020). System architecture for blockchain based transparency of supply chain social sustainability. *Robotics and Computer-integrated Manufacturing*, 63, 101896. DOI: 10.1016/j.rcim.2019.101896

Venkatesh, V., Thong, J. Y., & Xu, X. (2016). Digitalization and performance: How organizational, cultural, and technological factors shape digital adoption and new performance creation. *Management Information Systems Quarterly*, 40(1), 157–178. DOI: 10.2307/41410412

Venugopal, V., & Saleeshya, P. (2019, May 04). Manufacturing system sustainability through lean and agile initiatives. *International Journal of Sustainable Engineering*, 12(03), 159–173. DOI: 10.1080/19397038.2019.1566411

Vera-Baquero, A., Colomo Palacios, R., Stantchev, V., & Molloy, O. (2015). Leveraging big-data for business process analytics. *The Learning Organization*, 22(4), 215–228. DOI: 10.1108/TLO-05-2014-0023

Verhoef, P. C., Broekhuizen, T., Bart, Y., Bhattacharya, A., Dong, J. Q., Fabian, N., & Venkatesan, R. (2017). Digital transformation: A multidisciplinary reflection and research agenda. *Journal of Business Research*, 81, 236–246.

Verhoef, P. C., Broekhuizen, T., Bart, Y., Bhattacharya, A., & Dong, Qi, J., Fabian, N., & Haenlein, M. (2021). The Influence of Digital Transformation on Customer Experience. *Journal of Service Research*.

Verhoef, P. C., Kannan, P. K., & Inman, J. J. (2015). From multi-channel retailing to omni-channel retailing: Introduction to the special issue on multi-channel retailing. *Journal of Retailing*, 91(2), 174–181. DOI: 10.1016/j.jretai.2015.02.005

Verma, D. (2018). Analysis of Smart Manufacturing Technologies for Industry Using AI Methods. [TURCOMAT]. *Turkish Journal of Computer and Mathematics Education*, 9(2), 529–540. DOI: 10.17762/turcomat.v9i2.13857

-Vial, G. (2021). Understanding digital transformation: A review and a research agenda. *Managing digital transformation*, 13-66.

Vial, G. (2018). Digital innovation and the fourth industrial revolution: Epochal social changes? *Journal of Innovation Economics & Management*, 26(3), 3–14.

Vial, G. (2019). Building digital capabilities for transformative performance: A dynamic capabilities perspective. *Journal of Business Research*, 101, 638–650.

Villalonga, A., Negri, E., Biscardo, G., Castano, F., Haber, R. E., Fumagalli, L., & Macchi, M. (2021). A decision-making framework for dynamic scheduling of cyber-physical production systems based on digital twins. *Annual Reviews in Control*, 51, 357–373. DOI: 10.1016/j.arcontrol.2021.04.008

Vincent, A. A., Segun, I. B., Loretta, N. N., & Abiola, A. (2021). Entrepreneurship, agricultural value-chain and exports in Nigeria. *United International Journal for Research and Technology*, 2(08), 1–8.

Vogel-Heuser, B., Fay, A., Schaefer, I., & Tichy, M. (2015). Evolution of software in automated production systems: Challenges and research directions. *Journal of Systems and Software*, 110, 54–84. DOI: 10.1016/j.jss.2015.08.026

Volvo. (2023). *Volvo Group implements a new Internet of Things (IoT) network to make factories smarter*. https://www.volvogroup.com/en/news-and-media/news/2023/mar/volvo-group-implements-a-new-internet-of-things-iot-network-to-make-factories-smarter.html

Von Hippel, E., & von Krogh, G. (2016). Free revealing and the private-collective model for innovation incentives. *R & D Management*, 46(3), 438–451.

Vu, N., Ghadge, A., & Bourlakis, M. (2021). Blockchain adoption in food supply chains: A review and implementation framework. *Production Planning and Control*, 0(0), 1–18. DOI: 10.1080/09537287.2021.1939902

Wallace, A. S., Willis, F., Nwaze, E., Dieng, B., Sipilanyambe, N., Daniels, D., Abanida, E., Gasasira, A., Mahmud, M., & Ryman, T. K. (2017). Vaccine wastage in Nigeria: An assessment of wastage rates and related vaccinator knowledge, attitudes and practices. *Vaccine*, 35(48), 6751–6758. DOI: 10.1016/j.vaccine.2017.09.082 PMID: 29066189

Waller, M. A., & Fawcett, S. E. (2013). Data science, predictive analytics, and big data: A revolution that will transform supply chain design and management. *Journal of Business Logistics*, 34(2), 77–84. DOI: 10.1111/jbl.12010

Wamba, S. F., Gunasekaran, A., Akter, S., Ren, S. J. F., Dubey, R., & Childe, S. J. (2015). Big data analytics and firm performance: Effects of dynamic capabilities. *Journal of Business Research*, 70, 356–365.

Wang, L., & Alexander, C. (2015). Big data driven supply chain management and business administration. *American Journal of Economics and Business Administration*, 7(2), 60–67. DOI: 10.3844/ajebasp.2015.60.67

Wang, M., & Flessa, S. (2020). Modelling Covid-19 under uncertainty: What can we expect? *The European Journal of Health Economics*, 21(5), 665–668. DOI: 10.1007/s10198-020-01202-y PMID: 32494911

Wang, M., & Prajogo, D. (2024). The effect of supply chain digitalization on a firm's performance. *Industrial Management & Data Systems*, 124(5), 1725–1745. DOI: 10.1108/IMDS-09-2023-0629

Wang, R., & Strong, D. M. (1996). Beyond accuracy: What data quality means to data consumers. *Journal of Management Information Systems*, 12(4), 5–34. DOI: 10.1080/07421222.1996.11518099

Wang, Y., Gunasekaran, A., Ngai, E. W. T., & Papadopoulos, T. (2020). Big data analytics in logistics and supply chain management: Certain investigations for research and applications. *International Journal of Production Economics*, 229, 107852.

Wang, Y., Tiwari, M. K., & Wee, H. M. (2021). Impact of robotics and automation on productivity and labor: A quantitative study. *Journal of Manufacturing Systems*, 60, 225–239.

Webb, M. (2015). Overview of food safety standards. In *Food Safety, Market Organization, Trade and Development* (pp. 45-58). Springer International Publishing. DOI: 10.1007/978-3-319-15227-1_3

-Weill, P., & Ross, J. W. (2017). How Digital Transformation Creates New Business Value

Weinstein, R. (2005). RFID: A technical overview and its application to the enterprise. *IT Professional*, 7(3), 27–33. DOI: 10.1109/MITP.2005.69

-Westerman, G., Bonnet, D., & McAfee, A. (2014). Digital Transformation and the Creation of New Business Models

Westin, A. F. (1967). *Privacy and freedom*. Atheneum.

Wiese, T., Abicht, J., Friedrich, C., Hellmich, A., & Ihlenfeldt, S. (2022). Flexible skill-based control for robot cells in manufacturing. *Frontiers in Robotics and AI*, 9, 1014476. DOI: 10.3389/frobt.2022.1014476 PMID: 36246488

Williamson, O. E. (1985). *The economic institutions of capitalism*. Free Press.

Williams, T. J. (1989). *A reference model for computer integrated manufacturing (CIM)*. International Purdue Works.

Wiltshire, J., & Jaimurzina, A. (2017). Air transport as a driver of sustainable development in Latin America and the Caribbean: challenges and policy proposals. *Natural Resources and Infrastructure Division*. (https://hdl.handle.net/11362/43412)

Winasis, S., Djumarno, D., Riyanto, S., & Ariyanto, E. (2021). The effect of transformational leadership climate on employee engagement during digital transformation in Indonesian banking industry. *International Journal of Data and Network Science*, 5(2), 91–96.

Winkelhaus, S., Strauss, C., & Zühlke, D. (2020). Logistics 4.0: A definition for research and practice. *Decisions*, 58(5), 1285–1300.

Wouters, O. J., Shadlen, K. C., Salcher-Konrad, M., Pollard, A. J., Larson, H. J., Teerawattananon, Y., & Jit, M. (2021). Challenges in ensuring global access to COVID-19 vaccines: Production, affordability, allocation, and deployment. *Lancet*, 397(10278), 1023–1034. DOI: 10.1016/S0140-6736(21)00306-8 PMID: 33587887

Wu, G. C., Yue, W. T., Jin, Y., & Yen, H. (2016). Cloud computing in logistics service: Framework, simulation, and performance evaluation. *Journal of Computer Information Systems*, 56(4), 331–338.

Xia, F., Yang, L. T., Wang, L., & Vinel, A. (2012). Internet of Things. *International Journal of Communication Systems*, 25(9), 1101–1102. DOI: 10.1002/dac.2417

Xoliswa, F., Das, D. K., & Hassan, M. M. (2016). Sustainable road transportation: a critical reflection. *Interim: Interdisciplinary Journal, 15*(1), 87-96. (https://hdl.handle.net/10520/EJC-6cef893b3)

XSNET. (2017). *Updated for 2017: The V's of Big Data: Velocity*. Volume, Value, Variety, and Veracity.

Xu, C., Qu, Y., Luan, T. H., Eklund, P. W., Xiang, Y., & Gao, L. (2021). A lightweight and attack-proof bidirectional blockchain paradigm for internet of things. *IEEE Internet of Things Journal*, 9(6), 4371–4384. DOI: 10.1109/JIOT.2021.3103275

Xu, J., Gu, B., & Tian, G. (2022). Review of agricultural IoT technology. *Artificial Intelligence in Agriculture*, 6, 10–22. DOI: 10.1016/j.aiia.2022.01.001

Xu, J., Pero, M. E. P., Ciccullo, F., & Sianesi, A. (2021). On relating big data analytics to supply chain planning: Towards a research agenda. *International Journal of Physical Distribution & Logistics Management*, 51(6), 656–682. DOI: 10.1108/IJPDLM-04-2020-0129

Xu, L., Gao, R., Xie, Y., & Du, P. (2019). To be or not to be? Big data business investment decision making in the supply chain. *Sustainability (Basel)*, 11(8), 2298. DOI: 10.3390/su11082298

Xu, M., Chen, X., & Kou, G. (2019). A systematic review of blockchain. *Financial Innovation*, 5(1), 1–14. DOI: 10.1186/s40854-019-0147-z

Xu, X., Rodgers, M. D., & Guo, W. (2021). A hub-and-spoke design for ultra-cold COVID-19 vaccine distribution. *Vaccine*, 39(41), 6127–6136. DOI: 10.1016/j.vaccine.2021.08.069 PMID: 34509324

Yadav, A. K., & Kumar, D. (2022). A LAG-based framework to overcome the challenges of the sustainable vaccine supply chain: an integrated BWM–MARCOS approach. *Journal of Humanitarian Logistics and Supply Chain Management*. DOI: 10.1108/JHLSCM-09-2021-0091

Yadav, A. K., Shweta, , & Kumar, D. (2022, November). Shweta, & Kumar, D. (2023). Blockchain technology and vaccine supply chain: Exploration and analysis of the adoption barriers in the Indian context. *International Journal of Production Economics*, 255, 108716. DOI: 10.1016/j.ijpe.2022.108716

Yang, J., Wang, X., & Zhao, Y. (2022). Parallel Manufacturing for Industrial Metaverses: A New Paradigm in Smart Manufacturing. *IEEE/CAA Journal of Automatica Sinica, 9*(12), 2063–2070. DOI: 10.1109/JAS.2022.106097

Yang, S. (2022). Analysis for supply chain management: Evidence from toyota. *BCP Business & Management*, 34, 1204–1209. DOI: 10.54691/bcpbm.v34i.3160

Yang, Y., Bidkhori, H., & Rajgopal, J. (2020). Optimizing vaccine distribution networks in low and middle-income countries. *Omega*, 99, 102197. DOI: 10.1016/j.omega.2020.102197

Yawson, D. E., & Yamoah, F. A. (2022, November). Review of Strategic Agility: A Holistic Framework for Fresh Produce Supply Chain Disruptions. *Sustainability (Basel)*, 14(22), 14977. Advance online publication. DOI: 10.3390/su142214977

Yli-Huumo, J., Ko, D., Choi, S., Park, S., & Smolander, K. (2016). Where is current research on blockchain technology?—A systematic review. *PLoS One*, 11(10), e0163477. DOI: 10.1371/journal.pone.0163477 PMID: 27695049

Yoon, J., & Pyo, S. (2019). A Review of Mitigation Measures for Reducing Railway Rolling Noise from an Infrastructure Point of View. *International Journal of Railway*, 12(1), 1–9. DOI: 10.7782/IJR.2019.12.1.001

Yuan, H., Xu, W., Li, Q., & Lau, R. (2018). Topic Sentiment Mining for Sales Performance Prediction in e-Commerce. *Annals of Operations Research*, 270(1–2), 553–576. DOI: 10.1007/s10479-017-2421-7

Yu, Q., Wang, Y., Jiang, X., Zhao, B., Zhang, X., Wang, X., & Liu, Q. (2021). Optimization of Vehicle Transportation Route Based on IoT. *Mathematical Problems in Engineering*, 2021, 1–10. DOI: 10.1155/2021/1312058

Yushi, L., Fei, J., & Hui, Y. (2012). Study on application modes of military Internet of Things (MIOT). *2012 IEEE International Conference on Computer Science and Automation Engineering (CSAE)*, 630–634. DOI: 10.1109/CSAE.2012.6273031

Yu, Y., Zeng, H., & Zhang, M. (2024). Digital transformation for supply chain collaborative innovation and market performance. *European Journal of Innovation Management*. Advance online publication. DOI: 10.1108/EJIM-09-2023-0736

Zabeu, S. (2023, March). *Volvo adopts IoT to monitor autonomous vehicles on the production line*. NetworkKing The IT Monitoring Magazine. https://network-king.net/volvo-adopts-iot-to-monitor-autonomous-vehicles-on-the-production-line/

Zaffran, M., Vandelaer, J., Kristensen, D., Melgaard, B., Yadav, P., Antwi-Agyei, K. O., & Lasher, H. (2013). The imperative for stronger vaccine supply and logistics systems. *Vaccine*, 31(SUPPL2), B73–B80. DOI: 10.1016/j.vaccine.2012.11.036 PMID: 23598495

Zain, I., Rehan, A., & Ashraf, J. (2016). Internet of Things. *International Journal of Engineering Development and Research*, 4(3), 1088–1092.

Zangiacomi, A., Pessot, E., Fornasiero, R., Bertetti, M., & Sacco, M. (2020). Moving towards digitalization: A multiple case study in manufacturing. *Production Planning and Control*, 31(2–3), 143–157. DOI: 10.1080/09537287.2019.1631468

Zhang, P., & Yuan, A. Q. (2014). A study on CPFR inventory management technology. *4th International Conference on Frontiers of Manufacturing Science and Measuring Technology, ICFMM 2014. 599-601*, pp. 2079 - 2082. Trans Tech Publications Ltd. DOI: 10.4028/www.scientific.net/AMM.599-601.2079

Zhang, Z., & Fisac, J. F. (2021). *Safe Occlusion-aware Autonomous Driving via Game-Theoretic Active Perception*. DOI: 10.15607/RSS.2021.XVII.066

Zhang, Y., Wang, W., Wu, N., & Qian, C. (2016). IoT-Enabled Real-Time Production Performance Analysis and Exception Diagnosis Model. *IEEE Transactions on Automation Science and Engineering*, 13(3), 1318–1332. DOI: 10.1109/TASE.2015.2497800

Zhao, H., Wayne, S. J., Glibkowski, B. C., & Bravo, J. (2007). The impact of psychological contract breach on work-related outcomes: A meta-analysis. *Personnel Psychology*, 60(3), 647–680. DOI: 10.1111/j.1744-6570.2007.00087.x

Zheng, M., & Wu, K. (2017). Smart Spare Parts Management Systems in Semiconductor Manufacturing. *Industrial Management & Data Systems*, 116(2), 322–348. DOI: 10.1108/IMDS-06-2016-0242

Zheng, P., Wang, H., Sang, Z., Zhong, R. Y., Liu, Y., Liu, C., Mubarok, K., Yu, S., & Xu, X. (2018). Smart manufacturing systems for Industry 4.0: Conceptual framework, scenarios, and future perspectives. *Frontiers of Mechanical Engineering*, 13(2), 137–150. DOI: 10.1007/s11465-018-0499-5

Zhong, R. Y., Huang, G. Q., Lan, S., Dai, Q. Y., Chen, X., & Zhang, T. (2015a). A big data approach for logistics trajectory discovery from RFID-enabled production data. *International Journal of Production Economics*, 165, 260–272. DOI: 10.1016/j.ijpe.2015.02.014

Zhong, R. Y., Xu, X., & Wang, L. (2017). IoT-enabled smart factory visibility and traceability using laser-scanners. *Advanced Engineering Informatics*, 32, 243–252.

Zhou, K., Liu, T., & Zhou, L. (2015). Industry 4.0: Towards future industrial opportunities and challenges. *2015 12th International Conference on Fuzzy Systems and Knowledge Discovery (FSKD)*, 2147–2152. DOI: 10.1109/FSKD.2015.7382284

Zhou, H., Wang, Q., Li, L., Teo, S. H. H., & Yang, S. H. (2023). Supply chain digitalization and performance improvement: A moderated mediation model. *Supply Chain Management*, 28(6), 993–1008. DOI: 10.1108/SCM-11-2022-0434

Zhu, K., Kraemer, K. L., & Xu, S. (2006). The influence of institutional factors on e-business adoption in China. *Management Science*, 52(10), 1557–1576. DOI: 10.1287/mnsc.1050.0487

Zhu, W., Zhou, G., Yen, I. L., & Bastani, F. (2015). A PT-SOA Model for CPS/IoT Services, In *Proceedings of the 2015 IEEE International Conference on Web Services*, New York, NY, USA, 27 June – 2 July 2015. DOI: 10.1109/ICWS.2015.91

Zilker, M., Behler, K., Bluhm, T., Heimann, P., Hennig, C., Kroiss, H., Kühner, G., Laqua, H., Lewerentz, M., Maier, J., Neu, G., Raupp, G., Reich, M., Riemann, H., Schacht, J., Spring, A., Treutterer, W., Werner, A., & Zehetbauer, T. (2010). Development and implementation of real-time data acquisition systems for fusion devices with open source software. *Fusion Engineering and Design*, 85(3-4), 378–382. DOI: 10.1016/j.fusengdes.2010.02.014

About the Contributors

Manal BENATIYA ANDALOUSSI I am a professor at Chouaïb Doukkaly University, holding a PhD in Management Sciences. Currently, I am working on research themes related to innovation and management sciences, specifically focusing on supply chain management. I teach supply chain management and logistics at the multidisciplinary faculty, and I am supervising doctoral thesis on the use of ERPs in public institutions and the use of AI in organization management. I am leading a pedagogical innovation project on ERP-based teaching. I have served as a guest editor and reviewer for several indexed journals.

***

Anurag A. S. obtained his BE degree in Electrical and Electronics from Anna University in 2013, followed by an MBA degree in Operations from Indira Gandhi National Open University in 2017. Accumulating nearly a decade of practical working experience in both the Engineering and Management fields, Anurag has garnered invaluable insights within various organizations across two culturally diverse countries. His extensive professional journey has deepened his understanding of the global significance of management functions. Currently pursuing a Ph.D. at the Central University of Kerala within the Management Studies Department, Anurag's research revolves around the intersection of Management and Artificial Intelligence. Fueled by a unique blend of engineering and business acumen, Anurag is wholeheartedly committed to unraveling the intricacies of how technology, specifically Artificial Intelligence, can enhance and streamline various facets of management in the contemporary business landscape.

Manal Benatiya Andaloussi, Ph.D., is a distinguished academician at Chouaib Doukkali Université. Her scholarly endeavors focus on elucidating the synergies between digital innovation, supply chain optimization, and sustainable practices.

Bassem Chaker holds a Dr.Eng. in Logistics and Production from the University of Sfax, complementing his prior Dipl.Eng. in Mechanical Engineering. Since 2016, he has been an integral part of the OLID Research Lab at the Higher Institute of Industrial Management of Sfax, contributing significantly as a research associate and, more recently, as a key member of a research project initiated in 2021. Actively engaged in the Tunisian Operational Research Society since 2019, Dr. Chaker demonstrates a keen interest in advancing operational research practices. His research portfolio envelops a diverse range of topics, including Logistics, Supply Chain Optimization, Sustainable Development, Agro-industry, Quality Control, and Non-destructive Testing, reflecting his commitment to excellence and innovative problem-solving in industrial domains.

Sinan Çıkmak is a Lecturer in the Department of Administration and Organization at the Vocational School of Social Sciences at Duzce University, Turkey. He completed his PhD in 2020 and MSc in 2012 at Sakarya University in Business Administration, and his undergraduate studies in Industrial Engineering at Kırıkkale University in 2006. Sinan worked as a production engineer in a company for five years after completing his undergraduate education. His research interests include operations management, logistics, and supply chain management.

Chedli Damak, a proficient professional in the realms of Supply Chain and Operational Management, currently assumes the position of Logistics and Transportation Manager at Mellouli Steel & Galvanizing Industries in Sfax, Tunisia. His specialization in strategic planning is exemplified through the meticulous optimization of logistical processes, resulting in a commendable 30% enhancement in product efficiency. As a distinguished Internal Industry 4.0 Expert, Chedli implemented inventory processes with a notable 90% accuracy, concurrently effecting a discernible 30% reduction in associated costs. His adeptness in technology integration, cost reduction methodologies, and pursuit of heightened operational efficiency renders him well-suited for roles such as a Supply Chain Manager or an Industry 4.0 Consultant.

Yousra EL KRAMI, Doctor in Management sciences, she had her PhD in internal audit with highest honors, brings her expertise as a part time professor at Mohammed V University Agdal and in a Business School in Rabat.

Mayuri Kulkarni is a learned scholar and a teacher with a sharp mind and good research background in the field of supply chain management. She holds a Ph. D. with a thesis named "Analytical Study of Supply Chain Management of Food Tech Service Industries" which discusses overall efficiency & optimization in the food Industry. Mayuri has been teaching MBA students for the past 8 years and she is most committed to preparing young leaders. In terms of academic performance, she has recorded impressive results and has written many papers that have been published in UGC-listed journals. This dedication towards professionalism in academics and Supply Chain Management sets Mayuri in a respectable pedestal in the field. Apart from teaching and researching, she has presented several workshops and seminars with the objective of bring theories from the classroom to the real world. Mayuri has invited guest speakers from the different industries to ensure that what is taught is well grounded in practice. I also want to note that she has served as a tutor for many students and has helped them navigate their academic and career paths. Owing to her rounded education and research, she is a valuable commodity both to academia and to industrial sectors.

Johnpaul M is currently an Assistant Professor in the Department of Management Studies at the Central University of Kerala. Dr. John earned a Bachelor's Degree in Economics from the prominent Loyola College in Chennai, as well as a Master's Degree in Business Administration and MA Economics from Osmania University in Hyderabad. He earned his Ph.D. and cleared the AP SET and UGC NET in Management. From 2009 until June 2022, he was an Assistant Professor at Mahatma Gandhi University's Department of Management Studies in Nalgonda. He additionally served as a Hostel Warden, Coordinator for the Academic Audit Cell, NSS Programme Officer, and in a variety of other academic and administrative posts at MGU. To his credit, he has over 13 years of teaching experience. He has published 15 research papers in national and international journals. He has delivered 17 papers at national and international conferences. He has participated in various Faculty Development Programs. He has written one edited book, "Responsible Marketing for Sustainable Business". His teaching topics include marketing, marketing research, strategic management, international business strategy, and managerial economics

Devkumar Mahisekar, 13 years of experience in teaching management stream and 12 years of industry experience Ph. D (Marketing Management), Savitribai Phule Pune University, August 2022 M.B. A (Qualified with additional subjects in Production and Materials Management, University of Pune, May 2011, I class M.B.A. (Marketing Management) -University of Pune, May 1997, I class B.E. (Production) - Marathwada University, Aurangabad Text Books; Planning and Control of Operations World Class Manufacturing Co-Author- Operations strategy Research papers: • Determination of consumer purchase preference for star rated home appliances and outcome of energy efficiency initiatives. Lutheran University of Brazil, Jan 2024, pp. 91 ISSN:1517-4492 I E- ISSN:2178-7727 Vol. 6, No. 2 (2023) • A study of market dynamics and energy sustainability efforts analysis for electrical home appliances AFR, Ilfov, Romania, Nov 2022 • A study of consumer purchase decision of electrical home appliance with emphasize on marketing mix and electric energy sustainability International Journal of Mechanical Engineering, Feb 2022 - Co-author • A Study of Market Dynamics of Energy Efficient Electrical Home Appliances Journal of Natural Remedies, Dec 2020 • A Study on Consumer Perception towards Energy Efficient Electrical Appliances Test Engineering and Management, C.A, U.S.A., Feb 2020 .

Kamalendu Pal is currently associated with the Department of Computer Science, School of Science and Technology at City St Geroge's, University of London. He has a diverse academic background, having received a BSc (Hons) degree in Physics from Calcutta University, India, followed by a Postgraduate Diploma in Computer Science from Pune, India. He has also worked as a research assistant for the government of India's two research and development organizations, under the Council of Scientific and Industrial Research (CSIR). Later, Kamalendu graduated with his MSc in Software Systems Technology from the University of Sheffield, a Postgraduate Diploma in Artificial Intelligence from Kingston University, an MPhil in Computer Science from University College London, an MBA from the University of Hull, and a diploma in Higher Education teaching practice from City St George's, University of London, United Kingdom. Kamalendu is an accomplished researcher, having published over a hundred and twenty international research articles (including book chapters) in the scientific community. His research articles have been published in prestigious journals such as the ACM SIGMIS Database, Expert Systems with Applications, Decision Support Systems, and international conferences. His research interests include various fields of computer science - such as knowledge-based systems, decision support systems, teaching and learning practices, blockchain technology, software engineering, service-oriented computing, sensor network simulation, and supply chain management. Kamalendu is also on the editorial board of an international computer science journal. He is a member of the British Computer Society, the Institution of Engineering and Technology, and the IEEE Computer Society.

Mushtaq Ahmad Shah is a finance expert with a PhD in Infrastructure Finance. He teaches banking, finance and economics at Lovely Professional University in India. Dr. Shah has over 8 years of experience teaching and researching at various institutions. He's written articles in academic journals and presented his work at conferences on banking, partnerships between public and private sectors, and behavioral finance.

Divyeshkumar Vaghani is a Data Engineer with over 7 years of experience in software engineering, specializing in big data analytics and its application to supply chain optimization. His work focuses on leveraging advanced analytics, machine learning, and data integration techniques to solve complex engineering problems and enhance business operations. Divyeshkumar is actively involved in research related to digital transformation, software systems, and data-driven strategies in supply chain management. He holds a master's degree in a relevant field and has contributed to several publications and projects that bridge the gap between software engineering and real-world business applications.

Amit Kumar Yadav has submitted his doctoral thesis in the area of operations and supply chain management at Indian Institute of Technology Roorkee. His doctoral research focuses on the issues of sustainable vaccine supply chain in the Indian context. To model these issues and their solutions, he explored a number of operation management/research and supply chain tool and techniques. He holds an M.Tech in Industrial Management from the Indian Institute of Technology (BHU) Varanasi, where he studied and compared the supply chain efficiencies of various production systems. He has published papers in international reputed journals like International Journal of Production Economics (ABDC A, IF = 11.251), International Journal of Productivity and Performance Management (ABDC B) and Journal of Humanitarian Logistics and Supply Chain Management (ABDC C). He is serving as a reviewer in reputed journals such as Business Strategy and Environment, Australian Journal of Management and Journal of Humanitarian Logistics and Supply Chain Management.

Index

Symbols

A

B

C

D

E

F

G

H

I

J

L

M

N

O

P

Q

R

S

T

V

W

www.ingramcontent.com/pod-product-compliance
Lightning Source LLC
LaVergne TN
LVHW080348011026
849161LV00009B/2228